Memory Allocation Functions

calloc	Allocate storage
free	Free storage
malloc	Allocate storage

Miscellaneous Functions

bsearch	Binary search
clearerr	Clears end-of-file and error indicators
difftime	Compute difference between times
exit	Terminate program
qsort	Quicksort
signal	Invoke a function to handle a signal
system	Execute a command
time	Find time

Input/Output Functions

†close	Close a file	getchar	Read a character
†creat	Create a file	gets	Read a string
fclose	Close a file	†lseek	Move within a file
fgetc	Read a character	†open	Open a file
fgets	Read a string	printf	Write formatted output
fopen	Open a file	putc	Write a character
fprintf	Write formatted output	putchar	Write a character
fputc	Write a character	puts	Write a string
fputs	Write a string	†read	Read from a file
fread	Read several items	rewind	Move to beginning of file
fscanf	Read formatted input	scanf	Read formatted input
fseek	Move within a file	sprintf	Write formatted output
ftell	Find position within a file	sscanf	Read formatted input
fwrite	Write several items	ungetc	Return a character to a buffer
getc	Read a character	†write	Write to a file

†Input/output function not specified by the standard.

Type and Conversion Functions

atof	Convert string to double
atoi	Convert string to int
atol	Convert string to long
isalnum	Alphanumeric?
isalpha	Alphabetic character?
iscntrl	Control character?
isdigit	Decimal digit?
isgraph	Nonblank, printable character?
islower	Lowercase character?
isprint	Printable character?
ispunct	Punctuation character?
isspace	Space character?
isupper	Uppercase character?
isxdigit	Hexadecimal character?
tolower	Convert from uppercase to lowercase
toupper	Convert from lowercase to uppercase

String Functions

memchr	Find left-most character in object
memcmp	Compare objects
memcpy	Copy object
memmove	Copy object
strcat	Concatenate strings
strchr	Find leftmost character in string
strcmp	Compare strings
strcpy	Copy string
strcspn	Complement of span
strlen	Length of string
strncat	Concatenate strings
strncmp	Compare strings
strncpy	Copy string
strpbrk	First break character
strrchr	Find rightmost character in string
strspn	Span
strstr	Find substring

Applications Programming in ANSI C
Second Edition

Applications Programming in ANSI C

Second Edition

Richard Johnsonbaugh
Martin Kalin
DEPAUL UNIVERSITY, CHICAGO

Macmillan Publishing Company
NEW YORK

Maxwell Macmillan Canada
TORONTO

Maxwell Macmillan International
NEW YORK   OXFORD   SINGAPORE   SYDNEY

Editor: David Johnstone
Production Supervisor: Ron Harris
Production Manager: Nick Sklitsis
Text Designer: Susan Frankenberry
Cover Designer: Cathleen Norz
Cover photograph: Autograph score of Schubert's Great C major Symphony, Gesellschaft der Musikfreunde. Used by permission

This book was set in Times Roman by York Graphic Services, Inc., printed and bound by Arcata Graphics-Hawkins. The cover was printed by Phoenix Color Corp.

Macmillan Publishing Company
866 Third Avenue, New York, New York 10022

Macmillan Publishing Company is part
of the Maxwell Communication Group of Companies.

Maxwell Macmillan Canada, Inc.
1200 Eglinton Avenue East
Suite 200
Don Mills, Ontario M3C 3N1

Library of Congress Cataloging-in-Publication Data

Johnsonbaugh, Richard, 1941-
    Applications programming in ANSI C / Richard Johnsonbaugh, Martin
Kalin.
        p.   cm.
    Includes index.
    ISBN 0-02-360951-6
    1. C (Computer program language)   I. Kalin, Martin.   II. Title.
QA76.73.C15J653 1990
005.26—dc20   89-32661
                                                             CIP

ISBN 0-02-361131-6

Printing: 3 4 5 6 7 8   Year: 3 4 5 6 7 8 9 0 1

Trademark Notices

Preface

This book is intended for a one-term course in applications programming in C. It replaces R. Johnsonbaugh and M. Kalin, *Applications Programming in ANSI C,* first edition, and R. Johnsonbaugh and M. Kalin, *Applications Programming in C.* We assume no prior knowledge of C, but we do assume programming experience in some high-level language. A one-term course in a language such as Pascal, FORTRAN, or PL/I is sufficient.

The book and its supplements, an *Instructor's Guide* and a diskette, provide a comprehensive support system to help the reader master C. The book includes numerous examples, exercises, sample applications, programming exercises, lists of common programming errors, and figures.

Overview

C stands out among general-purpose programming languages for its unrivaled mix of portability, power, flexibility, and elegance. It is a language suited for projects of various sizes in both systems and applications programming. Although C achieved a high level of portability without the benefit of an official standard, such a standard was developed by the X3J11 Standardization Committee, which was convened by the American National Standards Institute (ANSI) in 1983. In December 1989, the standard was approved. The C language presented in this book is based on ANSI C, hereafter referred to simply as *standard C;* however, it can also be used with traditional C compilers, since most of the differences between the two versions of C are transparent to the user. Moreover, we highlight important differences within the text and at the ends of chapters in sections called *Changes from Traditional C.*

This book includes the following features:

- Examples and exercises that cover a wide range of applications (in every chapter).
- Sample applications (in every chapter).
- A broad variety of programming exercises (at the end of every chapter). The book contains over 170 programming exercises.

- A section on common programming errors (at the end of every chapter).
- Highlighting of the differences between traditional C and standard C (at the end of every chapter, except Chapter 3).
- Discussion of the standard C functions.
- Exercises so that readers can check their mastery of the section (at the end of almost every section). The book contains over 600 such exercises. Answers to the odd-numbered section exercises are presented in the back of the book.
- Pictures to facilitate the learning process. Two colors are used, not only to make the pictures more attractive but also to differentiate input from output, to show the flow of control in the basic C constructs, and to highlight components of syntax diagrams.
- A number of appendixes.
- An introduction to data structures (stacks, linked lists, trees, and graphs) (Chapter 10).
- A thorough discussion of recursion (Sections 4.8 and 4.9).
- Macros and header files used to write functions with an arbitrary number of arguments (Section 4.10).
- Full coverage of type qualifiers (Section 7.8).
- Topics grouped according to their use and their relationships to one another. This organization enables readers to write simple but useful programs immediately and to skip or postpone some of the less often used and more esoteric parts of the language.
- Understandable code. When forced to choose between clarity and conciseness, we have opted for clarity.

Changes from the First Edition

- Earlier coverage of arrays and pointers. We have moved the chapters on arrays and pointers forward so that they now follow Chapter 4 on functions. We introduce pointers in Chapter 5 (arrays) and cover pointers fully in Chapter 6.
- A more comprehensive *Instructor's Guide*. The *Instructor's Guide* now includes solutions to selected programming exercises and sample syllabi, as well as solutions to section review exercises and transparency masters.
- Expanded coverage of standard functions. For example, Example 7.8.8 shows how to use the sorting function `qsort`.
- New sample applications. We have added sample applications dealing with scheduling (Section 7.9) and converting infix expressions to postfix (Section 10.5).
- Expanded coverage of the C preprocessor. Section 4.6 is devoted to the preprocessor.
- New and improved section review exercises.
- Additional programming exercises.
- Expanded coverage of UNIX (see Appendix F).
- Updated information on Turbo C (see Appendix G).
- In the font used to display computer code, 1 (one) and l (lowercase "el") are now distinguished.
- The source code, header files, and data files for all of the book's sample applications, as well as the source code for some of the longer examples, are available via anonymous ftp (see *Instructor's Supplements* subsection).

Organization of the Book

Especially in the early chapters, we have grouped related topics. For example, in Chapter 1 we discuss integer variables, the `while` loop, the `do while` loop, the `if` statement, and simple file handling. In this way, readers can immediately begin writing simple, but useful, programs. In Chapter 2, we discuss character, integer, and real variables; arithmetic operations; relational and logical operators; the assignment operator in more detail; the `for` statement; and the increment and decrement operators. Less frequently used constructs such as the `goto` statement, labels, conditional expressions, and bitwise operators are discussed in Chapter 3. This organization contrasts with the organization of a manual in which one section is devoted to every data type available in C, another section is devoted to every C operator available, and so on. The sections that can be skipped or introduced later, as needed, have been marked with a dagger[†].

Chapter 4, which deals with functions and program structure, contains the most important departure from traditional C from the point of view of the programmer—function prototypes. Function prototypes allow the compiler to check for matches between arguments and parameters of functions. For readers using a traditional C compiler, a subsection of Section 4.1 shows how to translate standard function headers and declarations into traditional C and gives several examples. Two sections are devoted to recursion. Section 4.8 discusses recursion in general and provides several short examples. Section 4.9 is a sample application that is solved recursively. Functions with an arbitrary number of arguments are discussed in Section 4.10.

Chapters 5 and 6, on arrays and pointers, now follow Chapter 4 on functions. This order makes it possible to introduce more interesting examples and programs earlier.

Storage classes have been moved to Chapter 7. The discussion begins by assuming that the program resides in a single source file. (This is probably true of all the programs that the readers will have written to this point.) We then turn to storage classes in a program divided into two or more source files. In class testing this book, we have found this order of presentation to be the most successful. Section 7.8 discusses type qualifiers that are new with the standard. Type qualifiers are used to inform the compiler, especially an optimizing compiler, about what assumptions it can make about variables. Chapter 7 concludes with a new sample application dealing with scheduling (Section 7.9).

The basic input/output functions for the standard input and standard output (e.g., `printf`, `scanf`), as well as the input/output functions for files (e.g., `fprintf`, `fscanf`), are introduced in Chapter 1. In Chapter 8, we treat these functions in depth and introduce additional input/output functions. Chapter 8 concludes with a sample application that shows how to implement a random access file in C using hashing.

Chapter 9 treats structures, unions, and enumerated types. Chapter 10 introduces data structures in C, with an emphasis on stacks, linked lists, trees, and graphs. Recursion is used as a natural programming technique for processing data structures such as trees. As an example of the use of stacks, we have added a sample application that converts infix expressions to postfix.

This book is devoted to C independent of any particular operating system. However, the basic commands that one needs to compile, link, and run a C program are given in Appendix G for three major systems: Turbo C under MS-DOS (which has supported standard C for some time), VAX-11 C under VAX/VMS, and C under UNIX. In addition, redirection of input and output, so useful in C, is presented for each of these systems. Appendix F contains an extended discussion of C and UNIX.

We rely heavily on short examples, pictures, tables, and other figures to illustrate specific points about C's syntax and semantics. From our own experience in teaching C and other languages, we are convinced that no single method is appropriate for clarifying every aspect about a language.

Most of our students agree with us that learning and using C is fun. We have tried to incorporate this view by using interesting examples, sample problems, programming exercises, and short slices of code.

Chapter Structure

The chapters are organized as follows:

- Contents
- Overview
- Section
- Section Exercises
- Section
- Section Exercises

  .

  .

  .

- Changes from Traditional C
- Common Programming Errors
- Programming Exercises

In each chapter, several sections are devoted to sample applications. Each of these sections contains a statement of a problem, sample input and output, a solution to the problem, and a well-documented implementation of the problem in C. Most of these sections conclude with an extended discussion. In some of the examples, these sections include a line-by-line discussion of the C program.

The sample applications include the following:

- Financial computations (Section 1.6)
- Statistics (Section 2.6)
- Bar graphs (Section 2.9)
- Printing a calendar (Section 3.6)
- Game playing (Section 4.7)
- Tiling (Section 4.9)
- Text processing (Sections 5.5, 7.2, 10.3)
- Sorting and searching (Sections 5.10 and 6.6)
- Scheduling (Section 7.9)
- Random access files (Section 8.7)
- Pattern recognition (Section 9.2)
- Database applications (Section 9.7)
- Converting infix to postfix (Section 10.5)
- Artificial intelligence (Section 10.9)

The *Changes from Traditional C* sections discuss differences in the standard language as presented in that chapter from traditional C. The *Common Programming Errors* sections highlight those aspects of the language that are easily misunderstood. The book contains over 170 programming exercises drawn from a wide variety of applications.

Exercises

The book contains over 600 section review exercises, the answers to which are true or false, short answers, code fragments, and, in a few cases, entire programs. These exercises are suitable as homework problems or as self-tests. The answers to the odd-numbered exercises are given in the back of the book, and the answers to the even-numbered exercises are given in the *Instructor's Guide*. Class testing this book has convinced us of the importance of these exercises.

The applications covered in the programming exercises at the ends of the chapters include the following:

- Graphing (Programming Exercise 2.7)
- Power-lifting competitions (Programming Exercise 2.10)
- Game playing (Programming Exercises 4.29 and 5.18)
- Income tax (Programming Exercise 3.4)
- Property depreciation (Programming Exercise 3.5)
- Data validation (Programming Exercise 5.10)
- Digital picture processing (Programming Exercises 5.17 and 10.28)
- Grading exams (Programming Exercise 5.20)
- Sorting (Programming Exercise 6.9)
- Education (Programming Exercises 6.19 and 8.18)
- Syntax checking (Programming Exercise 7.6)
- Data processing (Programming Exercises 8.8 through 8.13)
- Binary search trees (Programming Exercises 10.17 and 10.18)
- Parallel processing (Programming Exercise 10.26)

Not every reader will be interested in all of these applications; however, we think that it is important to show the variety of problems that C can address.

Appendixes

Seven appendixes are provided for reference. Appendix A contains ASCII and EBCDIC tables. Appendix B reviews unsigned and two's complement integers. Appendix C contains a summary of the C language, consisting of descriptions of the major constructs of C (e.g., switch, while), as well as a description of constants in C, the C data types, a summary of how functions work in C, initializing in definitions, a list of keywords, a summary of pointers in C, a table of the precedence of C operators, a list of the standard headers and their purposes, a summary of C storage classes, a summary of structures in C, and a summary of type qualifiers in C.

Complete two-color syntax diagrams of standard C may be found in Appendix D. Appendix E contains a list of some of the most useful standard C functions. We describe the parameters and return values for each function, the header file to include, and what the function does.

For those readers using C under UNIX, we have included Appendix F on UNIX and C. In this edition, have expanded the coverage of UNIX. In addition to the cc command, the cb and make utilities, the file system, exception handling, and pipes, discussed in the first edition, we also discuss man (the on-line help utility), directories and several commands for navigating within directories (e.g., pwd, mkdir), commands for handling files (e.g., ls, cp), the grep and find utilities, and run-time libraries.

Appendix G tells how to compile, link, and run a C program in Turbo C, VAX / VMS, and UNIX. Explanations are included for single-file and multiple-file programs.

Instructor Supplements

An *Instructor's Guide* and a program diskette are available at no cost to adopters of this book. The *Instructor's Guide* contains answers to the even-numbered section review exercises, transparency masters, sample syllabi, and solutions to selected programming exercises.

The program diskette contains the source code, header files, and data files for all of the book's sample applications, as well as the source code for some of the longer examples. Some programming exercises ask for modifications of these programs. In any case, we assume that many readers will want to experiment with the code that we provide on the diskette. There is no charge for making copies of this diskette to distribute to students. These files also are available on Internet through anonymous ftp. The node is *kalin.depaul.edu* and the directory is */dist*. The directory holds standalone ASCII versions of the files as well as a compressed tar version, *code.tar.Z*.

Acknowledgments

For the preceding edition, we received helpful comments from many persons, including Mark Brucks, Edith Chang, John Crywood, Jerrold W. Grossman, Warren M. Krueger, George W. Mayleben, Carol M. Smith, Dain Smith, Travis Tull, and Steven P. Wartik. Special thanks go to the following users of the book who reviewed this edition: James Abele, Arkansas Tech University; Charles Black, Kansas State University; Robert Dependahl, Santa Barbara City College; Mary Edgington, Wichita State University; Maurice Eggen, Trinity College, San Antonio; John Franco, University of Cincinnati; David Frisque, University of Michigan; Julie Gwynn, California State University, Sacramento; Maylene Hu, West Liberty State College; Koichiro Isshiki, California State Polytechnic University, Pomona; Mark LeBlanc, University of New Hampshire; Zhongming Liang, Purdue University at Fort Wayne; Ruth Malstrom, Raritan Valley Community College; William Muellner, Elmhurst College; Mladen Vouk, North Carolina State University.

We thank our colleagues Bob Fisher and David Miller for several useful discussions concerning C compilers, Henry Harr for sharing his thoughts on teaching C, Jim Janossy for his comments on the line editor sample application in Section 10.3, and I-Ping Chu for his advice on the scheduling problem in Section 7.9. We also thank Hanyi Zhang for providing several solutions to programming exercises that appear in the *Instructor's Guide*.

We are indebted to the Department of Computer Science and Information Systems at DePaul University and its chairman, Helmut Epp, for providing time and encouragement for the development of this book.

We are grateful to the Borland Corporation for furnishing current versions of Turbo C.

We received consistent support from the people at Macmillan. Special thanks for their help in preparing this edition go to David Johnstone, senior editor, Bill Winschief, senior representative / field editor, and Ronald C. Harris, production supervisor.

R.J.
M.K.

Contents

1

Introduction

1

1.1   A First C Program   2
1.2   Sample Application: Conversion of Lengths   4
1.3   Identifiers   8
1.4   The while Statement   9
1.5   The do while Statement   11
1.6   Sample Application: Computing Income Tax   12
1.7   The if Statement   14
1.8   More on the if Statement   21
1.9   Redirecting Input and Output   26
1.10 Files   28
      Changes from Traditional C   30
      Common Programming Errors   30
      Programming Exercises   31

2

Variables, Operators, and Control Flow

33

2.1   Cells, the sizeof Operator, and the Address Operator   34
2.2   Characters and Integers   36
2.3   Real Variables   44
2.4   Arithmetic Operations   48

2.5   Relational and Logical Operators and the Assignment
       Operator   52
2.6   Sample Application: Statistical Measures   58
2.7   The for Statement and the Comma Operator   61
2.8   The Operators ++ and --   64
2.9   Sample Application: Printing a Bar Graph   68
       Changes from Traditional C   70
       Common Programming Errors   71
       Programming Exercises   72

3

More Operators and Control Flow   75

3.1   The break and continue Statements   76
3.2   Sample Application: Generating Prime Numbers   80
3.3   The switch Statement   83
3.4   The goto Statement and Labels   89
3.5   Conditional Expressions   90
3.6   Sample Application: Printing a Calendar   90
3.7   The Cast Operator   94
3.8   getchar and putchar   95
†3.9   Bitwise Operators   99
       Common Programming Errors   103
       Programming Exercises   104

4

Functions and Program Structure   107

4.1   Introduction   108
4.2   Arguments and Parameters   118
4.3   Call by Value   120
4.4   Sample Application: Computing Resistance in Ohms   124
4.5   The Scope of Variables   127
4.6   The Preprocessor   129
4.7   Sample Application: Simulating a Dice Game   140
4.8   Recursion   146
4.9   Sample Application: Recursive Tiling   156
†4.10 Functions with an Arbitrary Number of Arguments   164
       Changes from Traditional C   168
       Common Programming Errors   169
       Programming Exercises   173

† Flagged sections can be omitted without loss of continuity.

5

Arrays 179

5.1 Why Arrays? 180
5.2 Array Indexes and Cell Offsets 181
5.3 Sample Application: Tracking and Reporting Car Sales 189
5.4 Character Strings as Arrays of Characters 194
5.5 Sample Application: Formatting Text with a Given Line Length 199
5.6 Arrays as Function Arguments 201
5.7 String-Handling Functions 205
5.8 Sample Application: Computing a String's Length 214
5.9 Multidimensional Arrays 215
5.10 Sample Application: Sorting and Searching 219
     Changes from Traditional C 225
     Common Programming Errors 225
     Programming Exercises 227

6

Pointers 235

6.1 Pointer Variables 236
6.2 Levels of Indirection 244
6.3 Pointers and Arrays 248
6.4 Call by Reference 264
6.5 Sample Application: Reversing a String in Place 273
6.6 Sample Application: Sorting and Searching Revisited 276
6.7 Smooth and Ragged Arrays 282
6.8 Command Line Arguments 285
6.9 Pointers to Functions 287
6.10 Sample Application: Comparing Sorting Algorithms 289
     Changes from Traditional C 293
     Common Programming Errors 294
     Programming Exercises 296

7

Storage Classes and Type Qualifiers 303

7.1 Storage Classes in a Single-Source File: `auto`, `extern`, `static` 304
7.2 Sample Application: Breaking Text Into Pages 311
7.3 The Storage Class `register` 315

7.4 Storage Classes in Multiple-Source Files 316
7.5 Nested Blocks 322
7.6 Storage Classes for Functions 326
7.7 Sample Application: Savings Account Transactions 328
7.8 Type Qualifiers: `const` and `volatile` 331
7.9 Sample Application: A Scheduling Problem 339
Changes from Traditional C 344
Common Programming Errors 344
Programming Exercises 346

8

Input and Output 351

8.1 Opening and Closing Files 352
8.2 Character Input/Output 356
8.3 Sample Application: Determining a Source File's Size in Bytes 358
8.4 String Input/Output 359
8.5 Formatted Input/Output 364
8.6 Moving Around in a File: `fseek`, `ftell`, `rewind` 377
8.7 Sample Application: A Random Access File 381
†8.8 Nonstandard Input/Output 392
Changes from Traditional C 393
Common Programming Errors 394
Programming Exercises 395

9

Structures, Unions, and Enumerated Types 401

9.1 Introduction to Structures 402
9.2 Sample Application: Pattern Recognition 411
9.3 The `typedef` Construct 416
9.4 Operations on Structures 419
9.5 Pointers to Structures, Nested Structures, and Self-referential Structures 423
9.6 Structures and Functions 430
9.7 Sample Application: An Airline Flight Database 436
†9.8 Unions and Bit Fields 448
9.9 Enumerated Types 452
Changes from Traditional C 455
Common Programming Errors 455
Programming Exercises 457

†Flagged sections can be omitted without loss of continuity.

10

Introduction to Data Structures   461

    10.1 Compile-Time and Run-Time Storage Allocation   463
    10.2 Linked Lists   470
    10.3 Sample Application: A Text Editor   483
    10.4 Stacks and Queues   499
    10.5 Sample Application: Converting from Infix to Postfix   511
    10.6 Graphs and Trees   518
    10.7 Tree Traversals   523
    10.8 Breadth-First Search and Depth-First Search   529
    10.9 Sample Application: Heuristic Graph Search   539
          Changes from Traditional C   551
          Common Programming Errors   551
          Programming Exercises   552

Appendix   559

    A.   ASCII and EBCDIC Tables   560
    B.   Unsigned and Two's Complement Integers   566
    C.   Summary of the C Language   569
    D.   Syntax Diagrams of C   580
    E.   Some C Functions   596
    F.   C and UNIX   616
    G.   Compiling, Linking, and Running a C Program in Turbo C,
          VAX/VMS, and UNIX   631

Hints and Solutions to Odd-Numbered Exercises

                                                     637

Index

                                                     675

Introduction

1

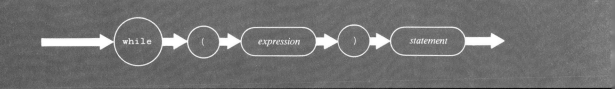

1.1   A First C Program
1.2   Sample Application: Conversion of Lengths
1.3   Identifiers
1.4   The `while` Statement
1.5   The `do while` Statement
1.6   Sample Application: Computing Income Tax
1.7   The `if` Statement
1.8   More on the `if` Statement
1.9   Redirecting Input and Output
1.10 Files
      Changes from Traditional C
      Common Programming Errors
      Programming Exercises

Why is it called C? This is usually one of the first questions asked by a newcomer to the C programming language. The answer is that C's predecessor was called B! B's predecessor was not A, but rather BCPL (Basic Combined Programming Language). BCPL, invented in 1967 by Martin Richards, was a typeless language that dealt directly with machine words and addresses. Inspired by BCPL, Ken Thompson in 1970 invented the typeless systems programming language B. B and assembly language were used to develop the first version of UNIX. In 1972, Dennis Ritchie designed C, which incorporates many of the ideas of BCPL and B but features typing (integers, real numbers, etc.).

Until 1989, the definition of C was that given in Brian W. Kernighan and Dennis M. Ritchie, *The C Programming Language* (Englewood Cliffs, N.J.: Prentice-Hall, 1978). We refer to this version of C as *traditional C*. Because of extensions to the language, some ambiguities in the original definition, and other concerns, in 1983 the American National Standards Institute (ANSI) convened a committee to "provide an unambiguous and machine-independent definition of the language C," and in December 1989 the standard was approved. The C language presented in this book is based on ANSI C, hereafter referred to simply as *standard C*. You can use this book even if you are using a traditional C compiler since most of the differences between the two versions of C are transparent to the user. Moreover, we highlight important differences within the text and at the end of chapters in a section called "Changes from Traditional C."

In this chapter we present programs that introduce some of the basic language constructs: the structure of a C program, identifiers, while and do while loops, the conditional statement (if–else), input, output, and files. We expand on all these topics in subsequent chapters.

1.1   A First C Program

The program in Figure 1.1.1 prints

```
ANSI--A kinder and gentler C!
```

to the video display.

```
/*   This program prints the message
          ANSI--A kinder and gentler C!
     to the video display.                          */
#include <stdio.h>
main()
{
     printf( "ANSI--A kinder and gentler C!\n" );
}
```

Figure 1.1.1 A first C program.

In C, /* marks the start of a comment, and */ marks the end of a comment. Comments are ignored by the compiler.

The line

```
#include <stdio.h>
```

is a **preprocessor directive** and requests some action before the program is actually translated into machine code. (The preprocessor, which processes directives before compilation, is discussed in detail in Section 4.6.) A preprocessor directive always begins with the pound sign #. The #include preprocessor directive causes the contents of the named file, *stdio.h* in this case, to be inserted precisely where the #include line appears. Such a file is called a **header file**. The *.h* extension derives from this nomenclature. Among other things, the file *stdio.h* provides the proper interface to the library output function printf. Appendix C lists the header files mandated by the standard, and Appendix E lists several useful library functions, as well as the necessary header files to include.

A C program consists of one or more **functions**, exactly one of which must be named main. Execution begins with main. Any function consists of statements enclosed in braces: { }. In this example the program consists of the single function main, made up of one statement:

```
printf( "ANSI--A kinder and gentler C!\n" );
```

Single statements in C, such as the statement

```
printf( "ANSI--A kinder and gentler C!\n" );
```

are terminated by semicolons (;).

Except for special characters such as \ (backslash), printf simply copies the characters within the double quotation marks to the video display. Thus the statement

```
printf( "ANSI--A kinder and gentler C!\n" );
```

writes

```
ANSI--A kinder and gentler C!
```

to the video display. The backslash character \ acts as a special escape character. The combination \n is interpreted as a newline and causes the next output, in this case the system prompt, to begin in column 1 of the next line.

Like most modern, high-level language compilers, the C compiler does not require the statements of a program to appear in any particular format. We format our programs, especially by using indentation, to help document them.

Appendix G describes how to compile, link, and run a C program in three common C environments: Turbo C under MS-DOS, VAX-11 C under VMS, and C under UNIX. Appendix F discusses the UNIX C compiler in more detail.

Exercises

1. Run the program in this section on your system.
2. Run modifications of the program in this section. Experiment by leaving out parts of the program. For example, omit the line

   ```
   #include <stdio.h>
   ```

   Omit a brace. Omit one of the double quotation marks. What errors, if any, result? Can you explain the errors?

1.2   Sample Application: Conversion of Lengths

Problem

Read a length in yards (yd) from the keyboard, convert the length to feet (ft) and inches (in), and write the converted lengths to the video display. It is assumed that the length is a nonnegative integer (i.e., one of 0, 1, 2, . . .). The program is terminated by entering a negative integer (i.e., one of −1, −2, . . .). The relationships among these units are

$$1 \text{ yd} = 3 \text{ ft}$$
$$1 \text{ yd} = 36 \text{ in}$$

Sample Input/Output

Input is in color; output is in black.

```
Enter next length 2

2 yd =
6 ft
72 in
Enter next length 30

30 yd =
90 ft
1080 in
Enter next length −99
*** END OF PROGRAM ***
```

C Implementation

```c
/*   This program reads a length in yards from the
     keyboard, converts the length to feet and inches,
     and writes the converted length to the video
     display. It is assumed that the length is a
     nonnegative integer. The program terminates when
     a negative integer is entered.                    */

#include <stdio.h>

main( )
{
    int yard, foot, inch;

    printf( "Enter next length " );
    scanf( "%d", &yard );

    while ( yard >= 0 ) {
        foot = 3 * yard;
        inch = 36 * yard;
        printf( "\n%d yd =\n", yard );
        printf( "%d ft\n", foot );
        printf( "%d in\n", inch );
        printf( "Enter next length " );
        scanf( "%d", &yard );
    }
```

```
        printf( "*** END OF PROGRAM ***\n" );
}
```

Discussion

In C, all variables must be **defined**. To define a variable in C is to request storage for a particular data type and to give the storage a name. This program begins by defining the variables `yard`, `foot`, and `inch`. Because these variables are defined to be of type `int`, each can hold one integer (one of 0, ±1, ±2, . . .).

To prompt the user to enter a length, we use the function `printf` introduced in Section 1.1. We call the string delimited by double quotation marks a **format string**. Since the format string contains no special characters (e.g., backslash), the statement

```
printf( "Enter next length " );
```

simply writes

```
Enter next length
```

to the video display.

Next, we use the library function `scanf` to read one integer from the keyboard. The function `scanf` also requires a format string. The `scanf` format string describes the type of data read. The descriptor %d says: Interpret the next input value as a decimal integer. Following the format string are the variables, each prefixed by &, in which the values are stored.† Thus the statement

```
scanf( "%d", &yard );
```

says: Read the next value; interpret it as a decimal integer; and store the value in the variable `yard`.

We then encounter the `while` loop. Notice that the body of the `while` loop

```
foot = 3 * yard;
inch = 36 * yard;
printf( "\n%d yd =\n", yard );
printf( "%d ft\n", foot );
printf( "%d in\n", inch );
printf( "Enter next length " );
scanf( "%d", &yard );
```

is enclosed in braces and that a semicolon is *not* used after the right brace. If the body of a `while` loop consists of one statement, the enclosing braces can be omitted.

As long as the condition

```
yard >= 0
```

in the `while` loop is true, the body of the `while` loop executes.

When we execute the body of the `while` loop, we first execute the statement

```
foot = 3 * yard;
```

The assignment operator is =, and the multiplication operator is *; thus, this statement

---

†Certain variables (e.g., pointer variables, to be discussed later) are not prefixed by & in `scanf`; however, all variables to be used in the early chapters (e.g., variables of type `int`) must be prefixed by &.

stores the product of 3 and the value of `yard` in the variable `foot`. Next, we store the product of 36 and the value of `yard` in the variable `inch`.

Next, we use the function `printf` again. However, this time the format string

```
\n%d yd =\n
```

contains the special characters \ and %. As we saw in the previous section, the presence of the characters \n (newline) in a `printf` format string causes the next output to begin in column 1 of the next line. The descriptor %d says: Interpret the variable in `printf` (`yard` in this case) as an integer, and write its value. The next characters

```
yd =
```

have no special meaning and are simply copied to the video display. We then skip again to column 1 of the next line. For example, if the value of `yard` is 2, the statement

```
printf( "\n%d yd =\n", yard );
```

causes the following action: We skip to column 1 of the next line. We write

```
2 yd =
```

and we then skip to column 1 of the next line.

Notice that & is required before variable names in `scanf` but that we do *not* write & before variable names in `printf`. This apparent anomaly will be clarified in Section 2.1.

When we execute the next line

```
printf( "%d ft\n", foot );
```

we write the value of `foot`. We then write

```
ft
```

and conclude by skipping to column 1 of the next line. For example, if the value of `foot` were 6, we would write

```
6 ft
```

and skip to column 1 of the next line.

When we execute the next line

```
printf( "%d in\n", inch );
```

we write the value of `inch`. We then write

```
in
```

and conclude by skipping to column 1 of the next line. For example, if the value of `inch` were 72, we would write

```
72 in
```

and skip to column 1 of the next line.

We then issue the prompt again and use the function `scanf` to read the next value of `yard`. Whenever the user enters a negative integer, the condition

```
yard >= 0
```

in the `while` loop is false, and so the `while` loop terminates. At this point we skip to the statement

```
printf( "*** END OF PROGRAM ***\n" );
```

following the while loop, which writes

```
*** END OF PROGRAM ***
```

Because this is the last statement in the function main, the program terminates.

Long strings may be broken into individual pieces, each delimited by double quotation marks, which the compiler will stick together. For example, the output of the program of Figure 1.2.1 is

```
Life with Mary was like being in a phone
booth with an open umbrella. No matter which
way you turned, you got it in the eye.

from Mary, Mary
```

In addition to >= (greater than or equal to), C provides the relational operators

> greater than
< less than
<= less than or equal to

and equality operators

== equal
!= not equal

```
#include <stdio.h>

main()
{
    printf( "Life with Mary was like being "
            "in a phone\nbooth with an open "
            "umbrella. No matter which\nway "
            "you turned, you got it in the eye.\n\n"
            "from Mary, Mary\n" );
}
```

Figure 1.2.1 A program with a long string.

Exercises†

1. Write a program that reads from the keyboard a weight in pounds, converts the weight to ounces, and writes the converted weight to the video display. It is assumed that the weight is a nonnegative integer. The program is terminated by entering a negative integer.

2. Write a program that prompts the user for integers. When the user enters a negative integer, the program stops reading numbers and writes the sum of all the nonnegative integers entered. Assume that at least one nonnegative integer is entered.

†Solutions to odd-numbered exercises are given in the back of the book.

1.3 Identifiers

When we write a program, we must select names for variables, functions, and so on. **Identifier** is the official word for *name* in a high-level language. An identifier in C must satisfy the following requirements:

- It must start with a letter (A through Z or a through z) or the underscore character (_).
- It must consist of only letters (A through Z or a through z), digits (0 through 9), and the underscore character (_).
- It must not be a keyword. A **keyword** is a word such as int or while that has a special meaning. A complete list of keywords is given in Appendix C.

Example 1.3.1. The following are legal identifiers:

```
total
total_cars
_sum
column3
TOTAL
```

Except for global names, which we will not encounter until Section 7.4, at least the first 31 characters of an identifier are significant, and uppercase characters are distinguished from lowercase characters. Thus total and TOTAL are distinct identifiers. The system typically uses identifiers that have an underscore as the first character. For this reason, we advise not using the underscore as the first character of any user-defined identifier, as there might be a conflict between the user-defined identifier and a system identifier.

Example 1.3.2. The following are *not* legal identifiers:

```
total$              (Illegal character $)
2nd_sum             (Begins with a digit)
long                (Keyword)
second sum          (Cannot use blank as a character)
TOTAL-CARS          (Illegal character −)
```

Exercises

1. Are the identifiers name and NAME different? Explain.

2. What advantages are there in allowing identifiers with long names?

State whether each name in Exercises 3 through 10 is a legal identifier. If the name is not a legal identifier, explain why it is not.

3. sum_of_credits   **4.** _type_of_car

5. while   **6.** SECTION_6

7. bingo-square   **8.** 3_4_87

9. initial tree   **10.** final_#

11. Are the identifiers

```
chapter_3_section_xi_example_3_6
chapter_3_section_xi_example_3_3
```

necessarily distinct? Explain.

1.4 The `while` Statement

We briefly introduced the `while` statement in Section 1.2. In this section, we discuss `while` loops in more detail.

The form of the `while` statement is

> `while` (*expression*)
>   *action*

To execute a `while` statement (see Figure 1.4.1), we first determine whether *expression* is true or false. C requires that *expression* be enclosed in parentheses. If *expression* is true, we execute *action* and return to the top of the loop. We again test *expression*, and if *expression* is true, we execute *action* and return to the top. We repeat this process. But if at any time we are at the top of the loop and *expression* is false, we skip to the statement immediately following *action*. The part of the `while` loop that we have designated *action* consists of one statement without braces or one or more statements enclosed in braces.

> *Example 1.4.1.*   When the program slice
>
> ```
> int x;
> x = 0;
> while ( x != 2 )
>      x = x + 1;
> printf( "x = %d\n", x );
> ```

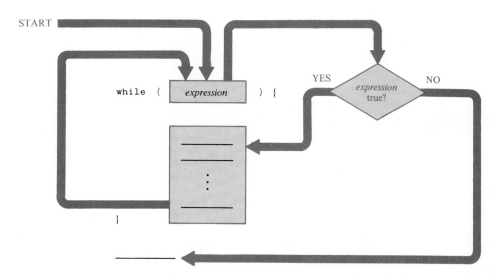

Figure 1.4.1 The `while` statement.

is executed, the output is

```
x = 2
```

The statement

```
x = 0;
```

sets x to 0. Since != is the relational operator "not equal to," the expression x != 2 evaluates to true; thus, we execute the statement

```
x = x + 1;
```

which adds 1 to x. We then return to the top of the while loop. At this point, x is 1. The expression x != 2 is true; thus, we again add 1 to x and return to the top of the while loop. At this point, x is 2. The expression x != 2 is now false; thus, we terminate the while loop. We then execute the statement

```
printf( "x = %d\n", x );
```

which writes

```
x = 2
```

Exercises

1. What is the output?

```
int x;
x = 7;
while ( x >= 0 ) {
      printf( "%d\n", x );
      x = x - 2;
}
```

2. What is the output?

```
int x;
x = 7;
while ( x >= 0 ) {
      x = x - 2;
      printf( "%d\n", x );
}
```

3. What is the output?

```
int x;
x = 7;
while ( x >= 0 )
      x = x - 2;
printf( "%d\n", x );
```

4. What is the output?

```
int x;
```

```
    x = 1;
    while ( x == 1 ) {
        x = x - 1;
        printf( "%d\n", x );
    }
```

5. What is the output?

```
    int x;
    x = 1;
    while ( x == 1 )
        x = x - 1;
        printf( "%d\n", x );
```

6. Where is the syntax error?

```
    while ( x > 0 ) do
        x = x - 1;
    printf( "%d", x );
```

1.5 The do while Statement

The do while statement is similar to the while statement; the only difference is that
the expression controlling the loop is tested at the bottom of the loop. For this reason, the
body of the loop is always executed at least once. The form of the do while statement is

```
    do
            action
    while ( expression );
```

To execute a do while statement (see Figure 1.5.1), we first execute *action*. We then
determine whether *expression* is true or false. If *expression* is true, we return to the top of
the loop and repeat this process. That is, we execute *action* and then determine whether
expression is true or false. If *expression* is true, we return to the top of the loop. Any time
we are at the bottom of the loop and *expression* is false, we skip to the statement immedi-

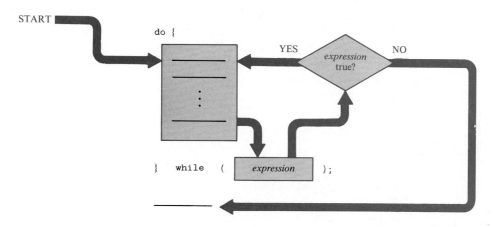

Figure 1.5.1 The do while statement.

ately following `while ( `*expression*` )`. The part of the `do while` loop that we have designated *action* consists of one statement without braces or one or more statements enclosed in braces.

> *Example 1.5.1.*   The `do while` loop is useful whenever the test naturally occurs at the bottom of the loop. Such an example is that of verifying user input. In this situation, the user enters a value and *then* the input is checked. The following segment asks the user for a positive integer and then checks for valid input. If the input is invalid, the user is prompted again to enter a value.

```
do {
     printf( "Enter a positive integer: " );
     scanf( "%d", &response );
} while ( response <= 0 );
```

Exercises

1. What is printed?

```
x = 4;
do {
     x = x - 2;
     printf( "x = %d\n", x );
} while ( x >= 1 );
```

2. Rewrite the segment of Example 1.5.1 using a `while` loop instead of a `do while` loop.

1.6   Sample Application: Computing Income Tax

Problem

New Freedonia has a particularly simple system of taxation. Income under 6000 greenbacks (the basic unit of currency in New Freedonia) is taxed at 30 percent, and income greater than or equal to 6000 greenbacks is taxed at 60 percent. Write a program that reads incomes and prints the taxes due. The program should read incomes until the user signals "end-of-file." Assume that the income is an integer. Drop the fractional part of the tax so that it is written as an integer.

Sample Input/Output

Input is in color; output is in black.

```
1000
Income = 1000 greenbacks
Tax = 300 greenbacks
7000
Income = 7000 greenbacks
Tax = 4200 greenbacks
```

```
2904
Income = 2904 greenbacks
Tax = 871 greenbacks
32067
Income = 32067
Tax = 19240
Exit
```

After the line Tax = 19240, a control character is entered to signal the end of the input file, and in the sample input/output the system prints Exit (see the following Discussion section).

Solution

We use a while loop to read incomes repeatedly. The condition in the while loop is a test for end-of-file. Within the while loop, we test whether the income is above or below 6000 and compute the tax accordingly.

C Implementation

```
/*   This program reads incomes until end-of-file and
     prints the tax due. Income under 6000 greenbacks
     is taxed at 30 percent, and income greater than or
     equal to 6000 greenbacks is taxed at 60 percent.
     We assume that the income is an integer. The tax
     is written as an integer.                       */

#include <stdio.h>

main()
{
     int income, tax;

     while ( scanf( "%d", &income ) != EOF ) {
          printf( "Income = %d greenbacks\n", income );
          if ( income < 6000 )
               tax = 0.3 * income;
          else
               tax = 0.6 * income;
          printf( "Tax = %d greenbacks\n", tax );
     }
}
```

Discussion

The file *stdio.h* contains the definition of the constant EOF. The value of EOF is usually defined to be 0 or −1, but by including *stdio.h*, we get the correct value of EOF for our particular system.

When scanf successfully reads a value, scanf returns a value that is not equal to EOF. In this case, the expression

```
scanf( "%d", &income ) != EOF
```

is true, so we execute the body of the while loop. When scanf encounters the end of the file, scanf returns the value EOF. In this case, the expression

```
scanf( "%d", &income ) != EOF
```

is false, so we terminate the `while` loop.

It is possible to signal the end of the file from the keyboard by typing some control character. In UNIX, control-D signals the end of the file; in VAX/VMS or Turbo C, control-Z is the signal. When end-of-file is signaled from the keyboard, the system writes some characters to the screen to confirm receipt of the control character. For example, in VAX/VMS, when the user types control-Z, the system writes `Exit`; in UNIX, when the user types control-D, the system writes $^\wedge$D; and in MS-DOS, when the user types control-Z, the system writes $^\wedge$Z.

In the `if–else` statement

```
if ( income < 6000 )
      tax = 0.3 * income;
else
      tax = 0.6 * income;
```

if the condition

```
income < 6000
```

is true, we execute the statement

```
tax = 0.3 * income;
```

But if the condition

```
income < 6000
```

is false, we execute the statement

```
tax = 0.6 * income;
```

In either case, we correctly compute the tax.

Notice that the `if` statement does not include the word *then*. Notice also that no semicolon follows the word `else`.

In either of the statements

```
tax = 0.3 * income;
```

or

```
tax = 0.6 * income;
```

the result of the multiplication is a decimal number. However, because the result is assigned to the variable `tax`, which is of type `int`, the fractional part is truncated.

1.7   The `if` Statement

We introduced the `if` statement in Section 1.6. In this section, we discuss the `if` statement in more detail.

The `if` statement is used to execute conditionally a segment of code. One form of the `if` statement is

```
if ( expression )
      action
```

As with the while statement, *expression* must be enclosed in parentheses. To execute an if statement (see Figure 1.7.1), we first determine whether *expression* is true or false. If *expression* is true, we execute *action* and proceed to the statement immediately following *action*. But if *expression* is false, we do *not* execute *action* but skip it and proceed to the statement immediately following. The part of the if statement that we have designated *action* consists of one statement without braces or one or more statements enclosed in braces.

Example 1.7.1. When the program slice

```
int code;
code = 1;
if ( code == 1 )
     printf( "The water was too warm\n" );
printf( "*** End of fishing excuses ***" );
```

is executed, the output is

```
The water was too warm
*** End of fishing excuses ***
```

Recall that to test for equality, we use == and *not* =. Using a single equals sign = when a double equals sign == is intended is a frequent error and a difficult one to detect. A single equals sign is the assignment operator; the double equals sign is the test for equality. It is syntactically correct to write

```
if ( x = 1 )
     .
     .
     .
```

but the way the system interprets this command is usually not what the user intended (see Example 2.5.7).

Example 1.7.2 shows an if statement in which the action consists of multiple statements.

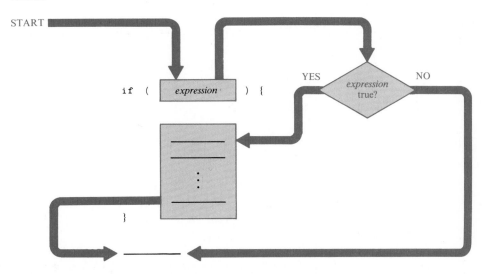

Figure 1.7.1 The if statement.

Example 1.7.2.   When the program slice

```
int code;
code = 1;
if ( code == 1 ) {
    printf( "The water was too warm\n" );
    printf( "The waters were all fished out\n" );
    printf( "It was too late in the season\n" );
}
printf( "*** End of fishing excuses ***" );
```

is executed, the output is

```
The water was too warm
The waters were all fished out
It was too late in the season
*** End of fishing excuses ***
```

The other form of the if statement is

```
if ( expression )
        action 1
else
        action 2
```

When this form of the if statement is executed (see Figure 1.7.2), we first determine whether *expression* is true or false. If *expression* is true, we execute *action 1* and proceed to the statement immediately following *action 2*; in this case, we do *not* execute *action 2*. But if *expression* is false, we execute *action 2* and proceed to the statement immediately following it; in this case, we do *not* execute *action 1*. Either *action 1* or *action 2* consists of one statement without braces or one or more statements enclosed in braces.

Example 1.7.3.   When the program slice

```
int code;
code = 1;
if ( code == 1 )
    printf( "The water was too warm\n" );
else
    printf( "The waters were all fished out\n" );
printf( "*** End of fishing excuses ***" );
```

is executed, the output is

```
The water was too warm
*** End of fishing excuses ***
```

Example 1.7.4.   When the program slice

```
int code;
code = 2;
if ( code != 2 ) {
    printf( "The water was too warm\n" );
    printf( "The waters were all fished out\n" );
}
```

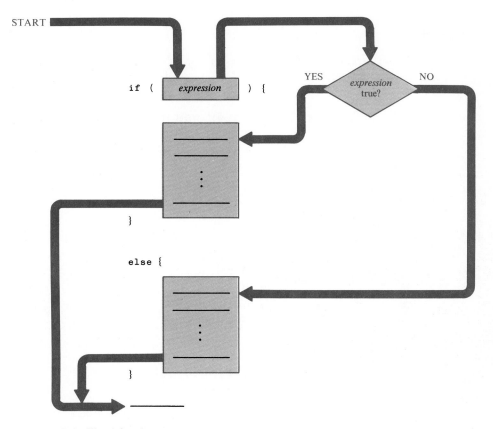

Figure 1.7.2 The if—else statement.

```
else {
     printf( "It was too late in the season\n" );
     printf( "The bait was wrong\n" );
}
printf( "*** End of fishing excuses ***" );
```

is executed, the output is

```
It was too late in the season
The bait was wrong
*** End of fishing excuses ***
```

Because if or if—else is itself a statement, if or if—else can be the action of another if or if—else statement.

Example 1.7.5. The program slice

```
if ( no_fish == 1 )
     if ( code < 2 )
          printf( "The water was too warm\n" );
     else
          printf( "The waters were all fished out\n" );
```

is interpreted as one "outer" if statement with one action statement that happens to be an if—else statement. That is, this segment is of the form

```
if ( no_fish == 1 )
    action
```

where *action* is the *single* statement (an if-else statement is considered to be a single statement):

```
if ( code < 2 )
    printf( "The water was too warm\n" );
else
    printf( "The waters were all fished out\n" );
```

When we execute

```
int no_fish, code;
no_fish = 1;
code = 2;
if ( no_fish == 1 )
    if ( code < 2 )
        printf( "The water was too warm\n" );
    else
        printf( "The waters were all fished out\n" );
printf( "*** End of fish story ***" );
```

the output is

```
The waters were all fished out
*** End of fish story ***
```

We first set no_fish to 1 and code to 2. Because no_fish == 1 is true, we execute the action statement

```
if ( code < 2 )
    printf( "The water was too warm\n" );
else
    printf( "The waters were all fished out\n" );
```

Because the expression code < 2 is false, we execute the statement

```
printf( "The waters were all fished out\n" );
```

following else. We then execute

```
printf( "*** End of fish story ***");
```

The compiler is insensitive to indentation. Thus if we rewrite the preceding program slice as

```
int no_fish, code;
no_fish = 1;
code = 2;
if ( no_fish == 1 )
    if ( code < 2 )
        printf( "The water was too warm\n" );
else
    printf( "The waters were all fished out\n" );
printf( "*** End of fish story ***" );
```

the output is still

```
The waters were all fished out
*** End of fish story ***
```

The indentation of the preceding slice implies that the programmer intended that if no_fish == 1 is true, we are to execute

```
if ( code < 2 )
    printf( "The water was too warm\n" );
```

and if no_fish == 1 is false, we are to execute

```
printf( "The waters were all fished out\n" );
```

To achieve this result, we must use braces and write

```
int no_fish, code;
no_fish = 1;
code = 2;
if ( no_fish == 1 ) {
    if ( code < 2 )
        printf( "The water was too warm\n" );
}
else
    printf( "The waters were all fished out\n" );
printf( "*** End of fish story ***" );
```

The output of the preceding program slice is

```
*** End of fish story ***
```

Example 1.7.6. The program slice

```
int no_fish;
no_fish = 1;
if ( no_fish == 1 )
    printf( "The water was too warm\n" );
else ;
    printf( "The waters were all fished out\n" );
```

prints

```
The water was too warm
The waters were all fished out
```

The semicolon after else is probably a logical error. In any case, the else action statement consists of the semicolon all by itself:

```
;
```

We call the statement that consists of a lonely semicolon a **null statement**. When a null statement is executed, nothing happens. Consider now what happens when the preceding program slice executes. The condition no_fish == 1 is true, so we execute the statement between if and else. The output is

```
The water was too warm
```

We skip the statement (namely, the null statement) that follows `else`. We then continue by executing the statement

```
printf( "The waters were all fished out\n" );
```

which prints

```
The waters were all fished out
```

We continue our discussion of the `if` statement in the following section.

Exercises

1. What is the output?

```
int x, y;
x = 3;
y = 5;
if ( x < 2 )
    printf( "%d\n", x );
else
    printf( "%d\n", y );
```

2. What is the output?

```
int x, y;
x = 3;
y = 5;
if ( x > 2 )
    printf( "%d\n", x );
else
    printf( "%d\n", y );
```

3. What is the output?

```
int x, y;
x = 3;
y = 5;
if ( x == 3 )
    printf( "%d\n", x );
else ;
    printf( "%d\n", y );
```

4. Where is the syntax error?

```
if ( x >= 2 ) then
    printf( "%d\n", x );
```

5. Where is the syntax error?

```
if x >= 2
    printf( "%d\n", x );
```

6. What is the output?

```
code = 2;
if ( code == 1 ) {
```

```
            printf( "Mathematician\n" );
            if ( code == 2 )
                printf( "Artist\n" );
            else
                printf( "Computer Scientist\n" );
    }
    else
            printf( "Public Relations Representative\n" );
```

7. What is the output?

```
    code = 1;
    if ( code == 1 ) {
            printf( "Mathematician\n" );
            if ( code == 2 )
                printf( "Artist\n" );
            else
                printf( "Computer Scientist\n" );
    }
    else
            printf( "Public Relations Representative\n" );
```

1.8 More on the if Statement

By nesting if–else statements, we obtain a particularly useful multiway decision structure. We discuss this use of the if statement in this section.

Nested if–else statements are typically written

```
    if ( expression 1 )
        action 1
    else if ( expression 2 )
        action 2
    else if ( expression 3 )
        action 3
        .
        .
        .
    else if ( expression n )
        action n
```

To execute this construct (see Figure 1.8.1), we find the *first* expression that is true, if any. If *expression i* is the first true condition, we execute *action i* and next the statement following *action n*. Only *action i* is executed; all other *actions* are skipped. If no expression is true, no *action* is executed; we simply skip to the statement following *action n*.

Example 1.8.1. The segment

```
    int code;
    code = 2;
    if ( code == 1 )
            printf( "The bait was wrong\n" );
```

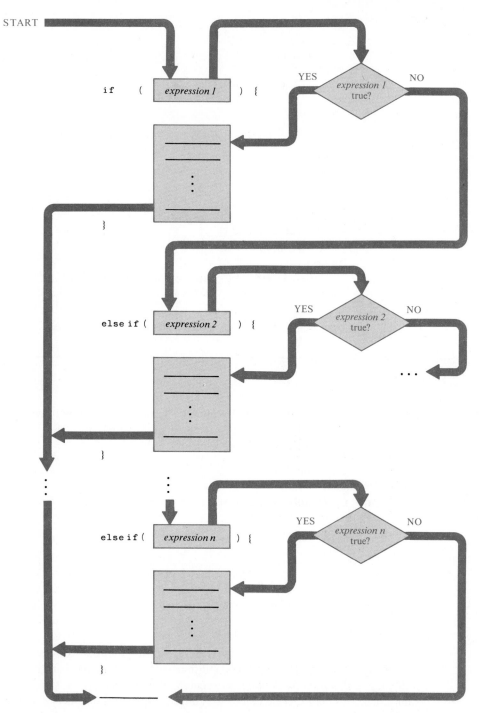

Figure 1.8.1 The if else-if ... else-if construct.

```
    else if ( code == 2 )
        printf( "The water was too warm\n" );
    else if ( code <= 3 )
        printf( "The waters were all fished out\n" );
    printf( "*** End of fishing excuses ***" );
```

prints

```
    The water was too warm
    *** End of fishing excuses ***
```

After setting code to 2, we find that the first true expression is code == 2. Thus we execute the statement

```
    printf( "The water was too warm\n" );
```

We do *not* execute the statement

```
    printf( "The waters were all fished out\n" );
```

even though the expression code <= 3 is also true. We execute only the action that follows the *first* true expression. We then execute

```
    printf( "*** End of fishing excuses ***" );
```

Another useful form of if–else statements is

```
    if ( expression 1 )
        action 1
    else if ( expression 2 )
        action 2
    else if ( expression 3 )
        action 3
            .
            .
            .
    else if ( expression n )
        action n
    else
        action
```

To execute this construct (see Figure 1.8.2), we find the first expression that is true, if any. If *expression i* is the first true condition, we execute *action i* and next the statement following *action*. Only *action i* is executed; all other *action*s are skipped. If no expression is true, we execute *action* and next the statement following *action*. *Only action is executed*; all other *action*s are skipped.

Example 1.8.2.   The segment

```
    int code;
    code = 10;
    if ( code == 1 )
        printf( "The bait was wrong\n" );
    else if ( code == 2 )
        printf( "The water was too warm\n" );
    else if ( code <= 3 )
        printf( "The waters were all fished out\n" );
```

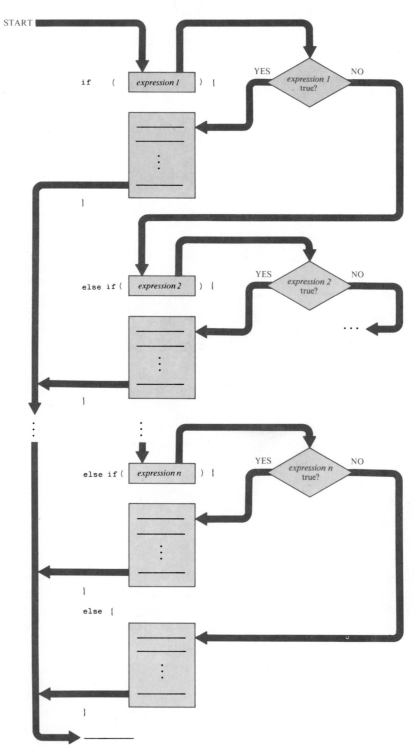

Figure 1.8.2 The if else−if ... else−if else construct.

```
else                                      te in the season\n" );
    pri                                       excuses ***" );
prints
    It                                    on
    *** End of fishing excuses ***
```

After setting code to 10, we find that all of the expressions are false. Thus we execute the statement

```
printf( "It was too late in the season\n" );
```

following the final else. We do *not* execute any other action statements. We then execute

```
printf( "*** End of fishing excuses ***" );
```

In an if else–if else–if···else–if else construct such as that of Example 1.8.2, the action following else at the end is called the **default** action. If none of the expressions is true, the default action is executed. By including a default action, we are guaranteed that *some* action is executed. This fact is often useful in debugging programs and making programs crash resistant.

Exercises

1. What is printed?

```
int x = 5;
if ( x < 2 )
    printf( "%d", x );
else if ( x < 4 )
    printf( "%d", 2 * x );
else if ( x < 6 )
    printf( "%d", 3 * x );
else
    printf( "%d", 4 * x );
```

2. What is printed?

```
int x = 6;
if ( x < 2 )
    printf( "%d", x );
else if ( x < 4 )
    printf( "%d", 2 * x );
else if ( x < 6 )
    printf( "%d", 3 * x );
else
    printf( "%d", 4 * x );
```

3. Do the two code fragments always produce the same output given the same input? Explain.

```
if ( code == 1 )                        if ( code == 1 )
    printf("Freshman\n");                    printf("Freshman\n");
else if ( code == 2 )                   if ( code == 2 )
    printf("Sophomore\n");                   printf("Sophomore\n");
else if ( code == 3 )                   if ( code == 3 )
    printf("Junior\n");                      printf("Junior\n");
```

If the fragments are logically the same, is one form preferable to the other? Explain.

4. Do the two code fragments always produce the same output, provided that `code` is restricted to one of the three values 1, 2, or 3? Explain.

```
if ( code <= 1 )                        if ( code == 1 )
    printf("Freshman\n");                    printf("Freshman\n");
else if ( code <= 2 )                   if ( code == 2 )
    printf("Sophomore\n");                   printf("Sophomore\n");
else if ( code <= 3 )                   if ( code == 3 )
    printf("Junior\n");                      printf("Junior\n");
```

If the fragments are logically the same, is one form preferable to the other? Explain.

5. Do the two code fragments always produce the same output provided that `code` is restricted to one of the three values 1, 2, or 3? Explain.

```
if ( code <= 1 )                        if ( code <= 1 )
    printf("Freshman\n");                    printf("Freshman\n");
else if ( code <= 2 )                   if ( code <= 2 )
    printf("Sophomore\n");                   printf("Sophomore\n");
else if ( code <= 3 )                   if ( code <= 3 )
    printf("Junior\n");                      printf("Junior\n");
```

If the fragments are logically the same, is one form preferable to the other? Explain.

6. Do the two code fragments always produce the same output given the same input? Explain.

```
if ( code == 1 )                        if ( code == 1 )
    printf("Freshman\n");                    printf("Freshman\n");
else if ( code == 2 )                   if ( code == 2 )
    printf("Sophomore\n");                   printf("Sophomore\n");
else if ( code == 3 )                   if ( code == 3 )
    printf("Junior\n");                      printf("Junior\n");
else                                    else
    printf("Senior\n");                      printf("Senior\n");
```

If the fragments are logically the same, is one form preferable to the other? Explain.

1.9 Redirecting Input and Output

We frequently refer to **standard input** and **standard output**. Normally, standard input refers to the keyboard, and standard output refers to the video display. The programs in the previous sections read from the standard input and write to the standard output.

Modern operating systems consider the keyboard and video display as files. This is reasonable, as the system can read from the keyboard just as it can read from a disk or tape file. Similarly, the system can write to the video display just as it can write to a disk or tape file. Suppose that, in the tax program of Section 1.6, we decided to read the incomes from the disk file *incomes.dat* instead of from the keyboard. We could still use our tax program if we told the system to replace input from the keyboard, considered now as a file, by input from another file, namely, the disk file *incomes.dat*. Every system has some method of redefining the standard input and the standard output. This process of changing the standard input or standard output is called **input redirection** or **output redirection**.

Example 1.9.1 **Redirection in MS-DOS or UNIX.** Input or output redirection in MS-DOS or UNIX is effortless. We use < to redirect the input and > to redirect the output. Suppose that the executable version of the tax program of Section 1.6 is called *tax* (UNIX) or *tax.exe* (MS-DOS). Now

```
% tax <incomes.dat
```

executes the program `tax` using as input the file *incomes.dat*. (We are using % as the system prompt.) Because the output was not redirected, the output appears on the video display. To redirect both the input and the output, we write

```
% tax <incomes.dat >out.dat
```

Now the program `tax` uses as input the file *incomes.dat*. The output is placed in the file *out.dat*. To redirect only the output, we write

```
% tax >out.dat
```

Now the program `tax` uses the keyboard as input. The output is placed in the file *out.dat*.

Example 1.9.2 **Redirection in VAX/VMS.** To redirect the input in VAX/VMS, we first issue the command

```
$ define/user sys$input infile.dat
```

and then run the program. (We are using $ as the system prompt.) The standard input is then replaced by the file *infile.dat*. To redirect the output in VAX/VMS, we first issue the command

```
$ define/user sys$output outfile.dat
```

and then run the program. The standard output is then replaced by *outfile.dat*. To redirect both the input and the output, we first issue the commands

```
$ define/user sys$input infile.dat
$ define/user sys$output outfile.dat
```

and then run the program. The standard input is then replaced by *infile.dat*, and the standard output is then replaced by *outfile.dat*.

Suppose that the executable version of the tax program of Section 1.6 is called *tax.exe*. Now

```
$ define/user sys$input incomes.dat
$ run tax
```

executes the program `tax` using as input the file *incomes.dat*. Because the output was not redirected, the output appears on the video display. To redirect both the input and the output, we issue the commands

```
$ define/user sys$input incomes.dat
$ define/user sys$output out.dat
$ run tax
```

Now the program `tax` uses as input the file *incomes.dat*. The output is placed in the file *out.dat*. To redirect only the output, we issue the commands

```
$ define/user sys$output out.dat
$ run tax
```

Now the program `tax` uses the keyboard as input. The output is placed in the file *out.dat*.

Exercises

1. Assume a UNIX environment. Write a command that executes the file *convert* using the input file *data.dat* and the output file *outfile.dat*.

2. Assume an MS-DOS environment. Write a command that executes the file *convert.exe* using the input file *data.dat* and the output file *outfile.dat*.

3. Assume a VAX/VMS environment. Write commands that execute the file *convert.exe* using the input file *data.dat* and the output file *outfile.dat*.

1.10   Files

In Section 1.9 we saw that one way to manipulate files in a program is to redirect the standard input and output. It is also possible to manipulate directly files within a program. This section introduces handling files in a program. In Chapter 8 we discuss this topic in much more detail.

Each file to be handled in a program must be associated with a **file pointer**. The file pointer is a variable that tells the system where to find the information necessary to read from or write to the file. To define file pointers, such as `fin` and `fout`, we write

```
FILE *fin, *fout;
```

(The star * designates a pointer. Pointers are discussed in Chapter 6. `FILE` is a structure defined in *stdio.h*. Structures are discussed in Chapter 9. For now, just follow the syntax.)

To open a file, we use the library function `fopen`. For example, to open the file *infile.dat* for reading, we write

```
fin = fopen( "infile.dat", "r" );
```

after first defining `fin` as a file pointer, as described previously. To open the file *outfile.dat* for writing, we write

```
fout = fopen( "outfile.dat", "w" );
```

after first defining `fout` as a file pointer, as described previously. To read from and write to files using file pointers, we replace `scanf` by `fscanf` and `printf` by `fprintf`. The function `fscanf` is the same as `scanf` except that the first argument is the file pointer that specifies the file to be read. The second argument is the format string, and the remaining arguments are the variables. The function `fprintf` is the same as `printf` except that the first argument is the file pointer that specifies the file to be written. The second argument is the format string, and the remaining arguments are the variables.

To show how file pointers, fscanf, and fprintf work, we rewrite the tax program of Section 1.6. This revised version reads incomes from the file *incomes.dat* and writes the output to the file *out.dat*.

```
/*    This program reads incomes from the file incomes.dat
      until end-of-file and writes the taxes due
      to the file out.dat. Income under 6000 greenbacks
      is taxed at 30 percent, and income greater
      than or equal to 6000 greenbacks is taxed at 60
      percent. We assume that the income is an integer.
      The tax is written as an integer.             */

#include <stdio.h>

main()
{
        int income, tax;
        FILE *fin, *fout;
        fin = fopen( "incomes.dat", "r" );
        fout = fopen( "out.dat", "w" );

        while ( fscanf( fin, "%d", &income ) != EOF ) {
            fprintf( fout, "Income = %d greenbacks\n",
                    income );
            if ( income < 6000 )
                    tax = 0.3 * income;
            else
                    tax = 0.6 * income;
            fprintf( fout, "Tax = %d greenbacks\n", tax );
        }
}
```

Because the function fscanf (and scanf, too) skips over white space (newlines, tabs, and blanks), the integers to be read by fscanf can be placed in the file *incomes.dat* in any way whatever, as long as at least one white space separates one integer from the next. Several white space characters can separate two integers. For example, the file *incomes.dat* could be

```
8900          6400
        2500
   32000          23600   9000
```

To the reader who wonders about closing files, two comments are in order. First, when a program terminates, each file that was opened is automatically closed. Second, a file can be closed in a program by using the function fclose. To close the files that we opened in the preceding program, we would write

```
fclose( fin );
fclose( fout );
```

After we execute

```
fclose( fp );
```

the file pointer `fp` is no longer associated with any file and the input/output buffer is flushed.

Exercises

1. Write statements that open the file *infile.dat* for reading.
2. Write statements that open the file *outfile.dat* for writing.
3. Write statements that write

   ```
   Delinquent Taxpayer
   ```

   to the file *output.dat*.
4. Write statements that read an integer from the file associated with the file pointer `fp1` into the `int` variable `id_numb`.
5. Modify the program of Section 1.2 so that it reads lengths from the file *length.dat* and writes the converted lengths to the file *cvt.dat*. Remove the prompts. Use EOF to read all the values in *length.dat*.
6. Write a program that reads weights in pounds from the file *weight.dat*, converts the weights to ounces, and writes the converted weights to the file *out.dat*. It is assumed that the weights are nonnegative integers. Use EOF to read all the values in *weight.dat*.
7. Write a program that reads integers from the file *scores.dat*. After all the integers have been read, the program writes the sum of all the nonnegative integers to the video display. Assume that the file *scores.dat* contains at least one integer.

Changes from Traditional C

1. In traditional C, fewer system header files, such as *stdio.h*, are available, and in some cases, their use is optional. Standard C specifies a header file to be included for each system function (see Appendix E). Each system constant, such as EOF and FILE, requires that a system header file be included (in traditional or standard C).
2. Traditional C requires that the pound sign that introduces a preprocessor directive be written in column 1. This requirement has been dropped in standard C.
3. Automatic concatenation of string constants is new.
4. The requirement that at least the first 31 characters of an identifier be significant has been added. C has always distinguished between uppercase and lowercase characters, however.

Common Programming Errors

1. An ampersand (&) is required before each (nonpointer) variable in `scanf`, but not in `printf`. For this reason,

   ```
   int x;
   scanf( "%d", x ); /***** ERROR *****/
   ```

   is an error.

2. To provide a proper interface to library input and output functions, the line

```
#include <stdio.h>
```

should appear before `main`.

3. It is an error to use EOF in a program without the line

```
#include <stdio.h>
```

4. It is an error to use `FILE` in a program without the line

```
#include <stdio.h>
```

5. The `while` statement does not include the word `do`. For this reason, it is a logical error to write

```
while ( condition ) do /***** ERROR *****/
     action
```

6. The `if` statement does not include the word `then`. For this reason, it is an error to write

```
if ( condition ) then /***** ERROR *****/
     action
```

7. In the `if` statement, the condition must be enclosed in parentheses. For this reason, it is an error to write

```
if condition /***** ERROR *****/
     action
```

8. In the `if` statement, no semicolon follows the word `else`. For this reason, it is a logical error to write

```
if ( condition )
     action 1
else ;              /***** PROBABLE ERROR *****/
     action 2
```

9. Using a single equals sign = when a double equals sign == is intended is a logical error. It is syntactically correct to write

```
if ( x = 1 )    /***** PROBABLE ERROR *****/
      .
      .
      .
```

but the way the system interprets this command is usually not what the user intended.

Programming Exercises

In Exercises 1.1 through 1.7, the input is read from the standard input, and the output is written to the standard output.

1.1. Write a program that reads a list of dry measures in pints until end-of-file and then converts each measure into quarts and pecks.

1.2. Write a program that reads positive integers m and n and then prints m^n.

1.3. Write a program that reads integers until end-of-file and then prints the largest and smallest values.

1.4. Write a program that reads integers until end-of-file and then prints the largest and second largest values.

1.5. Write a program that reads integers until end-of-file and then prints Yes if the numbers do not decrease and No otherwise. *Examples:*

If the input is

```
  -6   0   14   14   27
```

the output is

```
  Yes
```

If the input is

```
  -8   0   3   1   7   29
```

the output is

```
  No
```

1.6. Write a program that reads a list of integer test scores until end-of-file and then prints each test score together with Pass, if the score is greater than or equal to 60, and Fail otherwise.

1.7. Write a program that reads integers until end-of-file and then prints the maximum sum of consecutive values. *Example:*

If the input is

```
  27   6   -50   21   -3   14   16   -8   42   33   -21   9
```

the output is

```
  115
```

the sum of

```
  21   -3   14   16   -8   42   33
```

If all of the numbers in the input are negative, the maximum sum of consecutive values is defined to be 0.

1.8. Rewrite the programs of Exercises 1.1 through 1.7. Read from and write to files that are opened in the program.

Variables, Operators, and Control Flow

2

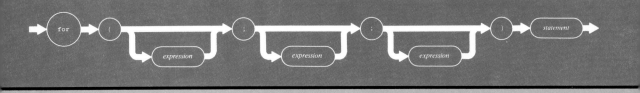

2.1   Cells, the `sizeof` Operator, and the Address Operator
2.2   Characters and Integers
2.3   Real Variables
2.4   Arithmetic Operations
2.5   Relational and Logical Operators and the Assignment Operator
2.6   Sample Application: Statistical Measures
2.7   The `for` Statement and the Comma Operator
2.8   The Operators ++ and --
2.9   Sample Application: Printing a Bar Graph
      Changes from Traditional C
      Common Programming Errors
      Programming Exercises

In this chapter we discuss data types for characters, integers, and real numbers. In addition, we examine several operators, some of which were briefly mentioned in Chapter 1, and we introduce the `for` statement.

2.1 Cells, the `sizeof` Operator, and the Address Operator

Programs manipulate data that ultimately are stored in the computer's memory. A **cell** is a section of memory that can store one data item of a particular type at a time. (The term *cell* is not a keyword in C.) For example, certain cells may hold integers. Other cells may hold real numbers—numbers with decimal points such as -67.3, 9020.33, $68.$, and 47.2003.

When we define a variable, a cell is allocated to hold items of the type specified. For example, if we write

```
int i;
```

one cell capable of holding an integer is allocated. We draw a cell as a rectangular box and write its name to the left. Figure 2.1.1 shows the result of defining the variable i of type `int`. We show a data item stored in a cell within the box that represents the cell. For example, Figure 2.1.2 shows the result of defining the variable i of type `int` and executing the assignment statement

```
i = 4;
```

It is possible to define and initialize simultaneously a variable by writing

```
int i = 4;
```

This definition and initialization also result in the situation shown in Figure 2.1.2. We can create several variables by writing

```
int i, j, k;
```

The result is shown in Figure 2.1.3.

Although a cell holds one data item at a time, it has a **size** that determines how many distinct items of the data type may be stored in the cell. For example, in some implementations, a particular integer cell has a size of eight bits. Because there are 256 eight-bit strings, such a cell can store 256 different integers (one at a time). In some implementations, these 256 combinations of bits are interpreted as the integers from 0 to 255 inclusive; in other implementations, these 256 combinations of bits are interpreted as the integers from -128 to 127 inclusive. We often refer to the set of all possible values of a data type as its **range**.

C measures storage in bytes. C *defines* one **byte** to be the amount of memory required to store one character (e.g., uppercase R, the symbol $, etc.). Fortunately, most machines also define byte in the same way, and so the terminology coincides.

C provides the `sizeof` operator, whose value is the amount of storage required by an object. (`sizeof` is a keyword.) `sizeof` is *not* a function whose value is determined at

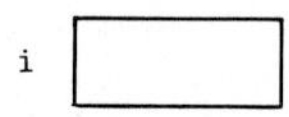

i [   ]

Figure 2.1.1 Allocating one cell to hold an `int`.

i [4   ]

Figure 2.1.2 Executing the assignment statement i = 4;

run time but, rather, an *operator* whose value is determined by the compiler. More precisely, the value of

sizeof (*object*)

is the amount of memory in bytes required to store *object*. A cell of type char (to be discussed in detail in Section 2.2) can hold one character; therefore, on any C system the value of

sizeof (char)

is 1. The values of sizeof for other data types vary from system to system. For example, in VAX-11 C, the value of sizeof (int) is 4, whereas in Turbo C, the value of sizeof (int) is 2. The sizeof operator tells us that in VAX-11 C, an int cell occupies four bytes but that in Turbo C, an int cell occupies only two bytes.

If k is a variable (i.e., the name of a cell), &k is the **address** or location of the cell in memory. We call & the **address operator**.

Example 2.1.1. The definition

int k = 8;

allocates a cell named k and initializes the cell to 8. Suppose that the address of the cell happens to be 6941 (see Figure 2.1.4). Then

- The name of the cell is k.
- The cell contains 8, or equivalently, the value of k is 8.
- The address of the cell is 6941, or equivalently, the value of &k is 6941.

The function scanf reads data and stores them in memory. In order to store data, scanf must be given the addresses of the cells in which the data are to be deposited. For this reason, scanf requires the address operator with its variables. On the other hand, to write data stored in simple variables (e.g., the int variable k in Example 2.1.1), we pass printf the variable rather than its address. All of these topics are explored thoroughly in Chapters 4 and 6.

Exercises

1. In an implementation in which certain cells of type integer can hold six bits, how many integers can be represented?
2. Assuming the situation of Exercise 1, if we represent consecutive integers starting with 0, which integers are represented?
3. Assuming the situation of Exercise 1, if we represent consecutive integers starting with −32, which integers are represented?

i [   ]   j [   ]   k [   ]

Figure 2.1.3 Allocating three cells to hold ints.

6941

Figure 2.1.4 A cell, its name, its contents, and its address.

2.2   Characters and Integers

The definition

```
char c;
```

creates one cell large enough to store one character. To store lowercase x in the variable c, we can write

```
c = 'x';
```

Notice that the character referenced is enclosed in single quotation marks. To print a character using the function `printf`, we use the format descriptor %c.

Example 2.2.1.   The program

```
#include <stdio.h>
main( )
{
    char d;
    d = 'x';
    printf( "The character is: %c.", d );
}
```

prints

```
The character is: x.
```

The function `scanf` can be used with the format descriptor %c to read one character. In this case, `scanf` reads the *next character*. The behavior of `scanf` with the %c format descriptor differs from the situation when we use the %d format descriptor. When we use the %d format descriptor, we skip white space until an integer is found. But we do *not* skip any white space when we use the %c format descriptor; the next character, white space or not, is read. Example 2.2.2 illustrates.

Example 2.2.2.   For the input

```
97 354
```

the program

```
#include <stdio.h>
main( )
{
    char d1, d2, d3, d4;
    int x;
    scanf( "%d%c%c%c%c", &x, &d1, &d2, &d3, &d4 );
```

```
        printf( "%d%c%c%c%c", x, d1, d3, d2, d4 );
    }
```

prints

```
97 534
```

The format descriptor for the variable x is %d; thus, after the white space is skipped, the next integer (namely, 97) is read into x. The format descriptor for the variable d1 is %c; thus, the next character (namely, blank) is read into d1. Then the next character, 3, is read into d2; the next character, 5, is read into d3; and the next character, 4, is read into d4. The printf statement first prints 97, the value of the variable x, after which the values of the variables d1, d3, d2, and d4 (blank, 5, 3, and 4) are printed.

For scanf to work properly, when we use the %c format descriptor, the corresponding argument must be the address of a char, and when we use the %d format descriptor, the corresponding argument must be the address of an int. It is a logical error to write, for example,

```
    int i;
    scanf( "%c", &i ); /***** ERROR *****/
```

(see Exercise 11).

To understand exactly how the data type char works, it is essential to realize that characters are represented internally as integers. To represent characters using integers, a table has been created that gives the correspondence between integers and characters. The most common methods of representing characters are known as **ASCII** (American Standard Code for Information Interchange) and **EBCDIC** (Extended Binary Coded Decimal Interchange Code). As an example, the decimal number 76 represents the character L in ASCII and the character < in EBCDIC. The complete tables for both ASCII and EBCDIC are given in Appendix A.

Assuming that the ASCII system is being used and that the variable c is of type char, the assignment statement

```
    c = 'L';
```

internally assigns c the integer value 76. Using the format descriptor %c with scanf says: Store the ASCII code of the next character in the input in the next variable. Using the format descriptor %c with printf says: Print the character whose ASCII code is stored in the next variable (see Figure 2.2.1).

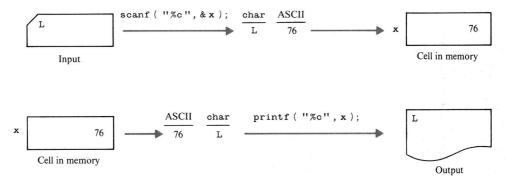

Figure 2.2.1 Reading and writing chars using scanf and printf.

Example 2.2.3.   The program

```
#include <stdio.h>
main( )
{
    char d;
    d = 76;
    printf( "%c", d );
}
```

prints L if ASCII is used and < if EBCDIC is used. The assignment statement

```
d = 76;
```

assigns the integer value 76 to d. The %c format descriptor in the print f statement causes the character corresponding to the value 76 to be printed.

The function print f can print a char variable ch or an int variable i using either %c or %d as the format descriptor. If we use %c, we print the character whose code is ch or i. If we use %d, we print the decimal value of ch or i. The reason that printf (unlike scanf) can interchange char and int is that the system converts char to int before passing the value to printf. Whether we start with char or int, printf receives an int.

Example 2.2.4.   The output of the program of Example 2.2.3 does not change if we define d as int rather than char; the format descriptor %c in printf still says: Print the character whose integer code is stored in the next variable.

Example 2.2.5.   Assuming that ASCII is used, the program

```
#include <stdio.h>
main( )
{
    char d;
    d = 'L';
    printf( "%c %d", d, d );
}
```

prints

```
L 76
```

The assignment statement

```
d = 'L';
```

assigns the character L to d. Internally, the ASCII code 76 is assigned to d. In the printf statement, the first format descriptor %c says: Print the character whose ASCII code is stored in the variable d; L is written. The second format descriptor %d says: Interpret the next variable d as an integer and print the integer; 76 is written.

There is a significant difference between '0' and 0 (zero). On an ASCII system, the code

```
char c, d;
c = '0';
d = 0;
```

assigns c the value decimal 48 (the ASCII value of the character 0) and d the value decimal 0. In EBCDIC, the same code assigns c the value decimal 240 (the EBCDIC value of the character 0) and d the value decimal 0. Thus the assignment statement

```
c = '0';
```

finds the integer code for the character 0 by consulting the appropriate table of character codes (ASCII, EBCDIC, or some other table) and assigns that value to the variable c. By contrast, the assignment statement

```
d = 0;
```

simply assigns the value decimal 0 to the variable d; the system does not have to consult any table of character codes.

The codes of certain special characters are given in Figure 2.2.2. (The complete list of special characters is given in Appendix C.) In addition, we can write ' \– ' where – is one, two, or three octal digits or ' \x– ' where – is one or two hexadecimal digits. The hexadecimal symbols for 10 through 15 may be written in either uppercase or lowercase. For example, if we write

```
c = '\134';
```

the (octal) value 134 is stored in c. Assuming ASCII representation, if we then execute

```
printf( "%c", c );
```

we print the backslash

```
\
```

because the code for the character \ is octal 134. (The notation ' \0 ' is a special case.) If we write

```
c = '\x5d';
```

the (hexadecimal) value 5d is stored in c. Assuming ASCII representation, if we then execute

```
printf( "%c", c );
```

we print the right bracket

```
]
```

because the code for the character] is hexadecimal 5d.

Even though the constants in Figure 2.2.2 contain more than one symbol between the single quotation marks, each has *one* integer value and represents *one* character. For example, ' \t ' represents the single tab character whose ASCII decimal code is 9. The notation ' \t ' designates a single character—tab—even though it contains a backslash and a lowercase t.

The following table shows how the printer reacts to the special characters given in Figure 2.2.2 when each is printed using the printf function with the %c format descriptor:

Value of c	Action When We Execute printf("%c", c);
'\a'	Bell rings. Printer prints nothing.
'\b'	Printer moves left one column.
'\f'	Printer skips to column 1, line 1, of next page.
'\n'	Printer skips to column 1 of the next line.
'\t'	Printer skips to next tab position.
'\0'	Printer prints nothing. (The null character is unprintable.)
'\\'	Printer prints one backslash \.
'\''	Printer prints one single quotation mark '.

Constant	Interpretation	ASCII (decimal)	EBCDIC (decimal)
'\a'	bell	7	47
'\b'	backspace	8	22
'\f'	form feed	12	12
'\n'	newline	10	21
'\t'	tab	9	5
'\0'	null	0	0
'\\'	\ (backslash)	92	177
'\''	' (single quote)	39	125

Figure 2.2.2 Codes of special characters.

The importance of the null character '\0' derives not from the action when it is printed (after all, it is unprintable) but, rather, from its use as a terminator in a data structure such as a string (see Section 5.4).

Example 2.2.6.   The program

```
#include <stdio.h>
main( )
{
        char d1, d2, d3, d4, d5, d6;
        d1 = 'x';
        d2 = '\t';
        d3 = '\\';
        d4 = 'x';
        d5 = '\n';
        d6 = '\'';
        printf( "%c%c%c%c%c%c", d1, d2, d3, d4, d5, d6 );
}
```

prints

```
x       \x
'
```

A reasonable question is, "If variables of type int or char are really just integers, why have two data types?" The answer is that because there are relatively few characters, variables of type char can use smaller cells than the cells used to store variables of type int. Indeed, C offers the programmer a choice of cell sizes to store integers:

```
char, short int, int, long int
```

Moreover, C guarantees that

```
sizeof ( char ) <= sizeof ( short int )
                 <= sizeof ( int )
                 <= sizeof ( long int ).
```

The type `short int` can be abbreviated to `short`, and `long int` can be abbreviated to `long`.

The header file *limits.h* defines the constants shown in Figure 2.2.3. These constants specify the range of the various integer types for a particular implementation. Typical values are as follows:

Constant	Value on a VAX	Value on an IBM PC
CHAR_MIN	−128	−128
CHAR_MAX	127	127
SHRT_MIN	−32768	−32768
SHRT_MAX	32767	32767
INT_MIN	−2147483648	−32768
INT_MAX	2147483647	32767
LONG_MIN	−2147483648	−2147483648
LONG_MAX	2147483647	2147483647

Constant	Interpretation
SCHAR_MIN	Smallest value of a `signed char`
SCHAR_MAX	Largest value of a `signed char`
UCHAR_MAX	Largest value of an `unsigned char`
CHAR_MIN	Smallest value of a `char`
CHAR_MAX	Largest value of a `char`
SHRT_MIN	Smallest value of a `short`
SHRT_MAX	Largest value of a `short`
USHRT_MAX	Largest value of an `unsigned short`
INT_MIN	Smallest value of an `int`
INT_MAX	Largest value of an `int`
UINT_MAX	Largest value of an `unsigned int`
LONG_MIN	Smallest value of a `long`
LONG_MAX	Largest value of a `long`
ULONG_MAX	Largest value of an `unsigned long`

Figure 2.2.3 Some constants defined in *limits.h*.

Any of the integer types (`char`, `short`, `int`, `long`) can be preceded by either `signed` or `unsigned`. Each of the data types

```
signed char, signed short, signed int, signed long
```

is interpreted as a signed, two's complement integer. Each of the data types

```
unsigned char, unsigned short, unsigned int,
unsigned long
```

is interpreted as an unsigned binary integer and *not* as a two's complement, signed integer. The data type unsigned int may be abbreviated to unsigned. The types signed short and short coincide, as do signed int and int, and signed long and long. The type char coincides with either signed char or unsigned char; the choice is implementation dependent. (Appendix B discusses unsigned and two's complement integers.)

A decimal integer constant is written using the digits 0 through 9, except that the first digit must *not* be 0. An octal integer constant is written using the symbols 0 through 7, except that the first symbol *must* be 0. A hexadecimal integer constant is written using the symbols 0 through 9, a through f, and A through F, preceded by 0x or 0X (the first symbol is zero).

Example 2.2.7. Each constant denotes the decimal integer 2599:

   2599   05047   0xA27

An integer constant may be terminated by u or U, to indicate that it is unsigned, or by l or L, to indicate that it is long. If a decimal constant is not terminated with either u, U, l, or L, it is the first of the types int, long, or unsigned long in which its value can be represented. If an octal or hexadecimal constant is not terminated with either u, U, l, or L, it is the first of the types int, unsigned int, long, or unsigned long in which its value can be represented. If a decimal, octal, or hexadecimal constant is terminated with either u or U, it is the first of the types unsigned int or unsigned long in which its value can be represented. If a decimal, octal, or hexadecimal constant is terminated with either l or L, it is the first of the types long or unsigned long in which its value can be represented. If a decimal, octal, or hexadecimal constant is terminated with either l or L and u or U, it is of type unsigned long.

Exercises

1. Write a one-line definition of variables a, b, and c of type int.
2. Write a one-line definition of variables a, b, and c of type char.
3. Write a one-line definition of variables a, b, and c of type int that assigns a the value 9, b the value −23, and c the value 0.
4. Write a one-line definition of variables a, b, and c of type char that assigns a the value '5', b the value '\n', and c the value 10.
5. State the principal difference between a variable of type int and a variable of type char.

In Exercises 6 through 10, tell what is printed. Assume ASCII representation of the characters.

6.
```
#include <stdio.h>
main( )
{
    char x;
    x = 90;
    printf( "%c", x );
}
```

7.
```c
#include <stdio.h>
main( )
{
    int x;
    x = 90;
    printf( "%c", x );
}
```

8.
```c
#include <stdio.h>
main( )
{
    char x;
    x = 90;
    printf( "%d", x );
}
```

9.
```c
#include <stdio.h>
main( )
{
    int x;
    x = 90;
    printf( "%d", x );
}
```

10.
```c
#include <stdio.h>
main( )
{
    char z1, z2, z3, z4, z5, z6, z7;
    z1 = 'z';
    z2 = '\n';
    z3 = 'Z';
    z4 = '\\';
    z5 = '\t';
    z6 = '\'';
    z7 = 'y';
    printf( "%c%c%c%c%c%c%c", z1, z2, z3, z4,
        z5, z6, z7 );
}
```

11. Explain the peculiar output produced by one system. Assume that ASCII is used and that sizeof (int) is 2. The program

```c
#include <stdio.h>
main( )
{
    int i = '2';
    scanf( "%c", &i );
    printf( "%c\n", i );
    printf( "%d\n", i );
}
```

prints

```
2
13106
```

when the input is

3

12. Write and run a program that prints the value of each constant in Figure 2.2.3.

2.3   Real Variables

C provides three types of real numbers: `float`, `double`, and `long double`. Use of the type `double` normally provides a larger cell size than does `float`. Use of the type `long double` may provide a larger cell size than does `double`, although on some systems, the types `double` and `long double` are identical.

The differences among the real number types is, not surprisingly, implementation dependent, although C guarantees that

```
sizeof ( long double) >= sizeof ( double )
                        >= sizeof ( float )
```

on any system. For example, in Turbo C the range of a `float` number is 0.0 and values approximately from 10^{-38} to 10^{38} in absolute value; the range of a `double` number is 0.0 and values approximately from 10^{-308} to 10^{308} in absolute value; and the range of a `long double` number is 0.0 and values approximately from 10^{-4932} to 10^{4932} in absolute value. In Turbo C, the type `float` provides about 6 significant digits, the type `double` provides about 15 significant digits, and the type `long double` provides about 19 significant digits.

Example 2.3.1.   The definitions

```
float x;
double y;
```

enable a cell named x to hold a number of type `float` and a cell named y to hold a number of type `double`.

Given these definitions, we may write

```
x = 6.89;
x = 8;
y = 6.89;
y = 8;
x = 736.901e15;
y = 88.268842E-12;
```

The first statement assigns the real number 6.89 to x. In the second statement, the constant 8 is an integer. The system converts 8 to the real number 8.0 and assigns 8.0 to x. Similar comments apply to the next two statements involving y. Constants containing e or E are said to be written in **exponential** or **scientific notation**. (The meaning is the same whether we write e or E.) The integer following e or E gives the exponent for 10. For example,

```
736.901e15 = 736.901 x 10¹⁵ =
736,901,000,000,000,000.0
```

and

$$88.268842E{-}12 = 88.268842 \times 10^{-12} =$$
$$0.000000000088268842$$

If x is of type double and y is of type float, we may assign the value of y to x with no surprises, as double includes all of the float values. On the other hand, if we assign the value of x to y and y has more significant digits than type float can hold, some precision will be lost due to truncation.

To print the value of a variable of type double or float using printf, we use the format descriptor %e, %E, or %f. If we use %e, the value of the next variable in the variable list is obtained and printed in the form

m.n···ne±x

The number is preceded by − if it is negative. The descriptor %E is identical to %e except that the number is printed with an uppercase E. If we use %f, the value of the next variable in the variable list is obtained and printed in the form

m···m.n···n

The number is preceded by − if it is negative.

To print the value of a variable of type long double using printf, we use the format descriptor %Le, %LE, or %Lf. The descriptor %Le (respectively, %LE, %Lf) behaves similarly to %e (respectively, %E, %f), which is used to print a variable of type double or float.

Example 2.3.2. The program

```
#include <stdio.h>
main( )
{
     float x, y;
     double v, w;

     x = 42.4907;
     y = 3.8872e-12;
     v = -55.23289108;
     w = -84.3002669e17;
     printf( "x = %e, y = %e\n", x, y );
     printf( "x = %E, y = %E\n", x, y );
     printf( "x = %f, y = %f\n", x, y );
     printf( "v = %e, w = %e\n", v, w );
     printf( "v = %E, w = %E\n", v, w );
     printf( "v = %f, w = %f\n", v, w );
}
```

in Turbo C prints

```
x = 4.249070e+001, y = 3.887200e-012
x = 4.249070E+001, y = 3.887200E-012
x = 42.490700, y = 0.000000
v = -5.523289e+001, w = -8.430027e+018
v = -5.523289E+001, w = -8.430027E+018
v = -55.232891, w = -8430026690000000000.000000
```

(The output y = 0.000000 results from writing only the first six digits to the right of the decimal point.)

If we use the format descriptor %f in scanf, we skip white space and interpret the next number as a real number. This value is placed in the next variable, which must be of type float. If we use the format descriptor %lf in scanf, we also skip white space and interpret the next number as a real number; however, in this case, the value is placed in the next variable, which must be of type double. Finally, if we use the format descriptor %Lf in scanf, we again skip white space and interpret the next number as a real number; in this case, the value is placed in the next variable, which must be of type long double.

Example 2.3.3.   Assuming that the standard input is

```
47.304       -38.30026452e5
```

the program

```
#include <stdio.h>
main( )
{
     float x;
     double y;
     scanf( "%f%lf", &x, &y );
     printf( "x = %f\ny = %f\n", x, y );
     printf( "x = %e\ny = %e\n", x, y );
}
```

in Turbo C prints

```
x = 47.304001
y = -3830026.452000
x = 4.730400e+001
y = -3.830026e+006
```

(The extraneous digits result from changing between decimal and binary.)

The header file *float.h* defines the constants shown in Figure 2.3.1. These constants specify the range of various real number types for a particular implementation. Values in Turbo C are as follows:

Constant	Value in Turbo C
FLT_DIG	6
DBL_DIG	15
LDBL_DIG	19
FLT_EPSILON	1.19209290e-07
DBL_EPSILON	2.2204460492503131e-16
LDBL_EPSILON	1.084202172485504e-19
FLT_MAX	3.40282347e38
DBL_MAX	1.797693134862316e308
LDBL_MAX	1.18973149535723e4932
FLT_MAX_10_EXP	38
DLB_MAX_10_EXP	308
LDLB_MAX_10_EXP	4932

Constant	Interpretation
FLT_DIG	Number of digits of precision for float
DBL_DIG	Number of digits of precision for double
LDBL_DIG	Number of digits of precision for long double
FLT_EPSILON	Smallest positive float x such that $1.0 + x \neq 1.0$
DBL_EPSILON	Smallest positive double x such that $1.0 + x \neq 1.0$
LDBL_EPSILON	Smallest positive long double x such that $1.0 + x \neq 1.0$
FLT_MAX	Largest float
DBL_MAX	Largest double
LDBL_MAX	Largest long double
FLT_MAX_10_EXP	Largest base 10 exponent allowed for float
DLB_MAX_10_EXP	Largest base 10 exponent allowed for double
LDLB_MAX_10_EXP	Largest base 10 exponent allowed for long double

Figure 2.3.1 Some constants defined in *float.h*.

A real constant may be terminated by f or F to indicate that it is a float or by l or L to indicate that it is a long double. If a real constant is not terminated with either f, F, l, or L, it is of type double. Notice that if x is of type float and we write

```
x = 4.293;
```

the constant 4.293 is of type double. When the assignment statement is executed, 4.293 is automatically converted to type float and the value is then stored in x. If, on the other hand, we write

```
x = 4.293f;
```

the constant 4.293f is of type float. This time, when the assignment statement is executed, since the constant is already of type float, no conversion occurs; the value is simply copied to the float variable x.

Exercises

In Exercises 1 through 4, express each number in exponential notation as used in C.

1. 399481.772   **2.** -9987768791.19002

3. .00000000022815   **4.** $-.00000005983$

5. What is printed? (Assume ASCII representation.)

```
#include <stdio.h>
main( )
{
     int i;
     char c;
     float x;
     i = 8;
     c = '\n';
     x = 42.4907;
     printf( "i = %d%c", i, c );
     printf( "%c\tc = %d%c", c, c, c );
```

```
        printf( "x = %e\tx = %f", x, x );
}
```

6. Write and run a program that prints the value of each constant in Figure 2.3.1.

2.4 Arithmetic Operations

C supplies the binary arithmetic operators

+	add
−	subtract
*	multiply
/	divide
%	modulus

(A **binary operator** has two operands.) C does not have an exponential operator, although the library function pow(x,y) can be used to compute x^y. Except for the modulus operator that requires integer operands, the arithmetic operators may be applied to expressions of any arithmetic type (char, int, float, double, etc.). The two arguments need not be of the same type.

Example 2.4.1. Given the definitions

```
char c, d;
int i, j;
float w, x;
double y, z;
c = 8;
d = 'R';
i = 76;
w = 7.9;
y = 23.4891e8;
```

we show the results of various arithmetic operations.

The assignment

```
j = i * i;
```

sets j to 5776 (= 76 · 76).

In the assignment

```
j = i * c;
```

we multiply a variable of type int by a variable of type char. The rule in such mixed computations is that the result is of the most general type; in this case, the result is of type int. Thus we assign the value 608 (= 76 · 8) to j.

Division of positive integers truncates the fractional part; thus, in the statement

```
j = i / c;
```

we set j to 9: 76 divided by 8 is 9.5, and dropping the fractional part gives 9. The result of dividing integers, one of which is negative, depends on the particular C implementation.

Assuming ASCII representation, the statement

```
j = i * d;
```

sets j to 6232, the product of 76 and 82. (82 is the ASCII code of the character R.)
The statement

```
x = i / w;
```

sets x to 9.6202532 (= 76/7.9).
In the statement

```
j = i / w;
```

the result of dividing i by w is 9.6202532. However, this number is to be assigned to the variable j of type int, which means that the fractional part is dropped; j is thus 9.
The statement

```
z = w * y;
```

sets z to 18556389000.0 (= $7.9 \cdot 23.4891 \times 10^8$).
The statement

```
z = c * i * w;
```

sets z to 4803.2 (= $8 \cdot 76 \cdot 7.9$).

The binary operator % is called the **modulus operator**. The value of the expression a % b is the remainder when a is divided by b. The operands a and b must be integers.

Example 2.4.2. If a, b, c, and d all are of type int and we execute

```
a = 3;
b = 8;
c = 0;
```

the statement

```
d = b % a;
```

sets d to 2, as the remainder when 8 is divided by 3 is 2. The statement

```
d = a % b;
```

sets d to 3, as the remainder when 3 is divided by 8 is 3. However, the statement

```
d = a % c;
```

is illegal because we cannot divide by zero.

C also has a unary plus operator + and a unary minus operator −. (A **unary operator** has one operand.) Applying the unary minus operator to the variable a changes the sign of a.

Example 2.4.3. If a and b are variables of type int, the value of a is 45, and we execute

```
b = -a;
```

the value of b is −45.

In an unparenthesized expression involving some or all of +, −, *, /, %, we first evaluate unary + and −, then *, /, and %, and finally binary + and −. The precedence of all C operators is given in Figure 2.4.1. Some of these operators will be introduced in later chapters.

Example 2.4.4. The value of the expression

```
5 + 3 * 4
```

is 17. The value of the expression

```
5 + -3 * 4
```

is −7. The value of the expression

```
(5 + 3) * 4
```

is 32. The value of the expression

```
5 + 8 % 3
```

is 7.

C has special kinds of operators that combine arithmetic operations with an assignment. For example, the operator += combines addition with an assignment. The statement

```
x += 3;
```

is equivalent to

```
x = x + 3;
```

We can think of the result of executing x += 3; as "increment x by 3."

In general, if *op* is a binary arithmetic operator (or a bitwise operator, to be discussed in Section 3.9), the statement

```
x op= y;
```

is equivalent to

```
x = x op y;
```

In addition to the operator += already mentioned, the operators

```
-=  *=  /=  %=
```

are available. For example, executing

```
y *= x + z;
```

is equivalent to executing

```
y = y * ( x + z );
```

We can think of the result of executing y *= x + z; as "multiply the current value of y by x + z."

The operators *op*= have the same precedence as does the assignment operator = (see Figure 2.4.1).

Exercises

Give the value of the variable on the left side of the assignment operator in each of Exercises 1 through 13. The statements are *not* executed sequentially. Assume that just before each statement, we have

```
int i, j, k;
float x, y, z;
i = 3;
```

```
j = 5;
x = 4.3;
y = 58.209;
```

1. k = j * i;   **2.** k = j / i;
3. z = x / i;   **4.** k = x / i;
5. z = y / x;   **6.** k = y / x;
7. i = 3 + 2 * j;   **8.** k = j % i;
9. k = i % j;   **10.** k = j % i * 4;
11. i += j;   **12.** j -= x;
13. i %= j;

Description	Operator	Associates from the	Precedence
Function expr	( )	left	High
Array expr	[ ]		(Evaluated first)
struct indirection	->		
struct member	.		
Incr/decr	++ --	right	
One's complement	~		
Unary not	!		
Address	&		
Dereference	*		
Cast	(*type*)		
Unary plus	+		
Unary minus	-		
Size in bytes	sizeof		
Multiplication	*	left	
Division	/		
Modulus	%		
Addition	+		
Subtraction	-		
Shift left	<<		
Shift right	>>		
Less than	<		
Less than or equal	<=		
Greater than	>		
Greater than or equal	>=		
Equal	==		
Not equal	!=		
Bitwise and	&		
Bitwise exclusive or	^		
Bitwise inclusive or	|		
Logical and	&&		
Logical or	||		
Conditional	? :	right	
Assignment	= %= += -= *= /=		
	>>= <<= &= ^= |=		(Evaluated last)
Comma	,	left	Low

Figure 2.4.1 Precedence of all C operators (operators between horizontal lines have the same precedence).

2.5 Relational and Logical Operators and the Assignment Operator

We previously introduced the **relational operators**

==	equal
!=	not equal
>	greater than
>=	greater than or equal
<	less than
<=	less than or equal

that are used to compare two values. In this section, we discuss the relational operators and the **assignment operator** = in greater detail and introduce the **logical operators**

&&	and
||	or
!	not

The value of an expression involving a relational operator is either true or false. For example, if the value of x is 3 and the value of y is −9, the value of the expression x == y is false. If the value of x is 312 and the value of y is 312, the value of the expression x == y is true. Unlike some languages, C does not use a special data type to represent true and false. Instead, false is represented by the value 0, and true is represented by any value other than 0. For example, each of the following while loops executes indefinitely:

```
while ( 1 ) {
      .
      .
      .

}
while ( 312 ) {
      .
      .
      .

}
while ( -8.3591 ) {
      .
      .
      .

}
```

But the body of the while loop

```
while ( 0 ) {
      .
      .
      .

}
```

never executes.

Example 2.5.1. Sometimes it is desirable to skip temporarily a section of code. This action is sometimes referred to as *bracketing out code*. For example, we might want to skip a print statement that was inserted for debugging purposes. The code

```
if ( 0 ) {
        code to be skipped
}
```

accomplishes this task. Since 0 is interpreted as false, the body of the if statement will not execute. The alternative of commenting out code:

```
/*
        code to be skipped
*/
```

may not work if the code to be skipped itself contains a comment, since the standard does not permit comments to nest (although many systems do allow nested comments).

When the system evaluates a logical expression, the value assigned is 1 if the expression is true and 0 if the expression is false.

Example 2.5.2. Assuming that the value of x is 1, the value of y is 4, and the value of z is 14, the following table gives the values of various expressions. In expressions involving arithmetic and relational operators, the arithmetic operations are performed first (see Figure 2.4.1).

Expression	Value	Interpretation
x < y + z	1	True
y == 2 * x + 3	0	False
z <= x + y	0	False
z > x	1	True
x != y	1	True

Suppose that c1 and c2 are of type char and each has as its value one of the lowercase letters a through z. In both ASCII and EBCDIC, if the character c1 precedes the character c2 in the alphabet, the expression c1 < c2 is true. This also applies if c1 and c2 each has as its value one of the uppercase letters A through Z.

Example 2.5.3. The expression

```
'c' < 'g'
```

is true. The expression

```
'T' > 'Y'
```

is false.

C provides the logical operators *and, or,* and *not.* The logical and is denoted &&; the logical or is denoted ||; and the logical not is denoted !. The results of using these operators are given in the following table:

x	y	x && y	x || y	!x
True	True	True	True	False
True	False	False	True	False
False	True	False	True	True
False	False	False	False	True

Notice that according to Figure 2.4.1, unary not (!) is evaluated *before* the relational operators (<, <=, etc.), which, in turn, are evaluated *before* the logical operators && and \|\|. Notice also that && is evaluated before \|\|.

In evaluating either a logical and expression (*expr1* && *expr2*) or a logical or expression (*expr1* \|\| *expr2*), C guarantees that *expr1* is evaluated before *expr2*. Moreover, in determining the value of the expression

   expr1 && *expr2*

if *expr1* is false, then *expr2* is *not* evaluated. (After *expr1* is found to be false, *expr1* && *expr2* is false regardless of the value of *expr2*, so there is no need to evaluate *expr2*.) Similarly, in determining the value of the expression

   expr1 \|\| *expr2*

if *expr1* is true, then *expr2* is *not* evaluated. (After *expr1* is found to be true, *expr1* \|\| *expr2* is true regardless of the value of *expr2*, so there is no need to evaluate *expr2*.)

The programmer can often take advantage of the way that C evaluates logical expressions. For example, the statement

```
if ( x != 0.0 && y/x > 3.0 ) {
    .
    .
    .

}
```

does not cause an execution error when x equals 0.0. If x equals 0.0, the expression x != 0.0 is false and the expression y/x > 3.0 is not evaluated. In a high-level language that always evaluates x != 0.0 and y/x > 3.0, if x equals 0.0, an execution error results.

Example 2.5.4.   Assuming that the value of x is 1, the value of y is 4, and the value of z is 14, the following table gives the values of various logical expressions:

Expression	Value
x <= 1 && y == 3	0
x <= 1 || y == 3	1
!(x > 1)	1
!x > 1	0
!(x <= 1 || y == 3)	0
x >= 1 && y == 3 || z < 14	0

In the expression x <= 1 && y == 3, we first evaluate x <= 1 (which is true) and then y == 3 (which is false). Because the logical and of a true expression and a false expression is false, the expression x <= 1 && y == 3 is false (0).

In the expression x <= 1 || y == 3, we first evaluate x <= 1, which is true; therefore, the expression y == 3 is *not* evaluated. The value of the expression x <= 1 || y == 3 is true (1).

In the expression ! (x > 1), the parentheses force us to evaluate the expression x > 1 first, which is false. Negating the false expression gives the value true (1).

In the expression !x > 1, ! is the unary not operator and is evaluated first. Because x is 1 (true), !x is false (0). Because the expression 0 > 1 is false, the expression !x > 1 is false (0).

We have already observed that the expression x <= 1 || y == 3 is true. Negating a true expression gives the value false (0).

Because && is evaluated before ||, the expression

    x >= 1 && y == 3 || z < 14

has the same value as

    (x >= 1 && y == 3) || z < 14

To determine the value of the expression x >= 1 && y == 3, we first evaluate x >= 1, which is true. We then evaluate y == 3, which is false. Thus the expression x >= 1 && y == 3 is false. Finally, we evaluate z < 14, which is false. Thus the expression

    x >= 1 && y == 3 || z < 14

is false (0).

In C, as in other high-level languages, the assignment operator = assigns a value to a variable. For example, the statement

    x = y;

assigns the value of the variable y to the variable x. However, in C, unlike most other high-level languages, the *expression* x = y has a value—namely, the value assigned (see Figure 2.5.1). For example, if y has the value 6, the statement

    x = y;

assigns x the value 6. The value of the expression x = y is 6 (the value assigned).

Example 2.5.5. Suppose that the value of z is 10. When we execute the statement

    x = (y = z);

the parentheses make it clear that we first evaluate the expression

    y = z

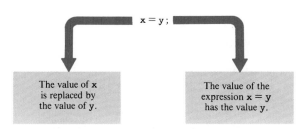

Figure 2.5.1 The assignment operator.

Thus we first assign 10, the value of z, to y. Because the expression y = z has the value 10, the right side of the assignment statement

```
x =  . . .
```

is 10. Therefore x is also assigned the value 10.

The parentheses in Example 2.5.5 are unnecessary, however. The statement

```
x = ( y = z );
```

is the same as

```
x = y = z;
```

because the assignment operator associates from the right (see Figure 2.4.1). The effect of writing

```
x1 = x2 = x3 = ··· = xn;
```

is to assign the value of xn to x1 and x2 and x3. . . .

The assignment operator has a lower precedence than any of the arithmetic operators, logical operators, or relational operators (i.e., the assignment operator is evaluated after all of the arithmetic operators, logical operators, and relational operators, unless, of course, parentheses are used to override the normal order of evaluation).

Example 2.5.6.   Assuming that the value of x is 1 and the value of y is 4, the expression

```
y == ( x = 3 ) + 1
```

is true and so has the value 1.

The value of the expression x = 3 is 3, the value assigned. The value 3 is then added to 1. Thus the value of the expression

```
( x = 3 ) + 1
```

is 4. Because the value of y is 4, the expression

```
y == ( x = 3 ) + 1
```

is true.

Example 2.5.7.   Assuming that the value of x is 1 and the value of y is 4, the expression

```
x <= 1 && ( y = 3 )
```

is true and so has the value 1.

The expression x <= 1 is true. The value of the assignment y = 3 is 3, which is interpreted as true. (Remember that *any* nonzero value is interpreted as true.) Finally, the logical and of the true values x <= 1 and y = 3 gives the value true.

Example 2.5.8.   The output of the program

```
#include <stdio.h>
main()
{
     int x = 2;
```

```
        if ( x = 3 )
              printf( "true" );
        else
              printf( "false" );
   }
```

is

```
   true
```

The value of the expression

```
   x = 3
```

is 3 (the value assigned). Because a nonzero value is interpreted as true, we execute the statement

```
   printf( "true" );
```

which prints true. This example shows that problems arise when = is used when == was intended.

In C, any *expression* followed by a semicolon is a *statement*. For example, the expression x = y followed by a semicolon becomes the statement

```
   x = y;
```

Even the expression x + y followed by a semicolon is the legal statement

```
   x + y;
```

although its usefulness is unclear. The other C statements, some of which will be discussed subsequently, are iteration statements (while, do while, and for statements), selection statements (if and switch statements), jump statements (goto, continue, break, and return statements), compound statements (a sequence of statements enclosed in braces), and labeled statements (a statement preceded by a label). The detailed syntax is given in Appendix D.

Exercises

1. Assuming that the value of x is 21, the value of y is 4, the value of z is 8, the value of c is 'A', and the value of d is 'H', fill in the missing entries in the following table. Also, give the values of all the variables. Assume that ASCII representation is being used. In some cases, you may need to refer to the ASCII table in Appendix A.

Expression	Value
x + y >= z	1
y == x - 2 * z - 1	
6 * x != x	
c > d	
x = y == 4	
(x = y) == 4	
(x = 1) == 1	
2 * c > d	

2. Assuming that the value of x is 11, the value of y is 6, the value of z is 1, the value of c is 'k', and the value of d is 'y', fill in the missing entries in the following table. Also, give the values of all the variables. Assume that ASCII representation is used. In some cases, you may need to refer to the ASCII table in Appendix A.

Expression	Value
x > 9 && y != 3	1
x == 5 || y != 3	
!(x > 14)	
!(x > 9 && y != 23)	
x <= 1 && y == 6 || z < 4	
c >= 'a' && c <= 'z'	
c >= 'A' || c <= 'Z'	
c != d && c != '\n'	
5 && y != 8 || 0	
x >= y >= z	

3. What is the likely logical error?

```
if ( code == 1 & flag == 0 )
    printf( "OK\n" );
```

4. What is the likely logical error?

```
if ( code == 1 | flag == 0 )
    printf( "ERROR\n" );
```

2.6   Sample Application: Statistical Measures

Problem

Read a series of real numbers from the standard input, and print a statistical summary of the data that includes the largest value input, the smallest value input, the sum of all values read, the mean (average) of all values input, the population variance, and the standard deviation. The population variance measures the spread of the values and is given by the formula

$$\frac{\sum_{i=1}^{n} x_i^2}{n} - \bar{x}^2$$

where $\bar{x}$ is the mean of the n values $x_1, x_2, \ldots, x_n$ read. The standard deviation is the square root of the variance.

Sample Input/Output

```
2.0   3.0   4.0
```
    Input

```
3 data items read
maximum value read = 4.000000
minimum value read = 2.000000
```

```
sum of all values read = 9.000000
mean = 3.000000
variance = 0.666667
standard deviation = 0.816497
```

Output

Solution

We step through the input. After we read a value,

1. We count it.
2. If it is larger than any value seen so far, we record it as a new high.
3. If it is smaller than any value seen so far, we record it as a new low.
4. We update the sum of all values read.
5. We update the sum of squares of all values read.

After reading all the values, we compute the mean, variance, and standard deviation and print the statistical summary.

C Implementation

```c
/*   This program reads a series of real numbers from
     the standard input and prints a statistical
     summary of the data that includes the largest
     value input, the smallest value input, the sum of
     all values read, the mean (average) of all values
     input, the population variance, and the standard
     deviation.                                         */

#include <stdio.h>
#include <math.h>

main()
{
     float x, /* current value input */
           max, /* largest value seen so far */
           min, /* smallest value seen so far */
           sum, /* sum of all values seen so far */
           mean, /* mean of all values read */
           sum_of_squares, /* sum of squares of all
                                values seen so far */
           variance; /* variance of all values read */
     int   count; /* number of values read so far */

     if ( scanf( "%f", &x ) == EOF ) /* empty? */
          printf( "0 data items read\n" );
     else {
          max = min = sum = x;
          count = 1;
          sum_of_squares = x * x;
          while ( scanf( "%f", &x ) != EOF ) {
               count += 1;
               if ( x > max ) /* new high? */
                    max = x;
```

```
                    if ( x < min ) /* new low? */
                        min = x;
                    sum += x;
                    sum_of_squares += x * x;
                }
                printf( "%d data items read\n", count );
                printf( "maximum value read = %f\n", max );
                printf( "minimum value read = %f\n", min );
                printf( "sum of all values read = %f\n", sum );
                mean = sum / count;
                printf( "mean = %f\n", mean );
                variance = sum_of_squares / count - mean * mean;
                printf( "variance = %f\n", variance );
                printf( "standard deviation = %f\n",
                    sqrt( variance ) );
            }
        }
```

Discussion

We use `scanf` to read the standard input. We first execute the `if` statement

```
    if ( scanf( "%f", &x ) == EOF ) /* empty? */
```

to test whether there are any numbers in the input. If there are no values in the input, we simply print

```
    0 data items read
```

and terminate the program. Otherwise, we initialize `max`, `min`, and `sum` to the value of x. The value of the variable `max` is equal to the largest value read so far. The value of the variable `min` is equal to the smallest value read so far. The value of the variable `sum` is equal to the sum of all values read so far. We initialize `count` to 1. The value of the variable `count` is equal to the number of values read so far. We initialize `sum_of_squares` to x * x. The value of the variable `sum_of_squares` is equal to the sum of the squares of all values read so far.

We use the `while` loop

```
    while ( scanf( "%f", &x ) != EOF ) {
        .
        .
        .
    }
```

to read the input and to test for end-of-file. After reading a new number x, we increment `count`. If x is larger than `max` (the largest value seen so far), we update `max`. If x is smaller than `min` (the smallest value seen so far), we update `min`. We also update `sum` and `sum_of_squares`. After reading all of the data, we print the statistical summary. To compute the square root, we use the library function `sqrt`. We include the math header file *math.h* in order to use mathematical functions such as `sqrt`.†

---

†When compiling a C program in UNIX that uses mathematics functions, the flag −lm (load referenced modules from the mathematics library) must be added to the compile command.

Exercise

1. Can we replace the lines

```
if ( x > max )
        max = x;
if ( x < min )
        min = x;
```

by the lines

```
if ( x > max )
        max = x;
else
        min = x;
```

2.7 The for Statement and the Comma Operator

The for statement, like the while and do while statements, is used to execute repeatedly a segment of code. The C for loop is similar to the for loop of Pascal or BASIC and the do loop of FORTRAN or PL/I, but as we shall see, the C for loop is considerably more general than are the analogous loops of these other languages.

The form of the for statement is

> for (*expr1*; *expr2*; *expr3*)
>   *action*

In the for loop, *expr1* is used to initialize the loop; *expr2* is used to test for continued looping; *expr3* is used to update the loop; and *action* is the body of the loop.

To execute a for statement (see Figure 2.7.1), we first evaluate *expr1*; *expr1* is evaluated once and only once, at the beginning of the loop. We next evaluate *expr2*. If

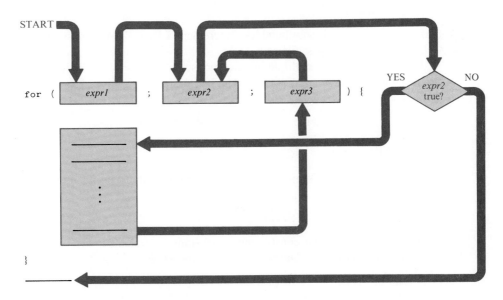

Figure 2.7.1 The for statement.

expr2 is false, the `for` loop terminates, and we next execute the statement following *action*. If *expr2* is true, we execute *action* and then evaluate *expr3*. We then repeat the test / action / update process. That is, we evaluate *expr2*. If *expr2* is false, the `for` loop terminates, and we next execute the statement following *action*. If *expr2* is true, we execute *action* and then evaluate *expr3*. We continue until *expr2* is false, at which point we skip to the statement following *action*.

The body of the `for` loop consists of one statement without braces or one or more statements enclosed in braces.

Example 2.7.1.   When the segment

```
sum = 0;
for ( i = 1; i <= 4; i += 1 )
    sum += i;
printf( "sum = %d", sum );
```

is executed, we print the sum of the first four positive integers.

We first set `sum` to 0. At the start of the `for` loop, we set `i` to 1 (initialization). Because `i <= 4` is true (test), we execute `sum += i`, which sets `sum` to 1 (action). We next execute `i += 1` (update), which sets `i` to 2. The test / action / update process is then repeated. Because `i <= 4` is true, we execute `sum += i`, which sets `sum` to $1 + 2 = 3$. We next execute `i += 1`, which sets `i` to 3. The process is then repeated. Because `i <= 4` is true, we execute `sum += i`, which sets `sum` to 6. We next execute `i += 1`, which sets `i` to 4. The process is then repeated. Because `i <= 4` is true, we execute `sum += i`, which sets `sum` to 10. We next execute `i += 1`, which sets `i` to 5. The process is then repeated. Because `i <= 4` is false, we terminate the `for` loop. We then print

```
sum = 10
```

Experienced C programmers write the `for` loop of Example 2.7.1 as

```
for ( i = 1; i <= 4; i++ )
    sum += i;
```

The expression `i++` is shorthand for "increment i by 1." We discuss the operator `++` in detail in the following section.

It is possible to have multiple initializations in a `for` loop. The individual assignments are separated by commas. For example, the program segment of Example 2.7.1 may be written

```
for ( i = 1, sum = 0; i <= 4; i++ )
    sum += i;
printf( "sum = %d", sum );
```

In fact, the preceding segment is an application of the **comma operator**. When the expression

   expr1, expr2, . . . , exprn

is evaluated, each of the constituent expressions is evaluated; first *expr1*, then *expr2*, . . . , and finally *exprn*. The value of the expression

   expr1, expr2, . . . , exprn

is equal to the value of the last constituent expression *exprn*.

In the `for` loop

```
for ( expr1; expr2; expr3 )
      action
```

any of *expr1*, *expr2*, or *expr3* may be missing (though the two semicolons must always be present). For example,

```
for ( i = 1; i <= 4; ) {
     sum += i;
     i++;
}
```

is logically equivalent to the `for` loop of Example 2.7.1.

If *expr2* is missing, the condition is regarded as true. For example,

```
for ( ; ; )
      action
```

is an infinite loop.

If the body of the `for` loop contains no `continue` statement (to be discussed in Section 3.1)

```
for ( expr1; expr2; expr3 )
      action
```

is logically equivalent to

```
expr1;
while ( expr2 ) {
      action
      expr3;
}
```

The `while` loop

```
while ( expression )
      action
```

is logically equivalent to

```
for ( ; expression; )
      action
```

We see that `while` loops may be rewritten as `for` loops and that `for` loops may be rewritten as `while` loops. The decision on whether to write a `for` loop or a `while` loop should be based on considerations of clarity and style.

Exercises

1. What is printed?

```
for ( i = 1; i <= 5; printf( "%d\n", i ) )
      i++;
```

2. What is printed?

```
for ( i = 1; i <= 5; i++ ) {
    printf( "%d\n", i );
    i += 2;
}
```

3. What is printed?

```
for ( i = 1; i <= 5; i++ ) ;
    printf( "%d\n", i );
printf( "%d\n", i );
```

4. What is the error?

```
for ( i = 1, i <= 5, i++ )
    printf( "%d\n", i );
```

5. Using a `for` loop, write a program that computes and prints the value of the sum $2 + 4 + \cdots + 100$.

6. On one system, when the program

```
#include <stdio.h>

main()
{
        float x;

        for ( x = 0; x <= 1.0; x += 0.1 )
            printf( "%.1f  ", x );
}
```

is run, the output is

```
0.0   0.1   0.2   0.3   0.4   0.5   0.6   0.7   0.8   0.9
```

(The format descriptor `%.1f` causes one digit after the decimal to be printed.) Where's the missing `1.0`?

2.8 The Operators ++ and --

The unary operators `++` and `--` are unlike those in any other programming language. The increment operator `++` adds 1, and the decrement operator `--` subtracts 1. Like the assignment operator, the increment and decrement operators have a value. We now describe the situation in more detail.

When we execute

```
x++;
```

two things happen (see Figure 2.8.1):

- The value of the variable x is increased by 1.
- The value of the expression x++ is equal to the original value of x.

Example 2.8.1. If the value of x is 3, after we execute

```
y = x++;
```

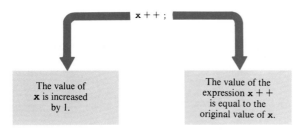

Figure 2.8.1 The postincrement operator.

the value of x is 4 (because ++ causes x to be incremented), and the value of y is 3 (the value of the *expression* x++).

When we execute

++x;

two things also happen (see Figure 2.8.2):

- The value of the variable x is increased by 1.
- The value of the expression ++x is 1 more than the original value of x.

Example 2.8.2.   If the value of x is 3, after we execute

    y = ++x;

x has the value 4 (because ++ causes x to be incremented) and y has the value 4 (the value of the *expression* ++x).

Simultaneously attempting to increment a variable and store a value in the same variable, while syntactically correct, may result in unpredictable behavior. For example, the statement

    i += i++; /***** Danger *****/

which attempts to double i and then increment it, may result in different behavior in different systems. Of course, a statement such as

    j += i++;

results in clearly defined behavior—j is incremented by the original value of i, and i is incremented by 1.

When we execute

    x--;

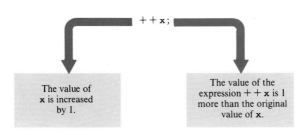

Figure 2.8.2 The preincrement operator.

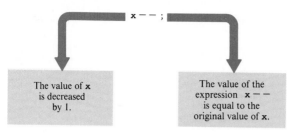

Figure 2.8.3 The postdecrement operator.

two things happen (see Figure 2.8.3):

- The value of the variable x is decreased by 1.
- The value of the expression x−− is equal to the original value of x.

Example 2.8.3.   If the value of x is 4, after we execute

   y = x−−;

x has the value 3 (because −− causes x to be decremented) and y has the value 4 (the value of the *expression* x−−).

When we execute

   −−x;

two things also happen (see Figure 2.8.4):

- The value of the variable x is decreased by 1.
- The value of the expression −−x is 1 less than the original value of x.

Example 2.8.4.   If the value of x is 4, after we execute

   y = −−x;

x has the value 3 (because −− causes x to be decremented) and y has the value 3 (the value of the *expression* −−x).

Notice that the increment and decrement operators have two effects: First, the value of the variable is incremented or decremented, and second, the expression has a value. The value of the variable is incremented or decremented regardless of whether ++ or −− is placed before or after the variable. The value of the *expression* is dependent on whether ++ or −− is placed before or after the variable. If ++ or −− is placed before the variable, the value of the expression is equal to the incremented or decremented value of the

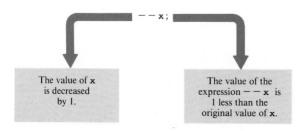

Figure 2.8.4 The predecrement operator.

variable. If ++ or -- is placed after the variable, the value of the expression is equal to the original value of the variable.

The operators ++ and -- have the same precedence as the logical not and the unary plus and minus operators (see Figure 2.4.1).

Example 2.8.5. Assuming that the value of x is 1 and that of y is 4, the expression

```
--y == 3 && !( x++ <= 1 )
```

is false and so has value 0.

Because the value of the expression --y is 3, the new value of y, the expression --y == 3 is true. The value of the expression x++ is 1, the original value of x. Because the value of the expression x++ is less than or equal to 1, the expression x++ <= 1 is true. The logical not of a true expression is false. Thus the expression !(x ++ <= 1) is false. The logical and of a true expression and a false expression is false, thus the expression

```
--y == 3 && !( x++ <= 1 )
```

is false.

The plus and minus signs have several different meanings in C. For example, - can be unary minus, binary subtraction, or part of the decrement operator. To break up a program (the official term is *parse*) into its constituent parts (*tokens*), each sequence of symbols that represents a token is taken to be as long as possible. Using this convention, the expression

```
x---y
```

is parsed as

```
x-- - y
```

The first token is the identifier x; the second token is the decrement operator -- (not -, as a longer token is possible); the third token is the binary subtraction operator -; and the last token is the identifier y.

Exercises

Give the value of i and k after each statement is executed in Exercises 1 through 5. The statements are *not* executed sequentially. Assume that just before each statement, we have

```
int i, j, k;
i = 3;
k = 0;
```

1. k = ++i;   **2.** k = i++;

3. k = --i;   **4.** k = i--;

5. i = j = k--;

6. Assuming that ASCII representation is used, the value of c is 'k', and the value of d is 'y', find the value of the expression

```
--c == 'j' && d++ == 'y'
```

7. What is printed?

```
int x = 7;
if ( x-- < 2 )
    printf( "%d", x );
else if ( x-- < 4 )
    printf( "%d", 2 * x );
else if ( x-- < 6 )
    printf( "%d", 3 * x );
else
    printf( "%d", 4 * x );
```

8. Do the two code fragments always produce the same output given the same input? Explain.

```
if ( code++ <= 3 )                  if ( code++ <= 3 )
    printf("%d\n", code);               printf("%d\n", code);
else if ( code++ <= 5 )             if ( code++ <= 5 )
    printf("%d\n", code);               printf("%d\n", code);
else if ( code++ <= 7 )             if ( code++ <= 7 )
    printf("%d\n", code);               printf("%d\n", code);
```

If the fragments are logically the same, is one form preferable to the other? Explain.

9. How is the expression

```
x-----y
```

parsed? Is it a legal expression?

2.9   Sample Application: Printing a Bar Graph

Problem

Print a bar graph that shows the worth of various comic books. The input data are the names of the comic books and the values of the books in thousands of dollars.

Sample Input/Output

```
Action Comics
48
Marvel Mystery Comics
43
Detective Comics
40
More Fun Comics
29
Superman
28
```

Input

```
Action Comics
*******************************************
Marvel Mystery Comics
****************************************
Detective Comics
**************************************
More Fun Comics
***************************
Superman
**************************
```

Output

Solution

The bar graph is created by printing a number of stars equal to the value of each comic in thousands of dollars. We can use a for loop to print the appropriate number of stars. We print the name of the comic simply by echoing the input to the output a character at a time.

C Implementation

```c
/*   This program prints the names of comic books and
     a bar graph to show the values of the books in
     thousands of dollars.                            */

#include <stdio.h>

main( )
{
    char c;
    int value; /* value in thousands of comic */
    int i;   /* loop counter */

    while ( scanf( " %c", &c ) != EOF ) {
        do { /* print title of comic */
            printf( "%c", c );
            scanf( "%c", &c );
        } while ( c != '\n' );
        printf( "\n" );
        scanf( "%d", &value ); /* get value of comic */
        for ( i = 1; i <= value; i++ ) /* print stars */
            printf( "*" );
        printf( "\n" );
    }
}
```

Discussion

In the line

```c
while ( scanf( " %c", &c ) != EOF ) {
```

we attempt to read the first character of a title. If no more input remains, the program terminates. Notice that the format string " %c" has a blank before %c. A blank in a scanf format string causes white space to be skipped before the next directive, %c in this case, is processed. The format string "%c" without the blank would cause the next character to be read regardless of whether it was a white space character or not. The reason for including the blank in this format string will be explained shortly.

If we have not reached end-of-file, we execute the do while loop to copy the title of the comic to the output. We use the test

```
c != '\n'
```

as we assume that a newline marks the end of each title. We then print a newline so that the row of stars begins on the following line.

We execute

```
scanf( "%d", &value );
```

to read the value of the comic. We then execute the for loop to print the stars. At this point, the next character to be read in the input is the newline that follows the integer representing the value of the comic. The blank in the scanf format string " %c" at the top of the while loop causes any white space, including this newline, to be skipped before reading a nonwhite space character or detecting end-of-file. It is instructive (see Exercise 3) to consider what would happen if the blank in this format string were omitted.

Exercises

1. Which, if any, of the three input files works correctly with the bar graph program? Explain. [The last lines of (a) and (b) are terminated by newlines, but the last line of (c) is not terminated by a newline.]

   (a) Action Comics 48
   Marvel Mystery Comics 43

   (b) Action Comics
   48 Marvel Mystery Comics
   43

   (c) Action Comics
   48
   Marvel Mystery Comics
   43

2. Rewrite the bar graph program using format strings of the form "%c" and "%d" (with no blanks in the format strings).

3. Explain what would happen if the blank in the scanf format string " %c" were omitted.

Changes from Traditional C

1. The constant '\a' (bell) is new.

2. The header files *limits.h* and *float.h* are not specified in traditional C. Of course, the constants defined therein (see Figures 2.2.3 and 2.3.1) have also been added.

3. The signed integer and long double data types are new. The term long float, which is a synonym for double, has been deleted. The designation of

unsigned constants by writing u or U, the designation of float constants by writing f or F, and the designation of long double constants by writing l or L have all been added by the standard. The format descriptors, %Lf, %Le, and %LE (used to read and write a value of type long double) are new.

4. Traditional C has no unary plus operator.

5. Although many compilers use the rule that one should take the longest sequence of symbols that represents a token, the standard makes it an official requirement of the language.

Common Programming Errors

1. Except for the specially denoted characters '\n', '\t', and so on, which represent one character, only one symbol may be placed between the single quotation marks. Do not place multiple characters between single quotation marks, such as 'ralph' or 'computer_science'.

2. To assign the *character* zero to the variable c, write

    ```
    c = '0';
    ```

    not

    ```
    c = 0;
    ```

3. It is a logical error to mismatch a format descriptor and its corresponding argument in scanf. For example, it is an error to write

    ```
    int i;
    scanf( "%c", &i );  /***** LOGICAL ERROR *****/
    ```

    because %c requires as its corresponding argument the address of a char.

4. The logical and operator is && rather than &. The unary operator & is the address operator (see Section 2.1), and the binary operator & is the bitwise and operator (see Section 3.9).

5. The logical or operator is || rather than |. The operator | is the bitwise or operator (see Section 3.9).

6. It is illegal to write x % y if either x or y is float, double, or long double. The operands of % must be integers.

7. The three expressions in a for statement are separated by semicolons, not commas or some other symbol. It is an error to write

    ```
    for ( expression 1, expression 2, expression 3 ) { /** ERROR **/
        .
        .
        .
    }
    ```

8. Do not place a semicolon between for (−) and the body of the for loop. The code

    ```
    /***** PROBABLE ERROR *****/
    for ( i = 0; i < 10; i++ ) ;
        printf( "i = %d\n", i );
    ```

is syntactically correct but logically erroneous, assuming that the programmer intends the statement

```
printf( "i = %d\n", i );
```

to be the body of the `for` loop.

Programming Exercises

2.1. The standard input contains the opening balance of a checking account followed by a list of transactions. Write a program that prints the opening balance followed by the closing balance. For example, if the input is (a negative number represents a withdrawal, and a positive number represents a deposit)

```
324.56   420.32   -3.54   -87.56
```

the output is

```
Opening Balance = $324.56
Closing Balance = $653.78
```

2.2. The cost of one type of phone service is $7.03 plus 4.5 cents for each unit used. Write a program that reads the standard input that lists the units used and prints the bill for each customer. The standard input looks like

```
88290        46
31556         7
             .
             .
             .
```

Each line gives the customer's identification number followed by the number of units used. The output is of the form

```
88290    $ 9.10
31556    $ 7.35
           .
           .
           .
```

Each line gives the customer's identification number followed by the bill. (To print exactly two places after the decimal point, use `%.2f` instead of `%f`. Complete details on formatting are given in Section 8.5.)

2.3. The cost of one type of phone service is $9.38 plus 4.5 cents for each unit used over 65 units. Write a program that reads the standard input that lists the units used and prints the bill for each customer. Follow the format specification of Exercise 2.2.

2.4. Write a program that copies the standard input to the standard output, except that each newline character is preceded by the two characters `\n` and each tab is replaced by the two characters `\t`. (In this way, newlines and tabs become visible.)

2.5. Write a program that reads the standard input and prints the code of each character in decimal. Separate the decimal codes with blanks and print 10 codes per line.

2.6. Write a program that reads a list of test scores and prints the test scores together with the letter grades according to the scale

90–100	A
80–89	B
70–79	C
60–69	D
0–59	F

2.7. Write a program to graph the function

$$y = \frac{x}{1 + x^2}$$

on the interval from 0 to 2 in increments of 0.1. As in the bar graph program, print a number of stars proportional to y for the requested values of x.

2.8. Write a program to graph the function $y = \sin(x)$ on the interval from 0 to π in increments of $\pi/20$. As in the bar graph program, print a number of stars proportional to y for the various values of x. The function $\sin(x)$ is available as a library function.

2.9. Opponents of the late Chicago Mayor Harold Washington presented petitions containing 196,000 signatures seeking a referendum on a nonpartisan mayoral election. (The opponents of Mayor Washington felt that they had a better chance to unseat him if the election were nonpartisan.) To the charge by Mayor Washington's supporters that many of the signatures were invalid, the opposition leader, Rep. William Lipinski, replied, "Normally, petitions are 10 to 15 percent forged. Maybe this, since it is so large, will go 20 percent."

Assume that for each increase of 50,000 signatures, the percentage of forged signatures increases by 5 percent. Write a program that lists the number of signatures, the percentage forged, and the number of forged signatures beginning with 50,000 signatures with 5 percent forged and ending when all (100 percent) signatures are forged. The output is in increments of 50,000.

2.10. A handicapping system is used to determine the winner in power-lifting competitions. For male body weights over 125 kg and less than or equal to 165 kg, a coefficient C is determined from the following table:

Bodyweight (B)	Coefficient (C)
$125.1 \leq B < 135$	$0.5208 - 0.0012(B - 125)$
$135 \leq B < 145$	$0.5088 - 0.0011(B - 135)$
$145 \leq B < 155$	$0.4978 - 0.0010(B - 145)$
$155 \leq B < 165$	$0.4878 - 0.0009(B - 155)$

(There are other formulas for women's competition and for persons whose weights are less than 125 kg.) Each lifter is then assigned the value

$$C(S + BP + D)$$

where S is the weight lifted in the squat position, BP is the weight bench pressed, and D is the deadlift. The winner is the person with the largest value.

Write a program that reads a body weight, squat weight, weight bench pressed, and deadlift for a lifter and prints the value assigned to the lifter.

2.11. This programming exercise is derived from an example originally due to Mitchell Feigenbaum and adapted by John Allen Paulos in *Beyond Numeracy* (New York: Alfred A. Knopf, 1990). Consider the deceptively simple formula

$$\text{NextYr} = \text{Rate} * \text{CurrentYr} * \left(1 - \frac{\text{CurrentYr}}{1000000}\right)$$

which calculates next year's population of, say, egrets on the basis of the current population and the growth rate. The variable `Rate` controls the growth rate and takes on values between 0 and 4. The variable `CurrentYr` gives the current value of the egret population and is assumed to have a value between 0 and 1,000,000. The variable `NextYr` gives the value of the egret population one year later. The formula guarantees that `NextYr` will also have a value between 0 and 1,000,000. For example, if `CurrentYr` is 100,000 and `Rate` is 2.6, `NextYr` is 234,000.

Now suppose that we initialize `CurrentYr` to 100,000 and `Rate` to 2.6 and compute the egret population 25 years hence by solving for `NextYr`, setting `CurrentYr` to `NextYr`, solving again for `NextYr`, and so on for 25 iterations. The egret population turns out to be roughly 615,385. We get the same result if we initialize `CurrentYr` to, say, 900,000 but leave `Rate` set to 2.6. In fact, the population stabilizes at roughly 615,385 for any value of `CurrentYr` so long as `Rate` is 2.6! For some values of `Rate`, the population oscillates. For example, if `Rate` is 3.14, then after about 40 years the egret population takes on this pattern from one year to the next: 538,007 to 780,464 to 538,007 to 780,464, and so on indefinitely. For `Rate` equal to approximately 3.57, however, the population does not stabilize or oscillate but rather varies randomly from one year to the next.

Write a program that prompts the user for `Rate`, an initial `CurrentYr`, and a number of iterations. On each iteration, the program prints the year and the current egret population.

2.12. Amend the program of Exercise 2.11 so that it prompts the user for a number of iterations, an initial `Rate`, an initial `CurrentYr`, a `Rate` increase, and a `Rate` limit. For example, if the user enters 25 for the number of iterations, 100,000 for `CurrentYr`, 3.5 for `Rate`, 0.1 for the `Rate` increase, and 3.9 for the `Rate` limit, then the program iterates 25 times with `Rate` set to 3.5; 25 times with `Rate` set to 3.6; and so on until `Rate` is set to 3.9. On each iteration, the program prints the year, the `Rate`, and the current egret population.

More Operators
and Control Flow

3

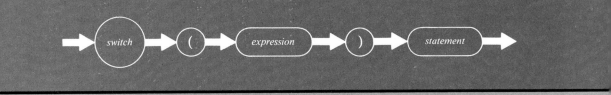

switch → (→ expression →) → statement

3.1 The break and continue Statements
3.2 Sample Application: Generating Prime Numbers
3.3 The switch Statement
3.4 The goto Statement and Labels
3.5 Conditional Expressions
3.6 Sample Application: Printing a Calendar
3.7 The Cast Operator
3.8 getchar and putchar
†3.9 Bitwise Operators
     Common Programming Errors
     Programming Exercises

†This section can be omitted without loss of continuity.

In this chapter, we conclude our discussion of the basic operators and control flow constructs of C.

3.1 The `break` and `continue` Statements

The `break` statement causes an immediate exit from the innermost `while`, `do while`, or `for` loop (or from a `switch` statement, to be introduced in Section 3.3).

Example 3.1.1.   When the segment

```
for ( i = 1; i <= 10; i++ ) {
    printf( "%d\n", i );
    if ( i == 3 )
        break;
    printf( "bottom of loop\n" );
}
printf( "out of loop" );
```

is executed, the output is

```
1
bottom of loop
2
bottom of loop
3
out of loop
```

We first set i to 1. Because i <= 10 is true, we execute the body of the `for` loop. We first execute

```
printf( "%d\n", i );
```

Because i == 3 is false, we next execute

```
printf( "bottom of loop\n" );
```

We increment i so that i is now 2. Because i <= 10 is true, we execute the body of the `for` loop. We first execute

```
printf( "%d\n", i );
```

Because i == 3 is false, we next execute

```
printf( "bottom of loop\n" );
```

We increment i so that i is now 3. Because i <= 10 is true, we execute the body of the `for` loop. We first execute

```
printf( "%d\n", i );
```

Because i == 3 is true, we execute

```
break;
```

which causes an immediate exit from the `for` loop. We execute

```
printf( "out of loop" );
```

Example 3.1.2.   The following program illustrates a typical use of the break statement. The program tests whether the standard input (assumed to consist of integers) is sorted in ascending order. As soon as we find a pair of integers, i followed by after_i with i > after_i, we can stop checking the integers since, at this point, we know the input is *not* in ascending order. The break statement is used to terminate the body of the while loop where the order of the input is tested. If we read to the end of the file, we know that the file is sorted.

```
#include <stdio.h>

main( )
{
    int i,         /* an int in the standard input */
        after_i,   /* the int that follows i in the
                                   standard input */
        eof_flag;  /* flag to signal whether EOF was
                                   encountered */

    scanf( "%d", &i );
    while ( ( eof_flag = scanf( "%d", &after_i ) )
              != EOF )
        if ( i > after_i )  /* order OK? */
            break;          /* if not, terminate
                                          loop */
        else                /*if so, update i &
                                  check next pair */
            i = after_i;

    if ( eof_flag != EOF )
        printf( "\nfile is not sorted\n" );
    else
        printf( "\nfile is sorted\n" );
}
```

The continue statement is similar to the break statement in that the continue statement also terminates the body of the loop, but instead of exiting the loop, we consider resuming execution of the loop. More precisely, if we encounter a continue statement in a while loop, we immediately jump to the top of the loop and test the expression to determine whether to execute the body of the loop again. If we encounter a continue statement in a do while loop, we immediately jump to the bottom of the loop and test the expression to determine whether to execute the body of the loop again. If we encounter a continue statement in a for loop

```
for ( expression 1; expression 2; expression 3 )
    action
```

we immediately execute *expression 3* and then test whether *expression 2* is true or false to determine whether to execute *action* again.

Example 3.1.3.   When the segment

```
for ( i = 1; i <= 3; i++ ) {
    printf( "%d\n", i );
    if ( i == 2 )
```

```
        continue;
     printf( "bottom of loop\n" );
}
printf( "out of loop" );
```

is executed, the output is

```
1
bottom of loop
2
3
bottom of loop
out of loop
```

We first set i to 1. Because i <= 3 is true, we execute the body of the for loop. We first execute

```
printf( "%d\n", i );
```

Because i == 2 is false, we next execute

```
printf( "bottom of loop\n" );
```

We increment i so that i is now 2. Because i <= 3 is true, we execute the body of the for loop. We first execute

```
printf( "%d\n", i );
```

Because i == 2 is true, we execute

```
continue;
```

This causes us to begin immediately the next iteration of the loop. We skip the rest of the statements in the body of the loop. In this case, we do *not* execute

```
printf( "bottom of loop\n" );
```

We jump immediately to the expression i++.

We increment i so that i is now 3. Because i <= 3 is true, we execute the body of the for loop. We first execute

```
printf( "%d\n", i );
```

Because i == 2 is false, we next execute

```
printf( "bottom of loop\n" );
```

We increment i so that i is now 4. Because i <= 3 is false, we terminate the for loop. We execute

```
printf( "out of loop" );
```

Example 3.1.4. The following program illustrates a typical use of the continue statement. The program computes the average of the *positive* numbers in the standard input; it skips the nonpositive numbers by using the continue statement.

```
#include <stdio.h>

main()
{
```

```
float x, sum;
int count;

sum = 0.0;
count = 0;

while ( scanf( "%f", &x ) != EOF ) {
    if ( x <= 0.0 )
        continue; /* skip nonpositive input */
    sum += x;
    count++;
}

if ( count > 0 ) /* any positive numbers read? */
    printf( "\naverage = %f\n", sum / count );
else
    printf( "\nno positive numbers read\n" );
}
```

Exercises

1. What is printed?

```
for ( i = 1; i <= 6; i++ ) {
    if ( i % 2 )
        continue;
    else
        printf( "%d\n", i );
    printf( "bottom of loop\n" );
}
```

2. What is printed?

```
for ( i = 1; i <= 6; i++ ) {
    if ( i % 2 )
        printf( "%d\n", i );
    else
        break;
    printf( "bottom of loop\n" );
}
```

1
bottom of loop

3. What is printed?

```
i = 0;
while ( i < 5 ) {
    if ( i < 2 ) {
        i += 2;
        continue;
    }
    else
        printf( "%d\n", ++i );
    printf( "bottom of loop\n" );
}
```

4. What is printed?

```
i = 0;
while ( i < 5 ) {
      if ( i < 3 ) {
            i += 2;
            printf( "%d\n", i );
            continue;
      }
      else {
            printf( "%d\n", ++i );
            break;
      }
      printf( "bottom of loop\n" );
}
```

5. What is printed?

```
i = 0;
do {
      if ( i < 3 ) {
            i += 2;
            printf( "%d\n", i );
            continue;
      }
      else {
            printf( "%d\n", ++i );
            break;
      }
} while ( i < 5 );
```

6. Rewrite the program of Example 3.1.2 without using a `break` statement.

7. Rewrite the program of Example 3.1.4 without using a `continue` statement.

3.2 Sample Application: Generating Prime Numbers

Problem

Write a program that prints all positive prime integers less than or equal to n. (A positive integer i is **prime** if $i > 1$ and the only divisors of i are 1 and i itself.) The value of n is supplied by the user.

Sample Input/Output

Input is in color; output is in black.

```
This program lists all primes <= n
Input n: 12
      Primes <= 12:
2
3
5
7
11
```

Solution

We begin by prompting the user for a value of n. We then use a `for` loop to step through the integers 2 through n. When we find a prime, we print it. To test whether the integer `possible_prime` is prime, we use another `for` loop to see if any of the integers 2 through `possible_prime` − 1 divide `possible_prime`. (This is not a very efficient way to test whether an integer is prime; see Exercises 1 and 2 for a better method.) If we find a divisor of `possible_prime`, we can immediately terminate the `for` loop using the `break` statement. If we find no divisors of `possible_prime`, we know the integer is prime.

C Implementation

In this example and some subsequent examples, we number certain lines in the source code for reference.

```
/*   This program prints all positive prime integers less than or
     equal to the user-supplied value n.                         */

#include <stdio.h>

main()
{
      int possible_prime, n, possible_divisor;

      printf( "\tThis program lists all primes <= n\n\n\n" );
      printf( "Input n: " );
      scanf( "%d", &n );
      printf( "\n\n\tPrimes <= %d:\n\n", n );
1     for ( possible_prime = 2; possible_prime <= n;
                  possible_prime++ ) {
            /* try to find a divisor of possible_prime */
2           for ( possible_divisor = 2;
                  possible_divisor < possible_prime;
                  possible_divisor++ )
3                 if ( possible_prime % possible_divisor == 0 )
                        /* found a divisor so possible_prime is not
                           prime */
                        break;
4           if ( possible_divisor == possible_prime )
                  /* exhausted possible divisors, so possible_prime
                     is prime */
                  printf( "%d\n", possible_prime );
      }
}
```

Discussion

We trace the prime number program when n is 4. At line 1, we set `possible_prime` to 2. Because `possible_prime <= n` is true, we execute the body of the first `for` loop. At line 2, we set `possible_divisor` to 2. Because `possible_divisor < possible_prime` is false, we do not execute the body of the second `for` loop. At line 4, the condition `possible_divisor == possible_prime` is true, so we print the first prime 2.

At line 1, we increment `possible_prime` so that the value of `possible_prime` is now 3. Because `possible_prime` <= n is true, we execute the body of the first `for` loop. At line 2, we set `possible_divisor` to 2. Because it is true that `possible_divisor` < `possible_prime`, we execute the body of the second `for` loop. At line 3, we compute `possible_prime` % `possible_divisor` = 3 % 2 = 1. Because this expression is not 0, we return to line 2, where we increment `possible_divisor`. The value of `possible_divisor` is now 3. Because `possible_divisor` < `possible_prime` is now false, we exit the second `for` loop. At line 4, the condition `possible_divisor` == `possible_prime` is true, so we print the second prime 3.

At line 1, we increment `possible_prime` so that the value of `possible_prime` is now 4. Because `possible_prime` <= n is true, we execute the body of the first `for` loop. At line 2, we set `possible_divisor` to 2. Because it is true that `possible_divisor` < `possible_prime`, we execute the body of the second `for` loop. At line 3, we compute `possible_prime` % `possible_divisor` = 4 % 2 = 0. Because this expression is 0, we execute the `break` statement, which causes an immediate exit from the `for` loop. In this case, we terminate the second `for` loop (but we remain in the first `for` loop). (In general, the `break` statement terminates the *innermost* loop only.) At line 4, the condition `possible_divisor` == `possible_prime` is false, so we do not execute the `printf` statement. At line 1, we increment `possible_prime` so that the value of `possible_prime` is now 5. Because `possible_prime` <= n is now false, the program terminates.

Exercises

1. Show that the integer $i \geq 2$ is prime if and only if no integer k, $2 \leq k \leq \sqrt{i}$, divides i.

2. Use the result of Exercise 1 to speed up the prime number program given in this section.

3. Can you suggest additional methods to speed up the prime number program given in this section?

4. A student reported that when the following program was run on a desktop computer, it ran perfectly, but when it was run on a super-minicomputer, no output was produced. Explain.

```
#include <stdio.h>

main()
{
        int possible_prime, is_prime, possible_divisor;

        for ( possible_prime = 2; possible_prime <= 4500;
                possible_prime++ ) {
          is_prime = 1;
          for ( possible_divisor = 2;
                possible_divisor < possible_prime;
                possible_divisor++ )
            if ( possible_prime % possible_divisor == 0 )
                is_prime = 0;
```

```
                    if ( is_prime != 0 )
                        printf( "%d  ", possible_prime );
                }
                printf( "\n\n" );
        }
```

3.3 The switch Statement

The switch statement can be regarded as a special instance of the if else−if else−if ⋯ else−if else statement (see Section 1.8) in which the conditions for branching have integer values. One form of the switch statement is

```
switch ( integer expression ) {
case constant 1:
        statements 1
case constant 2:
        statements 2
        .

        .

        .
case constant n:
        statements n
}
```

To execute this form of the switch statement (see Figure 3.3.1), we first evaluate *integer expression*. We then compare the value of *integer expression* with *constant 1*, then *constant 2*, then *constant 3*, and so on. (All the constants must be different.) If the value of *integer expression* equals *constant i*, execution begins with *statements i*. If the value of *integer expression* does not equal any of the constants, execution begins with the statement following the terminating brace of the switch statement. As in the case of loops, break causes an immediate exit from the switch construct. Normally, in every instance, *statements i* concludes with break. Braces need not enclose *statements i*.

Example 3.3.1. When the segment

```
char filing_code;
filing_code = 'm';
switch ( filing_code ) {
case 's':
        printf( "Single\n" );
        break;
case 'm':
        printf( "Married filing joint return\n" );
        break;
case 'h':
        printf( "Head of household\n" );
        break;
}
printf( "*** End of filing status ***\n" );
```

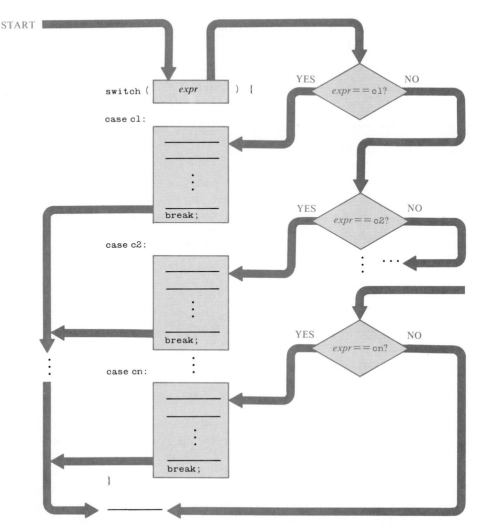

Figure 3.3.1 The `switch` statement.

is executed, the output is

```
Married filing joint return
*** End of filing status ***
```

We first set `filing_code` to the value `'m'`. When we execute the `switch` statement, we compare the value `filing_code` with the constants `'s'`, `'m'`, and `'h'`. Because `filing_code` equals `'m'`, execution resumes with the statement following `case 'm':`. We then execute

```
printf( "Married filing joint return\n" );
break;
```

The `break` statement causes an exit from the `switch` statement. Thus we conclude by executing

```
printf( "*** End of filing status ***\n" );
```

If we were to execute the code of Example 3.3.1 with the break statements removed,

```
char filing_code;
filing_code = 'm';
switch ( filing_code ) {
case 's':
     printf( "Single\n" );
case 'm':
     printf( "Married filing joint return\n" );
case 'h':
     printf( "Head of household\n" );
}
printf( "*** End of filing status ***\n" );
```

the output would be

```
Married filing joint return
Head of household
*** End of filing status ***
```

In this code, we first set filing_code to the value 'm'. When we execute the switch statement, we compare the value filing_code with the constants 's', 'm', and 'h'. Because filing_code equals 'm', execution resumes with the statement following case 'm':. We then execute

```
printf( "Married filing joint return\n" );
```

Because no break statement follows, we simply execute the next statements

```
printf( "Head of household\n" );
printf( "*** End of filing status ***\n" );
```

A second form of the switch statement is

```
switch ( integer expression ) {
case constant 1:
     statements 1
case constant 2:
     statements 2
         .
         .
         .
case constant n:
     statements n
default:
     statements
}
```

To execute this form of the switch statement (see Figure 3.3.2), we first evaluate *integer expression*. We then compare the value of *integer expression* with *constant 1*, then *constant 2*, then *constant 3*, and so on. (All the constants must be different.) If the value of *integer expression* equals *constant i*, execution begins with *statements i*. If the value of *integer expression* does not equal any of the constants, execution begins with *statements*. As in the case of loops, break causes an immediate exit from the switch construct. Normally, in every instance, all *statements* conclude with break. Braces need not enclose *statements i* or *statements*.

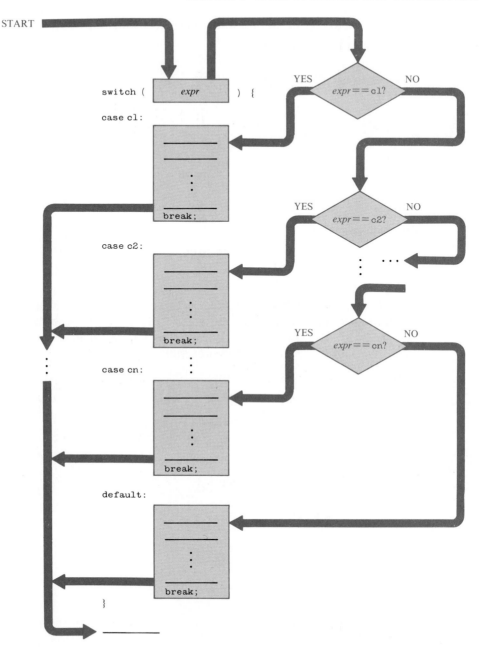

Figure 3.3.2 The switch statement with default.

Example 3.3.2. When the segment

```
char filing_code;
filing_code = 'z';
switch ( filing_code ) {
case 's':
    printf( "Single\n" );
    break;
```

```
case 'm':
     printf( "Married filing joint return\n" );
     break;
case 'h':
     printf( "Head of household\n" );
     break;
default:
     printf( "Filing status missing\n" );
     break;
}
printf( "*** End of filing status ***\n" );
```

is executed, the output is

```
Filing status missing
*** End of filing status ***
```

We first set filing_code to the value 'z'. When we execute the switch statement, we compare the value filing_code with the constants 's', 'm', and 'h'. Because filing_code does not equal any of these constants, execution resumes with the statement following default:. We then execute

```
printf( "Filing status missing\n" );
break;
```

The break statement causes an exit from the switch statement. We execute

```
printf( "*** End of filing status ***\n" );
```

Exercises

1. What is printed?

```
ball_club = 1;
switch ( ball_club ) {
case 0:
     printf( "Mets\n" );
     break;
case 1:
     printf( "Cubs\n" );
     break;
case 2:
     printf( "Royals\n" );
     break;
}
printf( "*** End of baseball team listing\n" );
```

2. What is printed?

```
ball_club = 1;
switch ( ball_club ) {
case 0:
     printf( "Mets\n" );
```

```
case 1:
    printf( "Cubs\n" );
case 2:
    printf( "Royals\n" );
}
printf( "*** End of baseball team listing\n" );
```

3. What is printed?

```
ball_club = 5;
switch ( ball_club ) {
case 0:
    printf( "Mets\n" );
    break;
case 1:
    printf( "Cubs\n" );
    break;
case 2:
    printf( "Royals\n" );
    break;
default:
    printf( "No team\n" );
    break;
}
printf( "*** End of baseball team listing\n" );
```

4. What is printed?

```
ball_club = 5;
switch ( ball_club ) {
case 0:
    printf( "Mets\n" );
case 1:
    printf( "Cubs\n" );
case 2:
    printf( "Royals\n" );
default:
    printf( "No team\n" );
}
printf( "*** End of baseball team listing\n" );
```

5. What is printed?

```
for ( ball_club = 0; ball_club < 7; ball_club += 2 )
    if ( ball_club < 3 ) {
        switch ( ball_club ) {
        case 0:
            printf( "Mets\n" );
            break;
        case 1:
            printf( "Cubs\n" );
            break;
```

```
            case 2:
                 printf( "Royals\n" );
                 break;
            default:
                 printf( "No team\n" );
                 break;
            }
            printf( "*** End of baseball team listing\n" );
    }
    else
            printf( "Strike three!\n" );
```

3.4 The goto Statement and Labels

The goto statement causes an unconditional transfer to some other part of a program. One place in which the goto statement is useful is in exiting from a loop that is contained in several other loops. Because of its ability to jump about, the goto statement is easily abused. Thus we rarely use the goto statement in this book.

A **label** is an identifier followed by a colon:

identifier:

A label is a target of a goto statement.

Example 3.4.1. When the segment in which out is a label

```
    for ( i = 0; i < 5; i++ )
        for ( j = 0; j < 5; j++ )
            for ( k = 0; k < 5; k++ )
                if ( i + j + k == 2 )
                    goto out;
    out: printf( "i = %d, j = %d, k = %d\n", i, j, k );
```

is executed, the output is

i = 0, j = 0, k = 2

The first for loop sets i to 0. The second for loop sets j to 0. The third for loop sets k to 0. Because the expression

i + j + k == 2

is false, we increment k and again execute the body of the third for loop.
At this point, k is 1. Because the expression

i + j + k == 2

is false, we increment k and again execute the body of the third for loop.
At this point, k is 2. Because the expression

i + j + k == 2

is true, we jump to the label out. At this point, we have exited all three for loops. We conclude by executing the printf statement.

3.5   Conditional Expressions

The statement

```
x = flag ? y : y * y;
```

is short for

```
if ( flag )
        x = y;
else
        x = y * y;
```

In general, to obtain the value of the conditional expression

> *expr 1 ? expr 2 : expr 3*

we first determine whether *expr 1* is true or false. If *expr 1* is true, the value of the conditional expression

> *expr 1 ? expr 2 : expr 3*

is *expr 2*; if *expr 1* is false, the value of the conditional expression is *expr 3*. For example, if flag is true, the value of the conditional expression

```
flag ? y : y * y
```

is y; if flag is false, the value of the conditional expression is y * y. Therefore, if flag is true and we execute

```
x = flag ? y : y * y;
```

we assign x the value y; if flag is false, we assign x the value y * y.

Example 3.5.1.   When we execute the statement

```
x = ( i > j ) ? j : i;
```

x is set to the minimum of i and j.

Exercise

1. What is printed?

```
for ( i = 1; i < 4; i++ )
            printf( "%d\n", ( i % 2 ) ? i : 2 * i );
```

3.6   Sample Application: Printing a Calendar

Problem

Write a program that prints a calendar for a year. Prompt the user for which day of the week January 1 is on and whether the year is a leap year. The day that January 1 is on is coded as

```
0 Sunday
1 Monday
2 Tuesday
3 Wednesday
4 Thursday
5 Friday
6 Saturday
```

The leap year condition is coded as

```
0 no leap year
1 leap year
```

Sample Input/Output

Input is in color; output is in black.

```
Enter day and leap year codes: 4 0

January

Sun    Mon    Tue    Wed    Thu    Fri    Sat
                                    1      2      3
  4      5      6      7      8      9     10
 11     12     13     14     15     16     17
 18     19     20     21     22     23     24
 25     26     27     28     29     30     31

February

Sun    Mon    Tue    Wed    Thu    Fri    Sat
  1      2      3      4      5      6      7
  8      9     10     11     12     13     14
 15     16     17     18     19     20     21
 22     23     24     25     26     27     28

              .    .    .
```

Solution

We begin by prompting the user for the January 1 and leap year codes. The variable day_code is initialized to the January 1 code. Before continuing, we check to be sure that day_code is at least 0 and less than 7. If day_code does not satisfy this test, we ask the user for new codes. Because this test comes after the prompt and the user input, we may use a do while loop. (We do not check for a correct code for leap year; 0 is interpreted as a nonleap year and any other value as a leap year. Exercise 1 asks for a version that also checks that the leap year code is either 0 or 1.)

We then step through a for loop to print the 12 months. We use a switch statement to print the name of the month and to set the variable days_in_month to the number of days in the month. We print the name of the month followed by the names of the days:

```
Sun   Mon   Tue   Wed   Thu   Fri   Sat
```

We allocate two columns for the date, regardless of whether it is 1 through 9 or 10 or greater, by using the format descriptor %2d in printf. This format descriptor makes it easy to align the dates correctly. (In Section 8.5, we describe in detail the use of format descriptors with printf and scanf.)

We print 1 for January after skipping

```
1 + day_code * 5
```

spaces. (This formula takes into account our skipping one space to obtain the correct position for a Sunday date and the names being five columns apart; see Figure 3.6.1.) After positioning the print head at the correct position for printing 1 in January, we print the dates for January. If the last date printed is day, we can test the value of

```
( day + day_code ) % 7
```

to decide whether we are at the end of the week and must begin a new line. To reset day_code to the proper value for the next month, we can execute

```
day_code = ( day_code + days_in_month ) % 7;
```

C Implementation

```
/*   This program prints a calendar for a year. The user enters a
code for the day of week for Jan 1 to begin and a code to indicate
whether or not the calendar is to be a leap year calendar.

    The codes are: day_code (0 = Sun, 1 = Mon, etc.)
                       leap_year (0 = no leap year, 1 = leap year)  */
#include <stdio.h>

main()
{
    int day_code, /* day_code = 0 means the month starts on Sun
                     day_code = 1 means the month starts on Mon
                     day_code = 2 means the month starts on
                                  Tues, etc.   */
        days_in_month,     /* number of days in month currently
                              being printed */
        leap_year, /* 1 means leap year; 0 means no leap year */
        day,       /* counter for day of month */
        month;     /* month = 1 is Jan, month = 2 is Feb, etc. */
    do {
        printf( "Enter day and leap year codes: " );
        scanf( "%d%d", &day_code, &leap_year );
    } while ( day_code < 0 || day_code > 6 );

    for ( month = 1; month <= 12; month++ ) {
        switch ( month ) { /* print name and set days_in_month */
        case 1:
            printf( "\n\nJanuary" );
```

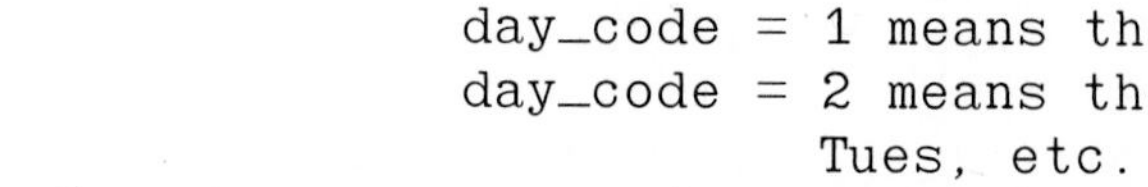

```
Sun⎵⎵ Mon⎵⎵ Tue⎵⎵ Wed⎵⎵ Thu⎵⎵ Fri⎵⎵ Sat⎵⎵
 xx     xx     xx     xx     xx     xx     xx
                      ↑
```

⎵ denotes one blank.
xx denotes the print position for the date.
The arrow shows the print position for 1 in January if day_code = 3.

Figure 3.6.1 Formatting a calendar.

```
        days_in_month = 31;
        break;
    case 2:
        printf( "\n\nFebruary" );
        days_in_month = leap_year ? 29 : 28;
        break;
    case 3:
        printf( "\n\nMarch" );
        days_in_month = 31;
        break;
    case 4:
        printf( "\n\nApril" );
        days_in_month = 30;
        break;
    case 5:
        printf( "\n\nMay" );
        days_in_month = 31;
        break;
    case 6:
        printf( "\n\nJune" );
        days_in_month = 30;
        break;
    case 7:
        printf( "\n\nJuly" );
        days_in_month = 31;
        break;
    case 8:
        printf( "\n\nAugust" );
        days_in_month = 31;
        break;
    case 9:
        printf( "\n\nSeptember" );
        days_in_month = 30;
        break;
    case 10:
        printf( "\n\nOctober" );
        days_in_month = 31;
        break;
    case 11:
        printf( "\n\nNovember" );
        days_in_month = 30;
        break;
    case 12:
        printf( "\n\nDecember" );
        days_in_month = 31;
        break;
    }
printf( "\n\nSun  Mon  Tue  Wed  Thu  Fri  Sat\n" );
/* advance printer to correct position for first date */
for ( day = 1; day <= 1 + day_code * 5; day++ )
    printf( " " );
```

```
/* print the dates for one month */
for ( day = 1; day <= days_in_month; day++ ) {
    printf( "%2d", day );
    if ( ( day + day_code ) % 7 > 0 ) /* before Sat? */
        /* move to next day in same week */
        printf( "    " );
    else /* skip to next line to start with Sun */
        printf( "\n " );
}
/* set day_code for next month to begin */
day_code = ( day_code + days_in_month ) % 7;
    }
}
```

Exercise

1. Write a version of the calendar program that checks that the leap year code supplied by the user is either 0 or 1.

3.7 The Cast Operator

It is possible to convert explicitly one data type to another by using the **cast operator**. The data type to which the value of the original item is converted is written in parentheses to the left of the item. For example, if x is of type int, the value of the expression

```
( float ) x
```

is the original value of x converted to float. (The type and value of x are unchanged.)

Example 3.7.1. Suppose that the value of the int variable hits is the number of hits that a baseball player has made and the value of the int variable at_bats is the number of official at bats by the player. To calculate the player's batting average to several decimal places and to store the average in the float variable average, we could write

```
average = ( float ) hits / ( float ) at_bats;
```

If we simply write

```
average = hits / at_bats;
```

C discards the fractional part of the quotient

```
hits / at_bats
```

because hits and at_bats are of type int. Writing

```
( float ) hits / ( float ) at_bats
```

causes the system first to convert hits and at_bats to float and then to compute the quotient.

Exercise

1. Suppose that the variables x and y are of type `float` and z is of type `double`. Write a statement that stores the quotient x/y in z. Use casts to force the computation to be carried out with `doubles`.

3.8 getchar and putchar

As an alternative to using the format descriptor %c with `scanf` and `printf` to read and write a single character, we may use the functions `getchar` and `putchar`.

The function `getchar` reads one character from the standard input, and the function `putchar` writes one character to the standard output. If we invoke `getchar` and there is no character to read, `getchar` returns the value EOF.

Every C implementation guarantees that the value of EOF is different from the integer code of every character used by that system. This allows us to detect the end of the file without confusing the end-of-file code with the code of a character.

Example 3.8.1. The following program reads the standard input and writes it to the standard output:

```
#include <stdio.h>

main()
{
    int c;

    while ( ( c = getchar () ) != EOF )
        putchar( c );
}
```

We shall trace this program, assuming ASCII coding of characters and -1 as the value for EOF. Suppose that the standard input consists of the three characters

```
xyz
```

The first time we arrive at the `while` loop, `getchar` returns the integer code of the first character, x, in the standard input. Because the ASCII decimal code of x is 120, 120 is assigned to the variable c. (Recall that the value of the expression

```
c = getchar()
```

is the value assigned.) Thus, the expression

```
( c = getchar() ) != EOF
```

becomes

```
120 != -1
```

Because 120 is not equal to -1, the expression is true. In fact, as we previously pointed out, no character code is equal to EOF. Next, the body of the `while` loop is executed. The statement

```
putchar( c );
```

writes the character x to the standard output.

The second time we arrive at the top of the `while` loop, `getchar` returns the integer code of the next character, y, in the standard input. This value is assigned to the variable c. Again the expression

```
( c = getchar( ) ) != EOF
```

is true. The body of the `while` loop is again executed. The statement

```
putchar( c );
```

writes the character y to the standard output.

The third time we arrive at the top of the `while` loop, `getchar` returns the integer code of the last character, z, in the standard input. This value is assigned to the variable c. Once again the expression

```
( c = getchar( ) ) != EOF
```

is true, and we again execute the body of the `while` loop

```
putchar( c );
```

which writes the character z to the standard output.

The fourth time we arrive at the `while` loop, `getchar` attempts to return the code of another character in the standard input, but none exists; so `getchar` returns the value EOF, which is -1 in this example. The expression

```
( c = getchar( ) ) != EOF
```

becomes

```
-1 != -1
```

Because the expression is false, the `while` loop terminates and the program ends.

We emphasize that when `getchar` is invoked and there are no more characters to read in the standard input, `getchar` returns the value EOF. This value is *not* in the standard input. The function `getchar` was written so that when it detects the end of the file, it simply returns the value EOF—a value that does not represent an actual character in the system, whether the system uses ASCII, EBCDIC, or some other encoding of characters as integers.

Because not equal `!=` has a higher precedence than the assignment operator `=`, it is necessary to enclose c = `getchar( )` in parentheses, as shown in Example 3.8.1. If we omit the parentheses and write

```
c = getchar( ) != EOF
```

we first evaluate

```
getchar( ) != EOF
```

If there is a character to read, the value of

```
getchar( ) != EOF
```

is 1 (true) and c is assigned the value 1. In this case, the value of the expression

```
c = getchar( ) != EOF
```

is 1 (true). If we are at the end of the file, the value of

```
getchar( )  != EOF
```

is 0 (false) and c is assigned the value 0. In this case, the value of the expression

```
c = getchar( )  != EOF
```

is 0 (false).

Many systems do not write the output to the video display until a carriage return is typed. In this case, a typical session with this program at the terminal might look like this:

```
That plane's dustin' crops where
That plane's dustin' crops where
there ain't no crops.
there ain't no crops.
```

(Input is in color, and output is in black.) When the first line

```
That plane's dustin' crops where
```

is typed, the system writes the output to a **buffer**, a temporary holding area. The characters in the buffer are not copied to the video display until a carriage return is typed. It appears that

```
That plane's dustin' crops where
```

is typed and there is no output. Actually, after each character is typed, putchar writes the character to the buffer. Immediately after putchar writes the carriage return to the buffer, the buffer is copied to the video display. Similarly, when

```
there ain't no crops.
```

is typed, the characters are placed one by one in a buffer. Following the carriage return, the buffer is copied to the video display. (To signal end-of-file from the keyboard, a control character is typed [see Section 1.6].)

Other systems write each character to the video display immediately after it is typed. In such a system, a typical session with this program at the terminal might look like this:

```
TThhaatt ppllaannee''ss dduusstiinn'' ccrroopps
wwhheerree tthheerree aaiinn''tt nnoo ccrroopps..
```

(Input is in color, and output is in black.)

If we redirect the standard input to a disk file and leave the standard output as the video display and then run the program of Example 3.8.1, the file will appear at the video display. This is equivalent to issuing a type command in VAX/VMS or MS-DOS or issuing a cat command in UNIX.

If we leave the standard input as the keyboard and redirect the standard output to a disk file and then run the program of Example 3.8.1, we will copy whatever we type at the keyboard to the disk file.

If we redirect the standard input to disk file *file1* and we redirect the standard output to disk file *file2* and then run the program of Example 3.8.1, we will copy *file1* to *file2*. This is equivalent to issuing a copy command in VAX/VMS or MS-DOS or a cp command in UNIX.

Notice that in the program of Example 3.8.1, the variable c used to handle the characters was defined as type int. The program may not work properly if c is of type char.

On some systems, the range of char does not include the value EOF. In this case, the expression

```
( c = getchar() ) != EOF
```

is never false, and the loop

```
while ( ( c = getchar() ) != EOF ) {
        .

        .

        .

}
```

never terminates. C ensures that the range of int includes all character codes in addition to the value EOF.

Exercises

1. Assuming ASCII representation of the characters, what is printed when the following program is run and the standard input consists of the following?

   ```
   abc

   #include <stdio.h>

   main()
   {
        int c;
        while ( ( c = getchar() ) != EOF )
             putchar ( c + 10 );
   }
   ```

2. Write a program that prints the number of occurrences of the character ! in the standard input.

3. Write a program that tests whether there are the same number of left brackets, [, as right brackets,], in the standard input.

4. Write a program that tests whether there are the same number of left braces, {, as right braces, }; whether there are the same number of left brackets, [, as right brackets,]; and whether there are the same number of left parentheses, (, as right parentheses,), in the standard input.

5. Assuming ASCII representation of the characters, what is the output if the standard input is the following?

   ```
   abc

   #include <stdio.h>

   main()
   {
        int c;

        while ( c = getchar() != EOF )
             printf( "%d\n", c );
   }
   ```

†3.9 Bitwise Operators

Although C can be used on a variety of computer systems, C lets the programmer interact directly with the hardware of a particular system through bitwise operators and expressions. These operators and expressions also make possible a highly efficient use of storage. The operators work only with integral data types such as char and int. To use bitwise operators and expressions, the programmer must know several things about the underlying hardware:

- The number of bits that make up a byte on the particular system. (On many commonly used systems there are eight bits in a byte.)
- The number of bytes in the integer data types (char, int, etc.).
- The system's character code (e.g., ASCII).
- The type of representation used for integers (e.g., two's complement). (Two's complement is discussed in Appendix B.)

We assume an 8-bit byte, ASCII character representation, a 16-bit cell for storing an int, and two's complement representation.

Bitwise Complement Operator

The **bitwise complement** (or **one's complement**) **operator** ~ (called *tilde*) changes each 1 bit in its operand to 0 and changes each 0 bit to 1.

Example 3.9.1. If the int variable x has the value 6, which in binary is 0000000000000110, the bitwise complement ~x is

    1111111111111001

The decimal value of ~x is -7 (assuming two's complement). Notice that the complement operator does *not* change 6 into -6. The operator ~ merely complements each bit. The decimal values of both the original bit string and the complemented string depend on the system's method of representing integers.

Bitwise Logical Operators

Given two bits b_1 and b_2, we can *and* b_1 and b_2, we can *or* b_1 and b_2, and we can *exclusive or* b_1 and b_2. The following table defines these three operators (*exclusive or* is abbreviated to *exor*):

b_1	b_2	b_1 and b_2	b_1 or b_2	b_1 exor b_2
1	1	1	1	0
1	0	0	1	1
0	1	0	1	1
0	0	0	0	0

The bit

b_1 *and* b_2

†This section can be omitted without loss of continuity.

is 1 if both b_1 and b_2 are 1, and 0 otherwise. The bit

b_1 *or* b_2

is 0 if both b_1 and b_2 are 0, and 1 otherwise. The bit

b_1 *exor* b_2

is 1 if exactly one of b_1 and b_2 is 1, and exactly one is 0. The bit

b_1 *exor* b_2

is 0 if both b_1 and b_2 are 1 or both are 0.

C supports three logical operations on bitwise expressions: the **and operator** &, the **or operator** |, and the **exclusive-or operator** ^. Each operator expects two operands. The result is obtained by using the preceding table to bitwise *and*, *or*, or *exor* the operands.

Example 3.9.2. Given the definitions

```
/* integer variables to be treated as bitwise
   expressions */
int  bitstr1 = 12;
int  bitstr2 = -35;
```

we have

Expression	Binary Representation	Decimal Representation
bitstr1	0000000000001100	12
bitstr2	1111111111011101	− 35
~bitstr1	1111111111110011	− 13
~bitstr2	0000000000100010	34
bitstr1 & bitstr2	0000000000001100	12
~bitstr1 & bitstr2	1111111111010001	− 47
~bitstr1 & ~bitstr2	0000000000100010	34
~(bitstr1 & bitstr2)	1111111111110011	− 13
bitstr1 | bitstr2	1111111111011101	− 35
~(bitstr1 | bitstr2)	0000000000100010	34
bitstr1 ^ bitstr2	1111111111010001	− 47
~(bitstr1 ^ bitstr2)	0000000000101110	46

Example 3.9.3. Recall that ASCII uses seven bits to represent a character. If we are using a computer with an eight-bit byte, one bit is unused when we encode a character in ASCII. Some word processors use this bit to indicate something special about the text, such as a font change or an underline. It is sometimes necessary to convert such files to ordinary ASCII files by setting each leading bit to 0. Notice that if x is the eight-bit string 01111111 and y is any string of eight bits whatever, the leading bit in x & y is 0, and the remaining seven bits are identical to the bits in y. We may use this observation to write the following program that echoes the standard input to the standard output, except that the leading bit in each byte is set to 0:

```
#include <stdio.h>

main()
{
    int c;
    int mask = 127; /* mask is 01111111 in binary */
```

```
        while ( ( c = getchar() ) != EOF )
            putchar( c & mask );
    }
```

Bitwise Shift Operators

The **bitwise shift operators** move bits right or left. The first (or left) argument to a shift operator holds the bits to be shifted, and the second (or right) argument tells how far to shift the bits. The left shift operator is denoted <<, and the right shift operator is denoted >>. Before shifting the bits, if the first operand is of type char or short, it is converted to int. If the first operand is of type unsigned char or unsigned short, it is converted to int, provided that int can represent all the values of the original type; otherwise, it is converted to unsigned int. If the first operand is of type int, unsigned int, long, or unsigned long, it is not converted. The shift expression as a whole has the data type of the converted first operand.

Example 3.9.4.   The code segment

```
int x = 'A'; /* ASCII for 'A' is 65 decimal. */
int y = 3;
printf( "%d", x << y );
```

prints

    520

The ASCII code for 'A' is 65 in decimal and

    0000000001000001

in binary. The expression

    x << y

shifts the bits in x left y positions. In this case, we shift the bits in x left three places. When we execute a left shift operation, we always fill the vacated positions on the right with zeros. The bit string's length remains fixed; in this case, it stays at 16. Thus the value of x << y is

    0000001000001000

which has the value 520 in decimal. The effect of this shift is to drop three bits from the left end and add three zeros to the right end.

Because of the rule about converting the type of the first operand in a shift expression, the output in Example 3.9.4 is unchanged if we define x to be of type char rather than of type int.

We next show what happens if we right shift 'A'.

Example 3.9.5.   The code segment

```
int x = 'A'; /* ASCII for 'A' is 65 decimal. */
int y = 2;
printf( "%d", x >> y );
```

prints

    16

The expression

```
x >> y
```

shifts the bits in x right y positions. In this case, we shift the bits 0000000001000001 right two places. If the leftmost bit is 0, we always fill the vacated positions on the left with zeros. (We will discuss what happens if the leftmost bit is 1 after this example.) As with the left shift operator, the bit string's length remains fixed; in this case, it stays at 16. Thus the value of x >> y is

```
0000000000010000
```

which has the value 16 in decimal. The effect of this shift is to drop two bits from the right end and add two zeros to the left end.

The action of the right shift operator is not standard across systems except for unsigned types. If we right shift bits in an unsigned type, the bits added at the left are zero on any system. Systems vary in how they pad for the other data types. Some always add zeros at the left (such a shift is called a *logical shift*), whereas others add zeros if the preshifted integer is positive, or ones if the preshifted integer is negative (such a shift is called an *arithmetic shift*).

The right operand for either shift operator should be a positive integer, because this operand indicates how far the bit string is shifted. The right operand should not be greater than the bit string's length. It would not make sense to shift, say, a string of 16 bits 20 positions in either direction.

Exercises

Exercises 1 through 4 assume that ints are stored in 16-bit cells, chars are stored in 8-bit cells, ASCII is used to represent characters, and integers are represented using two's complement.

1. What is printed?
   ```
   int   bitstring1 = 111;
   int   bitstring2 = -67;
   printf( "\n%d", bitstring1 | ~bitstring2 );
   printf( "\n%d", ~bitstring2 | bitstring1 );
   printf( "\n%d", ~bitstring1 | bitstring2 );
   ```

2. What is printed?
   ```
   int char1 = 'a';
   int char2 = 'z';
   printf( "\n%d", char1 << 1 );
   printf( "\n%d", char2 << 1 );
   ```

3. What is printed?
   ```
   char char1 = 'a';
   char char2 = 'z';
   printf( "\n%d", char1 << 1 );
   printf( "\n%d", char2 << 1 );
   ```

4. What is printed?
   ```
   int char1 = 'a';
   int char2 = 'z';
   ```

```
printf( "\n%c", char1 >> 1 );
printf( "\n%d", char1 >> 1 );
printf( "\n%c", char2 >> 1 );
printf( "\n%d", char2 >> 1 );
```

5. Explain how the following program tests for odd and even integers:

```
#include <stdio.h>

main()
{
    int mask = 1;
    int input;
    while ( scanf( "%d", &input ) != EOF )
        if ( input & mask )
            printf( "\n\nodd" );
        else
            printf( "\n\neven" );
}
```

6. Explain how the following program slice sets `min_int` to the least `int` (i.e., the negative `int` with the largest absolute value) on whatever system is used. Assume two's complement representation of integers.

```
int min_int = 1;
while ( min_int > 0 )
    min_int <<= 1;
```

7. Write a program slice that sets `max_int` to the largest `int` on whatever system is used. Assume two's complement representation of integers.

8. Given the definition

```
int x;
```

how are the decimal values of x and ~x related?

9. Assume that both a and b are of type `int`. What are the values of a and b after the following code is executed?

```
a = a ^ b;
b = a ^ b;
a = a ^ b;
```

10. Write a program that tests a 16-bit `int` to see whether the bits alternate between 1 and 0. Assume two's complement representation of integers.

11. Write a program that reads 16-bit `int`s and prints the bit string representation of each value read. Assume two's complement representation of integers.

Common Programming Errors

1. The `break` and `continue` statements affect the *innermost* loop only. For example, in

```
1      for ( ... )
2              for ( ... ) {
               .

               .
```

```
            break;
                .
                .
                .
        }
```

the `break` statement causes an exit from `for` loop 2 but *not* from `for` loop 1.

2. In the `switch` construct, the integer expression that follows `switch` must be enclosed in parentheses. Thus it is an error to write

```
    switch i {  /***** ERROR *****/
            .
            .
            .
    }
```

3. In the `switch` construct, the term following `case` must be a constant expression of integer type (and not a variable). Thus it is an error to write

```
    case i:    /***** ERROR *****/
```

when `i` is a variable.

4. Normally, in the `switch` construct, each group of statements following `case` or `default` concludes with `break`. If `break` is omitted, execution continues with the statements in the next `case` or `default`.

5. When using the expression

```
    ( c = getchar() ) != EOF
```

enclose `c = getchar()` in parentheses, as shown. When the expression

```
    c = getchar() != EOF
```

is evaluated, `=` is evaluated *after* `!=`. Thus `getchar()` retrieves the next character from input, which is then compared with EOF. The value of the expression `getchar() != EOF` is either 0 or 1. Thus either 0 or 1 is assigned to `c`.

6. When using the expression

```
    ( c = getchar() ) != EOF
```

define `c` to be of type `int`. On some systems, the loop

```
    while ( ( c = getchar() ) != EOF ) {
            .
            .
            .
    }
```

never terminates if `c` is of type `char`. (The loop never terminates if `c` of type `char` and the range of `char` does not include the value EOF.)

Programming Exercises

3.1. Write a program that converts uppercase characters to lowercase and passes non-uppercase characters unchanged.

3.2. Twin primes are two primes that differ by 2 (e.g., 3 and 5, 101 and 103). Write a program that prints all twin primes less than 1000. (An unsolved problem is whether there are infinitely many twin primes.)

3.3. Write a program that replaces two or more consecutive blanks by a single blank. For example, if the input is

        Let's   go to   the   movies.

the output is

        Let's go to the movies.

3.4. The tax for single taxpayers earning up to $15,610 is shown in the following table:

	Amount	
Over	*But not over*	*Tax*
$0	$2,390	$0
$2,390	$3,540	11% of amount over $2,390
$3,540	$4,580	$126.50 + 12% of amount over $3,540
$4,580	$6,760	$251.30 + 14% of amount over $4,580
$6,760	$8,850	$556.50 + 15% of amount over $6,760
$8,850	$11,240	$870.00 + 16% of amount over $8,850
$11,240	$13,430	$1,252.40 + 18% of amount over $11,240
$13,430	$15,610	$1,646.60 + 20% of amount over $13,430

Write a program that reads the taxable incomes of single taxpayers and lists the taxable incomes and the taxes.

3.5. Using the 15-year property-accelerated method of depreciation, property bought in January is depreciated 12 percent in the first year, then 10 percent, 9 percent, 8 percent, 7 percent, then 6 percent for four years, and then 5 percent for the remaining six years. For example, property worth $40,000 would be depreciated according to the following schedule:

Year	*Amount*
1	$4,800 (= 12% of $40,000)
2	$4,000 (= 10% of $40,000)
3	$3,600 (= 9% of $40,000)
4	$3,200 (= 8% of $40,000)
5	$2,800 (= 7% of $40,000)
6	$2,400 (= 6% of $40,000)
7	$2,400 (= 6% of $40,000)
8	$2,400 (= 6% of $40,000)
9	$2,400 (= 6% of $40,000)
10	$2,000 (= 5% of $40,000)
11	$2,000 (= 5% of $40,000)
12	$2,000 (= 5% of $40,000)
13	$2,000 (= 5% of $40,000)
14	$2,000 (= 5% of $40,000)
15	$2,000 (= 5% of $40,000)
Total Depreciation $40,000	

Write a program that reads a sequence of property values and, for each amount read, prints a table similar to the preceding table.

3.6. Rewrite the calendar program (Section 3.6) so that it prints two months side by side. (In this way, the calendar for one year will fit on one $8\frac{1}{2} \times 11$ inch page.)

3.7. Rewrite the calendar program (Section 3.6) so that the user provides only a year. The program should print a calendar for the given year to the file *calendar.dat*. The first line of output should be the year. Print two months side by side so that the calendar will fit on one $8\frac{1}{2} \times 11$ inch page. For year x, the value of the variable day_code of the program of Section 3.6 is given by

$$\text{day\_code} = \left(x + \left\lfloor \frac{x-1}{4} \right\rfloor - \left\lfloor \frac{x-1}{100} \right\rfloor + \left\lfloor \frac{x-1}{400} \right\rfloor \right) \bmod 7$$

where $\lfloor a \rfloor$ denotes the greatest integer less than or equal to a. Year x is a leap year if and only if

x is divisible by 4 and not by 100

or

x is divisible by 400

3.8. Write a program in which the user enters a year and the output is a list of months with a Friday the thirteenth. (The formulas of Exercise 3.7 may be useful.)

Functions and Program Structure

4

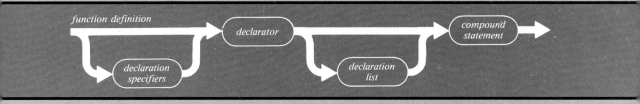

function definition

declaration specifiers

declarator

declaration list

compound statement

4.1   Introduction

4.2   Arguments and Parameters

4.3   Call by Value

4.4   Sample Application: Computing Resistance in Ohms

4.5   The Scope of Variables

4.6   The Preprocessor

4.7   Sample Application: Simulating a Dice Game

4.8   Recursion

4.9   Sample Application: Recursive Tiling

†4.10   Functions with an Arbitrary Number of Arguments

       Changes from Traditional C

       Common Programming Errors

       Programming Exercises

†This section can be omitted without loss of continuity.

A C program consists of one or more functions. Even a small program typically has several component functions, for C encourages the decomposition of a program into multiple component functions. In this chapter, we cover the fundamentals of functions and program structure.

4.1 Introduction

A C program is made up of one or more component functions, exactly one of which must be named `main`. Execution begins with `main`, and the program as a whole terminates when `main` does.† Because a program is an automated solution to a problem, each function solves a part of the problem. Just as a problem decomposes into its parts, a C program decomposes into its component functions.

Example 4.1.1. The program of Figure 4.1.1 reads a midterm grade, a final grade, and a weight, computes a weighted average, and assigns the course grade P (for pass) if the weighted average is greater than 7.0 or F (for fail) if the weighted average is less than or equal to 7.0. The exam scores, `exam1` and `exam2`, are integers between 0 and 10, inclusive, and `exam1_weight` is a real number between 0.0 and 1.0. The weighted average is computed using the formula

```
exam1_weight * exam1 + ( 1.0 - exam1_weight ) * exam2
```

For example, if `exam1` is equal to 8, `exam2` is equal to 6, and `exam1_weight` is equal to 0.76, the weighted average is

```
0.76 * 8 + 0.24 * 6 = 7.52
```

and the course grade is P.

The function `grade` computes the weighted average and determines the course grade. When the function `grade` is invoked in `main`

```
letter_grade = grade( mid_term, final, weight );
```

the value of `mid_term` (in main) is assigned to `exam1` (in grade), the value of `final` (in main) is assigned to `exam2` (in grade), and the value of `weight` (in main) is assigned to `exam1_weight` (in grade), after which the statements in grade begin executing. When a `return` statement executes in grade, a value (either `'P'` or `'F'`) is sent back to `main`. The execution of main's statements resumes at the line where it was suspended:

```
letter_grade = grade( mid_term, final, weight );
```

The assignment statement is completed by assigning the returned value from `grade` to the variable `letter_grade`, after which the line

```
printf( "\nGrade is: %c", letter_grade );
```

executes.

---

†It is possible to invoke certain library functions (such as `exit`) to terminate a program anywhere, but in this chapter we will not use any of these special functions.

```
#include <stdio.h>

main( )
{
    int ans, mid_term, final;

    float weight;
    char letter_grade;

    char grade( int exam1, int exam2, float exam1_weight );

    do {
        printf( "\n\nCompute another grade (1 = Yes, 0 = No)? " );
        scanf( "%d", &ans );
        if ( ans == 1 ) {
            printf( "\nEnter mid term, final, weight: " );
            scanf( "%d%d%f", &mid_term, &final, &weight );
            letter_grade = grade( mid_term, final, weight );
            printf( "\nGrade is: %c", letter_grade );
        }
    } while ( ans == 1 );
}

char grade( int exam1, int exam2, float exam1_weight )
{

    float average;

    average = exam1_weight * exam1 + ( 1.0 - exam1_weight ) * exam2;
    if ( average > 7.0 )
        return ( 'P' );
    else
        return ( 'F' );
}
```

Figure 4.1.1 A program with two functions.

Function Terminology

There are a number of terms that refer to functions with which we must become familiar. Some of the terminology introduced here is developed in the following sections.

Any C function can be **invoked** or **called** by another. For example, in Figure 4.1.1, `main` invokes `grade`. The invoking function may **pass** information to the invoked function, and the invoked function may **return** information to its invoker. By passing and returning information, functions communicate with one another.

An invoking function passes information by passing **arguments**.[†] In C, any expression can be an argument. In the invoking function, arguments are evaluated, and the values are passed to the invoked function. In Figure 4.1.1, the arguments to `grade` are `mid_term`, `final`, and `weight`. The arguments are passed when `grade` is invoked in `main`:

```
    letter_grade = grade( mid_term, final, weight );
```

[†]Certain functions expect an arbitrary number of arguments; `printf` is an example. In Sections 4.1 through 4.9, we assume that each user-defined function expects a fixed number of arguments.

An invoked function has **parameters** that catch the information passed to it. In Figure 4.1.1, the parameters in grade are exam1, exam2, and exam1_weight. We see that arguments and parameters need not have the same names.

Every function has a **header** and a **body**. (Somehow the metaphor was corrupted, and so we talk about a function's ''body'' and its ''header,'' not its ''head.'') In C we **define** a function by giving its header and body.

A function's header consists of

- The data type returned, or the keyword void if the function does not return a value.
- The function's name.
- In parentheses, a list of parameters and their types separated by commas, or the keyword void if the function has no parameters.

Specifying the data type returned is optional; if it is omitted, it defaults to int. The right parenthesis that terminates the parameter list is *not* followed by a semicolon. There is no limit to the number of parameters a function can have, except that the number of parameters must be the same as the number of arguments in any invocation of the function.

The header is followed by the body. A function's body consists of a group of statements enclosed in a pair of braces. The left brace indicates where the body starts, and the right brace indicates where the body ends.

Example 4.1.2.   The header of the function grade of Figure 4.1.1 is

```
char grade( int exam1, int exam2, float exam1_weight )
```

The keyword char indicates that grade returns to its invoker a value of type char. The parameter list

```
int exam1, int exam2, float exam1_weight
```

shows that grade has three parameters: exam1 of type int, exam2 also of type int, and exam1_weight of type float.

The body of grade is

```
{
    float average;

    average = exam1_weight * exam1 + ( 1.0 - exam1_weight ) * exam2;
    if ( average > 7.0 )
        return ( 'P' );
    else
        return ( 'F' );
}
```

Example 4.1.3.   The function echo_line has no parameters and returns a value of type int.

```
int echo_line( void )
{
        .
        .
        .
}
```

Example 4.1.4. The function `print_stars` has one parameter `size` of type `int` and returns no value.

```
void print_stars ( int size )
{
    .
    .
    .
}
```

Example 4.1.5. The function `print_prompt` has no parameters and returns no value.

```
void print_prompt( void )
{
    .
    .
    .
}
```

The `return` Statement

If a C program is very simple, it may consist of just one function, `main`; but `main` usually invokes other functions, some of which invoke others. Obviously, some functions must invoke no others, or the process would continue indefinitely. A function always returns to its invoker. When a function is invoked, the statements in its body begin executing and continue until either a `return` statement or the last statement in its body is executed, after which the statements in the invoking function resume execution in their regular sequence.

The `return` statement is optional in a function that does not return a value but, if used, it is written

```
return;
```

If a function that does not return a value contains no `return` statement, the function returns to its invoker after the last statement in the function's body is executed.

A function that returns a value must have at least one `return` statement, which is written

```
return ( exprn );
```

or

```
return exprn;
```

where *exprn* is any legal C expression. The two forms have exactly the same meaning. When either is executed, the function returns the value *exprn* to its invoker. A function can return at most *one* value per invocation. For example,

```
return ( 45 * 6 + add1( x ) );   /* common * /
```

and

```
return 45 * 6 + add1( x );        /* legal */
```

are equivalent. When either is executed, the function returns the value of the expression

```
45 * 6 + add1( x )
```

to its invoker. The expression

```
45 * 6 + add1( x )
```

is complex, involving even a call to the function add1. The expression's complexity does not violate the rule that the function may return just a single value, for even the most complicated expression evaluates to just one value.

A function may contain any number of return statements. Of course, only one return statement is executed per invocation, because the return statement returns control, and perhaps a value, to the invoking function. In Figure 4.1.1, the function grade has two return statements. Using multiple return statements in if—else or switch constructs is common. As a rule of thumb, we suggest keeping the number of return statements small; otherwise, functions become hard to understand, hard to debug, and hard to alter.

Function Declarations

A function's declaration is different from its definition. To *define* a function is to create it by giving its header and its body. To *declare* a function is to give the data type of the value that the function returns (or void if the function does not return a value), its name, and in parentheses the data types of its parameters separated by commas (or void if the function has no parameters). Unlike a function definition, a function declaration is terminated by a semicolon. The standard style of writing function definitions and declarations in which the data types are included within parentheses is called **function prototype form**.

The declaration of a function f occurs inside each function that invokes f or outside all functions and before the first function that invokes f. A function declaration inside a function g serves as a declaration only for g. A function declaration outside all functions serves as a declaration for all functions that follow it in the same file.

Example 4.1.6. In Figure 4.1.1, the declaration for grade

```
char grade( int exam1, int exam2, float exam1_weight );
```

occurs in main because main invokes grade. We could also have declared grade outside of and before main:

```
#include <stdio.h>
char grade( int exam1, int exam2, float exam1_weight );
main()
{
        .
        .
        .
}
```

Example 4.1.7. To declare the functions of Examples 4.1.3 through 4.1.5, we could write

```
int echo_line( void );
void print_stars( int size );
void print_prompt( void );
```

In a declaration, the names that follow the data types of the parameters are optional and are ignored by the compiler. (In a *definition*, the parameters must always be named.) Names are typically included in a declaration to help document the function. These names need not be the same as the names of the parameters. In Figure 4.1.1, either

```
char grade( int, int, float );
```

or

```
char grade( int mid, int fin, float wt );
```

could serve as a declaration of grade.

The compiler can use a function declaration to check for matches between arguments and parameters of functions and issue appropriate warnings and error messages if it detects problems. In Figure 4.1.1, if we replace the header

```
char grade( int exam1, int exam2, float exam1_weight )
```

by

```
char grade( int exam1, int exam2, int exam1_weight )
```

the Turbo C compiler generates the message

```
Type mismatch in redeclaration of 'grade'
```

If we replace the statement

```
letter_grade = grade( mid_term, final, weight );
```

by

```
letter_grade = grade( mid_term, final );
```

the Turbo C compiler generates the message

```
Too few parameters in call to 'grade' in function main
```

If a function is invoked without being declared, the system will assume (possibly incorrectly) that it returns an int, and no checking for matches of parameters and arguments will occur.

Traditional C

For readers using a traditional C compiler, this subsection will explain how to translate standard function headers and declarations into traditional C.

In traditional C, a function header is written differently than in standard C. The data types are not written within the parentheses; instead, the names of the parameters are repeated after the parentheses with the data types. For example, in traditional C the header of the function grade in Figure 4.1.1 is written

```
char grade( exam1, exam2, exam1_weight )
int exam1;
int exam2;
float exam1_weight;
```

Also, traditional C does not allow the inclusion of parameter names and data types in function declarations, although the data type returned can be indicated. (If the returned data type is omitted in a function declaration, it is assumed to be int.) The returned data type and function name are followed by an empty set of parentheses (to indicate that it is a function and not a variable). For example, in traditional C the declaration of `grade` in Figure 4.1.1 is written

```
char grade( );
```

Since traditional C does not provide information about parameter data types in function declarations, the traditional C compiler is unable to check for matches between arguments and parameters. Figure 4.1.2 shows how the program of Figure 4.1.1 is written in traditional C.

```c
#include <stdio.h>

main( )
{
    int ans, mid_term, final;
    float weight;
    char letter_grade;

    char grade( );

    do {
        printf( "\n\nCompute another grade (1 = Yes, 0 = No)? " );
        scanf( "%d", &ans );
        if ( ans == 1 ) {
            printf( "\nEnter mid term, final, weight: " );
            scanf( "%d%d%f", &mid_term, &final, &weight );
            letter_grade = grade( mid_term, final, weight );
            printf( "\nGrade is: %c", letter_grade );
        }
    } while ( ans == 1 );
}

char grade( exam1, exam2, exam1_weight )
int exam1;
int exam2;
float exam1_weight;
{
    float average;

    average = exam1_weight * exam1 + ( 1.0 - exam1_weight ) * exam2;
    if ( average > 7.0 )
        return ( 'P' );
    else
        return ( 'F' );
}
```

Figure 4.1.2 The program of Figure 4.1.1 written in traditional C.

Functions in Source Files

Unless stated otherwise, we assume throughout this chapter that all of the functions that make up a program are in one file. Other variations, which we explore in Chapter 7, are possible: Each component function in a program may be defined in its own file; or some function definitions can share a file, whereas others do not. However, the entire definition for each function must reside in one file. For example, we cannot put a function's header in one file and its body in a different file. Finally, one function's definition cannot occur in another function's body. The following is *illegal* in C:

```
void fun1( int size )
{   .
    .
    .
    int fun2( char c )      /* ILLEGAL! */
    {   .
        .
        .
    }
    .
    .
    .
}
```

Functions and Program Design

Big problems may require big programs—too big to be written all at one time or to be written by a single programmer. Thus, by decomposing a program into functions, we can divide the work among several programmers. Then it is even possible for the programmers to write the functions at different times. There are other advantages. We can test one function separately from the rest. We can change one function without changing other parts of the program. We can make the program more readable by delegating intricate or otherwise specialized tasks to the appropriate functions.

For example, consider the bar graph program of Section 2.9. This program repeatedly reads the title of a comic book, followed by its value in thousands of dollars, and prints the title followed by a line of stars equal in length to the value. In Section 2.9, we solved this problem using a program consisting of a single function, main. By using multiple functions, we can achieve a better design. If we decompose the problem into the tasks

1. Read and print the title
2. Print the stars

and write functions to solve these tasks, we obtain a program like that shown in Figure 4.1.3.

The function main in Figure 4.1.3 is short and clear because it delegates most of the work to other functions. The function main simply invokes the function echo_line to print the title, and if not at end-of-file reads the value and invokes the function print_stars. The functions echo_line and print_stars handle the details. If not at end-of-file, the function echo_line copies the input to the output until it encounters a newline. The function print_stars prints a line of size stars.

```
#include <stdio.h>

main()
{
    int value;
    int echo_line( void );
    void print_stars( int size );
```

```
    while ( echo_line() != EOF ) {
        scanf( "%d", &value );
        print_stars( value );
    }
}

int echo_line( void )
{
    int c;

    if ( scanf( " %c", &c ) == EOF )
        return ( EOF );

    for ( ; ; c = getchar() ) {
        putchar( c );
        if ( c == '\n' )
            return ( c );
    }
}

void print_stars( int size )
{
    int i;

    for ( i = 1; i <= size; i++ )
        putchar( '*' );
    putchar( '\n' );
}
```

Figure 4.1.3 The bar graph program revisited.

Exercises

1. (True / False) A C program must have a function called `main`.
2. (True / False) If a C program has two component functions, `main` and `mystery`, it is possible that `mystery` invokes `main`.
3. (True / False) An invoking function must pass arguments to the invoked function.
4. (True / False) An argument and its corresponding parameter must have the same name.
5. (True / False) Every function returns a value to its invoker.
6. (True / False) Parameters are declared in the function's header.
7. (True / False) Every function must be defined in its own separate file.
8. (True / False) A function's header and body must be defined within the same file.
9. (True / False) A function may contain more than one `return` statement.
10. (True / False) A function may return more than one value at a time.
11. (True / False) A `return` statement may include an expression that invokes a function.
12. Is the following syntax correct?

    ```
    return;
    ```

13. Explain the difference between the definition of a function and the declaration of a function.

14. What information is given by the following function declaration?

```
int type( float x );
```

15. What is the syntax error in the following function definition?

```
void fun1( int parm1, float parm2 );
{          .
           .
           .
}
```

16. What is the syntax error in the following function definition?

```
void fun1( int, float )
{          .
           .
           .
}
```

17. What is the syntax error in the following function declaration?

```
int status( code char, time float );
```

18. Write the header of a function power with two parameters, base of type double and exponent of type int, which returns a value of type double. How would power be declared in another function that invokes it?

19. Write a function echo_chars with no parameters. The function echo_chars copies the standard input to the standard output and returns the number of characters copied.

20. Write a function main that invokes the function echo_chars of Exercise 19 once. Be sure to declare echo_chars in main. After invoking echo_chars, main prints a message that tells the number of characters copied.

21. Write a function echo_some_chars, with one parameter max_echo, which copies at most max_echo chars from the standard input to the standard output and returns the number of characters copied. The function may copy fewer than max_echo characters if end-of-file is encountered. If at least one character was copied, echo_some_chars returns the number of characters copied; otherwise, echo_some_chars returns EOF.

22. Write a function main that repeatedly invokes the function echo_some_chars of Exercise 21 until end-of-file. First, invoke echo_some_chars with the argument equal to 2, then 4, then 8, and so on. Be sure to declare echo_some_chars in main. After each invocation, have main print a message that tells the number of characters copied.

23. If the function h is invoked as

```
h( ( a, b, c ) );
```

how many arguments are passed to h?

24. Is the following syntactically correct? Explain.

```
return ( val1, val2 );
```

4.2 Arguments and Parameters

A function is invoked with zero or more arguments. The values of the arguments, which represent information passed from the invoking to the invoked function, are obtained from expressions. The arguments are enclosed in parentheses and separated by commas if there is more than one. In the bar graph program (Figure 4.1.3), the function `main` invokes `print_stars` with one argument:

```
print_stars( value );
```

If a function has no arguments, it is invoked with an empty argument list. In the bar graph program, the function `main` invokes `echo_line` with no arguments:

```
while ( echo_line() != EOF ) {
```

Functions can be invoked in two different ways. If a function does not return a value, the function is invoked as was `print_stars`—it is simply named. On the other hand, if a function returns a value, the function's name can appear anywhere a simple variable can appear. For example, in the bar graph program, `echo_line` appears in the expression

```
echo_line() != EOF
```

Within an expression, we invoke a function by naming it. The value returned replaces the function's name in the expression, after which the evaluation of the expression continues. So if `echo_line` returns EOF, the preceding expression evaluates to false; otherwise, it evaluates to true.

Matching Parameters with Arguments

Although arguments and parameters may have different names, a function's parameters should match the function's arguments in number and data type. For example, if a function is invoked with two arguments, it should have two parameters. If the arguments are of type `int` and `char`, respectively, the first parameter should be of type `int` and the second of type `char`. The match between arguments and parameters is important, for parameters are simply variables that are initialized to the values of the arguments when the function is invoked.

> *Example 4.2.1.* The function `human_surface_area` has two parameters, `weight` and `height`, both of type `float`, and returns a value of type `float`. If we want to invoke `human_surface_area` in the function `health`, we should include the declaration
>
> ```
> float human_surface_area( float weight, float height );
> ```
>
> in `health`. We could then invoke `human_surface_area` in `health` by using two arguments that evaluate to `float`. For example, we might have

```
void health (...)
{
    float w, h, hsa1, hsa2, hsa3;
    float human_surface_area( float weight, float height );
        .
        .
        .
```

```
hsa1 = human_surface_area( 100.0, 8.0 );
printf( "Human surface area = %f\n", hsa1 );
scanf( "%f%f", &w, &h );
hsa2 = human_surface_area( w, h );
printf( "Human surface area = %f\n", hsa2 );
scanf( "%f%f", &w, &h );
hsa3 = human_surface_area( w * 0.4536,
                           h * 0.3048 );
printf( "Human surface area = %f\n", hsa3 );
      .
      .
      .
}
```

When a function is invoked and the data type of an argument is different from the data type declared for the parameter, the system converts the data type of the argument to the data type declared, if possible. If the system is unable to convert the data type, an error message is issued.

Order of Evaluation of Arguments

When a function is invoked, all the function's arguments are evaluated before control is passed to the invoked function; however, C does *not* guarantee the *order* of evaluation of the arguments.

Example 4.2.2. Consider a function fun that expects, as arguments, two integer expressions. Suppose that we invoke it, dangerously, as follows:

```
int  num1 = 5;
void fun( int i, int j );
fun( ++num1, ++num1 );  /* caution! */
```

The values passed to fun need *not* be

```
fun( 6, 7 );
```

because C does *not* guarantee any particular order of argument evaluation. C does *not* guarantee a left-to-right, a right-to-left, or any other order of argument evaluation. C guarantees only that all the arguments passed to a function will be evaluated before control passes to the function.

Exercises

1. (True/False) A function is invoked with a call statement, as in

   ```
   call check( guess );
   ```

2. (True/False) In the following slice of code

   ```
   z = 111;
   fun( ++z, ++z, ++z );
   ```

   fun's three arguments must evaluate to 112, 113, and 114 in that order.

3. (True/False) In Exercise 2, fun's three arguments are evaluated before control passes to fun.

4. How is a function that does not return a value invoked?

5. What is the general rule for evaluating a function's arguments?

4.3 Call by Value

Every argument to a function is an expression, which has a value. C passes an argument to an invoked function by making a copy of the expression's value, storing it in a temporary cell, and making the corresponding parameter this cell's identifier. This method of passing arguments is known as **call by value**.

Example 4.3.1. The function `main` in Figure 4.3.1 invokes the function `square`. When invoked, the function `square` multiplies the passed value by itself and returns the result. We show two calls to `square` to illustrate both a simple variable and a complex expression as an argument.

Because `square` returns a value of type `int`, its header

```
7    int  square( int numb )
```

includes the word `int` in front of the function's name. By declaring a single parameter `numb`, we indicate that `square` expects a single argument of type `int` when invoked. The parameter `numb` becomes the identifier of the special cell used to hold a copy of `square`'s argument.

The function `square` is declared in the function `main` that invokes it:

```
4    int  square( int numb );
```

The variables `num1`, `num2`, `ans1`, and `ans2`, defined in lines 1 through 3,

```
1    int    num1 = 5;
2    int    num2 = 2;
3    int    ans1, ans2;
```

```
     main()
     {
1        int num1 = 5;
2        int num2 = 2;
3        int ans1, ans2;
4        int square( int numb );

5        ans1 = square( num1 );
6        ans2 = square( num1 + num2 );
     }

7    int square( int numb )
     {
8        numb = numb * numb;
9        return ( numb );
     }
```

Figure 4.3.1 Call by value.

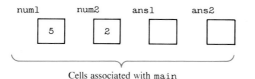

Cells associated with main

Figure 4.3.2 Beginning execution of main.

are the *only* variables defined in the function main. When main begins executing, storage is allocated for these variables (see Figure 4.3.2).

When square is invoked at line 5,

    5   ans1 = square(num1);

a temporary cell for the parameter numb is created (see Figure 4.3.3). The variable num1 is the single argument. A variable is an expression, though a simple one; its value is its contents. Next, num1's value, 5, is copied into the cell numb (see Figure 4.3.4). Notice that the function square works on a *copy* of the argument and not on the argument itself. After num1's contents have been copied into the special cell, nothing happens to num1 at all. Because square works only with a copy of num1's contents and not with num1's original contents, num1 is protected from whatever might occur in the function square.

Execution of square begins at line 8,

    8   numb = numb * numb;

where the item in numb is replaced by 25 (see Figure 4.3.5). When we execute line 9

    9   return (numb);

the value of numb, 25, is returned to the invoking function main, and the temporary cell numb vanishes (see Figure 4.3.6). Execution of the assignment statement 5

    5   ans1 = square(num1);

is completed when the computed value of square, 25, is copied into ans1 (see Figure 4.3.7). The item in num1 remains the same after the call to square.

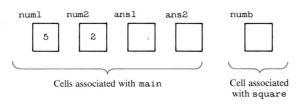

Cells associated with main   Cell associated
                                     with square

Figure 4.3.3 Beginning the first invocation of square.

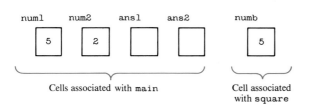

Cells associated with main   Cell associated
                                     with square

Figure 4.3.4 Copying the value of an argument to a parameter.

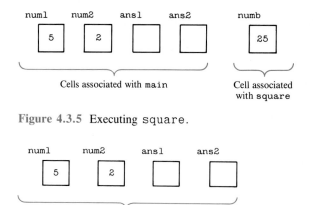

Figure 4.3.5 Executing square.

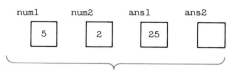

Figure 4.3.6 After square executes the first time.

The function square can access the argument passed to it because its parameter, numb, becomes the identifier of the special cell that holds a copy of the argument. Thus call by value lets us pass arguments to a function but with a guarantee that the original arguments will remain unchanged, no matter what the invoked function does to the copies.

We now move to line 6

6   ans2 = square(num1 + num2);

The key difference between line 6 and line 5 is that the argument to square is now a complex expression rather than a simple one. When we execute line 6, the value, 7, of the argument

num1 + num2

is computed. Again, a temporary cell numb is created, and the value of the argument is copied to numb (see Figure 4.3.8). Note that num1's contents have not changed from the first call to square and that this call also does not alter the contents of either num1 or num2.

Execution of square begins at line 8,

8   numb = numb * numb;

where the item in numb is replaced by 49. When we execute line 9

9   return (numb);

the value, 49, of numb is returned to the invoking function main, and the temporary cell numb vanishes. Execution of the assignment statement 6

Figure 4.3.7 Completion of the first assignment statement.

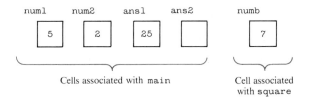

Figure 4.3.8 Beginning the second invocation of square.

```
6    ans2 = square( num1 + num2 );
```

is completed when the computed value of square, 49, is copied into ans2 (see Figure 4.3.9). At this point, the program terminates.

Incidentally, lines 8 and 9

```
8    numb = numb * numb;
9    return ( numb );
```

normally would be reduced to a single line

```
return ( numb * numb );
```

A benefit of call by value is that it protects the values of the arguments in the invoking function from being changed by the invoked function. (In some programming languages, functions work directly on the arguments and not on copies, so that it is easy to change the values of the arguments.) What if the C programmer wants the invoked function to change some values? For example, suppose for some reason that we want to pass square the variable num1 as its argument in Figure 4.3.1, have the function square the argument, and then have the function replace num1's contents by its square. This can be done in C by passing num1's address to square; **call by reference** describes this method of passing arguments to a function. Chapters 5 and 6 go into the details of call by reference. Here we simply mention that C supports call by value and enables the effect of call by reference.

Exercises

1. (True/False) The phrase *call by value* means that a C function always returns a value.

2. (True/False) Call by value ensures that an invoked function cannot change the contents of any variable that occurs as an argument.

3. Suppose that the function fun has three arguments

```
fun( arg1, arg2, arg3 );    /* invoking function fun */
```

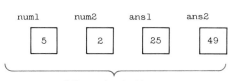

Figure 4.3.9 After square executes the second time.

and the three parameters, as specified in fun's header

```
fun( char parm1, char parm2, char parm3 )   /* fun's header */
```

Using storage cells, explain the relationship between each argument and parameter.

4. Suppose that we add the line

```
    ans1 = square( ans2 );
```

to main after line 6 in Figure 4.3.1. By drawing storage cells like those of Figures 4.3.2 through 4.3.9, show how this assignment statement is executed.

4.4   Sample Application: Computing Resistance in Ohms

Problem

Given single character codes for the colored bands that mark a resistor, compute its resistance in ohms. The color codes are as follows:

Color	Code
Black	0
Brown	1
Red	2
Orange	3
Yellow	4
Green	5
Blue	6
Violet	7
Gray	8
White	9

If the integer codes of the bands are (in order) color1, color2, and color3, the resistance in ohms is

$$\text{resistance} = (10 * \text{color1} + \text{color2}) * 10^{\text{color3}}$$

Sample Input/Output

Input is in color; output is in black.

```
The colored bands are coded as follows:
COLOR                   CODE
─────                   ────
    Black─────────> B
    Brown─────────> N
    Red───────────> R
    Orange────────> O
    Yellow────────> Y
    Green─────────> G
    Blue──────────> E
    Violet────────> V
    Gray──────────> A
    White─────────> W
```

```
        Enter three codes.  ERO
        Resistance in ohms: 62000.000000
```

Solution

We code the colors as single characters: 'B' for black, 'N' for brown, and so forth. We then use a separate function to look up the corresponding numeric values and compute the resistance. If the user enters a bad code, the function decode_char returns the value − 999.0 to flag the bad code. We use the mathematics function pow to compute the exponential. The function pow expects the double values x and y and returns the double value x^y. To provide proper access to the mathematics functions, we include the file *math.h*.

C Implementation

```
/*   This program computes the resistance in ohms for a resistor.
     It prints a menu of colors of bands that mark a resistor and
     asks the user to enter character codes for each brand; for
     example, the user might enter 'B' for black. The program
     decodes the characters, computes the resistance, and prints
     the result.

     The function main invokes print_codes to print the codes,
     getchar to read three such codes from the keyboard, and
     decode_char to do the decoding. main uses a standard library
     function pow, which raises a number to a power to help
     compute the resistance; main then prints the resistance as a
     floating-point number.                                      */
#include <stdio.h>
#include <math.h>
main()
{
        char      code1, code2, code3;      /* one code per band */
        double    resistance;
        double    color1, color2, color3;   /* decoded values */
        int       flag;

        void      print_codes( void );      /* menu of codes */
        double    decode_char( char code );

        /* Print codes and prompt for user input. */
        print_codes();
        printf( "\n\n\tEnter three codes. " );

        /* Read three character codes. */
        code1 = getchar();
        code2 = getchar();
        code3 = getchar();

        /* Decode each character code. */
        color1 = decode_char( code1 );
        color2 = decode_char( code2 );
        color3 = decode_char( code3 );
```

```
      /* Check whether codes were legal. */
      if ( color1 == -999.0  ||  color2 == -999.0  ||
           color3 == -999.0 )
           printf( "\n\n\tBad code -- cannot compute resistance\n" );

      /* If codes were legal, compute and print resistance in ohms. */
      else {
           resistance = ( 10.0 * color1  +  color2 )
                          * pow( 10.0, color3 );
           printf( "\n\n\tResistance in ohms:\t%f\n", resistance );
      }
}

/*   This function prints a menu of color codes to guide the user
     in entering input. */
void  print_codes( void )
{

   printf( "\n\n\tThe colored bands are coded as follows:\n\n\n\t" );
   printf( "COLOR\t\t\tCODE\n\t" );
   printf( "-----\t\t\t----\n\n" );
   printf( "\tBlack----------> B\n" );
   printf( "\tBrown----------> N\n" );
   printf( "\tRed------------> R\n" );
   printf( "\tOrange---------> O\n" );
   printf( "\tYellow---------> Y\n" );
   printf( "\tGreen----------> G\n" );
   printf( "\tBlue-----------> E\n" );
   printf( "\tViolet---------> V\n" );
   printf( "\tGray-----------> A\n" );
   printf( "\tWhite----------> W\n" );
}

/*   This function expects a character (color code) and returns a
     double precision floating-point number as its value. If the
     code is not legal, it returns a value that signals this fact. */
double decode_char( char code )
{
     switch ( code ) {
     case 'B':
          return ( 0.0 );
     case 'N':
          return ( 1.0 );
     case 'R':
          return ( 2.0 );
     case 'O':
          return ( 3.0 );
     case 'Y':
          return ( 4.0 );
     case 'G':
          return ( 5.0 );
```

```
     case 'E':
          return ( 6.0 );
     case 'V':
          return ( 7.0 );
     case 'A':
          return ( 8.0 );
     case 'W':
          return ( 9.0 );
     default:
          return ( -999.0 );/* illegal code */
     }
}
```

Exercises

1. Modify the program of this section to take into account the possibility that the third band of a resistor can be any of the listed colors or silver (whose code is −2) or gold (whose code is −1).

2. Modify the program of Exercise 1 to decode a fourth band, if present. If there is no fourth band, the tolerance (that is, the percentage by which the rated resistance might vary) is 20 percent. If the fourth band is silver, the tolerance is 10 percent. If the fourth band is gold, the tolerance is 5 percent. The program should print the smallest possible resistance (in ohms) and the largest possible resistance.

4.5 The Scope of Variables

In addition to parameters, functions usually use variables. Every variable has a **scope**—the region of the program in which it is **visible**. A variable is visible in a region if it can be referenced in that region. For example, the program of Section 4.4 has a variable code1 defined in the first line of main's body. The scope of the variable code1 extends from this line to the last line in main, but it does not extend to other functions. Thus code1 can be accessed in main but not in print_codes.

Variables Local to a Function

The variables that we have been defining are **local** to the functions in which they reside. In other words, a variable of the type we have been using is visible only within the function that contains its definition, and it may be accessed only within this function. (It is possible for a variable to have scope larger or smaller than an entire function. We discuss these options in Chapter 7.)

Example 4.5.1. Suppose that we have two functions, move_left_leg and move_right_leg, that are components of the same program and that each has two variables named i and j:

```
void  move_left_leg( void )
{
     /* This i and j are local to move_left_leg. */
          int i, j;
```

.
.
.
```
}
void  move_right_leg( void )
{
    /* This i and j are local to move_right_leg. */
    int i, j;
        .
        .
        .

}
```

The variables i and j in move_left_leg are local to move_left_leg, and the variables i and j in move_right_leg are local to move_right_leg. We have four *distinct* variables, although two happen to be named i and the other two j. If one programmer writes move_left_leg and another writes move_right_leg, neither has to worry about what the other uses as names for local variables; hence, each programmer can use variables named i and j. The compiler ensures that the variables named i and j in one function are distinct from the variables named i and j in the other.

In general, any legal identifier may be used for a function variable. However, it is illegal to define two variables that have the same scope and the same name. Also, it is illegal to define a variable within a function with the same name as one of its parameters.

Exercises

1. (True / False) C allows distinct variables to have the same names.
2. Explain the relationship between the variables f1 and f2 in the functions main and fun1.

```
main()
{
    float f1, f2;
    char  c1;
    int   fun1( float p1, float p2 );
    .
    .
    .

}
int  fun1( float p1, float p2 )
{
    float  f1, f2;
    .
    .
    .

}
```

3. What is the error?

```
int schedule( char activity )
{
        int i;
        float time;
        int activity;
        .
        .
        .
}
```

4.6 The Preprocessor

The C preprocessor processes a C source file before the compiler translates the program into object code:

C Source Code $\rightarrow$ Preprocessor $\rightarrow$ Compiler

The preprocessor follows the programmer's *directives*, which are commands that start with the character #. We previously introduced the #include directive. C programs typically include the preprocessor directive

```
#include <stdio.h>
```

to provide a proper interface to the standard input / output libraries. The preprocessor also provides a **macro** facility. Macros resemble functions but are handled by the system quite differently than functions. In this section, we treat the #include directive in more detail, introduce macros, and explain the other directives of the preprocessor (Figure 4.6.1 lists all the directives with brief explanations).

Directive	*Meaning*
#include	Include the contents of a text file.
#define	Define a macro.
#undef	Cancel a previous #define.
#if	If a test succeeds, take specified actions.
#ifdef	If a macro is defined, take specified actions.
#ifndef	Opposite of #ifdef—if a macro is not defined, take specified actions.
#else	If the previous #if, #ifdef, or #ifndef fails, take specified actions.
#endif	Mark the end of an #if, #ifdef, or #ifndef body.
#elif	"Else if"—a way around nested #if–#else constructs.
#line	Set line number for the compiler to use when issuing warning or error messages.
#error	Specify a compile-time error and an accompanying message.
#pragma	Provide implementation-specific information to the compiler.
#	Ignore this line.

Figure 4.6.1 Preprocessor directives.

Preprocessor directives may start in any column, although they traditionally start in column 1. Directives may occur on any line inside or outside function definitions, but they typically occur at the beginning of a file so that they take effect in all succeeding lines. Although directives can be quite elaborate, our examples are straightforward. The programmer must keep in mind that the preprocessor follows directives literally. It knows nothing about C's syntax or semantics, much less about the programmer's intentions.

File Inclusions

The #include directive

```
#include <stdio.h>
```

instructs the preprocessor to include the contents of the file *stdio.h*. The angle brackets indicate that this file is to be found in a directory already known to the operating system. The brackets typically are used to #include any standard header files, as well as any other header files provided by the local implementation. The preprocessor searches the directory for the file, and when it finds the file, it replaces the #include line by the specified file. An #included file may have any name but traditionally carries a *.h* extension to underscore its status as a header file, namely, a file to be #included at the head of some other file.

The #include directive

```
#include "mydefs.h"
```

with the file name in double quotation marks, directs the preprocessor to include the contents of a file to be found in the working (generally the current) directory.

Every standard C implementation furnishes libraries of functions, as well as header files that enable the use of these libraries and contain definitions of several macros. (Macros are discussed later in this section.) The actual code for the system functions resides in system run-time libraries; the system header files contain declarations of these functions. By using system functions and macros, the programmer is relieved of the responsibility for writing his or her own. Figure 4.6.2 lists some useful system header files, brief descriptions of the files, and the section in this book where each file is introduced. Appendix E lists the header files needed to use a number of standard functions. Appendix F discusses run-time libraries.

System Header File	Purpose
ctype.h	Functions for testing and modifying characters (see Section 8.5)
float.h	Describes local floating point conditions (see Section 2.3)
limits.h	Describes local integer conditions (see Section 2.2)
math.h	Math functions (see Section 2.6)
stdarg.h	Functions with an arbitrary number of arguments (see Section 4.10)
stdio.h	Input and output (see Section 1.1)
stdlib.h	General utilities (see Section 4.9)
string.h	String-handling functions (see Section 5.7)
time.h	Time functions (see Section 6.10)

Figure 4.6.2 Some useful system header files.

Using One File Inclusion

A file may contain any number of #include directives. Further, the directives may be nested: One #included file may #include another, which #includes another, and so on. At least eight levels of nesting are guaranteed. A good way to manage #include directives is to consolidate them in one file and then to include this file wherever needed. For example, suppose that our program has six component functions, each of which needs access to *stdio.h*, access to the same user-defined constants, and access to the mathematics library. We could build one file called *all.h*, which contains

```
/* file inclusions */
#include <stdio.h>
#include <math.h>

/* user-defined constants */
#include "defs.h"
```

The program would contain the line

```
#include "all.h"
```

which would then be replaced by the files *stdio.h*, *math.h*, and *defs.h*.

Care must be taken when recompiling programs whose component functions have #include directives. Suppose that *defs.h* is included in six different files, each holding one or more functions. If we later change the contents of *defs.h*, we must be sure to recompile all the functions that the #include directive affects. If we forget to recompile all the affected functions, some functions may work with the old contents of *defs.h*, whereas others may work with the new version. This is almost sure to cause a run-time error that may be very hard to track down.

Macros

In Section 1.6 we introduced the symbolic constant EOF, which represents end-of-file. The file *stdio.h* contains a preprocessor directive that might look like this:

```
#define EOF (-1)
```

This #define directs the preprocessor to replace subsequent occurrences of EOF with (-1), a C expression that evaluates to the negative integer -1. The technical name for the #defined EOF is **macro**, and it is common to say that the macro EOF *expands* into (-1), which is its value. The use of parentheses in the #define for EOF is a habitual precaution to ensure that the preprocessor correctly expands EOF.

> *Example 4.6.1.* Consider this series of #defines, which shows how a macro, once #defined, can be used in the #define of a subsequent macro. The example also shows that #defines can be documented in the normal C style.

```
#define NormalMeetings    3   /* with Boss1, Boss2, Boss3 */
#define SpecialMeetings   2   /* morning nap and afternoon
                                    cocktail */
#define TimePerMeeting   20   /* in minutes */
/** Caution! **/
#define TotalMeetings    NormalMeetings + SpecialMeetings
#define TotalTime        TotalMeetings * TimePerMeeting
```

The value of `TotalTime` is 43, not the expected 100. The macro `TotalMeetings` expands into

```
NormalMeetings + SpecialMeetings
```

and these macros expand into

```
3 + 2
```

`TotalTime` expands into `TotalMeetings` multiplied by `TimePerMeeting`, or

```
3 + 2 * 20
```

In C, the multiplication operator has higher precedence than the addition operator, so multiplication occurs before addition. In effect, `TotalTime` expands into

```
3 + ( 2 * 20 )
```

which evaluates to 43. The problem can be avoided by parenthesizing the `#define` for `TotalMeetings`:

```
#define TotalMeetings ( NormalMeetings + Special Meetings )
```

`TotalTime` now expands into the expression

```
( 3 + 2 ) * 20
```

which has 100 as its value. Of course, it would be prudent to use parentheses in the `#define` for `TotalTime` as well:

```
#define TotalTime ( TotalMeetings * TimePerMeeting )
```

It is illegal to change the definition of a macro by using a second `#define` statement (unless the macro is first undefined using the `#undef` directive). It is legal to repeat a `#define` statement. For example, many versions of *stdio.h* contain the definition

```
#define TRUE 1
```

Even if this definition appears in *stdio.h*, it is still legal to write

```
#include <stdio.h>
#define TRUE 1
```

A `#define` may occur on more than one line if the backslash is used. For example,

```
#define TotalMeetings  \          /* carry over to next line */
       ( NormalMeetings + \   /* ditto */
         SpecialMeetings )
```

allows the `#define` to occur on three lines in all.

Parameterized Macros

Macros may be `#defined` with parameters, which act as placeholders for actual arguments. A parameterized macro begins with `#define`. Next comes the name of the macro and then parentheses containing the parameters. The parameters are separated by commas. No white space is allowed between the macro name and the left parenthesis. (When white space follows the macro name, the macro is assumed to be an unparenthesized macro like those in the preceding subsection.) The macro name and parentheses are followed by the macro's definition. In the code that follows a macro definition, the preprocessor substitutes each occurrence of the macro by its definition.

For example, suppose that our program repeatedly needs a `printf` statement with three arguments: two character expressions and an integer expression. Suppose also that we want the arguments printed on a new line, separated by tabs. We can write a macro to do this printing, as follows:

```
#define PRINT3( e1, e2, e3 ) \
        printf( "\n%c\t%c\t%d", (e1), (e2), (e3) )
```

We show how the preprocessor will handle the code:

```
#include <stdio.h>

#define PRINT3( e1, e2, e3 ) \
        printf( "\n%c\t%c\t%d", (e1), (e2), (e3) )

main()
{
    char char1 = 'A';
    char char2 = 'Z';
    int num = 999;

    PRINT3( char1, char2, num + 1 );
}
```

The macro PRINT3 expects three arguments, as indicated by the three parameters e1, e2, and e3 in its definition. We use PRINT3 in the function's body with char1, char2, and num + 1 as the actual arguments:

```
PRINT3( char1, char2, num + 1 );
```

Notice again that we supply the semicolon, as it is not included in PRINT3's definition. Substituting the three actual arguments char1, char2, and num + 1 in PRINT3's definition gives

```
printf( "\n%c\t%c\t%d", (char1), (char2), (num + 1) )
```

for the expansion. The output is

```
A       Z       1000
```

In the `printf`, we enclosed each of PRINT3's parameters in parentheses because, as noted previously, in certain contexts omitting the parentheses may cause problems.

Parameterized Macros Versus Functions

The similarity in syntax between parameterized macros and functions should not obscure important differences between them.

Example 4.6.2. The code

```
#include <stdio.h>

#define min( x, y )  ( ( (x) < (y) ) ? (x) : (y) )

main()
{
    int num1, num2,
        max( int x, int y );
```

```
    /* Read two integers. */
    printf( "\n1st num: " ); scanf( "%d", &num1 );
    printf( "\n2nd num: " ); scanf( "%d", &num2 );

    /* Print their min and max. */
    printf( "\n\nMin: %d\tMax: %d\n",
        min( num1, num2 ),              /* macro */
        max( num1, num2 ) );           /* function */
}

int max( int x, int y )
{
    return ( ( x > y ) ? x : y );
}
```

implements `min` as a parameterized macro and `max` as a function. Although it is common to say that a parameterized macro such as `min` is invoked (within the last `printf` statement), this is technically wrong. No arguments are passed to `min` and `min` returns no value. Instead, the preprocessor merely replaces

```
min( num1, num2 )
```

with

```
( ( (num1) < (num2) ) ? (num1) : (num2) )
```

before the code is even compiled, let alone run. By contrast, `max` is implemented as a function. Function calls have an associated overhead when a program is executed because the system must make copies of any arguments passed to the function, keep track of where to resume program execution when the function returns, and so on. Macros do not incur such run-time overhead and, in this sense, are more efficient than functions.

There are other subtle differences between macros and functions. No type checking of arguments in macros is done. This is sometimes an advantage. For example, the macro `min` in Example 4.6.2 can find the minimum of any two numeric data types (`float`, `int`, `long double`, etc.). At the same time, this lack of type checking can introduce errors that are difficult to uncover. For example, the macro `min` in Example 4.6.2 also produces some value, presumably useless, when one argument is a string and the other a `float`.

Macros can produce surprising and unpredictable side effects. For example, consider the macro `square` defined as

```
#define square( x ) (x) * (x)
```

When the following code is preprocessed

```
a = 3;
b = square( a++ );
```

the second line is expanded as

```
b = (a++) * (a++);
```

When the code is executed, if the implementation evaluates one (`a++`) to obtain the value 3, then increments a, next evaluates the other (`a++`) to obtain the value 4, and then increments a again, the value of a becomes 5 and the value of b becomes 12. (This is the behavior in our VAX-11 C.) On the other hand, if the implementation first evaluates each (a++) so that each receives the value 3, and then twice increments a, the value of a again becomes 5, but this time the value of b becomes 9. (This is the behavior in Turbo C and in some UNIX systems.)

If square is implemented as a function

```
int square( int x )
{
        return ( x * x );
}
```

after the code

```
a = 3;
b = square( a++ );
```

is executed, the value of a is 4 and the value of b is 9 irrespective of the particular implementation.

The Convenience of Macros

Parameterized macros resemble functions, especially if the macros are written in lower-case letters. For example, getchar looks like a function, although it is usually implemented as a macro by a #define directive in the file *stdio.h*. The macro getchar can be defined by writing

```
#define     getchar()      fgetc( stdin )
```

The function fgetc(fp) reads a single character from the file referenced by the file pointer fp (see Section 1.10). The file pointer stdin is defined in *stdio.h* so as to reference the standard input. In particular, fgetc(stdin) reads one character from the standard input. Thus, when getchar() is expanded to fgetc(stdin), whenever we encounter getchar() we read one character from the standard input. putchar is also usually implemented as a macro. The macros getchar and putchar are defined for convenience; they are somewhat simpler to use than the functions fgetc and fputc, by which they are replaced when the macro is expanded.

Miscellaneous Directives

We conclude this section by briefly clarifying and illustrating each of the remaining preprocessor directives.

The #undef directive

```
#undef      TRUE
```

instructs the preprocessor to cancel any definition of TRUE. An #undef can be used to guard against conflicts between two macros or between a macro and a variable. For example, if a programmer intends to define a variable named TRUE, he or she first might #undef TRUE as a precaution.

The #ifdef directive

```
#ifdef      BIG_TABLE
#define     ROWS          10000
#define     COLUMNS       10000
#define     TAB_SIZE      ( ROWS * COLUMNS )
#endif
```

instructs the preprocessor to define macros ROWS, COLUMNS, and TAB_SIZE if the macro BIG_TABLE is already defined. So if the preprocessor first encounters

```
#define    BIG_TABLE
```

it then #defines ROWS, COLUMNS, and TAB_SIZE. Note that the #endif directive marks the end of the conditional directive. In this example, the #define does not specify a value for BIG_TABLE. The #ifdef test does not check whether a macro has a particular value but, rather, whether it has been #defined at all.

The #ifndef directive is the opposite of #ifdef. The #ifndef directive

```
#ifndef    INTEGER
#define    INTEGER       short int
#endif
```

instructs the preprocessor to define INTEGER as short int if INTEGER has *not* been defined already. The directive says, in effect: Use this definition of INTEGER if you do not have one already.

The #ifndef directive

```
#ifndef    BIG_TABLE
#define    ROWS          10000
#define    COLUMNS       10000
#define    TAB_SIZE      ( ROWS * COLUMNS )
#endif
```

directs the preprocessor to define ROWS, COLUMNS, and TAB_SIZE if BIG_TABLE has *not* been defined already.

The preprocessor also recognizes the term defined. The code

```
#if defined( BIG_TABLE )  &&   !defined( SMALL_TABLE )
#define   ROWS          10000
#define   COLUMNS       10000
#define   TAB_SIZE      ( ROWS * COLUMNS )
#endif
```

shows how the #if directive, together with the defined construct, accomplishes what otherwise would require an #ifndef nested in an #ifdef:

```
#ifdef    BIG_TABLE
#ifndef   SMALL_TABLE
#define   ROWS          10000
#define   COLUMNS       10000
#define   TAB_SIZE      ( ROWS * COLUMNS )
#endif
#endif
```

The two examples have the same effect, but the first is more concise. Both #ifdef and #ifndef are restricted to a *single* expression as a test, but the #if combined with defined allows compound expressions.

The following code

```
#include <stdio.h>
#define   TRACE   1
main( )
{
```

```
int    current_count;
float  percentage;
               .
               .
               .

#if TRACE
printf( "\n\nCurrent count == %d\n", current_count );
printf( "\n\nPercentage == %f\n", percentage );
#endif
               .
               .
               .

}
```

illustrates *conditional compilation*. Imagine that you are programming in an environment that has no built-in tracing or debugging facilities and that you want to trace the values of the variables current_count and percentage. You can use the #if directive to implement your own tracer. In our example, the tracer can be turned on by defining TRACE as any nonzero value and turned off by defining TRACE as 0. If TRACE is nonzero, the compiler compiles the lines

```
printf( "\n\nCurrent count == %d\n", current_count );
printf( "\n\nPercentage == %f\n", percentage );
```

If TRACE is 0, these lines are not compiled. If we no longer need the tracer, we simply #define TRACE as zero instead of deleting the printf statements. (In Section 2.5.1, we showed an alternative way to skip code by using the if statement.)

The #else directive has the expected meaning. Suppose that we know that a program will be run either on a VAX, which implements a short int as a 16-bit cell, or on an IBM PC, which implements an int as a 16-bit cell. If we want our integer variables to be implemented as 16-bit cells on either machine, we can define them as INTEGER data types; for example,

```
INTEGER count;
```

and include the following directives at the beginning of the program:

```
#ifdef    VAX_COMPUTER
#define   INTEGER   short int
#else
#define   INTEGER   int
#endif
```

If the program is to run on a VAX, we #define the macro VAX_COMPUTER; otherwise, we leave it undefined.

The #ifdef and #else directives can be used to customize code. Consider an example from Turbo C. If the user #defines the macro UNIX_matherr, the code that defines a UNIX C error handler is compiled; otherwise, the code that defines an alternative, and less powerful, error handler is compiled. The construct may be outlined as

```
#ifdef UNIX_matherr
       /* definition of the UNIX error handler */
#else
       /* definition of the alternate error handler */
#endif
```

More than one line can follow the #else directive, just as more than one can follow the #ifdef directive. Note that we always conclude with #endif. The #else also can be used with the #if and the #ifndef.

The #elif directive is short for "else if" and gives an alternative to nested #if directives. In the code

```
#if          defined( VAX )
#define      GREETING  printf( "\n\n\t\tWelcome to VAX C!\n" )
#elif        defined( IBM )
#define      GREETING  printf( "\n\n\t\tWelcome to IBM C!\n" )
#elif        defined( ATT )
#define      GREETING  printf( "\n\n\t\tWelcome to ATT C!\n" )
#else
#define      GREETING  printf( "\n\n\t\tWelcome C, PERIOD!\n" )
#endif
```

the preprocessor checks whether VAX is #defined, and if so, it #defines GREETING with a VAX message. If not, it checks whether IBM is #defined; and if so, it #defines GREETING with an IBM message; and so on. Note that we terminate with #endif and use #else to complete the construct.

Suppose that the file *prog1.c* is

```
#include "mydefs.h"
main( )
{         .
          .
          .
}
```

If *mydefs.h* contains 24 lines of text and the 13th line of *prog1.c* contains a syntax error, the typical C compiler issues a message that an error has occurred at line 37, not line 13, because the preprocessor includes the 24 lines from *mydefs.h* before passing the *prog1.c* file along to the compiler. The experience can be very frustrating, especially if you look at line 37 in *prog1.c*. Indeed, there may be no line 37 in *prog1.c*! The #line directive directs the compiler how to number lines and, optionally, which file name to use in reporting an error.

If we change *prog1.c* to

```
#include "mydefs.h"
#line 1
main( )
{         .
          .
          .
}
```

the #line directive instructs the compiler to treat the following line as number 1, the next as line 2, and so on. Now, when the compiler detects the syntax error at line 13 of *prog1.c*, it reports the error as occurring at line 13 of *prog1.c*.

The #line directive has an optional second argument, a character string, that should be the name of a file. For example, the directive

```
#line   25   "oldprog1.c"
```

instructs the compiler to treat the following line as number 25 and to report any errors as originating in the file *oldprog1.c*.

The #error directive

```
#if  defined( ATT )  &&  defined( IBM )
#error "You can't be on two computers at once!!!"
#endif
```

instructs the compiler to generate an error and to display a corresponding message. The directive lets the programmer extend the compiler's own error-detection and error-message capabilities.

The #pragma directive gives the compiler implementation-specific instructions. One simply writes #pragma and then the name of the instruction. For example, we might write

```
#pragma    inline
```

to tell the compiler that the file contains in-line assembly code. If the compiler does not understand the instruction in a #pragma line, it simply ignores it.

A line containing only # is called a *null directive* and is simply ignored by the compiler.

Exercises

1. (True/False) A single #include directive may name several files.
2. Write an #include directive to include the system file *time.h*.
3. Write an #include directive to include the user file *structures.h*.
4. Write the #include directive necessary to use the library function rand (see Appendix E).
5. Where does the C preprocessor put the contents of the file that it has been directed to include in another file?
6. In #include directives, why are some file names enclosed in double quotation marks, whereas others are enclosed in angle brackets?
7. (True/False) A macro, which is created through a #define directive, must be written in uppercase letters.
8. (True/False) Each macro requires a separate #define directive to create it.
9. What is the output?

```
#include <stdio.h>
#define min( x, y ) ( (x) < (y) ) ? (x) : (y)
main()
{
    printf( "%d\n", min( 3, 6 ) + 1 );
}
```

10. Find the syntax error.

```
#define        PLUS
          +
```

11. Write a macro dbl with one parameter x that multiplies x by 2.

12. Show an expansion of the macro

```
#define TIMES2( num ) 2 * num
```

that does not give the intended result.

13. The following are two definitions for a macro that picks the maximum of two numbers. Which is better, and why? Give an example to illustrate your preference.

```
#define MAX1( num1, num2 ) ( num1 > num2 ? num1 : num2 )
#define MAX2( num1, num2 ) ( (num1) > (num2) ? (num1) : (num2) )
```

14. One version of the VAX-11 C compiler automatically #defines the macro vax11c as 1 but does not #define EXIT_SUCCESS and EXIT_FAILURE, although these macros are specified by the standard. Write code that #defines EXIT_SUCCESS as 1 and EXIT_FAILURE as 0 (the correct values for VAX-11 C) when the program is compiled using the VAX-11 C compiler and is ignored otherwise. (The values EXIT_SUCCESS and EXIT_FAILURE are used by the library function exit.)

15. What is the error in the following attempt to define a parameterized macro max?

```
#define max ( x, y ) ( x > y ? x : y )
```

16. Macro definitions typically do not include a semicolon at the end. Can you think of any advantage in not including it?

17. Why is it misleading to talk about a parameterized macro "call"?

4.7 Sample Application: Simulating a Dice Game

Problem

Simulate the following dice game. A player bets on the outcome of rolling a pair of dice. The first roll of the dice is the player's *mark*. The rules are as follows:

- If the player's mark is 7 or 11, the player wins his or her bet immediately.
- If the player's mark is not 7 or 11, the player keeps rolling until he or she matches the mark for a win or rolls 7 or 11 for a loss. The amount won or lost is equal to the amount of the bet unless the player wins with a mark of 2 ("snake eyes") or 12 ("box cars"), in which case the amount won is equal to twice the amount of the bet.

Sample Input / Output

Input is in color; output is in black.

```
        Your bankroll stands at 500
Want to play? (1: yes, 0: no) 1
Your bet in dollars? 100
        Your current mark is: 6.
        Roll 'em again!

        You rolled a 6.
        You win 100 dollars.
        Your bankroll stands at 600
```

```
Want to play? (1: yes, 0: no) 1

Your bet in dollars? 300
      Your bet of 300 exceeds the limit of 250.
      Please enter your bet again. 250

      Your current mark is: 8.
      Roll 'em again!

      You rolled a 7.
      You lost a trifling 250 bucks.
      Your bankroll stands at 350

Want to play? (1: yes, 0: no) 1

Your bet in dollars? 50

      Your current mark is: 4.
      Roll 'em again!

      You rolled a 4.
      You win 50 dollars.
      Your bankroll stands at 400

Want to play? (1: yes, 0: no) 1

Your bet in dollars? 200

      Your current mark is: 5.
      Roll 'em again!

      You rolled a 10.
      Roll 'em again!

      You rolled a 9.
      Roll 'em again!

      You rolled a 10.
      Roll 'em again!

      You rolled a 6.
      Roll 'em again!

      You rolled a 6.
      Roll 'em again!

      You rolled a 9.
      Roll 'em again!

      You rolled a 7.
      You lost a trifling 200 bucks.
      Your bankroll stands at 200

Want to play? (1: yes, 0: no) 0

      You're winning -- don't quit now!
      Your bankroll stands at 200
```

Solution

The player's bankroll is initialized to NESTEGG, defined as 500. The player is asked whether he or she wants to continue playing. The player is allowed to play as long as the bankroll exceeds zero. Each bet must be less than the LIMIT, defined as 250. To simulate the roll of one die, we write a function ran, which returns a random integer between 1 and k, inclusive, and invoke it with k = 6.

The function roll_them_bones handles the details of rolling the dice, interpreting the rolls, and updating the bankroll.

To illustrate the use of #defines, we use several macros. We handle most of the input and output with macros. All of the #defines are placed in two files, which are then included in main and roll_them_bones.

C Implementation

```
/* main.h -- #defines included in main */

#define    TRUE       1
#define    FALSE      0
#define    NL         putchar( '\n' )
#define    TAB        putchar( '\t' )
#define    FORMAT     NL, NL, TAB
#define    FORMAT2    NL, TAB, TAB
#define    NESTEGG    500
#define    LIMIT      250
#define    PLAY_PROMPT     FORMAT, \
           printf( "Want to play? (1: yes, 0: no) " )
#define    READ_ANS( ans )  scanf( "%d", (&ans) )

#define    BET_PROMPT      FORMAT, \
           printf( "Your bet in dollars? " )
#define    BET_REPROMPT    FORMAT2, \
           printf( "Please enter your bet again. " )
#define    READ_BET( bet )  scanf( "%d", (&bet) )

#define    WARN1( bet, lmt ) FORMAT, TAB, \
           printf( "\aYour bet of %d exceeds the limit of %d.", \
               (bet), (lmt) )
#define    WARN2( bet, bnk ) FORMAT, TAB, \
           printf( "\aYou bet %d; you have %d.", (bet), (bnk) )

#define    WINNER_MSG      FORMAT, TAB, \
           printf( "\aYou're winning -- don't quit now!" )
#define    LOSER_MSG       FORMAT, TAB, \
           printf( "You're losing -- don't quit now!" )
#define    BANKROLL_MSG( r ) FORMAT2, \
           printf( "Your bankroll stands at %d", (r) )
/* end of main.h */

/* roll.h -- #defines included in roll_them_bones */
#define    SNAKE_EYES      2
#define    BOX_CARS        12

#define    PRINT_MARK( mark )     NL, FORMAT2, \
           printf( "Your current mark is: %d.", (mark) )
```

```
#define    PRINT_ROLL_MSG           FORMAT2, \
               printf( "Roll 'em again!" )
#define    PRINT_DICE( dice )       FORMAT2, \
               printf( "You rolled a %d.", (dice) )
#define    WIN_MSG( bet )           FORMAT2, \
               printf( "Take %d dollars, but don't run!", \
                   (bet) )
#define    POSSIBLE_DOUBLE_MSG      FORMAT2, \
               printf( "Win and you win double!" )
#define    DOUBLE_WIN_MSG( amt )    FORMAT2, \
               printf( "You win double -- %d dollars!", (amt) )
#define    REGULAR_WIN_MSG( amt ) FORMAT2, \
               printf( "You win %d dollars.", (amt) )
#define    CONSOLE_MSG( bet )       FORMAT2, \
               printf( "You lost a trifling %d bucks.", (bet) )
#define    SHUT_EYES      3
/* end of roll.h */


/*            main program                */
#include <stdio.h>
#include <stdlib.h>
#include <limits.h>
#include "main.h"

main()
{
    int    bankroll = NESTEGG;
    int    ans;              /* 1: play; 0: halt */
    int    bet;              /* player's bet in dollars */
    /* roll_them_bones simulates a game & returns a new bankroll */
    int    roll_them_bones( int bet, int bankroll );

    /* Play until desire or money runs out */
    do {
        BANKROLL_MSG( bankroll );
        PLAY_PROMPT;
        READ_ANS( ans );
        if ( ans == TRUE ) {
            BET_PROMPT;
            READ_BET( bet );
            while ( bet > LIMIT ) {
                WARN1( bet, LIMIT );
                BET_REPROMPT;
                READ_BET( bet );
            }
            while ( bet > bankroll ) {
                WARN2( bet, bankroll );
                BET_REPROMPT;
                READ_BET( bet );
            }
            /* Update bankroll after a game's played. */
```

```
                    bankroll = roll_them_bones( bet, bankroll );
            }
    } while ( ans == TRUE && bankroll > 0 );
    if ( bankroll > 0 ) {
        WINNER_MSG;
        BANKROLL_MSG( bankroll );
    }
    else
        LOSER_MSG;
}

/* ROLL_THEM_BONES -- simulates one game */

#include "roll.h"

int roll_them_bones( int bet, int bankroll )
{
    void sleep( int how_long ); /* pause for time proportional to
                                    how_long */
    int  ran( int k ); /* random number generator: ran(k) returns
                           an integer in the range 1 through k */
    int  mark;   /* sum of dice on 1st roll */
    int  dice;   /* sum of dice after 1st roll */
    int  double_flag = FALSE; /* TRUE if dice equals 2 or 12 */

    /* Roll the dice the first time to get the player's "mark". */
    mark = ran( 6 ) + ran( 6 );
    PRINT_MARK( mark );

    /* Check for 7 or 11. */
    if ( mark == 7  ||  mark == 11 ) {
        WIN_MSG( bet );
        bankroll += bet;
        return ( bankroll );   /* Exit a winner. */
    }

    /* Check for possibility of double payoff on bet. */
    if ( mark == SNAKE_EYES  ||  mark == BOX_CARS ) {
        double_flag = TRUE;
        POSSIBLE_DOUBLE_MSG;
    }
    /* Roll until DICE equals either MARK or 7 or 11. */
    do {
        dice = ran( 6 ) + ran( 6 );
        PRINT_ROLL_MSG;
        NL;
        sleep( SHUT_EYES ); /* pause a bit to simulate time
                               between rolls of the dice. */
        PRINT_DICE( dice );
    } while ( dice != mark  &&  dice != 7  &&  dice != 11 );

    if ( dice == mark )
        if ( double_flag ) {
```

```
                    bankroll += 2 * bet;
                    DOUBLE_WIN_MSG( 2 * bet );
                }
                else {
                    bankroll += bet;
                    REGULAR_WIN_MSG( bet );
                }
        else {
            bankroll -= bet;
            CONSOLE_MSG( bet );
        }
        return ( bankroll );
}

/*   ran returns a random integer in the range 1 to k.

     ran invokes the library function rand which returns a random
     integer in the range 0 to RAND_MAX (defined in stdlib.h).   */

int ran( int k )
{
    double x = RAND_MAX + 1.0;
    int y;

    y = 1 + rand() * (k / x);
    return ( y );
}

/* sleep pauses for time proportional to how_long */
void sleep( int how_long )
{
    int i, j;

    for ( i = 0; i < how_long; ++i )
        for ( j = 0; j < INT_MAX; ++j ) /* INT_MAX is defined in
                                           limits.h */
            ;
}
```

Discussion

The macros used in the program are distributed between the files *main.h* and *roll.h*. The file *main.h* is included before the function main so that all of the macros are available to main and roll_them_bones. The file *roll.h* is included just before roll_them_bones, as *roll.h* includes only macros needed by roll_them_bones.

If the player attempts to bet more than the limit or bankroll, we sound the bell (\a) and print a warning message:

```
#define   WARN1( bet, lmt ) FORMAT, TAB, \
              printf( "\aYour bet of %d exceeds the limit of %d.", \
                      (bet), (lmt) )
#define   WARN2( bet, bnk ) FORMAT, TAB, \
              printf( "\aYou bet %d; you have %d.", (bet), (bnk) )
```

To write the function `ran`, we use the library function `rand`. The function `rand`, which requires the header file *stdlib.h*, returns a random integer in the range 0 to RAND_MAX. The macro RAND_MAX is defined in *stdlib.h*. Since

$$0 \leq \text{rand()} \leq \text{RAND\_MAX},$$

multiplying by k and dividing by RAND_MAX + 1, we find that

```
0 ≤ rand() * k/(RAND_MAX + 1)
  ≤ RAND_MAX * k/(RAND_MAX + 1)
  = k * (RAND_MAX/(RAND_MAX + 1))
  < k.
```

Thus

```
1 ≤ 1 + rand() * k/(RAND_MAX + 1)
  < k + 1.
```

If we now convert `1 + rand() * k / (RAND_MAX + 1)` to an `int` by dropping the fractional part, the resulting integer, which is returned by `ran`, is in the range 1 to k.

For example, if k is 6, RAND_MAX is 2147483647, and `rand` returns the value 733976916,

```
1 + rand() * k / (RAND_MAX + 1)
  = 1 + 733976916 * (6 / 2147483648)
  = 1 + 2.050708 = 3.050708.
```

The function `ran` returns the truncated value 3.

As written, each time the program is run we obtain identical sequences of random integers from the function `rand`. Consequently, each time the program is run we obtain the same sequence of rolls of the dice. To change the sequence of random integers obtained, we must provide a different *seed*, or start-up value, for the random integer generator `rand`. The library function `srand` can be used to provide a new starting value for `rand`. The interested reader may want to incorporate this enhancement into the program (see Programming Exercise 4.16).

We write a function `sleep` to simulate the pause that occurs between two rolls of the dice. The function `sleep` has one argument, `how_long`. We simply loop `how_long * INT_MAX` times to obtain a pause. The macro INT_MAX, which is defined in *limits.h*, is the largest `int` on the local system. Many systems supply a function, `sleep`, which when invoked with the argument `how_long` pauses `how_long` seconds; however, the existence of `sleep` is not guaranteed by the standard.

The dice game program shows how the `#define` directive allows us to tailor C to a particular application. Although this does not eliminate the need for documentation, the example illustrates how a specialized language can be built on top of C.

4.8   Recursion

A **recursive function** is a function that invokes itself. C supports recursive functions; any C function can invoke itself. Recursion is a powerful, elegant, and natural way to solve a large class of problems. A problem in this class can be solved by decomposing it into subproblems of the same type as the original problem. Each subproblem, in turn, can be decomposed further until the process yields subproblems that can be solved in a straight-forward way. Finally, solutions to the subproblems can be combined to obtain a solution to the original problem.

Example 4.8.1. The **factorial** of n (written $n!$) is defined as:

$$n! = \begin{cases} 1, & \text{if } n = 0 \\ n(n-1)(n-2) \cdots 2 \cdot 1, & \text{if } n \geq 1 \end{cases}$$

That is, if $n \geq 1$, $n!$ (read "n factorial") is equal to the product of all the integers between 1 and n inclusive. (For technical reasons, $0!$ is defined to be 1.) As examples,

$$3! = 3 \cdot 2 \cdot 1 = 6,$$
$$6! = 6 \cdot 5 \cdot 4 \cdot 3 \cdot 2 \cdot 1 = 720.$$

Let us define the *factorial function* as

$$\text{factorial}(\,n\,) = n!$$

Notice that the factorial function can be written "in terms of itself" since, if we "peel off" n, the remaining product is simply $(n-1)!$; that is,

$$\begin{aligned} \text{factorial}(\,n\,) &= n! \\ &= n(n-1)(n-2) \cdots 2 \cdot 1 \\ &= n(n-1)! \\ &= n \cdot \text{factorial}(\,n-1\,). \end{aligned}$$

Problem	Simplified Problem
5!	5 * 4!
4!	4 * 3!
3!	3 * 2!
2!	2 * 1!
1!	None

Figure 4.8.1 Decomposing the factorial problem.

For example,

$$\begin{aligned} \text{factorial}(\,5\,) &= 5! \\ &= 5 \cdot 4 \cdot 3 \cdot 2 \cdot 1 \\ &= 5 \cdot 4! \\ &= 5 \cdot \text{factorial}(\,4\,). \end{aligned}$$

The equation

$$\text{factorial}(\,n\,) = n \cdot \text{factorial}(\,n-1\,)$$

shows how to decompose the original problem (compute $n!$) into increasingly simpler subproblems [compute $(n-1)!$, compute $(n-2)!$, . . .] until the process reaches the straightforward problem of computing $1!$. The solutions to these subproblems can then be combined, by multiplying, to solve the original problem.

For example, the problem of computing $5!$ is reduced to computing $4!$; the problem of computing 4! is reduced to computing 3!; and so on. Figure 4.8.1 summarizes this process.

Once the problem of computing 5! has been reduced to solving subproblems, the solution to the simplest subproblem can be used to solve the next simplest subproblem, and so on, until the original problem has been solved. Figure 4.8.2 shows how the subproblems are combined to compute 5!.

Next, we write a recursive function that computes factorials. (Exercise 1 is to write a nonrecursive function that computes factorials.) The code is a direct translation of the equation

$$\text{factorial}(\ n\ ) = n \cdot \text{factorial}(n - 1).$$

Problem	Solution
1!	1
2!	2 * 1! = 2
3!	3 * 2! = 3 * 2 = 6
4!	4 * 3! = 4 * 6 = 24
5!	5 * 4! = 5 * 24 = 120

Figure 4.8.2 Combining subproblems to compute 5!.

```
#include <stdio.h>

main( )
{
     int   fact( int num ),
           num;

     printf( "\nPlease enter a number:   " );
     scanf( "%d", &num );

     if ( num < 0 )        /* legal input? */
        printf( "\nERROR-number must be >= 0." );
     else
        printf( "\nFactorial of %d is %d.", num,
               fact( num ) );
}

int   fact( int num )
{
     if ( num <= 1 )                /* base cases */
        return ( 1 );
     else                           /* recursive call */
        return ( num * fact( num - 1 ) );
}
```

Figure 4.8.3 gives a trace of the execution when the user enters the value 5. We label the calls to `fact` "`fact-1st`," "`fact-2nd`," and so on to aid in the clarification.

Invoking Function	Invoked Function	Argument	Value Returned
main	fact-1st	5	5 * fact(4) to main
fact-1st	fact-2nd	4	4 * fact(3) to fact-1st
fact-2nd	fact-3rd	3	3 * fact(2) to fact-2nd
fact-3rd	fact-4th	2	2 * fact(1) to fact-3rd
fact-4th	fact-5th	1	1 to fact-4th

Figure 4.8.3 Tracing the recursive factorial function.

When main calls fact-1st with 5 as the argument, the condition

    num <= 1

is false; thus, fact-1st invokes fact-2nd with 4 as the argument. In this call to fact-4th, the condition

    num <= 1

is again false; thus, fact-2nd invokes fact-3rd with 3 as the argument. The recursive calls continue until num is 1 when the condition

    num <= 1

is true. In this case, fact-5th invokes no functions but simply returns 1 [the value of fact(1)] to its invoker fact-4th. Next, fact-4th returns 2 [the value of 2 * fact(1)] to its invoker fact-3rd. Next, fact-3rd returns 6 [the value of 3 * fact(2)] to its invoker fact-2nd. Next, fact-2nd returns 24 [the value of 4 * fact(3)] to its invoker fact-1st. Finally, fact-1st returns 120 [the value of 5 * fact(4)] to its invoker main.

Three points need emphasis. First, there must be some situations in which a recursive function does *not* invoke itself; otherwise, it would invoke itself forever. In the function fact, if n $\le$ 1, fact does not invoke itself. We call the values for which a recursive function does not invoke itself the *base cases*. To summarize, every recursive function must have base cases.

Second, in any function invocation, recursive or not, *the function invoked always returns to its invoker*. When main invokes fact, fact returns to main. When fact invokes itself, the invoked fact returns to the invoking fact. So when fact-1st invokes fact-2nd with 4 as the argument, fact-2nd returns to fact-1st 4 multiplied by the value of 3!. It is thus a bit misleading to say that a recursive function "invokes itself." It would be better to say that a recursive function invokes a *copy* of itself; however, we use the standard terminology and say that a function invokes itself.

The third point is that when a function invokes itself, *the values used in testing for the base cases must change*. For example, suppose that we mistakenly wrote the else statement in the function fact as

```
if ( num <= 1 )            /* base cases */
   return ( 1 );
else                       /* recursive call */
   return ( num * fact( num ) );   /* TROUBLE!!! */
```

Every recursive call to the function fact passes the same value as it received; so unless num is less than or equal to 1, the condition

```
num <= 1
```

is never true. In this case, the function `fact` will keep invoking itself. We say that "infinite recursion" results. In the correct version, the function `fact` always invokes itself with a different argument from the one it received; `fact` receives `num` and passes `num − 1`. This changes the value in the test for the base cases.

A key challenge in writing recursive functions is to avoid infinite recursion. A recursive function must test for base cases in which no recursive call occurs. In the function `fact`, the base case occurs when the parameter is less than or equal to 1. Since each recursive call decrements the argument it receives before passing it along, the base case eventually is satisfied.

> **Example 4.8.2.**   The **Tower of Hanoi** is a puzzle consisting of three pegs mounted on a board and n disks of various sizes with holes in their centers (see Figure 4.8.4). If a disk is on a peg, only a disk of smaller diameter can be placed on top of it. Given all the disks properly stacked on one peg as in Figure 4.8.4, the problem is to transfer the disks to another peg by moving one disk at a time.
>
> The Tower of Hanoi puzzle was invented by Édouard Lucas in the late nineteenth century. The following myth was also created to accompany the puzzle (and, one assumes, to help market the puzzle). The puzzle was said to be derived from a mythical gold tower which consisted of 64 disks. The 64 disks were to be transferred by monks according to the rules set forth previously. It was said that before the monks finished moving the tower, the tower would collapse and the world would end in a clap of thunder. Since at least 18,446,744,073,709,551,615 moves are required to solve the 64-disk Tower of Hanoi puzzle, we can be fairly certain something would happen to the tower before it was completely moved.
>
> For small values of n, the solution is evident; however, if n is as large as 7 or 8, the solution is not immediately obvious. Fortunately, if we think recursively, the problem is much less forbidding.
>
> Consider the n-disk problem. Assume that, as in the factorial example (Example 4.8.1), we can reduce the original problem to a subproblem of the same type. Specifically, assume that we can solve the $(n − 1)$-disk problem. Now, suppose that we fix the bottom disk. We can then recursively move the $n − 1$ top disks from peg 1 to peg 2 (see Figure 4.8.5). Next, we move the remaining disk on peg 1 to peg 3. Finally, we

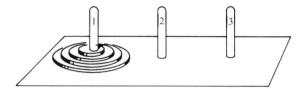

Figure 4.8.4   The Tower of Hanoi puzzle.

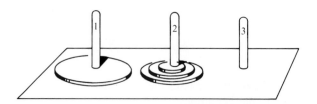

Figure 4.8.5   The first moves in a recursive solution to the Tower of Hanoi puzzle.

again solve the ($n - 1$)-disk problem; we move the $n - 1$ disks on peg 2 to peg 3. We have succeeded in moving all n disks from peg 1 to peg 3. The base case is the 1-disk problem. Figure 4.8.6 contains a listing of a program that solves the puzzle.

```c
#include <stdio.h>
main()
{
      void  hanoi( char peg1, char peg2, char peg3, int how_many );

      char  peg1 = 'A',    /* origin */
            peg2 = 'B',    /* destination */
            peg3 = 'C';    /* spare */

      int   how_many;  /* number of disks initially on the origin */

      /* Prompt for and warn about the number of disks
         to be moved. */
      printf( "\n\tHow many disks initially on peg A?"
              "\n\tIf more than 7, the solution may seem to "
              "take forever!\n\t" );
      scanf( "%d", &how_many );

      /* Anything to move? */
      if ( how_many < 1 )
          printf( "\n\tThere's nothing to move!" );
      /* Otherwise solve with:                    */
      /*    -- peg1 as the origin                 */
      /*    -- peg2 as the destination            */
      /*    -- peg3 as the spare                  */
      else
          hanoi( peg1, peg2, peg3, how_many );
}
void  hanoi( char p1, char p2, char p3, int how_many )
/*    p1 -- origin
      p2 -- destination
      p3 -- spare
      how_many -- number of disks to move */

{

      /* If there is only 1 disk on p1, then move it to p2 */
      /* and quit as the problem is solved.                */
      if ( how_many == 1 ) {
          printf( "\n\n\tMove top disk from peg %c to peg %c.",
                  p1, p2 );
          return;
      }
      /* Otherwise:                                             */
      /*    (1) Move how_many - 1 disks from p1 to p3:          */
      /*        p1 is the origin, p3 is the destination.        */
      /*        and p2 is the spare.                            */
      /*                                                        */
      /*    (2) Move the top disk from p1 to p2.                */
      /*                                                        */
```

```
/*    (3) Move how_many - 1 disks from p3 to p2:           */
/*        p3 is the origin, p2 is the destination,         */
/*        and p1 is the spare.                             */
hanoi( p1, p3, p2, how_many - 1 );
printf( "\n\n\tMove top disk from peg %c to peg %c.",
        p1, p2 );
hanoi( p3, p2, p1, how_many - 1 );
}
```

Figure 4.8.6 Solving the Tower of Hanoi puzzle.

Example 4.8.3. A robot can take steps of 1 meter or 2 meters. Write a function to calculate the number of ways the robot can walk n meters. As examples:

Distance	Sequence of Steps	Number of Ways to Walk
1	1	1
2	1, 1 or 2	2
3	1, 1, 1 or 1, 2 or 2, 1	3
4	1, 1, 1, 1 or 1, 1, 2 or 1, 2, 1	
	or 2, 1, 1 or 2, 2	5

Let walk(n) denote the number of ways the robot can walk n meters. We have observed that

$$walk(1) = 1$$
$$walk(2) = 2.$$

Now suppose that $n > 2$. The robot can begin by taking a step of 1 meter or a step of 2 meters. If the robot begins by taking a 1-meter step, a distance of $n - 1$ meters remains; but, by definition, the remainder of the walk can be completed in walk($n - 1$) ways. Similarly, if the robot begins by taking a 2-meter step, a distance of $n - 2$ meters remains and, in this case, the remainder of the walk can be completed in walk($n - 2$) ways. Since the walk must begin with either a 1-meter or a 2-meter step, all of the ways to walk n meters are accounted for. We obtain the formula

$$walk(n) = walk(n - 1) + walk(n - 2).$$

For example,

$$walk(4) = walk(3) + walk(2) = 3 + 2 = 5.$$

We can write a recursive function `walk_recur` (see Figure 4.8.7) to compute walk(n) by translating the equation

$$walk(n) = walk(n - 1) + walk(n - 2)$$

```
#include <stdio.h>
main()
{
    int   walk_recur( int dist ),
          distance,        /* how far to walk */
          count_walks;     /* how many ways to walk distance meters */
```

```
    printf( "\nHow far to walk?  " );
    scanf( "%d", &distance );
    if ( distance < 1 )       /* distance must be positive */
       printf( "\n\n\tERROR--distance must be positive." );
    else {
       count_walks = walk_recur( distance );
       printf( "\n\n\tThe robot can walk %d meters in %d ways.\n",
           distance, count_walks );
    }
}

int  walk_recur( int dist )
{
    /* base cases: 1 meter--1 way, 2 meters--2 ways */
    if ( dist <= 2 )
       return ( dist );

    /* recursive call--walk( dist - 1 ) + walk( dist - 2 ) */
    return ( walk_recur( dist - 1 ) + walk_recur( dist - 2 ) );
}
```

Figure 4.8.7   Solving the robot walking problem.

directly into a program. The base cases are $n = 1$ and $n = 2$.

The body of walk_recur contains a conditional statement that tests for the base cases: dist equals 1 or dist equals 2. The recursion occurs within the return statement. If dist is greater than 2, walk_recur returns the sum of the values obtained by recursive calls with argument dist $- 1$ and argument dist $- 2$.

The sequence

$$walk(1), \ walk(2), \ walk(3), \ . \ . \ .$$

whose values begin

$$1, \ 2, \ 3, \ 5, \ 8, \ 13, \ . \ . \ .$$

is called the **Fibonacci sequence** in honor of Leonardo Fibonacci (ca. 1170–1250), an Italian merchant and mathematician. After returning from the Orient in 1202, he wrote his most famous work *Liber Abaci*, which, in addition to containing what we now call the Fibonacci sequence, advocated the use of Hindu-Arabic numerals and was a major factor in Western Europe's adoption of the decimal number system. Fibonacci signed much of his work Leonardo Bigollo. *Bigollo* translates as "traveler" or "blockhead." There is some evidence that Fibonacci enjoyed having his contemporaries consider him a blockhead for advocating the new number system.

Our examples show that recursive functions provide a natural and elegant way to solve certain problems. In the factorial and robot examples, the C code practically copies the mathematical descriptions of the functions. Yet the robot example in particular also illustrates a problem that sometimes arises with recursion—inefficiency.

Figure 4.8.8 shows how many times walk_recur computes walk(2) and walk(1), the two base cases, in the course of computing walk(6). The value walk(2) is computed five times and walk(1) is computed three times. Thus the base cases are computed a total of eight times. (Other cases, in turn, are repeatedly recomputed.) Notice that walk(5) is

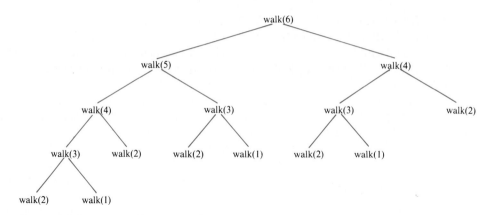

Figure 4.8.8 Counting the number of base cases computed during recursion.

also equal to eight. In general, when `walk_recur` is passed the argument $n \geq 2$, it computes the base cases walk($n-1$) times (see Exercise 6). Since walk(n) grows exponentially with n (see Exercise 7), as n gets large, it becomes infeasible to use `walk_recur` to compute the walk function.

Of course, it is more efficient to compute walk(1) and walk(2) once each. We can write a nonrecursive function that does just this.

Example 4.8.4.   The function `walk_non_recur` also computes the number of ways a robot can walk n meters by taking steps of 1 meter or 2 meters, but more efficiently than does `walk_recur`. We assume that `walk_non_recur` also is invoked from `main`, which passes only positive integers to it.

```
/* iterative version of the walk function */

int   walk_non_recur( int dist )
{
      int   previous,      /* walk(n - 1) */
            current,       /* walk(n)     */
            temp;

      if ( dist <= 2 )
            return ( dist );

      previous = 1;   /* starts as walk(1) */
      current = 2;    /* starts as walk(2) */

      /* compute walk(3), then walk(4),...,
         until walk(dist) */
      --dist;
      while ( --dist ) {
            temp = previous;
            previous = current;
            current += temp;
      }
      return ( current );
}
```

During one invocation, `walk_non_recur` computes each member of the sequence walk(1), walk(2), . . . one time, for it works "from the bottom up"—walk(1) to walk(2) to walk(3) and so on up to walk(n). If $n > 2$, the function `walk_non_recur` is more efficient than `walk_recur`, which during a single invocation computes the base cases several times. Notice that `walk_recur` works "from the top down"—from walk(n) to walk($n - 1$) and walk($n - 2$) and so on down to walk(2) and walk(1).

A recursive function in which the recursive call occurs in the last statement is said to be *tail recursive*. For example, both the factorial function (Example 4.8.1) and the function to solve the robot walking problem (Figure 4.8.7) are tail recursive. A tail recursive function can always be rewritten as an iterative function (see, e.g., Example 4.8.4). On most systems, a tail recursive function runs more slowly and uses more memory than the corresponding iterative version.

Should we *always* rewrite a recursive function nonrecursively? The answer is an emphatic "No!" On some systems, certain recursive functions (e.g., the function `quicksort` in Section 9.7) may run *faster* than versions from which the recursion has been removed. Such systems are designed to optimize the performance of certain kinds of recursive functions. Tail recursive functions are typically *not* optimized.

Finally, recursion is the most natural way to solve some problems. For example, the code for `walk_recur` follows straightforwardly from the formula, whereas the code for `walk_non_recur` does not. Even though we may eventually code a function nonrecursively, we still may begin with a recursive version to be sure that the function is correct.

The goal in this chapter is to introduce and illustrate recursion in C. In the remainder of the book, we use recursion where it arises naturally (e.g., sorting, tree traversal, graph search).

Exercises

1. Write a nonrecursive function that computes factorials.
2. Trace the execution of the Tower of Hanoi program for the case of three disks.
3. Write a recursive function that computes

$$S(n) = 2 + 4 + 6 + \cdots + 2n.$$

   [*Hint:* $S(n) = S(n - 1) + 2n.$]
4. If the standard input is

   ```
   abcd
   ```

   what is the output?

   ```
   #include <stdio.h>

   main()
   {
           void mystery( void );
           mystery();
   }

   void mystery( void )
   {
   ```

```
int c;
if ( ( c = getchar() ) != EOF ) {
    mystery();
    putchar( c );
}
}
```

5. A robot can take steps of 1 meter, 2 meters, or 3 meters. Write a recursive function to calculate the number of ways the robot can walk n meters.

6. [For readers comfortable with mathematical induction.] Prove that the number of times that walk_recur computes the base cases, when the argument is $n \geq 1$, is walk($n - 1$). Define walk(0) = 1.

7. [Also for readers comfortable with mathematical induction.] Prove that for $n \geq 5$,

$$\text{walk}(n) > \left(\frac{3}{2}\right)^n.$$

4.9 Sample Application: Recursive Tiling

Problem

Given n, a power of 2, tile with right trominoes an $n \times n$ board with one square missing. A **right tromino** (hereafter shortened to *tromino*) is composed of three 1×1 squares joined as shown in Figure 4.9.1. By a *tiling*, we mean an exact covering of the board, except for the missing square, without having any of the trominoes overlap one another or extend outside the figure. A tiling of a 4×4 board with one square missing is shown in Figure 4.9.2.

Sample Input / Output

We assume that the board to be tiled is placed in the standard xy-coordinate system with the lower-left corner at (0,0), as shown in Figure 4.9.3. The position of the missing square is entered by giving the coordinates of its lower-left corner. For example, the missing square in Figure 4.9.3 is given by entering 1 2.

The output gives the coordinates of the trominoes and the orientation of the trominoes. The output a b specifies the corner of the tromino shown in Figure 4.9.4. The four possible orientations, designated LL, UL, LR, and UR, are shown in Figure 4.9.5. (The terminology arises from the orientation of the trominoes if they are placed in the corners of a square: LL is lower left, UL is upper left, etc.) The tiling of Figure 4.9.3 is given as (see Figure 4.9.6)

Figure 4.9.1 A tromino.

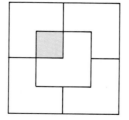

Figure 4.9.2 A tiling of a 4×4 board with a missing square.

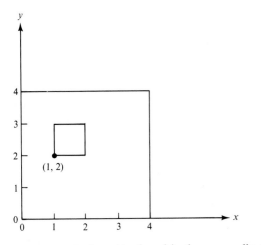

Figure 4.9.3 An $n \times n$ board in the xy-coordinate system.

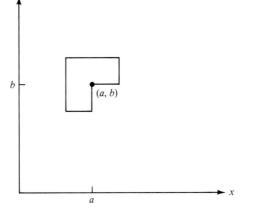

Figure 4.9.4 A tromino in the xy-coordinate system.

```
2 2 LR
1 3 UL
3 3 UR
3 1 LR
1 1 LL
```

Sample Interactive Session

Input is in color; output is in black.

```
------------------------------------------
Enter size of board (0 to quit): 2
Enter coordinates of missing square: 0 0
Tiling
------
```

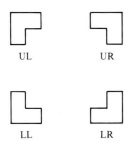

Figure 4.9.5 Oriented trominoes.

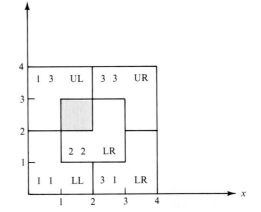

Figure 4.9.6 Tiling a 4 × 4 board in the xy-coordinate system.

```
1 1 UR
------------------------------------
Enter size of board (0 to quit): 2
Enter coordinates of missing square: 1 0
Tiling
------
1 1 UL
------------------------------------
Enter size of board (0 to quit): 4
Enter coordinates of missing square: 0 0
Tiling
------
2 2 UR
1 3 UL
3 3 UR
3 1 LR
1 1 UR
------------------------------------
Enter size of board (0 to quit): 4
Enter coordinates of missing square: 3 2
Tiling
------
2 2 LL
1 3 UL
3 3 UL
3 1 LR
1 1 LL
------------------------------------
Enter size of board (0 to quit): 8
Enter coordinates of missing square: 3 5
Tiling
------
4 4 LR
2 6 UL
1 7 UL
3 7 UR
3 5 LL
1 5 LL
6 6 UR
5 7 UL
7 7 UR
7 5 LR
5 5 UR
6 2 LR
5 3 LR
7 3 UR
7 1 LR
5 1 LL
2 2 LL
1 3 UL
```

```
3 3 LL
3 1 LR
1 1 LL
_____
Enter size of board (0 to quit): 0
```

Solution

Recursion can be used to solve the tiling problem because we can reduce the original problem to simpler instances of the same problem.

Consider the $2^k \times 2^k$ board with one square missing in Figure 4.9.7. If we subdivide this board into four equal portions, we obtain four $2^{k-1} \times 2^{k-1}$ boards. One of these boards contains the missing square. Using recursion, we may tile this board. If we place one tromino as shown in Figure 4.9.7, we may consider each of the three untiled boards as having one missing square; the missing square is the square covered by the tromino. We may then use recursion to tile of each of the three remaining boards. The problem is solved!

C Implementation

```c
/*  This program tiles with right trominoes an nxn board with one
    square missing, assuming that n is a power of 2.             */

#include <stdio.h>

main()
{
    int board_size,
        x_missing,   /* x coordinate of missing square */
        y_missing;   /* y coordinate of missing square */

    void tromino               /* function to do tiling */
            ( int x_board,     /* x coordinate of board */
              int y_board,     /* y coordinate of board */
              int x_missing,    /* x coordinate of missing square */
```

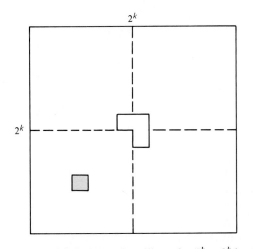

Figure 4.9.7 Recursive tiling of a $2^k \times 2^k$ board.

```
              int y_missing,      /* y coordinate of missing square */
              int board_size ); /* size of board */

        do {
            printf( "\n--------------------------------------" );
            printf( "\nEnter size of board (0 to quit): " );
            scanf( "%d", &board_size );
            if ( board_size ) {
                printf( "\nEnter coordinates of missing square: " );
                scanf( "%d%d", &x_missing, &y_missing );
                printf( "\n\nTiling\n------\n" );
                tromino( 0, 0, x_missing, y_missing, board_size );
            }
        } while ( board_size );
}

void tromino( int x_board,      /* x coordinate of board */
              int y_board,      /* y coordinate of board */
              int x_missing,    /* x coordinate of missing square */
              int y_missing,    /* y coordinate of missing square */
              int board_size )  /* size of board */

{
        int half_size = board_size / 2, /* size of subboard */
            x_center,  /* x coordinate of center of board */
            y_center,  /* y coordinate of center of board */
            x_upper_left,   /* x coordinate of missing square in upper
                                                      left subboard */
            y_upper_left,   /* y coordinate of missing square in upper
                                                      left subboard */
            x_upper_right,  /* x coordinate of missing square in upper
                                                     right subboard */
            y_upper_right,  /* y coordinate of missing square in upper
                                                     right subboard */
            x_lower_right,  /* x coordinate of missing square in lower
                                                     right subboard */
            y_lower_right,  /* y coordinate of missing square in lower
                                                     right subboard */
            x_lower_left,   /* x coordinate of missing square in lower
                                                      left subboard */
            y_lower_left;   /* y coordinate of missing square in lower
                                                      left subboard */
        if ( board_size == 2 ) {    /* 2x2 board */
            /* print position of tromino */
            printf( "%d%d ", x_board + 1, y_board + 1 );
            /* find and print orientation of tromino */
            if ( x_board == x_missing )
                /* missing square in left half */
                if ( y_board == y_missing )
                    /* missing square in lower left */
                    printf( "UR\n" );
```

```
                    else
                         /* missing square in upper left */
                         printf( "LR\n" );
              else
                   /* missing square in right half */
                   if ( y_board == y_missing )
                        /* missing square in lower right */
                        printf( "UL\n" );
                   else
                        /* missing square in upper right */
                        printf( "LL\n" );
         return;
    }

    /* compute x and y coordinates of center of board */
    x_center = x_board + half_size;
    y_center = y_board + half_size;

    /* print position of special, center tromino */
    printf( "%d%d ", x_center, y_center );

    /* Find and print orientation of center tromino.
       Also, set x_upper_left, y_upper_left, ... . */
    if ( x_missing < x_center) {
         /* missing square in left half */
         x_upper_right = x_lower_right = x_center;
         y_upper_right = y_center;
         y_lower_right = y_center - 1;
         if ( y_missing < y_center ) {
              /* missing square in lower left quadrant */
              printf( "UR\n" );
              x_upper_left = x_center - 1;
              y_upper_left = y_center;
              x_lower_left = x_missing;
              y_lower_left = y_missing;
         }
         else {
              /* missing square in upper left quadrant */
              printf( "LR\n" );
              x_upper_left = x_missing;
              y_upper_left = y_missing;
              x_lower_left = x_center - 1;
              y_lower_left = y_center - 1;
         }
    }
    else {
         /* missing square in right half */
         x_upper_left = x_lower_left = x_center - 1;
         y_upper_left = y_center;
         y_lower_left = y_center - 1;
         if ( y_missing < y_center ) {
```

```
            /* missing square in lower right quadrant */
            printf( "UL\n" );
            x_upper_right = x_center;
            y_upper_right = y_center;
            x_lower_right = x_missing;
            y_lower_right = y_missing;
        }
        else {
            /* missing square in upper right quadrant */
            printf( "LL\n" );
            x_upper_right = x_missing;
            y_upper_right = y_missing;
            x_lower_right = x_center;
            y_lower_right = y_center - 1;
        }
    }

    /* tile the four subboards */
    tromino( x_board, y_board + half_size,
         x_upper_left, y_upper_left, half_size );
    tromino( x_board + half_size, y_board + half_size,
         x_upper_right, y_upper_right, half_size );
    tromino( x_board + half_size, y_board,
         x_lower_right, y_lower_right, half_size );
    tromino( x_board, y_board,
         x_lower_left, y_lower_left, half_size );
}
```

Discussion

The function `tromino` has five parameters: `x_board`, `y_board`, `x_missing`, `y_missing`, and `board_size`. The pair (`x_board`, `y_board`) gives the coordinates of the lower-left corner of the board to be tiled (which can be anywhere in the *xy*-plane). Figure 4.9.8 shows the meaning of the parameters and local variables if the missing square is in the upper-right quadrant. The pair (`x_missing`, `y_missing`) gives the coordinates of the missing square. The parameter `board_size` is the size of the board.

The local variable `half_size` is equal to `board_size/2` so that `half_size` is the size of the subboards to be tiled recursively. The pair (`x_center`, `y_center`) gives the coordinates of the center of the board. By comparing `x_missing` with `x_center` and `y_missing` with `y_center`, we can determine which quadrant contains the missing square. The pair (`x_upper_left`, `y_upper_left`) gives the coordinates of the missing square in the upper-left subboard. If the missing square is in the upper-left subboard, `x_upper_left` = `x_missing` and `y_upper_left` = `y_missing`. Otherwise, (`x_upper_left`, `y_upper_left`) gives the coordinates of one square of the special tromino that we position at the center of the original board. Similarly, (`x_upper_right`, `y_upper_right`) gives the coordinates of the missing square in the upper-right subboard; (`x_lower_right`, `y_lower_right`) gives the coordinates of the missing square in the lower-right subboard; and

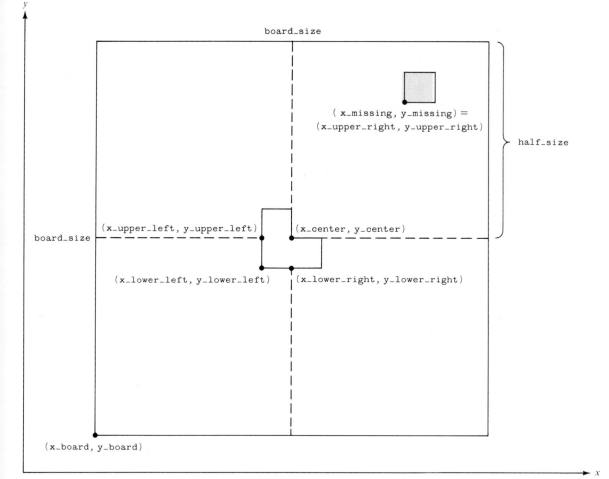

Figure 4.9.8 Notation for the function `tromino`.

(`x_lower_left,y_lower_left`) gives the coordinates of the missing square in the lower-left subboard.

The base case occurs when `board_size` is equal to 2, in which case, we solve this trivial case directly (without a recursive call). If `board_size` > 2, we determine which quadrant contains the missing square and then initialize `x_upper_left`, `y_upper_left`, ... We then recursively call `tromino` four times to tile each of the four subboards.

The sample program does no error checking. To make the program crash proof, one should check whether `board_size` is a power of 2 and whether the coordinates that the user provides for the missing square actually describe a square within the board. Programming Exercise 4.24 requests this enhancement.

In "Tiling deficient boards with trominoes" (*Math. Mag.* 59 [1986]: 34–40), I. P. Chu and R. Johnsonbaugh show that if $n \neq 5$, it is possible to tile with trominoes an $n \times n$ board with one square missing if and only if 3 does not divide n. Algorithms are given to construct the tilings. Programming Exercise 4.26 is to write a C program to tile arbitrary boards.

†4.10 Functions with an Arbitrary Number of Arguments

Normally, the number of parameters of a function is equal to the number of arguments passed in any invocation of the function. However, C does allow functions that expect an arbitrary number of arguments. The library function `printf` is a familiar example; `printf` expects a format string followed by an arbitrary number of arguments to be formatted and printed. It is also possible for programmers to write their own functions with an arbitrary number of arguments.

The standard provides the header file *stdarg.h*, which contains definitions and macros that facilitate writing a function with an arbitrary number of arguments of arbitrary types. In this section, we explain the syntax for such functions and discuss how to use *stdarg.h*.

The header of a function that expects an arbitrary number of arguments consists of

- The data type returned, or the keyword `void` if the function does not return a value.
- The function's name.
- In parentheses, a nonempty list of *named parameters* and their types separated by commas, terminated by three periods.

The named parameters are ordinary parameters, and the three periods indicate that a varying number of arguments follows the last named parameter. There must be at least one named parameter.

Example 4.10.1. The header

```
int max( int how_many,... )
```

indicates that the function `max` expects one argument of type `int` followed by an arbitrary number of arguments. The function returns an `int`.

Example 4.10.2. The header of `printf` may be written

```
int printf( char *format_string,... )
```

The header indicates that `printf` expects one argument, the format string, followed by an arbitrary number of arguments (the values to be formatted and printed). The type of the first argument, `char *`, pointer to `char`, is simply the address of the format string. (Pointers are thoroughly discussed in Chapter 6.)

Example 4.10.3. The header of `fprintf` may be written

```
int fprintf( FILE *fp, char *format_string,... )
```

The header indicates that `fprintf` expects two arguments, a file pointer and a format string, followed by an arbitrary number of arguments (the values to be formatted and printed).

In the body of a function that expects an arbitrary number of arguments, the named parameters are accessed in the usual way—by using their names. To access the arguments that follow the last named parameter, we must first define a variable of type `va_list`. Such a variable can be used to hold the address of an argument that follows the last named parameter. The type `va_list` is defined in *stdarg.h*. For example, if we define the variable `arg_addr` of type `va_list` by writing

†This section can be omitted without loss of continuity.

```
va_list arg_addr;
```

it is then possible for `arg_addr` to hold the address of one of the arguments that follows the last named parameter. To set `arg_addr` to the address of the first argument that follows the last named parameter, we use the macro `va_start`. Two arguments must be furnished to `va_start`; the first is a variable of type `va_list`, and the second is the last named parameter.

Example 4.10.4. Suppose that the header of the function `max` is

```
int max( int how_many, ... )
```

To define a variable `arg_addr` of type `va_list` and store in `arg_addr` the address of the first argument after `how_many`, we would write

```
va_list arg_addr;
va_start( arg_addr, how_many );
```

Example 4.10.5. Suppose that the header of the function `fprintf` is

```
int fprintf( FILE *fp, char *format_string, ... )
```

To define a variable `arg_ptr` of type `va_list` and store in `arg_ptr` the address of the first argument after `format_string`, we would write

```
va_list arg_ptr;
va_start( arg_ptr, format_string );
```

Suppose that, as in Example 4.10.4, we have defined a variable `arg_addr` of type `va_list` and stored in `arg_addr` the address of one of the arguments `arg` that follows `how_many`. To obtain the value of `arg` and to advance `arg_addr` to the argument after `arg`, we use the macro `va_arg`. Two arguments must be furnished to `va_arg`; the first is the variable `arg_addr` and the second is the data type of `arg`.

Example 4.10.6. Suppose that the header of the function `max` is

```
int max( int how_many, ... )
```

After the statements

```
va_list arg_addr;
va_start( arg_addr, how_many );
```

execute, `arg_addr` holds the address of the first argument after `how_many`. Suppose that the first argument after `how_many` is of type `int`. To obtain the value of this argument, store it in the variable `next_int`, and advance `arg_addr` to the next argument, we write

```
next_int = va_arg( arg_addr, int );
```

At this point, `arg_addr` holds the address of the second argument after `how_many`.

We should *never* specify `char`, `short`, or `float` as a second argument to `va_arg` since arguments of type `char` and `short` are converted to `int` and an argument of type `float` is converted to `double`.

After reading all the arguments that follow the last named parameter, we must invoke the macro `va_end` with one argument—the variable that accessed the special argument list. The macro `va_end` provides the proper cleanup operations.

Example 4.10.7. After using the variable `arg_addr` of type `va_list` to read all the arguments that follow the last named parameter, we must write

```
va_end( arg_addr );
```

The declaration of a function that expects an arbitrary number of arguments follows the standard syntax. For example, to declare the function `max` of Example 4.10.1, we would write

```
int max( int how_many,... );
```

We could declare `printf` by writing

```
int printf( char *format_string,... );
```

The compiler stops checking for matches between arguments and parameters when it encounters the ellipses . . . .

Example 4.10.8. Figure 4.10.1 shows a complete program that invokes the user-written function `max` that expects an arbitrary number of arguments. The function `max` returns the maximum of an arbitrary number of integers. The first argument to `max` must be the number of integers over which to take the maximum. The integers over which to take the maximum follow the first argument. For example, the value of

```
max( 3, 4, 16, -4)
```

is 16.

The function `main` prompts the user to enter one to four integers. Then `main` invokes `max` to compute the maximum of the integers entered and prints the maximum.

```c
#include <stdio.h>
#include <stdarg.h>
#include <limits.h>

main()
{
    int max_int;
    int i1, i2, i3, i4;  /* arguments to test max function */

    int max( int how_many,... );

    printf( "Enter one to four integers\n"
            "generate EOF when done\n" );

    scanf( "%d", &i1 );

    if ( scanf( "%d", &i2 ) == EOF )
        max_int = max( 1, i1 );
    else if ( scanf( "%d", &i3 ) == EOF )
        max_int = max( 2, i1, i2 );
    else if ( scanf( "%d", &i4 ) == EOF )
        max_int = max( 3, i1, i2, i3 );
    else
        max_int = max( 4, i1, i2, i3, i4 );

    printf( "\nMaximum integer = %d\n", max_int );
}
```

```
/*   max -- Returns the maximum of a list of ints. The first
     argument is the number of ints over which to take the
     maximum. The ints over which to take the maximum follow
     the first argument.   */

int max( int how_many,... )
{
     int largest = INT_MIN; /* low value so first comparison is
                               correct */
     int i;
     va_list arg_addr;   /* gives location of argument after
                            how_many in max */
     int next_int;

     va_start( arg_addr, how_many ); /* set arg_addr to the address
                                        of the first argument after
                                        how_many in max */

     for ( i = 0; i < how_many; i++ )
         /* va_arg returns the value of the next argument
            in max and updates arg_addr. The second argument to
            va_arg is the data type of argument being read
            (in max). */
         if ( ( next_int = va_arg( arg_addr, int ) ) > largest )
             largest = next_int;

     va_end( arg_addr ); /* mop up */

     return ( largest );
}
```

Figure 4.10.1 A function that expects an arbitrary number of arguments.

A function that expects an arbitrary number of arguments must have some way to determine the number of arguments actually passed. In the function max of Figure 4.10.1, the first argument is a value that max can use to determine the number of arguments passed. The functions printf and fprintf determine the number of arguments passed by examining the format string. (For example, if the format string is

```
"i = %d, x = %f"
```

printf and fprintf expect two arguments after the format string.) The standard does not specify a macro that gives the number of arguments passed. However, some C systems (e.g., VAX-11 C) provide a macro that gives the number of arguments passed.

Exercises

1. What value does the function max in Figure 4.10.1 return if the first argument is zero?
2. Write a header for scanf.
3. Write a declaration for scanf.
4. Write a declaration for fprintf.

5. Write a function `min` that returns the minimum of a list of `int`s. The first argument is the number of `int`s over which to take the minimum. The `int`s over which to take the minimum follow the first argument.

6. Write a function `prod` that multiplies a list of `int`s. The list is terminated by 0, which is not multiplied. For example, the value of

```
prod( 3, 6, 2, 0 )
```

is 36. There is one named parameter, the first integer to be multiplied. It is assumed to be nonzero.

7. How do you think that `va_arg` determines the address of the next argument so that it properly updates its first argument?

Changes from Traditional C

1. As was already pointed out, the use of function prototypes is new with the standard and, from the perspective of the programmer, represents the greatest change made by the standard. For now, the standard supports function prototypes as well as the traditional way of declaring functions and writing function headers. The standards committee apparently would eventually like to permit only function prototypes. For the time being in standard C, if a function is not declared in prototype form, the compiler does no checking for matches between arguments and parameters and issues no warning or error messages when mismatches occur.

2. In traditional C, arguments of type `char` or `short` are automatically converted to `int` and arguments of type `float` are automatically converted to `double` before being passed to the invoked function. With the addition of function prototypes, if the data types of an argument and its corresponding parameter differ, C converts the data type of the argument to the data type declared for the parameter, if possible. If the conversion cannot be made, C issues an error message.

3. Traditional C does not require the keyword `void`, but most implementations have supported it for some time.

4. The header file *stdlib.h* is new with the standard.

5. In traditional C, it is an error to repeat a macro definition. For example, if *stdio.h* contains the line

```
#define TRUE 1
```

the following is an error in traditional C (but legal in standard C):

```
#include <stdio.h>
#define TRUE 1
```

The problem in traditional C can be corrected by writing

```
#include <stdio.h>
#ifndef TRUE
#define TRUE 1
#endif
```

6. The directives `#elif`, `#error`, and `#pragma` and the `defined` operator may not be available in traditional C.

Common Programming Errors

1. It is an error to have a C program without a function named `main`. The program as a whole begins with the execution of `main` and ends with the termination of `main`.

2. It is an error to define, in the same program, functions with the same name.

3. There are no semicolons in a function's header. For example, the following is an error:

   ```
   /* ILLEGAL header for print_report */
   void print_report( int file_code,
                      int number_of_records );
   {
          .
          .
          .
   }
   ```

4. Unless a function is defined and declared as expecting an arbitrary number of arguments, it is an error to have unequal numbers of parameters and arguments. For example, the following is an error:

   ```
   main( )
   {
        void print_report( int file_code,
                          int number_of_records );
        int fc;
        .
        .
        .
        print_report( fc );   /***** ERROR *****/
        .
        .
        .
   }
   void print_report( int file_code,
                      int number_of_records )
   {
        .
        .
        .
   }
   ```

5. A function's body is enclosed in braces, but its header is not. Note the difference:

   ```
   /***** ERROR -- header enclosed in braces *****/
   { void print_report( int file_code,
                       int number_of_records ) }
   {
        /* function's body */
   ```

```
         .
         .
         .
    }
    /***** correct syntax *****/
    void print_report( int file_name,
                       int number_of_records )
    {
        /* function's body */
         .
         .
         .

    }
```

6. Because a function may return at most one value, the following is an error:

```
    /***** ERROR -- attempt to return two values *****/
    int  count_animals( int speciesl, int species2 )
    {
        int   count1, count2;
         .
         .
         .

        return ( count1 count2 );   /***** ERROR *****/
    }
```

However, a returned value may be any legal C expression (including a function invocation), and so the following is legal:

```
    int  count_animals( int species1, int species2 )
    {
        int   count1, count2;
         .
         .
         .

        return ( count1 + count2 );
    }
```

7. Definitions for a program's component functions may be spread across different files. However, the entire definition of a particular function must occur in one file, and so it is an error to put the function's header in one file and its body in another.

8. It is an error to define one function inside another. For example:

```
    /**** ERROR -- attempt to nest the definition of one
          function inside another function     ****/
    void  fun1( float x, float y )
    {
         .
         .
         .

        void  fun2( int p )      /***** ERROR *****/
```

```
        {

                    .
                    .
                    .

        }
    }
```

Although one function cannot be *defined* inside another, it can and should be *declared* inside or before whatever functions invoke it. For example:

```
/* declaring one function inside another */
void fun1( float x, float y )
{
        /* declaration of fun2 */
        void  fun2( int count );
                    .
                    .
                    .

}
```

9. It is an error to omit the parentheses and data types of the parameters when declaring a function. For example, the following is an incorrect declaration of the function strength:

```
/* ERRONEOUS way to declare the function strength */
float strength;
```

The preceding is interpreted as the definition of a *variable* strength as distinct from the *function* strength. The proper declaration is

```
/*  CORRECT way to declare the function strength */
float strength( float power_coeff );
```

10. When a function is invoked, all its arguments are evaluated before control passes to it. However, the arguments need not be evaluated in any particular order (e.g., left to right). So it is an error to depend on left-to-right, right-to-left, or some other evaluation.

11. Because C passes arguments using the call by value convention in which a function receives a *copy* of the argument, it is an error to assume that the value of an argument can be changed by the invoked function. For example, the output of the following program is y = 5.

```
#include <stdio.h>

main()
{
        void square( int x )
        int y = 5;

        square( y );
        printf( "y = %d", y );
}

void square( int x )
{
```

```
        x = x * x;
    }
```

12. A variable defined inside a function is visible only in that function. For this
    reason, the following is an error:

```
    main()
    {
        int x = 4;
        void square( void );

        square();
    }

    void square( void )
    {
        /***** ERROR: x is not visible in square *****/
        x = x * x;
    }
```

13. It is illegal to define two variables that have the same scope and the same name
    or to define a variable within a function with the same name as one of its
    parameters. For example, the following is an error:

```
    int match( int person1, int person2 )
    {
        /***** ERROR: same name as parameter *****/
        int person1;

            .
            .
            .

    }
```

14. It is an error to extend a #define across more than one line without including
    the symbol \. For example:

```
    /***** ERROR -- #define on two lines without the
           \ continuation symbol *****/
    #define  EQUALS
             ==
```

15. In the definition of a parameterized macro, no white space is allowed between
    the macro's name and the left parenthesis that precedes the parameter list. For
    this reason, the following attempt to define a parameterized macro square is an
    error:

```
    #define square ( x ) ( (x) * (x) ) /* ERROR */
```

16. An #include file must be enclosed either in double quotation marks, for
    example,

```
    #include "defs.h"
```

    or in angle brackets, for example,

```
    #include <stdio.h>
```

It is an error to omit such delimiters. For example:

```
/***** ERROR -- no delimiters around defs.h *****/
#include defs.h
```

17. It is an error to write #define or #include with any uppercase letters:

```
#INCLUDE "defs.h"   /***** ERROR *****/
```

18. It is an error to #include a file in itself.

19. In every recursive function, there must be some situations in which the function does not invoke itself. For this reason, the following is an error:

```
int fact( int num )
{
    /*** ERROR-no base cases ***/
    return ( num * fact( num - 1 ) );
}
```

20. It is an error to use the definitions and macros in *stdarg.h* to write a function that expects an arbitrary number of arguments without writing the ellipses (, . . .) in its header. For example, the following is an error:

```
#include <stdarg.h>

int max( int how_many ) /* ERROR: ,... missing */
{
    va_list arg_addr;
    .

    .

    .
    va_start( arg_addr, how_many );
    .

    .

    .
}
```

Programming Exercises

4.1. Write a program with three component functions: main, make_pos, and make_neg. The function main prompts the user for an integer and checks whether the integer is negative or positive. If the integer is negative, main invokes the function make_pos, which multiplies the integer by itself and prints the result. If the integer is positive, main invokes the function make_neg, which multiplies the integer by itself, then by −1, and prints the result.

4.2. Write a program in which the function main prompts the user for one of the six letters a, b, p, q, x, y. The function main then invokes one of the six functions print_a, print_b, print_p, print_q, print_x, print_y. Each prints a large uppercase version of the letter made out of the corresponding lowercase letter. (None has any arguments.) For example, if the user enters the letter p, print_p prints something like

```
ppppppppp
ppp     ppp
ppp     ppp
ppp     ppp
ppppppppp
ppp
ppp
ppp
ppp
ppp
```

4.3. Write a program that prompts the user for two integers and one of the letter codes a, s, m, or d. The interpretation is given by the following table:

Letter	Meaning
a	add
s	subtract
m	multiply
d	divide

The function main issues the prompt and stores the user's input in the variables num1, num2, and operator. Then main checks the letter code. If the letter code is a, main invokes the function add with arguments num1 and num2 and similarly for s, m, and d. Each of the functions add, subtract, multiply, and divide invokes the function print_result, which prints the result of the arithmetic operation.

4.4. Write symbolic constants for the binary operators *, /, %, +, −, <, >, <=, and >=; then, using the symbolic constants, write a short program consisting of statements like

```
printf( "\n\tPLUS example:\t%d", 3 PLUS 2 );
```

one for each operator.

4.5. Write a function color_band with one parameter that holds a resistance. The function color_band prints the color codes that represent the resistance (see Section 4.4). Write a main function that reads a resistance and passes it to color_band. You may write some auxiliary functions if you wish.

4.6. The expression $C(n, r)$ denotes the number of r-element subsets of an n-element set. For example, $C(4, 2)$ is 6 because there are six 2-element subsets of a 4-element set. The value of $C(n, r)$ is given by the formula

$$C(n, r) = n! / (r! * (n − r)!)$$

Write a program that computes $C(n, r)$ using the following component functions:

(a) main: prompts the user for two numbers, storing them in variables n and r, respectively.

(b) check: compares r and n. If r > n, check invokes the function err_msg, which prints an error message.

(c) comb: computes $C(n, r)$.

(d) fact: computes factorial.

The function main prints the result.

4.7. Write a program that prompts the user for a letter from the alphabet and then generates and prints its Morse code symbol. Define a macro PRINT_DOT, which prints a period, and a macro PRINT_DASH, which prints the underscore symbol. Then define macros PRINT_A, PRINT_B, ... , PRINT_Z. Each of these macros is defined in terms of other macros. For example, the definition for PRINT_A might be

```
#define   PRINT_A     PRINT_DOT,  PRINT_DASH
```

The macro PRINT_H can be defined in terms of PRINT_I because the Morse code for the letter H is four dots, and the code for the letter I is two dots:

```
#define   PRINT_H     PRINT_I,  PRINT_I
```

The complete Morse code table follows:

```
A . _          J . _ _ _        S . . .
B _ . . .      K _ . _          T _
C _ . _ .      L . _ . .        U . . _
D _ . .        M _ _            V . . . _
E .            N _ .            W . _ _
F . . _ .      O _ _ _          X _ . . _
G _ _ .        P . _ _ .        Y _ . _ _
H . . . .      Q _ _ . _        Z _ _ . .
I . .          R . _ .
```

4.8. Write a function power that expects two arguments, x and n, and returns x to the power n. The argument x is of type double and n is of type int.

4.9. Write a function that returns the square root of the argument x passed to it. Use *Newton's method*. Repeatedly replace the approximate square root r with

$$\frac{x/r + r}{2}$$

Begin by setting r to 1. Stop when $|r^2 - x| < 0.0001$.

4.10. Redo Exercise 4.9, stopping when the absolute difference of two successive approximations to the square root differs by at most 0.0001.

4.11. Write a program that computes the net pay for a wage earner. Assume that each wage earner can be identified through a unique five-digit identification code, ranging from 00000 to 99999. Use the following simplified formulas, with lowercase names as variables that you define and uppercase names as macros:

```
gross_pay = ( REG_HRS * wage ) + ( overtime * OT_WAGE )
soc_secur_tax = SOC_SECUR_RATE * gross_pay
deductions = DEPENDENT_DEDUCTION * dependents
fed_inc_tax = FIT_RATE * ( gross_pay - deductions )
union_dues = UNION_DUES_RATE * gross_pay
net_pay = gross_pay - soc_secur_tax - fed_income_tax
          - union_dues
```

Choose realistic values for the macros. For example, SOC_SECUR_RATE should be about 6 percent; FIT_RATE should be at least 15 percent; and DEPENDENT_DEDUCTION should be about $2000. The function main should prompt the user for the required data, including the wage earner's unique numeric identification code, and print the net pay.

4.12. The following table gives the monthly cost of financing $1000 over 30 years for a home loan at various rates of interest:

Rate	Monthly Cost
6.0%	$ 6.00
7.0%	$ 6.66
8.0%	$ 7.34
9.0%	$ 8.05
10.0%	$ 8.78
10.5%	$ 9.15
11.0%	$ 9.52

Write a program that prompts the user for the price of a home, the current interest rate, and the percentage of the total price made as a down payment. Print the amount of the down payment, the amount to be financed, the monthly payment, and the total amount of interest paid over 30 years. For example, if the input is

```
Price of home:           100000
Interest rate:           9
Percent as down payment: 20
```

the output is

```
Down payment:     20000
Amount financed:  80000
Monthly payment:  644
Total interest:   131840
```

All input/output operations should be done in the function `main` and all calculations in whatever other functions seem appropriate.

4.13. Write the program of Exercise 4.12 using only one function, `main`. Replace the others with macros.

4.14. Write a program that computes the sum

$$\sum_{i=1}^{n} \frac{1}{i^2}$$

in two ways: first, in the order

$$1 + \frac{1}{2^2} + \frac{1}{3^2} + \cdots$$

then in the order

$$\frac{1}{n^2} + \frac{1}{(n-1)^2} + \cdots$$

Use two different functions to compute the sums. Write a function `main` that invokes each function for $n = 10, 100, 1000, 10000$.

4.15. For the program of Exercise 4.14, if the two functions give different values, answer the following questions:

(a) Why are the sums different?

(b) Which do you think is more accurate, and why?

4.16. Each time the program in Section 4.7 is run, the function `rand` produces identical sequences of random integers. Modify the program by using the library function `srand` to correct this defect.

4.17. The greatest common divisor (*gcd*) of two integers greater than zero can be computed as follows, where *mod*(M, N) is the remainder when M is divided by N:

$$gcd(\ M,\ N\ ) = \begin{cases} N, & \text{if } mod(\ M,\ N\ ) = 0 \\ gcd(\ N,\ R\ ), & \text{if } mod(\ M,\ N\ ) = R,\ R > 0. \end{cases}$$

Write a recursive function that computes the greatest common divisor.

4.18. Suppose that we have a $2 \times n$ rectangular board divided into $2n$ squares. Write a function that computes the number of ways to cover exactly this board by 1×2 dominoes.

4.19. A robot can take steps of 1 meter or 2 meters. Write a function that lists all of the ways the robot can walk n meters.

4.20. A robot can take steps of 1 meter, 2 meters, or 3 meters. Write a function that lists all of the ways the robot can walk n meters.

4.21. One version of Ackermann's function is defined as follows:

$$ack(\ M,\ N\ ) = \begin{cases} N + 1, & \text{if } M = 0 \\ ack(\ M - 1,\ 1\ ), & \text{if } M \neq 0 \text{ and } N = 0 \\ ack(\ M - 1,\ ack(\ M,\ N - 1)\ ), & \text{if } M \neq 0 \text{ and } N \neq 0. \end{cases}$$

Write a recursive function that computes Ackermann's function.

4.22. Although the Tower of Hanoi puzzle is most easily solved by using recursion, there is a nonrecursive solution (see, for example, E. R. Berlekamp, J. H. Conway, and R. K. Guy, *Winning Ways*, Vol. 2, New York: Academic Press, 1982: 753–754). Write a nonrecursive function that solves the Tower of Hanoi puzzle.

4.23. Write a recursive function to solve a modified version of the Tower of Hanoi puzzle. The modified puzzle consists of *four* pegs mounted on a board and n disks of differing sizes with holes in their centers; otherwise the rules are the same. Given all the disks stacked on one peg, the problem is to transfer the disks to another peg by moving one disk at a time. Your function should use fewer moves than the function of Example 4.8.2. (*Hint:* Use the method described in Example 4.8.2 except begin by fixing the *two* bottom disks.)

4.24. Modify the tromino tiling program of Section 4.9 so that it checks whether the board size entered is a power of 2 and whether the coordinates that the user provides for the missing square describe a square within the board.

4.25. [For programmers with access to Turbo C or a similar system that provides a library of graphics functions.] Write a program that uses a graphics display to show a tiling with trominoes of a $2^n \times 2^n$ board with one square missing.

4.26. Write a program that tiles with trominoes an $n \times n$ board with one square missing, provided that $n \neq 5$ and 3 does not divide n. The algorithms are given in I. P. Chu and R. Johnsonbaugh, "Tiling deficient boards with trominoes," *Math. Mag.* 59 (1986): 34–40.

4.27. Write a program to simulate throwing darts (see the following figure):

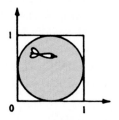

Use a random number generator to obtain 1,000 pairs of real numbers (x, y) satisfying $0 < x < 1$, $0 < y < 1$. Print the proportion P of throws that hit the dart board, that is, the proportion of pairs (x, y) that are inside the circle. Also, print $4 * P$. Notice that the geometry of the problem leads us to expect P to be about $\pi/4$. Thus $4 * P$ provides an approximation of π.

4.28. Modify the calendar program (Section 3.6) by writing four functions:

- `main`—Prompts the user for a year; invokes `get_day_code`; invokes `get_leap_year`; and invokes `print_calendar`.
- `get_day_code`—Has one parameter `year` and returns the `day_code` for this year.
- `get_leap_year`—Has one parameter `year` and returns FALSE if the year is not a leap year and TRUE if the year is a leap year. `#define FALSE` as a macro having value 0, and TRUE as a macro having value 1.
- `print_calendar`—Has parameters `year`, `day_code`, and `leap_year`. It prints the year and calendar to the file *calendar.dat*.

Programming Exercise 3.7 contains useful formulas.

4.29. Simulate the Monty Hall puzzle, which gets its name from the host of the television game show *Let's Make a Deal*. The puzzle involves a game played as follows. A contestant picks one of three doors; behind one of the doors is a car, and behind the other two are goats. After the contestant picks a door, the host opens an unpicked door that hides a goat. (Because there are two goats, the host can open a door that hides a goat no matter which door the contestant first picks.) The host then gives the contestant the option of abandoning the picked door in favor of the still closed and unpicked door. The puzzle is to determine which of three strategies the contestant should follow:

- Always stay with the door initially picked.
- Randomly stay or switch (e.g., by flipping a coin to decide).
- Always switch to the unpicked and unopened door.

The user should be prompted as to which strategy he or she wishes to follow, as well as for how many times the game should played. Use a random number generator to place the car at the start and to simulate the contestant's initial pick. If the contestant follows the second strategy, use the random number generator to determine whether the contestant stays or switches. The program should print the number of games played and the percentage of games won. (A game is won if the contestant gets the car.) Before running the simulation, try to determine whether any of the three strategies is better than the others. You then can use the simulator to test your answer. The results may surprise you. (For a technical discussion of this puzzle, see L. Gillman, "The car and the goats," *Amer. Math. Mo.* 99 (1992): 3–7.)

Arrays

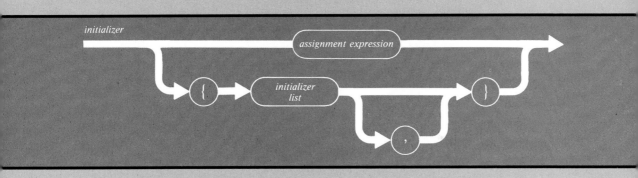

5.1 Why Arrays?
5.2 Array Indexes and Cell Offsets
5.3 Sample Application: Tracking and Reporting Car Sales
5.4 Character Strings as Arrays of Characters
5.5 Sample Application: Formatting Text with a Given Line Length
5.6 Arrays as Function Arguments
5.7 String-Handling Functions
5.8 Sample Application: Computing a String's Length
5.9 Multidimensional Arrays
5.10 Sample Application: Sorting and Searching
     Changes from Traditional C
     Common Programming Errors
     Programming Exercises

Arrays, pointers, and strings are related topics in C. We divide the topics between this chapter and the next. In this chapter, we introduce arrays and pointers and explain how C implements a character string as an array of characters. In Chapter 6, we expand on these topics.

5.1 Why Arrays?

Suppose that we have a used-car business with a dozen brands in stock, and we want a program to track daily sales and then generate a report. To simplify matters, let us use integer codes for each brand, as illustrated in Figure 5.1.1. For each brand, we need a variable to track the number of cars in stock and the number of cars sold. The number-of-cars-sold variable for each brand is initialized to zero in the morning and incremented with each sale. At night, we can update the inventory by subtracting the number of cars sold from the number of cars in stock for each brand. Our program might take a brute-force approach by defining two variables for each brand, as shown in Figure 5.1.2. This gives us two dozen distinctly named variables. The approach is inelegant and confusing, for it requires so many variables. If our business booms and we start selling two dozen brands, we will need to add another two dozen variables. Processing so many variables will be messy, and the code will likely be confusing. The computer staff will dread the prospect of adding any more brands.

```
 0   BMW
 1   BUICK
 2   CHEVY
 3   FORD
 4   GEO
 5   HONDA
 6   JAGUAR
 7   MERCEDES
 8   NISSAN
 9   OLDS
10   PLYMOUTH
11   TOYOTA
```

Figure 5.1.1 Integer codes for a dozen car brands.

```
int   cars_in_stock_bmw,         total_cars_sold_bmw;
int   cars_in_stock_buick,       total_cars_sold_buick;
int   cars_in_stock_chevy,       total_cars_sold_chevy;
int   cars_in_stock_ford,        total_cars_sold_ford;
int   cars_in_stock_geo,         total_cars_sold_geo;
int   cars_in_stock_honda,       total_cars_sold_honda;
int   cars_in_stock_jaguar,      total_cars_sold_jaguar;
int   cars_in_stock_mercedes,    total_cars_sold_mercedes;
int   cars_in_stock_nissan,      total_cars_sold_nissan;
int   cars_in_stock_olds,        total_cars_sold_olds;
int   cars_in_stock_plymouth,    total_cars_sold_plymouth;
int   cars_in_stock_toyota,      total_cars_sold_toyota;
```

Figure 5.1.2 Brute-force approach to variables for the cars program.

In many applications, we use an array to group related variables under a single name. Instead of having a dozen distinctly named variables to track car sales, we have a dozen variables under a single name:

```
/* two arrays, each with 12 integer variables */
int   cars_in_stock[ 12 ], total_cars_sold[ 12 ];
```

The number enclosed in square brackets specifies the number of distinct variables created under the single name. If we need to track sales for more or less than a dozen brands, we simply alter the numbers in the square brackets.

Example 5.1.1.   The definition

```
int   cars_in_stock[ 12 ];
```

defines 12 integer variables. The definition

```
int   cars_in_stock[ 24 ];
```

defines 24 integer variables. The definition

```
int   cars_in_stock[ 1200 ];
```

defines 1,200 integer variables.

Exercises

Exercises 1 through 3 assume the definition

```
int   trucks_in_stock[ 25 ];
```

1. How many different variables are in the array?
2. Suppose that we change 25 in the definition to 55. How many different variables are now in the array?
3. What is the data type for each variable in trucks_in_stock?
4. Why do you think that the designers of C chose brackets [ ] rather than parentheses ( ) for dealing with arrays?

5.2   Array Indexes and Cell Offsets

A definition reserves one or more cells in memory and associates a name with the cell or cells that the programmer can use to access the cells. For example, the definition

```
int cars_sold;
```

reserves one cell in memory and associates the name cars_sold with that cell (see Figure 5.2.1). On the other hand, the definition

```
int cars_in_stock[ 12 ];
```

reserves 12 contiguous cells in memory and associates the name cars_in_stock with the 12 cells (see Figure 5.2.1). All of the cells in an array are of the same data type so that each of the 12 cells in the array cars_in_stock can hold one int.

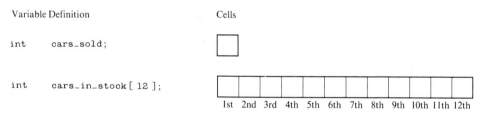

Figure 5.2.1 Variable names and associated cells.

Consider the difference between accessing the single cell associated with the variable cars_sold and the dozen cells associated with the array cars_in_stock. To access the cell associated with the variable cars_sold, we simply use the name cars_sold. For the array cars_in_stock, we must specify an index to indicate exactly which cell among the dozen we wish to access. The expression cars_in_stock[0] designates the first cell; the expression cars_in_stock[1] designates the second cell; the expression cars_in_stock[2] designates the third cell; and so on. In accessing a cell in an array, the integer enclosed in the square brackets is the index, which indicates the offset, or the distance between the cell to be accessed and the first cell. Thus the first cell in cars_in_stock has index 0 because its distance from the first cell is 0, that is, it is the first cell. The second cell has index 1 because its distance from the first cell is 1. The third cell has index 2 because its distance from the first cell is 2. We need to be careful when translating from English into C. An array's *first* element has *index* 0; its *second* element has *index* 1; its *third* element has *index* 2; and so on.

In dealing with arrays, we use square brackets in two quite different ways. When we *define* an array, the number of cells is specified in square brackets. For example, the statement

    int cars_in_stock[12];

defines cars_in_stock to be an array consisting of 12 elements. When we *access* a specific array element, we use the array's name together with an index enclosed in square brackets. Assuming the preceding definition for cars_in_stock, all of the expressions

    cars_in_stock[0]
    cars_in_stock[1]
    cars_in_stock[2]
                .
                .
                .
    cars_in_stock[11]

are legal references to the cells created under the name cars_in_stock. Notice that

    cars_in_stock[12]

is *not* a legal reference to a cell under the name cars_in_stock. The expression cars_in_stock[12] attempts to reference a cell at a distance 12 from the first cell, that is, the 13th cell. Because there are only 12 cells, this is an error. Your C system may not warn you when your program contains a meaningless index, such as cars_in_stock[12] or cars_in_stock[−999]. It is up to the programmer to ensure that index expressions remain within the array's bounds.

The number of cells in an array is given as a bracketed expression only once, in the definition; thereafter, the bracketed expression is an index. For example, `cars_in_stock[ 12 ]` occurs only in the definition to indicate that this array has 12 elements. Thereafter, expressions such as `cars_in_stock[ 0 ]`, `cars_in_stock[ 10 ]`, and so on identify particular elements in this array. Such references occur as often as needed.

Example 5.2.1.   Given the definitions

```
int cars_in_stock [ 12 ];
int ind1 = 1;
int ind2 = 2;
```

the expression

```
cars_in_stock[ 2 ]
```

has index 2 and so references the third element in the array `cars_in_stock`. The cell that is referenced is a distance 2 from the first. The expression

```
cars_in_stock[ ind2 ]
```

also references the third element in the array.
   The expression

```
cars_in_stock[ ind1 ]
```

has index 1 and so references the second element in the array.
   The expression

```
cars_in_stock[ ind1 + ind2 ]
```

has index 3 and so references the fourth element in the array.
   The expression

```
cars_in_stock[ ind2 - ind1 ]
```

has index 1 and so references the second element in the array.
   The expression

```
cars_in_stock[ ind1 - ind2 ]
```

has the meaningless index -1. What happens when such an expression is used is system dependent. Some systems do not give a warning that a senseless index was used.
   The expression

```
cars_in_stock[ ind2 * ind2 ]
```

has index 4 and so references the fifth element in the array. The expression

```
cars_in_stock[ ind2 + ind1 * ind2 ]
```

also has index 4 and so also references the fifth element in the array.

In defining an array, the number of cells is normally given as an integer constant, but an expression is permitted if the value of the expression is known at compile time. For example, if MAX is #defined as some integer constant, the definition

```
int array[ MAX + 1 ];
```

is permitted because the compiler can determine the value of MAX + 1. Any expression whatsoever is permitted as an index into an array as long as the expression evaluates to an integer and the index has a value that actually refers to a cell in the array. The value of an index may not be known until run time. In the reference

```
cars_in_stock[ ind2 + ind1 * ind2 ],
```

the value of the index

```
ind2 + ind1 * ind2
```

is not known until the values of the variables ind1 and ind2 are determined, which occurs at run time. The *definition*

```
int cars_in_stock[ ind2 + ind1 * ind2 ];
```

is illegal.

An array can be initialized in the definition. The initial values are enclosed in braces and separated by commas. Arrays of type char can also be initialized in another way in the definition; see Section 5.4.

Example 5.2.2. The definition

```
int id[ 4 ] = { 45, 2, 800, 81 };
```

creates and initializes the array id, as shown in Figure 5.2.2.

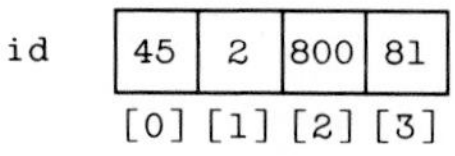

Figure 5.2.2 Initializing the array id in the definition.

If, in a definition, fewer initial values are given than there are cells, the cells beginning with the first are initialized with the given values. After the initial values supplied are exhausted, each of the remaining cells is initialized to 0. It is an error to supply more initial values than there are cells.

Example 5.2.3. The definition

```
char name[ 9 ] = { 'D', 'i', 'c', 'k' };
```

creates and initializes the array name, as shown in Figure 5.2.3.

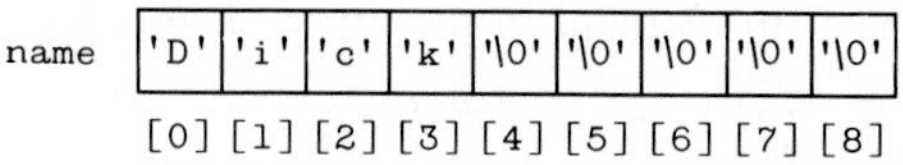

Figure 5.2.3 Initializing the array name in the definition.

If we define and initialize arrays, we can omit the integers that specify the number of cells. The compiler allocates exactly as many cells as are needed to store the initial data. We can omit the number of cells in a definition *only* if the array is initialized.

Example 5.2.4. The definition

```
int age[] = { 6, 0, 1, 7, 3 };
```

creates and initializes the array `age`, as shown in Figure 5.2.4.

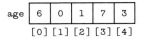

Figure 5.2.4 Initializing the array `age` in the definition.

Arrays and Pointers

To access a specific element in an array, we can use the array's name together with an index. The array's name provides the address of its first cell, and the index provides the offset from this first cell.

Example 5.2.5. The code

```
#include <stdio.h>

main()
{
    int lucky_nums[] = { 1, 3, 5, 7 };

    /* Print 3rd lucky number. */
    printf( "%d\n", lucky_nums[ 2 ] );
}
```

prints 5, the contents of the third cell in the array `lucky_nums`. The system locates the third cell by using `lucky_nums` as a pointer to a base address (i.e., the address of the array's first cell) and the index 2 as an offset from this base address. Figure 5.2.5 illustrates and assumes that the first cell in `lucky_nums` is located at address 534. The address is shown above the first cell and indexes, as offsets from the first cell, are shown below the cells.

Figure 5.2.5 An array's name as a pointer to the first cell in the array.

There are two equivalent ways to characterize `lucky_nums`: first, as a pointer to the first cell in the array with this name; second, as an expression whose value is the address of the first cell in the array (in this example, address 534). The expression

```
lucky_nums
```

is thus shorthand for the expression

```
&lucky_nums[ 0 ]
```

because each expression gives the address of the first cell in the array named `lucky_nums`.

An array's name is a **pointer constant**; its value is set to the address of the first cell of the array when the array is defined and cannot be changed thereafter. In Example 5.2.5, we assume that the array `lucky_nums` begins at the `int` cell with address 534, which means that the name `lucky_nums` points to this cell throughout the program. It would be an error to try to change the value of `lucky_nums`. Any expression of the form

```
lucky_nums = ...              /*** ERROR ***/
```

is an error because an array's name, as a pointer constant, cannot have its value changed through an assignment operation. Accordingly, an array's name never can occur alone as the left-hand side of an assignment statement. Of course, an expression such as

```
lucky_nums[ 0 ] = 777; /* OK */
```

is correct because `lucky_nums[ 0 ]` specifies a particular `int` cell within the array, and it is perfectly legal to change the contents of this or any other cell in the array.

C supports **pointer variables** in addition to pointer constants. Like a pointer constant, a pointer variable holds the address of some cell; but unlike a pointer constant, a pointer variable can have its value set through an assignment operation. Because pointer variables are so important in C, we devote Chapter 6 to them. For now we conclude with a example that sketches the syntax of pointer variables and shows that a pointer variable may have its value reset. By the way, you have seen pointer variables already with reference to file input/output (see Section 1.10).

Example 5.2.6.   The code

```
#include <stdio.h>

main()
{
    int lucky_nums[] = { 1, 3, 5, 7 };
    int *ptr;                  /* ptr's definition */

    ptr = lucky_nums;          /* ptr --> 1st cell */
    ptr = &lucky_nums[ 0 ]; /* ditto */

    ptr = &lucky_nums[ 2 ]; /* ptr --> 3rd cell */
}
```

defines `ptr` as a variable of type pointer to `int`, which means that `ptr` can hold the address of an `int` cell. Because `lucky_nums` is defined as an array of four `ints`, `ptr` can hold the address of any cell in this array. The first two assignment statements store in `ptr` the address of the first cell in the array `lucky_nums` (see Figure 5.2.6). The last assignment statement stores in `ptr` the address of the third cell in the array `lucky_nums` (see Figure 5.2.7). Note that the pointer variable `ptr`, unlike the pointer constant `lucky_nums`, can occur as the left-hand side of an assignment statement. The code does not show how `ptr` might be used in a C program. We leave this expansive topic to the next chapter.

Implementation Issues: What the C Programmer Can Ignore

The C programmer can access any element in an array without knowing how big each element is. For example, suppose that we want to access the third element in

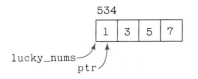

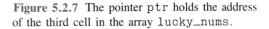

Figure 5.2.6 The pointer ptr holds the address of the first cell in the array lucky_nums.

Figure 5.2.7 The pointer ptr holds the address of the third cell in the array lucky_nums.

cars_in_stock, an array of ints. On one computer system, an int might occupy 16 bits of storage, whereas on another system, an int might occupy 32 bits of storage. On *either* system, we can access the third element as cars_in_stock[2]. The index says: Give me the element that lies two away from the first, regardless of how many bits each element has.

There is a related point. On one system, int variables might require twice as many bits of storage as do char variables; on another system, int variables might require four times as many bits as do char variables. Yet we access, say, the fourth element in either an array of integers or an array of characters on any system by using 3 as the index, regardless of whether and how the elements differ in number of bits.

The sizeof Operator and Arrays

The sizeof operator (see Section 2.1) may be used with arrays, as the following example illustrates:

Example 5.2.7. We assume a computer system that uses four bytes to store an int. Given the definition

```
int disease_codes[ 30 ];
```

the value of

```
sizeof ( disease_codes )
```

is

```
30 * 4 = 120
```

This means that the array disease_codes occupies 120 bytes.

Exercises

Exercises 1 through 9 assume the definition

```
char  letters[ 26 ];
```

1. (True/False) The array letters has 26 elements.

2. Which element in the array does the expression letters[1] designate?

3. Does the expression letters[26] reference an element in the array?

4. (True/False) The expression

```
c = letters[ 3 ];
```

assigns to the variable c the contents of the fourth element in letters. Assume that c is of type char.

5. Suppose that the variable letters[0] has the character A as its contents, and letters[25] has the character Z as its contents. Also assume that the variable temp is of type char. What results from the following slice of code?

```
temp = letters[ 25 ];
letters[ 25 ] = letters[ 0 ];
letters[ 0 ] = temp;
```

6. How many cells are in the array letters?

7. What are legal indexes for letters?

Exercises 8 and 9 assume the definition

```
int digits[ 100 ];
```

8. Do the expressions digits[23] and letters[23] both reference the 24th element in the respective arrays?

9. Must the elements of the array digits and the array letters have the same number of bits?

10. Explain the relationship between an offset and an array index.

11. What is the error in the following definition statement?

```
/* mixed has some char and some int variables */
int  char mixed[ 100 ];
```

12. What is the error in the following definition statement?

```
/* numbers has 100 elements, 0 through 99 */
int  numbers[ 0:99 ];
```

13. What is the error in the following definition statement?

```
/* reals has 500 floating-point elements */
float  reals( 500 );
```

14. What is the error in the following definition statement?

```
int s[ 3 ] = { 4, 33, 20, -9, 70 };
```

15. What is the error in the following definition statement?

```
main()
{
    double score[ ];
        .
        .
        .
}
```

16. Show what is stored in the cells of the array when we write

```
int a[ 5 ] = { 26, -1003 };
```

17. Show what is stored in the cells of the array when we write

```
int x[ 5 ] = { 8, -2, 20, 26, -1003 };
```

18. Show what is stored in the cells of the array when we write

```
char x[ ] = { 'R', 'a', 'm', 's' };
```

Assume that an int occupies two bytes and that a float occupies four bytes. Given the definition

```
int disk[ 500 ];
float weight[ 40 ];
```

find the value of each expression in Exercises 19 through 22.

19. sizeof (weight)

20. sizeof (disk)

21. sizeof (weight[0])

22. sizeof (disk[100])

23. Suppose that a is an array of type int and that each cell in the array holds either 1 or 0. Suppose also that i and j are valid indexes into a. Do the two fragments always produce the same output? Explain.

```
v = a[ i ];                    if ( ( v = a[ i ] ) &&
w = a[ j ];                         !( w = a[ j ] ) || !v && w )
if ( v && !w || !v && w )           printf( "Yes\n" );
        printf( "Yes\n" );    else
else
        printf( "No\n" );           printf( "No\n" );
```

24. The following code is supposed to set i to the first occurrence of a positive number in

```
a[ 0 ],a[ 1 ], . . . ,a[ n ]
```

or to n + 1 if there are no positive numbers; however, the code is incorrect. Explain what the problem is and write a correct version.

```
for ( i = 0; a[ i ] <= 0 && i <= n; i++ )
    ;
```

5.3 Sample Application: Tracking and Reporting Car Sales

Problem

Track sales for a used-car business with one dozen brands in stock, each with an integer code, and generate a daily report that indicates

- Inventory by brand at day's start.
- Total cars sold by brand at day's end.
- Sales as a percentage of inventory, by brand.

Sample Input/Output

Input is in color; output is in black.

```
Cars in stock for brand: 0   10
Cars in stock for brand: 1   13
```

```
Cars in stock for brand: 2  5
Cars in stock for brand: 3  23
Cars in stock for brand: 4  38
Cars in stock for brand: 5  4
Cars in stock for brand: 6  20
Cars in stock for brand: 7  25
Cars in stock for brand: 8  5
Cars in stock for brand: 9  27
Cars in stock for brand: 10  17
Cars in stock for brand: 11  13

Which brand was sold? 3
How many cars in sale? 6

Which brand was sold? 9
How many cars in sale? 5

Which brand was sold? 10
How many cars in sale? 7

Which brand was sold? -1

DAILY REPORT
----- ------
Brand #:                0
Inventory at day's start:     10
Total sales:         0
Inventory at day's end:           10
Sales as percentage of inventory:  0.000000

Brand #:                1
Inventory at day's start:     13
Total sales:         0
Inventory at day's end:           13
Sales as percentage of inventory:  0.000000

Brand #:                2
Inventory at day's start:      5
Total sales:         0
Inventory at day's end:            5
Sales as percentage of inventory:  0.000000

Brand #:                3
Inventory at day's start:     23
Total sales:         6
Inventory at day's end:           17
Sales as percentage of inventory:  26.086957

Brand #:                4
Inventory at day's start:     38
Total sales:         0
Inventory at day's end:           38
Sales as percentage of inventory:  0.000000
```

```
Brand #:                 5
Inventory at day's start:      4
Total sales:             0
Inventory at day's end:              4
Sales as percentage of inventory:  0.000000

Brand #:                 6
Inventory at day's start:          20
Total sales:             0
Inventory at day's end:             20
Sales as percentage of inventory:  0.000000

Brand #:                 7
Inventory at day's start:          25
Total sales:             0
Inventory at day's end:             25
Sales as percentage of inventory:  0.000000

Brand #:                 8
Inventory at day's start:       5
Total sales:             0
Inventory at day's end:              5
Sales as percentage of inventory:  0.000000

Brand #:                 9
Inventory at day's start:          27
Total sales:             5
Inventory at day's end:             22
Sales as percentage of inventory:  18.518519

Brand #:                10
Inventory at day's start:          17
Total sales:             7
Inventory at day's end:             10
Sales as percentage of inventory:  41.176471

Brand #:                11
Inventory at day's start:          13
Total sales:             0
Inventory at day's end:             13
Sales as percentage of inventory:  0.000000
```

Solution

Inside a `for` loop, we ask the user how many cars are in stock for each brand and initialize to zero the number of cars sold for each. Inside a `while` loop, we ask which brand was involved in a sale and how many cars of that brand were sold. We check to make sure that the brand falls within the array's bounds. This `while` loop terminates when the user enters any negative integer for a brand. We then use another `for` loop to generate the daily report for each brand. For precision in computing sales as a percentage of inventory, we cast the integer variables `cars_sold` and `cars_in_stock` to `floats`.

C Implementation

```
/*  This program tracks sales and inventory for a dozen brands */
/*  of cars in a used-car business. The brands are coded as in */
/*  Figure 5.1.1.                                              */
/*                                                             */
/*  At each day's start, the user initializes the array        */
/*  cars_in_stock[ brand ] to total inventory for a given      */
/*  brand and total_cars_sold[ brand ] to zero. With each      */
/*  sale, the program updates total_cars_sold[ brand ] by      */
/*  cars_sold. At day's end, the user enters a negative         */
/*  integer for a brand, which causes the program to generate  */
/*  a summary report.                                          */

0   #include <stdio.h>

1   #define  NUM_BRANDS  12   /* number of brands currently handled */

    main( )
    {
2         int   cars_in_stock[ NUM_BRANDS ];
3         int   total_cars_sold[ NUM_BRANDS ];
4         int   cars_sold;
5         int   brand;

          /* Initialize cars_in_stock and total_cars_sold for each
             brand. */
6         for ( brand = 0; brand < NUM_BRANDS; ++brand ) {
7             printf( "\n\n\tCars in stock for brand: %d  ", brand );
8             scanf( "%d", &cars_in_stock[ brand ] );
9             total_cars_sold[ brand ] = 0;
          }

          /*  Record sales, updating total_cars_sold, until user
              signals halt.*/
          printf( "\n\n\n" );

          /*  Loop until user signals halt by setting brand less
              than zero. */
10        while ( brand >= 0  ) {
11            printf( "\n\n\t Which brand was sold? " );
12            scanf( "%d", &brand );
              /* BRAND in bounds? */
13            if ( brand >= 0 && brand < NUM_BRANDS ) {
14                printf( "\n\t How many cars in sale? " );
15                scanf( "%d", &cars_sold );
16                total_cars_sold[ brand ] += cars_sold;
              }
          }

          /* Generate daily report for each brand. */
          printf( "\n\n\n\n\t\tDAILY REPORT" );
          printf( "\n\t\t----- ------" );
```

```
17          for ( brand = 0; brand < NUM_BRANDS; ++brand ) {
                printf( "\n\n\t\tBrand #:\t\t\t%d", brand );
                printf( "\n\t\tInventory at day's start:\t%d",
                    cars_in_stock[ brand ] );
                printf( "\n\t\tTotal sales:\t\t\t%d",
                    total_cars_sold[ brand ] );
                printf( "\n\t\tInventory at day's end:\t\t%d",
                    cars_in_stock[ brand ] - total_cars_sold[ brand ] );
18              printf( "\n\t\tSales as percentage of inventory:\t\t%f",
                    100 * ( ( float ) total_cars_sold[ brand ] /
                    ( float ) cars_in_stock[ brand ] ) );
            }
    }
```

Discussion

```
        /* Lines 1, 2, and 3 */
1   #define NUM_BRANDS 12 /* number of car brands currently handled */
2           int   cars_in_stock[ NUM_BRANDS ];
3           int   total_cars_sold[ NUM_BRANDS ];
```

The macro NUM_BRANDS is defined as the number of brands we currently handle. If our business grows to 50 or even 5,000 brands, we can change the macro NUM_BRANDS and leave the rest of the code alone. The definitions allocate NUM_BRANDS variables under the array name `cars_in_stock`. Recall that the bracketed expression, used in a definition statement, indicates the number of cells allocated rather than a particular element in the array.

```
        /* Lines 6, 7, 8, 9 */
6           for ( brand = 0; brand < NUM_BRANDS; ++brand ) {
7               printf( "\n\n\tCars in stock for brand: %d  ", brand );
8               scanf( "%d", &cars_in_stock[ brand ] );
9               total_cars_sold[ brand ] = 0;
            }
```

The `for` loop initializes each variable in the `cars_in_stock` and `total_cars_sold` arrays. The integer variable `brand`, used as an index into the two arrays, controls the loop. It is initialized to zero and incremented on each iteration. Because the last element in each array has the index NUM_BRANDS $-$ 1, the `for` loop terminates when `brand` equals NUM_BRANDS. For example, if NUM_BRANDS is 12, we initialize `cars_in_stock[ 0 ]` through `cars_in_stock[ 11 ]`. In this case, the `for` loop terminates when `brand` equals 12.

The car brands have integer codes; hence the integer variable `brand` can be used to prompt the user for a given brand's inventory. The function `scanf` works just as it would with a nonarray variable; we provide a format string `"%d"` and then attach the address operator, &, to the variable `cars_in_stock[ brand ]`, whose value is to be read from the terminal. Finally, each variable in the array `total_cars_sold` is initialized to zero. The assignment statement behaves just as it would for a nonarray variable. An array variable can be processed just as any other ordinary variable would.

```
        /* Lines 10 through 16 */
10          while ( brand >= 0 ) {
11              printf( "\n\n\tWhich brand was sold? " );
```

```
12          scanf( "%d", &brand );
            /* BRAND in bounds? */
13          if ( brand >= 0 && brand < NUM_BRANDS ) {
14              printf( "\n\t How many cars in sale? " );
15              scanf( "%d", &cars_sold );
16              total_cars_sold[ brand ] += cars_sold;
            }
        }
```

The variable brand, besides being used as index into the arrays cars_in_stock and total_cars_sold, controls the for loops in lines 6 and 17 and the while loop in line 10. The while loop ends when the user enters a negative integer and brand becomes negative.

Line 11 prompts the user to enter a brand, and line 12 reads the brand. Line 13 checks whether the user has entered a legal index, that is, a value between 0 and NUM_BRANDS − 1. If brand < 0 or brand > NUM_BRANDS − 1, we skip the update (lines 14 through 16). If brand is a legal index, we ask how many cars of that brand were sold and then update the variable total_cars_sold[brand].

As part of the daily report, for each brand, line 18

```
18      printf( "\n\t\tSales as percentage of inventory:\t\t%f",
            100 * ( ( float ) total_cars_sold[ brand ] /
            ( float ) cars_in_stock[ brand ] ) );
```

prints total_cars_sold divided by cars_in_stock, thus showing the user what percentage of inventory was sold that business day. The variables in both cars_in_stock and total_cars_sold are of type int; so to gain precision in computing the percentage, they are coerced into type float with the cast operator (float). Array variables of a given type, like ordinary variables, may be cast into some other type.

5.4 Character Strings as Arrays of Characters

C supplies the data type char but no data type for character strings. Instead, the C programmer must represent a string as an array of characters. The array uses one cell for each character in the string and a final cell to hold the null character ' \0 ', which marks the end of the string. (Recall that the expression ' \0 ' designates *one* character.)

Figure 5.4.1 shows how we can represent the names of the Three Stooges as character strings. The array stooge1 is initialized character by character using the assignment operator; the array stooge2 is initialized by using the function scanf; and the array stooge3 is initialized in the definition.

```
/*  This program illustrates character strings. It uses three
    arrays of characters to hold the names of the Three Stooges,
    entering the names in three different ways; it then prints
    all three names using printf and the string conversion
    specification %s.                                           */

#include <stdio.h>

main()
{
```

```
1       char    stooge1[ 4 ];           /* Moe */
2       char    stooge2[ 6 ];           /* Curly */
3       char    stooge3[ 6 ] = "Larry"; /* Larry */

        /* Initialize array stooge1, character by character. */
4       stooge1[ 0 ] = 'M';
5       stooge1[ 1 ] = 'o';
6       stooge1[ 2 ] = 'e';
7       stooge1[ 3 ] = '\0';

        /* Initialize array stooge2 with scanf. */
        printf( "\n\n\tPlease enter the second Stooge's name: " );
8       scanf( "%s", stooge2 );

        /* Print each string, using printf and the %s conversion
           specification. */
9       printf( "\n%s", stooge1 );
10      printf( "\n%s", stooge2 );
11      printf( "\n%s", stooge3 );
}
```

Figure 5.4.1 stooges program.

The definitions in lines 1 through 3

```
1       char    stooge1[ 4 ];
2       char    stooge2[ 6 ];
3       char    stooge3[ 6 ] = "Larry";
```

show how C treats character *strings* as arrays of characters. Even though the name "Moe" has three characters, the array stooge1 has four cells—one cell for each letter in Moe's name and one for the null character. Similarly, the names "Curly" and "Larry" have five characters apiece, but the arrays stooge2 and stooge3 each have six cells.

In Section 5.2, we showed how to initialize arrays in the definition by listing the initial values in braces. There is an alternative to the brace notation for character arrays, as line 3 shows:

```
3    char    stooge3[ 6 ] = "Larry";
```

Here we define stooge3 as an array of six cells and initialize it to the string "Larry". The result is

stooge3 | 'L' | 'a' | 'r' | 'r' | 'y' | '\0' |
        [0] [1] [2] [3] [4] [5]

When the number of initializers is smaller than the size of the array, the system fills the remaining cells with the null character ('\0').

Line 3 could also have been written in a simpler fashion:

```
3'   char    stooge3[] = "Larry";
```

Line 3' specifies no number of cells for the array stooge3 but, rather, lets the compiler determine the number from the initialization string. In this case, the system automatically adds the null terminator. Line 3′ is thus easier on the programmer, and safer as well; the programmer does not have to count the number of characters or worry about miscounting.

Lines 4 through 7

```
4    stooge1[ 0 ] = 'M';
5    stooge1[ 1 ] = 'o';
6    stooge1[ 2 ] = 'e';
7    stooge1[ 3 ] = '\0';
```

offer another (tedious) way to initialize a character string. Here we initialize the array's variables one at a time, including the last variable, which holds the null character. The characters are entered as characters, *not as strings*. For example, we write

```
stooge1[ 0 ] = 'M'; /* a single character, 'M' */
```

and *not*

```
stooge1[ 0 ] = "M"; /* ERROR: a string of two
                       characters, 'M' and '\0' */
```

There is a big difference. The single-quoted M—'M'—is *one* character. By contrast, the double-quoted M—"M"—is a *character string*, in this case, a string with two characters— the character M followed by the character \0. We need a single character variable to hold 'M' but an array of two cells to hold "M".

To read a string using scanf,

```
8    scanf( "%s", stooge2 );
```

we use the conversion specification %s, which directs scanf to skip white space and then to read into the character array stooge2 *all* characters up to the next white space. The system adds a null terminator. The array must be large enough to hold the characters read and the terminating '\0'. If we type

```
Curly
```

and then a carriage return, line 8 initializes the array stooge2 as

```
stooge2 |'C'|'u'|'r'|'l'|'y'|'\0'|
         [0] [1] [2] [3] [4] [5]
```

When we type a string to be read by scanf with the %s conversion specification, we must *not* enclose the string in double quotation marks. If we incorrectly type

```
"Curly"
```

to initialize the array using scanf, we do *not* initialize the array to Curly. The double quotation marks themselves are considered a character and are read into the array. Thus the array is initialized as

```
stooge2 |'"'|'C'|'u'|'r'|'l'|'y'|
         [0] [1] [2] [3] [4] [5]
```

At this point, the system reads the next character " and attempts to store it in the next available cell in the array stooge2. Because no more cells are available in stooge2, an error occurs. If we define stooge2 as

```
char stooge2[ 8 ];
```

and we type

```
"Curly"
```

using `scanf`, the array `stooge2` is initialized as

stooge2	'"'	'C'	'u'	'r'	'l'	'y'	'"'	'\0'
	[0]	[1]	[2]	[3]	[4]	[5]	[6]	[7]

When we use `scanf` with the %s conversion specification, we must *not* prefix the name of the array that is used to store the characters with the address operator &. (However, as we saw in Section 1.2, we *must* prefix the name of an ordinary variable with &.) The function `scanf` *always* requires address expressions so that it knows where to store the data. However, an array's name, unlike a simple variable's name, *is an address expression*—the address of the first element in the array (see Section 5.2). In line 8,

```
8    scanf( "%s", stooge2 );
```

writing `stooge2` causes the address of the array to be passed to `scanf`. For this reason, `scanf` knows where to store the characters. Line 8 is equivalent to

```
scanf( "%s", &stooge2[ 0 ] );
```

Here `stooge2[ 0 ]` is a simple (`char`) variable that is the name of the first cell in the array `stooge2`. Prefixing the address operator & gives the address of the first cell in the array. That is, `stooge2` and `&stooge2[ 0 ]` have the same interpretation: Both give the address of the array `stooge2`.

Recall that the %c conversion specification reads just *one* character. If we write

```
scanf( "%c", stooge2 );
```

or

```
scanf( "%c", &stooge2[ 0 ] );
```

the %c conversion specification directs `scanf` to read one character and store it in the first cell of the array. If we type

```
Curly
```

and execute either of the preceding `scanf` statements, we obtain

stooge2	'C'	Uninitialized				
	[0]	[1]	[2]	[3]	[4]	[5]

The function `printf`, with the %s conversion specification, expects the corresponding argument to be the address of some character in a character string. In this case, `printf` writes all the characters beginning with the character whose address is given and ending with the character preceding the terminating null character, '\0'. Because we want to print each stooge's name, we give `printf` the address of the first element in each array:

```
9     printf( "\n%s", stooge1 );
10    printf( "\n%s", stooge2 );
11    printf( "\n%s", stooge3 );
```

Because each array name is the address of its first element, it is simplest to use the name as the `printf` argument. Nonetheless, lines 9 through 11 could have been written as follows:

```
printf( "\n%s", &stooge1[ 0 ] );
printf( "\n%s", &stooge2[ 0 ] );
printf( "\n%s", &stooge3[ 0 ] );
```

Exercises

1. (True / False) C requires that the programmer explicitly enter a null character at the end of every character string.

2. Explain the error in this slice of code:

   ```
   char c = "A";   /* define and initialize c */
   ```

3. What is printed?

   ```
   char   c[ 2 ] = "A";
   printf( "%c\n", c[ 0 ] );
   printf( "%s", c );
   ```

   In Exercises 4 through 6, assume that the arrays `stooge1`, `stooge2`, and `stooge3` are initialized as in Figure 5.4.1.

4. What is printed?

   ```
   for ( i = 0; i < 3; ++i )
      putchar( stooge1[ i ] );
   ```

5. What is printed?

   ```
   printf( "%s\n", &stooge2[ 1 ] );
   printf( "%c", stooge2[ 1 ] );
   ```

6. Explain the difference between the two uses of `scanf`.

   ```
   scanf( "%c", &stooge3[ 0 ] );
   scanf( "%s", &stooge3[ 0 ] );
   ```

   Exercises 7 through 15 assume the definition

   ```
   char   s[] = "Alfred Hitchcock";
   ```

7. How many cells are in the array `s`?

   Which of Exercises 8 through 15 are likely errors? Explain. If the expression is acceptable, what will be printed?

8. `printf( "%s", s[ 2 ] );`
9. `printf( "%s", &s[ 2 ] );`
10. `printf( "%s", s );`
11. `printf( "%s", &s );`
12. `printf( "%c", s[ 2 ] );`
13. `printf( "%c", &s[ 2 ] );`
14. `printf( "%c", s );`

15. `printf( "&c", &s );`

Exercises 16 through 23 assume the definition

`char s[ 15 ];`

Which of Exercises 16 through 23 are likely errors? Explain. If the expression is acceptable, show the contents of the array `s` if the input is

`Bob`

16. `scanf( "%s", s[ 2 ] );`
17. `scanf( "%s", &s[ 2 ] );`
18. `scanf( "%s", s );`
19. `scanf( "%s", &s );`
20. `scanf( "%c", s[ 2 ] );`
21. `scanf( "%c", &s[ 2 ] );`
22. `scanf( "%c", s );`
23. `scanf( "%c", &s );`

5.5 Sample Application: Formatting Text with a Given Line Length

Problem

Reformat text so that no line exceeds a given length. The first line of input specifies the length.

Sample Input/Output

```
35
Doctor, I'm going to tell you something I've never told anyone in
this world before, not even Myrtle Mae. Every once in a while, I see
this big white rabbit myself. Now, isn't that terrible? And, what's
more, he's every bit as big as Elwood says he is.
```

Input (From *Harvey*)

```
Doctor, I'm going to tell you
something I've never told anyone in
this world before, not even Myrtle
Mae. Every once in a while, I see
this big white rabbit myself. Now,
isn't that terrible? And, what's
more, he's every bit as big as
Elwood says he is.
```

Output

Solution

After reading the maximum line length for the output file, we repeatedly read words using `scanf`. A word is read into an array of `char`s. We determine the length of the word by counting the number of characters preceding the null terminator. If the length of the word exceeds the maximum line length, we print an error message to that effect but continue to format the file. In general, after an error it is best to print an error message and continue, if possible. If there is room for the word on the current output line, we add it to the current line; otherwise, we begin a new line. If we are processing the *first* word in the file, we begin on the first line of the output file. Thereafter, to begin a new line in the output file, we must print a newline character, '\n' (which is not counted as part of the line length). To add a word to an existing line of the output file, we must print a blank to separate the new word from the previous word.

C Implementation

```c
/*    This program reformats the standard input, except for the
      first line which contains the new maximum line length,
      line_length, to at most line_length characters per line. The
      program writes to the standard output. Lines are broken at
      spaces.                                                      */

#include <stdio.h>
#define MAX_WORD_LENGTH 80          /* max length of word in input */

main()
{
      int line_length,              /* max length of line in output */
          curr_line_length = 0,     /* number of chars printed so far
                                                    in current line */
          word_length;              /* length of current word */
      char word[ MAX_WORD_LENGTH + 1 ]; /* buffer to read word
                                      +1 is for terminating '\0' */

      scanf( "%d", &line_length );   /* 1st line of input has line
                                                        length */
      while ( scanf( "%s", word ) != EOF ) {
          /* determine length of current word */
          for ( word_length = 0; word[ word_length ] != '\0';
                word_length++ )
               ;
          if ( word_length > line_length )
              printf( "\nERROR: word length exceeds line length" );
          if ( curr_line_length == 0 ) { /* first word to write? */
              printf( "%s", word );
              curr_line_length = word_length;
          }
          else {
              /* +1 is for space */
              curr_line_length += word_length + 1;
              /* if word won't fit on current line,
                 start a new line */
              if ( curr_line_length > line_length ) {
                  printf( "\n%s", word );
                  curr_line_length = word_length;
              }
```

```
        else
            /* word fits, add space and word to current line */
            printf( " %s", word );
    }
}
}
```

5.6 Arrays as Function Arguments

An array can be passed as an argument from one function to another. Because arrays as function arguments can be discussed in full only after more on pointers, we begin the topic in this chapter and expand it in Chapter 6.

Consider, for example, a function sum that computes the sum of the array elements

```
a[ 0 ],a[ 1 ],...,a[ n ]
```

Two parameters are required—an array parameter a to catch the array passed and a parameter n to catch the index of the last item in the array to be summed. If we assume that the array is an array of ints and that the index n is of type int, the parameters in sum can be described as

```
/* sum's header */
int sum( int a[], int n )
```

The parameter declaration for the array includes square brackets to signal the function sum that a is an *array name* and not the name of an ordinary parameter. Note that the number of cells is *not* enclosed in square brackets. Of course, the simple parameter n is declared as we have previously described.

If in some other function we want to invoke the function sum to compute

```
b[ 0 ] + b[ 1 ] + ··· + b[ m ]
```

and store the result in x, we write

```
/* invoking a function with an array argument */
x = sum( b, m );
```

To pass the array b, we simply enter its name as the argument. Figure 5.6.1 gives a complete program in which we initialize an array and invoke the function sum to sum its entries.

In passing an array's name to a function, we pass the address of the array's first element. The expression

```
b    /* the name of the array b */
```

is shorthand for

```
&b[ 0 ] /* address of an array's 1st element */
```

We thus can invoke the function sum in two equivalent ways:

```
x = sum( b, m );
```

or

```
x = sum( &b[ 0 ], m );
```

```
#include <stdio.h>

#define MAX_ELEMENTS 100

main()
{
     int b[ MAX_ELEMENTS ], x, m = 0, sum( int a[], int n );
     while ( m < MAX_ELEMENTS && scanf( "%d", &b[ m ] ) != EOF )
          m++;
     /* reset m so it is the index of the last item in the array b */
     m--;
     printf( "%d item(s) input\n", m + 1 );
     if ( m >= 0 ) {
          x = sum( b, m );
          printf( "sum = %d", x );
     }
}
int sum( int a[], int n )
{
     int partial_sum = 0, i;
     for ( i = 0; i <= n; i++ )
          partial_sum += a[ i ];
     return ( partial_sum );
}
```

Figure 5.6.1 A function to sum an array.

In either case, within the function sum we can access every cell in the array b. We can access the first cell because we are given its address specifically. We can access any other cell by using the appropriate index that gives the desired cell's offset from the first cell.

> **Example 5.6.1.** The cars program of Section 5.3 has only one component function, main. Suppose that we use a separate function, print_report, to generate the report on inventory and daily sales, and pass to print_report the arrays cars_in_stock and total_cars_sold as arguments (see Figure 5.6.2). We invoke print_report from main by writing
>
>   print_report(cars_in_stock, total_cars_sold);
>
> To pass the arrays, we simply enter their names as arguments. To receive the arrays, we need a parameter for each. The parameters in print_report are described as
>
>   /* print_report's header */
>   void print_report(int inventory[], int sales[])

```
#include <stdio.h>

#define  NUM_BRANDS 12 /* number of car brands currently handled */
main()
{
        int  cars_in_stock[ NUM_BRANDS ];
        int  total_cars_sold[ NUM_BRANDS ];
```

```
        int   cars_sold;
        int   brand;

        void print_report( int inventory[], int sales[] );

        /*  Initialize cars_in_stock and total_cars_sold for each
            brand. */
        for ( brand = 0; brand < NUM_BRANDS; ++brand ) {
            printf( "\n\n\tCars in stock for brand: %d", brand );
            scanf( "%d", &cars_in_stock[ brand ] );
            total_cars_sold[ brand ] = 0;
        }
        /* Record sales, updating total_cars_sold, until user
           signals halt.*/
        printf( "\n\n\n" );

        /*  Loop until user signals halt by setting brand less
            than zero. */
        while ( brand >= 0 ) {
            printf( "\n\n\t Which brand was sold? " );
            scanf( "%d", &brand );
            /* BRAND in bounds? */
            if ( brand >= 0 && brand < NUM_BRANDS ) {
                printf( "\n\t How many cars in sale? " );
                scanf( "%d", &cars_sold );
                total_cars_sold[ brand ] += cars_sold;
            }
        }

        /* Generate daily report for each brand. */
        print_report( cars_in_stock, total_cars_sold );
}
void print_report( int inventory[], int sales[] )
{
        int brand;

        printf( "\n\n\n\n\t\tDAILY REPORT" );
        printf( "\n\t\t----- ------" );

        for ( brand = 0; brand < NUM_BRANDS; ++brand ) {
            printf( "\n\n\t\tBrand #:\t\t\t%d", brand );
            printf( "\n\t\tInventory at day's start:\t%d",
                inventory[ brand ] );
            printf( "\n\t\tTotal sales:\t\t\t%d",
                sales[ brand ] );

            printf( "\n\t\tInventory at day's end:\t\t%d",
                inventory[ brand ] - sales[ brand ] );
            printf( "\n\t\tSales as percentage of inventory:\t\t%f",
                    100 * ( (float) sales[ brand ] /
                    ( float ) inventory[ brand ] ) );
        }
}
```

Figure 5.6.2 The cars program revisited.

The body of the function print_report requires only slight changes from the original for loop in main. The variable brand must be defined in print_report's body. Also, the parameter inventory must be substituted for cars_in_stock, and the parameter sales must be substituted for total_cars_sold. (We use different names for the arguments and the parameters only for emphasis. The parameters could just as well have been named cars_in_stock and total_cars_sold.) Except for the new names, the printf statements remain unchanged. For example, the line

```
printf( "\n\t\tInventory at day's end:\t\t%d",
    cars_in_stock[ brand ] - total_cars_sold[ brand ] );
```

becomes

```
printf( "\n\t\tInventory at day's end:\t\t%d",
    inventory[ brand ] - sales[ brand ] );
```

In Chapter 6, we investigate other methods of passing arrays and of declaring array parameters.

Exercises

1. Suppose that we have an array sample1 defined as

```
float    sample1[ 10 ];
```

Explain the difference between what is passed to the functions fun1 and fun2.

```
fun1( sample1 );
fun2( sample1[ 2 ] );
```

2. What is the error?

```
main()
{
    double    bignums[ 20 ];
    void      fun( double bigs[] );

    /* invoke fun with bignums as argument */
    fun( bignums );
        .
        .
        .
}
void  fun( double bigs )
{       .
        .
        .
}
```

3. What is printed?

```
#include <stdio.h>

main()
{
```

```
        int a[ 5 ], b, i;
        void f( int x[], int y );

        for ( i = 0; i < 5; i++ )
            a[ i ] = 2 * i;

        b = 16;
        f( a, b );

        for ( i = 0; i < 5; i++ )
            printf( "%d\n", a[ i ] );

        printf( "%d", b );
    }
    void f( int x[], int y )
    {
        int i;

        for ( i = 0; i < 5; i++ )
            x[ i ] += 2;

        y += 2;
    }
```

4. (True/False) The following function returns 1 if

```
    v[ low ],...,v[ high ]
```

   is in ascending order, and 0 otherwise. Explain.

```
    int order( int v[], int low, int high )
    {
        int flag = 1;
        for ( ; low < high; low++ )
            if ( v[ low ] <= v[ low + 1 ] )
                flag = 1;
            else
                flag = 0;
        return ( flag );
    }
```

5. Explain how the program of Figure 5.6.1 would behave if the last lines of the function main were changed to

```
    if ( m >= 1 ) {
        x = sum( &b[ 1 ], m - 1 );
        printf( "sum = %d", x );
        .
        .
        .
```

5.7 String-Handling Functions

Because strings are a derived rather than a basic data type in C, it is not surprising that C has no built-in operators for string handling. Thus a programmer either writes his or her own string-handling functions or draws them from the standard library. In this section, we discuss some string-handling functions, which require the header file *string.h*. (Appendix E summarizes these and other library functions.)

strcat, strncat

The function names strcat and strncat are short for *string concatenation*. To **concatenate** two strings, s_1 and s_2, is to form the single string s_1 followed by s_2. For example, if we concatenate

"The Sound " and "of Music"

we obtain the string

"The Sound of Music"

The function strcat expects two arguments, which should be character strings. In more precise terms, each argument should be the address of a character in a null-terminated array of characters, and an *array's name* is just such an address. The function strcat concatenates the strings and puts the result, properly null terminated, into the first argument. Finally, strcat returns the address of the first string.

> **Example 5.7.1.** The result of the definitions and initializations
>
> ```
> char   string1[ 17 ] = "The ";
> char   string2[ 13 ] = "Caine Mutiny";
> ```
>
> is shown in Figure 5.7.1. The changes to the array string1 after executing
>
> ```
> strcat( string1, string2 );
> ```
>
> are shown in Figure 5.7.2. The array string2 is unchanged. If we then execute
>
> ```
> printf( "The concatenated string is:\t%s", string1 );
> ```
>
> the output is
>
> ```
> The concatenated string is   The Caine Mutiny
> ```

The function strncat is like strcat except that there is a third argument, which specifies the maximum number of characters to be included from the second string.

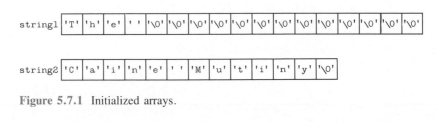

Figure 5.7.1 Initialized arrays.

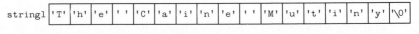

Figure 5.7.2 Using strcat.

Figure 5.7.3 Using `strncat`.

Example 5.7.2. Given the definitions in Example 5.7.1, the changes to the array `string1` after executing

```
strncat( string1, string2, 5 );
```

are shown in Figure 5.7.3. The array `string2` is unchanged. If we then execute

```
printf( "The concatenated string is:\t%s", string1 );
```

the output is

```
The concatenated string is    The Caine
```

strcmp, strncmp

The function names `strcmp` and `strncmp` are short for *string comparison*. When we compare two different strings, there are two possibilities:

- Each character in the shorter string is identical to the corresponding character in the longer string.
- At some position, the characters in the strings differ.

If the first possibility holds, the shorter string precedes the longer. For example, *dog* precedes *doghouse*. If the second possibility holds, we locate the leftmost position, p, in the string at which the characters differ. The order of the strings is determined by the order of the characters at position p, and the order of the characters is defined by the table that encodes the characters (e.g., ASCII, EBCDIC). For example, *gladiator* precedes *gladiolus* (see Figure 5.7.4). At the leftmost position at which the characters differ, we find *a* in *gladiator* and *o* in *gladiolus*, and *a* precedes *o* in every encoding system. This method of ordering strings is called **lexicographic order**.

```
Index:  0 1 2 3 4 5 6 7 8
        g l a d i a t o r
        g l a d i o l u s
        ‾‾‾‾‾‾‾‾‾  ‾‾
        identical  different
```

Figure 5.7.4 Lexicographic order.

The function `strcmp` expects two arguments, the addresses of null-terminated character strings. It compares them and returns

- 0 if the two are equal.
- A negative integer if the first string is lexicographically less than the second.
- A positive integer if the first string is lexicographically greater than the second.

Example 5.7.3. Suppose that we define and initialize two strings as

```
char string1[] = "gladiator";
char string2[] = "gladiolus";
```

If we then execute

```
if ( strcmp( string1, string2 ) < 0 )
        printf( "string1 < string2" );
else if ( strcmp( string1, string2 ) == 0 )
        printf( "string1 == string2" );
else
        printf( "string1 > string 2" );
```

the output is

```
string1 < string2
```

because the value of the expression

```
strcmp( string1, string2 )
```

is negative.

The function `strncmp` is like `strcmp` except that there is a third argument, which specifies the maximum number of characters to be used in the comparison. If this argument is negative or zero, `strncmp` returns 0.

Example 5.7.4.   Suppose that we define and initialize two strings as

```
char string1[] = "gladiator";
char string2[] = "gladiolus";
```

The value of the expression

```
strncmp( string1, string2, 4 )
```

is 0, as the first four characters of `string1` are equal to the first four characters of `string2`.

strcpy, strncpy

The function names `strcpy` and `strncpy` are short for *string copy*. Each copies all or part of the second argument into the first argument. The two arguments should be addresses of null-terminated character strings. Each returns the address of the first argument.

Example 5.7.5.   The result of the definitions and initializations

```
char    string1[] = "My One and Only";
char    string2[] = "South Pacific";
```

is shown in Figure 5.7.5. The changes to the array `string1` after executing

```
strcpy( string1, string2 );
```

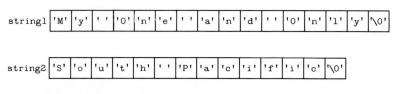

Figure 5.7.5 Initialized arrays.

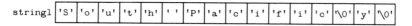

string1 | 'S' | 'o' | 'u' | 't' | 'h' | ' ' | 'P' | 'a' | 'c' | 'i' | 'f' | 'i' | 'c' | '\0' | 'y' | '\0'

Figure 5.7.6 Using `strcpy`.

are shown in Figure 5.7.6. The array `string2` is unchanged. If we execute

```
printf( "%s", string1 );
```

the output is

```
South Pacific
```

The function `strncpy` has a third argument, which specifies the number of characters to copy. More precisely, when

```
strncpy( string1, string2, max_len );
```

is executed, exactly `max_len` characters are copied from `string2` to `string1`. If the number of nonnull characters in `string2` is less than `max_len`, null terminators are used to fill `string1`. The resulting string is *not* null terminated if the number of nonnull characters in `string2` is greater than or equal to `max_len`.

Example 5.7.6. Given the definitions in Example 5.7.5, the changes to the array `string1` after executing

```
strncpy( string1, string2, 5 );
```

are shown in Figure 5.7.7. The array `string2` is unchanged. If we execute

```
printf( "%s", string1 );
```

the output is

```
Southe and Only
```

strlen

The function name `strlen` is short for *string length*. This function brings relief after the preceding functions, for it is straightforward. It expects the address of a null-terminated character string and returns the number of nonnull characters up to the null terminator.

Example 5.7.7. The result of the definitions and initializations

```
char   string[] = "Follies";
char   null_string[] = "";
```

is shown in Figure 5.7.8. Because the length of `string` is 7 and the length of `null_string` is 0, if we execute

```
printf( "string has length %d\n", strlen( string ) );
printf( "null_string has length %d\n",
        strlen( null_string ) );
```

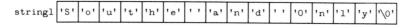

string1 | 'S' | 'o' | 'u' | 't' | 'h' | 'e' | ' ' | 'a' | 'n' | 'd' | ' ' | 'O' | 'n' | 'l' | 'y' | '\0'

Figure 5.7.7 Using `strncpy`.

string

| 'F' | 'o' | 'l' | 'l' | 'i' | 'e' | 's' | '\0' |

null_string | '\0' |

Figure 5.7.8 Using `strlen`.

the output is

```
string has length 7
null_string has length 0
```

strstr, strchr, strrchr

The function name `strstr` is short for *string in string* and the function names `strchr` and `strrchr` are short for *string has character*. The three functions are similar in that they all search a string for a specified component. They differ in that `strstr` searches for a substring, whereas `strchr` and `strrchr` search for a single character: `strchr` searches for the first occurrence and `strrchr` for the last occurrence of the specified character.

Example 5.7.8   The output for the program

```
#include <stdio.h>
#include <string.h>

main()
{
  /* strstr example */
  printf( "strstr: %s\n",
          strstr( "photon spin", "on sp" ) );

  /* strchr example */
  printf( "strchr: %s\n",
          strchr( "photon spin", 'n' ) );

  /* strrchr example */
  printf( "strrchr: %s\n",
          strrchr( "photon spin", 'n' ) );
}
```

is

```
strstr: on spin

strchr: n spin

strrchr: n
```

All three functions return the address of the search substring or character if the string contains it and NULL otherwise. NULL, which is #defined in the standard header file *stddef.h* and, for convenience, in some other system header files as well (e.g., *stdio.h*, *string.h*), is an implementation-dependent value guaranteed not to be an actual address. In the `strstr` example, the function returns the address of the second `'o'` in "photon spin" because this is where the substring "on sp" begins in "photon spin". In the `strrchr` example, the function returns the address of the rightmost 'n' in 'photon spin'. In a call such as

```
strstr( "photon spin", "tons" );
```

the function would return NULL because "photon spin" does not contain "tons" as a substring.

The header *string.h* also declares several functions that begin mem. These functions, fully described in Appendix E, process data of arbitrary type. In all cases, the number of bytes to process is specified, so the null terminator is not used. The functions `memcpy` and `memmove` copy *n* bytes from one object to another; `memcmp` compares *n* bytes of one object with *n* bytes of a second object; `memchr` searches for the first occurrence of a character within the first *n* bytes of an object; and `memset` copies a character into the first *n* bytes of an object. Since these functions need not check for a null terminator, the intent is to provide functions that can be implemented to run faster than their `str`−counterparts.

Exercises

1. What is printed?

```
#include <stdio.h>
#include <string.h>

main()
{
    char   part1[] = "Base 8 is ";
    char   part2[] = "just like base 10 ";
    char   part3[] = "if you have no thumbs.";
    char   result[ 80 ] = "";

    strcat( result, part1 );
    strcat( result, part2 );
    strcat( result, part3 );
    printf( "%s", result );
}
```

2. Given

```
char   s1[] = "abc";
char   s2[] = "aBc";
```

is the value of the expression

```
strcmp( s1, s2 )
```

positive, negative, or zero? Assume ASCII coding of the characters.

3. Given

```
char   s1[] = "abc";
char   s2[] = "aBc";
```

is the value of the expression

```
strcmp( s1, s2 )
```

positive, negative, or zero? Assume EBCDIC coding of the characters.

4. What is printed?

```
#include <stdio.h>
#include <string.h>

main( )
{
    char  str1[ 11 ] = "lousy ";
    char  str2[] = "mousie";

    printf( "%s", strncat( str1, str2, 4 ) );
}
```

5. What is printed?

```
#include <stdio.h>
#include <string.h>

main( )
{
    char str1[ 20 ] = "Far Out ";
    char str2[ 20 ] = "";

    strcat( str1, str2 );
    printf( "%s\n%s", str1, str2 );
}
```

6. What is printed?

```
#include <stdio.h>
#include <string.h>

main( )
{
    char str1[ 20 ] = "Far Out ";
    char str2[ 20 ] = "";

    strcat( str2, str1 );
    printf( "%s\n%s", str1, str2 );
}
```

7. What is printed?

```
#include <stdio.h>
#include <string.h>

main( )
{
    char str1[] = "Great Deals";
    char str2[] = "Shady Lane";

    printf( "%s", strncpy( str1, str2, 5 ) );
}
```

8. What is printed?

```
#include <stdio.h>
#include <string.h>
```

```
main( )
{
    char string1[] = "doghouse";
    char string2[] = "dog";

    if ( strcmp( string1, string2 ) < 0 )
        printf( "string1 < string2" );
    else if ( strcmp( string1, string2 ) == 0 )
        printf( "string1 == string2" );
    else
        printf( "string1 > string2" );
}
```

9. What is printed?

```
#include <stdio.h>
#include <string.h>

main( )
{
    char string1[] = "doghouse";
    char string2[] = "";

    if ( strcmp( string1, string2 ) < 0 )
        printf( "string1 < string2" );
    else if ( strcmp( string1, string2 ) == 0 )
        printf( "string1 == string2" );
    else
        printf( "string1 > string 2");
}
```

10. What is printed?

```
#include <stdio.h>
#include <string.h>

main( )
{
    char str[ 14 ] = "The Big Sleep";

    strcpy( &str[ 4 ], "Men" );
    printf( "%s\n", str );
}
```

11. What is printed?

```
#include <stdio.h>
#include <string.h>

main( )
{
    char str[] = "My Brother Was an Only Child";

    printf( "%d\n", strlen( str ) );
    printf( "%d", strlen( &str[ 5 ] ) );
}
```

12. What is printed?

```
#include <stdio.h>
#include <string.h>

main()
{
  printf( "%s\n",
          strstr( "Miami Blues", "Blue" ) );

  printf( "%s\n",
          strchr( "Miami Blues", 'i' ) );

  printf( "%s\n",
          strrchr( "Miami Blues", 'i' ) );
}
```

13. Test what happens on your system when you pass `strlen` an array of characters that does not have a null terminator.

5.8 Sample Application: Computing a String's Length

Problem

Write a function to determine a character string's length.

Sample Input/Output

```
"otter"        5
""             0
"a"            1
```

      Input   Output

Solution

We call our function `length` to distinguish it from the function `strlen` in the standard library. We initialize the variable `count` to 0 and step through the string (which is an array of characters) one character at a time until we find the null terminator. Each time we increment `count` by 1.

C Implementation

```
/* function to compute a string's length */
/* length expects an array of characters */
int  length( char string[] )
{
    int  count;      /* string's length */

    for ( count = 0; string[ count] != '\0'; ++count )
        ;
    return ( count );
}
```

Exercises

1. Write an alternative version of the function `length`, using a `while` loop instead of a `for` loop.

2. Write a function `cat` that concatenates two strings and puts the result into the first argument.

3. Write a function `compare` that compares two strings and returns a positive value (respectively, zero value, negative value) when `strcmp` returns a positive value (respectively, zero value, negative value).

4. Write a function `copy` that copies the string in the second argument into the first argument.

5.9 Multidimensional Arrays

The number of indexes used to access a particular element in an array is called the **dimension** of the array. All of the arrays that we have discussed so far are **one-dimensional arrays**, for they need only one index to access a specific element. An array's definition shows how many dimensions it has. An array with one pair of brackets [ ] is one-dimensional; an array with two pairs of brackets [ ] [ ] is two-dimensional; and so on. Arrays of more than one dimension are called **multidimensional arrays**.

Example 5.9.1. The statement

```
float tolerance[ 12 ][ 50 ];
```

defines `tolerance` as a two-dimensional array of `float`s. Two indexes are needed to access a specific element. Examples of legal references are

```
tolerance[ 5 ][ 30 ];
tolerance[ 11 ][ 49 ];
tolerance[ 0 ][ 0 ];
```

The array `tolerance` of Example 5.9.1 creates the cells

```
tolerance[ 0 ][ 0 ],tolerance[ 0 ][ 1 ],...,tolerance[ 0 ][ 49 ]
tolerance[ 1 ][ 0 ],tolerance[ 1 ][ 1 ],...,tolerance[ 1 ][ 49 ]
                           .
                           .
                           .
tolerance[ 11 ][ 0 ],tolerance[ 11 ][ 1 ],...,tolerance[ 11 ][ 49 ]
```

Because each row has 50 cells, there are

```
600 = 50 * 12
```

cells. In general, if we multiply together the numbers in brackets in the definition of an array, we obtain the total number of cells created.

Example 5.9.2. The following table gives the definitions of several arrays, the number of dimensions of each, and the number of cells created.

Array Definition	Dimensions	Number of Cells
int tape[100];	one	100
int cars[10][10];	two	100
char address[100][10];	two	1,000
float temperature[10][10][10];	three	1,000
int count[20][10][10];	three	2,000

The Convenience of Multidimensional Arrays

A personnel department wants a program to help process job applicants. Specifically, the department wants to show an applicant a list of available jobs, to ask the applicant to choose one or more items from the list, and then to have a program print for every choice the starting salary per year, the required credentials (e.g., high school diploma), the job location, and the package of benefits (e.g., retirement and profit-sharing plans). This information can be represented as a table whose rows are the available jobs and whose columns are the job attributes (see Figure 5.9.1).

Let us assume that the company has 100 different jobs, each with an integer code: 0 for accountant, 1 for auditor, and so on. We also assume that the credentials have integer codes: 0 for high school diploma, 1 for bachelor's degree in recreation management, and so on. Salary, benefits, and location have integer codes as well. Thus each row and column entry is an integer (see Figure 5.9.2). The job table can be represented as a two-dimensional array whose elements are of type int by defining

```
/* rows-jobs; columns-job attributes */
int  job_table[ 100 ][ 4 ];
```

Multidimensional Arrays as Arrays of Arrays

The definition of job_table suggests that a two-dimensional array can be seen as a one-dimensional array, each of whose elements is itself an array. Indeed, this is C's

```
CODES:    R  == retirement
          PS == profit sharing
          MM == major medical
          LS == limo service
          HSD == high school diploma
          BSA == bachelor of science in accounting
          MSA == master of science in accounting
          -- == open
```

ATTRIBUTES / JOB	CREDENTIAL	SALARY	BENEFITS	LOCATION
ACCOUNTANT	BSA	19,700	RPSMM	27 East Oak
AUDITOR	MSA	28,340	RPSMM	27 East Oak
CUSTODIAN	HSD	16,000	RMM	14 Technology Drive
.	.	.	.	.
.	.	.	.	.
.	.	.	.	.
SALES_MANG.	--	37,900	RPSMM	121 Yellowbrick Road

Figure 5.9.1 Job table.

```
INTEGER CODE          TRANSLATION
Job 25:               Computer Programmer
Credential 4:         Bachelor of Science, Computer Science
Salary 72:            27,200 per year
Benefits 1101:        Retirement, Profit Sharing, No Medical,
                      Limo Service
Location 6:           14 Technology Drive
```

	CREDENTIAL	SALARY	BENEFITS	LOCATION
Row 25	4	72	1101	6

Figure 5.9.2 Integer codes for the job of computer programmer.

official interpretation; job_table is an array of arrays. Specifically, job_table is a one-dimensional array of 100 elements, as given in the first pair of brackets, and each of these 100 elements is an array of four elements, as given in the second pair of brackets. Suppose that job_table[25] represents the row entry for the job of computer programmer, which has an associated credential, salary, benefits, and location (see Figure 5.9.2). Then job_table[25] has as its value an array of four elements, one variable for credential, one variable for salary, one variable for benefits, and one variable for location.

Figure 5.9.3 shows how the cells in the array job_table might be allocated in internal memory and suggests how a multidimensional array could be replaced by a one-dimensional array. We could define a **cell-mapping function** that computes, for every cell in a given multidimensional array, the corresponding cell in a one-dimensional array. Figure 5.9.4 illustrates in the case of the two-dimensional array job_table and the one-dimensional array new_job_table.

If multidimensional arrays can be converted into one-dimensional arrays, why bother with the multidimensional arrays? There are applications, such as the job table example, in which a multidimensional array is more natural or convenient than a one-dimensional array. Section 5.10 gives another example.

Multidimensional Arrays as Arguments

Suppose that we want to pass the array job_table, whose definition is

```
int  job_table[ 100 ][ 4 ];
```

to the function print_table, which prints each entry in the job table. We can pass the multidimensional job_table just as we pass a one-dimensional array—by giving its name as an argument:

```
print_table( job_table );
```

Figure 5.9.3 Layout of cells in the two-dimensional array job_table.

```
TWO-DIMENSIONAL                          ONE-DIMENSIONAL
job_table[ 0 ][ 0 ]        ↔        new_job_table[ 0 ]
job_table[ 0 ][ 1 ]        ↔        new_job_table[ 1 ]
job_table[ 0 ][ 2 ]        ↔        new_job_table[ 2 ]
job_table[ 0 ][ 3 ]        ↔        new_job_table[ 3 ]
job_table[ 1 ][ 0 ]        ↔        new_job_table[ 4 ]

              .                  .              .
              .                  .              .
              .                  .              .

job_table[ 99 ][ 0 ]       ↔        new_job_table[ 396 ]
job_table[ 99 ][ 1 ]       ↔        new_job_table[ 397 ]
job_table[ 99 ][ 2 ]       ↔        new_job_table[ 398 ]
job_table[ 99 ][ 3 ]       ↔        new_job_table[ 399 ]
```

Figure 5.9.4 Representing a two-dimensional array as a one-dimensional array.

However, the parameter declaration in `print_table` is more complicated than the declaration for a one-dimensional array. *To declare a parameter for a multidimensional array, we must specify the number of cells in all dimensions beyond the first.* Thus `print_table`'s header is

```
/* parameter for a 2-dimensional array */
void  print_table( int jobs[][ 4 ] )
```

If another array, `job_table3`, has three dimensions

```
int  job_table3[ 100 ][ 4 ][ 6 ];
```

and we pass it to `print_report`, the parameter declaration in `print_report` looks like

```
/* parameter for a 3-dimensional array */
void  print_table( int jobs3[][ 4 ][ 6 ] )
```

Although our concern here is with the mechanics of passing and receiving multidimensional arrays, we can at least outline the reason that the parameter declaration is more complex. Every array, no matter how many dimensions it has, is implemented as a one-dimensional array. Now consider the contrast between locating, say, the third element in the one-dimensional array `cars_in_stock` and the third element in the two-dimensional array `job_table`. Both arrays consist of integer variables. However, each element in `cars_in_stock` is a single integer variable, whereas each element in `job_table` is an array of integer variables. Thus the third element in the array `cars_in_stock` is the third integer variable in this array, but the third element in the array `job_table` is an array of four integer variables, the first cell of which lies in the ninth position (see Figure 5.9.5). When we pass a multidimensional array to a function, we tell the receiving function (through the parameter declaration) the size of each element,

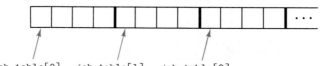

Figure 5.9.5 The array `job_table` as an array of arrays.

which consists of several cells. In the case of job_table, the declaration says, in effect: Each element in this array is itself an array of four integer variables. The receiving function then is able to compute where each element begins in the one-dimensional implementation of the multidimensional array.

Exercises

1. Do the following two definitions allocate the same number of cells?

   ```
   char   characters[ 1000 ];
   int    numbers[ 10 ][ 100 ];
   ```

2. Do the arrays of Exercise 1 have the same number of dimensions?
3. How do we compute the number of cells in a multidimensional array?
4. How do we determine the dimension of a multidimensional array?
5. (True/False) The parameter declaration for a multidimensional array must include the size for every dimension.
6. Given the definition

   ```
   char   arr4[ 100 ][ 7 ][ 5 ][ 120 ];
   ```

   show
   (a) A call to a function fun1, with the array arr4 as the only argument.
   (b) fun1's header.

7. Suppose that we define

   ```
   int   numbs[ 100 ][ 100 ];   /* array of 10,000 ints */
   ```

   and store in each cell the sum of the two indexes that reference the cell. For example, the contents of numbs[5][87] would be 92. Now assume that we map numbs into a one-dimensional array new_numbs, which also has 10,000 integer variables, in such a way that each cell in new_numbs has the same contents as the corresponding cell in numbs. What is printed?

   ```
   printf( "%d", new_numbs[ 67 ] );
   printf( "%d", new_numbs[ 0 ] );
   printf( "%d", new_numbs[ 876 ] );
   printf( "%d", new_numbs[ 777 ] );
   printf( "%d", new_numbs[ 2 ] );
   ```

8. Find the index of the cell in new_job_table that corresponds to the cell job_table[i][j] (see Figure 5.9.4).
9. Write a program that copies each cell's contents in a three-dimensional array into the corresponding cell in a one-dimensional array.

5.10 Sample Application: Sorting and Searching

Problem ⎯⎯⎯⎯⎯⎯⎯⎯⎯⎯⎯⎯⎯⎯⎯⎯⎯⎯⎯⎯⎯⎯⎯⎯⎯⎯⎯⎯⎯⎯⎯⎯⎯⎯⎯

Read the names and phone numbers of students from the file *students.dat*. The file consists of one record per line. The last name is in columns 1–25, the first name is in columns 26–50, and the phone number is in columns 51–62. Sort the records into ascending order, and then search the file for a last name requested by a user. If the name is found, print the entire record; if the name is not found, print a message to that effect.

Sample Input/Output

Assume that the file *students.dat* is

Turner	Tina	638–321–8989
Springsteen	Bruce	618–454–9871
Lauper	Cindi	708–123–9091

.
.
.

Input is in color; output is in black.

```
Enter a student's name, or signal EOF to halt:  Lauper
Record:  Lauper                Cindi                    708-123-9091

Enter a student's name, or signal EOF to halt:  Turner
Record:  Turner                Tina                     638-321-8989

Enter a student's name, or signal EOF to halt:  Springsteen
Record:  Springsteen           Bruce                    618-454-9871

Enter a student's name, or signal EOF to halt:  Hitchcock
      Hitchcock is not in our directory.

Enter a student's name, or signal EOF to halt:  Exit
```

In response to the last prompt, a control character is entered.

Solution

This program illustrates several topics from this chapter and introduces some topics to be developed in the next chapter.

We partition the program among four functions: main, selection_sort, swap, and binary_search.

The function main reads records from *students.dat* into the two-dimensional array students, invokes selection_sort to do the sorting and binary_search to do the searching, and does all prompting and printing.

The function main uses the library function fgets to read records from *students.dat*. The function fgets expects three arguments: the address of an array in which to store a character string, the maximum number of characters to store, and a file pointer. The function fgets reads the next line from the file referenced by the file pointer and stores it in the array. If max_line denotes the second argument, the "next line" consists of

The next max_line − 1 characters.

or

All characters up to and including the next newline character.

or

All characters up to the end of the file.

whichever is shortest. If at least one character is stored, fgets adds a terminating null to the end of the line. Notice that fgets stores the newline character if it was read and that fgets never stores more than max_line characters (including the newline character and the null terminator). If no characters are stored or an error occurs, fgets returns NULL. In our program, we use fgets to read strings of length 63 (including the newline) and store them in the two-dimensional array students. We reserve 64 cells for each record—63 for the string and 1 for the null terminator. We also use fgets to read the name of the student to find.

The function selection_sort sorts the student records into ascending order. The documentation explains how the sort works. Our implementation of the selection sort algorithm is inefficient, for it uses strcpy to move character strings around in the array students. In Chapter 6 we show how to avoid such inefficiency by using pointers.

The function swap swaps two records.

The function binary_search searches for a given record, using the student's name as a key. It returns either the corresponding record's index in the array students or a flag to indicate that the record was not found. The documentation explains how binary_search works.

The user ends the program by generating an EOF when prompted for a student's last name.

C Implementation

```
/*    The PHONE program reads NUMB_RECS records from
      the file students.dat into the two-dimensional
      array students. The records occur one to a line,
      with a maximum length of MAX_REC_SIZE and fields
      formatted as follows:

          25 chars      25 chars        12 chars
        <last name> <first name> <phone number>
            ↑             ↑              ↑
      Column 1      Column 26      Column 51

      MAX_REC_SIZE is thus LNAME_SIZE + FNAME_SIZE + PNUM_SIZE.
      One record occurs per line.

      PHONE sorts the records--as character strings--in ascending
      order and then does lookups. It prompts for a last name,
      padding it if necessary with blanks to LNAME_SIZE, and then
      searches the array. If the name is found, the entire record
      is written to the terminal in data-processing format, i.e.,
      the fields are printed in their file column positions. If the
      name is not found, a message is written.

      PHONE uses selection sort for the sorting and binary search
      for the searching. The program consists of the functions:
      main, selection_sort, binary_search, and swap.          */

#include   <stdio.h>
#include   <string.h>

#define    NUMB_RECS      30 /* number of records in students.dat */
#define    LNAME_SIZE     25 /* first 25 chars */
#define    FNAME_SIZE     25 /* next 25 chars */
#define    PNUM_SIZE      12 /* last 12 chars */
#define    MAX_REC_SIZE (LNAME_SIZE + FNAME_SIZE + PNUM_SIZE)
```

```
#define    NO_FIND         (-999) /* flag to signal lookup failure */
#define    BLANK           ' '    /* used to pad candidate name so
                                     it, too, has LNAME_SIZE chars */

main()
{
    /* student records (+2 is for the newline and the
       null terminator) */
    char students[ NUMB_RECS ][ MAX_REC_SIZE + 2 ];

    /* candidate in search (+2 is for the newline and the
       null terminator) */
    char candidate[ LNAME_SIZE + 2 ];

    int cand_len; /* length of candidate's name */
    int index; /* index into students */
    int i;

    void selection_sort( char array[][ MAC_REC_SIZE + 2 ],
                         int size1 );

    /* returns NO_FIND or index of found item into students */
    int binary_search( char candidate[],
                       char array[][ MAX_REC_SIZE + 2 ],
                       int size );
    FILE *fp;

    /*  read the names of NUMB_RECS records into array students */
    fp = fopen( "students.dat", "r" );

    for ( i = 0; i < NUMB_RECS; ++i )
        fgets( students[ i ], MAX_REC_SIZE + 2, fp );

    /* sort the records into ascending order, by name */
    selection_sort( students, NUMB_RECS );

    /*  Prompt the user for a student's name and look for it in the
        array students. Halt when the user signals EOF at the
        prompt. */
    printf( "\n\n\Enter a student's name, "
            "or signal EOF to halt:  " );
    while ( fgets( candidate, LNAME_SIZE + 2, stdin ) != NULL ) {
        /* Pad candidate with blanks to LNAME_SIZE chars. */
        cand_len = strlen( candidate ) - 1; /* -1 for newline
                                               stored by fgets */
        for ( i = cand_len; i < LNAME_SIZE; i++ )
            candidate[ i ] = BLANK;
        candidate[ LNAME_SIZE ] = '\0'; /* null terminate */

        index = binary_search( candidate, students, NUMB_RECS );
        if ( index != NO_FIND )
            printf( "\nRecord:  %s", students[ index ] );
        else {
            candidate[ cand_len ] = '\0'; /* knock off blanks */
```

```
                  printf( "\n\t%s is not in our directory.",
                         candidate);

           }
           printf( "\n\n\Enter a student's name, "
                   "or signal EOF to halt:  " );
       }
}

/*   selection_sort ( array, size1 )

     The function expects an array and its size. It sorts the
     elements into ascending order. It does not return a value.

     The algorithm can be sketched as follows:

         1. Repeat steps 2 and 3 for ind equals 0, 1,..., size1 - 2.

         2. Select the smallest item among

            array[ ind ], array[ ind + 1 ],..., array[ size1 - 1 ].

         3. Swap the smallest with array[ ind ].

                                                                    */

void selection_sort( char array[][ MAX_REC_SIZE + 2 ], int size1 )
{
     int    smallest_index; /* index of smallest string seen */
     int    i, j;
     void swap( char array[][ MAX_REC_SIZE + 2 ],
                int current,
                int low );

     /*  loop size1 - 1 times, selecting smallest string each time */
     for ( i = 0; i < size1 - 1; ++i ) {
         /* assume ith string is smallest */
         smallest_index = i;
         /* compare smallest against remaining strings */
         for ( j = i + 1; j < size1; ++j )
             /* look for smaller string */
             if ( strcmp( array[ j ], array[ smallest_index ] ) < 0 )
              smallest_index = j;

         /* put smallest at index i */
         if ( i != smallest_index )
             swap( array, i, smallest_index );
     }
}

/* Swap array[ current ] and array[ low ]. */

void swap( char array[][ MAX_REC_SIZE + 2 ], int current, int low )
{
     char   temp[ MAX_REC_SIZE + 2 ];
```

```
        strcpy( temp, array[ current ] );
        strcpy( array[ current ], array[ low ] );
        strcpy( array[ low ], temp );
}
/*    binary_search( candidate, array, size )

    The function searches the sorted array

            array[ 0 ], array[ 1 ],..., array[ size - 1 ]

    for candidate, returning the appropriate index if
    candidate is found, and the NO_FIND flag otherwise.

    The algorithm can be sketched as follows:

        1. Repeat steps 2 through 4 until either the candidate
           is found or there is nothing left to search.

        2. Find the (approximate) midpoint in the array. (This
           is an index into the array.)

        3. Compare the array's midpoint item with candidate: if
           they match, return the midpoint value and halt
           (success).

        4. If the candidate is less than the midpoint item,
           search the first half of the array, discarding the
           second half; otherwise, search the second half,
           discarding the first.

        5. Return NO_FIND (failure).                              */
int binary_search( char candidate[],
                   char array[][ MAX_REC_SIZE + 2 ],
                   int size )
{
    int    first = 0;        /* first position in array */
    int    last = size - 1;  /* last position in array */
    int    mid;              /* midpoint in array */
    int    flag;             /* holds result of string comparison */

    /* search until list is empty */
    while ( first <= last ) {
        /* find (approximate) midpoint */
        mid = ( first + last ) / 2;
        flag = strncmp( candidate, array[ mid ], LNAME_SIZE );
        if ( flag == 0 ) /* candidate == array[ mid ] */
            return  ( mid ); /* signal success--candidate found */
        if ( flag > 0 ) /* candidate > array[ mid ] */
            first = mid + 1;   /* search right half */
        else /* candidate < array[ mid ] */
            last = mid - 1;    /* search left half */
    }

    return ( NO_FIND );
}
```

Exercises

1. For the sample input file *students.dat* tell what the output will be if in response to

```
Enter a student's name, or signal EOF to halt:
```

we respond by entering Lauper followed by two blanks.

2. What is wrong with the following attempt to implement binary search recursively?

```
int b_search( int a[], int l, int r, int key )
{
    int mid = ( l + r ) / 2;
    if ( a[ mid ] == key )
        return( mid );
    if ( l == r )
        return ( -1 ); /* fail */
    if ( a[ mid ] < key )
        return ( b_search( a, mid + 1, r, key ) );
    else
        return ( b_search( a, l, mid - 1, key ) );
}
```

3. Rewrite the function binary_search so that it is recursive.

Changes from Traditional C

1. In traditional C, an array must have storage class `static` or `extern` (see Chapter 7) to be initialized at definition time. For example,

```
char    stooge1[] = "Larry";   /* auto */
```

is not allowed in most implementations of traditional C. Instead, we would have to use either a `static` array

```
static char    stooge1[] = "Larry"; /* static */
```

or an `extern` array

```
char    stooge1[] = "Larry";   /* extern */
```

For the `extern` array, the definition and initialization must occur outside all function bodies.

Common Programming Errors

1. It is an error to reference an array element that does not exist. Given the following definition,

```
/* array of five elements, indexed 0 through 4 */
int    numbers[ 5 ];
```

it is an error to reference numbers[5], numbers[10], or numbers[-1]; only the indexes 0 through 4 may be used.

2. It is an error to supply more values in an initialization than there are cells in the array. For this reason, the following is an error:

```
int a[ 3 ] = { 90, -73, 8, 661 };   /* ERROR */
```

3. It is an error to use an array's name as the left-hand side of an assignment statement. Note the difference:

```
int  numbers[ 5 ];
numbers[ 0 ] = 999; /* correct */
numbers = 777;         /*** ERROR ***/
```

4. It is an error to assign a character string, even a string with only one nonnull character, to a `char` variable, because every character string is an array. Note the difference:

```
char  string[ 2 ];
string[ 0 ] = 'A';  /* correct */
string[ 1 ] = "B";  /*** ERROR ***/
```

"B" is not a single character but, rather, an array that consists of 'B' and the terminating null character; 'A', by contrast, is a single character.

5. In using the library functions for formatted input and output, such as `printf` or `scanf`, it is an error to use the %s format descriptor for any argument other than an expression that evaluates to the address of a character array. Note the difference:

```
char string[ 2 ];
char character;
printf( " Enter a string: " );
scanf( "%s", string );       /* correct */
printf( " Enter a string: " );
scanf( "%s", &string );      /*** ERROR ***/
printf( " Enter a character: " );
scanf( "%s", character );  /*** ERROR ***/
```

Library functions that handle strings typically expect addresses of character arrays. The name of any array of type `char` is an address expression, for it gives the address of the first character in the array.

6. If multidimensional arrays are passed as arguments to a function, the size for all but the array's first dimension must be included in the parameter declaration. Note the difference:

```
main()
{
        /* 2-dimensional array */
        int   numbers[ 10 ][ 10 ];

                .

                .

                .

        add1( numbers );
        sub1( numbers );
```

```
           .
           .
            .
}
void  add1( int array[][ 10 ] )  /* correct */
{    .
         .
         .
}
void  sub1( int array[][] )      /*** ERROR ***/
{    .
         .
         .
}
```

Programming Exercises

5.1. Write a program with an array `numbs` defined and initialized as

```
int  numbs[ 100 ] = { 1, 3, 5 };
```

Although `numbs` can hold 100 integers, only three cells have been initialized. Your program is to store integers in the remaining cells according to the formula

```
numbs[ i ] = numbs[ 0 ] + numbs[ 1 ] + ··· + numbs[ i - 1 ],
```

for i = 3, . . . , 99. For example:

```
numbs[ 3 ] = numbs[ 0 ] + numbs[ 1 ] + numbs[ 2 ] = 1 + 3 + 5 = 9,
numbs[ 4 ] = numbs[ 0 ] + numbs[ 1 ] + numbs[ 2 ] + numbs[ 3 ]
           = 1 + 3 + 5 + 9 = 18
```

After computing the values, print the array.

5.2. Write a program that prints your name at the terminal in the style

```
TTTTTTTTTT    IIIIIIIIII    N      N        A
    T             I         N N    N        A A
    T             I         N  N   N       A   A
    T             I         N   N  N     A AAA A
    T             I         N    N N    A       A
    T         IIIIIIIIII    N      N   A         A
```

Use a 6 × 10 array (i.e., a two-dimensional array, with 6 as the size of the first dimension and 10 as the size of the second dimension) to represent each oversized letter. Each array contains a mix of uppercase alphabetic characters and blanks.

5.3. Write a program that prompts the user for a string that contains, at most, 30 characters. Store the string in an array using the function `scanf` with the `%s`

conversion specification. Write a function that prints a string in reverse, and pass the user's string (and whatever other argument(s) you think appropriate) to this function.

5.4. Write a program that reads words from a file, computes their length, stores them in a two-dimensional array if the length is not equal to 4 (we want to discourage four-letter words), and prints the words stored in the array. Assume that no word has a length greater than 80 characters.

5.5. A string that reads the same either backward or forward is called a **palindrome**. Examples are *anna* and *otto*. Write a program that prompts the user for a string, tests whether it is a palindrome, and prints an appropriate message. The test should be done in a separate function.

5.6. Write a function `check` with two parameters: `str` and `c`. The parameter `str` is a `char` array, and the parameter `c` is a `char`. The function `check` returns 1 if `c` is in `str` and 0 otherwise. Write a `main` function that calls `check` several times to demonstrate that `check` is working properly.

5.7. Write a function `substring` with four parameters: `str`, `substr`, `i`, and `len`. The parameters `str` and `substr` are `char` arrays. The parameters `i` and `len` are `int`s. The function `substring` normally copies `len` consecutive characters from `str`, beginning at index `i`, into `substr`; however, if the null terminator is encountered in `str`, the function stops copying characters into `substr`. Assume that `substr` is large enough to hold the characters copied and the null terminator. *Example*: If

```
str is "He has his future ahead of him"
i is 7
len is 3
```

after

```
substring( str, substr, i, len );
```

`substr` is "his".

Write a `main` function that invokes `substring` several times to demonstrate that it is working properly.

5.8. Write a function `insert` with three parameters: `str`, `substr`, and `i`. The parameters `str` and `substr` are `char` arrays. The parameter `i` is an `int`. The function `insert` inserts the string `substr` into `str` immediately after index `i`. Assume that `str` is large enough to hold the added characters. *Example*: If

```
str is "He has his ahead of him"
substr is " future"
i is 9
```

after

```
insert( str, substr, i );
```

`str` is "He has his future ahead of him".

Write a `main` function that invokes `insert` several times to demonstrate that it is working properly.

5.9. Write a function `find` with two parameters: `str` and `substr`. The parameters `str` and `substr` are `char` arrays. The function `find` returns the index of the first occurrence of `substr` in `str`; or if `substr` does not occur in `str`, `find` returns −1. *Examples*: If

```
str is "He has his future ahead of him"
substr is "future"
```

`find` returns the value 11. If

```
str is "He has his future ahead of him"
substr is "Future"
```

`find` returns the value −1.

Write a `main` function that invokes `find` several times to demonstrate that it is working properly.

5.10. An International Standard Book Number (ISBN) is a code of 10 characters separated by dashes such as 0-8065-0959-7. An ISBN consists of four parts: a group code, a publisher code, a code that uniquely identifies the book among those published by the particular publisher, and a check character. For the ISBN 0-8065-0959-7, the group code is 0, which identifies the book as one from an English-speaking country. The publisher code 8065 identifies the book as one published by Citadel Press. The code 0959 uniquely identifies the book among those published by Citadel Press (Brode: *Woody Allen: His Films and Career*, in this case). The check character is computed as follows: First, compute the sum of the first digit plus two times the second digit plus three times the third digit, . . . , plus nine times the ninth digit. The last character is the remainder when the sum is divided by 11. If the remainder is 10, the last character is X. For example, the sum for the ISBN 0-8065-0959-7 is

$$0 + 2*8 + 3*0 + 4*6 + 5*5 + 6*0 + 7*9 + 8*5 + 9*9 = 249$$

The remainder when 249 is divided by 11 is 7, the last character in the ISBN. The check character is used to validate an ISBN.

Write a function with one parameter `s` that is an array of characters. The function returns 1 (true) if the array represents a valid ISBN and 0 (false) otherwise. Write a `main` function that calls the function several times to show that it is working properly.

5.11. Write a program that begins by defining the arrays

```
int    integer1[ 5 ];
int    integer2[ 5 ];
int    sum[ 6 ];
```

The program asks for five single-digit integers (selected from {0, 1, . . . , 9}, repetitions allowed). As the program reads the digits, it stores each in one of `integer1`'s cells. Next, the program asks for and stores in `integer2` five more single-digit integers. The program then treats each array as if it represented a single integer. For example, if we read 2, 3, 0, 3, 5 into `integer1`, `integer1` is then interpreted as the five-digit integer 23,035. The program adds the five-digit integers `integer1` and `integer2` and stores the sum in the array `sum`. (The array `sum` has one more cell than do the other two so that it can hold a carry.) For example, if we read

$$4\ 5\ 0\ 7\ 1\ 9\ 2\ 9\ 8\ 7$$

the arrays `integer1`, `integer2`, and `sum` are:

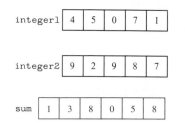

integer1 | 4 | 5 | 0 | 7 | 1

integer2 | 9 | 2 | 9 | 8 | 7

sum | 1 | 3 | 8 | 0 | 5 | 8

If there is no carry, the cell `sum[ 0 ]` must hold a zero.

5.12. Modify Exercise 5.11 by adding an extra cell to the arrays `integer1`, `integer2`, and `sum`. The first cell in each array holds either 1 to indicate a negative integer or 0 to indicate a positive integer.

5.13. Modify Exercise 5.11 to compute the product rather than the sum of two integers. The program should handle both positive and negative integers.

5.14. Write a program that uses `fgets` to read a line at a time from a file and encodes the line using the arrays

```
int    code1[] = "JMARTYVWBDLQNCXGZEKIPUFOHS";
int    code2[] = "abcdefghijklmnopqrstuvwxyz";
```

The program then prints the encoded line. Assume that each line in the input file contains, at most, 60 characters.

The encoding works as follows: Each uppercase letter occurs somewhere in array `code1`. The program searches this array for the letter, notes the index of the variable in which the letter occurs, and then uses this index in array `code2` to find the corresponding lowercase letter that encodes the uppercase one. For example, suppose that the line contains the letter R. Because R is stored at index 3 in `code1`, R is encoded as d—the character stored at index 3 in `code2`. Characters in the input file that are not in the array `code1` are unchanged.

5.15. Figures 5.9.3 and 5.9.4 illustrate how a job table might be implemented using a two-dimensional array of integer variables. The integers are codes for either different jobs, such as accountant and computer programmer, or attributes of a given job, such as required credential (e.g., B.S.C.S), salary, benefits (e.g., 110 means retirement, profit sharing, no major medical coverage), and location (e.g., 23 means Marketing Headquarters Building). Construct appropriate codes for 10 different jobs, each with four attributes, and construct codes for each attribute as well. Then read character strings such as

```
computer_programmer
major_medical_coverage
```

from an input file, and encode the strings as integers to be stored in the appropriate cells in the array `job_table`.

5.16. Add a module to Exercise 5.15. This module prompts the user for a character string such as

```
computer_programmer
```

and then looks up, in the array `job_table`, all the attributes. It decodes the integers stored in `job_table` and prints the appropriate strings. If the input string is `computer_programmer`, for example, the output might be

```
Credential        B.S.C.S
Salary:           29750
Benefits:         Retirement*Profit_Sharing
Location:         Turing_Center
```

5.17. A **binary (digital) picture** is a two-dimensional array, each of whose entries is 0 or 1. The image is interpreted as light (1) on a dark (0) background. For example, the following is a binary picture of a football:

```
0 0 0 0 0 0 0
0 0 1 1 1 0 0
0 1 1 1 1 1 0
0 0 1 1 1 0 0
0 0 0 0 0 0 0
```

In analyzing a binary picture, it is often necessary to identify the edges. Let us define an element of the picture (called a *pixel*) to be an edge pixel if it is 1 and at least one of the pixels immediately above, below, left, or right is 0. We can then show the edges by setting each edge pixel to 1 and all other pixels to 0. After identifying the edges in the preceding picture, we obtain

```
0 0 0 0 0 0 0
0 0 1 1 1 0 0
0 1 0 0 0 1 0
0 0 1 1 1 0 0
0 0 0 0 0 0 0
```

Write a program that reads a binary picture and prints the picture showing the edges.

5.18. John H. Conway (*Scientific American*, October 1970, p. 120) invented a game called *Life* to model the process of birth, survival, and death. The idea is that organisms require others in order to survive and procreate but that overcrowding results in death.

We can use a two-dimensional array, whose dimensions have the same size, to implement the game. We start with a 10 × 10 array:

```
char  life[ 10 ][ 10 ];
```

Each cell in the array holds either a star * or a blank. The star represents the presence of an organism, the blank its absence. The game starts with an initial generation, which consists of any mix of stars and blanks; however, the game becomes interesting only with certain mixes of stars and blanks.

Three rules govern the transition from one generation to the next:

(a) *Birth Rule*: An organism is born into any empty cell that has exactly three living neighbors.

(b) *Survival Rule*: An organism with either two or three living neighbors survives from one generation to the next.

(c) *Death Rule*: An organism with four or more neighbors dies from overcrowding. An organism with fewer than two neighbors dies from loneliness.

A *neighbor* of a cell C is any of the cells that touch C. For example, the cells labeled with an X are the neighbors of cell A.

	X	X	X
	X	A	X
	X	X	X

A cell that does not lie along any edge has exactly eight neighbors. Because of the rules, it is relatively easy for an organism along an edge to die and relatively hard for either an edge organism to survive or a new organism to be born into an edge cell.

Write a program that reads an initial generation into the array `life` and then produces N new generations, N > 20. Print each generation.

5.19. Write a program that converts Roman numerals into decimal equivalents. The program prompts the user for a Roman numeral, which is entered as a character string. The program first converts the Roman numeral to decimal and then prints the decimal numeral. The program halts when the user enters a string that is not a valid Roman numeral. Assume that each Roman numeral has a length of, at most, 10. The following table gives the Roman symbols and their decimal equivalents:

Roman	Decimal
M	1000
D	500
C	100
L	50
X	10
V	5
I	1

The algorithm for converting a Roman numeral

$$R_1R_2 \cdots R_n$$

to decimal is as follows:

1. Set i to 1 (i is the position of the symbol currently being scanned).
2. Set *convert* to 0 (at the conclusion of the algorithm, *convert* will be the decimal value of the Roman numeral).
3. If $i = n$, add the decimal value of R_n to *convert* and stop.
4. If the decimal value of R_i is greater than or equal to the decimal value of R_{i+1}, add the decimal value of R_i to *convert*, set i to $i + 1$, and go to step 3.
5. If the decimal value of R_i is less than the decimal value of R_{i+1}, subtract the decimal value of R_i from *convert*, set i to $i + 1$, and go to step 3.

Example: The decimal value of the Roman numeral XIV is 14. Initially, *convert* is 0. Because X's value is greater than I's, we add 10 to *convert* to obtain *convert* = 10. Because I's value is less than V's, we subtract 1 from *convert* to obtain *convert* = 9. Because V is the last numeral, we add 5 to *convert* to obtain the final value, *convert* = 14.

5.20. Write a program that grades a true/false exam, converts the numeric scores into letter grades, and prints the letter grade for each student. Assume a class of 30 students, each identified by a social security number. The exam has 25 questions, and the correct answers are stored in the array `correct`:

```
char    correct[] = "FFTFTFTTTFFFTFTFFTFFTTFTT";
```

The social security numbers and test results are read from a file, which is formatted as follows:

```
/* social security number        test results */
   234567601                 TFFFTFTFFFTTFTFFTTFTFTTTF
   446367211                 FFFTFTTTFTFTFFFTFTFTFTFTF
   421987612                 TTFTFTFTTFTFFTFTFTFFTFTFT
      .                               .
      .                               .
      .                               .
```

The instructor, a bit on the strict side, curves the results using these rules:

- The top 10 percent get *A*'s.
- The next highest 15 percent get *B*'s.
- The next highest 50 percent get *C*'s.
- The next highest 15 percent get *D*'s.
- The bottom 10 percent get *F*'s.

Write a function to grade a student's exam. Write another function to print each student's social security number and letter grade.

5.21. Write a program to multiply two 5 × 5 matrices of integers. The result is to be stored in another 5 × 5 matrix. Represent the 5 × 5 matrix as a two-dimensional array of type `int`. If A and B are the matrices to be multiplied, the product C = AB is defined as follows:

$$C[row][column] = \sum_{k=0}^{4} A[row][k] * B[k][column]$$

Read integers from an input file into the arrays A and B; store the product AB in C; and then print the three arrays.

5.22. Find a newspaper article containing approximately 500 words, and write a program that
(a) Stores each word in the article in the two-dimensional array `words`.
(b) Counts how many times each word occurs in the article.
A word such as *the* presumably will occur many times in the article. Store it once, but count the number of times it occurs. Print both the stored words and their respective counts.

5.23. Goldbach's conjecture in mathematics is that every even integer greater than 2 can be expressed as the sum of two prime numbers. Write a program that prompts the user for a number, checks whether it is even and positive, and prints two primes that sum to it. For example, if the input is 52, the output might be 47 and 5, two primes that sum to 52.

5.24. This programming exercise is based on Lewis Carroll's system for encoding and decoding text. We assume ASCII representation of characters. The encoding and decoding use the following table:

	bl	!	"	#	·	·	·	|	}	~
bl	bl	!	"	#	·	·	·	|	}	~
!	!	"	#	$	·	·	·	}	~	bl
"	"	#	$	%	·	·	·	~	bl	!
#	#	$	%	&	·	·	·	bl	!	"
·						·				
·						·				
|	|	}	~	bl	·	·	·	y	z	{
}	}	~	bl	!	·	·	·	z	{	|
~	~	bl	!	"	·	·	·	{	|	}

Across the top and along the side we list, in order, the (printable) ASCII characters blank (bl) through ~. The first row inside the table is identical to the list across the top. Thereafter, each row is the same as the previous row, except that each character is shifted one position to the left and the last character of a row is the first character of the preceding row.

To encode text, a string, called a *code string*, is chosen arbitrarily. To illustrate the encoding method, we assume that the code string is Walrus and the text to encode is

    Meet me in St. Louis

Characters other than blank through ~ are not altered. We write the code string, repeated as often as necessary, on top of the text to be encoded:

    WalrusWalrusWalrusWa
    Meet me in St. Louis

The pairs of characters WM, ae, le, . . . , one on top of the other, are used as indexes into the preceding table. The encoded text results from finding the entries in the table that correspond to these pairs. The entry in row W and column M is %, so the first character of the encoded text is %. The entry in row a and column e is G; the entry in row l and column e is R, and so on. Thus the text is encoded as

    %GRgua=aVauGLol?eiAU

To decode text, we reverse this process.

Write a program that repeatedly prompts the user to encode text, decode text, or quit. If the user chooses to either encode or decode text, he or she is prompted for a code string, a file to encode or decode, and an output file.

Pointers

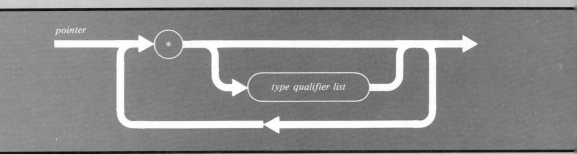

pointer

*

type qualifier list

6.1   Pointer Variables
6.2   Levels of Indirection
6.3   Pointers and Arrays
6.4   Call by Reference
6.5   Sample Application: Reversing a String in Place
6.6   Sample Application: Sorting and Searching Revisited
6.7   Smooth and Ragged Arrays
6.8   Command Line Arguments
6.9   Pointers to Functions
6.10 Sample Application: Comparing Sorting Algorithms
      Changes from Traditional C
      Common Programming Errors
      Programming Exercises

Because pointers, arrays, and strings are closely related topics in C, this chapter can be considered an extension of Chapter 5. Pointers lend efficiency, power, and flexibility to C programs. It is by mastering pointers that the programmer fully exercises the muscles of C.

6.1   Pointer Variables

A straightforward way to access a variable is through its name. For example, if we want to increment the `int` variable `num1` by 100, we can access `num1` by name:

```
num1 += 100;   /* access num1 through its name */
```

Another, and often more convenient and efficient, way to access a variable is through a second variable that holds the address of the variable that we want to access. We illustrate with an example.

> *Example 6.1.1.*   Suppose that we have an `int` variable `x` and another variable `pt` that can hold the *address* of an `int`. (We will shortly discuss how to define such a variable.) We may assign the address of `x` to `pt` by writing
>
> ```
> pt = &x;
> ```
>
> Recall (see Section 2.1) that if we write & immediately to the left of a variable, the value of the expression obtained is the address of the variable. A variable that holds an address, such as `pt`, is called a **pointer variable** (or, more simply, a **pointer**).
>   Suppose that the address of the `int` variable `x` is 9640 (see Figure 6.1.1). If we write
>
> ```
> pt = &x;
> ```
>
> the address of `x` is assigned to `pt` (see Figure 6.1.1). We say that the variable `pt` *points to* `x`. This situation is often drawn as shown in Figure 6.1.2. The arrow is drawn from the cell that stores the address to the cell whose address is stored.

Figure 6.1.1 A pointer variable.

Figure 6.1.2 The variable `pt` points to `x`.

We can access the contents of the cell whose address is stored in pt by writing *pt. To **dereference** the pointer pt is to use the expression *pt. For example, if we execute

```
pt = &x;
*pt = 3;
```

the value of the cell named x is 3 (see Figure 6.1.3). The reference *pt is not to the cell named pt but, rather, to the cell whose address is stored in pt. Alternatively, we can think of * as a directive to follow the arrow (as in Figure 6.1.3) to find the cell to reference. Notice that if pt holds the address of x,

```
x = 3;
```

and

```
*pt = 3;
```

both have the same effect; that is, both store the value 3 in x.

C requires a definition for each variable. To define a pointer variable pt that can hold the address of an int variable, we write

```
int *pt;
```

The syntax is a bit misleading. The data type is

```
int *
```

and the variable is

```
pt
```

The asterisk means "pointer to." That is, the data type

```
int *
```

is pointer to int.

In C, unlike some high-level languages, a pointer holds the address of a particular data type. For example, a variable of type

```
char *
```

(pointer to char) is a data type distinct from a variable of type

```
int *
```

(pointer to int).

There is also the data type

```
void *
```

Figure 6.1.3 Assignment using a pointer.

(pointer to `void`), which can be characterized as the data type for a generic pointer variable. A pointer to `void` may be converted, with a cast operation, to a pointer to any other data type; and any pointer whatever may be converted to a pointer to `void`. (In Sections 7.8 and 10.1 we show why such a conversion is useful in C.)

It is illegal to define a pointer to one data type and then to use it, without a cast operation, to point to some other data type.

Example 6.1.2.   The program slice defines `num_ptr` as a pointer to an `int` but erroneously uses it to hold the address of a `float`.

```
int *num_ptr;        /* pointer to int */
float real = 77.7;
num_ptr = &real;     /***** ERROR *****/
```

Example 6.1.3.   The following program slice swaps the contents of the variables `char1` and `char2` but uses the address and dereferencing operators to do so. Figures 6.1.4 through 6.1.9 show how the C statements affect the contents of the cells.

```
Line
1        char char1 = 'A';
2        char char2 = 'Z';
3        char temp;
4        char *char_ptr;
5        char_ptr = &char1;
6        temp = *char_ptr;
7        *char_ptr = char2;
8        char2 = temp;
```

Lines 1 through 3

```
1        char char1 = 'A';
2        char char2 = 'Z';
3        char temp;
```

are standard definitions and initializations. Each allocates a cell to hold a `char` and gives the cell a name. In the case of `char1` and `char2`, the cells are initialized. We assume that the cell named `char1` is located at address 1293, that the cell named `char2` is located at address 7757, and that the cell named `temp` is located at address 2131 (see Figure 6.1.4).

In line 4

```
4        char *char_ptr;
```

we define `char_ptr` to be a pointer to a `char` variable. This definition also results in the allocation of a cell (see Figure 6.1.5). We assume that the cell named `char_ptr`

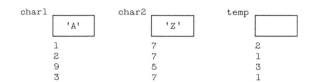

Figure 6.1.4 Allocation and initialization of cells.

Figure 6.1.5 Allocation of a cell to hold an address.

is located at address 4455. The star *, together with the data type char, indicates that char_ptr can hold the *address* of a char cell. Because char_ptr has not been initialized, it does not yet point to any particular char variable.

In line 5

5   char_ptr = &char1;

the expression &char1 is equal to char1's address, 1293; thus, the variable char_ptr is assigned the address of char1 (see Figure 6.1.6).

In line 6

6   temp = *char_ptr;

the expression *char_ptr accesses the contents of the cell to which char_ptr points—char1. Thus the character A is stored in the variable temp (see Figure 6.1.7). If the star operator were not attached to char_ptr, the assignment statement would attempt illegally to store the contents of char_ptr, the address 1293, in the char cell temp, and an error would result.

In line 7

7   *char_ptr = char2;

the left-hand side is the variable to which char_ptr points, char1. The result is that char1 is assigned the value 'Z' (see Figure 6.1.8).

In line 8

8   char2 = temp;

we copy the contents of temp into char2 (see Figure 6.1.9). We have indeed swapped the contents of char1 and char2.

Figure 6.1.6 Assignment to a pointer variable.

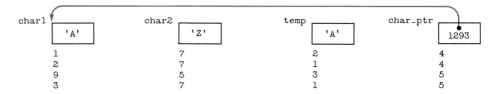

Figure 6.1.7 Assignment using a pointer.

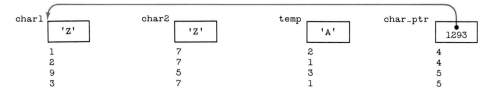

Figure 6.1.8 Another assignment using a pointer.

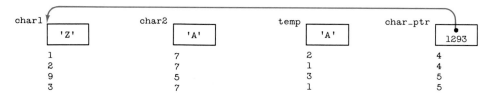

Figure 6.1.9 An ordinary assignment.

The star in the definition of the variable `char_ptr` of Example 6.1.3 indicates that we can access a character only *indirectly* through `char_ptr`. Notice the contrast between the variables `char_ptr` and `char1`. The variable `char1` holds a character, and so we can access a character directly through `char1`. For instance, if we want to print `char1`'s contents, we simply write

```
putchar( char1 );
```

On the other hand, to access a character through `char_ptr`, we must do so indirectly; in other words, we must dereference the pointer. If `char_ptr` holds the address of the variable `char1`, to print `char1`'s contents, we write

```
putchar( *char_ptr );
```

The expression `*char_ptr` says, in effect: Give us the contents of the variable whose address is in `char_ptr`.

Example 6.1.4. The output of the program

```
#include <stdio.h>
main()
{
       char c = 'O', d = 'H';
       char *p1, *p2, *temp;

       p1 = &c;
       p2 = &d;
       temp = p1;
       p1 = p2;
       p2 = temp;
       printf( "%c%c", *p1, *p2 );
}
```

is

```
HO
```

If we assume that the address of c is 941 and that the address of d is 6940, after the lines

```
char c = '0', d = 'H';
char *p1, *p2, *temp;

p1 = &c;
p2 = &d;
```

execute, we have the situation shown in Figure 6.1.10.

Executing

```
temp = p1;
```

copies the contents of p1 into temp so that both temp and p1 point to c (see Figure 6.1.11).

Executing

```
p1 = p2;
```

copies the contents of p2 into p1 so that both p1 and p2 point to d (see Figure 6.1.12).

Executing

```
p2 = temp;
```

copies the contents of temp into p2 so that both p2 and temp point to c (see Figure 6.1.13).

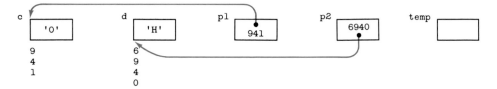

Figure 6.1.10 Initial status of the program of Example 6.1.4.

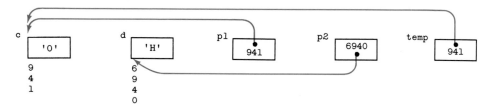

Figure 6.1.11 After temp = p1;

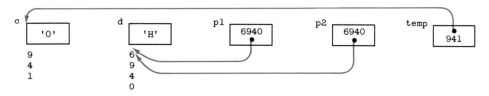

Figure 6.1.12 After p1 = p2;

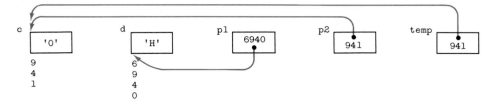

Figure 6.1.13 After p2 = temp;

Because the value of *p1 is 'H' and the value of *p2 is 'O', when we execute

```
printf( "%c%c", *p1, *p2 );
```

we print

```
HO
```

Initializing a Pointer

A pointer, like any other variable, can be initialized in its definition. For example, the definitions

```
int i;
int *ptr = &i;
```

allocate storage for two cells, i and ptr. The variable i is an ordinary int variable and ptr is a pointer to an int. Further, the pointer variable ptr is initialized to the address of i (see Figure 6.1.14). The syntax is somewhat misleading; we are *not* initializing *ptr but, rather, ptr. The statement

```
int *ptr = &i;
```

is equivalent to

```
int *ptr;
ptr = &i;
```

In the preceding definitions, we can initialize ptr to the value of an expression that involves the variable i, as i is defined *before* ptr is. In general, to initialize a variable v to the value of an expression that involves variables w, x, . . . , the variables w, x, . . . must be defined before v.

Example 6.1.5.   The program

```
#include <stdio.h>
main()
{
     char c1 = 'J';
     char c2 = 'O';
     char c3 = 'G';
     char *p1 = &c1;
     char *p2;

     p2 = &c2;
     printf( "%c%c%c", *p1, *p2, c3 );
}
```

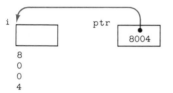

Figure 6.1.14 Initializing a pointer.

initializes the pointer p1 to the address of the char variable c1. The pointer p2 is assigned the address of the char variable c2. To print the characters to which p1 and p2 point, we use the dereferencing operator *. The ordinary (nonpointer) char variable c3 requires no dereferencing. The output of the program is

```
JOG
```

Restrictions on the Address Operator

The address operator cannot be applied to every C expression. In particular, the address operator cannot be applied to a constant. For example,

```
&77   /***** ERROR *****/
```

is illegal.

The address operator cannot be applied to an expression involving operators such as + and /. Given the definition

```
int num = 5;
```

the reference

```
&( num + 11 )   /***** ERROR *****/
```

is illegal.

Exercises

1. What is the error in this slice of code?

```
char var1, ptr1;
var1 = 'X';
ptr1 = &var1;
```

2. Given the definitions

```
double    var1, *ptr1, *ptr2;
float     *ptr3;
int       var2, *var4;
```

what are the data types of var1, ptr1, *ptr1, ptr2, *ptr2, ptr3, *ptr3, var2, var4, and *var4?

3. What is the error in this slice of code?

```
char  c = 'A';
char  *p;
p = c;
```

4. What is printed?

```
char    var1 = 'S';
char    var2 = 'X';
char    *ptr1, *ptr2;
ptr1 = &var1;
ptr2 = &var2;
*ptr2 = *ptr1;
printf( "%c\t%c", *ptr1, var2 );
```

In Exercises 5 through 7, assume the definitions

```
int   var1 = 2323;
int   *ptr;
ptr = &var1;
```

and that var1's address is 55555.

5. What is the value of var1?

6. What is the value of ptr?

7. What is the value of *ptr?

Assume the definitions and initializations

```
char c = 'T';
char d = 'S';
char e;
char *p1 = &c;
char *p2 = &d;
char *p3;
```

Assume further that the address of c is 6940, that the address of d is 9772, and that the address of e is 2224. Give the values of the expressions in Exercises 8 through 16 after we execute

```
p1 = &c;
p2 = &d;
p3 = p1;
p1 = p2;
p2 = p3;
p3 = &e;
*p3 = *p1;
*p1 = *p2;
*p2 = *p3;
```

8. &c	**9.** d	**10.** e
11. c	**12.** p2	**13.** p3
14. *p1	**15.** *p2	**16.** *p3

6.2   Levels of Indirection

It is possible to define a variable using multiple stars as, for example,

```
int **pt;
```

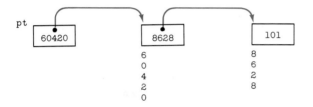

Figure 6.2.1 A pointer to a pointer to an `int`.

The variable `pt` is of type

    `int **`

Each star is read "pointer to." Thus, the preceding statement defines `pt` to be a pointer to a pointer to an `int`. That is, the cell named `pt` can contain an address of a cell that contains an address of a cell that contains an `int` (see Figure 6.2.1). The number of arrows that we must follow to access the datum or, equivalently, the number of stars that must be attached to the variable to reference the value to which it points is called the **level of indirection** of the pointer variable. We see that the definition of a C pointer is brief but loaded with information. A pointer's level of indirection determines how much dereferencing must be done to access the data type given in the definition.

Example 6.2.1. Figure 6.2.2 illustrates variables with levels of indirection from 0 to 3. In line 1

    1   `char char1 = 'A';`

because the variable `char1` is defined with no stars, its level of indirection is zero. To access a `char` through `char1`, we need not dereference it at all; `char1` itself holds a `char`, the character A.

LINE	C PROGRAM	CELL NAME	CELL	CELL ADDRESS
	`/*levels of indirection*/`			
	`    main( )`			
	`    {`			
1	`char char1 = 'A';`	char1	'A'	4433
2	`char *ptr1;`	ptr1		1990
3	`char **ptr2;`	ptr2		2727
4	`char ***ptr3;`	ptr3		9994
5	`ptr1 = &char1;`	char1	'A'	4433
		ptr1	4433	1990
6	`ptr2 = &ptr1;`	ptr2	1990	2727
7	`ptr3 = &ptr2;`	ptr3	2727	9994
	`    }`			

Figure 6.2.2 Levels of indirection.

In line 2

```
2     char *ptr1;
```

because the variable `ptr1` is defined with one star, its level of indirection is one. To access a `char` through `ptr1`, we need to dereference it just once, or equivalently, the expression *ptr1 evaluates to a `char`. Line 5

```
5     ptr1 = &char1;
```

is an assignment statement that uses the address operator. The expression &char1 gives us `char1`'s address, which happens to be 4433; this address becomes `ptr1`'s contents. Figure 6.2.2 shows a single arrow from `ptr1` to `char1`, indicating that we can access a `char`, namely, the contents of `char1`, by dereferencing `ptr1` exactly once.

In line 3

```
3     char **ptr2;
```

because the variable `ptr2` is defined with two stars, its level of indirection is two. To access a `char` through `ptr2`, we need to dereference it twice, or equivalently, the expression **ptr2 evaluates to a `char`. Line 6

```
6     ptr2 = &ptr1;
```

and Figure 6.2.2 illustrate the double indirection. After the assignment operation, `ptr2` holds the address of `ptr1`; so `ptr2` points to `ptr1`, which in turn points to `char1`. We must follow two arrows to get from `ptr2` to a `char`, namely, the value `'A'` stored in `char1`.

In line 4

```
4     char ***ptr3;
```

because the variable `ptr3` is defined with three stars, its level of indirection is three. To access a `char` through `ptr3`, we need to dereference it three times, or equivalently, the expression ***ptr3 evaluates to a `char`. Line 7

```
7     ptr3 = &ptr2;
```

and Figure 6.2.2 illustrate the triple indirection. After the assignment operation, `ptr3` holds the address of `ptr2`, and `ptr2` holds the address of `ptr1`; so `ptr3` points to `ptr2`, which points to `ptr1`, which in turn points to `char1`. We must follow three arrows to get from `ptr3` to a `char`, namely, the value `'A'` stored in `char1`.

The lines 4 and 7 could be combined into

```
char ***ptr3 = &ptr2;
```

for C allows a pointer, like any other variable, to be initialized at definition time. This definition and initialization contain several pieces of information:

- The expression ***ptr is of type `char` rather than, say, `int` or `float`.
- Through the triple dereferencing of `ptr3`, we can access a `char`, or equivalently, `ptr3` should point to a pointer that points to a pointer that points to a `char`.
- The variable `ptr3` is initialized to the *address,* not the contents, of `ptr2`. This address happens to be 2727. The equivalent assignment statement is thus

```
ptr3 = &ptr2;
```

and *not*

```
***ptr3 = &ptr2;   /***** ERROR *****/
```

The expression ***ptr3 evaluates to a char, *not* to a pointer. So, whenever the expression ***ptr3 occurs as the left-hand side of an assignment, the right-hand side likewise should be an expression that evaluates to a char. For example, we could write

```
***ptr3 = 'Z';
```

which has the effect of storing the character Z in cell char1.

The definition

```
char   ***ptr3;
```

tells us directly that the expression ***ptr3 is of type char; it also tells us indirectly about the data types of the related expressions **ptr3, *ptr3, and ptr3, even though none of these is defined explicitly. To simplify the discussion, we say simply that the expression ***ptr3 is a char.

- If ***ptr3 is a char, then **ptr3 must be a pointer to a char.
- If **ptr3 is a pointer to a char, then *ptr3 must be a pointer to a pointer to a char.
- If *ptr3 is a pointer to a pointer to a char, then ptr3 must be a pointer to a pointer to a pointer to a char.

Exercises

1. (True/False) An expression with the star operator, such as *ptr, cannot occur on the left-hand side of an assignment statement.

2. Explain why it makes no sense for an expression with the address operator, such as &var, to occur on the left-hand side of an assignment statement.

3. If the pointer variable ptr holds the address of a char, what is the data type of *ptr?

4. What is the error in this slice of code?

```
char first = 'A';
char last = 'Z';
char *ptr1, *ptr2;
ptr1 = &first;
ptr2 = &last;
*ptr1 = &ptr2;
```

5. What is printed?

```
float fnum = 1234.56;
float *fptr1 = &fnum;
float **fptr2 = &fptr1;
printf( "%f", **fptr2 );
```

6. What is the error in this slice of code?

```
float fnum = 1234.56;
float *fptr1;
```

```
float **fptr2 = &fptr1;
printf( "%f", **fptr2 );
```

7. What is printed?

```
char char1 = 'P';
char char2 = 'Q';
char *p, *q;
p = &char1;
q = &char2;
*p = *q;
printf( "%c", char1 );
```

8. What is the error in this slice of code?

```
float num = 999.99;
float ptr1;
float *ptr2;
ptr1 = &num;
ptr2 = &ptr1;
```

9. What is the error in this slice of code?

```
float **p1, *p2;
p2 = &p1;  /* store p1's address in p2 */
```

10. Given the definition

```
double ****ptr;
```

what are the data types of `***ptr`, `**ptr`, `*ptr`, and `ptr`?

11. What is the error in this slice of code?

```
char c = 'Z';
char **p, *q;
q = &c;
p = &q;
printf( "%c", *p );
```

6.3 Pointers and Arrays

Pointers and arrays are closely related, as we see in this section. We begin by restating (see Section 5.2) a fact that, if forgotten or not clearly understood, can be a frequent source of errors and misunderstandings:

> An array's name is a *constant* whose value is the address of the array's first element. For this reason, the value of an array's name cannot be changed by an assignment statement or by any other means.

Example 6.3.1. Given the definitions

```
float  on_time_rate[ 100 ];
float  *ptr;
```

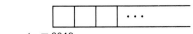

on_time_rate = 6042

Figure 6.3.1 An array of 100 real numbers.

the array's name, on_time_rate, is a constant whose value is the address of the first element of the array of 100 floats (see Figure 6.3.1). We may assign ptr the address of the first element of the array by writing

```
ptr = on_time_rate;
```

(see Figure 6.3.2). An equivalent way to assign ptr the address of the first element of the array is to write

```
ptr = &on_time_rate[ 0 ];
```

If ptr holds the address of a float, we may *not* write

```
on_time_rate = ptr;          /******* ERROR *******/
```

The preceding statement attempts to assign a value to the constant on_time_rate. Such a statement is akin to writing

```
30 = x;          /******* ERROR *******/
```

For the same reason, we may *not* write

```
&on_time_rate[ 0 ] = ptr;          /******* ERROR *******/
```

Pointers to char and Arrays of Type char

A string constant such as

```
"My Mother, the Car"
```

is stored as an array (see Figure 6.3.3). Just as the value of an array's name is the address of the array's first cell, a reference to a string constant produces the address of the cell that holds the first character. We illustrate with several examples.

Example 6.3.2. Because a char pointer can hold the address of a char, it is appropriate to define and initialize simultaneously such a variable. The statement

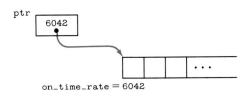

on_time_rate = 6042

Figure 6.3.2 A pointer to an array.

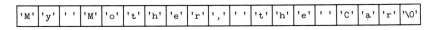

Figure 6.3.3 Storing a string constant.

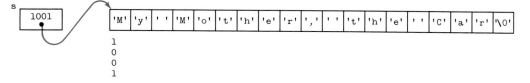

Figure 6.3.4 Defining and initializing a `char` pointer.

```
char *s = "My Mother, the Car";
```

defines the `char` pointer s and initializes it to the address of the first character in the string "My Mother, the Car". More precisely, storage is allocated for the string "My Mother, the Car" and the address of the first cell is stored in s (see Figure 6.3.4). Notice that the statement does *not* copy a string. (The assignment operator *cannot* be used to copy a string. Rather, a function such as `strcpy` is used.)

The statement

```
char *s = "My Mother, the Car";
```

is equivalent to the pair of statements

```
char *s;
s = "My Mother, the Car";
```

In either statement, we assign s (*not* *s) a value. Again, despite the syntax of the assignment statement, no string is copied. Only the *address* of a string is copied.

The statement

```
char *s1 = "My Mother, the Car";
```

defines s1 to be a `char` pointer; s1 is *not* an array. To define an *array* s2 and initialize it to the string "My Mother, the Car", we could write

```
char s2[] = "My Mother, the Car";
```

The principal difference between the two definitions is that the value of s1 can be changed (s1 is a pointer *variable*), but the value of s2 cannot be changed (s2 is a pointer *constant*).

Example 6.3.3. It is an error to write

```
char s[ 80 ];
s = "My Mother, the Car";   /***** ERROR *****/
```

Although the syntax resembles the correct code of Example 6.3.2, the second line attempts to copy the *address* of the string "My Mother, the Car" (or, more precisely, the address of the first cell of storage for the string) into s. Because s is a pointer constant, an error results.

The next example highlights a common error that results from not distinguishing carefully between pointers and arrays.

Example 6.3.4. The following attempt to read a string results in an error because the pointer s has not been initialized:

```
char *s;
scanf( "%s", s );   /***** ERROR *****/
```

To correct the problem, we must reserve storage and initialize s to the address of the first cell of the storage:

```
char string[ 10 ];
char *s = string;
scanf( "%s", s );
```

The value of string is the address of the first cell of the array (see Figure 6.3.5). The statement

```
char *s = string;
```

allocates storage for the pointer s and copies the address of the first cell in the array into s (see Figure 6.3.5). The statement

```
scanf( "%s", s );
```

passes the address s of the first cell to scanf, which then stores the string read (see Figure 6.3.5).

While it is legal to take the address of an array s, the result is typically equal to the address of the first element of s. This fact can produce surprises. For example, the following code prints garbage since *p references the *contents* of the array s:

```
char s[] = "Hi", **p;
p = &s;
printf( "%s\n", *p ); /* ERROR: p equals &s equals s */
```

The preceding code can be corrected by defining a variable t of type pointer to char that can hold the address of the first cell of s, and then taking the address of non-array variable t. The following code correctly prints Hi:

```
char s[] = "Hi", **p, *t;
t = s;
p = &t;
printf( "%s\n", *p );
```

Arrays and Pointer Arithmetic

Throughout Chapter 5, we accessed the individual cells in an array by using the array's name together with an index. C offers an alternative syntax that involves pointer variables and limited arithmetic operations on them. We illustrate the alternative ways of processing an array with an example that prints an array's elements in reverse order (see Figure 6.3.6). Program 1 uses the array's name together with an index to access each element. We call this method of accessing an array **array syntax**. Program 2 accesses the cells in the array by using a pointer. We call this method of accessing an array **pointer syntax**. Program 1 is the familiar approach from Chapter 5; program 2 requires some clarification.

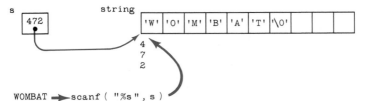

Figure 6.3.5 Using a pointer to read a string.

```
/*    Each program reads five characters into an array
      using getchar and then prints them in reverse
      order using putchar.

      The first program uses an array's name with
      indexes to access the array elements. The second
      program uses a pointer variable.                  */

/***************** PROGRAM 1 **************/

#include <stdio.h>
main( )
{
      char letters[ 5 ];
      int ind;

      /* read five characters into letters */
      for ( ind = 0; ind < 5; ++ind )
          letters[ ind ] = getchar( );

      /* print the characters in reverse order */
      for ( ind = 4; ind >= 0; --ind )
          putchar( letters[ ind ] );
}
/*************** END PROGRAM 1 *************/


/***************** PROGRAM 2 **************/

#include <stdio.h>
main( )
{
1     char letters[ 5 ];
2     char *ptr;
3     int count;

      /* initialize ptr to the address of
         letters[ 0 ] */
4     ptr = letters;

      /* read five characters into letters */
5     for ( count = 0; count < 5; ++count ) {
6         *ptr = getchar( );
7         ++ptr;
      }

      /* print the characters in reverse order */
8     for ( count = 0; count < 5; ++count ) {
9         --ptr;
10        putchar( *ptr );
      }
}
/*************** END PROGRAM 2 *************/
```

Figure 6.3.6 Two simple array programs.

At line 2 of program 2 (Figure 6.3.6),

```
2    char  *ptr;
```

we define `ptr` to be a pointer to `char`. Because each cell in the array `letters` holds a `char`, `ptr` is suitable for pointing to each.

At line 4,

```
4    ptr = letters;
```

we store the address of the first cell of `letters` in the variable `ptr`.

The `for` loop, lines 5 through 7, reads five characters and stores them in the array `letters`. In line 6

```
6    *ptr = getchar();
```

the dereferencing operator `*` ensures that the target (i.e., the left-hand side) of this assignment is the cell to which `ptr` points, not `ptr` itself. The idea is to store a character in each cell of `letters`, not to store it in `ptr`. At line 4, we stored the address of `letters[ 0 ]` in `ptr`; so line 6 stores the first character in `letters[ 0 ]`. For example, if the first character in the standard input is R, `getchar` fetches the character R. This character is then stored in the cell `letters[ 0 ]` to which `ptr` points (see Figure 6.3.7).

C supports—indeed, encourages—basic arithmetic operations on pointers. For instance, pointers can be incremented and decremented using the operators `++` and `--`. The result of incrementing a pointer is that the pointer points to the *next* cell in the array, regardless of the size of the cell. The programmer need not worry about how big the cell is; C handles this detail. For example, if `ptr` points to `letters [ 0 ]`, after line 7

```
7    ++ptr;
```

`ptr` points to `letters[ 1 ]` (see Figure 6.3.8).

In the `for` loop of lines 8 through 10, we access the elements in `letters` in reverse order and print each. After the `for` loop of lines 5 through 7 finishes executing, `ptr` points one cell beyond the end of the array `letters`; thus, in the `for` loop of lines 8 through 10, we decrement `ptr`

```
9    --ptr;
```

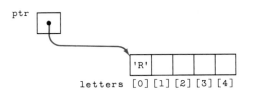

Figure 6.3.7 Executing `*ptr = getchar();`

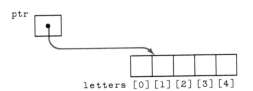

Figure 6.3.8 Executing `++ptr;`

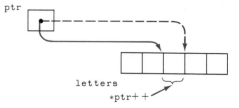

Figure 6.3.9 Executing *ptr++;

so that ptr points to the *previous* cell before dereferencing ptr and printing the value to which it points. As was the case for the increment operator, the programmer need not worry about how big the cell is; C handles this detail.

Lines 6 and 7 can be combined into one line as follows:

    *ptr++ = getchar( );

The star and increment operators associate right to left and have the same precedence; so the expression *ptr++ is equivalent to

    *(ptr++)

When we evaluate the expression ptr++, ptr is incremented (so that ptr then points to the next cell in the array), and because ++ occurs on the right side of ptr, the *original* value of ptr becomes the value of the *expression* ptr++. The dereferencing operator * thus applies to the original value of ptr; that is, we follow the arrow from the *original* address stored in ptr, *not* the updated address (see Figure 6.3.9). (In Figure 6.3.9, the dotted line shows where ptr points after executing *ptr++.) To summarize, the effect of evaluating the expression *ptr++ is to increment ptr and to reference the cell to which ptr originally pointed. Thus, when we execute

    *ptr++ = getchar( );

we read the next character, store it in the cell to which ptr *currently* points, and increment ptr so that it points to the next cell in the array letters.

If we incorrectly wrote

    (*ptr)++

we first access the item in the cell to which ptr points and then increment that item (see Figure 6.3.10). The address stored in ptr would be unchanged.

In a similar fashion, lines 9 and 10 could be combined into the single line

    putchar(*--ptr);

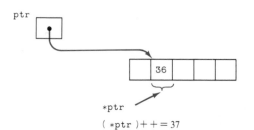

Figure 6.3.10 Executing (*ptr)++;

Pointer Operations

We have already given examples to show the effect of incrementing and decrementing pointers using the operators ++ and --. Other operations may also be applied to pointers:

- Adding an integer to a pointer, for example, ptr + 2.
- Subtracting an integer from a pointer, for example, ptr - 2.
- Subtracting two pointers, for example, ptr2 - ptr1.
- Comparing pointers using a relational operator, for example, ptr1 >= ptr2.

We illustrate the use of pointer operations in several examples.

Example 6.3.5. Suppose that we define a char array

```
char alpha[] = { 'A', 'B', 'C', 'D', 'E' };
```

two pointers to char

```
char *p1, *p2;
```

and an ordinary char variable

```
char x;
```

Figure 6.3.11 shows the array alpha, consisting of five contiguous cells, as well as the variables p1, p2, and x.

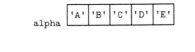

Figure 6.3.11 Allocating an array, pointer variables, and an ordinary variable.

When we execute

```
p1 = alpha;
```

we copy the address of the first cell of the array alpha into p1 (see Figure 6.3.12). If we add 2 to the pointer p1, the value is the address of the cell two beyond the cell pointed to by p1. The effect of executing the statement

```
p2 = p1 + 2;
```

is shown in Figure 6.3.13. If we dereference the pointer p2, we obtain the contents 'C' of the cell pointed to by p2. For example, if we execute

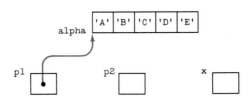

Figure 6.3.12 Executing p1 = alpha;

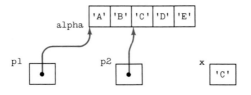

Figure 6.3.13 Executing p2 = p1 + 2; x = *p2;

```
x = *p2;
```

we copy the value 'C' into x (see Figure 6.3.13).
We could also have copied 'C' into x by writing

```
x = *( p1 + 2 );
```

Notice that both

```
*( p1 + 2 )
```

and

```
alpha[ 2 ]
```

reference the value in the third cell of the array alpha. We discuss the equivalence of
the pointer and array syntax in more detail later in this section.

Similarly, if we subtract a positive integer i from a pointer p, the value is the
address of the cell i units before the cell pointed to by p.

When using pointer arithmetic, we need not worry about the physical size of the
elements. For example, incrementing a pointer changes the address to the next cell in an
array, regardless of whether the data type of the array is char, int, or some other
type. C can take into account the cell size in computing the new address because every
pointer is defined as pointing to a specific type of variable and, because the data type is
known, the physical size of the array's elements is also known.

Example 6.3.6. Suppose that we define a float array

```
float share[] = { 21.4, 33.0, 5.1, 8.8 };
```

and two pointers to float

```
float *pf1, *pf2;
```

After we execute

```
pf1 = pf2 = share;
```

both pf1 and pf2 point to the first cell in the array share (see Figure 6.3.14). If we
execute

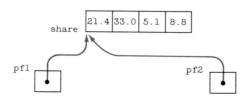

Figure 6.3.14 Executing pf1 = pf2 = share;

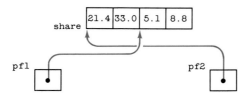

Figure 6.3.15 Executing `pf1++; pf1++;`

```
pf1++;
pf1++;
```

`pf1` points to the third cell in the array `share` (see Figure 6.3.15). It is not surprising that the value of the expression `pf1 - pf2` is 2. In general, if p1 and p2 are pointers, the expression p1 - p2 measures the gap between the cell pointed to by p1 and the cell pointed to by p2. More precisely, if p1 - p2 is zero, p1 and p2 point to the same cell. If p1 - p2 is positive, p1 points to a cell beyond the cell pointed to by p2, and the value p1 - p2 gives the offset. If p1 - p2 is negative, p1 points to a cell before the cell pointed to by p2 and the value p2 - p1 gives the offset.

Example 6.3.7. Suppose that we define an `int` array

```
int filing_code[] = { 2, 5, 1, 3, 3 };
```

and two pointers to `int`

```
int *q1, *q2;
```

After we execute

```
q1 = filing_code;
q2 = q1 + 4;
```

q1 points to the first cell in the array `filing_code`, and q2 points to the last cell in the array `filing_code` (see Figure 6.3.16). The expression

```
q1 < q2
```

is true; C assumes that if a is an array and i < j, the address of a[i] is less than the address of a[j].

After we execute

```
q1++;
q2--;
```

the expression

```
q1 < q2
```

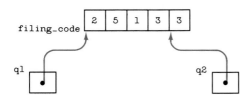

Figure 6.3.16 Executing `q1 = filing_code; q2 = q1 + 4;`

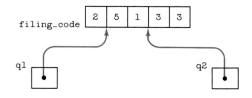

Figure 6.3.17 Executing q1++; q2--;

is still true (see Figure 6.3.17).
After we execute

```
q1++;
q2--;
```

again, the expression

```
q1 < q2
```

is false (see Figure 6.3.18).

Our examples have represented addresses as integers, which may suggest that a C pointer is of type int. It is not. A pointer holds the address of a particular type of variable (e.g., int, float), but a pointer itself is not one of the primitive data types int, float, and the like.

Not all arithmetic operations on pointers are allowed. For instance, it is illegal to add two pointers, to multiply two pointers, or to divide one pointer by another.

Range for Pointers to Array Cells

With respect to a pointer to an array, the standard requires that the pointer must point either to a cell in the array or, at most, to one cell beyond the array. Of course, it is still a logical error to dereference a pointer that points beyond the end of the array. For example, given the definition

```
float  array[ 10 ], *ptr;
```

with respect to array, the only legal values for ptr are

```
array, array + 1, array + 2,..., array + 10
```

Although ptr may hold the value array + 10, it would be a logical error to dereference ptr if it had this value.

The Equivalence of Array and Pointer Syntax

The relationship between array indexes and pointers runs deep in C. Given the definition

```
char publisher[ 20 ];
```

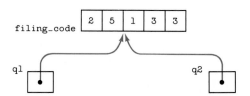

Figure 6.3.18 Executing q1++; q2--; again.

we may use an array index to reference the item in the 13th cell by writing

```
publisher[ 12 ]
```

The index 12 gives the offset from the first element in an array and thus indeed locates the item in the 13th cell. We can also use pointer syntax to reference the item in the 13th cell by writing

```
*( publisher + 12 )
```

Because the value of `publisher` is the address of the first cell, the value of `publisher + 12` is the address of the 13th cell. By dereferencing `publisher + 12`, we obtain the item in the 13th cell. Though differing syntactically, the two notations have the same meaning.

Mixing Array and Pointer Syntax

C lets the programmer use array syntax, pointer syntax, or a mixture of the two in processing arrays. Figure 6.3.19 illustrates this flexible approach. The program, though simple, uses operations that are typical of C programs.

Line 1

```
1    char  blocks[ 3 ] = { 'A', 'B', 'C' };
```

allocates contiguous storage for the array `blocks` and provides initial values.

Line 2

```
2    char  *ptr = &blocks[ 0 ];
```

defines `ptr` to be a pointer to `char`. The initialization assigns to `ptr` the address of the first cell in the array `blocks`. We are initializing `ptr`, *not* `*ptr`.

Line 4

```
4    temp = blocks[ 0 ];
```

stores the contents of the variable `blocks[ 0 ]`, the character A, in the variable `temp`.

The name `blocks` is a pointer constant whose value is the address 4434 of the first cell in the array `blocks`. Thus the expression `blocks + 2` evaluates to 4436, the address of the third cell in the array `blocks`. By dereferencing this expression, we obtain the character C. Therefore line 5

```
5    temp = *( blocks + 2 );
```

assigns the character C to `temp`. Notice that the expression `*( blocks + 2 )` is equivalent to `blocks[ 2 ]`.

In line 2, the variable `ptr` was initialized to the address 4434 of the first cell in `blocks`. Thus the expression `ptr + 1` is the address of the next cell in `blocks`, namely, 4435. Dereferencing the pointer expression yields the contents of the second cell—the character B. The assignment in line 6

```
6    temp = *( ptr + 1 );
```

stores `'B'` in `temp`.

Because the value of `*ptr` is `'A'`, in line 7

```
7    temp = *ptr;
```

we store `'A'` in `temp`.

LINE	C STATEMENT	CELL NAME	CELL(S)	CELL ADDRESS
	main( )			
	{			
1	char blocks[3] = { 'A', 'B', 'C' };	blocks	'A' 'B' 'C'	4434-4435-4436
2	char *ptr = &blocks[0];	ptr	4434	1101
3	char temp;	temp		9999
4	temp = blocks[0];	temp	'A'	9999
5	temp = *(blocks + 2);	temp	'C'	9999
6	temp = *(ptr + 1);	temp	'B'	9999
7	temp = *ptr;	temp	'A'	9999
8	ptr = blocks + 1;	ptr	4435	1101
9	temp = *ptr;	temp	'B'	9999
10	temp = *(ptr + 1);	temp	'C'	9999
11	ptr = blocks;	ptr	4434	1101
12	temp = *++ptr;	ptr	4435	1101
		temp	'B'	9999
13	temp = ++*ptr;	ptr	4435	1101
		temp	'C'	9999
14	temp = *ptr++;	temp	'C'	9999
		ptr	4436	1101
15	temp = *ptr;	temp	'C'	9999
	}			

Figure 6.3.19 Review of arrays and pointers.

The value of the pointer expression blocks + 1 is 4435, the address of the second cell in the array blocks. Thus after line 8

    8   ptr = blocks + 1;

ptr points to blocks[1].

Because of line 8, the expression *ptr now evaluates to the contents of blocks[1], the character B. Thus line 9

    9   temp = *ptr;

copies 'B' into temp.

Because `ptr` currently holds the address of `blocks[ 1 ]`, the pointer expression `ptr + 1` evaluates to the address of the third cell in the array `blocks`. So the expression `*( ptr + 1 )` gives the contents of `blocks[ 2 ]`, the character C. Thus line 10

```
10    temp = *( ptr + 1 );
```

copies `'C'` into `temp`.

In line 11

```
11    ptr = blocks;
```

the pointer variable `ptr` is again set to the address of `blocks[ 0 ]`.

Because `*` and `++` have the same precedence and associate from the right, the expression

```
*++ptr
```

is equivalent to

```
*( ++ptr )
```

To evaluate this expression, we first increment `ptr`. We then dereference the expression `++ptr`. Because the value of the expression `++ptr` is the new value of `ptr`, we access the item using the updated value of `ptr`. Before executing line 12

```
12    temp = *++ptr;
```

`ptr` pointed to `blocks[ 0 ]`. After line 12 increments `ptr`, `ptr` points to `blocks[ 1 ]`. Dereferencing gives us the contents of `blocks[ 1 ]`, the character B, which is then stored in the variable `temp`.

The expression

```
++*ptr
```

is equivalent to

```
++( *ptr )
```

To evaluate this expression, we first dereference `ptr`. We then increment the item obtained by dereferencing. Before executing line 13

```
13    temp = ++*ptr;
```

`ptr` pointed to `blocks[ 1 ]`, which equals the character B. Thus `*ptr` accesses `'B'`. Therefore the item in the second cell of blocks is incremented. Incrementing the character B really means incrementing the integer code for this character, thus generating the code for the character that comes after B, namely, C. Finally, we assign the value `'C'` to `temp`.

The expression

```
*ptr++
```

is equivalent to

```
*( ptr++ )
```

To evaluate this expression, we first increment `ptr`. We then dereference the expression `ptr++`. Because the value of the expression `ptr++` is the original value of `ptr`, we access the item using the original value of `ptr`. Before executing line 14

```
14    temp = *ptr++;
```

the value of `ptr` is 4435, the address of `blocks[ 1 ]`. Thus the expression `*ptr++` references `'C'`, the contents of `blocks[ 1 ]`. This character is stored in `temp`. After `ptr` is incremented, its value becomes 4436, the address of `blocks[ 2 ]`.

Because `ptr` currently points to `blocks[ 2 ]`, whose value is the character C, after we execute line 15

```
15    temp = *ptr;
```

we store `'C'` in `temp`.

Exercises

1. (True/False) An array's name is a pointer constant.
2. (True/False) An array's name is a pointer variable.
3. Explain the difference between a pointer variable and a pointer constant.
4. Explain why an array's name by itself cannot occur as the left-hand side of an assignment statement.
5. Given the definitions

   ```
   int t[ 30 ];
   int *p;
   ```

   one of the statements

   ```
   t = p;
   p = t;
   ```

   is correct and the other incorrect. Which is which? Explain what happens when the correct statement is executed. What is the error in the incorrect statement?
6. Write statements that successively
   (a) Define and initialize a `char` pointer `str` to the address of the first character in the string `"It's deja vu all over again"`.
   (b) Define a `char` pointer `ptr`.
   (c) Define an array a of size 20 of `chars`.
   (d) Copy the address of the string `"It's deja vu all over again"` into `ptr`.
   (e) Copy the string `"It's deja vu all over again"` into a.
   (f) Copy the address of the first cell of the array a into `str`.
7. (True/False) Given the definitions and initializations

   ```
   double s[ 10 ];
   double *p = s;
   ```

   if we next execute

   ```
   p += 10;
   ```

   an error will result because p does not point to a cell in the array s.
8. What is printed?

   ```
   int nums[ 5 ] = { 11, 22, 33, 44, 55 };
   int *ptr = nums + 5;
   ```

```
int i;
for ( i = 0; i < 5; ++i )
    printf( "\n%d", *--ptr );
```

9. What is the error?

```
float   reals[ 3 ];
float   *ptr;
reals[ 0 ] = 123.4;
reals[ 1 ] = 432.1;
reals[ 2 ] = 214.3;
ptr = &reals;
printf( "%f", *ptr );
```

10. Given the definitions

```
int   numbs[ 10 ];
int   *ptr = numbs;
```

which of the following expressions are equivalent?
(a) numbs[3]
(b) numbs + 3
(c) *(numbs + 3)
(d) *(ptr + 3)
(e) *ptr + 3

11. Suppose characters is an array of 10 char variables. Explain the difference between the expressions

```
characters + 5            *( characters + 5 )
```

12. What is the error?

```
char letters[] = { 'p', 'q', 'r', 's', 't' };
char *p;
*p = &letters[ 4 ];
```

13. What is printed?

```
float reals[ 2 ];
*( reals + 1 ) = 111.1;
*reals = *( reals + 1 );
printf( "%f", reals[ 0 ] );
```

14. What is the error?

```
char stuff[] = { 'X', 'Y', 'Z' };
char *p = stuff;
printf( "%c\t%c", *stuff[ 0 ], *p );
```

15. What is printed?

```
int   numbs[ 2 ];
int   *ptr = numbs;
numbs[ 0 ] = 10;
numbs[ 1 ] = 1000;
printf( "%d\n", ++*ptr );
printf( "%d", *ptr );
```

16. Suppose that the program in Figure 6.3.19 is continued beyond line 15, as shown. Explain what happens when each line executes.

```
--ptr;
--ptr;
temp = ++*ptr++;
temp = *--ptr;
temp = --*ptr;
```

17. What is the error?

```
int val[] = { 6,9 };
int *ptr = val + 1;
while ( ptr >= val )
    printf( "%d\n", *ptr-- );
```

18. The following is correct. What is the meaning?

```
printf( "%c", *( "xyz" + 1 ) );
```

19. Given the definitions

```
int a[ 10 ], i;
```

the expressions a[i] and i[a] are both legal. Explain.

6.4 Call by Reference

In Chapter 4, we discussed how C uses **call by value**, in which an argument is communicated to a function by passing the value of the argument. More precisely, the parameter that matches a particular argument references a cell that contains a *copy* of the value of the

```
main()
{
        char    char1 = 'A';    /* char1 is at address 99999 */
        char    *ptr = &char1; /* ptr has 99999 as its contents */
        void    fun( char *p );
            .
            .
            .

        fun( ptr );    /* char1's address is passed to fun */
            .
            .
            .

}

void fun( char *p )
{
            .
            .
            .

}
```

Figure 6.4.1 Passing a pointer to a function.

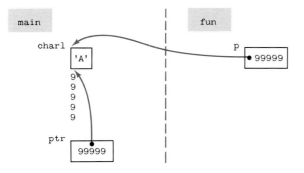

Figure 6.4.2 Passing a pointer to a function.

argument. We also mentioned that C also supports **call by reference**, in which an argument is communicated to a function by passing not the value of the argument but, rather, the address of the argument.

Consider the situation in Figure 6.4.1, in which the argument to fun is a pointer and so has an address as its value. When the function fun is invoked, C makes a copy of ptr's value, the address 99999, and stores it in a cell named p (see Figure 6.4.2). Because the function fun has only a copy of ptr, fun cannot alter ptr's value. With respect to ptr, the call to fun remains call by value. However, because fun knows the address of char1, fun can alter the value of char1. We say that with respect to char1, the call to fun is call by reference. Even though fun receives only a copy of char1's address, this copy is as good as the original because fun can use the address to access char1 itself and so can alter char1's value.

Example 6.4.1. In this example, we consider two versions of a program: The first uses call by value, and the second uses call by reference.

```
          /*  Version 1: Call by Value */
          main( )
          {
1              int num1 = 25;
2              int num2;
3              int add1( int number );

4              num2 = add1( num1 );
          }

5         int add1( int number )
          {
6              return ( ++number );
          }
```

After the definitions and initializations in lines 1 and 2

```
1      int num1 = 25;
2      int num2;
```

we have the situation shown in Figure 6.4.3. When we invoke add1 in line 4

```
4      num2 = add1( num1 );
```

a copy of the argument num1 is stored in the cell named number (see Figure 6.4.4). Control passes to line 6

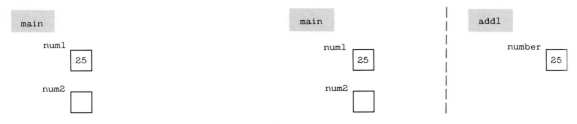

Figure 6.4.3 After definitions and initializations.   **Figure 6.4.4** Call by value.

```
6      return ( ++number );
```

in the function `add1`. The result of evaluating

```
++number
```

is that the value of the cell `number` is incremented by 1. We then return the value of the expression `++number` to `main`, where in line 4 it is copied into `num2` (see Figure 6.4.5). The value of `num1` is unchanged. Indeed, because `add1` received only a copy of the value of `num1`, `add1` could not change `num1`'s value.

The second version uses call by reference.

```
       /*  Version 2:  Call by Reference */
       main( )
       {
1              int num1 = 25;
2              int num2;
3              int *ptr = &num1;
4              int add1( int *p );

5              num2 = add1( ptr );
       }

       /* add1 expects the address of an int, not an int */
6      int add1( int *p )
       {
7              return ( ++*p );
       }
```

After the definitions and initializations in lines 1 through 3

```
1      int num1 = 25;
2      int num2;
3      int *ptr = &num1;
```

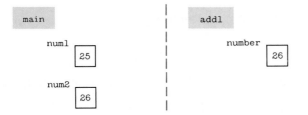

Figure 6.4.5 Conclusion of version 1.

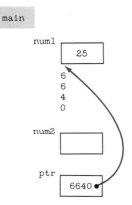

Figure 6.4.6 After definitions and initializations.

we have the situation shown in Figure 6.4.6. Line 3 defines `ptr` to be a pointer to an `int` and initializes `ptr` to the address of `num1`. The pointer `ptr` now points to `num1`.

The header of `add1` in line 6

6   int add1(int *p)

states that `add1` has one parameter p—a pointer to an `int`.

When we invoke `add1` in line 5

5   num2 = add1(ptr);

a copy of the argument `ptr`, the address of `num1`, is stored in a cell named p (see Figure 6.4.7). The function `add1` can now access the variable `num1` because `add1` has `num1`'s address.

Control passes to line 7

7   return (++*p);

The operator * dereferences p, giving `num1`'s contents, after which the increment operator ++ adds one. The value of `num1` is changed from 25 to 26. Then `add1`

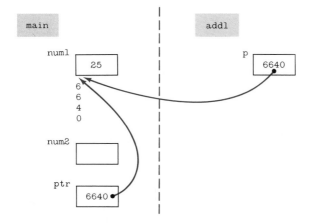

Figure 6.4.7 Call by reference.

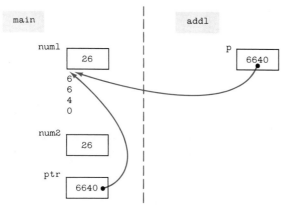

Figure 6.4.8 Conclusion of version 2.

returns the value 26 to `main`, which is assigned to `num2` (see Figure 6.4.8). After line 5 executes, both `num1` and `num2` hold 26. With respect to the variable `num1`, the call to `add1` is call by reference.

When we pass an array to a function, C always uses call by reference; that is, when an array `s` is passed to a function, C passes the address of the first cell in `s`.

Example 6.4.2.   Given the function `main`

```
main( )
{
          int s[ 10 ];
          void f( int a[] );
          .
          .
          .

          f( s );
          .
          .
          .

}
```

when the statement

```
f( s );
```

executes, the address of the first cell in the array `s` is passed to `f`.

The header of the function `f` could be written

```
void f( int a[] )
```

When the function `f` is invoked by `main`, the address of the first cell in the array `s` is passed to `f`, where it is copied into a cell named `a`.

An equivalent way to write the header is

```
void f( int *a )
```

Here `a` is declared to be a pointer to an `int`. But a pointer to an `int` simply references a cell that can hold the address of an `int`. Thus, `f` again can receive the address of the first cell of an array of `int`s. The two parameter declarations have exactly the same meaning; the difference is only syntactic.

In Chapter 5, we used the form

```
int a[]
```

to declare an array parameter. The equivalent form

```
int *a
```

is probably more common.

Given either of the equivalent parameter declarations

```
int a[]
```

or

```
int *a
```

in the body of the function, we may use either array syntax

```
a[ i ]
```

or pointer syntax

```
*( a + i )
```

to access a cell. Because a is a pointer variable and *not* a pointer constant, we may use any of the legal arithmetic operations such as a++ or a--.

To illustrate the use of pointer syntax, we rewrite the function of Section 5.8 that computes the length of a string.

Example 6.4.3. The function `new_length` computes the length of a string represented as a null-terminated array of `char`s.

```
int new_length( char *str )
{
     char *ptr = str;
     while ( *str )
          ++str;
     return ( str - ptr );
}
```

We trace the execution of `new_length` for the invocation

```
i = new_length( s );
```

given the definition and initialization

```
char s[] = "Hi";
```

The result of the definition and initialization

```
char s[] = "Hi";
```

is shown in Figure 6.4.9. When we invoke `new_length`

```
i = new_length( s );
```

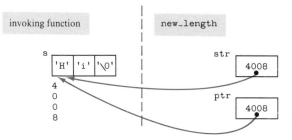

Figure 6.4.9 After definitions and initializations.   **Figure 6.4.10** Passing an array to a function.

the address of the first cell in the array s is passed to `new_length`, where it is copied into a cell named `str` (see Figure 6.4.10). The parameter declaration

```
char *str
```

in `new_length` properly states that `str` can hold the address of a `char`.

The result of the definition and initialization

```
char *ptr = str;
```

is to allocate a cell named `ptr` and to copy the value of `str` into it (see Figure 6.4.10). Now `str`, `ptr`, and s all point to the first cell in the array s.

The value of `*str` is the code (e.g., ASCII) of the character H. Because this code is not equal to 0, we execute the body of the `while` loop where `str` is incremented; `str` now points to the second cell in the array s (see Figure 6.4.11).

Now the value of `*str` is the code of the character i. Because this code is not equal to 0, we execute the body of the `while` loop where `str` is again incremented; `str` now points to the third cell in the array s (see Figure 6.4.12).

Because the value of `*str` is 0 (= '\0'), the `while` loop terminates. The value of the expression

```
str - ptr
```

is 2, the distance (in cells) from the cell pointed to by `ptr` to the cell pointed to by `str`. Thus the function `new_length` correctly returns 2, the length of the string `"Hi"`.

Notice that in Example 6.4.3 we are *not* incrementing the pointer *constant* s, as this would, of course, be an error. Rather, we are incrementing the pointer *variable* `str`, which initially contains a *copy* of s.

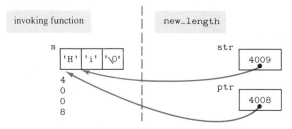

Figure 6.4.11 After `++str;`

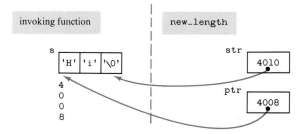

Figure 6.4.12 After ++str;

Call by value and call by reference have different advantages. Call by value protects the arguments. Because the function receives a copy of the argument's value and not the argument's address, the function cannot alter the value of the argument. Yet programmers sometimes want an invoked function to alter the value of a variable in the invoking function, and call by reference provides the means.

Exercises

1. To use call by reference, must the C programmer invoke a function with an address expression?
2. Explain how call by value prevents an invoked function from modifying the arguments in the invoking function.
3. Does call by reference prevent an invoked function from modifying the arguments in the invoking function?
4. If we invoke a function with an array's name as its argument, do we use call by reference with respect to the cells in the array?

Exercises 5 through 8 refer to the following program slice:

```
char char1, *ptr;
void fun( char *ptr );
char1 = 'Z';
ptr = &char1;
fun( ptr );
```

5. (True/False) The call to `fun` involves call by reference with respect to `ptr`.
6. (True/False) The call to `fun` involves call by reference with respect to `char1`.
7. (True/False) The function `fun` could change the contents of `ptr`.
8. (True/False) The function `fun` could change the contents of `char1`.
9. What is printed?

```
#include <stdio.h>
main( )
{
        char    characters[] = { 'A', 'B', 'C' };
        char    *ptr = characters;
```

```
        char  next_char( char *p );
        int   i;

        next_char( ptr++ );
        next_char( ptr++ );
        next_char( ptr );

        for ( i = 0; i < 3; ++i )
                printf( "\n%c", characters[ i ] );
}
char  next_char( char *p )
{
        return ( ++*p );
}
```

10. What is printed?

```
#include <stdio.h>

main()
{
        char s[] = "Hi";
        int f( char *str );
        printf( "%d", f( s ) );
}

int f( char *str )
{
        char *ptr = str;
        while ( *++str )
                ;
        return ( str - ptr );
}
```

11. What is printed?

```
#include <stdio.h>

main()
{
        char s[] = "Hi";
        int f( char *str );
        printf( "%d", f( s ) );
}
int f( char *str )
{
        char *ptr = str;
        while ( *str++ )
                ;
        return ( str - ptr );
}
```

12. Write a function cat that concatenates two strings and puts the result into the first argument. Use pointer syntax.

13. Write a function `compare` that compares two strings and then returns a positive value (respectively, zero value, negative value) when `strcmp` returns a positive value (respectively, zero value, negative value). Use pointer syntax.

14. Write a function `copy` that copies the string in the second argument into the first argument. Use pointer syntax.

6.5 Sample Application: Reversing a String in Place

Problem

Write a program that reads a string and prints it in reverse.

Sample Input/Output

Input is in color; output is in black.

```
Enter a string: STAR
Reversed string: RATS
```

Solution

The function `main` issues the prompt, reads the string, invokes a function `rev` that reverses the string, and writes the reversed string. The function `rev` reverses the string in place and uses pointer syntax.

The function `rev` expects a single argument, the address of the first cell in an array of `char`s. The function `rev` uses two pointers: the parameter `s`, which initially points to the first character, and an auxiliary pointer `end`, which initially points to the last character (the character just before the null terminator). (We want to leave the null character in place.) As long as `s` is less than `end`, we swap the characters to which `s` and `end` point, increment `s`, and decrement `end`.

C Implementation

```c
/*   This program reads a string of up to 100
     characters with no embedded blanks and writes the
     reversed string. The function rev, invoked with
     the array as its single argument, does the work.
     The original and reversed strings occupy the same
     storage.                                           */
#include <stdio.h>
#include <string.h>
main()
{
        char str[ 101 ]; /* storage for up to 100 chars
                            and a null terminator */
        void rev( char *s );

        printf( "\n\nEnter a string:\t" );
        scanf( "%s", str );
        rev( str );
        printf( "\n\nReversed string:\t%s", str );
}
```

```
/*    rev expects a pointer to a character string. It
      reverses the characters in the string leaving the
      null terminator in place. */
void rev( char *s )
{
      char temp, *end;
      end = s + strlen( s ) - 1; /* end points to
                                       last nonnull
                                       character in s */

      while ( s < end ) {
          temp = *s;
          *s++ = *end;
          *end-- = temp;
      }
}
```

Discussion

We show how the program executes if the string

STAR

is passed to rev.

When rev is invoked, we copy the address str into s (see Figure 6.5.1). Because

strlen(s) - 1 = 4 - 1 = 3

when we execute

end = s + strlen(s) - 1;

we set the pointer end to the cell three beyond the cell pointed to by s (see Figure 6.5.1). We have indeed set end to the last nonnull character.

The condition

s < end

is true, and so we execute the body of the while loop.

When we execute

temp = *s;

we copy the contents 'S' of the cell to which s points into temp (see Figure 6.5.1). Because temp must hold a char, temp is defined as type char rather than as a pointer to a char.

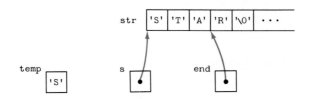

Figure 6.5.1 The beginning of rev.

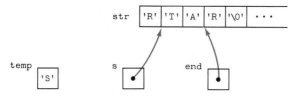

Figure 6.5.2 After *s++ = *end;

When we execute

```
*s++ = *end;
```

we copy the contents 'R' of the cell to which end points into the cell to which s *currently* points. We then increment s (see Figure 6.5.2).

When we execute

```
*end-- = temp;
```

we copy the contents 'S' of temp into the cell to which end *currently* points. We then decrement end (see Figure 6.5.3).

We see that when we execute the body of the while loop, we swap *s and *end, increment s, and decrement end.

The condition

```
s < end
```

is still true, so we execute the body of the while loop again. The result is shown in Figure 6.5.4. Now the condition

```
s < end
```

is false, so we return from the function rev. We have indeed reversed the string.

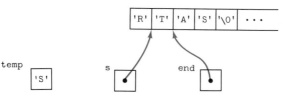

Figure 6.5.3 After *end-- = temp;

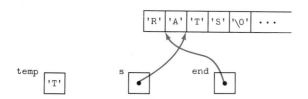

Figure 6.5.4 After another iteration of the while loop.

Exercises

1. Trace the program of this section when the input is RAW.

2. Will the function `rev` work properly if the line

```
while ( s < end ) {
```

is replaced with

```
while ( s <= end ) {
```

6.6   Sample Application: Sorting and Searching Revisited

Problem

The program of Section 5.10 sorts the file *students.dat*, which contains names and phone numbers of students, and then searches the file for names requested by a user. Section 5.10 contains a more complete description of the program, as well as sample input and output.

In this section, we revise the phone program so that it is more efficient. More specifically, after reading each record from *students.dat* into the two-dimensional array `students`, we store the address of the record in the array `students_add`. To sort the array `students`, we move the pointers in the array `students_add` rather than move the strings around in the array `students`. In most situations, it is faster to move addresses than it is to move strings. Figures 6.6.1 and 6.6.2 contrast the two methods of sorting. In Figure 6.6.1, the strings are sorted by physically moving them around in the array. In Figure 6.6.2, the strings are sorted by moving the pointers. In the latter case, the sorted order is obtained by accessing the record `*students_add[ 0 ]`, then the record `*students_add[ 1 ]`, and so on. We use the array of pointers `students_add` for searching as well as sorting. The underlying algorithms are unchanged from Section 5.10; we use selection sort for sorting and binary search for searching.

C Implementation

```
/*   The NEW_PHONE program improves the efficiency of the
     sort in the PHONE program of Section 5.10 by moving
     pointers to data rather than the data themselves.
     The NEW_PHONE program also uses pointer syntax rather than
     array syntax to contrast the difference.

     The NEW_PHONE program uses the same data file, students.dat,
     as the PHONE program and NEW_PHONE also stores student
     records in the two-dimensional array named students. As
```

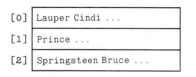

Figure 6.6.1 Data in physical order.   **Figure 6.6.2** Data sorted using pointers.

each record is stored, NEW_PHONE copies its address in the array students to the array students_add, which is an array of pointer to char. NEW_PHONE, like PHONE, uses selection sort for sorting except that NEW_PHONE moves the pointers in students_add rather than the strings in students. The strings in the array students never change position once they are read from the file students.dat. NEW_PHONE, again like PHONE, uses binary search to search for student records; but the difference again is that NEW_PHONE accesses the array of strings through the array of pointers.   */

```
#include <stdio.h>
#include <string.h>

#define   NUMB_RECS      30 /* number of records in students.dat */
#define   LNAME_SIZE     25 /* first 25 chars */
#define   FNAME_SIZE     25 /* next 25 chars */
#define   PNUM_SIZE      12 /* last 12 chars */
#define   MAX_REC_SIZE (LNAME_SIZE + FNAME_SIZE + PNUM_SIZE)
#define   NO_FIND  (-999) /* flag to signal lookup failure */
#define   BLANK       ' ' /* used to pad candidate name so it,
                             too, has LNAME_SIZE chars */

main()
{
      /* student records (+2 is for the newline and the
         null terminator because fgets is used to read) */
1     char students[ NUMB_REC ][ MAX_REC_SIZE + 2 ];

      /* addresses of records */
2     char *students_add[ NUMB_RECS ];

      /* candidate in search */
3     char candidate[ LNAME_SIZE + 2 ];

4     int index; /* index into students */
5     int i;
6     int cand_len;

7     void selection_sort( char *array_add[], int size1 );

      /* returns NO_FIND or index of found item */
8     int  binary_search( char *candidate,
                          char *array_add[],
                          int size );

9     FILE *fp;

    /* read the names of NUMB_RECS records into the array
       students and store the addresses in students_add */

10    fp = fopen( "students.dat", "r" );

11    for ( i = 0; i < NUMB_RECS; ++i ) {
12         fgets( *( students + i ), MAX_REC_SIZE + 2, fp );
```

```
13              *( students_add + i ) = *( students + i );
           }

        /* sort the records into ascending order by moving
           pointers */
14      selection_sort( students_add, NUMB_RECS );

        /* Prompt the user for a student's name and look for it in
           the array students. Halt when the user signals EOF at
           the prompt. */
15      printf( "\n\nEnter a student's name, "
                "or signal EOF to halt:  " );
16      while ( fgets( candidate, LNAME_SIZE + 2, stdin ) != NULL ) {

            /* Pad candidate with blanks to LNAME_SIZE chars.
               -1 for newline stored by fgets. */
17          cand_len = strlen( candidate ) - 1;
18          for ( i = cand_len; i < LNAME_SIZE; i++ )
19                  candidate[ i ] = BLANK;
20          candidate[ LNAME_SIZE ] = '\0';   /* null terminate */

21          index = binary_search( candidate, students_add,
                                   NUMB_RECS );
22          if ( index != NO_FIND )
23              printf( "\n\tRecord:  %s", students_add[ index ] );
24          else {
25              candidate[ cand_len ] = '\0';   /* remove blanks */
26              printf( "\a\n\t%s is not in our directory.",
                        candidate );
            }
27          printf( "\n\nEnter a student's name, "
                    "or signal EOF to halt:  " );
        }
    }


    /*   selection_sort( array_add, size1 )

         The function expects an array and its size. It sorts the
         elements (in this case, the dereferenced pointers to
         strings) into ascending order. It returns no value. */
    void  selection_sort( char *array_add[], int size1 )
    {
28      int    smallest_index; /* index of smallest string seen */
29      int    i, j;
30      void   swap( char *array_add[], int current, int low );

        /* loop size1 - 1 times, selecting smallest string each
           time */
31      for ( i = 0; i < size1 - 1; ++i ) {
            /* assume ith string is smallest */
32          smallest_index = i;
            /* compare smallest against remaining strings */
33          for ( j = i + 1; j < size1; ++j )
                /* look for smaller string */
```

```
34                    if ( strcmp( *( array_add + j ),
                            *( array_add + smallest_index ) ) ) < 0 )
35                       smallest_index = j;
                /* put smallest at index i */
36               if ( i != smallest_index )
37                   swap( array_add, i, smallest_index );
           }
   }

   /* Swap array_add[ current ] and array_add[ low ]. */
   void swap( char *array_add[], int current, int low )
   {
38       char   *temp;

39       temp = *( array_add + current );
40       *( array_add + current ) = *( array_add + low );
41       *( array_add + low ) = temp;
   }

   /*   binary_search( candidate, array_add, size )

        The function searches the sorted list of strings whose
        addresses are

        array_add[ 0 ],array_add[ 1 ],...,array_add[ size - 1 ]

        for candidate, returning the appropriate index if candidate
        is found and the NO_FIND flag otherwise.                    */

   int   binary_search( char *candidate,
                        char *array_add[],
                        int size )
   {
42       int   first = 0;          /* first position in array */
43       int   last = size - 1;    /* last position in array */
44       int   mid;                /* midpoint in array */
45       int   flag;               /* holds result of string compare */

         /* search until list is empty */
46       while ( first <= last ) {
                 /* find (approximate) midpoint */
47           mid = ( first + last ) / 2;
48           flag = strncmp( candidate, *( array_add + mid ),
                            LNAME_SIZE );
49           if ( flag == 0 )
50               return ( mid ); /* candidate found */
51           if ( flag > 0 )
52               first = mid + 1;  /* search right half */
53           else
54               last = mid - 1;   /* search left half */
         }

55       return ( NO_FIND );
   }
```

Discussion

In line 1

```
1   char students[ NUMB_RECS ][ MAX_REC_SIZE + 2 ];
```

we define a two-dimensional array to hold the character strings that represent the student records, just as we did in the original version of the program. However, the strings are stored permanently in the order in which they are read.

In line 2

```
2   char *students_add[ NUMB_RECS ];
```

we define an array of pointers to hold the addresses of the records. Each pointer is initialized to the address of the corresponding element in `students`. The brackets have higher precedence than does the star operator, which means that `students_add` is being defined as an array of pointers to characters and not as a pointer to an array. Line 2 is equivalent to

```
char  *( students_add[ NUMB_RECS ] );
```

To define a pointer to an array of characters, we would write

```
char ( *array_pointer )[ NUMB_RECS ];
```

The loop in lines 11 through 13

```
11   for ( i = 0; i < NUMB_RECS; ++i ) {
12       fgets( *( students + i ), MAX_REC_SIZE + 2, fp );
13       *( students_add + i ) = *( students + i );
     }
```

reads NUMB_RECS character strings from the file *students.dat* into the two-dimensional array `students`. Line 13 then stores the address of each cell in the array `students` in the corresponding cell in the pointer array `students_add`. The value of `students[ 0 ]`, which is the address of the first string, is stored in `students_add[ 0 ]`; the value of `students[ 1 ]`, which is the address of the second string, is stored in `students_add[ 1 ]`; and so on.

Lines 12 and 13 use pointer syntax instead of the equivalent array syntax:

```
fgets( students[ i ], MAX_REC_SIZE + 2, fp );
students_add[ i ] = students[ i ];
```

In line 14

```
14   selection_sort( students_add, NUMB_RECS );
```

we pass `students_add`, not `students`, to `selection_sort`. As previously discussed, the sort orders the array `students` by moving the pointers in the array `students_add`.

Because `students_add` contains the sorting information about `students`, in line 21

```
21   index = binary_search( candidate, students_add,
                            NUMB_RECS );
```

`binary_search` uses `students_add` rather than `students` as its second argument.

In selection_sort, we store the address of the smallest string in array_add[0]; then we store the address of the second smallest string in array_add[1]; and so on. At the ith, stage, we begin by assuming that the ith string is the smallest among

```
array_add[ i ],...,array_add[ size - 1 ]
```

The variable smallest_index, which stores the index of the smallest string seen so far, is initialized in line 32:

```
32    smallest_index = i;
```

Whenever we find a smaller string, we update smallest_index.

Line 32 resembles the corresponding line in the original program and serves essentially the same purpose. In the revised program, smallest_index holds an index into an array of pointers to strings, whereas in the original program, it held an index into an array of strings.

Line 34

```
34    if ( strcmp( *( array_add + j ),
                 *( array_add + smallest_index ) ) < 0 )
```

uses strcmp, as in the original program, to compare two strings. The function strcmp expects as arguments the addresses of two character strings. The first argument, *(array_add + j), evaluates to the address of a string in students. The second argument, *(array_add + smallest_index), holds the address of the smallest string found so far.

In line 37

```
37    swap( array_add, i, smallest_index );
```

we swap pointers in array_add.

As can be seen by consulting the header for swap,

```
void swap( char *array_add[], int current, int low )
```

swap's first argument is the address of the first element in an array of pointers to character strings. Notice the similarity between the parameter declaration for array_add and the definition of students_add in line 2.

In lines 39 through 41

```
39    temp = *( array_add + current );
40    *( array_add + current ) = *( array_add + low );
41    *( array_add + low ) = temp;
```

we exchange the contents of the cells in array_add using the dereferencing operator.

The function binary_search expects three arguments: a pointer to a string (a student's name), an array of pointers (to entries in the array students), and the array's size. If the function binary_search finds the desired string, it returns the index of the pointer to the string. If the string is not found, binary_search returns NO_FIND, whose value is −999.

The library function strncmp, which is used in line 48,

```
48    flag = strncmp( candidate, *( array_add + mid ),
                   LNAME_SIZE );
```

compares character strings. The first two arguments are the addresses of the strings to be compared, and the third is the maximum number of characters to use in the comparison. In line 48, `candidate` points to a string that the user enters; `*( array_add + mid )` points to the string in the array `students` whose address is `array_add[ mid ]`.

6.7 Smooth and Ragged Arrays

Suppose that a program needs to store in an array the names of all 50 U.S. states as character strings. One way to store the states is to use a two-dimensional array (see Figure 6.7.1). The size of the first dimension must be 50 to accommodate all 50 states. The size of the second dimension must be equal to one more than the length of a longest state. (We need one extra cell to store the null terminator.) Because there are 14 letters in a longest state (South Carolina or North Carolina), the size of the second dimension must be 15. We call a two-dimensional array of `chars` a **smooth array**. As shown in Figure 6.7.1, the right edge of our array is "smooth," as the same number of cells are allocated per line.

Smooth arrays waste space when the strings to be stored vary in length. For example, in Figure 6.7.1 "Ohio" uses only 5 of the allocated 15 cells. An alternative to a smooth array is a **ragged array**, in which the number of cells allocated for each string is exactly equal to one more than the length of the string (see Figure 6.7.2). The smooth array in Figure 6.7.1 is a standard two-dimensional array, with each element an array of fixed size 15. By contrast, the ragged array in Figure 6.7.2 is an array of pointers to character strings. The string `"Ohio"` (with the null terminator) uses 5 cells, whereas the string `"South Carolina"` uses 15 cells. As shown in Figure 6.7.2, the right edge of our array is "ragged," as the number of cells allocated per line varies.

The following example illustrates the differences in how data are accessed in smooth and ragged arrays.

```
main( )
{
        char  states1[ 50 ][ 15 ] =
            { "Ohio" , "South Carolina" , "Illinois" ... };
        .
        .
        .
}
```

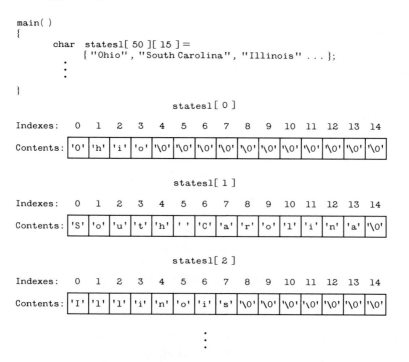

Figure 6.7.1 A smooth array.

```
main( )
{
        char  *states2[ 50 ] =
           .      { "Ohio", "South_ Carolina", "Illinois" , ... };
           .
           .

}
```

                          states2[0]

Indexes: 0   1   2   3   4

Contents: |'O'|'h'|'i'|'o'|'\0'|

                          states2[1]

Indexes: 0   1   2   3   4   5   6   7   8   9 10 11 12 13 14

Contents: |'S'|'o'|'u'|'t'|'h'|' '|'C'|'a'|'r'|'o'|'l'|'i'|'n'|'a'|'\0'|

                          states2[2]

Indexes: 0   1   2   3   4   5   6   7   8

Contents: |'I'|'l'|'l'|'i'|'n'|'o'|'i'|'s'|'\0'|

                              .
                              .
                              .

Figure 6.7.2 A ragged array.

Example 6.7.1.   Consider simplified versions of arrays states1 and states2, in which each has three elements:

```
char    states1[ 3 ][ 9 ] =
        { "Wyoming", "Ohio", "Illinois" };
char    *states2[ 3 ] =
        { "Wyoming", "Ohio", "Illinois" };
```

To access the character n in "Illinois", we can use the expressions

```
/* access n in "Illinois" */
states1[ 2 ][ 4 ]
states2[ 2 ][ 4 ]
```

The "2" in the expression

```
states1[ 2 ][ 4 ]
```

requests the third element in the array states1. Because states1 is an array of arrays, each with nine cells, the system must add $2 \cdot 9 = 18$ to the address of the first cell to obtain the address of the string "Illinois" (see Figure 6.7.3). The "4" in the expression

```
states1[ 2 ][ 4 ]
```

requests the fifth element in states1[2]. Thus the system adds

```
2 · 9 + 4
```

to the address of the first cell of states1 to access n (see Figure 6.7.3). The "2" in the expression

```
states2[ 2 ][ 4 ]
```

states1 = 5904

'W'	'y'	'o'	'm'	'i'	'n'	'g'	'\0'	

'O'	'h'	'i'	'o'	'\0'				

5904 + 2 · 9 = 5922

'I'	'l'	'l'	'i'	'n'	'o'	'i'	's'	'\0'

$$5926 = 5922 + 4$$
$$= 5904 + 2 \cdot 9 + 4$$

Figure 6.7.3 Accessing a character in a smooth array.

requests the third element in the pointer array `states2`. The system adds $2 \cdot S$, where S is the size of a cell that holds an address, to the address of the first cell to obtain the address of the cell `states2[ 2 ]`. This cell contains the address of the string `"Illinois"` (see Figure 6.7.4, in which we assume that $S = 4$). Thus to locate n in `states2`, we compute the offset from the starting address given by `states2[ 2 ]`; that is, we add 4 to `states2[ 2 ]` (see Figure 6.7.4).

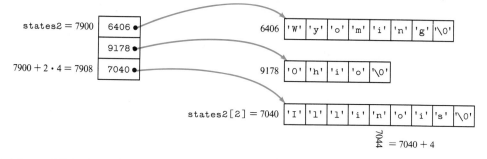

Figure 6.7.4 Accessing a character in a ragged array.

Exercises

1. Which is the smooth array, and which is the ragged array?

```
char *silly1[ 2 ] =
     { "awhopbobalooba", "yowee" };
char silly2[ 2 ][ 35 ] =
     { "awhopbobalooba", "yowee" };
```

2. How much storage is allocated for `silly1` in Exercise 1?

3. How much storage is allocated for `silly2` in Exercise 1?

4. What is printed?

```
char  str1[ 25 ] = "Texas";
char  *str2 = "Texas";
printf( "%s\n%s", str1, str2 );
printf( "%c", *str2 );
```

5. Explain the computation needed to find X in the array `string`

```
char string[ 2 ][ 30 ] =
     { "ZZZZZZZZZZZZ", "AAAAAAAXAAAAAAA" };
```

6. Where does X occur in the one-dimensional realization of the array `string` in Exercise 5?

For each expression in Exercises 7 through 12, indicate which character is referenced, or if the expression is illegal, explain why it is illegal. The arrays are defined in Figures 6.7.1 and 6.7.2.

7. `states1[ 0 ][ 2 ]`   **8.** `states2[ 0 ][ 2 ]`
9. `states1[ 1 ][ 13 ]`   **10.** `states2[ 1 ][ 13 ]`
11. `states1[ 2 ][ 14 ]`   **12.** `states2[ 2 ][ 14 ]`

6.8 Command Line Arguments

The function `main` can have two parameters, traditionally named `argv` and `argc`. The parameter `argv` is an array of pointers to strings, and `argc` is an `int` whose value is equal to the number of strings to which `argv` points. The parameters `argc` and `argv` catch arguments passed to `main` when it begins executing.

When we specify parameters for `main`, the parameter declarations, as for any C function, occur in the header. We write

```
/* command line arguments */
main( int argc, char *argv[] )
/* argc holds argv's size */
/* argv holds pointers to strings */
{
      .

      .

      .
}
```

Suppose that we compile the preceding program. Assuming that the executable program is in a file called *TEST*, we run the program by typing

```
$ TEST
```

where $ is the system prompt. We call the preceding line the **command line**. When a program is run, in addition to executing it, the operating system passes the strings on the command line to `main`. More precisely, the operating system stores the strings on the command line in memory and sets `argv[ 0 ]` to the address of the first string on the command line, `argv[ 1 ]` to the address of the second string on the command line, and so on. The argument `argc` is set to the number of strings on the command line. The value of `argc` is always at least 1, for the command line contains the name of the file that holds the program to be executed, in this case *TEST*. We call the strings on the command line the **command line arguments**.

Example 6.8.1. For the command line

```
$ TEST
```

`argc` is equal to 1, as there is one string on the command line. The parameter `argv[ 0 ]` is equal to the address of the string TEST.

The use of command line arguments becomes more interesting and useful when the command line contains more than one argument, as the following example illustrates.

Example 6.8.2.   Suppose that the files

```
customers.dat   /* file 1 */
suppliers.dat   /* file 2 */
creditors.dat   /* file 3 */
deadbeats.dat   /* file 4 */
```

hold records, one per line, with information such as name, address, and phone number. The program in Figure 6.8.1 prints the data files that we specify on the command line. We show how this program executes after we issue the command

```
$ print_files customers.dat suppliers.dat creditors.dat deadbeats.dat
```

Because the function `main` expects two arguments, line 2

```
2     main( int argc, char *argv[] )
```

declares parameters `argc` and `argv`. The parameter `argc` catches the number of command line arguments, which in this case is five. The parameter `argv` holds pointers to character strings, which in this case are

```
argv[ 0 ] /* pointer to the string "print_files" */
argv[ 1 ] /* pointer to the string "customers.dat" */
argv[ 2 ] /* pointer to the string "suppliers.dat" */
argv[ 3 ] /* pointer to the string "creditors.dat" */
argv[ 4 ] /* pointer to the string "deadbeats.dat" */
```

The command line holds five strings: the name of the file in which the program resides and the names of four data files to print. Thus our program prints $argc - 1$ files.

```
1     #include <stdio.h>
2     main( int argc, char *argv[] )
      {
3          char record[ 80 ];   /* input buffer */
4          int i;
5          FILE *fp;
6          printf( "\n\n\tNumber of files to be "
                   "printed:\t%d\n", argc - 1 );

           /* print each file */
7          for ( i = 1; i < argc; ++i ) {
8               printf( "\n\tFile:\t%s\n", argv[ i ] );
9               fp = fopen( argv[ i ], "r" );

                /* print each record in one file */
10              while ( fgets( record, 80, fp ) != NULL )
11                   printf( "%s", record );

12              fclose( fp );
      }
      }
```

Figure 6.8.1 `print_files` program.

Line 6

```
6      printf( "\n\n\tNumber of files to be "
               "printed:\t%d\n", argc - 1 );
```

reports the number of files to be printed.

In lines 7 through 9

```
7      for ( i = 1; i < argc; ++i ) {
8          printf( "\n\tFile:\t%s\n", argv[ i ] );
9          fp = fopen( argv[ i ], "r" );
```

we initialize the loop counter i to 1 instead of 0, because we want to print the names of data files only; argv[0] contains the address of the string "print_files", the program file's name. The function printf with the %s format descriptor expects the address of character string, and each element in the array argv is a pointer to a string. The function fopen expects two arguments, both addresses of strings. The first string gives the name of a file, and the second gives the mode in which the file is to be opened. The expression argv[i] gives the address of a string that names a file.

Exercises

1. What is printed if the command line is

```
$ myprogram file1.dat file2.dat file3.dat file4.dat
```

when we execute

```
printf( "\n%d\t%s\t%s\n", argc, argv[ 4 ], argv[ 2 ] );
```

2. How might one use the string argv[0]?

3. Test the program of Figure 6.8.1 on your system.

4. Rewrite the program of Figure 6.8.1 using pointer syntax.

6.9 Pointers to Functions

A function's name, like an array's name, is a *pointer constant*. The value of such a pointer constant can be regarded as the address of the code that represents the function. For example, if score is a function that returns an int, the value of score can be regarded as the address of the code that represents the function score.

It is possible to define variables and to declare parameters that can contain addresses of functions (pointers to functions). One use of pointers to functions is to pass a function as an argument to another function.

To define the variable ptr to be of type "pointer to a function that has one parameter of type char and returns an int," we write

```
int ( *ptr )( char );
```

The definition begins with the data type (int in this example) returned by a function to which the variable can point. This data type is followed by the variable's name prefixed by an asterisk (*ptr in this example). As usual, the asterisk signals a pointer. The asterisk and name *must* be enclosed in parentheses. The definition concludes with the data types of the parameters of a function to which the variable can point. In this example, `ptr` can point to a function with a single parameter of type `char`. The parameter data type list is enclosed in parentheses and terminated by a semicolon. The syntax is cumbersome, but no parentheses can be omitted. If, for example, we write

```
int *ptr( char );
```

we are declaring `ptr` to be a function (as opposed to a pointer to a function) that has one parameter of type `char` and returns a pointer to an `int`; the parentheses have a higher precedence than the star does.

If `ptr` is a pointer to a function that has one parameter of type `char` and returns an `int`, we can invoke the function to which `ptr` points with the argument `letter` by dereferencing `ptr` and supplying the argument:

```
( *ptr )( letter );
```

The standard also allows this last statement to be written without the star:

```
ptr( letter );
```

The two forms have identical meanings; each invokes the function to which `ptr` points with the argument `letter`.

A parameter of type pointer to function is described in the usual way. For example, suppose that `sum` is a function that returns no value and that `sum` has one parameter `ptr` of type "pointer to a function that has one parameter of type `char` and returns an `int`." The header of sum would be written

```
void sum( int ( *ptr )( char ) )
```

The expression

```
int ( *ptr )( char )
```

characterizes `ptr` as a pointer to a function that has one parameter of type `char` and returns an `int`.

Section 6.10 contains a program that illustrates the use of pointers to functions.

Exercises

1. (True/False) A function's name is a pointer constant.
2. What is the meaning of each statement?

```
float   *fun1( int );
float   ( *fun2 )( int );
```

3. Given the slice of code

```
void    fun1( int i, char c );
void    fun2( int *ptr );
int     fun3( float x, float y );

/* invoke fun99 with 3 functions as arguments */
fun99( fun1, fun2, fun3 );
```

write the header for `fun99`. How would `fun99` be declared in a function that invokes it?

6.10   Sample Application: Comparing Sorting Algorithms

Problem

Write a program to compare the times needed to execute several sorting functions for various input sizes. For each set of items to sort, print the number of items to sort and then the times required by the various functions.

Sample Output

(This program receives no input.)

```
Sort 100 items
    Algorithm: Selection sort
        Time = 0.000000 seconds
    Algorithm: Quicksort
        Time = 0.000000 seconds

Sort 200 items
    Algorithm: Selection sort
        Time = 1.000000 seconds
    Algorithm: Quicksort
        Time = 0.000000 seconds

Sort 500 items
    Algorithm: Selection sort
        Time = 1.000000 seconds
    Algorithm: Quicksort
        Time = 1.000000 seconds

Sort 1000 items
    Algorithm: Selection sort
        Time = 5.000000 seconds
    Algorithm: Quicksort
        Time = 1.00000 seconds

Sort 2000 items
    Algorithm: Selection sort
        Time = 21.000000 seconds
    Algorithm: Quicksort
        Time = 1.000000 seconds

Sort 3000 items
    Algorithm: Selection sort
        Time = 57.000000 seconds
    Algorithm: Quicksort
        Time = 1.000000 seconds

Sort 4000 items
    Algorithm: Selection sort
        Time = 101.000000 seconds
    Algorithm: Quicksort
        Time = 2.000000 seconds
```

```
Sort 5000 items
      Algorithm: Selection sort
            Time = 260.000000 seconds
      Algorithm: Quicksort
            Time = 5.000000 seconds
```

Solution

The function main repeatedly invokes the function timer, passing to timer the sorting function to time and the array to sort. The function timer receives as arguments the name of the sort, so that timer can print its name; the data to sort; the number of items to sort; and the address of the sorting function, so that timer can invoke the sort. More precisely, the last argument to timer is a pointer to a function that performs a sort. The function timer uses the library function time to read the time, invokes the sorting function, and then again reads the time. Finally, timer prints the elapsed time.

To initialize the array a, main invokes the function fill_array to write random numbers into a. The function timer copies the data in a into the array b defined in timer. Since timer does not change the array a, when timer is invoked in main with another sorting function, it sorts exactly the same data as the previous function. In this way, we compare the times of the sorting functions for the same input.

We leave to the reader the choice of which sorting functions to time and the task of writing the functions.

C Implementation

```
/*  This program times various sorting functions; main invokes
    the function timer which invokes and times a sort. The
    arguments to timer are

        --the name of the algorithm
        --an array that holds the ints to sort
        --the number of items to sort
        --a pointer to the function that sorts            */
#include <stdio.h>
#include <time.h>
#include <stdlib.h>

#define NUMB_OF_ARRAY_SIZES   8
#define MAX_SIZE_TO_SORT   5000

main()
{
        int i;  /* loop counter */
        /* sort arrays of size 100, 200, 500, 1000, 2000,
            3000, 4000, 5000 */
        int numb[] = { 100, 200, 500, 1000, 2000, 3000,
                        4000, 5000 };
        int a[ MAX_SIZE_TO_SORT ]; /* holds ints to sort */

        /* fills an array with random ints */
        void fill_array( int a[], int count );
        void selection_sort( int a[], int count );
        void quicksort( int a[], int count );
```

Line numbers in left margin: 1, 2, 3, 4, 5, 6

```
7            void timer( char *alg_name,
                         int a[],
                         int size,
                         void ( *sort_alg )( int [], int ) );

8        for ( i = 0; i < NUMB_OF_ARRAY_SIZES; i++ ) {
9            printf( "\n\n\nSort %d items\n", numb[ i ] );
10           fill_array( a, numb[ i ] );
11           timer( "Selection sort", a, numb[ i ],
                     selection_sort );
12           timer( "Quicksort", a, numb[ i ], quicksort );
        }
    }

    /*   timer receives four arguments

             --the name of the algorithm
             --an array that holds the ints to sort
             --the number of items to sort
             --a pointer to the function that sorts
```

timer first copies the array that holds the ints to sort
to the local array b, so that the data passed are not
changed. After printing the name of the sorting algorithm,
the function is invoked and the time to sort is printed.
The time is measured by invoking the system functions
time, which returns the current calendar time, and
difftime, which returns the difference in seconds between
two calendar times. */

```
13   void timer( char *alg_name, /* string with name of algorithm */
14               int a[],        /* data to sort */
15               int size,       /* number of ints to sort */
16               void ( *sort_alg )( int [], int ) ) /* pointer to
                                              sort function */

     {
17       int i; /* loop counter */
18       int b[ MAX_SIZE_TO_SORT ]; /* array to sort */
19       time_t start; /* time when sort begins */
20       time_t stop;  /* time when sort ends */

         /* Copy a to b. b will be sorted. */
21       for ( i = 0; i < size; i++ )
22           b[ i ] = a[ i ];
23       printf( "\tAlgorithm: %s\n", alg_name );
24       start = time( NULL );
         /* sort b[ 0 ],..., b[ size - 1 ] */
25       ( *sort_alg )( b, size );
26       stop = time( NULL );
27       printf( "\t\tTime = %f seconds\n",
                 difftime( stop, start ) );
     }
```

```
        /*  fill_array writes random ints into a[ 0 ],..,
            a[ count - 1 ]. The library function rand is used, and
            rand returns a random integer. */
28      void fill_array( int a[], int count )
        {
29          int i;
30          for ( i = 0; i < count; i++ )
31              a[ i ] = rand();
        }

32      void selection_sort( int a[], int count )
        /* a[] is the array to sort */
        /* sort a[ 0 ],..., a[ count - 1 ] */
        {
            /* code to implement selection_sort */
        }

33      void quicksort( int a[], int count )
        /* a[] is the array to sort */
        /* sort a[ 0 ],..., a[ count - 1 ] */
        {
            /* code to implement quicksort */
        }
```

Discussion

In line 2 in main,

```
2   int numb[] = { 100, 200, 500, 1000, 2000, 3000,
                   4000, 5000 };
```

for convenience, we store the sizes of the lists to sort. In line 8

```
8   for ( i = 0; i < NUMB_OF_ARRAY_SIZES; i++ ) {
```

we step through the various lists. We print the number of items to sort, invoke fill_array to write random numbers into the array a, and then time the various sorting functions by invoking timer.

In line 11,

```
11  timer( "Selection sort", a, numb[ i ],
           selection_sort );
```

we pass the name "Selection sort", the array a, the size numb[i], and the pointer constant selection_sort to timer. Since timer receives the address of the function selection_sort, it can invoke this function and time it. In line 12,

```
12  timer( "Quicksort", a, numb[ i ], quicksort );
```

we pass the name "Quicksort", the array a, the size numb[i], and the pointer constant quicksort to timer. Because timer receives the address of the function quicksort, it can now invoke quicksort and time it. (We discuss quicksort in Section 9.7.)

The header of timer, lines 13 through 16,

```
13  void timer( char *alg_name,  /* string with name of algorithm */
14              int a[],          /* data to sort */
```

```
15          int size,         /* number of ints to sort */
16          void ( *sort_alg )( int [], int ) ) /* pointer to
                                           sort function */
```

declares four parameters: alg_name, a, size, and sort_alg. Because alg_name is a pointer to char, it can receive the address of a string—the name of the algorithm. In line 16, sort_alg is declared to be a pointer to a function that has two parameters, an array of ints and an int, and returns no value. When timer is invoked, sort_alg receives the address of a sorting function.

The function timer begins by copying the data in a to b, after which it prints the name of the algorithm. To time the sorts, we use the library functions time, which returns the current calendar time, and difftime, which returns the difference in seconds between two calendar times. We read the time just before we invoke the sort, and we read the time just after the sort concludes. By invoking difftime with the two times, we obtain the time for the sort. Because time returns a value of type time_t, and difftime expects arguments of type time_t, we define start and stop as type time_t. Information available in the header file *time.h* allows the system to replace the name time_t with an integer type appropriate to the particular implementation. For example, in Turbo C time_t is replaced by long.

At line 24,

```
24    start = time( NULL );
```

we read the time just before we invoke the sort. We invoke the sort at line 25

```
25    ( *sort_alg )( b, size );
```

by dereferencing the pointer and supplying the required arguments. The arguments to the function to which sort_alg points are b, the array to sort, and size, the number of items to sort. After finishing the sort, we read the time

```
26    stop = time( NULL );
```

and then print the elapsed time:

```
27    printf( "\t\tTime = %f seconds\n",
            difftime( stop, start ) );
```

The library function difftime returns the difference of the calendar times stop and start.

The values to sort are randomly generated. We isolate the activity of filling the array a with random numbers in the function fill_array. The function fill_array uses the library function rand, which is declared in the header file *stdlib.h*. The function rand returns a random integer between 0 and RAND_MAX, which is defined in *stdlib.h*. The program concludes with stubs for the various sorting functions to be timed.

Changes from Traditional C

1. Traditional C does not have the data type void * (pointer to void).
2. Traditional C does not restrict the range of legal values of pointers to array cells.
3. If ptr is a pointer to a function, traditional C requires that ptr be explicitly dereferenced in order to invoke the function to which it points:

```
( *ptr ) ( ... );
```

The equivalent syntax

```
( ptr ) ( ... );
```

is new with the standard.

Common Programming Errors

1. It is an error to assign an address to any variable except a pointer:

```
int  *ptr1;
int  num1, num2;
num1 = &num2; /***** ERROR *****/
ptr1 = &num2; /***** correct *****/
```

2. It is an error to assign the address of one type to a pointer to different type (e.g., to assign the address of a char to a pointer to int):

```
int *ptr1, *ptr2;
char *cptr;
            .
            .
            .
ptr1 = cptr; /***** ERROR *****/
ptr1 = ptr2; /***** correct *****/
```

3. It is an error to assign a nonpointer variable to a pointer variable:

```
char c;
char *ptr;
ptr = c;  /***** ERROR *****/
ptr = &c; /***** correct *****/
```

4. It is an error to multiply two pointers, to add two pointers, or to divide two pointers.

5. It is an error to apply the address operator & to a constant. For example, the expression &77 is illegal.

6. The statement

```
char *ptr = "Old Songs Deranged";
```

is *not* equivalent to the pair of statements

```
char *ptr;
*ptr = "Old Songs Deranged";    /***** ERROR *****/
```

The last statement attempts to copy the address of the string into the cell to which ptr points rather than into ptr itself. The two statements

```
char *ptr;
ptr = "Old Songs Deranged";
```

are equivalent to the statement

```
char *ptr = "Old Songs Deranged";    /** correct **/
```

7. The code

```
char s[ 20 ];
s = "Old Songs Deranged";    /***** ERROR *****/
```

tries to copy the address of the string into s. Because s is a pointer constant, an error results. The programmer was probably trying to copy the string into the array s. A string can be copied using a library function

```
strcpy( s, "Old Songs Deranged" );
```

8. It is an error to attempt to access an item at an address given by a pointer if either the pointer has no value or the cell it references has not been given a value. For example:

```
int   num, *ptr;

/*** ERROR—ptr points nowhere ***/
printf( "%d", *ptr );

ptr = &num;
/*** ERROR—num has no value ***/
printf( "%d", *ptr );
```

9. It is an error to attempt to store an item at an address given by a pointer if the pointer does not contain an address of proper storage. For example:

```
char *ptr, *a[30];

/*** ERROR—ptr points nowhere ***/
scanf( "%s", ptr );

/*** ERROR—a[ 0 ] points nowhere ***/
scanf( "%s", a[ 0 ] );
```

10. The *definitions*

```
char s[ 10 ];
char *s;
```

are *not* the same. The first definition allocates 10 cells, each of which can hold one char, and assigns s the value (which cannot be changed) of the address of the first cell. The first definition makes s a pointer constant. The second definition allocates one cell named s that can hold the *address* of a cell that holds a char. The second definition makes s a pointer variable. On the other hand, the parameter *declarations* char s[ ] and char *s are identical. Both declare s to be the name of a cell that can contain the address of a cell that holds a char; s is a pointer variable.

11. The definition and initialization

```
char *ptr = "I'm a bagel on a plate of onion rolls.";
```

does *not* copy a string but, rather, copies an address. Storage is reserved for the string

```
"I'm a bagel on a plate of onion rolls."
```

and the *address* of this string is stored in the cell named ptr.

12. It is an error to omit the parentheses in defining or declaring a pointer to a function, as in

```
char ( *p )( void );
```

If we write

```
char *p( void );
```

we are declaring p to be a function that returns a pointer to a char.

Programming Exercises

6.1. Write a function flip_sign that expects a pointer to an array of integers and an integer that gives the array's size. The function flip_sign multiplies each number in the array by −1. Use pointer syntax throughout.

6.2. Write a function check with two parameters: str and c. The parameter str is a pointer to a char, and the parameter c is a char. The function check returns 1 if c is in the string pointed to by str, and 0 otherwise. Write a main function that calls check several times to demonstrate that check is working properly.

6.3. Write a function substring with three parameters: str, substr, and len. The parameters str and substr are pointers to char. The parameter len is an int. The function substring normally copies len consecutive characters, beginning with the character pointed to by str, into storage pointed to by substr. However, if the null terminator is encountered, the function stops copying characters. *Example:* If str points to the seventh character in the string

```
"Let's talk about the black bird."
```

and len is 4, after

```
substring( str, substr, len );
```

substr points to storage that contains "talk".

Write a main function that invokes substring several times to demonstrate that it is working properly.

6.4. Write a function find with two parameters: str and substr. The parameters str and substr are pointers to char. The function find returns the address of the first occurrence of the string pointed to by substr in the string pointed to by str. If the string pointed to by substr does not occur in the string pointed to by str, find returns NULL. *Examples:* If str points to

```
"Let's talk about the black bird."
```

and substr points to "black", then find returns a pointer to the character b (in black) in the string pointed to by str.

If str points to

```
"Let's talk about the black bird."
```

and substr points to "blue", then find returns the value NULL.

Write a main function that invokes find several times to demonstrate that it is working properly.

6.5. Write your own version of `strncat` (see Section 5.7). Use only pointer syntax. Write a `main` function that invokes your function several times to demonstrate that it is working properly.

6.6. Write your own version of `strncmp` (see Section 5.7). Use only pointer syntax. Write a `main` function that invokes your function several times to demonstrate that it is working properly.

6.7. Write your own version of `strncpy` (see Section 5.7). Use only pointer syntax. Write a `main` function that invokes your function several times to demonstrate that it is working properly.

6.8. Write a program that reads up to 100 integers from a file, computes the mean m, and then computes and stores in an array, for each integer n in the file, the difference n − m. Distribute the tasks among different functions and use pointer syntax throughout.

6.9. Write a function `insertion_sort` that sorts strings. The parameters are an array of pointers to `char` and the number of strings to sort. Use the following algorithm to sort

```
array[ 0 ],...,array[ SIZE − 1 ].
```

    1. Initialize COUNT to 1.
    2. Repeat steps 3 through 7 until COUNT equals SIZE.
    3.   Set IND to COUNT.
    4.   Repeat steps 5 and 6 as long as IND ≥ 1 and array[IND] < array[IND − 1].
    5.   Swap array[IND] and array[IND − 1].
    6.   Decrement IND by 1.
    7.   Increment COUNT by 1.

Use only pointer syntax. As sample input, use an array of 20 character strings.

6.10. Modify `insertion_sort` (Exercise 6.9) so that it sorts by moving pointers rather than by moving the strings.

6.11. Amend the PHONE program (Section 6.6) by replacing selection sort with insertion sort (see Exercise 6.9).

6.12. Write a function that computes the median of a set of integers. If the integers are stored in an array that is then sorted, the median occurs at the array's midpoint. If there are an even number of integers, we average the two middle numbers to obtain the median. For example, the median of

```
88  34  9  23  −2
```

is 23. Use either selection sort or insertion sort. Use pointer notation throughout.

6.13. Most time-sharing computer systems require the user to log in by giving a user name and a password. Write a program that simulates this activity. The program begins by giving the user a list of available computers (e.g., IBM-1, CYBER-6, VAX-4, ATT-1). After the user selects a given computer, the program prompts for a user name and checks to see whether such a name is valid. If not, it issues an error message, and the program terminates. If the name is found, the program asks for a password. If the password is valid, a welcome message is printed; otherwise, an error message is printed, and the program terminates. *Hint:* Use two arrays of character strings, `username` and `password`, so that the index into `username` is also the index into the corresponding `password`. Use ragged arrays to hold all character strings.

6.14. Expand the program of Exercise 6.13 by allowing the user to change the password. Assume that no password may be longer than 32 characters.

6.15. A *stack* is a structure that has a *top* and four standard operations:

- Test for *empty*, which determines whether there are any items on the stack.
- Test for *full*, which determines whether any items can be added to the stack.
- *Push*, which adds an item to the stack at the top.
- *Pop*, which removes an item from the top of the stack.

A familiar example of a stack is a spring-loaded stack of trays in a cafeteria.

Stacks have other uses, as in simulation. Imagine a rail yard in which cars not in use are kept on a single siding:

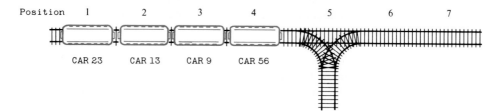

We can move CAR56 directly to, say, position 7. What if we want to move CAR13 to position 7? Obviously, we first must move CAR56 and CAR9 to the rail siding that connects at position 5. We can first push CAR56 onto it, and then CAR9. Note that, in effect, we have stacked the two cars. After the stacking, CAR9 is at the top; to get it back to the original rail, we pop the stack once. To get CAR56 back on the main siding, we pop the stack a second time.

Write a program that initializes an array of 10 character strings to "CAR1", "CAR2", ..., "CAR5" so that five elements have strings and five remain empty. A second array of pointers to strings, with size 3, simulates the stack, namely, the siding onto which cars can be pushed. The user enters a series of commands such as push, pop, and move_to_position N, where N is a number designating one of the 10 positions on the main rail. By using these commands, the user can move cars to different positions.

Can any car be moved to any position given the preceding restrictions?

6.16. Write a program TRANSLATION that translates sentences from English into the foreign language of your choice. The program uses a table-lookup method. There are two ragged arrays—one for words in English, the other for words in the foreign language. To translate an English word, we find the index of the English word and use this index in the array of foreign words. For example, suppose that we translate from English into German, and our English sentence is

    One is what one eats.

We locate the word One in the English table and use its index to find the German translation. After translating all the words, we might obtain

    Man ist was man isst.

Write a program that has a vocabulary of at least 30 words in each language. The program's input is a sentence in English, and its output is a translation into the foreign language.

6.17. Write a program that reads an integer n and several lines of text. The text that follows the integer n is printed right-justified, n characters per line, by adding extra spaces as evenly as possible. *Example:* If the input is

```
30
What's the difference between a mathematician and a
computer scientist? Answer: A mathematician has
all the theories and no answers. A computer scientist
has all the answers and no theories.
```

The output is

```
What's  the  difference  between
a mathematician and a computer
scientist?      Answer:       A
mathematician  has  all   the
theories  and  no  answers.   A
computer scientist has all the
answers   and   no    theories.
```

6.18. Write a program to shuffle a deck of cards and deal a hand of bridge. (A bridge deal divides a deck of cards into four hands of 13 cards each. The hands are labeled North, East, South, and West.)

Use an array of `int`s with 52 cells. Initialize the array to 1 in the first cell, 2 in the second cell, . . . , and 52 in the 52nd cell. Now swap the entry in the first cell with the entry in a cell at a random position; next, swap the entry in the second cell with the entry in a cell at a random position; and so on; and finally, swap the entry in the 52nd cell with the entry in a cell at a random position. Print the hands using the following conversion table:

Integer n	Suit	Value ($1 = Ace$, $11 = Jack$, $12 = Queen$, $13 = King$)
$1 \leq n \leq 13$	Club	n
$14 \leq n \leq 26$	Diamond	$n - 13$
$27 \leq n \leq 39$	Heart	$n - 26$
$40 \leq n \leq 52$	Spade	$n - 39$

Major bridge tournaments play with computer-generated hands.

6.19. Book Bingo is a game used by junior high teachers to spur interest in reading. A sample Book Bingo card follows:

```
Science     Poetry        Dog             Supernatural  Fantasy
Detective   Travel        Other Animals   Horse         Romance
How-To      Autobiog      Your Choice     Hist Fiction  Sports
Mystery     Sci Fiction   Adventure       Myths         Teens
Hobbies     Careers       Short Stories   History       Biography
```

After a student reads a book, he or she places a token in the square for the appropriate category. The first person to get five tokens in a row—

horizontally, vertically, or diagonally—wins. Write a program to create 30 Book Bingo cards using the preceding categories. The positions should be randomly assigned, except that Your Choice should always be in the position shown. Use a variant of the card-shuffling algorithm of Exercise 6.18 to assign random positions for the categories.

6.20. For the purpose of forming car pools, the region in which the employees of Hearty Hanna's Healthfood Hutch live was divided into 16 regions, and each region was assigned a number:

```
 1   2   3   4
 5   6   7   8
 9  10  11  12
13  14  15  16
```

Write a program that lists each employee, followed by a list of all other employees who live nearby. You must define "nearby." The input is a list of employees and their coded locations:

```
Joe Kusinski
2
Ming Lee
11
James O'Brien
12
     .
     .
     .
```

6.21. A *magic square* is a square matrix (i.e., a two-dimensional array in which each dimension has the same size) of integers. If SIZE is the size of each dimension, the magic square's elements are the integers 1 through SIZE^2. The square is "magic" in that every row, column, and diagonal has the same sum. *Example:*

6	1	8
7	5	3
2	9	4

is a magic square with SIZE = 3. Each row, column, and diagonal sums to 15.

The following is an algorithm for generating a magic square when SIZE is odd:

Start with 1 in the middle of the top row; then move up and left on a diagonal, assigning numbers in increasing order to empty spots. If a spot is occupied, move to the spot immediately under the present spot. After visiting the spot in the upper left-hand corner, move to the spot immediately under it. Otherwise, if you fall off the top of the square, move to the bottom of the column immediately to the left of the present column; if you fall off the side of the square, move to the far right of the row immediately above the present row.

Write a program that generates a magic square for SIZE = 5.

6.22. In this exercise, we assume that one `char` is stored per eight-bit byte.

A *leading separate numeric string* is a string whose first character is one of blank, −, or +. Each character following the first is one of the digits 0 through 9. *Example:*

`"−9037"`

is a leading separate numeric string. It is interpreted as representing the integer −9,037.

A *packed decimal array* is an array p of `chars`

in which each hexadecimal value $h_0, h_1, \ldots, h_{2k}$ is one of 0 through 9. The hexadecimal value h_{2k+1} is one of A through F. The packed decimal array p is interpreted as the decimal number

$$sign\ h_0 h_1 h_2 h_3 h_4 h_5 \cdots h_{2k}$$

where *sign* is + if h_{2k+1} is A, C, E, or F, and *sign* is − if h_{2k+1} is B or D. *Examples:* The packed decimal array

`90 32 1C`

represents the decimal number +90,321. The packed decimal array

`06 72 4D`

represents the decimal number −6,724. Packed decimal arrays are used when exact arithmetic is necessary. Many large computers provide machine instructions to compute with packed decimal arrays.

Write functions `lsn_to_packed` and `packed_to_lsn` to convert between leading separate numeric and packed decimal arrays. Write a `main` function that calls `lsn_to_packed` and `packed_to_lsn` several times to demonstrate that your functions are working.

6.23. Write several different sorting functions, and then use the program of Section 6.10 to compare the times of the sorting functions.

Storage Classes and Type Qualifiers

7

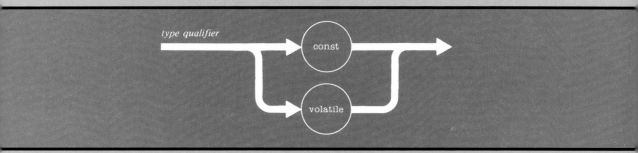

7.1 Storage Classes in a Single-Source File: `auto`, `extern`, `static`

7.2 Sample Application: Breaking Text into Pages

7.3 The Storage Class `register`

7.4 Storage Classes in Multiple-Source Files

7.5 Nested Blocks

7.6 Storage Classes for Functions

7.7 Sample Application: Savings Account Transactions

7.8 Type Qualifiers: `const` and `volatile`

7.9 Sample Application: A Scheduling Problem

Changes from Traditional C

Common Programming Errors

Programming Exercises

In this chapter, we examine storage classes for both variables and functions and show how a programmer can use storage classes to advantage. A variable's storage class determines when the cell is allocated and how long the cell remains in existence. The storage class of a variable or a function influences its visibility—that is, where in a program the variable or function can be referenced. The chapter concludes with a discussion of type qualifiers. A type qualifier advises the compiler about how a variable is expected to be accessed.

7.1   Storage Classes in a Single-Source File: `auto`, `extern`, `static`

We first discuss the storage classes `auto`, `extern`, and `static` for program variables, assuming that the entire program is in one source file. In Section 7.4 we treat storage classes in a program divided among two or more source files.

Before examining the various storage classes, we must introduce a couple of definitions. A **block** is a section of C code bounded by braces { }. For example, the body of a function is a block. A variable can be defined inside a block or outside all blocks. All the variable definitions that we have met so far were contained in blocks. If the definition of a variable is contained in a block, the smallest block that contains the definition is called its **containing block**.

Example 7.1.1.   In the program

```
#include <stdio.h>

int i = 0;

main()
{
        char c;

        while ( scanf( "%c", &c ) != EOF )
             i++;
        printf( "file length = %d\n", i );
}
```

the definition of the variable i is not contained in any block. The containing block of the variable c is the body of `main`.

We now discuss each of the storage classes `auto`, `extern`, and `static`.

`auto`

When we write

```
int num;
```

inside the body of a function, the variable num receives the default storage class `auto`. Further, an `auto` variable must be defined inside a function's body. It is legal to specify explicitly the storage class `auto` by writing

```
auto int num;
```

but it is more common to omit the storage class and write

```
int num;
```

For any storage class, if both the storage class and the data type are given, the storage class must come first.

Storage for an `auto` variable is allocated when control enters the variable's containing block and is released when control leaves its containing block. The term `auto` underscores the fact that storage is allocated and released automatically.

An `auto` variable is visible only in its containing block.

Example 7.1.2.   In the following slice of code, the `auto` variable `err_code` is defined:

```
/* allocation and release of storage
   for an auto variable */
void  err_handle( void )
{
     int  err_code;
       .
       .
       .

}
```

Storage for `err_code` is allocated when the function `err_handle` is invoked and is released when `err_handle` returns to the invoking function. If `err_handle` is invoked several times during the course of the program's execution, storage for `err_code` is allocated and released several times. The variable `err_code` is visible only in the function `err_handle`.

If an `auto` variable is simultaneously defined and initialized, the initialization is repeated each time storage is allocated. If an `auto` variable is defined but not initialized, the variable has an undefined value when control enters its containing block.

Example 7.1.3.   Suppose that we want to count the number of times the function `err_handle` of Example 7.1.2 is invoked in our program. The following approach

```
void  err_handle( void )
{
     int  err_code;
     int  count = 0;   /* dubious */

     ++count;
       .
       .
       .

}
```

does *not* work because the variable `count` has `auto` as its storage class. Each time `err_handle` is invoked, storage for `count` is allocated anew, and `count` is reset to zero. Each time `err_handle` returns, `count`'s storage cell is released, and the value of `count` is lost. After discussing the storage class `static`, we can modify this example so that it does count the number of times that `err_handle` is invoked.

extern

The default storage class for a variable defined outside a function's body is `extern`. Moreover, an `extern` variable must be defined *outside* all function bodies. Storage for an `extern` variable is allocated for the life of the program—conceptually just before the program as a whole begins executing. If an `extern` variable is simultaneously defined and initialized, it is initialized only once—when storage is allocated. If an `extern` variable is defined but not initialized, the system initializes it to zero once—when storage is allocated. An `extern` variable is visible in all functions that follow its definition.

Example 7.1.4.   In the following code, the variables `table` and `err_flag` have storage class `extern`. The variable `table` is visible in `main`, `read_table`, and `verify_table`. The variable `err_flag` is visible only in `read_table` and `verify_table` since it is defined before these functions; it is *not* visible in `main` since it is defined after `main`. Storage is allocated for `table` and `err_flag` once— just before the program as a whole begins executing. Since `table` and `err_flag` are not initialized in the program, the system initializes each of `table`'s 80 cells to zero and `err_flag` to zero.

```
#include <stdio.h>

int table[ 80 ];

main( )
{
        .
        .
        .
}

char err_flag;

char read_table( void )
{
        .
        .
        .
}

char verify_table( void )
{
        .
        .
        .
}
```

static

A `static` variable may be defined either inside or outside a function's body; the term `static` must be included in the definition. In this section we consider only `static` variables that are defined inside a function's body. In Section 7.4, we deal with `static` variables that are defined outside a function's body.

To define the `static` variable `i` to be of type `int`, we write

```
static int i;
```

Storage for a `static` variable is allocated for the life of the program—conceptually just before the program as a whole begins executing. If a `static` variable is simultaneously defined and initialized, it is initialized only once—when storage is allocated. If a `static` variable is defined but not initialized, the system initializes it to zero once—when storage is allocated. A `static` variable that is defined inside a function's body is visible only in its containing block.

> *Example 7.1.5.* In the following code, the variables `ptr` and `list` have storage class `static`. Storage is allocated for `ptr` and `list` once—just before the program as a whole begins executing. Since `list` is not initialized in the program, the system initializes each of `list`'s 100 cells to zero.

```
main( )
{
      static char *ptr = "Never trust anyone over 30.";
      static short list[ 100 ];
      .
      .
      .
}
```

In Example 7.1.3, we illustrated an unsuccessful attempt to count the number of times the function `err_handle` was invoked using the `auto` variable `count`. Each time `err_handle` was entered, storage for `count` was allocated anew, and each time `err_handle` was exited, storage was released and `count`'s value was lost. We can correct this problem with a `static` variable.

> *Example 7.1.6.* The following code successfully counts the number of times that `err_handle` is invoked:

```
void  err_handle( void )
{
   static  int  count = 0; /*  Initialize once only. */
   ++count;   /*  Count times err_handle is entered. */
      .
      .
      .
}
```

Storage for `count` is allocated once—for the life of the program—and `count` is initialized only once. Because storage for `count` remains for the life of the program, the value of `count` is not lost each time `err_handle` is exited. At the first invocation of `err_handle`, `count` is incremented to 1. When we leave `err_handle`, `count`'s cell and its contents remain in existence. The second time that `err_handle` is invoked, `count` is incremented to 2. Again, when we leave `err_handle`, `count`'s cell and its contents remain in existence. We see that `count` does indeed count the number of times that `err_code` is invoked.

Because `count` is defined *inside* a function's body, it is visible only in its containing block; that is, `count` is visible throughout `err_handle`, but nowhere else.

An `auto` or `static` variable that is defined inside a block is visible only in its containing block. For this reason, we can have identically named yet distinct variables in different functions.

Example 7.1.7. Each of the functions `compute_fed_tax` and `compute_state_tax` contains a variable named `taxes`:

```
float compute_fed_tax( float gross, float rate )
{
     float taxes;

          .
          .
          .

}
float compute_state_tax( float gross, float rate )
{
     float taxes;

          .
          .
          .

}
```

Although the two variables `taxes` have the same name, they reference different storage cells. The programmer does not have to be worried about whether a variable in one function shares a name with a variable in some other function.

A reference to an `auto` or `static` variable defined inside a block that has the same name as an `extern` variable is resolved in favor of the `auto` or `static` variable. The following example illustrates.

Example 7.1.8. In the program

```
#include <stdio.h>

int i = 0;

main( )
{
     void val( void );

     printf( "main's i = %d\n", i++ );
     val( );
     printf( "main's i = %d\n", i );
     val( );
}
void val( void )
{
     static int i = 100;
     printf( "val's i = %d\n", i++ );
}
```

the `extern` variable `i` is visible in `main` and ordinarily would be visible in `val`; however, because `val` has an identically named variable `i`, the reference in `val` to `i` is to the `static` variable defined in `val`.

When the program executes, we first print

```
main's i = 0
```

When `main` invokes `val` and we execute

```
printf( "val's i = %d\n", i++ );
```

because the reference is to the `static` variable i defined inside `val`, we print

```
val's i = 100
```

and i is incremented. When control returns from `val` to `main`, the cell for i in `val` remains because the variable i in `val` has storage class `static`. The program concludes by printing

```
main's i = 1
val's i = 101
```

Exercises

1. What is the error?

```
/* the file starts here */
auto   int   x, y, z;

void fun1( void )
{   .
       .
       .
}
```

2. In a variable definition, in what order do the variable's data type and storage class appear if both are given?

3. What is printed?

```
#include <stdio.h>

int i = 0;

main()
{
      void val( void );

      printf( "main's i = %d\n", i++ );
      val();
      printf( "main's i = %d\n", i );
      val();
}

void val( void )
{
      int i = 100;

      printf( "val's i = %d\n", i++ );
}
```

4. What is printed?

```c
#include <stdio.h>

main( )
{
    int i;
    int g( int x );

    for ( i = 1; i < 5; i++ )
        printf( "%d\n", g( i ) );
}

int g( int x )
{
    static int v = 1;
    int b = 3;

    v += x;
    return ( v + x + b );
}
```

5. What is printed?

```c
#include <stdio.h>

float x = 4.5;

main( )
{
    float y;
    float f( float a );

    x *= 2.0;
    y = f( x );
    printf( "%f\t%f", x, y );
}

float f( float a )
{
    a += 1.3;
    x -= 4.8;
    return ( a + x );
}
```

6. What is printed?

```c
#include <stdio.h>

main( )
{
    int y, z, s = 2;
    int f( int a ), g( int a );
```

```
            s *= 3;
            y = f( s );
            z = g( s );
            printf( "%d\t%d\t%d", s, y, z );
      }

      int t = 8;

      int f( int a )
      {
            a += -5;
            t -= 4;
            return ( a + t );
      }

      int g( int a )
      {
            a = 1;
            t += a;
            return ( a + t );
      }
```

7. What is printed?

```
      #include <stdio.h>

      main()
      {
            static int count = 5;
            printf( "count = %d\n", count-- );
            if ( count )
                  main();
      }
```

8. What happens in the program of Exercise 7 if `static int` is changed to `int`?

9. Write a function `walk_dynamic` that computes the Fibonacci sequence (see Example 4.8.3) by storing the value of `walk(i)` in an `extern` array at index `i`. Instead of using recursion to compute the previous values as in Figure 4.8.7, `walk_dynamic` simply looks the values up in the array. This method of computing a recursive sequence is known as *dynamic programming* (see, e.g., T. H. Cormen, C. E. Leiserson, and R. L. Rivest, *Introduction to Algorithms*, Cambridge, Mass.: MIT Press, 1990).

7.2 Sample Application: Breaking Text Into Pages

Problem

Write a program that writes the standard input to the standard output with a fixed number of lines per page. Print a page number at the top of each page.

Sample Input/Output _____

Assume that we write 54 lines per page: one line with the page number, a blank line, and 52 lines from the standard input.

```
Page 1

Line 1
Line 2
   .
   .
   .
Line 52
```

```
Page 2

Line 53
Line 54
   .
   .
   .
Line 104
```

```
             Page 3

             Line 105
             Line 106
                .
                .
Line 1          .
Line 2       Line 156
```

```
   .            .
   .            .
   .            .
```

Input   Output

Solution _____

A line is delimited by '\n'. We use the macro PAGE_LENGTH to denote the number of lines per page, not counting the page number line and the following blank line. We write two functions besides main. The first, print_page, prints the page number, a blank line, and up to PAGE_LENGTH lines. The function print_page returns FALSE (0) if end-of-file is encountered and TRUE (1) otherwise. (If nothing remains in the standard input, print_page prints nothing and returns FALSE.) The other function, echo_line, copies one line of the standard input to the standard output. It returns EOF if end-of-file was reached and a value different from EOF otherwise. The function main simply invokes print_page until print_page returns FALSE.

C Implementation

```
/*    This program writes the standard input to the standard output,
      PAGE_LENGTH + 2 lines per page. (The extra two lines are for
      the page number and one blank line.) A page consists of

      Page       <page number>
      <blank>

      followed by up to PAGE_LENGTH lines of text. */

#include <stdio.h>

#define TRUE 1

#define FALSE 0

#define PAGE_LENGTH 52

main()
{
        int print_page( void );

        /* print pages until standard input is exhausted */
        while ( print_page() )
                ;
}

/*    If no input remains, print_page simply returns FALSE;
      otherwise, it prints a page number and a blank line followed
      by PAGE_LENGTH lines (or fewer if end-of-file is reached) and
      finally a form feed. If end-of-file was reached, print_page
      returns FALSE; otherwise, it returns TRUE.
*/
int print_page( void )
{
        int line_no;
        int c;
        static int page_no = 1;
        int echo_line( void );

        if ( ( c = getchar() ) == EOF ) /* anything left? */
                return ( FALSE );

        /* Something was left. Put it back so echo_line works
           properly. */
        ungetc( c, stdin );
        printf( "Page      %d\n\n", page_no++ );

        for ( line_no = 0; line_no < PAGE_LENGTH; line_no++ )
                /* echo one line and check if end-of-file was
                   reached */
                if ( echo_line() == EOF ) {
                        putchar( '\f' ); /* form feed (jump to top of next
                                            page) */
```

```
                    return ( FALSE );
                }
        putchar( '\f' );
        return ( TRUE );
}
/*    echo_line copies one line (defined as everything up to and
      including the next newline) from the standard input to the
      standard output. It returns EOF if end-of-file was reached and
      non-EOF ('\n' actually) if end-of-file was not reached.
*/
int echo_line( void )
{
        int c;

        while ( ( c = getchar() ) != EOF && c != '\n' )
             putchar( c );

        if ( c == '\n' )
             putchar( '\n' );

        return ( c );
}
```

Discussion

The variable page_no in the function print_page is defined static, as the page number must be retained from one invocation of print_page to the next. This variable is initialized once to 1, at the start of the program's execution.

The function print_page invokes the library function ungetc. The function ungetc has two parameters: The first is a character and the second is a file pointer. The effect of ungetc is to return the character to the file referenced by the file pointer. After invoking ungetc, the next character read, by getchar for example, is the character returned by ungetc. If the second argument in ungetc is stdin (defined in *stdio.h*), the character is returned to the standard input. For example, if the standard input is

```
abc
```

the output when we execute

```
c = getchar();
putchar( c );
c = getchar();
putchar( c );
ungetc( c, stdin );
c = getchar();
putchar( c );
c = getchar();
putchar( c );
```

is

```
abbc
```

In print_page, if we encounter the end of the file immediately, we simply return FALSE:

```
if ( ( c = getchar() ) == EOF )
        return ( FALSE );
```

If we are not at end-of-file, c contains the character read. In this case, we return the character read to the standard input by invoking ungetc:

```
ungetc( c, stdin );
```

If we do not invoke ungetc, the character is lost and is not echoed by echo_line. We then print the page number.

We then use a for loop to print up to PAGE_LENGTH lines. If echo_line signals end-of-file, we print a form feed (which causes the next output to begin in column 1 of the next page) and return FALSE. If we print exactly PAGE_LENGTH lines, we print a form feed and return TRUE.

The function echo_line uses getchar to read data from the standard input. We read characters, and as long as we do not encounter end-of-file or '\n' (which signals the end of the line), we echo the standard input to the standard output. At the end of the while loop, the value of c is either '\n' or EOF. If c is equal to '\n', we echo the newline and return it:

```
if ( c == '\n' )
        putchar( '\n' );
```

If c is equal to EOF, we return EOF:

```
return ( c );
```

7.3 The Storage Class register

By defining a register variable, the programmer makes a recommendation to the C compiler that a CPU register is to be used as the storage cell. The recommendation is made for reasons of efficiency; the time required to access a CPU register is significantly less than the time required to access a cell in the computer's memory.

The C compiler is *not* required to follow the register recommendation. Indeed, some compilers (e.g., the VAX-11 C compiler) ignore the recommendation altogether, even though they may—for reasons of their own—use a register as the variable's storage cell. Optimizing compilers try to use registers for loop counters and other variables that are referenced frequently. These compilers may implement a variable as a register variable regardless of the programmer's instructions. If the compiler cannot or will not heed the register recommendation for a variable, the variable's storage class defaults to auto.

Example 7.3.1.   Because a programmer believes that the loop counter i will be accessed frequently in the program,

```
main()
{
        register int i;
                .
                .
                .
```

```
        for ( i = 0; i < 1000; i++ )
                    .
                    .
                    .

    }
```

i is defined as a register variable.

We may define a register *variable* only in a block, although the storage class register can be applied to the parameters of a function. Storage for register variables is allocated and released similarly to that for auto variables; storage is allocated when control enters the block containing the definition and is released when control exits this block. Thus a variable defined as register should have as narrow a scope as possible in order to maximize the number of registers available at any time. In Section 7.5, we discuss how to narrow a variable's scope within a function. Of course, the preceding comments assume a compiler willing and able to heed the register recommendation.

Because a register variable may be stored in a CPU register and not in memory, the address operator & cannot be applied to a register variable. It follows that, if a program needs a variable's address, the variable should not be defined as register.

Exercises

1. When is storage for a register variable allocated?
2. When is storage for a register variable released?
3. (True/False) A register variable may be defined either inside or outside a function's body.

7.4 Storage Classes in Multiple-Source Files

We have seen how blocks control the visibility of auto, static, and register variables within functions. We can use extern and static variables, defined outside blocks, to control the visibility of variables across functions. We begin with the storage class extern.

Recall from Section 7.1 that the definition of an extern variable occurs outside all blocks and that an extern variable is visible in all functions in the same file that follow the definition.

Example 7.4.1. Suppose that the following code resides in one file:

```
#include <stdio.h>

main()
{
    int p( void );
    int q( void );
    int k;
```

```
            k = p( );
            printf( "%d\n", k );
            k = q( );
            printf( "%d\n", k );
    }
    int count = 0;

    int p( void )
    {
            count++;
            return ( count );
    }
    int q( void )
    {
            count += 5;
            return ( count );
    }
```

The statement

```
    int count = 0;
```

is the definition of the `extern` variable `count`. This statement serves as a directive to allocate storage for `count` and to initialize `count` to 0. The variable `count` is visible in all functions that follow its definition in this file—namely, p and q. The variable `count` is *not* visible in `main`, and therefore a reference to `count` in `main` is illegal. The output of this program is

```
    1
    6
```

To extend the visibility of an `extern` variable beyond the functions that follow its definition, we write the keyword `extern`, then the data type, and then the variable's name. For example, to make the `extern` variable `count` of Example 7.4.1 visible in `main`, we write

```
    extern int count;
```

in `main`. We call

```
    extern int count;
```

a **declaration** of the `extern` variable `count`. An `extern` variable has exactly one *definition* that causes storage to be allocated for the variable and, optionally, an initialization of the variable. An `extern` variable may have several *declarations;* each makes the `extern` variable visible in its containing block, or if the declaration is not contained in a block, the `extern` variable is visible in all functions that follow the declaration.†

Example 7.4.2. If we add the declaration

```
    extern int count;
```

†Officially, a variable whose storage class is `auto`, `static`, or `register` also has a definition and a declaration. However, for such a variable, the definition and declaration coincide. Only for `extern` variables is the distinction apparent. For this reason, we refer to the definition/declaration of an `auto`, `static`, or `register` variable as the definition.

to main, the extern variable count will then be visible in main, and every reference to count in main will be to the variable count defined by the statement

```
int count = 0;
```

The output of the modified program

```
#include <stdio.h>
main( )
{
        extern int count;
        int p( void );
        int q( void );
        int k;

        count -= 10;
        printf( "%d\n", count );
        k = p( );
        printf( "%d\n", k );
        k = q( );
        printf( "%d\n", k );
}

int count = 0;

int p( void )
{
        count++;
        return ( count );
}

int q( void )
{
        count += 5;
        return ( count );
}
```

is

```
-10
-9
-4
```

Example 7.4.2 shows how we can declare an extern variable to extend its visibility to functions that precede its definition. A more common reason to declare an extern variable is to make it visible in another file, as Example 7.4.3 illustrates. (In Appendix G, we explain how to compile and link a program divided into two or more files.)

Example 7.4.3.   If we simply divide the program of Example 7.4.1 into files *A* and *B*, as shown, the reference to count in file *B* is illegal because count is unknown in file *B*.

```
/****************** BEGIN FILE A ******************/

#include <stdio.h>

main( )
{
```

```
        int p( void );
        int q( void );

        int k;

        k = p();
        printf( "%d\n", k );
        k = q();
        printf( "%d\n", k );
}

int count = 0;

int p( void )
{
        count++;

        return ( count );
}

/****************** END FILE A ********************/

/***************** BEGIN FILE B *******************/

int q( void )
{
        count += 5;       /* ILLEGAL reference to count */

        return ( count );
}

/****************** END FILE B ********************/
```

To make the extern variable count defined in file *A* visible in file *B*, we must declare count in file *B*:

```
/********* BEGIN REVISED FILE B *******************/

int q( void )
{
        extern int count;

        count += 5;         /* LEGAL reference to count */

        return ( count );
}

/************* END REVISED FILE B *****************/
```

The output of the program consisting of file *A* and revised file *B* is exactly the same as the output of the program of Example 7.4.1:

```
1
6
```

To summarize, the storage class extern may be used to allow different functions to access the same variable. Such a variable must be created exactly once by defining the variable outside all blocks. Although an extern variable must be defined outside all blocks, there are two syntactically legal ways to do so. First, the keyword extern must be omitted if the extern variable is not initialized at definition time. Second, the keyword `extern` may be either present or absent if the variable is initialized at definition time.

> *Example 7.4.4.* The definitions of the `extern` variables `inspection_date` and `max_capacity` illustrate the two legal ways to define an `extern` variable: `inspection_date` is defined without the keyword `extern` and `max_capacity` with the keyword `extern`. The attempted definition of `recommended_capacity` is illegal because the keyword `extern` is present but `recommended_capacity` is not initialized.

```
int              inspection_date;            /* legal definition */
extern float     max_capacity = 1200.50;     /* legal definition */
extern float     recommended_capacity;       /* ILLEGAL definition */

main( )
{
        .
        .
        .

}
```

Because the keyword `extern` is never required to define an `extern` variable, regardless of whether the `extern` variable is initialized at definition time, we recommend that the keyword `extern` be omitted when defining `extern` variables.

Once defined outside all blocks, an `extern` variable can be made visible in a block by declaring the variable in the block. If the variable is declared outside all blocks, it is visible in each of the functions that follow its declaration. Each declaration must include the keyword `extern`. Although an `extern` variable can be initialized in its definition, it cannot be initialized in any declaration.

By defining a `static` variable outside any block, we can achieve visibility in all functions that follow the definition just as if the variable were `extern`, but we can further guarantee that the variable will *not* be visible in any other file or in any function that precedes its definition in the same file. A `static` variable is *never* visible in more than one file.

> *Example 7.4.5.* Suppose that file *A* contains

```
    void clear( void )
    {
            .
            .
            .

    }

    static int dist;

    extern int pos;

    void draw( void )
    {
            dist = 222;
            pos = 333;
```

.
.
.

```
}
```

Both the `static` variable `dist` and the `extern` variable `pos` are visible in the function `draw`. (We assume that the `extern` variable `pos` has been defined in some other file.) However, `dist` is not visible in any function in any other file and cannot be made visible in another file by any declaration whatever. The storage class `static`, when used in this manner, protects the variable from being inadvertently accessed by some function in another file. By contrast, the `extern` variable `pos` is visible in `draw`, in the file where it is defined, and in any other file that contains the declaration

```
extern int pos;
```

Thus `pos`, unlike `dist`, may be visible across files.

In Appendix G, we tell how to compile, link, and run a C program divided among two or more source files in Turbo C under MS-DOS, VAX-11 C under VMS, and C under UNIX.

Exercises

1. Explain how a `static` variable may be made visible in several functions.
2. Can a `static` variable be visible in several files?
3. (True/False) The same `extern` variable may be defined in several different files.
4. Explain how an `extern` variable may be visible across several files.
5. In which of the following functions is each variable visible?

```
/***************** BEGIN FILE A *****************/

main( )
{
    extern int x;
    char c;
    .
    .
    .
}

float y;

void f1( void )
{
    .
    .
    .
}

/****************** END FILE A ********************/
```

```
/***************** BEGIN FILE B *******************/
char d;
float f2( int w )
{
     int v;
     .
     .
     .

}
int x;
void print_prompt( void )
{
     .
     .
     .

}
extern float y;
double far_out( int t )
{
     .
     .
     .

}
/****************** END FILE B *******************/
```

6. List some advantages and disadvantages of using variables that are visible in several functions.

7.5   Nested Blocks

So far, our examples have defined variables whose visibility is at least as large as the body of a function. This need not be the case; C allows us to restrict the visibility of a variable to a part of a function. We examine this situation in this section.

Recall that a block is a group of statements delimited by braces. A block may have other blocks nested in it; however, C forbids the nesting of one function's definition in another function's body. A variable defined in a block is visible in its containing block.

Example 7.5.1. Figure 7.5.1 shows nested blocks that contain definitions of variables. The variable var1 is the most widely visible; its scope extends from line 1 through line 19, thus encompassing the entire body of the function main. By contrast, the variable var2 is visible only in block 2, for it is defined after the opening left brace on line 6. Block 2 and therefore also var2's scope extend until the closing right brace on line 17. Finally, var3 is the least visible of the three variables, with its scope limited to block 3, which extends from line 12 through line 16.

An error would result from trying to access any of the three variables outside its scope. For example, var3 cannot be referenced before line 12 or after line 16, and

<u>Line</u>

```
      main( )
      /* block 1: lines 1 through 19 */

 1    {      int var1 = 10;
 2           var1 += 20;              /* Only var1 is visible here. */
 3
 4           /* block 2: lines 6 through 17 */
 5
 6           {    int  var2 = 100;
 7                var2 += 50;         /* var2 is visible in block 2. */
 8                var1 += 50;         /* var1 is visible in block 2. */
 9
10                /* block 3: lines 12 through 16 */
11
12                {   int  var3 = 500;
13                    var3 += 100;    /* var3 is visible in block 3. */
14                    var2 += 100;    /* var2 is visible in block 3. */
15                    var1 += 100;    /* var1 is visible in block 3. */
16                }
17           }
18           var1 += 100;            /* Only var1 is still visible. */
19    }
```

Figure 7.5.1 Variable scopes.

<u>Line</u>

```
      #include <stdio.h>
      main( )
      /* block 1: lines 1 through 20 */

 1    {    int  var1 = 10;
 2         var1 += 20;
 3         printf( "%d\n", var1 ):             /* Value printed-30 */
 4
 5         /* block 2: lines 7 through 17 */
 6
 7         {    int  var1 = 100;
 8              var1 += 50;
 9              printf( "%d\n", var1 );      /* Value printed-150 */
10
11             /* block 3: lines 13 through 16 */
12
13              {    int  var1 = 500
14                   var1 += 100;
15                   printf( "%d\n", var1 ); /* Value printed-600 */
16              }
17         }
18         var1 += 100;
19         printf( "%d\n", var1 );             /* Value printed-130 */
20    }
```

Figure 7.5.2 Variable scopes and variable name conflicts.

var2 cannot be referenced before line 6 or after line 17. The variable var1 cannot be referenced before line 1 or after line 19; that is, var1 cannot be referenced outside main's body.

Example 7.5.1 becomes more interesting and informative, but also somewhat contrived, if the variables in the three blocks have the same name (see Figure 7.5.2). (The program is slightly longer, for it includes print statements to aid clarification.) Although the three variables share a name, they are *distinct*. How does C resolve this conflict? It uses the definition in the "smallest" block. More precisely, a reference to a variable x is associated with the definition in the smallest block that contains both the reference to x and a definition of x.

Example 7.5.2.   In Figure 7.5.2, the smallest block that contains both the reference to var1 in line 2 and a definition of var1 is block 1; therefore, var1 referenced at line 2 is the variable defined in block 1 at line 1. This explains why we print 30 at line 3.

The smallest block that contains both the reference to var1 in line 8 and a definition of var1 is block 2; therefore, var1 referenced at line 8 is the variable defined in block 2 at line 7. This explains why we print 150 at line 9.

The smallest block that contains both the reference to var1 in line 14 and a definition of var1 is block 3; therefore, var1 referenced at line 14 is the variable defined in block 3 at line 13. This explains why we print 600 at line 15.

The smallest block that contains both the reference to var1 in line 18 and a defini-

Line

```
       #include <stdio.h>
       main()
       /* block 1: lines 1 through 20 */
 1     {    int   var1 = 10;
 2            var1 += 20;
 3            printf( "%d\n", var1 );              /* Value printed-30 */
 4
 5            /* block 2:  lines 7 through 17 */
 6
 7            {    int   var1 = 100;
 8                  var1 += 50;
 9                  printf( "%d\n", var1 );      /* Value printed-150 */
10
11                  /* block 3: lines 13 through 16 */
12
13                  {
14                      var1 += 100;
15                      printf( "%d\n", var1 ); /* Value printed-250 */
16                  }
17            }
18            var1 += 100;
19            printf( "%d\n", var1 );              /* Value printed-130 */
20     }
```

Figure 7.5.3 More variable scopes and variable name conflicts.

tion of var1 is block 1; therefore, var1 referenced at line 18 is the variable defined in block 1 at line 1. This explains why we print 130 at line 19.

Example 7.5.3. Suppose that var1 had not been defined in block 3 (see Figure 7.5.3). Now the smallest block that contains both the reference to var1 in line 14 and a definition of var1 is block 2; therefore, var1 referenced at line 14 is the variable defined in block 2 at line 7. This explains why we print 250 at line 15.

Example 7.5.4. Now suppose that we amend Figure 7.5.3 by defining an extern variable var1 outside main (see Figure 7.5.4). The extern variable is visible throughout the function main—*except* when it conflicts, in name, with an identically named variable defined inside a block. The result is that the output in Figure 7.5.4 is identical to that of Figure 7.5.3. The extern variable var1 conflicts in name with the auto variables named var1 defined in the various blocks, and in this case, the definition in the smallest block is still used.

Exercises

1. May any block in a C program contain a variable definition?

2. Explain how it is possible in C for different variables to have the same name.

Line

```
        #include <stdio.h>
        int var1;   /* yet another var1 */

        main()
        /* block 1: lines 1 through 20 */

 1      {    int  var1 = 10;
 2           var1 += 20;
 3           printf( "%d\n", var1 );          /* Value printed–30 */
 4
 5           /* block 2: lines 7 through 17 */
 6
 7           {    int  var1 = 100;
 8                var1 += 50;
 9                printf( "%d\n", var1 );    /* Value printed–150 */
10
11                /* block 3: lines 13 through 16 */
12
13                {
14                     var1 += 100;
15                     printf( "%d\n", var1 ); /* Value printed–250 */
16                }
17           }
18           var1 += 100;
19           printf( "%d\n", var1 );          /* Value printed–130 */
20      }
```

Figure 7.5.4 Even more variable scopes and variable name conflicts.

3. Is it legal to define, in the same block, two variables with the same name?

4. (True/False) Variables defined in the same function always have the same scope.

5. Does an `extern` variable always win a name conflict with a `static` variable?

6. What is printed?

```
#include <stdio.h>

int  x = 999;

main()
{
     int x = -999;

     {
          int x = 1;
          { int x = 2;

            printf( "%d\n", x );
          }
          printf( "%d\n", x );
     }
     printf( "%d\n", x );
}
```

7.6   Storage Classes for Functions

A function, like a variable, has a storage class, but the storage class of a function, unlike that of a variable, must be either `extern` or `static`. The default storage class for functions is `extern`, which typically is omitted from the function's definition. The syntax

```
/* explicit use of extern in a function's definition */
extern  int print_stock_market_tape( void )
{   .
     .
     .
}
```

is legal but clumsy. The preceding syntax says that `print_stock_market_tape` has `extern` as its storage class and returns an `int`; it does *not* say that `print_stock_market_tape` returns an `extern int`.

An `extern` variable can be visible across functions, even functions in different files. The same is true of an `extern` function, which can be invoked by any other function, whatever its storage class, in any file.

If we want to restrict the visibility of a function `f`, we must

* *Explicitly* define `f`'s storage class to be `static`.
* Place the functions that invoke `f` in the same file as `f`, either above or below it.
* Place the functions in which `f` is not to be visible in a different file from the file that contains `f`.

Example 7.6.1. Suppose that file *A* contains only the functions `main`, `bid`, and `deal`:

```
/* File A -- contains only main, bid, and deal */

main()
{
    void  bid( void );
    int   deal( void );
            .
            .
            .

}
void bid( void )
{   .
    .
    .
}
/* deal is visible only to main and bid */
static int deal( void )
{   .
    .
    .
}
```

Because `deal` is a `static` function, only the functions `main` and `bid` may invoke `deal`. No other function in any other file can invoke `deal`.

Many C programs get along without `static` functions, but if an application requires limited visibility for one or more functions, C can satisfy the requirement with `static` functions housed in a file with only those other functions meant to invoke it.

Exercises

1. What is the error?

```
auto int fun1( int parm1 )
{
    .
    .
    .

}
```

2. (True/False) In C, the default storage class for a function is `extern`.

3. Explain how we can ensure that the function `fun5` can be invoked only by the functions `fun1`, `fun2`, `fun3`, and `fun4`.

4. Is a `static` function visible only in functions defined after it in the same file?

7.7   Sample Application: Savings Account Transactions

Problem

Write a program that updates a savings account, given a sequence of deposits and withdrawals. After each transaction, ask for an interest rate; then calculate what the balance would be in a year's time if there were no more transactions during the year and if the interest rate did not change during the year. Assume that the interest on the account is compounded daily.

Sample Input/Output

A plus sign indicates a deposit, and a minus sign indicates a withdrawal. Input is in color; output is in black.

```
Make a transaction? (y/n)   y

Transaction? (+/-)   +
Amount?  500

Current interest rate (as a percentage)?   5.6

Balance of 500.000000 would be 528.796569 in one year.

Make a transaction? (y/n)   y

Transaction? (+/-)   -
Amount?  100

Current interest rate (as a percentage)?   4

Balance of 400.000000 would be 416.323397 in one year.

Make a transaction? (y/n)   n
```

C Implementation

```c
/* defs.h-symbolic constants and macros for the       */
/*       BANK_BALANCE program; included in savings.c. */
#define  YES                 'y'
#define  NO                  'n'

#define  PROMPT       printf( "\n\n\tMake a transaction? (y/n)   " )
#define  READ_RESPONSE( resp )  (   resp = getchar(), getchar(), \
                               resp = resp )

#define  ADD                 '+'
#define  SUBTRACT            '-'

#define  TRANSACTION_PROMPT  printf( "\n\n\tTransaction? (+/-)   " )
#define  READ_TYPE( trans )  trans = getchar(), getchar()

#define  AMOUNT_PROMPT       printf( "\n\tAmount?   " )
#define  READ_AMOUNT( amt )  scanf( "%f", (&amt) ), getchar()

#define  PRINT_ERROR     printf( "\n\n\tImproper transaction.\n" )

#define  INTEREST_PROMPT \
    printf( "\n\n\tCurrent interest rate (as a percentage)?   " )
```

```
#define   READ_RATE( rate )     scanf( "%f", (&rate) ), getchar()

#define   PRINT_YEAR_END_BALANCE( bal, year_end_bal ) \
    printf( "\n\n\tBalance of %f would be %f in one year.", \
            bal, year_end_bal )

        /* end of file defs.h */

        /* savings.c -- functions main and update */
/*                    BANK_BALANCE program --                        */
/*                                                                   */
/*   This program prompts the user for a bank transaction,           */
/*   either depositing or withdrawing from a savings account.        */
/*   It then asks for the amount by which to update the              */
/*   balance and the current interest rate to calculate the          */
/*   new balance in a year's time. (Interest is assumed to be        */
/*   compounded daily.)                                              */
/*                                                                   */
/*   In addition to the header files, the program is spread          */
/*   across two files. savings.c contains main and the static        */
/*   function update; calc_int.c contains the function              */
/*   calculate_interest. The variable balance is static and          */
/*   visible throughout savings.c.                                   */

#include <stdio.h>
#include "defs.h"

static float balance = 0.0; /* current amount in savings account */

main()
{
    char   transaction; /* either deposit (+) or withdraw (-) */
    char   response; /* either YES or NO */
    float  amount;
    float  interest_rate;
    float  year_end_balance;

    void   update( float amt ); /* updates account after a
                                    deposit or a withdrawal */
    float  calculate_interest( float balance, float rate );

    PROMPT;

    while ( READ_RESPONSE( response ) != NO ) {

      TRANSACTION_PROMPT;
      READ_TYPE( transaction );

      switch ( transaction ) {
      case ADD:
      case SUBTRACT:
          AMOUNT_PROMPT;
          READ_AMOUNT( amount );
          if ( transaction == ADD )
              update ( amount );
```

```
            else
                update( -amount );
            INTEREST_PROMPT;
            READ_RATE( interest_rate );
            interest_rate /= 100.0; /* convert percent to decimal */
            year_end_balance =
                calculate_interest( balance, interest rate );
            PRINT_YEAR_END_BALANCE( balance, year_end_balance );
            break;
        default:
            PRINT_ERROR;
            break;
        }
        PROMPT;

    }
}

/*  update( amount ) -- adds amount to balance; invoked */
/*                      by main                         */

static void update( float amt )
{
        balance += amt;
}
              /* end of file savings.c */

              /* calc_int.c */

/*  calculate_interest( balance, rate )  --              */
/*                                                        */
/*  The function expects a balance and an interest rate and */
/*  returns the balance in one year given the interest rate; */
/*  it assumes that the interest is compounded daily for 365 */
/*  days. For clarity, the function breaks down the        */
/*  computation into several steps.                        */

#include <math.h>

#define  DAYS_PER_YEAR   365.0

float   calculate_interest( float balance, float rate )
{
        double  year_end_bal;
        double  avg_rate;

        avg_rate = ( double ) rate / DAYS_PER_YEAR;

        year_end_bal =
            ( double ) balance * pow( 1 + avg_rate, DAYS_PER_YEAR );

        return ( ( float ) year_end_bal );
}
        /* end of file calc_int.c */
```

Discussion

In addition to *defs.h* and the system #include files, the program occupies two files: *savings.c* contains the functions main and update; and *calc_int.c* contains the function calculate_interest. Because the function update is static, it is visible only to main. We want to be sure that only main can invoke update. Because the variable balance is defined outside and before the functions main and update, it is visible in each of these functions. We want to be sure that each function in this file updates one and the same variable named balance. Because the variable balance is static, it is known *only* to these functions. We want to be sure that only the functions in *savings.c* can alter the variable balance.

The function calculate_interest computes the balance in a year's time, assuming that there are no more transactions during the year and that the interest rate does not change during the year. The balance at the end of a year, assuming that interest is compounded daily, is computed by the formula

$$YB = B * \left(1 + \frac{R}{365} \right)^{365}$$

where *YB* is the balance at the end of a year, *B* is the present balance, and *R* is the annual interest rate. The function calculate_interest explicitly uses the cast operator

    (double)

to convert the float parameters to double. We use the library function pow to compute the exponential, which is the reason that we include the header file *math.h*. The function pow expects both its arguments to be of type double and raises its first argument to the power of its second. Notice that we have divided the computation into steps for clarity. We explicitly cast the value returned, year_end_bal, to float.

The header file *defs.h* contains several macros to read user input and write messages. Notice that each input macro reads user input and then executes getchar() to throw away the trailing newline. For example, the macro READ_TYPE

```
#define  READ_TYPE( trans )  trans = getchar(), getchar()
```

reads one character, copies the value into the variable trans, and then reads and discards the trailing newline.

The macro READ_RESPONSE

```
#define  READ_RESPONSE( resp )  ( resp = getchar(), getchar(), \
                                  resp = resp )
```

reads one character, copies the value into the variable resp, reads and discards the trailing newline, and then executes

    resp = resp

The value of an expression that uses the comma operator is the value of the last expression; thus, the value of READ_RESPONSE(resp) is resp. If we omit resp = resp, the value of READ_RESPONSE(resp) is newline, the value read by the second expression getchar().

7.8 Type Qualifiers: const and volatile

Each variable has a *data type* such as char or int and a *storage class* such as auto or extern. (The official designation is *type specifier*, but we use the more familiar *data type*.) We explain in this section how a variable also may have a **type qualifier** such as `const` or `volatile`. (The names `const` and `volatile` are keywords.) We begin with the syntax of type qualifiers in general and then clarify what each means.

Each type qualifier is an option in a variable's definition. If a type qualifier occurs, it comes after the storage class and before the data type.

> *Example 7.8.1.* In the program
>
> ```
> volatile float  salary;
>
> main()
> {
>         static const int ssnum;
>
>                 .
>                 .
>                 .
>
> }
> ```

the variable `salary` has type qualifier `volatile` and the variable `ssnum` has type qualifier `const`. Any combination of storage class, data type, and type qualifier is possible. Figure 7.8.1 shows some possibilities.

Storage Class	Type Qualifier	Data Type
auto	const	int
auto	volatile	char
static	const	float
static	volatile	float
extern	volatile	double
extern	const	char

Figure 7.8.1 Some possible combinations of storage class, type qualifier, and data type.

A variable's definition can include both type qualifiers:

```
const volatile int   flag;
```

A variable with type qualifiers may be initialized when defined.

> *Example 7.8.2.* The code slice
>
> ```
> const float  life_long_salary = 256.45;
> ```

defines the `const` variable `life_long_salary` and initializes it to 256.45.

Finally, type qualifiers also can occur in parameter declarations.

> *Example 7.8.3.* The function definition
>
> ```
> void fun( const int n )
> {
>             .
>             .
>             .
>
> }
> ```

illustrates how a type qualifier can occur in a parameter declaration.

We clarify each type qualifier separately and then consider them in combination. We conclude with a discussion of type qualifiers and compiler optimization.

const

The keyword const stands for *constant* because it allows the programmer to define a *variable* as a constant—that is, to define a variable whose value, once assigned, is not to be changed. Recall that C also allows the programmer to #define a macro. The difference is that a const variable has an associated storage cell, whereas a macro has a value but no associated storage cell. A const variable's value is set when the program executes (e.g., by interactively assigning a value to the variable with a call to a function such as scanf), whereas a macro's value is set at compile time (when the preprocessor substitutes the value given in the #define directive for the macro).

> *Example 7.8.4.* The program slice
>
> ```
> const float     life_long_salary;   /* definition */
> life_long_salary = 256.45;          /* assignment */
>                        .
>                        .
>                        .
> life_long_salary = 300.99;              /*** ERROR ***/
> ```
>
> contains an error because life_long_salary, with const as a type qualifier, should not have its value of 256.45 updated to 300.99 or anything else. The compiler may generate an error message. For example, if the code slice of Example 7.8.4 is in the function main, the Turbo C compiler issues the error message
>
> ```
> Cannot modify a const object in function main
> ```
>
> when it tries to compile the statement
>
> ```
> life_long_salary = 300.99;
> ```
>
> By the way, the compiler would issue exactly the same error message even if we tried to update life_long_salary's value to the original value of 256.45. A const variable's value, once set, should not be reset to any value, including its initial one.

volatile

The type qualifier volatile indicates that a variable's storage cell might be referenced by something besides statements in the program that defines the variable.

> *Example 7.8.5.* In the code
>
> ```
> /* define and initialize an extern volatile int */
> volatile int    wait_flag = 1;
>
> /* main invokes the function busy_wait, which */
> /* references wait_flag.                      */
> ```

```
main()
{
        void  busy_wait( void );

        busy_wait();   /* wait awhile... */
                .

                .

                .
}

/* wait until system sets wait_flag to zero */
void busy_wait( void )
{
        /* not endlessly waiting, i hope... */
        while ( wait_flag )
                ;
}
```

the variable wait_flag is defined as volatile in order to signal the programmer's expectation that something outside the C program—for example, a routine from the machine's operating system—eventually alters wait_flag's value; otherwise, the while loop in busy_wait becomes an infinite loop. Exactly how the programmer knows that the operating system can reset wait_flag's value is not at issue here; the point is that the volatile type qualifier signals the programmer's expectation that wait_flag can be referenced by something besides the code in this program. Why the programmer would want to qualify a variable as volatile is clarified later.

Type Qualifiers in Combination

The type qualifiers may occur alone or together.

Example 7.8.6. Consider the variable definition:

```
static volatile const char    c;
```

The variable c is volatile, and so is expected to have its value set by something outside the program. As a const variable, c should have its value set but not reset.

Parameters with Type Qualifiers

Example 7.8.7. In the following program, the function main defines a variable num and passes it as an argument to the function fun that has a const parameter. The programmer is informing the system that after the value of num is copied to the parameter n, the value of n will not be changed. Notice that since the variable num in main is not qualified, its value can be changed in any way whatsoever.

```
main()
{
        int num = 25;
        void fun( const int n );
```

```
                           .
                           .
                           .
                fun( num );
                           .
                           .
                           .

        }
        void fun( const int n )
        {

                    .
                    .
                    .

        }
```

Example 7.8.8.   The following program shows how to use the library function qsort that sorts an array of arbitrary data type.

```c
#include <stdio.h>
#include <stdlib.h>

#define MAX_SIZE 100

int compare( const void *first, const void *second );

main()
{
    int seq[ MAX_SIZE ], how_many, i;

    for ( how_many = 0;
            how_many < MAX_SIZE
                && scanf( "%d", &seq[ how_many ] ) != EOF;
            how_many++ )
                ;

    qsort( seq, how_many, sizeof ( seq[ 0 ] ), compare );

    for ( i = 0; i < how_many; i++ )
        printf( "%d\n", seq[ i ] );
}

int compare( const void *first, const void *second )
{
    return ( *( ( int * ) first ) - *( ( int * ) second ) );
}
```

The program reads integers until end-of-file, sorts them, and then prints them. The function qsort uses the quicksort algorithm (to be explained in Section 9.7). The function qsort uses a pointer to a function. The function pointed to, in turn, uses const parameters.

The function qsort is declared in the standard header file *stdlib.h.* Its prototype declaration is

```c
void qsort( void *start, size_t no_elts, size_t size_elt,
        int ( *cmp ) ( const void *, const void * ) );
```

The parameter `start` is the address of the array to sort. Since `qsort` sorts arbitrary data, `start` is declared as pointer to `void`. The parameter `no_elts` is the number of elements in the array to sort, and `size_elt` is the size of one cell of the array in bytes. The type `size_t` is defined in *stdlib.h* to be one of the built-in types appropriate to the local implementation. For example, in Turbo C, `size_t` is `unsigned int`. The parameter `cmp` is a pointer to a function that compares two elements whose data type is the same as that of the array and returns an integer to signal the result of the comparison. Before invoking `qsort`, the programmer must supply a comparison function suitable for the data type to be sorted. The arguments to the comparison function `*cmp` are pointers to the two items to be compared. Since `qsort` must compare data of arbitrary type, the type of the parameters of `*cmp` is pointer to `void`. Specifying the type qualifier `const` indicates that `*cmp` will not change the data to which its parameters point. The value of the expression `*cmp( *first, *second )` is negative if `*first` is to the left of `*second` in the sorted order; `*cmp( *first, *second )` is zero if `*first` is equal to `*second`; and `*cmp( *first, *second )` is positive if `*first` is to the right of `*second` in the sorted order. Since `qsort` receives a pointer to a comparison function along with the start and size information, it can sort data of arbitrary size and type.

In the invocation of `qsort`, the argument `seq`, which is of type pointer to `int`, is automatically converted to pointer to `void` because in the declaration of `qsort` the first argument is of type pointer to `void`. We use the `sizeof` function to compute the size of one cell of the array in bytes. Recall (Section 6.9) that a function's name is a pointer constant that can be regarded as the address of the function; thus, placing `compare` in `qsort`'s argument list correctly passes a pointer to the function `compare`.

In the function `compare`, we must cast the arguments `first` and `second`, which are of type pointer to `void`, to pointer to `int` before subtracting them. If these arguments are not cast, we receive an error message informing us that we are attempting to subtract variables of an illegal data type.

To sort an array `seq` of type other than `int`, we need not alter the line

```
qsort( seq, how_many, sizeof ( seq[ 0 ] ), compare );
```

We need only change the definition of `seq` and write a new function `compare`.

Type Qualifiers and Compiler Optimization

The type qualifier `const` can benefit the programmer directly. If the programmer wants a variable to behave as a constant, he or she can guard against attempted updates to the variable by giving it the type qualifier `const`.

The type qualifier `volatile` also can benefit the programmer, but in a more subtle way. The programmer can discourage the compiler from optimizing a variable by qualifying it as `volatile`. A full discussion of optimization is beyond the scope of this book, so instead we sketch the basic ideas.

Modern computer systems typically have a *hierarchical storage system* and *optimizing compilers*. A storage system is hierarchical in the sense that storage is partitioned, for example, into CPU registers, read-only internal memory (ROM), read/write internal memory (random access memory or RAM), fast external storage (e.g., disks), slow external storage (e.g., tapes), and so on. Each of these partitions may contain further partitions. The important point is that access times to storage in these partitions can differ significantly. For example, access time to a CPU register is typically faster by a factor of at least 10 than access to a RAM storage cell. For this reason, an optimizing compiler tries to use CPU registers as storage for frequently accessed variables.

In order to optimize the code slice

```
for ( i = 0; i < limit; ++i ) {
        .

        .

        .
}
```

a compiler might reserve a CPU register rather than a RAM cell as storage for i because i is referenced in the for loop limit times. In Section 7.3, we saw that the programmer can recommend this action to the compiler by defining i with the storage class register.

The type qualifier const also serves as a *recommendation* to the compiler that it try optimizing the variable. The compiler knows that a const variable should be assigned a value once only; thereafter, the value should not be altered. A specific partition in the system's hierarchical memory may be especially suited for just this kind of reference to a storage cell.

The qualifier volatile warns the compiler against certain kinds of optimization. For example, suppose that the variable wait_flag in Example 7.8.5 did not have volatile as a type qualifier but that its value still could be altered by something outside the program that defines this variable. Suppose further that no statement in this program alters wait_flag's initial value of 1. An optimizing compiler, recognizing that wait_flag's value cannot be reset from within the program, might reserve storage for wait_flag in an area of hierarchical memory that prevents any further updates to wait_flag. The result is that the while loop in busy_wait becomes an infinite loop. By including the type qualifier volatile, we warn the compiler against this kind of optimization. In effect, the type qualifier volatile tells the compiler that a variable may be referenced in ways that are hidden from the compiler but known to the programmer.

We emphasize that type qualifiers serve only as *recommendations* to the compiler about whether to optimize. (However, the type qualifier const may cause the compiler to issue an error at any attempted update of a const variable.) The type qualifiers thus allow the programmer only to advise the compiler, not to coerce it, with respect to optimization. Further, even if the compiler does follow a recommendation to optimize, the compiler does so in system-dependent ways. It is legal to qualify a variable as const and volatile even though, on a particular system, the use of both type qualifiers might send conflicting signals to the compiler: The const qualifier might encourage the compiler to use a particular optimization, whereas the volatile qualifier might discourage the compiler from using that very optimization.

Exercises

1. What is the error?

```
volatile static int   fail_flag;
```

2. What is the error?

```
main( )
{
    static const float      real;
    char                    code = 'A';
    real = 99.9;
            .
            .
            .
    if ( code != 'A' )
        real = 0.0;      /* set to zero */
    else
        real = 99.9;     /* reset to initial value */
            .
            .
            .
}
```

3. Are the following variable definitions equivalent?

```
const volatile int  fail_flag; /* version 1 */
volatile const int  fail_flag; /* version 2 */
```

4. Is it legal for a parameter to be declared with a type qualifier?

5. Is it legal for a parameter to be declared with more than one type qualifier?

6. In the following code, is it legal for the function f to change the value of y?

```
main( )
{
        const int x = 1;
        void f( int y );
            .
            .
            .
        f( x );
            .
            .
            .
}
void f( int y )
{
        .
        .
        .
}
```

7. Rewrite the function compare of Example 7.8.8 so that when the program invokes qsort, the array of ints is sorted in decreasing order.

8. Write a program similar to that of Example 7.8.8 that reads strings into an array and sorts them in alphabetical order.

9. Write a program similar to that of Example 7.8.8 that reads strings into an array and sorts them in reverse alphabetical order.

10. Modify the program of Example 7.8.8 so that the program reads integers until encountering a negative integer (which is discarded). Then the program invokes `qsort` to sort the integers read in increasing order. Next, the program reads integers until end-of-file. After each integer is read, the program invokes the library function `bsearch` (see Appendix E) to determine whether the integer is in the array. If the integer is present, the program prints a message to that effect and also prints its index in the array. If the integer is not present, the program simply prints a message to that effect.

7.9   Sample Application: A Scheduling Problem

Problem

Given the start and finish times of each activity in a set, find a conflict-free subset of activities of maximum size. A conflict-free set of activities is one in which, given any two distinct activities, one always finishes before the other starts. For the set shown in the sample input, there is a schedule consisting of four nonconflicting activities, as shown in the output, but it is impossible to schedule five nonconflicting activities.

Sample Input/Output

Each line of input gives the start and finish times (in that order) of one activity.

```
 6  10     Optimal schedule:
 1   5         1    5
 1   6         5    7
 9  12         9   12
 5   7        13   16
 6  14
 3   7
10  14
13  16

  Input          Output
```

Solution

We use a greedy algorithm. A *greedy algorithm* is an algorithm that optimizes the choice at each iteration without regard to previous choices. The principle can be summarized as "doing the best locally." In this problem, since we want to choose the maximum number of conflict-free activities, at each iteration we choose an activity with the minimum finish time that does not conflict with the previously chosen activities. The idea is that minimizing the finish time at each iteration leaves the maximum number of activities to pick from at the next iteration. Optimizing at each iteration does *not* in general lead to an optimal solution (see Exercises 2 and 3); however, as we will show in the Discussion section, the greedy method does give an optimal solution to our scheduling problem.

We show how our greedy algorithm works for the sample input. Among all activities, 1,5 has the minimum finish time; thus it is chosen first. Since activities 1,6 and 3,7 conflict with 1,5, they are excluded from any further consideration. Thus, at the second iteration we select from among activities

$$6,10 \quad 9,12 \quad 5,7 \quad 6,14 \quad 10,14 \quad 13,16,$$

5,7, the one with the minimum finish time. At the third iteration the available activities are

$$9,12 \quad 10,14 \quad 13,16.$$

We choose activity 9,12 since it has the minimum finish time. At the fourth iteration we select activity 13,16 since it is the only one left. At this point the algorithm terminates with the optimal schedule

$$1,5 \quad 5,7 \quad 9,12 \quad 13,16.$$

We represent each activity as a string. The start time is right-justified within the field consisting of the first five characters, and the finish time is right-justified within the field consisting of the next five characters. Thus, to sort the activities on the finish field, we simply sort the strings on the second field of five characters. Since the integers are right-justified, sorting as strings is the same as sorting as numbers. We write a general sorting function that can sort any number of strings on a field of arbitrary size beginning at any specified index. We place this function in its own file and link it to the main file that implements the greedy scheduling algorithm. In this way, this general sorting function is available to any program that needs to sort strings.

C Implementation

```
              /* begin file: schedule.c */

/* This program finds a conflict-free, optimal schedule of
   activities. More precisely, given the start and finish times of
   a set of activities, the program finds a subset of activities
   of maximum size in which, given any two distinct activities,
   one always finishes before the other starts.

   This file must be linked to the file sort_str.c that contains
   the string-sorting function sort_str.

   The input is of the form

   sssssfffff
   sssssfffff
      . . .

   where each line gives the start and finish times of one
   activity. sssss is the start time (an integer) right-justified
   in columns 1-5, and fffff is the finish time (also an integer)
   right-justified in columns 6-10. The input file name is
   supplied on the command line.
 */

#include <stdio.h>
#include <string.h>

#define Max_No_Strings 100
#define Str_Len 12
#define Field_Width 5
```

```
/* select[ i ] = 0, if activity i is not selected.
   select[ i ] = 1, if activity i is selected. */
int select[ Max_No_Strings ];

/* count = number of activities */
int count;

char str[ Max_No_Strings ][ Str_Len ];

void sort_str( char **s, int num_elts,
               int str_size, int start, int length ),
     greedy_selector( void );

main( int argc, char **argv )
{
   int i;
   FILE *fp;
   fp = fopen( argv[ 1 ], "r" );

   for ( count = 0;
         count < Max_No_Strings &&
             fgets( str[ count ], Str_Len, fp ) != NULL;
         count++ )
      ;

   greedy_selector();

   printf( "\n\nOptimal schedule:\n\n" );

   for ( i = 0; i < count; i++ )
      if ( select[ i ] )
         printf( "%s", str[ i ] );
}

/* This function implements the greedy
   algorithm to find an optimal schedule. */
void greedy_selector( void )
{
   int i, j;

   /* Sort strings by finish time.
      The arguments to sort_str are:

          array of strings
          number of strings
          size in bytes of each string (all strings must
             be the same length)
          index of substring on which to sort
          length of substring on which to sort

      We are sorting on finish times that occur in columns
      6-10: begin at index Field_Width and of length
      Field_Width.
    */
   sort_str( str, count, sizeof ( str[ 0 ] ),
             Field_Width, Field_Width );
```

```
   /* always select activity with smallest finish time */
   select[ 0 ] = 1;

   for ( j = 0, i = 1; i < count; i++ )
      /* if start time of next activity i in list is
         >= finish time of last activity j picked,
         pick activity i */
      if ( strncmp( str[ i ], str[ j ] + Field_Width,
                    Field_Width ) >= 0 ) {
         select[ i ] = 1;
         j = i;
      }
}

                       /* end file: schedule.c */

                       /* begin file: sort_str.c */

/* sort_str sorts an array of strings. The sort
   is on substrings beginning at a given index
   and having a given length. The arguments to sort_str are:

         s -- array of strings to sort
         numb_elts -- number of strings
         str_size -- size in bytes of each string (all strings must
            be the same length)
         start -- index of substring on which to sort
         length -- length of substring on which to sort

 */

#include <stdlib.h>
#include <string.h>

static int strt, len;

static int cmp( const void *, const void * );

void sort_str( char **s, int numb_elts, int str_size,
               int start, int length )
{
   strt = start;
   len = length;

   /* qsort is the standard implementation of quicksort. */
   qsort( s, numb_elts, str_size, cmp );
}

static int cmp( const void *a, const void *b )
{
   return ( strncmp ( ( ( char * ) a ) + strt,
                      ( ( char * ) b ) + strt, len ) );
}

                       /* end file: sort_str.c */
```

Discussion

One line requires 12 bytes of storage—10 bytes of actual data, 1 byte for the terminating newline, and 1 byte for the terminating \0. For this reason, we #define Str_Len to be 12.

The function greedy_selector begins by invoking sort_str to sort the strings by finish time. The last two arguments to sort_str define the substring on which to sort. Since the finish time begins at index 5 and is of length 5, the last two arguments passed to sort_str have value Field_Width (#defined as 5).

After sorting the strings, greedy_selector steps through the sorted list, always picking the next activity whose start time equals or exceeds the last chosen activity's finish time. This guarantees a conflict-free schedule. We use strncmp to compare the start time of activity i with the finish time of activity j:

```
strncmp( str[ i ], str[ j ] + Field_Width, Field_Width ) >= 0
```

The start time in string i begins at index 0, and the finish time in string j begins at index 5 (Field_Width); thus the first two arguments to strncmp are str[i] and str [j] + Field_Width. The number of characters to compare is 5; thus, the last argument to strncmp is Field_Width.

To perform the actual sorting, we invoke the library function qsort (see Example 7.8.8). The substrings to compare begin at index strt; thus, we must add this value to the pointers to the beginnings of the two strings. Moreover, we must cast the pointers to their correct type, pointer to char:

```
strncmp( ( ( char * ) a ) + strt,
         ( ( char * ) b ) + strt, len )
```

We cannot pass start and length as arguments to the function cmp because its header is declared as containing exactly two arguments (pointers to two items to be compared) in the header *stdlib.h*. For this reason, we create the variables strt and len, visible to both sort_str and cmp, into which we copy the values of start and length before cmp is invoked. In this way, the values of start and length are available to cmp.

The storage class of the function cmp and the variables strt and len is static since we wish to restrict the visibility of cmp, strt, and len to the file *sort_str.c*.

We conclude the Discussion section by showing that the greedy scheduling algorithm is correct; that is, that it does produce an optimal schedule.

Suppose that we are given a set of activities. Denote the activities selected by the greedy algorithm as

$$sg_1, fg_1 \quad sg_2, fg_2 \ldots sg_m, fg_m,$$

where sg_i denotes the start time and fg_i denotes the finish time of activity i. Also, let

$$so_1, fo_1 \quad so_2, fo_2 \ldots so_n, fo_n$$

denote an optimal subset of activities where s and f again denote the start and finish times. We assume that both lists are sorted in increasing order of finish time. Since n is the optimal number of activities, $n \geq m$. We must show that $n \leq m$. The argument is by contradiction, so we assume that $n > m$.

We first show that $fg_i \leq fo_i$ for $i = 1, \ldots, m$. Since the greedy algorithm first chooses the activity having the minimum finish time, $fg_1 \leq fo_1$.

Because $fg_1 \leq fo_1$, none of $so_2, fo_2 \ldots so_n, fo_n$ conflicts with sg_1, fg_1. Since the greedy algorithm next chooses the activity with minimum finish time that does not conflict with

$sg_1, fg_1, fg_2 \leq fo_2$. The argument can be repeated, so we conclude that $fg_i \leq fo_i$ for $i = 1, \ldots, m$.

Because $fg_m \leq fo_m$, so_{m+1}, fo_{m+1} does not conflict with $sg_1, fg_1 \ldots sg_m, fg_m$. Therefore the greedy algorithm would choose another activity. This contradiction establishes the result.

Exercises

1. What is the output of the program of this section for the input 10,13 8,13 10,12 2,8 1,6 5,13 5,8 12,16 7,8?

2. The smallest unit of currency in Old Freedonia is the panny. Coins in Old Freedonia are available in denominations of 1, 8, 13, and 50 pannies. Consider a greedy algorithm to make change for n pannies that begins by using as many 50-panny pieces as possible, then uses as many 13-panny pieces, and so on. Show, by giving an example, that this algorithm does *not* minimize the number of coins for all values of n.

3. Selecting activities in order of increasing finish times is not the only possible greedy algorithm for the scheduling problem of this section. Give an example to show that choosing activities in order of increasing duration (duration = finish time − start time) does not necessarily maximize the number of nonconflicting activities.

4. Modify the program in this section so that when it reads data, it checks to make sure that the start time of an activity is always less than its finish time.

Changes from Traditional C

1. In traditional C, an `extern` variable never can be defined with the keyword `extern`. In standard C, an `extern` variable can be defined with the keyword `extern` if the variable is initialized at definition time. The following is legal in standard C but illegal in traditional C:

```
extern  int   num = 123;
```

2. Most implementations of traditional C do not support the type qualifiers `const` and `volatile`.

Common Programming Errors

1. Whenever both the storage class and the data type are given in a definition or declaration, the storage class must come first. It is an error to write, for example,

```
int extern i;   /* ERROR! */
```

2. An `auto` variable that is not initialized contains garbage. For this reason, the following is an error:

```
#include <stdio.h>

void f( void )
{
        int     i;    /* not initialized */
        printf( "%d", i );   /*** ERROR ***/
            .
            .
            .
}
```

3. An `extern` variable must be defined exactly one time outside a function's body. (Of course, multiple declarations are allowed.)

4. An `extern` variable can be initialized only in its definition, not in any of its declarations.

5. An `extern` variable is not visible in the functions that precede its definition (unless the variable is explicitly declared in or before these functions). For this reason, the reference to `i` in the function `f` is illegal:

```
void f( void )
{
    printf( "%d", i );    /***** ERROR *****/
}

int i = 0;

void g( void )
{
    .
    .
    .
}
```

6. An `extern` variable is not visible in the functions that occur in a file that does not contain its definition (unless the variable is explicitly declared in or before these functions). For this reason, the reference to `i` in the function `f` is illegal:

```
/***************** BEGIN FILE A *********************/
void f( void )
{
    printf( "%d", i ); /* ERROR */
}
/***************** END FILE A *********************/

/***************** BEGIN FILE B *********************/
int i = 0;

void g( void )
{
    .
    .
    .
}
/***************** END FILE B *********************/
```

7. A `register` variable must be defined inside a function's body. The following is illegal:

```
register float x; /* ERROR */

void g( void )
{
      .
      .
      .
}
```

8. A type qualifier must precede the data type. For this reason, the following is incorrect:

```
float volatile  real;   /*** ERROR ***/
```

9. A `const` variable should not have its value reset.

```
main()
{
      const int  my_birth_date = 22968 /* 2-29-68 */
          .
          .
          .
      my_birth_date = 22868;   /*** ERROR ***/
          .
          .
          .
}
```

10. It is an error to apply the address operator & to a variable of storage class `register`.

Programming Exercises

7.1. Programming Exercise 4.14 was to compute the sum

$$\sum_{i=1}^{n} \frac{1}{i^2}$$

in two ways: first, in the order

$$1 + \frac{1}{2^2} + \frac{1}{3^2} + \cdots$$

then in the order

$$\frac{1}{n^2} + \frac{1}{(n-1)^2} + \cdots$$

Repeat this exercise, using `register` variables where appropriate.

7.2. Write a program in which the `main` function reads an integer, positive or negative, from the standard input; invokes the function `flip` to change the integer's sign; and invokes the function `print_out` to print both the original and the altered integer. All the program's component functions must reside in the same file; the function `flip` must have no arguments; and all variables visible in `print_out` must be visible *only* in `print_out`.

7.3. Write a program CHECKBOOK that prompts the user for an amount and either + or −. If the user enters +, then `balance`, an `extern` variable, is incremented by the amount. If the user enters −, then `balance` is decremented by the amount. Two functions, `deposit` and `withdraw`, perform the updating operations.

7.4. Write a function `rnd` that generates random numbers using the mid-square method. The function `rnd` has a variable `seed`, which has an arbitrary initial value. With each call, `seed` is given a new value, and this new value is returned by `rnd`. To obtain the new value of `seed`, square `seed` and extract the middle three digits. Extraction can be done with the division and modulus operators. For example, to extract the middle three digits from 9988899, we can divide by 100 with truncation and mod by 1000:

$$9988899 / 100 \rightarrow 99888 \quad /* \text{ division } */$$
$$99888 \% 1000 \rightarrow 888 \quad /* \text{ modulus } */$$

7.5. Write a program that prompts the user to enter an indefinite number of positive or negative integers. The user signals the end of input by generating EOF. After *each* integer is entered, the program prints the mean (average) of all the positive integers entered so far and the mean of all the negative integers entered so far. The program should be organized as follows:

(a) The function `main` prompts the user for input, stores it in the variable `next`, invokes either `calc_pos_mean` or `calc_neg_mean`, and prints the means of both groups of integers.

(b) The function `calc_pos_mean` expects one argument, `next`. It updates `pos_mean` but returns no value to `main`.

(c) The function `calc_neg_mean` expects one argument, `next`. It updates `neg_mean` but returns no value to `main`.

The function `main` communicates with `calc_pos_mean` and `calc_neg_mean` through both `extern` variables (you decide which to use) and the argument `next`. Each function should be in a separate file.

7.6. An assignment statement consists of four parts:

(a) The left-hand side, which must be a variable.

(b) The assignment operator, =.

(c) The right-hand side, which can be any legal expression.

(d) A semicolon, which terminates the statement.

The most complicated part is the right-hand side, for C allows expressions of various sorts (e.g., function calls, variables, constants, expressions involving arithmetic operators). Suppose that we limit the right-hand side to one of the following:

(a) A constant.

(b) A variable.

(c) One function call, with only constants or variables as arguments.

(d) An expression with one binary arithmetic operator (+, −, *, /, %), in which the operands must be constant or variables.

The following are examples of legal right-hand sides of assignment operators under our rules:

```
x = 12;              /* legal */
x = y;               /* legal */
x = fun1( 12 );      /* legal */
x = y + z;           /* legal */
x = y + 12;          /* legal */
```

The following are examples of illegal right-hand sides of assignment operators under our rules:

```
x = fun1( fun2( x ) );    /* illegal—nested function
                             call */
x = y + z + 10;           /* illegal—two operators */
x = fun1( x ) + z;        /* illegal operand */
```

We allow any amount of white space to separate parts of the assignment statement. For example, a single assignment statement may be spread over two or more lines. We assume that no assignment statement consists of more than 50 characters, including white space. (Each tab, blank, and newline counts as a single character.)

Write a program that prompts the user to enter an assignment statement at the keyboard and then tests whether it is legal under our restricted syntax. Follow the C rules for identifiers under which, for example, a variable's name may not begin with a number. Use only getchar() for input.

The program echoes each assignment statement as it is read and then prints a message about its legality. The function main does only input and output; the rest of the work must be distributed to another function or functions.

Hint: The program needs to remember the *previous* character read when retrieving the *current* character so that the two can be compared. For example, the assignment statement's left-hand side may not consist of a letter, a white space, and another letter.

7.7. The dice program (Section 4.7) might be simplified by replacing some function arguments with extern variables. Amend the program so that it uses at least one extern variable, and justify your choice(s).

7.8. Rewrite the sorting and searching program of Section 5.10. Make the array students an extern array. Use two files—one containing only main, the other containing the remaining functions.

7.9. Rewrite the sorting and searching program of Section 6.6. Replace the given sorting and searching functions by the library functions qsort and bsearch (see Section 7.8).

7.10. A large company has a database program that allows any user (e.g., a manager, a fellow employee, a visitor) to enter a person's name and, if the name is in the database, to retrieve the person's department and position. For example, if Hector Cruz is chief auditor in the manufacturing department, then entering the name

```
Hector Cruz
```

at the appropriate prompt retrieves a record such as

```
Cruz, Hector: Chief Auditor, Manufacturing
```

If Hector Cruz's name is not in the database, a message to that effect is printed. Once the record has been displayed, the program then prompts the user as follows:

```
Password for confidential data or Return:
```

If the user hits the Return key, the program resumes by prompting for another name; but if the user enters the appropriate password, the program then displays the employee's salary and bonus:

```
Yearly Salary:  108,346.00
Bonus:           23,451.00
```

The database can be implemented as `extern` ragged arrays of `char` (see Section 6.7) such that the index into one array may be used to retrieve data from another. Here is a small example:

```
char *emp_names[] = { "Melanie Washington", "Rodney Podoski",
            "Eleanor Jan", "I-Ping Chu", "Hector Cruz" };

char *emp_positions[] = { "VP, Sales", "CFO", "Manager, MIS",
            "CEO", "Chief Auditor, Manufacturing" };
```

Note that the name Hector Cruz occurs as the fifth string in the ragged array `emp_names` and that his position also occurs as the fifth string in the ragged array `emp_positions`. These two arrays should be visible throughout the program. By searching the array `emp_names` with a function such as `strcmp` (see Section 5.7), the program can find the index for lookups into `emp_positions`. Two other ragged arrays, one for salaries and another for bonuses, should be visible only to functions in the file *security.c*. This file likewise contains the functions `check_password`, `display_salary`, and `display_bonus`. The functions `display_salary` and `display_bonus` are visible only to the function `check_password`; no other functions in the program may invoke them. Write a program to these specifications. The program should document the use of storage classes, as well as your decisions about which functions to place in which files.

7.11. Write a program that simulates a tic-tac-toe board. The program does not play, but only records the moves of two players and signals a winner, if any. (Those who insist on winning can play against themselves and deliberately lose.) The board is displayed before and after every move. At the start of play, the board looks like this:

After the first two moves, it might look like this:

Here is how the program determines whether anyone wins. Imagine that the board is a magic square (see Programming Exercise 6.21); that is, a matrix whose rows, columns, and diagonals sum to 15:

6	1	8
7	5	3
2	9	4

The program records the moves of the two players in `int` variables, `X_Player` and `O_Player`, which are initialized to zero. Now suppose that the **X** player enters an **X** in the cell marked 5. We update `X_Player` as follows:

```
X_Player += 5;
```

and then check whether `X_Player` equals 15 with three marks. (The qualification is needed because the **X** player could have marks in cells 1, 3, 4, and 7. The total is 15, but not with three marks.) Note that the variable `X_Player` can equal 15 with three marks only if there are **X**'s in winning positions: across a row, down a column, or along a diagonal. The program can determine a tie straightforwardly because only nine moves in all are possible. So if the total number of moves equals nine and no winner has emerged, then the game ends in a tie. Although the board is displayed as a matrix, it can be represented within the program as a nine-element one-dimensional array. A player is prompted to enter an index that represents the cell in which he or she wishes to place an **X** or an **O**. For example, a player would enter index 0 to place a mark in the uppermost, leftmost cell; index 4 to place a mark in the center cell; index 8 to place a mark in the bottommost, rightmost cell; and so on. Incidentally, the program must keep track of which cells are already occupied and thus prevent a player from entering a mark in an already occupied cell. The program also should track whose move it is. Finally, the program should prompt the players for input, display the board after every move, and declare either a win or a tie at the end.

7.12. Improve Programming Exercise 7.11 by adding an instant replay capability. Before any move, a player can ask to review a history of the game so far. The program responds by displaying the sequence of moves, one at a time, that led to the current situation. Instant replay may be invoked at the end to recap the entire game.

Input and Output

8.1 Opening and Closing Files

8.2 Character Input/Output

8.3 Sample Application: Determining a Source File's Size in Bytes

8.4 String Input/Output

8.5 Formatted Input/Output

8.6 Moving Around in a File: fseek, ftell, rewind

8.7 Sample Application: A Random Access File

†8.8 Nonstandard Input/Output

Changes from Traditional C

Common Programming Errors

Programming Exercises

†This section can be omitted without loss of continuity.

The C language itself has no input/output facilities but relies instead on libraries of input/output functions. In addition to the standard input/output functions, many implementations support other input/output functions. After discussing the standard input/output functions, we reserve one section (Section 8.8) for some widely available nonstandard input/output functions.

8.1   Opening and Closing Files

To use standard input/output functions, we must #include *stdio.h*. Some functions that perform standard input/output identify the file to read or write by using a **file pointer**. A file pointer can store the address of information required to access the file. To define a file pointer fp, we write

```
FILE *fp;
```

We regard

```
FILE *
```

pointer to FILE as a data type in the same sense that int, char, char *, and so on are data types. FILE is itself defined in *stdio.h* as a structure (to be discussed in Chapter 9).

The C programmer opens a file with the function fopen and closes it with the function fclose. The function fopen expects two arguments: the name of the file, given as a character string, and the mode, also given as a character string. The allowable values for modes and their interpretations are given in the following table:

Mode	If the file exists	If the file does not exist
"r"	Opens the file for reading	Error
"w"	Opens a new file for writing	Creates a new file
"a"	Opens the file for appending (writing at the end of the file)	Creates a new file
"r+"	Opens the file for reading and writing	Error
"w+"	Opens a new file for reading and writing	Creates a new file
"a+"	Opens the file for reading and writing at the end of the file	Creates a new file

If an already existing file is opened with mode "w" or "w+", the file's old contents are discarded.

The standard distinguishes between **text files** and **binary files** in support of those computer systems that have these different file types. The modes in the preceding table are used to open text files. A binary file may be opened by appending a 'b' to the mode string. For example, the mode string "wb" is used to open a binary file for writing, and the mode string "r+b" is used to open a binary file for reading and writing.

A binary file may be viewed as a sequence of characters, each addressable by the programmer as an offset from a fixed position (e.g., the first position) in the file. Moreover, a binary file may be viewed as holding only characters that the programmer enters into the file because the system does not add any special characters of its own except, perhaps, null characters appended at the end of the file. By contrast, a text file may contain, in addition to the characters that the user enters, control or informational characters from the system. The result is that input/output functions cannot always process binary and text files in the same way. This is especially true in the case of functions such as fseek and rewind (see Section 8.6), which enable the programmer to move around in a file. Finally, because different systems handle text files in different ways but binary files in essentially the same way, the processing of binary files can be standardized to a greater extent than the processing of text files.

If the file is successfully opened, fopen returns a pointer to FILE that references the opened file. If the file cannot be opened because, for example, it does not exist, fopen returns NULL. Only FOPEN_MAX files may be open at one time. (The macro FOPEN_MAX is defined in *stdio.h*.)

When a file is opened, a **file position marker** (not to be confused with a pointer to FILE) is set to some location in the file. The file position marker identifies the next place in the file to read or write data. When a file is opened in mode "r", "w", "r+", or "w+", the file position marker is set to the beginning of the file. When a file is opened in mode "a" or "a+", the file position marker is set to the end of the file. After each input/output operation, the file position marker is automatically repositioned just after the data that were read or written. As we shall see in Section 8.6, the file position marker can be explicitly set by the programmer using functions such as fseek and rewind.

The function fclose expects one argument, a pointer to FILE. The function fclose returns zero if it successfully closes the file and EOF otherwise, for example, if the file does not exist. A file can be opened in one mode, closed, and then reopened in another mode. Notice that fopen and fclose do not return the same type of value; fopen returns a pointer to FILE, and fclose returns an int. When a program terminates, all open files are automatically closed.

Example 8.1.1. The program

```
#include <stdio.h>
#define RECORD_LENGTH   60

main()
{
        FILE *fptr;
        char stock_price_shares[ RECORD_LENGTH + 1 ];

        /* attempt to open PORTFOLIO.DAT for reading */
        if ( ( fptr = fopen( "PORTFOLIO.DAT", "r" ) ) == NULL )
            printf( "\nCannot open the file: PORTFOLIO.DAT\n" );
        else {
            while ( fgets( stock_price_shares,
                        RECORD_LENGTH + 1, fptr ) != NULL )
                printf( "\n%s", stock_price_shares );
            fclose( fptr );        /* close the file */
        }
}
```

attempts to open, for reading, the file *PORTFOLIO.DAT*. If the file cannot be opened, fopen returns NULL. In this case, a message is printed and the program terminates. If the file *PORTFOLIO.DAT* is successfully opened for reading, the program copies records from *PORTFOLIO.DAT* to the standard output. After copying all the records, the program closes the file. Note that the file pointer `fptr` is defined as a variable of type pointer to FILE.

Each record has a maximum length of 60 characters. Thus we must reserve 61 cells in the array `stock_price_shares` to store a record of maximum length and its null terminator.

When a C program begins executing, three files are automatically opened: **standard input**, **standard output**, and **standard error**. Furthermore, pointer constants are defined for each of these files:

File	Pointer Constant
standard input	`stdin`
standard output	`stdout`
standard error	`stderr`

If not redirected, standard input is the keyboard; standard output is the video display; and standard error is also the video display. We have already discussed the standard input and the standard output (see Section 1.9). The third file, standard error, is the destination for all error messages. Because `stdin`, `stdout`, and `stderr` are pointer constants, they cannot occur as the target of an assignment operation. In this respect, they are analogous to array and function names.

Exercises

1. (True/False) `stdin` is a pointer variable.

2. Is the following correct? Explain.
```
char   stock_price_shares[ 61 ];

while ( fgets( stock_price_shares, 61, stdin )
        != NULL )
     printf( "\n%s", stock_price_shares );
```

3. Is the following correct? Explain.
```
FILE *ptr;
char   stock_price_shares[ 61 ];

ptr = stdin;

while ( fgets( stock_price_shares, 61, ptr ) != NULL )
     printf( "\n%s", stock_price_shares );
```

4. Is the following correct? Explain.
```
FILE *ptr;
char   stock_price_shares[ 61 ];

ptr = fopen( "portfolio.dat", "r" );

stdin = ptr;

while ( fgets( stock_price_shares, 61, stdin )
        != NULL )
     printf( "\n%s", stock_price_shares );
```

5. What is the error?

```
FILE file_ptr;

file_ptr = fopen( "test.dat", "a+" );
```

6. What is the error?

```
FILE *file_ptr;

file_ptr = fopen( "special_friends.dat", "r" );
        .
        .
        .
fclose( *file_ptr );
```

7. Explain the difference between the mode "r" and the mode "r+".

8. Explain the difference between the mode "w" and the mode "w+".

9. Explain the difference between the mode "a" and the mode "a+".

10. Explain the difference between the mode "a" and the mode "ab".

11. Interpret the declaration

```
FILE ( *ptr )( void );
```

12. Suppose that the file *PORTFOLIO.DAT* holds the following records:

```
ibm   108.77      50
att    27.98      100
dec   111.43      30
```

What does the file *PORTFOLIO.DAT* look like after the following program executes?

```
#include <stdio.h>
main()
{
    FILE *fptr;
    char stock_price_shares[ 61 ];
    int i, count;

    fptr = fopen( "PORTFOLIO.DAT", "r" );   /* reading */

    while ( fgets( stock_price_shares, 61, fptr ) != NULL )
        printf( "\n%s", stock_price_shares );

    fclose( fptr );      /* close for reading */

    printf( "\nHow many new records for PORTFOLIO.DAT?" );
    scanf( "%d ", &count );
    fptr = fopen( "PORTFOLIO.DAT", "w" );   /* writing */

    for ( i = 0; i < count; ++i ) {
        gets( stock_price_shares );
        fputs( stock_price_shares, fptr );
    }

    fclose( fptr );
}
```

The function `gets` reads characters from the standard input until it encounters a newline. The function `fputs` writes a character string to the file referenced by its second argument.

8.2   Character Input/Output

C supports input/output at the character level with the following functions:

Reading Characters	Examples
	`FILE *fp;`
	`char c;`
`fgetc`	`c = fgetc( fp );`
`getc`	`c = getc( fp );`
`getchar`	`c = getchar();`

Writing Characters	Examples
	`FILE *fp;`
	`char c;`
`fputc`	`fputc( c, fp );`
`putc`	`putc( c, fp);`
`putchar`	`putchar( c );`

fgetc, getc, getchar

The function `fgetc` expects a single argument, a pointer to the file to read; `fgetc` then returns the next character in the specified file or EOF if end-of-file is reached or if there is an error. The function `getc` is identical to the function `fgetc`, except that `getc` is frequently implemented as a macro. The function `getchar` expects no argument, as it automatically returns the next character from the standard input, or EOF if end-of-file is reached or if there is an error.

fputc, putc, putchar

The function `fputc` expects two arguments: a character to write and a pointer to the file to write. The function `putc` is identical to the function `fputc`, except that `putc` is frequently implemented as a macro. The function `putchar` expects a single argument, a character to write, as it automatically writes the character to the standard output. Each of these functions returns the character written or, if there is an error, EOF.

Example 8.2.1.   The file *INSTRUMENTS.LOG* contains characters generated by various laboratory instruments. (What the characters mean or how the instruments write them to a file need not concern us here.) The following program reads the characters from *INSTRUMENTS.LOG*, prints them to the terminal for inspection, and then writes them to the file *DAILY.LOG*.

```
#include <stdio.h>
main()
{
```

```
        FILE *fptr_read, *fptr_write;
        int   instru_char;
        fptr_read = fopen( "INSTRUMENTS.LOG", "r" );
        fptr_write = fopen( "DAILY.LOG", "w" );

        while ( ( instru_char = fgetc( fptr_read ) )
                != EOF ) {
            putchar( instru_char );
            fputc( instru_char, fptr_write );
        }
        fclose( fptr_read );
        fclose( fptr_write );
    }
```

Exercises

1. Find the errors.

```
#include <stdio.h>
main()
{
    FILE *fp;
    int c;
    fp = fopen( "out.dat", "r" );
    while ( ( c = getchar() ) != EOF )
        fputc( fp, c );
    fclose( "out.dat" );
}
```

2. Suppose that the standard input is

```
A
B
```

(Each of A and B is immediately followed by a newline.) Write a program that echoes these characters so that the standard output is

```
AB
```

3. The functions getchar and putchar can be used for character input/output involving files other than the standard input and standard output if the programmer redirects input/output at the operating system level. What advantages and disadvantages are there in using only getchar and putchar for character input/output?

4. Explain the output of the following program:

```
#include <stdio.h>
main()
{
    FILE    *fptr;
    int     catch_char;
    fptr = fopen( "silly.out", "w" );
```

```
            while ( ( catch_char = getchar() ) != EOF )
                  if ( catch_char == ' ' ||
                         catch_char == '\t' ||
                         catch_char == '\n' )
                         putc( catch_char, fptr );
            fclose( fptr );
      }
```

5. Assuming that the standard input is

```
Buffalo Bill's
defunct
        who used to
        ride a watersmooth-silver
                            stallion
and break onetwothreefourfive pigeonsjustlikethat
```

what will the file *poetry.out* look like after the following program is run? (The third and fourth lines each begin with one tab. The fifth line begins with three tabs.)

```
#include <stdio.h>
main()
{
      FILE    *fptr;
      int     c;
      fptr = fopen( "poetry.out", "w" );
      while ( getchar() != EOF )
            if ( ( c = getchar() ) != EOF )
                  fputc( c, fptr );
      fclose( fptr );
}
```

8.3   Sample Application: Determining a Source File's Size in Bytes

Problem

Write a program that prompts the user for the name of a C source file and then counts the number of bytes in the file. Assume that the user enters a file name with no extension. In the program, concatenate " . c" to the end of the file name before opening the file.

Sample Input/Output

Input is in color; output is in black.

```
File name (NO extension):    stock_analysis
Byte size:        8435
```

C Implementation

```
/*   This program counts the number of bytes in a C source file.
     The program prompts the user for a file name and then
     concatenates the ".c" extension to this name. It uses the
     function getc to read the characters.
*/
```

```
#include <stdio.h>
#include <string.h>

main()
{
        FILE   *fptr;
        char   extension[] = ".c";
        char   file_name[ FILENAME_MAX ]; /* defined in stdio.h */
        int    char_count;

        printf( "\n\n\tFile name (NO extension):\t" );
        scanf( "%s", file_name );
        strcat( file_name, extension );
        fptr = fopen( file_name, "r" );
        for ( char_count = 0; getc( fptr ) != EOF; ++char_count )
            ;
        printf( "\n\tByte size:\t%d", char_count );
        fclose( fptr );
}
```

Discussion

The program consists of one short function. We use the library function `strcat` to concatenate the file name with the extension. (FILENAME_MAX, defined in *stdio.h*, is the maximum length allowed for a file's name on a given system.) The program opens the file and uses the function `getc` to read each character in the file, including white spaces and comments. A counter is incremented after each character is read.

8.4 String Input/Output

In some applications, it is more natural to handle input/output in larger pieces than characters. For example, a file of stock portfolio records may contain one record per line, with each record consisting of three fields: the stock's name, its current price, and the number of shares owned, with white space separating the fields. It would be tedious to use character input/output. The organization of the file suggests that each record be treated as a single character string and read or written as a unit. The function `fgets`, which reads whole strings rather than single characters, is suited to this task. In addition to the function `fgets` and its inverse, `fputs`, this section covers the functions `gets`, `puts`, `fwrite`, and `fread`.

fgets, gets

The function `fgets` expects three arguments: the address of an array in which to store a character string, the maximum number of characters to store, and a pointer to a file to read. If `max` is the specified maximum number of characters to store, `fgets` reads characters from the file into the array until

- `max − 1` characters have been read
- all characters up to and including the next newline character have been reached
- end-of-file is reached

whichever occurs first. If `fgets` reads a newline, the newline is stored in the array. If at least one character was read, `fgets` adds the null terminator `'\0'` to the end of the string. Notice that fgets never stores more than max characters (including newline and '\0'). If no characters were stored or an error occurs, fgets returns NULL; otherwise, fgets returns the address of the array. By specifying a maximum number of characters to store, the user can ensure that fgets does not attempt to exceed the size of the array. If we format a file so that each line represents a record, fgets can be used to read one whole record.

Example 8.4.1.   Suppose that the file *PERSONNEL.DAT* contains the records

```
212-44-5412   Mary R. Hertog    123 N. Elm    Marketing Manager
331-78-6765   Leo B. Cruz    78 S. Tordo    Account Executive
                                  .
                                  .
                                  .
```

Assume further that we restrict the record length to a maximum of 80 characters, including the newline. The following program reads records from the file and writes them to the standard output:

```
#define MAX_REC_SIZE 80
#include <stdio.h>

main()
{
   FILE   *file_ptr;
   char   record[ MAX_REC_SIZE + 1 ]; /* + 1 for null terminator */
   file_ptr = fopen( "PERSONNEL.DAT", "r" );

   while ( fgets( record, MAX_REC_SIZE + 1, file_ptr ) != NULL )
      fputs( record, stdout );
   fclose( file_ptr );
}
```

Because the maximum record size is 80, we must reserve 81 cells in the array; the extra cell is to hold the null terminator '\0'. The program does not generate its own newline when it prints each record to the terminal but relies instead on the newline read into the array by fgets. The function fputs, discussed in more detail in the following subsection, writes the contents of the array (first argument) to the file specified by the file pointer (second argument).

The function gets is similar to fgets but differs from it in two ways. First, gets expects only one argument, the address of an array in which to store a character string. Because the function gets reads from the standard input, it needs no file pointer. Further, a maximum number of characters to store is not specified. Second, gets reads until it encounters a newline or end-of-file but *discards* the newline (if read) rather than storing it in the receiving array. If no characters were stored or an error occurred, gets returns NULL; otherwise, gets adds the null terminator '\0' and returns the address of the array.

If the value of the second argument to fgets is exactly the number of bytes of the array passed to it as the first argument, there is no way for fgets to write beyond the end of the array. Such functions are inherently safer than functions such as gets that have no way to check for an attempt to write beyond the end of the array. Indeed, in November 1988, Robert Morris, Jr., unleashed a self-reproducing program ("worm") throughout a computer network called Internet. Apparently, no data were destroyed, but some 6000 computers, to various degrees for differing lengths of time, were rendered useless when they were shut down or unable to function normally because they were overtaken by the worm. Among other things, Morris took advantage of the function `gets` used by some system code. He provided input to `gets` that exceeded the array used by it. In this way, he was able to fill some storage beyond the array with offending code. Needless to say, to guard against future attacks on Internet, `gets` was replaced by `fgets`.

fputs, puts

The function `fputs`, the inverse of `fgets`, writes to a file. It expects two arguments: the address of a null-terminated character string and a pointer to a file; `fputs` simply copies the string to the specified file. It does not add a newline to the end of the string.

The function `puts` is similar to `fputs` but differs from it in two ways. First, `puts` writes a string to the standard output and so expects only one argument: the address of a null-terminated string. Second, `puts` automatically adds a newline character to the end of the string. Neither `fputs` nor `puts` copies the terminating null character to their respective files. Both return a nonnegative value or, in case of error, EOF. (Recall that both `fgets` and `gets` return NULL in case of error.)

Figure 8.4.1 summarizes how these related functions handle newlines and what values they return in case of error or end-of-file. However, there is a way to figure out what an input/output function will *likely* return when encountering end-of-file or an error. Consider `fgets` and `scanf` as examples. The function `fgets`, if successful, returns a pointer to a `char`, specifically, the first cell in the array. Because EOF is *not* a character, `fgets` cannot return EOF; thus, `fgets` returns NULL when it encounters end-of-file. By contrast, `scanf` returns an `int`. Because EOF is an `int`, `scanf` can return EOF when it encounters end-of-file. This is only a rule of thumb, with important exceptions (e.g., `fread`).

Example 8.4.2. Example 8.4.1 uses `fgets` to read an employee record from a file and `fputs` to write the record to the standard output. Here we amend the example by using `gets` to read an employee record from the standard input, `puts` to echo the record to the standard output for verification, and `fputs` to write the verified record to the file *PERSONNEL.DAT*.

```
#include <stdio.h>

main()
{
    FILE *file_ptr;
    char record[ 80 ];
    char ans[ 2 ];
    file_ptr = fopen( "PERSONNEL.DAT", "a" );
```

Function	Source/Destination	How It Handles a Newline	What It Returns
fgets	any file	reads newline into string	string's address or NULL
gets	standard input	does not read newline into string	string's address or NULL
fputs	any file	does not append a newline	nonnegative value or EOF
puts	standard output	appends a newline	nonnegative value or EOF

Figure 8.4.1 Summary of string input/output functions.

```
      printf( "\nEnter record, or generate EOF to halt:   " );
      while ( gets( record ) != NULL ) {
          printf( "\nVerification:   " );
          puts( record );
          printf( "\nAppend record to PERSONNEL.DAT (y/n)?   " );
          gets( ans );
          if ( *ans == 'y' ) {
                fputs( record, file_ptr );
                fputc( '\n', file_ptr );
          }
          printf( "\nEnter record, or generate EOF to halt:   " );
      }
      fclose( file_ptr );
}
```

The body of the `while` loop includes `fputc` to write a newline to the file because the function `gets`, unlike the function `fgets`, does not add a newline character to the receiving array. We can delete the line

```
   fputc( '\n', file_ptr );
```

if we replace the condition in the `while` loop with

```
   fgets( record, 81, stdin ) != NULL
```

fread

The function `fread` is more specialized than `fgets`. It expects four arguments:

```
   fread( receiving_array, input_size,
          input_count, file_ptr );
```

The argument `receiving_array` must be large enough to hold `input_count` strings, each of size `input_size`, from the file pointed to by `file_ptr`. The function `fread` returns the number of strings it successfully reads into the receiving array. The following example illustrates how `fread` is used.

Example 8.4.3.   A warehouse tracks its inventory with codes that have exactly nine characters: the first is a lowercase letter; the next three are digits; the fifth is another lowercase letter; and the last four are digits. The first five characters identify the part, and the last four give the quantity in stock. For example, the code

```
   b110c0237
```

means that the warehouse has 237 of part b110c in stock. The file *INVENTORY.DAT* contains up to 100 codes, with exactly one blank or one newline following each code. No characters precede the first code. For example, if *INVENTORY.DAT* stores up to eight codes per line, it will look like this:

```
   b110c0237 r980d1298 p454g0081 ... g334p9899
   a997s8701 g767w0003 m221p1091 ... p231g8090
                     .
                     .
                     .
```

Within a line, a blank separates two codes. Between two lines, a newline separates two codes. The result is that each line in the file, except possibly the last, consists of 80 characters: 72 for the 8 codes and 8 for the separators. We thus need an array of size 1,000 to store up to 100 codes and separators. The following program stores the codes in an array and writes the codes to the standard output, one per line.

```c
#include <stdio.h>

#define  SIZE      9        /* length of one code */
#define  COUNT     100      /* maximum number of codes */
main()
{
     FILE *fptr;
     /* + 1 for blank or newline */
     char array[ ( SIZE + 1 ) * COUNT ];
     char *ptr = array;
     int  i, n;
     void print_code( char *pointer );

     fptr = fopen( "INVENTORY.DAT", "r" );
     n = fread( array, SIZE + 1, COUNT, fptr );
     printf( "\nCodes:\n\n" );
     for ( i = 0; i < n; ++i ) {
          print_code( ptr );
          ptr += SIZE + 1; /* next code */
     }
     fclose( fptr );
}

void  print_code( char *pointer )
{
     int   i;
     for ( i = 0; i < SIZE; ++i )
          putchar( *pointer++ );
     putchar( '\n' );
}
```

fwrite

The function `fwrite` is the inverse of `fread`. It, too, expects four arguments:

```c
fwrite( array, output_size, output_count, file_ptr );
```

The function tries to write `output_count` strings, each of size `output_size`, from `array` into the file pointed to by `file_ptr`. The function `fwrite` returns the number of strings successfully written.

Exercises

1. Fill in the blank with EOF or NULL to check correctly for end-of-file.

```c
while ( fgets( receiving_array, 50, file_ptr )
        != _____ )
```

2. What is the maximum number of bytes read by `fgets` in Exercise 1?

3. When we execute

```
while ( gets( input_record ) != NULL )
      fputs( input_record, file_ptr );
```

will each record automatically be placed on its own line in the file to which file_ptr points? Explain.

4. Example 8.4.1 uses the function fputs to write a record to the standard output. Is there any advantage to using fputs instead of puts?

5. Example 8.4.3 uses fread to read up to 100 records from the file *INVENTORY.DAT* into a receiving array. Amend the program by having fwrite write the first half of the codes in the receiving array to the file *FIRST.DAT* and the second half to the file *SECOND.DAT*. In both *FIRST.DAT* and *SECOND.DAT*, write one record per line.

6. Use fgetc to write a function fgetstr, which is equivalent to fgets except for error checking.

7. Use getchar to write a function getstr, which is equivalent to gets except for error checking.

8. Use fputc to write a function fputstr, which is equivalent to fputs except for error checking.

9. Use putchar to write a function putstr, which is equivalent to puts except for error checking.

10. Use fgetc to write a function new_read, which is equivalent to fread except for error checking.

11. Use fputc to write a function new_write, which is equivalent to fwrite except for error checking.

8.5   Formatted Input/Output

Functions such as scanf and printf perform formatted input/output. To format input or output is to control where data are read or written, to convert input to the desired type (int, char, float, etc.), and to write output in the desired manner. In this section, we discuss scanf and printf in detail and introduce the related functions fscanf, sscanf, fprintf, and sprintf. All take a variable number of arguments, which enhances their power and flexibility. We divide these functions into two groups: the scanning or reading functions and the printing or writing functions.

scanf, fscanf, sscanf

The functions scanf, fscanf, and sscanf provide formatted input. Except for different sources of input, they are identical. The following tables describe the arguments to these functions:

Function	Input Source
scanf(format_str, ptr1,..., ptrN)	standard input
fscanf(file_ptr, format_str, ptr1,..., ptrN)	a file
sscanf(array, format_str, ptr1,..., ptrN)	array of char

Abbreviation	Meaning
format_str	format string
ptr	pointer to storage
file_ptr	pointer to a file
array	array of char

Because sscanf reads from a character string rather than a file, it is not an input/output function, but it is convenient to discuss sscanf here, as it otherwise resembles scanf and fscanf. The functions scanf and fscanf differ in that scanf reads from the standard input, whereas fscanf reads from an arbitrary file. For this reason, fscanf requires a pointer to a file as an argument.

Each scanning function expects a **format string** and an **address list**. Items in the format string and address list correspond: An item in the format string specifies which characters should be taken from the input and how they should be interpreted; the matching item in the address list specifies where the characters, if converted successfully, should be stored. The address list contains addresses of storage cells.

The format string may contain the following:

- White space, which can be any combination of blanks, tabs, and newlines. The presence of white space, except when it is included inside square brackets, [ ], (see Figure 8.5.1), causes any scanning function to ignore all consecutive white space characters up to the next character that is not a white space character.
- Characters other than white space or % (such as letters or digits) that must match the next non–white space character(s) in the input. If a match fails, the scanning function stops reading the input and returns the number of successful conversions that were stored.
- A conversion code composed of characters in the following order:
  1. The percent sign %.
  2. The optional assignment suppression operator *, which prevents the scanned expression from being stored in a variable.
  3. An optional positive number, which specifies the maximum field width of the datum to be read. (The actual width may be smaller if a delimiter is encountered.)
  4. A code (see Figure 8.5.1) that determines how the input is to be converted for storage in a variable.

Except for the codes %[ ], %c, and %n, the scanning functions skip white space in the input. In particular, the code %nc, where n is a positive integer, directs the scanning functions to read the next n characters in the input, even if the next n characters include white space. A terminating '\0' is *not* added when the %c code is used. On the other hand, the code %ns, where n is a positive integer, directs the scanning functions to read *at most* n characters. More precisely, when the %ns code is used, first any white space is skipped, then characters are read until n non-white space characters are read or white space is encountered, whichever occurs first. A terminating '\0' *is* added when the %s code is used. (Of course, if the end of the file is reached, the scanning functions stop reading regardless of what codes appear in the format string.)

Each scanning function returns EOF if it encounters end-of-file before any conversion; otherwise, it returns the number of successful conversions that were stored.

Code	Interpretation	Example of Input	Corresponding Argument Must Be
c	a character	p	address of `char`
s	a character string	pie	address of `char`
d	decimal integer converted to `int`	27649	address of `int`
hd	decimal integer converted to `short`	−6942	address of `short`
ld	decimal integer converted to `long`	2964775	address of `long`
o	octal integer converted to `int`	65777	address of `int`
ho	octal integer converted to `short`	5436	address of `short`
lo	octal integer converted to `long`	−7255547	address of `long`
x, X	hexadecimal integer converted to `int`	−6bff	address of `int`
hx, hX	hexadecimal integer converted to `short`	B2E	address of `short`
lx, lX	hexadecimal integer converted to `long`	2d3d27	address of `long`
i	integer [decimal, octal (leading 0), or hex (leading 0x or 0X)] converted to `int`	065702	address of `int`
hi	integer converted to `short`	0xB2E	address of `short`
li	integer converted to `long`	2964775	address of `long`
u	`unsigned int`	62548	address of `unsigned int`
hu	`unsigned short`	46927	address of `unsigned short`
lu	`unsigned long`	3694207846	address of `unsigned long`
e, f, g, E, G	floating-point number converted to `float`	4.13986e+03	address of `float`
le, lf, lg, lE, lG	floating-point number converted to `double`	3.141592654	address of `double`
Le, Lf, Lg, Le, LG	floating-point number converted to `long double`	3.14159265358979323846	address of `long double`
p	address	(implementation dependent)	address of a pointer to `void`
n	number of characters read so far (store in `int`)	(none)	address of `int`
hn	number of characters read so far (store in `short`)	(none)	address of `short`
ln	number of characters read so far (store in `long`)	(none)	address of `long`
[*chars*]	string that includes only *chars*	edit (if the conversion is [abcdefghit])	address of `char`
[^*chars*]	string that excludes only *chars*	edit (if the conversion is [^xyz])	address of `char`
%	match the character % in the input	%	(none)

Figure 8.5.1 Codes for `scanf`, `fscanf`, and `sscanf`.

Example 8.5.1. The following program uses each of the scanning functions to read the string

```
look_mom_no_hands
```

from their respective input sources:

```
#include <stdio.h>

main()
{
    FILE  *fptr;
    char string1[ 18 ], string2[ 18 ], string3[ 18 ];
    char   source[] = "look_mom_no_hands";

    fptr = fopen( "mom.dat", "r" );
    scanf( "%s", string1 );  /* read from stdin */
    fscanf( fptr, "%s", string2 );   /* read from file pointed
                                        to by fptr */
    sscanf( source, "%s", string3 ); /* read from array source */
    fclose( fptr );
}
```

Example 8.5.2. The program

```
    #include <stdio.h>

    main()
    {
        char      string[ 5 ];
        int       integer;
        float     real;
        scanf( "%2d%4s%4f", &integer, string, &real );
    }
```

scans the standard input for an integer whose decimal representation requires at most two characters (e.g., −9, 23); a string with maximum length 4, which leaves room in the receiving array for a terminating null; and a floating-point number whose decimal representation requires no more than four characters (e.g., 1.23). Given the input

```
    44mice2.97
```

the program stores 44 in the variable `integer`, the string "mice" in the array `string`, and 2.97 in the variable `real`. Because `scanf` successfully converted three items, it returns 3.

Example 8.5.3. Suppose that the input is

```
    one_two_three_o'clock_4_o'clock_rock
```

In the program

```
#include <stdio.h>

main()
{
    char rock_stanza[ 23 ];   /* input string + null terminator */
    int integer;
    int count;       /* number of successful scans */
    float real;
    count = scanf( "%22s%1d%12f", rock_stanza, &integer, &real );
}
```

scanf expects a character string of length 22, which is large enough to hold

```
one_two_three_o'clock_
```

It then expects a decimal integer in a field of width 1, which is large enough to hold the 4. However, it then expects a floating-point number in a field of width 12. Because scanf cannot convert the characters

```
_o'clock_rock
```

into a floating-point number, it stops reading. The variable count has a value of 2, the number of successful conversions.

Example 8.5.4.   The function

```
int getstrd( char *s )
{
     return ( scanf( " \"%[^\"]\"", s ) );
}
```

reads the next string, delimited by double quotation marks, from the standard input. If the file position marker is at end-of-file, getstrd returns EOF. Otherwise, getstrd first skips white space. If the character following the white space is not a double quotation mark, getstrd returns 0; otherwise, it reads all the characters up to, but not including, the next double quotation mark, into the storage pointed to by s. If getstrd successfully stores a string, it returns 1. The file position marker is left at the character just after the second double quotation mark.

The first character (blank) in the format string directs scanf to skip white space. The next two characters in the format string \" represent the single character " which must match " in the input. If scanf cannot match the double quotation mark, it terminates and returns 0. If scanf can match the double quotation mark, at this point we have skipped white space and found a double quotation mark.

In the next expression

```
[^\"]
```

the characters \" again represent the single character ". Because \" is preceded by ^, the expression matches characters as long as none is equal to ". Thus the conversion code

```
%[^\"]
```

is a directive to read and store all characters up to a double quotation mark.

The last two characters in the format string \" again represent the single character ", which must match " in the input. This match moves the file position marker to the character following " in the input.

The next example shows how sscanf can be used to convert a string (of digits) to an int. (The library function atoi performs the same conversion.)

Example 8.5.5.   If i is of type int and s is an array of char that holds a string of digits, when we execute

```
sscanf( s, "%d", &i );
```

the string s is converted to type int and the converted value is stored in i.

Sometimes it is convenient to replace one call to `scanf` by a call to `fgets` followed by a call to `sscanf`, as the next example shows.

Example 8.5.6. Suppose that we want to read an amount and then a line that describes the amount. The following approach does *not* work:

```
/***** ERROR *****/
scanf( "%d", &amount );
fgets( description, DESCR_SIZE, stdin );
```

Suppose that the user enters 625, a carriage return, and the description followed by a carriage return. After `scanf` reads `amount`, the file position marker is at the newline that follows 5. When `fgets` is invoked, it reads and stores only this newline.

The following code correctly reads the amount and description:

```
/***** CORRECT *****/
fgets( buffer, BUFF_SIZE, stdin );
sscanf( buffer, "%d", &amount );
fgets( description, DESCR_SIZE, stdin );
```

In this version, the first call to `fgets` reads the first line of input, *including the newline*, after which the file position marker is positioned at the first character of the description. The call to `sscanf` converts and stores the amount. When `fgets` is invoked the second time, it reads and stores the description.

printf, fprintf, sprintf

The functions `printf`, `fprintf`, and `sprintf` are the counterparts of `scanf`, `fscanf`, and `sscanf`; they provide formatted output. Except for different destinations of output, `printf`, `fprintf`, and `sprintf` are identical. The following tables describe the arguments to these functions:

Function	Output Destination
printf(format_str, arg1,..., argN)	standard output
fprintf(file_ptr, format_str, arg1,..., argN)	a file
sprintf(array, format_str, arg1,..., argN)	array of char

Abbreviation	Meaning
format_str	format string
arg	argument to print
file_ptr	pointer to a file
array	array of char

Because `sprintf` writes to an array rather than to a file, it—like its counterpart `sscanf`—is not an input/output function, but it is convenient to discuss `sprintf` here, as it otherwise resembles `printf` and `fprintf`. The function `printf` writes to the standard output and `fprintf` to a file. For this reason, `fprintf` requires a pointer to a file as an argument.

Flag	Interpretation
−	Left-justify in field
+	Begin a signed number with + or −
blank	If a signed number does not begin with + or −, add a space before printing it
#	For o conversion, begin number with 0 (zero)
	For x conversion, begin number with 0x
	For X conversion, begin number with 0X
	For e, E, f, g, and G conversions, use a decimal point
	For g and G conversions, do not remove trailing zeros
0 (zero)	Pad a number on the left with zeros

Figure 8.5.2 Flags used in the `printf` format string.

Each printing function expects a format string and an argument list. The argument list may contain any legal C expression, including a function call. Just as for the scanning functions, items in the format string and argument list correspond: An argument matches an item in the format string that specifies how the argument should be converted for output. (The function `sprintf` adds a null terminator.) The printing functions return the number of characters (digits, alphabetic characters, special characters, etc.) written. (In the case of `sprintf`, the added null terminator is not counted.) If an error occurs, the printing functions return a negative integer.

The format string may contain the following:

- Ordinary characters that are copied to the output.
- A conversion code composed of characters in the following order:
    1. The percent sign %.
    2. Optional flags (see Figure 8.5.2).
    3. An optional positive number, which specifies the minimum field width of the datum to be printed.†
    4. An optional period . which separates the field width from the precision.
    5. An optional positive number, which specifies the precision.‡
    6. A code (see Figure 8.5.3) that determines how the output is to be converted for printing.

The field width is the *minimum* number of columns in which to print the datum. If the item is larger than the specified field width, it is written anyway (using more columns than specified in the width), although for %s conversion, a precision value can specify the *maximum* number of characters to print. If the datum is smaller than the field width, it is right justified (unless a minus sign − specifies left justification). The extra columns are filled with blanks unless the width has a leading zero, in which case the extra columns are filled with zeros.

For floating-point numbers, the precision specifies the number of digits to print after the decimal point. As previously mentioned, for %s conversion, the precision specifies the maximum number of characters to print.

---

†The field width can be designated by *. In this case, the actual value is read from an argument in the argument list.

‡The precision can be designated by *. In this case, the actual value is read from an argument in the argument list.

Code	Interpretation	Example of Output	Corresponding Argument Must Be
c	a character	p	char, short, int
s	a character string	pie	address of char
d, i	integer written in signed decimal notation	−999	char, short, int
ld, li	long written in signed decimal notation	2964775	long
o	integer written in unsigned octal notation	7031	char, short, int
lo	long written in unsigned octal notation	7255547	long
x	integer written in unsigned hexadecimal notation (using a−f)	fe4	char, short, int
X	integer written in unsigned hexadecimal notation (using A−F)	FE4	char, short, int
lx	long written in unsigned hexadecimal notation (using a−f)	2d3d27	long
lX	long written in unsigned hexadecimal notation (using A−F)	2D3D27	long
u	unsigned decimal	287092	unsigned char, unsigned short, unsigned int
lu	unsigned long	3775287092	unsigned long
e	float or double written in the form m.nnnnnne±xx	3.141590e+03	float, double
E	float or double written in the form m.nnnnnnE±xx	3.141590E+03	float, double
f	float or double written in the form m.nnnnnn	2.718282	float, double
g	number written in the d, e, or f format, whichever is shortest	33.900000	float, double
G	number written in the d, E, or f format, whichever is shortest	33.900000	float, double
Le	long double written in the form m.nnnnnne±xx	3.141590423e+03	long double
LE	long double written in the form m.nnnnnnE±xx	3.141590423E+03	long double
Lf	long double written in the form m.nnnnnn	3.141592654	long double
Lg	number written in the d, Le, or Lf format, whichever is shortest	43.9000001	long double
LG	number written in the d, LE, or Lf format, whichever is shortest	43.9000001	long double
p	address	(implementation dependent)	pointer to void
n	number of characters written so far is stored in int whose address is passed	(none)	address of int
hn	number of characters written so far is stored in short whose address is passed	(none)	address of short
ln	number of characters written so far is stored in long whose address is passed	(none)	address of long
%	write the character %	%	(none)

Figure 8.5.3 Codes for printf, fprintf, and sprintf.

Example 8.5.7.   The following program uses each printing function to print the string

```
mom--next_time_with_hands
```

to its respective destination:

```
#include <stdio.h>
main()
{
      FILE *fptr;
      char string[] = "mom--next_time_with_hands";
      char destination[ 26 ]; /* 25 + null terminator */

      fptr = fopen( "hands.out", "w" );
      printf( "%s", string );
      fprintf( fptr, "%s", string );
      sprintf( destination, "%s", string );
      fclose( fptr );
}
```

Figure 8.5.4 illustrates some of the many possibilities available in formatting and converting using printf.

The next example shows how sprintf can be used to convert a value of type int to a string.

Program	Output

```
/* MFW stands for minimum field width. */
/* DP stands for decimal point. */
#include <stdio.h>
main()
{
   /* 1 character */
   char   big_A = 'A';

   /* 17 non-null characters */
   char hands[] = "look_mom_no_hands";

                                            Column 1 of Output

   /* 7 digits */                              |
   int    sevens = 7777777;                    |

   /* pi to 8 decimal places */                |
   double pi = 3.14159265;                      |

           /* conversion */                     |

   /* print numeric code for 'A' */             |
   printf( "\n%d", big_A );          65  <——

   /* print character with code 61 */
   printf( "\n%c", 61 );                 =

   /* print sevens in octal */
   printf( "\n%o", sevens );         35526761
```

Figure 8.5.4 Formatting using printf.

Program	Output
`/* print sevens in hexadecimal */` `printf( "\n%x", sevens );`	76adf1
`/* conversion and formatting */`	
`/* MFW is 1 automatically */` `printf( "\n%c", big_A );`	A
`/* MFW is 5; right-justified */` `printf( "\n%5c", big_A );`	A
`/* MFW is 5; left-justified */` `printf( "\n%-5c", big_A );`	A
`/* MFW is 17 automatically */` `printf( "\n%s", hands );`	look_mom_no_hands
`/* MFW is 17 */` `printf( "\n%17s", hands );`	look_mom_no_hands
`/* MFW is 2, but 17 columns provided */` `printf( "\n%2s", hands );`	look_mom_no_hands
`/* MFW is 20; right-justified */` `printf( "\n%20s", hands );`	look_mom_no_hands
`/* MFW is 20; left-justified */` `printf( "\n%-20s", hands );`	look_mom_no_hands
`/* MFW is 7 automatically */` `printf( "\n%d", sevens );`	7777777
`/* MFW is 7 */` `printf( "\n%7d", sevens );`	7777777
`/* MFW is 2, but 7 columns provided */` `printf( "\n%2d", sevens );`	7777777
`/* MFW is 10, right-justified */` `printf( "\n%10d", sevens );`	7777777

`/* MFW is 10, right-justified,`
`   pad with zeroes */`
`printf( "\n%010d", sevens );`
	0007777777

`/* MFW is 10, left-justified */` `printf( "\n%-10d", sevens );`	7777777

`/* MFW defaults to size needed to print`
`   the characters, the default number of`
`   digits to right of DP is system`
`   dependent */`
`printf( "\n%f", pi );`
	3.141593

`/* MFW is 10 in all (including DP),`
`   right-justified */`
`printf( "\n%10f", pi );`
	3.141593

`/* MFW is 30, right-justified */` `printf( "\n%30f", pi );`	3.141593

Figure 8.5.4 (continued)

Program	Output
/* MFW is 30, right-justified, pad with zeros */ printf("\n%030f", pi);	00000000000000000000003.141593
/* MFW is 30, left-justified */ printf("\n%-30f", pi);	3.141593
/* MFW is 30, left-justified, precision (number of significant digits) is 15, don't trim trailing zeros */ printf("\n%-#30.15g", pi);	3.14159265000000

```
        /* conversion and formatting with precision */
```

Program	Output
/* MFW is 17, print all 17 */ printf("\n%17.17s", hands);	look_mom_no_hands
/* MFW defaults to size needed to print characters (4) */ printf("\n%.4s", hands);	look
/* MFW is 17, print 4, right-justified */ printf("\n%17.4s", hands);	look
/* MFW is 17, print 4, left-justified */ printf("\n%-17.4s", hands);	look
/* MFW is 30, but print only 4 */ printf("\n%30.4s", hands);	look
/* MFW is 30, but print only 4, left-justified */ printf("\n%-30.4s", hands);	look
/* MFW is 20 (as an argument), print 8 (as an argument) */ printf("\n%*.*s", 20, 8, hands);	look_mom
/* MFW is 10, print 8 beyond DP */ printf("\n%10.8f", pi);	3.14159265
/* MFW defaults to size needed to print characters, print 2 beyond DP */ printf("\n%.2f", pi);	3.14
/* MFW is 20, print 2 beyond DP, left-justified */ printf("\n%-20.2f", pi);	3.14
/* MFW is 20, print 2 beyond DP, right-justified */ printf("\n%20.2f", pi);	3.14
/* MFW is 20, print 2 beyond DP, scientific notation, left-justified */ printf("\n%-20.2e", pi);	3.14e+00

```
}
```

Figure 8.5.4 (continued)

Example 8.5.8. If i is of type int and s is an array of char, when we execute

```
sprintf( s, "%d", i );
```

the value of i is converted to a null-terminated string of characters that is stored in the array s.

Character Conversion and Character Testing Functions

Although different systems may use different character sets (e.g., ASCII or EBCDIC), the standard provides functions, which are independent of any particular character set, for testing and converting characters. Use of these functions requires us to #include the header file *ctype.h*. (The standard allows these "functions" to be implemented as macros, but the standard still uses the term *function* to describe them.)

There are two character conversion functions, tolower and toupper. As the names suggest, they convert an uppercase character to a lowercase character or vice versa. Each expects an argument of type int, and each returns the int code for the converted character. The function tolower converts its argument from uppercase to lowercase and returns the converted value. If the argument is not an uppercase character, it returns the argument unchanged. The function toupper is the inverse of tolower. It converts its argument from lowercase to uppercase and returns the converted value. If the argument is not a lowercase character, it returns the argument unchanged.

Example 8.5.9. The program

```
#include <stdio.h>
#include <ctype.h>

main( )
{
        int lower_c, upper_C = 'C';
        lower_c = tolower( upper_C );
        printf( "\n%c", lower_c );
}
```

prints

```
c
```

The functions that check for specific characters return either a nonzero value (true) or zero (false) and are given in the following table. Each expects a single argument of type int.

Function	Returns True (Nonzero) If
isalpha(arg)	arg is a letter: A through Z or a through z
isupper(arg)	arg is an uppercase letter: A through Z
islower(arg)	arg is a lowercase letter: a through z
isdigit(arg)	arg is a decimal digit: 0 through 9
isxdigit(arg)	arg is a hexadecimal digit: 0 through 9, A through F, a through f
isalnum(arg)	arg is a digit or letter: 0 through 9, A through Z, a through z
isprint(arg)	arg is a printable character
isspace(arg)	arg is a white space
ispunct(arg)	arg is a punctuation character
iscntrl(arg)	arg is a control character
isgraph(arg)	arg is any printable character except for a blank

Exercises

1. Assume that the standard input is

   ```
   ABC1.23pqr34
   ```

   Describe the contents of string1, string2, and num after we execute

   ```c
   #include <stdio.h>
   main( )
   {
        char string1[ 4 ], string2[ 10 ];
        float    num;
        scanf( "%3s%4f%s", string1, &num, string2 );
   }
   ```

2. What is printed?

   ```c
   #include <stdio.h>
   main( )
   {
        char bad_news[] = "Dear John:";
        char letter[ 11 ];
        sscanf( bad_news, "%10s", letter );
        printf( "%s", letter );
   }
   ```

3. Suppose that the standard input is

   ```
   the cat sat on the mat 4 it wanted 2 nap
   ```

   What is printed?

   ```c
   #include <stdio.h>
   main( )
   {
        char word1[ 4 ], word2[ 4 ],
             word3[ 4 ], word4[ 3 ],
             word5[ 4 ], word6[ 4 ],
             word7[ 3 ], word8[ 7 ];
        int  num;
        scanf( "%3s%3s%*s%s%s%s%1d%s%s%*d%s",
             word1, word2, word3, word4, word5,
             &num, word6, word7, word8 );
        printf( "\n%.2s\n%.2s\n%10.2s\n%d",
             word1, word2, word8, num );
   }
   ```

4. In the program of Exercise 3, what value does scanf return?
5. In the program of Exercise 3, what value does printf return?
6. What is printed?

   ```c
   #include <stdio.h>
   #include <ctype.h>
   main( )
   {
   ```

```
                    char c1 = 'c';
                    char c2 = 'Z';
                    int num1 = 111;
                    int num2 = 55;
                    putchar( toupper( c1 ) );
                    putchar( tolower( c2 ) );
                    if ( ispunct( ']' ) )
                        printf( "\n] ispunct\n" );
                    if ( isalnum( num2 ) )
                        printf( "\n%c isalnum\n", num2 );
          }
```

7. Rewrite the function of Example 8.5.4 so that it receives two arguments, s and c. The argument s points to storage where the function copies the next string delimited by the non−white space character c from the standard input.

8. Write a line of code that uses `sscanf` to convert a string to a decimal of type `double`.

9. Write a line of code that uses `sscanf` to convert a string of hexadecimal digits to an integer of type `long`.

10. Write a line of code that uses `sprintf` to convert a decimal of type `float` to a string.

11. Write a line of code that uses `sprintf` to convert an integer of type `long` to a string of octal digits.

8.6 Moving Around in a File: `fseek, ftell, rewind`

The programmer can use the functions `fseek`, `ftell`, and `rewind` to determine or change the location of the file position marker. These functions work differently with binary and text files (see Section 8.1).

The header of `fseek` can be written

```
int fseek( FILE *file_pointer, long offset,
           int base_position )
```

If the file specified by `file_pointer` has been opened as a binary file, `fseek` resets the file position marker to `offset` bytes from the beginning of the file (base_position = SEEK_SET), from the current location of the file position marker (base_position = SEEK_CUR), or from the end of the file (base_position = SEEK_END). SEEK_SET, SEEK_CUR, and SEEK_END are defined in *stdio.h*. If the file specified by `file_pointer` has not been opened as a binary file, `fseek` loses much of its power: `offset` must be either 0L (zero) or a value returned by `ftell` (see the following subsection). In case of error (e.g., a NULL `file_pointer`), `fseek` returns a nonzero value; if successful, `fseek` returns zero.

Assuming that the file specified by `file_pointer` has been opened as a binary file, executing

```
fseek( file_pointer, 0L, SEEK_SET );
```

sets the file position marker zero bytes beyond the first byte, that is, to the first byte. Executing

```
fseek( file_pointer, 1L, SEEK_SET );
```

sets the file position marker one byte beyond the first byte, that is, to the second byte. Executing

```
fseek( file_pointer, 0L, SEEK_END );
```

sets the file position marker zero bytes from the end of the file, that is, to the end of the file (which is different from the last byte in the file). Executing

```
fseek( file_pointer, -1L, SEEK_END );
```

sets the file position marker one byte from the end of the file, that is, to the last byte in the file. Executing

```
fseek( file_pointer, -2L, SEEK_END );
```

sets the file position marker two bytes from the end of the file, that is, to the next to last byte in the file.
Executing

```
fseek( file_pointer, 0L, SEEK_CUR );
```

does not change the file position marker. Executing

```
fseek( file_pointer, 2L, SEEK_CUR );
```

sets the file position marker two bytes beyond (toward the end of the file) its current location. Executing

```
fseek( file_pointer, -2L, SEEK_CUR );
```

sets the file position marker two bytes before (toward the beginning of the file) its current location.

Example 8.6.1.   Assuming that the file specified by file_pointer has been opened as a binary file, when we execute

```
fseek( file_pointer, 5L, SEEK_SET );
```

we move the file position marker to the sixth byte from the beginning of the file. If we then execute

```
fseek( file_pointer, 15L, SEEK_CUR );
```

we move the file position marker 15 bytes beyond that location, that is, to the 21st byte from the beginning of the file. When we execute

```
fseek( file_pointer, -5L, SEEK_END );
```

we move the file position marker to the fifth byte from the end of the file.

The header of rewind can be written

```
void rewind( FILE *file_pointer )
```

The function rewind resets the file position marker in the file specified by file_pointer to the beginning of the file. Executing

```
rewind( file_pointer );
```

has the same effect as executing

```
fseek( file_pointer, 0L, SEEK_SET );
```

The function rewind works the same way for binary and text files.

The header of ftell can be written

```
long ftell( FILE *file_pointer )
```

In the case of binary files, the function ftell returns the location of the file position marker as an offset in bytes from the first position in the file specified by file_pointer. For binary files, ftell thus can be used to determine the number of characters—originally entered under programmer control—from the beginning of the file to the file position marker. In the case of text files, ftell is less useful. For text files, ftell returns a value that fseek can use later to move the file position marker to the position given by ftell; in effect, ftell can provide a position to which fseek later can return the file position marker. However, ftell cannot be used on text files to determine the number of nonsystem characters between the beginning of the file and the file position marker because text files may contain characters entered by the system rather than by the programmer. The function ftell returns −1L in case of error.

Example 8.6.2. The following program illustrates how fseek, rewind, and ftell may operate on a binary file. The file *test.dat* is VLSI.

```
#include <stdio.h>

main( )
{
    FILE *fptr;
    long spot;
    char letter;

    /* test.dat contains the string VLSI
       and is opened as a binary file. */
    fptr = fopen( "test.dat", "r+b" );

    letter = fgetc(  fptr  );              /* gets V */
    putchar(  letter  );                   /* prints V */
    letter = fgetc(  fptr  );              /* gets L */
    putchar(  letter  );                   /* prints L */
    spot = ftell(  fptr  );                /* marks S's spot */
    letter = fgetc(  fptr  );              /* gets S */
    putchar(  letter  );                   /* prints S */
    fseek(  fptr, spot, SEEK_SET  );  /* find S's spot */
    letter = fgetc(  fptr  );              /* gets S */
    putchar(  letter  );                   /* prints S */
    fseek(  fptr, spot, SEEK_SET  );  /* find S's spot again */
    fputc(  'Z', fptr  );                  /* put a Z in S's spot */
    fseek(  fptr, spot, SEEK_SET  );  /* find S's old spot */
    letter = fgetc(  fptr  );              /* gets Z */
    putchar(  letter  );                   /* prints Z */
    rewind(  fptr  );                      /* back to beginning */
    letter = fgetc(  fptr  );              /* gets V */
    putchar(  letter  );                   /* prints V */
}
```

Finally, the programmer can interleave reads from and writes to the same open file (e.g., a file opened in the mode "rb+" or "wb+") by using fseek and rewind to reset the file position marker. Reads and writes must not be interleaved without resetting the file position marker. Section 8.7 illustrates interleaved reads and writes with a random access file.

Exercises

1. Suppose that the file *TEST.DAT* is

```
ABC
```

What is printed?

```
#include <stdio.h>

main( )
{
        FILE *file;
        long position;

        file = fopen( "TEST.DAT", "r+b" );

        putchar( fgetc( file ) );
        position = ftell( file );
        putchar( fgetc( file ) );
        fseek( file, position, SEEK_SET );
        putchar( fgetc( file ) );
        fseek( file, position, SEEK_SET );
        fputc( 'Q', file );
        fseek( file, position, SEEK_SET );
        putchar( fgetc( file ) );
        fseek( file, 0L, SEEK_SET );
        putchar( fgetc( file ) );
}
```

2. Suppose that the file *data.dat* is

```
ABCDEFGHIJKLMNOPQRSTUVWXYZ
```

(The last byte in the file contains the character Z.) What is printed?

```
#include <stdio.h>

main( )
{
        int letter;
        FILE *fp;

        fp = fopen( "data.dat", "rb" );
        fseek( fp, 5L, SEEK_SET );
        letter = fgetc( fp );
        printf( "%c\n", letter );
        fseek( fp, 15L, SEEK_CUR );
        letter = fgetc( fp );
        printf( "%c\n", letter );
        fseek( fp, 0L, SEEK_END );
```

```
        if ( ( letter = fgetc( fp ) ) == EOF )
            printf( "EOF\n" );
        else
            printf( "%c\n", letter );
        fseek( fp, -5L, SEEK_END );
        letter = fgetc( fp );
        printf( "%c\n", letter );
    }
```

8.7 Sample Application: A Random Access File

Problem

Assume that a personnel department maintains employee records, each of which contains a social security number, name, department, and manager. Write a program that allows the user to add a record, to find a record, or to remove a record. Records are referenced by social security number. Use a random access file, that is, a file in which we can access records in any order whatever and not necessarily in physical order.

Sample Input / Output

Input is in color, output is in black.

```
                1  - add a record
                2  - find a record
                3  - remove a record
                0  - exit the program

                Please pick a number:  1

Please enter new record's key:  111333555
Please enter data:  Newman, Alfred E.  DP  Smith

                1  - add a record
                2  - find a record
                3  - remove a record
                0  - exit the program

                Please pick a number:  2

Please enter record's key:  111333555
Record:  Newman, Alfred E.  DP  Smith

                1  - add a record
                2  - find a record
                3  - remove a record
                0  - exit the program

                Please pick a number:  2

Please enter record's key:  999888777
There is no record with the key:  999888777

                1  - add a record
                2  - find a record
```

```
                  3  - remove a record
                  0  - exit the program

                  Please pick a number:  3

      Please enter record's key:  111333555
      Record has been deleted.

                  1  - add a record
                  2  - find a record
                  3  - remove a record
                  0  - exit the program

                  Please pick a number:  2

      Please enter record's key:  111333555
      There is no record with the key: 111333555

                  1  - add a record
                  2  - find a record
                  3  - remove a record
                  0  - exit the program

                  Please pick a number:  0
```

Solution

We use a **relative file**, in which a record's **relative address** (as opposed to its *physical* address) is its position in the file: first, second, ... Given a social security number, we can translate it into a relative address. Once we have the relative address, we can quickly determine approximately where the record is located in the file and then access it directly. A relative file is thus analogous to an array. Just as each of the array's elements has a position relative to the first, so each element in a relative file has a position relative to the first.

Conceptually, the records in a relative file are stored contiguously. We allow 47 bytes per record. The first byte holds a status flag that indicates whether a record is stored, whether a record was stored but deleted, or whether a record was never stored. The next nine bytes store the social security number. The remaining bytes hold the name, department, and manager. Thus we can imagine the first record as starting at position 0 and ending at position 46, the second record as starting at position 47 and ending at position 93, and so on:

```
T332112343Hopper, G. DP Wirth...    T502617496Johnsonbaugh, R. CS Epp...
↑                                    ↑
0 ← Byte                             47 ← Byte
0 ← Record's relative address        1  ← Record's relative address
```

To access a record, we designate the social security number as its **key**, and we define a hash function h that, given a *key*, produces a relative storage address:

$$h(\text{ key }) = \text{Record's relative address}$$

There are many different ways to define hash functions. Our implementation uses the division-remainder method, but we suggest an alternative method in Programming Exercise 8.16. We define the hash function h by the rule

$$h(\text{ key }) = \text{key \% divisor}$$

Figure 8.7.1 Inserting in a relative file.

where the modulo operation % yields the remainder after dividing *key* by *divisor*. For example, if *key* is 111111888 and *divisor* is 13, the record's relative address is 4. If *divisor* is *n*, the relative addresses range from 0 through $n - 1$.

When two *distinct* keys hash to the same relative storage address, we say that a **collision** occurs. For example, if our hash function is

$$h(\text{ key }) = \text{key} \% 13$$

we have

$$h(\text{ 111111888 }) = 4 = h(\text{ 332112343 })$$

There is a collision: The keys 111111888 and 332112343 map to the same relative address.

Any hashing system must provide a **collision resolution policy**—a way of handling collisions. Our collision resolution policy is called **linear probing**. When a collision occurs, we simply move to the next highest relative address (with the first record position assumed to follow the last record position). For example, if we insert the keys 42, 6, 31, and 14 in the relative file with relative addresses 0 through 12 using the hash function $h(\text{ key }) = \text{key} \% 13$, we obtain the situation shown in Figure 8.7.1. Now suppose that we insert the key 135. Because

$$h(\text{ 135 }) = 5 = h(\text{ 31 })$$

a collision occurs. Using linear probing, we insert 135 in the next highest unoccupied spot, 7. We obtain the situation shown in Figure 8.7.2.

Divisors should be chosen to minimize collisions. Research and experience show that divisors with no small prime factors do reasonably well at avoiding collisions. (Note that this rules out even numbers.) Avoiding collisions requires more than a good divisor, however. As more and more records are added to a relative file, collisions become more likely. A file's **load factor**, defined as

$$\text{load factor} = \frac{\text{number of records in file}}{\text{file's maximum capacity}}$$

is the percentage of occupied cells. Research and experience show that a relative file's load factor should not exceed 70 to 80 percent. Thus, if a relative file is to hold *N* records, the file should have capacity 1.25*N* so as not to exceed a load factor of 80 percent. Assume that we expect, at most, 330 employees. Because

$$1.25 * 330 = 412.5$$

Figure 8.7.2 Resolving a collision in a relative file.

we choose the next highest prime, 419, as our file size. Our hash function is

$$h(\ key\ )\ =\ key\ \%\ 419$$

To delete a record, we mark it rather than physically delete it. We reserve the first byte of the record to store either T (for taken), to indicate that the slot is occupied; F (for free), to indicate that the slot never held a record; or D (for deleted), to indicate that the slot holds a deleted record.

When we search for a record with a given key k, we first hash to relative address $addr$ = $k\ \%\ 419$. If the record at relative address $addr$ has status T (for taken), we check whether this record has key k. If so, the search terminates successfully; otherwise, we continue the search by checking the record at relative address

$$(\ addr\ +\ 1\ )\ \%\ 419$$

If the record at relative address $addr$ has status F (for free), the search terminates unsuccessfully, since if the record were present, we would have found it before reaching the free slot. If the record at relative address $addr$ has status D (for deleted), we must continue the search by checking the record at relative address

$$(\ addr\ +\ 1\ )\ \%\ 419$$

since the record we are searching for may have been inserted before the record at address $addr$ was deleted and would thus be found after further probing.

Distinguishing between free and deleted slots usually allows us to terminate the search for a nonexistent record before searching the entire file.

C Implementation

```
                  /***** RANDOM ACCESS FILE PROGRAM *****/
#include <stdio.h>
#include <stdlib.h>
#include <string.h>

#define  FILE_SIZE     419      /* slots 0 through 418 */
#define  RECORD_SIZE   47       /* 46 + status flag */
#define  KEY_SIZE      9        /* 9-digit unique identifier */
#define  TOTAL_BYTES   ( RECORD_SIZE * FILE_SIZE )
#define  INBUFF_SIZE   81       /* size of user buffer */
#define  TAKEN         'T'  /* slot that holds a record */
#define  FREE          'F'  /* slot that never held a record */
#define  DELETED       'D'  /* slot that holds a deleted record */
#define  FOUND         1
#define  NOT_FOUND     0
#define  BLANK         ' '

FILE   *fptr;
char    file[] = "records.dat";
char    inbuff[ INBUFF_SIZE ];   /* buffer for user input */
int     count;                   /* count of records in file */

main()
{
    void  add_record( void ), find_record( void ),
          remove_record( void ), initialize( void ),
```

```
                set_count( void );
    int    print_menu( void ), choice;

    /* open the file "records.dat" and count the number of
       records it contains, if it exists; otherwise, create and
       initialize it */
    if ( ( fptr = fopen( file, "r+b" ) ) != NULL )
        set_count();
    else {
        fptr = fopen( file, "w+b" );
        initialize();
    }

    /* Do file operations until user signals halt. */
    while ( ( choice = print_menu() ) != 0 )
        switch ( choice ) {
        case 1:
            add_record();
            break;
        case 2:
            find_record();
            break;
        case 3:
            remove_record();
            break;
        default:
            printf( "\a\n\n\t\t\tIllegal choice. "
                    "Please choose again.\n" );
            break;
        }
    fclose( fptr );
}

/* Create a relative file and indicate that FILE_SIZE record slots
   are open in it. */
void  initialize( void )
{
    int  i;
    char dummy[ RECORD_SIZE + 1 ];

    /* Create a dummy record to store repeatedly in file. */
    dummy[ 0 ] = FREE;           /* status unoccupied */
    for ( i = 1; i < RECORD_SIZE; ++i )
        dummy[ i ] = BLANK;
    dummy[ RECORD_SIZE ] = '\0';
    for ( i = 0; i < FILE_SIZE; ++i )
        fputs( dummy, fptr );
    count = 0;
}

/* Count occupied slots in file. */
void set_count( void )
```

```
{
    int   i;

    fseek( fptr, OL, SEEK_SET );

    for ( i = 0; i < FILE_SIZE; ++i ) {
        if ( fgetc( fptr ) == TAKEN )
            ++count;
        fseek( fptr, ( long ) ( RECORD_SIZE - 1 ), SEEK_CUR );
    }
}
/* Print a menu of choices, and return whichever the user picks. */
int  print_menu( void )
{
    int   choice;

    printf( "\n\n\n\t\t\t"
            "1    - add a record\n\t\t\t"
            "2    - find a record\n\t\t\t"
            "3    - remove a record\n\t\t\t"
            "0    - exit the program\n\n\t\t\t"
            "Please pick a number:   " );
    fgets( inbuff, INBUFF_SIZE, stdin );
    sscanf( inbuff, "%d", &choice );
    return ( choice );
}
/* Add a record to the file */
void  add_record( void )
{
    char   record[ RECORD_SIZE + 1 ];
    int    locate( char *key );

    if ( count >= FILE_SIZE )   /* full file? */
        printf( "\a\n\n\n\n  File is full.\n" );
    else {
        do {
            printf( "\n\nPlease enter new record's key: " );
            fgets( inbuff, INBUFF_SIZE, stdin );
            /* input must be KEY_SIZE + newline */
            if ( strlen( inbuff ) != KEY_SIZE + 1 )
                printf( "Key size must be %d", KEY_SIZE );
        } while ( strlen( inbuff ) != KEY_SIZE + 1 );

        if ( locate( inbuff ) == FOUND ) {
            printf( "\aThere is already a record with "
                    "the key: %s\n", inbuff );
            return;
        }

        strncpy( &record[ 1 ], inbuff, KEY_SIZE ); /* copy key */
        do {
            printf( "\nPlease enter data: " );
```

```
            fgets( inbuff, INBUFF_SIZE, stdin );
            /* input must be less than or equal to
               RECORD_SIZE - KEY_SIZE - 1 counting the
               newline */
            if ( strlen( inbuff ) > RECORD_SIZE - KEY_SIZE - 1 )
                printf( "\aRecord size must be less than"
                        " or equal to %d"
                        " counting the newline\n",
                        RECORD_SIZE - KEY_SIZE - 1 );
        } while ( strlen( inbuff ) > RECORD_SIZE - KEY_SIZE - 1 );
        strcpy( &record[ 1 + KEY_SIZE ], inbuff );
        record[ 0 ] = TAKEN;    /* mark status as taken */
        fputs( record, fptr );  /* store record */
        ++count;
    }
}

/* Return address to which a key hashes. */
long  get_address( char *key )
{
    long int_key, address;

    int_key = atol( key );  /* convert */
    address = ( int_key % FILE_SIZE ) * RECORD_SIZE; /* hash */
    return ( address );
}

/* Remove a record from the file by marking its slot DELETED. */
void  remove_record( void )
{
    char key[ KEY_SIZE + 1 ];
    long get_address( char *key );
    int locate( char *key );

    printf( "\n\nPlease enter record's key:  " );
    fgets( inbuff, INBUFF_SIZE, stdin );
    strncpy( key, inbuff, KEY_SIZE );
    key[ KEY_SIZE ] = '\0';
    if ( locate( key ) != FOUND )
        printf( "\a\nThere is no record with the key: %s\n", key );
    else {
        --count;
        fputc( DELETED, fptr );
        printf( "\nRecord has been deleted.\n" );
    }
}

/* Find a record with a given key and print it. */
void  find_record( void )
{
    char key[ KEY_SIZE + 1 ], record[ RECORD_SIZE + 1 ];
    int locate( char *key );
```

```
        printf( "\n\nPlease enter record's key:   " );
        fgets( inbuff, INBUFF_SIZE, stdin );
        strncpy( key, inbuff, KEY_SIZE );
        key[ KEY_SIZE ] = '\0';
        if ( locate( key ) == NOT_FOUND )
            printf( "\aThere is no record with the key: %s", key );
        else {
            fgets( record, RECORD_SIZE + 1, fptr ); /* read it */
            printf( "Record: %s", record + KEY_SIZE + 1 );
        }
}

/*    locate searches for the record with given key. locate returns
      1 if the record is found and 0 if the record is not found.
      Furthermore, if the record is found, locate sets the file
      position marker to the found record. If the record is not
      found, locate sets the file position marker to the unoccupied
      slot (DELETED or FREE), if any, to which key hashes, using
      linear probing to find such a slot if necessary. If the record
      is not found and the file is full, locate sets the file
      position marker to the hash address of key.
*/

int locate( char *key )
{
    long address,         /* current offset in file */
        start_address,    /* initial (hash) offset in file */
        unocc_address;    /* first DELETED offset in file, if any;
                             otherwise, equal to start_address */
    int  delete_flag = 0; /* 0 if no DELETED slot found;
                             1 otherwise */
    char stored_key[ KEY_SIZE + 1 ];
    long get_address( char *key );

    address = get_address( key );   /* hash to address */
    unocc_address = start_address = address;

    do {
        fseek( fptr, address, SEEK_SET );   /* find slot */
        switch ( fgetc( fptr ) ) { /* check status */
        case DELETED:
            /* if first visit to a DELETED slot,
               mark its location and set flag */
            if ( !delete_flag ) {
                unocc_address = address;
                delete_flag = 1;
            }
            break;

        case FREE:
            /* end of search. If first unoccupied slot is a
               DELETED slot, reset file position marker to that
```

```
                    slot; otherwise, reset file position marker to
                    present FREE slot which is the first unoccupied
                    slot. */
               if ( delete_flag )
                    fseek( fptr, unocc_address, SEEK_SET );
               else
                    fseek( fptr, address, SEEK_SET );
               return ( NOT_FOUND );
          case TAKEN:
               /* extract key */
               fseek( fptr, address + 1L, SEEK_SET );
               fgets( stored_key, KEY_SIZE + 1, fptr );
               /* key equals stored_key? */
               if ( strncmp( key, stored_key, KEY_SIZE ) == 0 ) {
                    /* restore file position marker */
                    fseek( fptr, address, SEEK_SET );
                    return ( FOUND );
               }
               break;
          }
          /* probe */
          address = ( address + RECORD_SIZE ) % TOTAL_BYTES;
     } while ( address != start_address );

     /* reset file position marker to first DELETED slot or
        to initial slot */
     fseek( fptr, unocc_address, SEEK_SET );
     return ( NOT_FOUND );
}
```

Discussion

The program begins by attempting to open the file *records.dat* as a binary file because the function `locate` uses the library function `fseek`:

```
    if ( ( fptr = fopen( file, "r+b" ) ) != NULL )
```

If the file exists, `fptr` returns a nonNULL pointer associated with the file. We then count the records in the file. (By maintaining a count of records in the file, we can quickly determine when the file is full.) If the file does not exist, `fptr` returns NULL. In this case, we create the (binary) file by executing

```
    fptr = fopen( file, "w+b" );
```

We then fill each slot with a dummy record whose status flag is set to F to indicate that the slot never held a record.

The `while` loop in `main` invokes the function `print_menu`, which displays a menu from which the user chooses among adding a record, finding a record given its key, deleting a record given its key, or exiting.

The major work in this program is assigned to the function `locate`, which searches the file for a record with a given key. The function `locate` returns 1 if the record is found and 0 if the record is not found. Furthermore, if the record is found, `locate` sets the file position marker to the slot containing the record. This makes it easy to write the functions `find_record` and `remove_record`. If the record is not found, `locate` sets the file position marker to the first deleted or free slot, if any, encountered during linear probing. This makes it easy to write the function `add_record` and to prevent distinct records from having identical keys.

The function `locate` begins by setting the variable `delete_flag` to 0. If we ever find a deleted slot, we reset `delete_flag` to 1. Next, `locate` invokes the function `get_address`, which calculates the relative address of the given key and returns the byte offset of the slot in the file. The function `get_address` converts the key as a character string to an integer and then uses the division-remainder method to hash to the relative address. The function `get_address` uses the library function `atol`, which expects a string of digits and returns the number represented by the string as an integer of type `long`.

The byte offset is stored in three variables: `address`, `unocc_address`, and `start_address`. The value of `start_address` does not change. The variable `address` is used to probe. The value of `unocc_address` is set to the first deleted slot in the file, if any; otherwise, it retains its original value, `start_address`.

We then execute a do while loop to search for the record. The file position marker is set to the current slot:

```
fseek( fptr, address, SEEK_SET );
```

A `switch` statement directs us to one of three sections of code corresponding to the status of the current slot. If the status is DELETED and the value of `delete_flag` is 0, we set `unocc_address` to the address of the first deleted slot and change the value of `delete_flag` to 1. If the status is FREE, we set the file position marker to the first deleted slot, if it exists; otherwise, we set the file position marker to the free slot. If the status is TAKEN, we extract the key and check if it is the desired key. If we find the record, we reset the file position marker to the present slot and return 1; otherwise, we continue the search.

At the bottom of the loop, we probe by resetting `address`:

```
address = ( address + RECORD_SIZE ) % TOTAL_BYTES;
```

We terminate the loop with a `return` statement if we reach a free slot (within `case` FREE) or if we find the record (within `case` TAKEN). We also terminate the loop if we search the entire file. The test for searching the entire file is the end-of-loop test:

```
} while ( address != start_address );
```

If we search the entire file without finding the record, we reset the file position marker to the first deleted slot, if it exists, or to the initial slot if there is no deleted slot. We then return 0.

We use `fgets` to read user input a line at a time. We then use `sscanf`, `strcpy`, or `strncpy` to format and copy the input to the appropriate place. To understand how `fgets` and `fputs` are used in this program, it is important to remember that if the second argument to `fgets` is MAX, `fgets` reads at most MAX − 1 characters or all characters up to and including the newline character, whichever occurs first. The function `fgets` always terminates the string with `'\0'`. The function `fputs` writes everything up to the null terminator, but does not write the null terminator itself, and does not add a newline (see Section 8.4). For example, in the function `add_record`, we read the line that should contain the new record's key using `fgets`:

```
fgets( inbuff, INBUFF_SIZE, stdin );
```

The user is expected to enter a 9-digit number followed by a newline. Thus `fgets` should read 10 characters, 9 digits and a newline, and store 11 characters, the 10 read followed by `'\0'`. We check whether the correct number (10 = KEY_SIZE + 1) of characters was entered by using the string length function:

```
if ( strlen( inbuff ) != KEY_SIZE + 1 )
```

If the correct number of characters was read, we check whether there is already a record with this key:

```
if ( locate( inbuff ) == FOUND ) {
```

If there is no record with this key, we store the key in `record` by using `strncpy`:

```
strncpy( &record[ 1 ], inbuff, KEY_SIZE );
```

Here we copy exactly nine characters into `record` and we do *not* write a null terminator in `record`; `strncpy` does not add a null terminator unless it reads a null terminator in the source string.

The next section of `add_record` is similar:

```
do {
    printf( "\nPlease enter data: " );
    fgets( inbuff, INBUFF_SIZE, stdin );
    /* input must be less than or equal to
       RECORD_SIZE - KEY_SIZE - 1 counting the newline */
    if ( strlen( inbuff ) > RECORD_SIZE - KEY_SIZE - 1 )
        printf( "\aRecord size must be less than"
                " or equal to %d"
                " counting the newline\n",
                RECORD_SIZE - KEY_SIZE - 1 );
} while ( strlen( inbuff ) > RECORD_SIZE - KEY_SIZE - 1 );
```

That is, we read a line that contains the name, department, etc., using `fgets`. Since the newline is considered to be part of the record, the line must have length less than or equal to

```
RECORD_SIZE - KEY_SIZE - 1
```

(We subtract 1 to account for the status flag.) We check whether an appropriate number of characters was entered by using the string length function. If a correct number of characters was read, we store the key in `record` by using `strcpy`:

```
strcpy( &record[ 1 + KEY_SIZE ], inbuff );
```

The function `strcpy` copies everything in `inbuff` up to and including `'\0'` into `record`. In particular, `strcpy` stores the newline in `record`. At this point, `record` is a null-terminated string appropriate as an argument to `fputs`. After marking the status as taken

```
record[ 0 ] = TAKEN;
```

we write the record to the file

```
fputs( record, fptr );
```

and count it

```
++count;
```

†8.8   Nonstandard Input / Output

The input / output functions discussed in this section were written originally for the UNIX operating system. Although these functions are not specified by the standard, they have been ported to many environments (e.g., Turbo C, VAX-11 C). To ensure code portability, the standard input / output functions should be used wherever possible.

To use the following functions, we must associate a nonnegative integer, called a **file descriptor**, with each file. The file descriptor is analogous to the file pointer used in the standard input / output functions. The standard files and their descriptors are as follows:

File	File Descriptor
stdin	0
stdout	1
stderr	2

The files accessed by functions in this section have an access mode, as do the files accessed by the standard input / output functions. For these nonstandard functions, the access modes are as follows:

Access Mode	Meaning
0	Read
1	Write
2	Read and write

We now describe some nonstandard input / output functions that are available in many implementations. The function

```
open( char *file_name, int access_mode )
```

returns a file descriptor if it succeeds in opening the file and −1 otherwise. An opened file then is referenced through the file descriptor. This function is the nonstandard version of `fopen`.

The function

```
close( int file_descriptor )
```

returns 0 if it succeeds in closing the file and −1 otherwise. It is the nonstandard version of `fclose`.

The function

```
read( int file_descriptor, char *destination, int size )
```

tries to read `size` bytes into `destination`, typically an array, from the file associated with `file_descriptor`. It returns the number of bytes actually read or −1 on failure. Like many standard functions, it does not try to read beyond end-of-file. The function `read` has several standard counterparts, but it most closely resembles `fread`.

†This section can be omitted without loss of continuity.

The function

```
write( int file_descriptor, char *destination, int size )
```

tries to write `size` consecutive bytes from `destination` into the file associated with `file_descriptor`. It returns the number of bytes actually written or −1 on failure. The function `write` has several standard counterparts, but it most closely resembles `fwrite`.

Example 8.8.1. The following program reads the string

```
look_mom_no_hands
```

from one file and prints it to the terminal:

```
/* CAUTION -- this program uses nonstandard functions */

#include <stdio.h>

#define   SIZE      17
#define   READ       0
#define   STDOUT     1

main()
{
        char    in_file[] = "input.dat";
        char    string[ SIZE ]; /* 17 chars */
        int     input; /* file descriptor */

        input = open( in_file, READ );
        read( input, string, SIZE );   /* read from
                                               input.dat */
        write( STDOUT, string, SIZE ); /* write to
                                           standard output */
        close( input );
}
```

Changes from Traditional C

1. Traditional C does not distinguish between standard and nonstandard input / output functions. However, traditional C often characterizes the standard functions as *high-level* functions and the nonstandard ones as *low-level* functions to reflect the fact that, in many implementations of traditional C, the low-level functions make calls directly to the operating system and the high-level functions are then implemented through calls to the low-level ones.

2. Traditional C implementations are not required to support any specific input /output functions, although many of them support all the standard functions.

3. Traditional C implementations are not required to support binary files. Accordingly, functions that move the file position marker (e.g., `fseek`) may behave differently from one implementation to another because text files themselves may differ from one implementation to the next. For this reason, functions such as `fseek` tend not to be portable in traditional C.

4. The file access modes r+, w+, a+, r+b, w+b, and a+b are new to standard C, although they are widely supported in traditional C.

5. Traditional C does not have all of the format descriptors (e.g., %p) of standard C.

6. In some traditional implementations of C, the scanning functions ignore white space in the format string.

7. SEEK_SET, SEEK_CUR, and SEEK_END are new to standard C. In traditional C they are, respectively, 0, 1, and 2.

Common Programming Errors

1. It is an error to use stdin, stdout, or stderr as targets of an assignment statement, because each is a pointer constant rather than a variable.

2. Input/output functions require the header file *stdio.h*. For example, it is an error to write

   ```
   FILE *fp;
   ```

   without including *stdio.h*, which contains the definition of FILE.

3. It is risky to use both standard and nonstandard input/output functions on the same open file. It is also risky to use nonstandard input/output functions when writing programs that must run in many different C environments.

4. It is an error to attempt input/output processing on an unopened file.

5. It is an error to read from a file that does not exist.

6. It is an error to open an already opened file to change its input/output mode. For example, if the file *records.dat* has been opened for reading only, it should be closed before being opened for writing. Of course, a file may be opened in the first place for both reading and writing.

7. It is an error to invoke input/output functions without the expected number of arguments in the proper order. Recall, for example, that fgets expects three arguments, the third of which is of type pointer to FILE. By contrast, fscanf expects a variable number of arguments, but the first must be of type pointer to FILE.

8. It is an error to invoke functions for formatted input/output without a format string. Further, every expression to be read or written should have a conversion or format directive in the string.

9. It is an error to invoke any of the scanning functions—scanf, fscanf, sscanf—with nonpointer arguments as targets for the input operations. These functions expect the addresses of storage cells, not their names. For example, if num is defined as an int variable,

   ```
   scanf( "%d", num ); /*** ERROR ***/
   ```

   is an error. The statement must be written

   ```
   scanf( "%d", &num ); /*** CORRECT ***/
   ```

10. It is an error to read from and then write to a file or to write to and then read from a file without an intervening call to a function that resets the file position marker.

Programming Exercises

8.1. Write a program that prompts the user to supply the names of a source file and a target file. The program checks to see that the names of the source file and the target file are not identical, and if they are not identical, it copies the source file to the target file. The program should print the size, in bytes, of the copied file.

8.2. Amend the program of Exercise 8.1 so that it also prompts the user as to whether he or she wants to include either a comment header of up to 60 characters at the beginning of the target file or line numbers in the target file (or both).

8.3. Write a program that prompts the user for a source file's name and an integer. The integer represents the column width of the target file into which the source file is copied. The program checks to see whether the integer falls within a reasonable range (e.g., between 1 and 80). The target file's name is the same as the source file's name, except that the extension is changed to *cw*. For example, if the source file is named *test.dat,* the target file is *test.cw*. The program then copies *test.dat* to *test.cw* using the new column width.

8.4. A pharmaceutical company maintains two testing laboratories in different parts of the country. The laboratories sometimes conduct the same tests, sometimes different ones. Each test has a unique identifying number, together with a two-character code for the outcome. Each laboratory maintains its own data file of test outcomes. A typical outcome file is

```
11254    BF
11254    XL
22398    XP
33365    AD
55121    GG
```

Each line represents one test and contains the identifying number followed by the two-character outcome code. The entries are sorted by identifying number. Once a day, the central office merges the two sorted files to produce a single sorted file. For example, if the first laboratory's data file is

```
11254 XL
11254 BF
22398 XP
33365 AD
55121 GG
```

and the second laboratory's data file is

```
10011 GH
21011 MM
22119 GM
22398 HJ
76111 AD
```

the merged file is

```
10011 GH
11254 XL
```

```
11254 BF
21011 MM
22119 GM
22398 XP
22398 HJ
33365 AD
55121 GG
76111 AD
```

Note that test results are sorted on the test number only. If two tests have the same identifying number, either may go before the other. Note, too, that the merged file is sorted. Write a program that merges the two sorted files.

8.5. Amend the program of Exercise 8.4 so that it merges three files.

8.6. Write a program that compares two files. If the files are identical, the program should print a message to that effect; otherwise, it should print the line number and column position at which the two first differ. Assume that lines are delimited by '\n'.

8.7. Write a program that prompts the user for a source file, a target file, and a character to be deleted from the source file as it is copied to the target file. For example, if the user enters

```
old.dat    new.dat    $
```

old.dat should be copied into new.dat, except for the dollar sign. Do not allow the deletion of any white space characters.

8.8. The BNPL ("Borrow Now, Pay Later") Credit Bureau maintains a master file that lists, for each of its customers, the social security number, name, current principal that the customer owes, and his or her credit limit. The master file might be

```
222-11-3349 Nancy Zoe 51.20 5000.00
333-22-1265 Willard Smith 2341.50 4500.00
                  .
                  .
                  .
```

The BNPL Credit Bureau also maintains a transaction file that tracks its customers' loans and payments. Each record in this file lists the customer's social security number, together with the transaction's amount and its date. A positive number indicates a payment, and a negative number indicates a loan. For example, the entries

```
333-22-1265 +25.00    9-7-93
222-11-3349 -1273.00 9-18-93
333-22-1265 -1350.50 9-18-93
```

mean that customer 333-22-1265 paid back $25.00 on 9-7-93 and borrowed $1,350.50 on 9-18-93 and that customer 222-11-3349 borrowed $1,273.00 on 9-18-93. Once a month the BNPL Credit Bureau updates its master file by processing entries in the transaction file. Assume that the master file entries are sorted by social security number but that the transaction file is not sorted.

Write one program that creates a transaction file, another that sorts the transaction file, and a third that updates the master file.

8.9. Amend the BNPL Credit Bureau program of Exercise 8.8 so that new customers may be added to the master file and current customers may be deleted. Remember that records in the master file are to be sorted by social security number.

8.10. Assume that you run a business and keep a computerized file of all your customers. The address file is formatted as follows:

```
Ms. Peggy March
Motown Recordings
888 E. Circle
Detroit, MI 54301
Mr. Rudolph Valentino
Hollywood Squares
21 Hollywood Avenue
Hollywood, CA 10201
        .
        .
        .
```

Assume that each entry for a customer takes exactly four lines. A separate file contains the body of a very polite "bill overdue" letter that asks the customer to pay up as soon as possible. Write a program that prompts the user for a customer's name; searches the address file for the customer's name; and, if successful, generates an output file that contains an individualized letter with the customer's name and address together with the body of the letter. The output file also contains the current date, which the user enters from the keyboard, as well as a line such as

```
Dear Ms. March:
```

following the address.

8.11. Expand the program of Exercise 8.10 in two ways. First, customer entries in the address file now may take anywhere from three to six lines, but a new customer entry line always begins with either "Mr." or "Ms." Second, assume that your business now maintains three input files. The first two are as in Exercise 8.10. The third contains credit information on each customer, as follows:

```
111–11–1111    March        12.30
223–11–9817    Valentino    6534.26
       .           .           .
       .           .           .
       .           .           .
```

The fields are social security number, last name, and amount due over 30 days. The program generates a letter that includes, at a selected spot in the body, the amount that has been due for more than 30 days. The generated letter is written to a fourth file.

8.12. A small stock exchange provides an on-line query system for its customers. Each stock traded on the exchange has a unique integer code that ranges from 1000 through 5999. The system maintains the following data on each stock:

```
1817     12.34     +0.16     17.89      9.21
1818      0.11     -0.04      4.32      0.05
1819     34.89        nc     21.50     18.76
                       .
                       .
                       .
```

The fields are stock number, current price, change, 52-week high, and 52-week low. The change field indicates the amount that the stock's price has changed since the last trading day; so, for example, stock 1817's price has gone up $0.16 since the last trading day. The entry nc means ''no change.''

Data are kept in five separate files. Stocks with numbers from 1000 to 1999 are in *File1,* those from 2000 to 2999 in *File2,* and so on. When the user enters a stock number, the system first determines the appropriate file and then prints the record of the stock. The system allows the user to ask about as many stocks as he or she wishes. Assume that the records in each file are sorted by stock number.

8.13. Assume that you are charged with printing reports on the weather for the National Weather Service. To save on storage, you compact your data files. Each day's entry consists of a three-character low temperature, a three-character high temperature, and a two-digit daily precipitation reading. Nine entries (72 characters) are stored per line. For example, the file

```
03404500-0900801...
```

shows that on the first day of the month, the low temperature was 34 degrees (034); the high was 45 degrees (045); and the precipitation was 0 inches (00). On the second day, the low was -9 degrees; the high was 8 degrees; and the precipitation was 1 inch. Each month's data are kept in their own file. To generate a report, the user simply enters a keyword such as DEC for December or MAR for March. The program then locates the appropriate file and prints a report formatted as follows:

```
Report on December
Date    Low    High    Precipitation
1       34     46      0
2       28     36      1
3       28     28      0
                .
                .
                .
```

8.14. Write a program TAIL that prompts the user for a file name and an integer, which is interpreted as a line offset from either the beginning or the end of the file. The program then writes the file to the standard output, starting at the specified offset. For example, if the user enters

```
/* file name */   /* offset */
party_animals.dat    35
```

TAIL prints the file *party_animals.dat,* starting at line 35. If the user enters

```
/* file name */   /* offset */
party_animals.dat −87
```

TAIL prints the file *party_animals.dat,* but starting 87 lines from the end of the file. If an error occurs (as, for example, if the file has only 20 lines and the user enters 35), print an error message.

8.15. During exercises at a military base, two different instruments track a missile's velocity at quarter-second intervals from its launch until it either strikes a target or is destroyed for safety reasons. The instruments store the data in separate files for later comparison by the CHECK program. Assume that the data consist of floating-point numbers separated by white space. The program CHECK prompts the user for a tolerance, which is the amount by which corresponding entries in the two files may differ. For example, suppose that the fifth entry in *File1* is 111.8356; the corresponding entry in *File2* is 111.8359; and the tolerance is 0.002. The program checks whether the absolute difference is less than or equal to the specified tolerance. In this example, the two numbers differ by 0.003, which exceeds the tolerance. The CHECK program reads corresponding numbers from the two files, averages them, and stores the average in a third file. In addition, whenever the difference between the two exceeds the tolerance, it does the following:

(a) Records, in the file *ERR.LOG,* which pairs exceed the tolerance. For example, if only the third and ninth pairs exceed the tolerance, only 3 and 9 are written to *ERR.LOG.*

(b) Writes to the standard error a message about any pair that exceeds the tolerance and the amount by which it exceeds it.

8.16. The random access file program of Section 8.7 uses the division-remainder method to hash a record's key to its relative address in the file. One competing method, known as **mid-square hashing**, works as follows: Given a key with N digits, to compute a relative address with K digits, we square the key and then extract the middle K digits from the squared key. For example, if N is 9 and K is 4, we have

```
Sample Key:          200120472
Key Squared:         40048203313502784
Middle 4 Digits:           3313
```

Revise the program of Section 8.7 so that it uses mid-square hashing.

8.17. Generate a list of 1,000 random keys, and use the hashing methods of Exercise 8.16 and Section 8.7 to generate addresses in the same range; then check for the relative frequency of collisions using each method.

8.18. The Cloze Procedure† is a method of estimating the suitability of instructional text for students. Given the text, we prepare a Cloze test as follows. Every fifth word is replaced by several underscores, and the student is asked to fill in the blanks. The percentage of correct responses is determined. (A response is counted correct only if it is identical to the omitted word, except possibly for a misspelling.) The suitability for instruction is estimated from the following table:

†The Cloze Procedure as described here is somewhat simplifed. Normally, the text is required to consist of at least 250 words, and no words are omitted from the first and last sentences.

Percent Correct	Suitability for Instruction
Less than 35%	Too hard
Between 35% and 65%	Suitable
More than 65%	Too easy

Write a program that reads in text and prepares a Cloze test. Define a word to be any sequence of letters *a* through *z* or *A* through *Z* delimited by nonletters. Replace every fifth word by 15 underscores.

Structures, Unions, and Enumerated Types

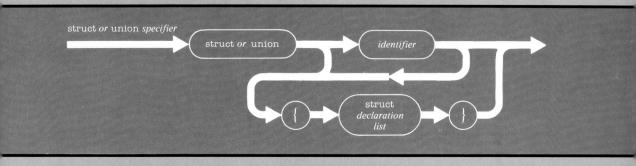

9.1 Introduction to Structures

9.2 Sample Application: Pattern Recognition

9.3 The `typedef` Construct

9.4 Operations on Structures

9.5 Pointers to Structures, Nested Structures, and Self-referential Structures

9.6 Structures and Functions

9.7 Sample Application: An Airline Flight Database

†9.8 Unions and Bit Fields

9.9 Enumerated Types

Changes from Traditional C

Common Programming Errors

Programming Exercises

†This section can be omitted without loss of continuity.

C supports not only built-in data types such as `char` and `int` but also user-defined data types that let the programmer tailor data representation to a particular application. C also supports both arrays that group variables of the same data type and structures that group variables of different data types.

After discussing structures, we turn to a related construct, `union`. We conclude with enumerated types, which are close in syntax to structures.

9.1 Introduction to Structures

The `PHONE` program of Chapter 5 (Section 5.10) uses character strings (arrays of `char`) to store names and phone numbers. Each string represents a record that has three fields: last name, first name, and phone number. A typical array element is a record such as

```
Lauper Cindi 708-123-9091
```

Suppose that we expand the record to include the additional fields of age, hobby, and annual income, so that a typical array element becomes

```
Lauper Cindi 708-123-9091 31 tiddly-winks 8432555.09
```

A record now has six fields: last name, first name, phone number, age, hobby, and annual income. We still could use a string to represent such a record by making each field a substring. Yet this approach has weaknesses. Suppose that we want to average the incomes of everyone in our database. We first must extract the incomes, which requires that we know exactly where each substring that represents the income begins and ends. After extracting each income substring, we must cast it into `float` before averaging. It would be better to represent income directly as a floating-point number. A **structure** furnishes the desired construct.

Example 9.1.1. The following structure declaration creates a user-defined data type named `struct personnel_record`:

```
/* declare a structure as a user-defined data type */
struct personnel_record {
     char   first_name[ 15 ];
     char   last_name[ 25 ];
     int    age;
     char   hobby[ 25 ];
     float  income;
};
```

A structure declaration begins with the keyword `struct` and is followed by a name (`personnel_record`, in this case) chosen by the user to identify the particular data type. The user-chosen name is called the **tag**. Next, in braces, are the **members** of the structure (`first_name`, `last_name`, `age`, `hobby`, and `income`, in this case). Notice that the terminating brace is followed by a semicolon.

A structure declaration, such as that of Example 9.1.1, allocates no storage but, rather, describes the structure and gives it a name. To allocate storage for a structure, we define variables just as for any other data type, as the following example illustrates.

Example 9.1.2. The following code defines three variables of type `struct per-sonnel_record` (declared in Example 9.1.1):

```
/* defining variables of a user-defined data type */
struct personnel_record   record1, record2, record3;
```

The preceding statement causes storage to be allocated for three variables, named `record1`, `record2`, and `record3`, each of type `struct person-nel_record`. Each of the variables `record1`, `record2`, and `record3` contains the members `first_name`, `last_name`, `age`, `hobby`, and `income`, as given in the structure declaration of Example 9.1.1 (see Figure 9.1.1). Before the three variables can be defined, the data type itself must be declared; that is, the code in Example 9.1.1 must *precede* the code in Example 9.1.2.

Notice that the syntax for defining variables is the same for both built-in and user-defined data types; that is, the definition

```
struct personnel_record   record1, record2, record3;
```

is syntactically identical to

```
char c1, c2, c3;
```

When we define structure variables, as in Example 9.1.2, the system uses the structure declaration as a template from which to construct instances of the structure. By referring to the structure declaration, the system can determine exactly how much storage to allocate.

Example 9.1.3. With built-in data types, we can define either individual variables or arrays of variables. The same is true for user-defined data types. The following code declares a user-defined data type named `struct inventory_list` and defines an array of 200 variables, each of type `struct inventory_list`:

```
/* declare a structure as a user-defined data type */
struct inventory_list {
        int    part_id;
```

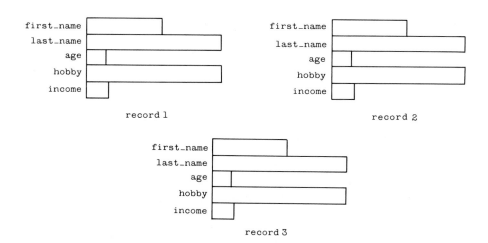

Figure 9.1.1 Three variables of type `struct personnel_record`.

```
        int    warehouse_id;
        int    quantity;
        char   part_name[ 20 ];
        char   supplier_name[ 40 ];
};

/* define an array of structure variables */
struct inventory_list  records[ 200 ];
```

We access variables in the array `records` by using an index in the standard fashion. For example, the expression

```
records[ 3 ]
```

references the fourth variable of type `struct inventory_list` in the array `records`.

To access a member of a structure, we write the structure variable name, a period (**member operator**), and then the member's name. For example, given the declaration and definitions in Examples 9.1.1 and 9.1.2, we can access the member `age` in the structure variable `record1` by writing

```
record1.age
```

The following example illustrates that any operation is legal on a structure member that is legal on an ordinary variable of the same type.

Example 9.1.4. Given the declaration and definitions

```
struct compact_disk {
     char   composer[ 30 ];
     char   work[ 30 ];
     int    id;
     float price;
};
struct compact_disk buffer, bin1[ 100 ];
```

the following code assigns values to each of the members of `buffer`:

```
strcpy( buffer.composer, "Ives, Charles" );
strcpy( buffer.work, "Three Places in New England" );
buffer.id = 9236;
buffer.price = 13.95;
```

The following code assigns values to each of the members of `bin1[ 14 ]`:

```
strcpy( bin1[ 14 ].composer, "Herrmann, Bernard" );
strcpy( bin1[ 14 ].work, "String Quartet \"Echoes\"" );
bin1[ 14 ].id = 3101;
bin1[ 14 ].price = 15.65;
```

To print the member `composer` in `bin1[ 14 ]`, we could write

```
printf( "Composer: %s", bin1[ 14 ].composer );
```

To decrease `price` by 2.00 in `bin1[ 14 ]`, we could write

```
bin1[ 14 ].price -= 2.00;
```

Although structure names must be distinct, we may use the same name for members in different structures. In fact, an ordinary variable may have the same name as a structure member. By using the member operator, the various variables are uniquely identified.

Example 9.1.5. The following code illustrates how the member operator is used to enforce unique variable names in a C program:

```
/* declare one structure */
struct yearly_income {
        float   full_time_job;    /* note the name */
        float   part_time_job;
        float   gross_income;
};

/* declare another structure */
struct taxes {
        float   full_time_job;    /* note the name */
        float   fed_rate;
        float   state_rate;
};

/* define variables of each type */
struct yearly_income fred, molly;
struct taxes curly, moe;

/* define a variable */
float    full_time_job;    /* note the name */

/* assign values to uniquely named variables */
fred.full_time_job  =   11010.23;
molly.full_time_job = 999999.99;
curly.full_time_job =     21.09;
moe.full_time_job   =      0.12;
full_time_job       =    111.11;
```

The variable named `fred.full_time_job` is one variable; the variable named `moe.full_time_job` is an altogether different variable; and the variable named `full_time_job` is yet another distinct variable.

C requires that the member operator be used in accessing any of a structure's members even if the member's name never appears in another definition.

To combine a declaration and definition of a structure, we simply list the variables to be defined between the terminating brace and the semicolon.

Example 9.1.6. The following code declares the data type `struct person-nel_record` and defines variables `record1`, `record2`, `record3`, and an array `records[ 200 ]` each of type `struct personnel_record`:

```
/* declaring a structure and defining
   variables of this type */
struct personnel_record {
        char   first_name[ 15 ];
        char   last_name[ 25 ];
        int    age;
```

```
        char   hobby[ 25 ];
        float income;
   }  record1, record2, record3, records[ 200 ];
```

The tag is not required. For example, Example 9.1.6 could be amended as shown in Example 9.1.7.

Example 9.1.7. The following code declares a structure without a tag and then defines 203 structure variables, as in Example 9.1.6:

```
/* declaring a structure without a tag and
   defining variables of this type */
struct {
        char   first_name[ 15 ];
        char   last_name[ 25 ];
        int    age;
        char   hobby[ 25 ];
        float income;
   }  record1, record2, record3, records[ 200 ];
```

We have 203 structure variables, just as in Example 9.1.6, but the data type has no identifying tag.

If we *declare* a structure without simultaneously defining any variables, it is important to include a tag because, without a tag, it will be impossible later to define any variables of the structure type declared! There is little advantage to untagged structures; indeed, they reduce the programmer's flexibility.

If a structure declaration is inside a block, it is visible only in its containing block. If a structure declaration is outside all blocks, it is visible throughout the rest of the file.

Example 9.1.8. In the following program, the structure declaration is visible only in the function `main`. For this reason, the attempt to define a variable of type `struct item` in the function `f` is illegal.

```
main()
{
     struct item {
          int id;
          int quantity;
          char name[ 20 ];
          char supplier[ 40 ];
     };
     .
     .
     .

}
void f( void )
{
     struct item temp;   /* ILLEGAL—struct item
                            is unknown */
     .
     .
     .

}
```

The error in Example 9.1.8 can be corrected by making the structure declaration visible throughout the file.

Example 9.1.9. In the following program, the structure declaration is visible throughout the file. For this reason, the definitions of variables of type `struct item` are legal in both `main` and the function `f`.

```
struct item {
      int   id;
      int   quantity;
      char name[ 20 ];
      char supplier[ 40 ];
};

main()
{
      struct item buffer;
      .
      .
      .

}
void f( void )
{
      struct item temp;
      .
      .
      .

}
```

It is common in C to declare tagged structures in a header file and then include the header file wherever needed.

Example 9.1.10. Suppose that the declaration of `struct person-nel_record` occurs in the file *structures.h*. The following code defines 200 variables of type `struct personnel_record` in the function `process_person-nel_records`:

```
#include "structures.h"
void  process_personnel_records( void )
{
      struct personnel_record  records[ 200 ];
          .
          .
          .

}
```

The `sizeof` operator (see Section 2.1) may be used with structures, as the next example illustrates.

Example 9.1.11. We assume a computer system that uses four bytes to store both an `int` and a `float`. Given the declaration

```
struct robot {
      char    name[ 15 ];
      int     limbs;
```

```
    int     joints;
    float   weight;
    float   max_speed;
    char    bad_habits[ 20 ][ 100 ];
} r2, robots[ 200 ];
```

the members of struct robot, when allocated, occupy the following space:

Member	Storage (in bytes)
name[15]	15
limbs	4
joints	4
weight	4
max_speed	4
bad_habits	2,000 = (20 * 100)
Total	2,031

If the members follow one another with no gaps, the value of sizeof (struct robot) is 2031. However, on many systems there *are* gaps between the members, since certain machine instructions require data types to be stored at particular addresses. On such systems, the value of sizeof (struct robot) exceeds 2031. If sizeof (struct robot) is 2031, the value of sizeof (robots) is

```
2031 * 200 = 406,200
```

In this case, the array robots occupies 406,200 bytes.

Exercises

1. What is the difference between a structure and an array?
2. Explain the difference between declaring a structure and defining a structure variable.
3. What is meant by saying that a structure declaration is a template?
4. What is a structure tag?
5. What advantage is there in declaring a structure with a tag?
6. Explain the difference between an array of structure variables and a structure variable that has an array as a member.
7. (True/False) Member variables of two different structures may have the same name.
8. In the following code, identify the tag, the members, and the structure variables:

```
struct new_years_resolutions {
    char    resolution1[ 20 ];
    char    resolution2[ 20 ];
    char    resolution3[ 20 ];
    float odds1; /* probability that resolution1
                    will be kept */
```

```
        float odds2; /* ditto for resolution2 */
        float odds3; /* ditto for resolution3 */
    } bob, carol, ted, alice;
```

Exercises 9 through 17 assume the declaration

```
struct animal {
    int    id;
    char   type[ 30 ];
    char   name[ 30 ];
    float  age;
};
```

9. Define a variable `temp` and an array `menagerie` with 200 cells, each of type `struct animal`.

   Exercises 10 through 17 assume the definitions of Exercise 9.

10. Write code that initializes each member of `temp` using the assignment operator and `strcpy`.

11. Write code that initializes each member of `menagerie[ 5 ]` using the assignment operator and `strcpy`.

12. Write code that initializes each member of `menagerie` using `scanf` and a loop.

    Exercises 13 through 17 assume that an `int` occupies two bytes and that a `float` occupies four bytes. Also, assume that the members follow one another with no gaps. Find the value of each expression in Exercises 13 through 17.

13. `sizeof ( struct animal )`

14. `sizeof ( temp )`

15. `sizeof ( menagerie )`

16. `sizeof ( menagerie[ 0 ].id )`

17. `sizeof ( menagerie[ 6 ].type )`

18. Declare a structure that represents a student record, including the student's name, age, address, social security number, grade-point average, current course load, courses taken, date of matriculation, major, and at least three other pieces of information that strike you as suitable for the record.

19. Define an array of 300 variables of the structure type of Exercise 18.

20. What errors, if any, occur in the following code?

```
struct wreck {
    char    *flotsam;
    char    *jetsam;
    int     number_of_crew_saved;
} wreck1;
flotsam = "a cracked flower pot";
jetsam = "two Persian carpets";
```

21. Explain the difference between `car.make` and `car.model` in the following code:

```
struct automobile {
    char   make[ 10 ];
```

```
        char   *model;
        int    number_of_doors;
        float price;
    } car;
```

22. Explain the error:

```
#include <stdio.h>

main()
{
    struct automobile {
        char   make[ 10 ];
        char   *model;
        int    number_of_doors;
        float price;
    } car;
    scanf( "%s", car.model );
        .
        .
        .
}
```

23. How does the system interpret the following code?

```
struct record {
    int id;
    char name[ 80 ];
}
main()
{
    .
    .
    .
}
```

24. Each record in an input file occupies one line and is terminated by a newline. Columns 1 through 29 contain the composer; columns 30 through 58 contain the work; columns 59 through 64 contain the id; and columns 65 through 70 contain the price:

```
Ives, Charles           Three Places in New England  302932 12.95
```

A structure cd is defined as

```
struct disc {
    char composer[ 30 ];
    char work[ 30 ];
    long id;
    float price;
} cd;
```

Which of the following (if any) will correctly read one record (including the terminating newline) from the standard input and store it in cd? (The data in cd.composer and cd.work need not be null terminated.)

(a) `scanf( "%29c%29c%6ld%6f", cd.composer,`
`cd.work, &cd.id, &cd.price );`

(b) `scanf( "%29c%29c%6ld%6f ", cd.composer,`
`cd.work, &cd.id, &cd.price );`

(c) `scanf( "%29c%29c%6ld%6.2f ", cd.composer,`
`cd.work, &cd.id, &cd.price );`

(d) `fgets( cd.composer, 30, stdin );`
`fgets( cd.work, 30, stdin );`
`scanf( "%6ld%6f ", &cd.id, &cd.price );`

(e) `fgets( cd.composer, 29, stdin );`
`fgets( cd.work, 29, stdin );`
`scanf( "%6ld%6f ", &cd.id, &cd.price );`

(f) `scanf( "%29s%29s%6ld%6f ", cd.composer,`
`cd.work, &cd.id, &cd.price );`

9.2 Sample Application: Pattern Recognition

Problem

Implement the *nearest neighbor method* to classify movies as hits or flops using a set (called a *sample set*) of movies, each of which is already classified as a hit or a flop. (A hit movie might be defined as one that made a profit.) For each film in the sample set, we are given the following data (see Figure 9.2.1):

- The percentage of hits of the director.
- The percentage of hits of the leading members of the cast.

These data are stored in the file *nearest_neighbor.dat*.

The nearest neighbor algorithm can be described as follows:

1. Compute the distance between the unclassified film and all films in the sample set.
2. Find the film in the sample set nearest the film to be classified.
3. Assign the unknown film the class of the nearest film.

Sample Input/Output

The file *nearest_neighbor.dat* has the format

`<hit percentage of director> <hit percentage of cast> <hit/flop>`

where 1 means hit and 0 means flop. The file is

```
10.0 20.0 0
10.0 30.0 0
20.0 50.0 0
20.0 60.0 1
30.0 10.0 0
40.0 10.0 0
40.0 40.0 0
40.0 60.0 0
40.0 70.0 1
60.0 30.0 0
```

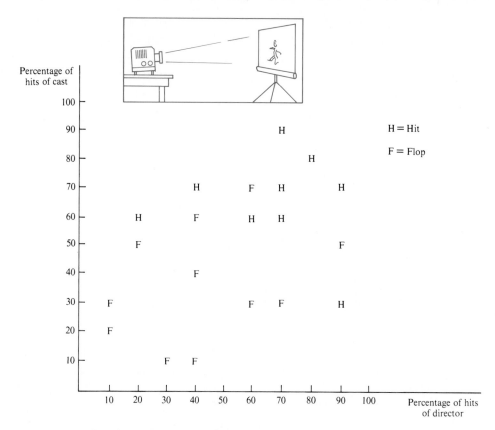

Figure 9.2.1 Sample set for a film classifier.

```
60.0 60.0 1
60.0 70.0 0
70.0 30.0 0
70.0 60.0 1
70.0 70.0 1
70.0 90.0 1
80.0 80.0 1
90.0 30.0 1
90.0 50.0 0
90.0 70.0 1
```

Sample Interactive Session

Input is in color; output is in black.

```
Enter name of file containing the sample set:
nearest_neighbor.dat

Enter the percentage of hits of the
director of the film to be classified or
generate EOF to terminate the program: 20

Enter the percentage of hits of the
leading members of the cast of the film
to be classified: 50
```

The film is a flop.

Enter the percentage of hits of the
director of the film to be classified or
generate EOF to terminate the program: 70

Enter the percentage of hits of the
leading members of the cast of the film
to be classified: 70

The film is a HIT!

Enter the percentage of hits of the
director of the film to be classified or
generate EOF to terminate the program: 70

Enter the percentage of hits of the
leading members of the cast of the film
to be classified: 50

The film is a HIT!

Enter the percentage of hits of the
director of the film to be classified or
generate EOF to terminate the program: 85

Enter the percentage of hits of the
leading members of the cast of the film
to be classified: 45

The film is a flop.

Enter the percentage of hits of the
director of the film to be classified or
generate EOF to terminate the program: Exit

(In the sample input / output, we assume that Exit is printed when EOF is generated.)

C Implementation

```
/*  This program classifies movies as hits or flops using the
    nearest neighbor algorithm.

    The program begins by prompting the user to provide the name
    of the file containing the sample set (set of already
    classified films). For each film, the data are the percentage
    of hits of the director and the percentage of hits of the
    leading members of the cast. The program then reads the data
    of at most MAX_NO_FILMS classified films. Next, the program
    prompts the user for data concerning unclassified films. The
    program finds the film nearest the unknown sample (by
    comparing the squares of Euclidean distances between the
    unclassified film and the classified films). The program
    assigns the unknown film the class of the film nearest it.

    The user terminates the program by generating EOF.          */

#include <stdio.h>
#include <float.h>
```

```
#define MAX_NO_FILMS 100 /* maximum number of classified films *
#define HIT 1

main()
{
    int numb_films = 0; /* number of films in sample set */
    int i;
    int nearest; /* index of nearest film */
    int eof_flag;
    double sdist; /* square of distance */
    double min_dist; /* minimum distance */
    FILE *fp;
    char file_name[ FILENAME_MAX ]; /* name of file containing
                                       sample set */
    struct hit_flop {
        double dir_hits; /* percentage of hits of the director */
        double cast_hits; /* percentage of hits of the leading
                             members of the cast */
        int code; /* 1 if a hit; 0 if a flop */
    };
    struct hit_flop film[ MAX_NO_FILMS ];
    double unknown_dir_hits; /* percentage of hits of the director
                                of a film to be classified */
    double unknown_cast_hits; /* percentage of hits of the leading
                                 members of the cast of a film to be
                                 classified */

    printf( "Enter name of file containing the sample set:\n" );
    scanf( "%s", file_name );
    fp = fopen( file_name, "r" );

    /* read sample file */
    while ( numb_films < MAX_NO_FILMS &&
            fscanf( fp, "%lf", &film[ numb_films ].dir_hits) != EOF ) {
        fscanf( fp, "%lf", &film[ numb_films ].cast_hits );
        fscanf( fp, "%d", &film[ numb_films ].code );
        numb_films++;
    }

    /* input values for unknown films and classify each using the
       nearest neighbor algorithm */
    do {
        printf( "\n\nEnter the percentage of hits of the\n"
                "director of the film to be classified or\n"
                "generate EOF to terminate the program: " );
        if ( ( eof_flag = scanf( "%lf", &unknown_dir_hits ) )
                != EOF ) {
            printf( "\n\nEnter the percentage of hits of the\n"
                    "leading members of the cast of the film\n"
                    "to be classified: ");
            scanf( "%lf", &unknown_cast_hits );
```

```
                    /* find the film nearest the unknown */
                    min_dist = DBL_MAX;
                    for ( i = 0; i < numb_films; i++ ) {
                         sdist = ( unknown_dir_hits - film[ i ].dir_hits )
                              * ( unknown_dir_hits - film[ i ].dir_hits )
                              + ( unknown_cast_hits - film[ i ].cast_hits )
                              * ( unknown_cast_hits - film[ i ].cast_hits );
                         if ( sdist < min_dist ) {
                              min_dist = sdist;
                              nearest = i;
                         }
                    }
                    printf( "\n\nThe film is a " );
                    if ( film[ nearest ].code == HIT )
                         printf( "HIT!\n" );
                    else
                         printf( "flop.\n" );
               }
          } while ( eof_flag != EOF );
}
```

Discussion

We define an array `file_name` of size `FILENAME_MAX` to store the name of the sample file. The macro `FILENAME_MAX` is defined in *stdio.h*, and its value is the maximum length of a file name for the particular implementation.

We define an array of `MAX_NO_FILMS` structures to hold the sample file. After prompting the user for the name of the sample file, we store the data in the array of structures. The variable `numb_films` counts the number of films in the sample file.

We continually prompt the user for the percentage of hits of the director and the percentage of hits of the cast of a film to classify. We locate the film in the array of structures nearest the unknown film. We compute the square of the (Euclidean) distance between each film in the array and the unknown film. Recall that the formula for the distance between the points (x_1, y_1) and (x_2, y_2) is

$$\sqrt{(x_1 - x_2)^2 + (y_1 - y_2)^2}$$

Because we are interested only in *comparing* distances (and not in computing the *actual* distances), we compare not the actual distances but, rather, the squares of the distances. Our program runs faster than a similar program that computes the actual distances, as computing square roots is time-consuming.

Before beginning the `for` loop that computes the squares of the distances, we set the variable `min_dist` to the largest possible double value `DBL_MAX`, defined in *float.h*. Each time we find a point closer to the unknown point, we update `min_dist` and the variable `nearest`, which is the index of the nearest point so far found. Choosing a large initial value for `min_dist` ensures that when we examine the first film in the array of structures, the variables `min_dist` and `nearest` receive correct initial values.

We then examine the code of the film nearest the film to be classified and classify the unknown film as the same type.

Pattern recognition is concerned with grouping data into classes based on the data's properties. (In real pattern recognition problems, as many as 100 or more properties may be considered.) Various techniques can be used to assign a class to an object based on a set of already classified data. We used the nearest neighbor method in its simplest incarnation. This method can be enhanced (see Programming Exercises 9.4 and 9.5) by, for example, replacing Euclidean distance by some other distance or by selecting the *k* nearest neighbors of the unknown and classifying the unknown as belonging to the class most frequently represented among the *k* samples. For more information on pattern recognition in general and the nearest neighbor method in particular, see K. Fukunaga, *Introduction to Statistical Pattern Recognition*, 2nd ed. (New York: Academic Press, 1990).

9.3 The `typedef` Construct

C provides the `typedef` construct, which lets the programmer provide a synonym for either a built-in or a user-defined data type. Although `typedef` may be used with any data type, its use with structures clarifies the definition of structure variables. We first illustrate the general use of `typedef` and then look at the specific use of `typedef` with structures.

> *Example 9.3.1.* If we write
>
> ```
> typedef int AGE;
> ```
>
> AGE becomes a synonym for `int`. Subsequently, we can substitute AGE for `int`. For example, we can define the `int` variable age_mary by writing
>
> ```
> AGE age_mary;
> ```
>
> The user-supplied name can be any mix of uppercase and lowercase characters.

Note the syntax of a `typedef`. First comes the keyword `typedef`, then the data type, and last the user-provided name for this data type.

A `typedef` is used only to create a synonym for a data type. In a `typedef`, no variables may be defined and no storage is allocated. For example, it is an error to write

```
typedef int AGE age_mary;   /* ERROR!!!! */
```

in an attempt to make AGE a synonym for `int` and to create an `int` variable named age_mary.

> *Example 9.3.2.* The following code makes AGE a synonym for `int` and SALARY a synonym for `float`. The code than defines variables using these names.
>
> ```
> main()
> {
>     typedef int AGE;
>     typedef float SALARY;
>     AGE     age_mary, age_bruce, age_lindsay;
>     SALARY  sal_mary, sal_bruce, sal_lindsay;
>         .
>         .
>         .
> }
> ```

> *Example 9.3.3.* The `typedef` construct is similar in purpose to the `#define` directive, but they are *not* identical. The `typedef` construct assigns a name to a data

type; the #define directive simply initiates text substitution without imposing any particular meaning. For example, the construct

```
typedef int * int_ptr;
```

assigns the name int_ptr to the data type pointer to int. Thus if we then write

```
int_ptr p, q;
```

the variables p and q are both of type pointer to int. On the other hand, the directive

```
#define int_p int *
```

causes subsequent occurrences of int_p to be replaced by int *. Thus if we then write

```
int_p r, s;
```

the preprocessor expands this to

```
int * r, s;
```

and r is of type pointer to int, whereas s is of type int.

typedef and Code Portability

The typedef can be used to promote code portability. Suppose that we have an application that assumes that all integers are represented by 16-bit storage cells. On computer system *A*, an int may be implemented as a 32-bit cell but a short int as a 16-bit cell; on system *B*, both an int and a short int are implemented as a 16-bit cell. Assume that we write our application on system *A* using the typedef:

```
/* on computer system A */
/* INTEGER has sixteen bits. */
typedef short int  INTEGER;
```

Throughout our application, we always use INTEGER instead of short int in defining variables. Now we port the code over to system *B*. We need to change only the typedef:

```
/* on computer system B */
/* INTEGER still has sixteen bits. */
typedef int  INTEGER;
```

This typedef could be put in a file such as *port.h* and then included in the files that need integer variables.

typedef and Structures

Our main concern in this section is the use of typedef in declaring structures. The syntax for a typedef when the data type is a structure remains the same:

```
typedef <data type> <user-provided name>;
```

Now, however, the data type is

```
struct <tag> { <members> }
```

Example 9.3.4.   The code

```
/*   associate the name PERSON with the
     data type struct personnel_record */
typedef  struct personnel_record {
         char   first_name[ 15 ];
         char   last_name[ 25 ];
         int    age;
         char   hobby[ 25 ];
         float  income;
} PERSON;
```

is a typedef for the data type struct personnel_record. PERSON is now the name for the user-defined data type struct personnel_record. After writing the preceding typedef, we can define variables of type PERSON as follows:

```
PERSON record1, record2, record3, records[ 200 ];
```

The preceding line is equivalent to

```
struct personnel_record record1, record2, record3,
       records[ 200 ];
```

The typedef name can be the same as the structure's tag. In Example 9.3.4, we could have used PERSONNEL_RECORD, even in lowercase, as the typedef name. Finally, although we can use the typedef with an untagged structure, we again recommend that structures be declared with tags.

Exercises

1. Rewrite the following declaration and definition using a typedef:

```
struct robot {
     char   name[ 15 ];
     int    limbs;
     int    joints;
     float  weight;
     float  max_speed;
     char   bad_habits[ 20 ][ 100 ];
} r2, d2;
```

2. Use a typedef to associate the name CAR with a structure that could be used to hold information about an automobile.

3. In the following code, clarify the difference between house and HOUSE:

```
struct house {
     char   address[ 25 ];
     int    rooms;
     float  asking_price;
};
typedef struct house HOUSE;
```

4. What is the value of sizeof (HOUSE) in Exercise 3, assuming that an int and a float each occupy four bytes? (Assume that the members follow one another with no gaps.)

5. Are the variable definitions in CASE 1 and CASE 2 equivalent? (We use the code of Exercise 3.)

```
/* CASE 1 */
struct house   homes_for_sale[ 1000 ];
/* CASE 2 */
HOUSE   homes_for_sale[ 1000 ];
```

6. For each of the definitions in Exercise 5, what is the data type of each variable in the array homes_for_sale?

7. What is the error?

```
typedef struct book {
     char   title[ 25 ];
     char   author[ 50 ];
     char   isbn[ 11 ];
     char   date_of_publication[ 8 ];
     float price;
} BOOK books[ 200 ];
```

8. (True/False) A typedef may be used only with a tagged structure.

9. (True/False) When using a typedef to declare a structure, the typedef name may be the same as a structure's tag.

10. What advantages are there in using a typedef in declaring a structure?

11. Print *stdio.h* and verify that FILE is defined by using a typedef.

12. Print *stdlib.h* and list the typedefs used there.

9.4   Operations on Structures

As we saw in Section 9.1, C supports all the appropriate operations on the members of a structure. At the same time, C provides limited operations on an entire structure. In this section, we explain how to assign one structure, as a whole, to another structure. In Section 9.6, we discuss passing a structure to a function and show how a function can return a structure. We begin by describing how to initialize members of a structure.

Initializing Members of Structures

A structure variable, like an array, can be initialized at definition time. Values for the members are enclosed in braces.

Example 9.4.1. The following code declares a structure, defines a structure variable, and initializes the structure's members:

```
/* declare a structure */
struct insur_policy {
     char   description[ 25 ];
```

```
        char   start_date[ 9 ];
        int    type;
        float  premium;
};

/* define a structure variable and initialize members */
struct insur_policy policy1 = {
        "auto insurance", "03/12/87", 22134, 476.09 };
```

Next, we rewrite Example 9.4.1 using a `typedef`.

Example 9.4.2. The following code uses a `typedef` to declare a structure, defines a structure variable, and initializes the structure's members:

```
/* give the typedef */
typedef struct insur_policy {
        char   description[ 25 ];
        char   start_date[ 9 ];
        int    type;
        float  premium;
} POLICY;

/* define a structure variable and initialize members */
POLICY policy1 =
        { "auto insurance", "03/12/87", 22134, 476.09 };
```

As shown in the following example, we can combine the declaration of `struct insur_policy`, the definition of the variable `policy1`, and the initialization of `policy1`'s members.

Example 9.4.3. The following code declares a structure, defines a structure variable, and initializes the members:

```
/* combining a structure's declaration, a structure
   variable's definition, and initialization of the
   members */
struct insur_policy {
        char   description[ 25 ];
        char   start_date[ 9 ];
        int    type;
        float  premium;
} policy1 = { "auto insurance", "03/12/87", 22134,
                476.09 };
```

To initialize an array of structures, we enclose in braces the set of values for each structure variable. All the sets of values for the structure variables themselves are inside braces.

Example 9.4.4. The following code declares a structure and then defines an array of structure variables whose members are initialized at definition time. To keep the example short, the array has only three elements.

```
/* give the typedef */
typedef struct insur_policy {
```

```
        char   description[ 25 ];
        char   start_date[ 9 ];
        int    type;
        float  premium;
    } POLICY;

    /* define an array of structure variables and
       initialize them */
       POLICY policies[ 3 ] =
       { { "auto insurance", "03/12/87", 22134, 476.09 },
         { "life insurance", "11/23/79", 55670,  78.51 },
         { "home insurance", "08/09/82", 99321,  12.32 } };
```

If an initialization provides fewer values than members, the remaining members are assigned the default value of zero. In Example 9.4.4, if we change

```
policies[ 3 ]
```

to

```
policies[ 4 ]
```

but leave the initial values the same, the members of policies[3]—namely, the fourth and last structure variable in the array—all have zero as their value.

The Assignment Operator Applied to Structure Variables

We conclude with a shortcut for assigning values to members of a structure. Suppose that we have two structure variables of the same type and that we want to assign all the values of the members in one variable to the members in the other variable. We can do so member by member, but as an alternative, we can apply the assignment operator to an entire structure. When the assignment operator is used in this way, the structure variables must be of the same data type.

Example 9.4.5. The following code shows two ways to assign values from all of one structure variable's members to another structure variable's members:

```
/* declare a structure and two structure variables */
typedef struct car {
    char   *make;
    char   *model;
    int    year;
    float  price;
} AUTO;

AUTO auto1, auto2;

/* assign values to auto1's members */
auto1.make = "Ford";
auto1.model = "Fiesta";
auto1.year = 1978;
auto1.price = 4001.89;

/* copy values to auto2's members */
/* the long way */
```

```
auto2.make = auto1.make;
auto2.model = auto1.model;
auto2.year = auto1.year;
auto2.price = auto1.price;

/* the short way */
auto2 = auto1;
```

Exercises

Exercises 1 and 2 assume the following declaration and definitions:

```
typedef struct bicycle {
        char    *brand_name;
        int     spokes_per_wheel;
        int     links_in_chain;
        float height;
        float length;
        float price;
} BIKES;
BIKES bike1, bike2;
```

1. Write code that assigns values to all the members of bike1 and then copies these values to the members of bike2. Assign each member of bike2 individually, using the assignment operator.

2. Write code that assigns values to all the members of bike1 and then copies these values to the members of bike2. Use one assignment statement to copy the values to bike2.

3. Is the following code legal?

```
struct race_horse {
        int     age;
        char    name[ 25 ];
        char    breed[ 15 ];
        float earnings;
};
struct race_horse  seattle_slew =
        { 3, "Seattle Slew", "thoroughbred" };
```

4. In Exercise 3, what is the value of seattle_slew.earnings?

5. Declare a structure that has as members a two-dimensional array of char, an int variable, and a float variable. Define two variables of this type and initialize them at definition time. (Keep the array small so that the initialization is not tedious.)

6. Write a typedef that declares a structure STEREO having fields id (of type int), brand (of type array of 80 chars), and cost (of type float). Write a program that reads records of type STEREO from the standard input until end-of-file or 100 records are read, sorts the records by id using the library function qsort (see Example 7.8.8), and then prints the sorted records.

7. Repeat Exercise 6 but sort the records by brand.

9.5 Pointers to Structures, Nested Structures, and Self-referential Structures

This section examines three more aspects of C structures: pointers to structures, nested structures, and self-referential structures.

Pointers to Structures

C supports pointers to structure variables and even has a special pointer operator for accessing members of structures.

Example 9.5.1. The following code illustrates one way to use pointers in accessing members of a structure variable:

```
/* declare a structure to represent a computer */
typedef  struct computer {
    char   brand[ 7 ];   /* manufacturer's name */
    char   model[ 10 ];  /* computer model id */
    char   cpu[ 10 ];    /* central processing unit's id */
    int    ram_size;     /* random access memory in bytes */
    int    disk_size;    /* auxiliary storage in bytes */
    float price;         /* price in dollars and cents */
} ELECTRIC_BRAIN;

/* define some variables of this type */
ELECTRIC_BRAIN  computer1, computer2, computer3;

/* define a pointer to this type */
ELECTRIC_BRAIN  *ptr;

/* assign computer1's address to ptr */
ptr = &computer1;

/* assign values to computer1's ram_size and price */
(*ptr).ram_size = 640;
(*ptr).price = 5678.98;
```

The code follows the familiar pattern of defining a pointer and assigning to it an address, in this case, the address of the structure variable `computer1`. To access a member of `computer1`, we must

- Dereference the pointer to `computer1` by attaching the indirection operator * to the pointer's name, which gives us `*ptr`.
- Use the member operator `.` together with the member's name to reference the member, which gives us `(*ptr).price` (see Figure 9.5.1).

We enclose the dereferencing expression `*ptr` in parentheses because the member operator has higher precedence than the instruction operator. Writing

```
(*ptr).price
```

ensures that the indirection operator * applies to `ptr` and not to `ptr.price`. The expression

```
*ptr.price
```

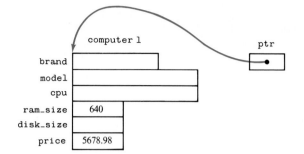

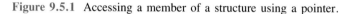

Figure 9.5.1 Accessing a member of a structure using a pointer.

which is equivalent to

```
*(ptr.price)
```

is meaningful only if `ptr` is a structure with a pointer member `price`.

It is very common in C to dereference a pointer to a structure and then to access a member. Because the syntax

```
(*ptr).price
```

is clumsy, an equivalent syntax

```
ptr -> price
```

is provided. We call `->` the **pointer operator**. The pointer operator consists of a minus sign followed by a greater-than sign. No white space is permitted between − and >, but white space is allowed between the pointer variable and the pointer operator, and between the pointer operator and the member. We emphasize that `(*ptr).price` and `ptr -> price` have exactly the same meaning. To use either, `ptr` must be a pointer to a structure, and `price` must be a member of the structure to which `ptr` points.

> *Example 9.5.2.*   We amend Example 9.5.1 by using the pointer operator to access two of `computer1`'s members, `ram_size` and `price`.
>
> ```
> /* assign computer1's address to ptr as before */
> ptr = &computer1;
>
> /* assign values to computer1's ram_size and price
>    using the alternate syntax */
> ptr -> ram_size = 640;
> ptr -> price = 5678.98;
> ```
>
> The four operators
>
> | | |
> |---|---|
> | pointer operator | -> |
> | member operator | . |
> | parentheses | ( ) |
> | square brackets | [ ] |

have the highest precedence in C, and each associates from left to right. We illustrate with an example.

Example 9.5.3. Assume the definitions and assignments

```
/* declare a structure; define two structure
   variables and two pointers to structures */
struct top_40_record {
     char  *title;
     char  *singer;
     int   chart_position;
     float price;
} record1, record2, *ptr1, *ptr2;

/* assign values to the pointers */
ptr1 = &record1;
ptr2 = &record2;

/* assign values to selected members */
record1.title = "Thunder Road";
record1.singer = "Bruce Springsteen";
record1.price = 1.78;
record2.title = "My Guy";
record2.singer = "Mary Wells";
record2.price = 2.78;
```

The value of each of the expressions

```
record1.title      (*ptr1).title      ptr1 -> title
```

is the address of the string "Thunder Road".
   The value of each of the expressions

```
record2.price      (*ptr2).price      ptr2 -> price
```

is 2.78.
   The member operator . and the brackets [ ] have equal precedence and associate from the left; thus, the expression

```
record2.singer[ 5 ]
```

is equivalent to

```
(record2.singer)[ 5 ]
```

Because the value of record2.singer is the address of the string "Mary Wells", the value of record2.singer[5] is character 5 or W (character 0 being the first).
   The pointer operator has a higher precedence than +, so the expression

```
ptr2 -> singer + 5
```

is equivalent to

```
(ptr2 -> singer) + 5
```

Because the value of ptr2 -> singer is the address of the string "Mary Wells", the value of ptr2 -> singer + 5 is the address of character 5. Dereferencing ptr2 -> singer + 5 yields the character W. Thus the value of the expression

```
*(ptr2 -> singer + 5)
```

is again W.

The pointer operator −> and the brackets [ ] have the same precedence and associate from the left. Thus the expression

```
ptr2 -> singer[ 5 ]
```

is equivalent to

```
(ptr2 -> singer)[ 5 ]
```

Because the value of `ptr2 -> singer` is the address of the string `"Mary Wells"`, the value of `ptr2 -> singer[ 5 ]` is again character 5 or W.

We have shown that each of

```
record2.singer[ 5 ]
*(ptr2 -> singer + 5)
ptr2 -> singer[ 5 ]
```

is equal to W.

The value of each of the expressions

```
*record2.singer    *ptr -> singer    *(ptr2 -> singer)
```

is M. Because . has a higher precedence than *, the expression

```
*record2.singer
```

is equivalent to

```
*(record2.singer)
```

The value of `record2.singer` is the address of the string `"Mary Wells"`. When we dereference `record2.singer`, we obtain the first character, M. Again, because −> has a higher precedence than *, the last two expressions

```
*ptr2 -> singer      *(ptr2 -> singer)
```

are equivalent. The value of `ptr2 -> singer` is the address of the string `"Mary Wells"`. When we dereference `ptr2 -> singer`, we again obtain the first character, M.

The value of each of the expressions

```
*record2.singer + 1
*ptr2 -> singer + 1
*(ptr2 -> singer) + 1
```

is N. For example, because * and . have a higher precedence than +, the expression `*record2.singer + 1` is equivalent to

```
(*record2.singer) + 1
```

Thus, we first evaluate `*record2.singer` to obtain M. When we add 1 to (the character code for) M, we obtain N.

Nested Structures

A structure can have members of any legal type, built-in or user defined; in particular, a structure may have structure variables as members.

Example 9.5.4. The following code declares the data type `struct robot`, which has a structure variable among its own members. The nested structure data type must be declared *before* a declaration of this type can occur within another structure.

```
/* the structure robot_arm */
struct robot_arm {
     char   manufacturer[ 30 ];
     int    joints[ 6 ];
     float degrees_of_motion[ 6 ];
     float length;
     float weight;
};

/* the structure robot, which has a member of */
/* type struct robot_arm                       */
struct robot {
     char              name[ 25 ];
     int               id;
     struct robot_arm  arm;
};
```

We could nest to further levels. For example, the structure `robot_arm` could have structure variables among its members.

To access a member of a nested structure variable, we use the member operator twice, once to access the nested structure variable and again to access a specific member of the nested structure.

Example 9.5.5. The following code defines structure variables of type `robot` and `robot_arm`, pointers to these structure variables, and assigns values using both the member operator and the pointer operator:

```
struct robot_arm {
     char   manufacturer[ 30 ];
     int    joints[ 6 ];
     float degrees_of_motion[ 6 ];
     float length;
     float weight;
};

struct robot {
     char   name[ 25 ];
     int    id;
     struct robot_arm arm, *armptr;
} r2d2, *ptr;

/* assign values to the pointers */
ptr = &r2d2;
r2d2.armptr = &r2d2.arm;

/* assign values to members of nested structure */
/* member operator syntax */
r2d2.arm.length = 56.4;
```

```
/* pointer operator syntax */
ptr -> armptr -> weight = 17.1;

/* mixed syntax */
(*ptr).armptr -> weight = 17.1;
```

C enforces one important restriction on nested structures: A structure of a given type cannot have, as a member, a structure variable of the same type.

Example 9.5.6.   The following declaration is illegal because the structure struct personnel_record has among its own members a variable of type struct personnel_record:

```
struct personnel_record {
   char                    first_name[ 15 ];
   char                    last_name[ 25 ];
   int                     age;
   char                    hobby[ 25 ];
   float                   income;
   struct personnel_record  manager;    /** ERROR **/
};
```

Self-referential Structures

A **self-referential structure** is a structure that includes, among its members, a *pointer* to itself. Self-referential structures are legal in C.

Example 9.5.7.   The declaration

```
/* declaring a self-referential structure */
struct personnel_record {
    char                    first_name[ 15 ];
    char                    last_name[ 25 ];
    int                     age;
    char                    hobby[ 25 ];
    float                   income;
    struct personnel_record  *rec_ptr;
};
```

furnishes an example of a self-referential structure. The data type struct personnel_record contains as a member rec_ptr, a pointer to itself.

A self-referential structure must be defined *with a tag*. Without a tag, there would be no way to identify the data type for the pointer. Self-referential structures lend great power to C and are treated in detail in Chapter 10.

Exercises

1. Given

```
typedef struct soldier {
    char   name[ 50 ];
```

```
      char    rank[ 15 ];
      int     serial_number;
   } SOLDIER;
   SOLDIER soldier1, soldier2, soldier3, *ptr;
```

write a statement that assigns to ptr the address of soldier3.

2. Assume the code of Exercise 1. Suppose that the character string "Captain" has been assigned to the array soldier3.rank and that ptr points to soldier3. Explain the error.

```
   printf( "%s", *ptr.rank );
```

3. Correct the statement of Exercise 2.

4. Are the following scanf statements equivalent?

```
   scanf( "%s", *(ptr).rank );
   scanf( "%s", ptr -> rank );
```

5. What is printed?

```
   typedef struct soldier {
       char    *name;
       char    *rank;
       int     serial_number;
   } SOLDIER;
   SOLDIER soldier1, soldier2, soldier3, *ptr;
   ptr = &soldier3;
   soldier3.name = "Audie Murphy";
   printf( "\n%s", (*ptr).name );
   printf( "\n%c", *ptr -> name );
   printf( "\n%c", *soldier3.name );
   printf( "\n%c", *(ptr -> name + 3) );
```

6. Declare structures department and employee. Nest struct employee in struct department. Be careful to declare the structures in the correct order.

7. Assume the declaration of Exercise 6. Define a variable of type struct department and assign values to all of its members, including the members of the nested structure.

8. Given

```
   typedef     struct engine {
       int     number_of_cyls;
       int     displacement;
       float   horsepower;
   } ENGINE;
   struct car {
       char    *make;
       char    *model;
       ENGINE motor, *motor_ptr;
   } car1, *ptr;
   ptr = &car1;
   car1.motor_ptr = &car1.motor;
```

```
ptr -> make = "Chevy";
car1.motor.number_of_cyls = 4;
```

access the string `"Chevy"` in three syntactically distinct ways.

9. Given the code of Exercise 8, access the integer 4 in three syntactically distinct ways.

10. Explain the error.

```
struct event {
        char            start_time[ 8 ];
        char            stop_time[ 8 ];
        float           duration;
        struct event    cause;
};
```

11. Explain why

```
struct node {
        int             contents
        struct node   *next, *last;
};
```

is a self-referential structure.

12. (True/False) A self-referential structure must be defined with a tag.

9.6   Structures and Functions

A structure can be passed to a function in two ways, by value or by reference (see Section 4.5).

Passing Structures by Value

Call by value behaves the same way for structure variables as for other variables: We do not pass the variable's contents but, rather, a copy of its contents. The invoked function can change the copy, but not the actual value of the variable that was passed. To pass a structure variable to a function, we place the variable in the invoked function's argument list. The invoked function must have a corresponding parameter to catch the argument. The parameter must be of the same data type as the argument passed.

Example 9.6.1.   The following program passes a structure to a function. Further, the invoked function returns a structure. We assume that the file *structures.h* contains the following declaration:

```
/* file structures.h */
typedef struct finances {
        char  *name;
        int   ssnum;
        int   deductions;
        float gross_income;
        float tax_rate;
```

```
            float taxes;
            float net_income;
        } FINANCES;
```

A second file contains the following code:

```
#define  DEDUCTION    650.00
#include "structures.h"

main()
{
    /* variables of type FINANCES */
    FINANCES poor_fred, rich_fred;

    /* function that returns a value of type FINANCES */
    FINANCES wishful_thinking( FINANCES poor_person );

    /* assign values to poor_fred's members */
    poor_fred.name = "Fred Flintstone";
    poor_fred.ssnum = 222003333;
    poor_fred.deductions = 2;
    poor_fred.gross_income = 9999.99;
    poor_fred.tax_rate = 0.27;

    /* compute poor_fred's actual taxes and net_income */
    poor_fred.net_income =
        poor_fred.gross_income - poor_fred.deductions * DEDUCTION;
    poor_fred.taxes = poor_fred.net_income * poor_fred.tax_rate;

    /*   assign rich_fred's members values returned from
         wishful_thinking */
    rich_fred = wishful_thinking( poor_fred );
}

FINANCES  wishful_thinking( FINANCES poor_person )
{
    /* compute make-believe taxes and net income */
    poor_person.tax_rate *= 0.1; /* decimate the tax rate */
    poor_person.gross_income *= 4; /* quadruple the gross income */
    poor_person.net_income =
      poor_person.gross_income - poor_person.deductions * DEDUCTION;
    poor_person.taxes =
      poor_person.net_income * poor_person.tax_rate;

    /* return all the structure's values */
    return ( poor_person );
}
```

As shown in Figure 9.6.1, the structure variable poor_fred's members all remain unchanged after the call to wishful_thinking. Call by value safeguards the original contents of structure variables, just as it does for other variables.

Call by value for structures has an interesting and important twist. Recall that because an array's name is a pointer constant that holds the first element's address, we pass an array by reference when we pass its name to the invoked function. The result is that the

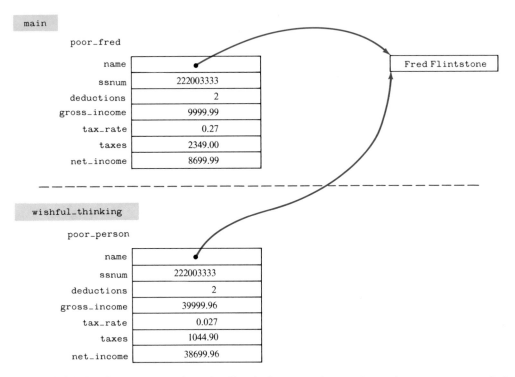
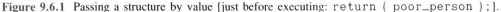

Figure 9.6.1 Passing a structure by value [just before executing: `return ( poor_person );`].

invoked function can access, and so alter, the original contents of any variable in the array. Yet if an array occurs as a member of a structure variable that is passed to a function, only a *copy* of the array's contents will be passed. In short, we can pass an array by value by making it a member of a structure.

Example 9.6.2.   The following code illustrates how we can pass an array by value. All changes made in the invoked function `double_each_cell` affect only the copies of the array's contents, not the original contents. We assume that the file *structs.h* contains the following declaration:

```
/* file structs.h */
struct sample {
    int  array[ 5 ];
};
```

The functions `main` and `double_each_cell` both occur in the same file. The two loops in `main` print exactly the same numbers, for the invoked function does not alter the original contents of the array passed as the member of a structure variable.

```
#include <stdio.h>
#include "structs.h"

main()
{
    struct sample sample1 = { 11, 22, 33, 44, 55 );
    int i;
    void double_each_cell( struct sample structure );
```

```
            /* print contents before invoking function */
            for ( i = 0; i < 5; ++i )
                printf( "\n%d", sample1.array[ i ] );

            double_each_cell( sample1 );

            /* print contents after invoking function */
            /* the original contents are printed again */
            for ( i = 0; i < 5; ++i )
                printf( "\n%d", sample1.array[ i ] );
    }

    void double_each_cell( struct sample structure )
    {
            int  i;

            for ( i = 0; i < 5; ++i )
                structure.array[ i ] *= 2;
    }
```

Passing Structures by Reference

Call by reference also works the same way for structure variables as for other variables. In C, we implement call by reference by passing a pointer to an object, whether the object is a variable, an array of variables, or a structure variable. The invoked function must have a parameter to catch the pointer, and the parameter must be declared as a pointer to the appropriate data type.

Example 9.6.3. We amend Example 9.6.1 so that the invoked function, changed from wishful_thinking to dreams_come_true, can alter the original contents of selected members in the structure variable (see Figure 9.6.2). We use the same declaration of the structure as in Example 9.6.1, and we assume that the declaration resides in the file *structures.h*.

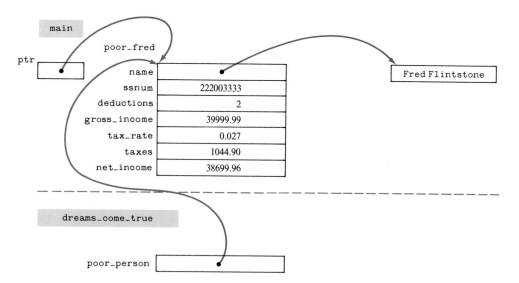

Figure 9.6.2 Passing a structure by reference [just after executing: dreams_come_true(ptr);].

```
#define DEDUCTION   650.00
#include "structures.h"

main()
{
     /* variables of type FINANCES */
     FINANCES poor_fred, rich_fred, *ptr;

     /* function that alters contents of a structure passed to it */
     void  dreams_come_true( FINANCES *poor_person );

     /* assign values to poor_fred's members */
     poor_fred.name = "Fred Flintstone";
     poor_fred.ssnum = 222003333;
     poor_fred.deductions = 2;
     poor_fred.gross_income = 9999.99;
     poor_fred.tax_rate = 0.27;

     /* compute poor_fred's actual taxes and net_income */
     poor_fred.net_income =
        poor_fred.gross_income - poor_fred.deductions * DEDUCTION;
     poor_fred.taxes = poor_fred.net_income * poor_fred.tax_rate;

     /* set pointer to poor_fred */
     ptr = &poor_fred;

     /* alter selected values in poor_fred's members */
     dreams_come_true( ptr );

     /* store the values, including the changed ones, in rich_fred */
     rich_fred = poor_fred;
}

void  dreams_come_true( FINANCES *poor_person )
{
     /* compute new taxes and net income */
     poor_person -> tax_rate *= 0.1; /* decimate the tax rate */
     /* quadruple the gross income */
     poor_person -> gross_income *= 4;
     poor_person -> net_income =
          poor_person -> gross_income
          - poor_person -> deductions * DEDUCTION;
     poor_person -> taxes =
          poor_person -> net_income * poor_person -> tax_rate;
}
```

Several points should be emphasized. The function `dreams_come_true` does not return a value because it alters the original contents of some members in `poor_fred`. The function can do so because it receives a pointer to this structure variable; accordingly, the parameter `poor_person` is now declared as a pointer to a structure of type FINANCES. After invoking the function, we can copy `poor_fred`'s values into `rich_fred`.

C's implementation of call by value and call by reference extend straightforwardly from simple variables to structures, and, as noted earlier, call by value for structures also enables call by value for arrays that are members of structure variables.

Exercises

1. Does the function f pass the variable tinker by value or by reference?

```
typedef struct job {
      char   *employer;
      char   *duties;
      float  wage;
} JOB;
JOB   tinker, tailor, soldier, spy;
void f( JOB  j  );
         .
         .
         .
f( tinker );
```

2. Does the function f pass the variable tinker by value or by reference?

```
typedef struct job {
      char   *employer;
      char   *duties;
      float  wage;
} JOB;
JOB   tinker, tailor, soldier, spy, *ptr;
void f( JOB  *p  );
ptr = &tinker;
         .
         .
         .
f( ptr );
```

3. Given the typedef

```
typedef struct tv_show {
      char title[ 50 ];
      char network[ 10 ];
      float rating;
      float share;
} TV_SHOW;
```

write a function get_tv_data1, with no parameters, which prompts the user for a title, network, rating, and share and returns a structure of type TV_SHOW initialized with the user's input.

4. Redo Exercise 3, but have the function return a pointer to a structure of type TV_SHOW. *Hint*: Define a static structure of type TV_SHOW in the function.

5. Using the typedef of Exercise 3, write a function get_tv_data2, with one parameter of type pointer to TV_SHOW, which prompts the user for a title, network, rating, and share and stores the user's input in the structure whose address was passed to the function.

6. Suppose that the typedef for struct job of Exercise 1 occurs in the file *structures.h*. What is printed?

```
#include <stdio.h>
#include "structures.h"
```

```
main( )
{
    JOB  tinker, *ptr;
    void double_wage( JOB *jobptr );

    ptr = &tinker;
    tinker.wage = 1.11;
    printf( "%f\n", ptr -> wage );
    double_wage( ptr );
    printf( "%f\n", ptr -> wage );
}

void double_wage( JOB *jobptr )
{
    jobptr -> wage *= 2.0;
}
```

7. Suppose that you come across another programmer's code, which contains the following:

```
struct array {
    int  numbers[ 1000 ];
} array1;
```

Why might the programmer object if you suggested replacing the preceding code with the following?

```
int  numbers[ 1000 ];
```

9.7 Sample Application: An Airline Flight Database

Problem

Implement a database on airline flights and answer various queries against the database. A user should be able to enter a flight number, an origin, or a destination and get a screen display of any flight that matches the data entered. The database consists of one record per flight. Each record has fields with the following information:

- a unique flight number
- the origin, an airport code
- the destination, an airport code
- the scheduled departure time
- the scheduled arrival time
- seat capacities
  - first class
  - second class
- fares
  - first class regular
  - first class discounted
  - second class regular
  - second class discounted

Sample Input/Output

The program prompts the user to enter a flight number, origin, or destination, and then it searches for a match. All records that match are displayed. Input is in color; output is in black.

```
Enter 1 to make a query, 0 to exit.
1

Do you wish to search for:
        FNUM :: 1
        ORIG :: 2
        DEST :: 3
1

Please enter item:
111

FNUM:           111
ORIGIN:         ord
DESTINATION:    lax
DEPARTURE:      11:02p
ARRIVAL:        2:07a
FARES:
        1ST REGULAR:    254.67
        1ST DISCOUNT:   219.87
        2ND REGULAR:    136.51
        2ND DISCOUNT:   90.00
CAPACITIES:
        1ST CLASS:      23
        2ND CLASS:      130

Enter 1 to make a query, 0 to exit.
1

Do you wish to search for:
        FNUM :: 1
        ORIG :: 2
        DEST :: 3
2

Please enter item:
ord

FNUM:           239
ORIGIN:         ord
DESTINATION:    nwk
DEPARTURE:      5:01p
ARRIVAL:        6:23p
FARES:
        1ST REGULAR:    197.88
        1ST DISCOUNT:   112.45
        2ND REGULAR:    115.98
        2ND DISCOUNT:   87.43
```

```
CAPACITIES:
        1ST CLASS:         18
        2ND CLASS:         215

FNUM:              111
ORIGIN:            ord
DESTINATION:       lax
DEPARTURE:         11:02p
ARRIVAL:           2:07a
FARES:
        1ST REGULAR:      254.67
        1ST DISCOUNT:     219.87
        2ND REGULAR:      136.51
        2ND DISCOUNT:     90.00
CAPACITIES:
        1ST CLASS:         23
        2ND CLASS:         130

Enter 1 to make a query, 0 to exit.
1

Do you wish to search for:
        FNUM :: 1
        ORIG :: 2
        DEST :: 3
3

Please enter item:
lax

FNUM:              111
ORIGIN:            ord
DESTINATION:       lax
DEPARTURE:         11:02p
ARRIVAL:           2:07a
FARES:
        1ST REGULAR:      254.67
        1ST DISCOUNT:     219.87
        2ND REGULAR:      136.51
        2ND DISCOUNT:     90.00
CAPACITIES:
        1ST CLASS:         23
        2ND CLASS:         130

Enter 1 to make a query, 0 to exit.
0
```

The origin and destination airports are coded. For example, `"ord"` is the standard airline code for O'Hare International Airport in Chicago, which is built on a former orchard; and `"lax"` stands for Los Angeles International Airport.

C Implementation

```
/*********** flights.h ***********/
#define  SIZE  600  /* number of FLIGHT structures in the array */
```

```
/* typedefs for FARE, SEAT, and FLIGHT */
typedef struct fare {
                float   regular1st, regular2nd;
                float   discount1st, discount2nd;
} FARE;

typedef struct seat {
                int     seats1st, seats2nd;
} SEAT;

typedef struct flight {
  char   fnum[ 4 ];            /* unique flight number */
  char   orig[ 4 ];            /* airport of origin */
  char   dest[ 4 ];            /* airport of destination */
  char   depart[ 8 ];         /* scheduled departure time */
  char   arrive[ 8 ];         /* scheduled arrival time */
  FARE   fares;               /* 1st & 2nd class fares */
  SEAT   seats;               /* 1st & 2nd class capacities */
} FLIGHT;
/***** end flights.h *****/

/***** main.c *****/

#include "flights.h"
#include <stdio.h>
#include <string.h>

FLIGHT    flights[ SIZE ];      /* array of flight structures... */
FLIGHT    *fnumptr[ SIZE ],     /*... sorted by fnum, */
          *origptr[ SIZE ],     /* origin, */
          *destptr[ SIZE ];     /* and destination */

main()
{
  void    input_flights( FILE *fptr ); /* reads data from file */
  void    sort_flights( void );     /* quicksorts flights on keys */
  void    query_flights( void );    /* performs lookups */
  FILE    *fptr;

  fptr = fopen( "flights.dat", "r" );

  input_flights( fptr ); /* read data into flights database */
  sort_flights();        /* sort on various keys for queries */
  query_flights();       /* perform queries */

  fclose( fptr );
}
/** Read input from FLIGHTS.DAT into array flights, storing  **/
/** address of each element in FNUMPTR, ORIGPTR, and DESTPTR **/
/** for later sorting.                                       **/

void  input_flights( FILE *fptr )
{
  int    i;
  FLIGHT  *ptr = flights;
```

```
  for ( i = 0; i < SIZE; ++i ) {
    /* read data into one structure variable */
    fscanf( fptr, "%s%s%s%s%s%f%f%f%f%d%d",
            ptr -> fnum,   ptr -> orig, ptr -> dest,
            ptr -> depart, ptr -> arrive,
            &ptr -> fares.regular1st,  &ptr -> fares.regular2nd,
            &ptr -> fares.discount1st, &ptr -> fares.discount2nd,
            &ptr -> seats.seats1st,    &ptr -> seats.seats2nd );
    fnumptr[ i ] = origptr[ i ] = destptr[ i ] = ptr++;
  }
}

/** Sort the arrays FNUMPTR, ORIGPTR, and DESTPTR by the keys **/
/** FNUM, ORIG, and DEST. Quicksort is used.                 **/

void  sort_flights( void )
{
  void  quicksort( FLIGHT *array[], int size, int flag );

  /* sort arrays by either FNUM, ORIG, or DEST. */
  quicksort( fnumptr, SIZE, 1 );
  quicksort( origptr, SIZE, 2 );
  quicksort( destptr, SIZE, 3 );
}

/** Quicksort an array of addresses to FLIGHT structures, using **/
/** either FNUM, ORIG, or DEST as a key.                        **/

void  quicksort( FLIGHT *array[], int size, int flag )
{
  int    find_pivot( FLIGHT *array[],
                     int size,
                     char pivot[],
                     int flag ),
         partition( FLIGHT *array[],
                     int size,
                     char pivot[],
                     int flag );
  int    part_spot;
  char   pivot[ 4 ];

  if ( find_pivot( array, size, pivot, flag ) != 0 ) {
    part_spot = partition( array, size, pivot, flag );
    /* lower */
    quicksort( array, part_spot, flag );
    /* upper */
    quicksort( array + part_spot, size - part_spot, flag );
  }
}

/** Compare the array's first item against the next item **/
/** that differs. PIVOT becomes the larger of the two.   **/
/** If all items the same, return 0; else return 1.      **/
```

```c
int  find_pivot( FLIGHT *array[], int size, char pivot[], int flag )
{
  int   i;
  char  *first; /* pointer to first item */

  switch ( flag ) {
  case 1:
    first = array[ 0 ] -> fnum;
    break;
  case 2:
    first = array[ 0 ] -> orig;
    break;
  case 3:
    first = array[ 0 ] -> dest;
    break;
  default:
    printf( "\n\nError in find_pivot -- bad flag.\n" );
    return ( 0 );
  }

  for ( i = 1; i < size; ++i )
    switch ( flag ) {
      /* fnum */
    case 1:
      if ( strcmp( first, array[ i ] -> fnum ) > 0 ) {
        strcpy( pivot, first );
        return( 1 );
      }
      if ( strcmp( array[ i ] -> fnum, first ) > 0 ) {
        strcpy( pivot, array[ i ] -> fnum );
        return( 1 );
      }
      break;
      /* orig */
    case 2:
      if ( strcmp( first, array[ i ] -> orig ) > 0 ) {
        strcpy( pivot, first );
        return( 1 );
      }
      if ( strcmp( array[ i ] -> orig, first ) > 0 ) {
        strcpy( pivot, array[ i ] -> orig );
        return( 1 );
      }
      break;
      /* dest */
    case 3:
      if ( strcmp( first, array[ i ] -> dest ) > 0 ) {
        strcpy( pivot, first );
        return( 1 );
      }
      if ( strcmp( array[ i ] -> dest, first ) > 0 ) {
```

```c
          strcpy( pivot, array[ i ] -> dest );
          return( 1 );
        }
        break;
    }
  return ( 0 );    /* all items the same */
}
/** Partition the array so that addresses of all        **/
/** keys < PIVOT are to the left, and                   **/
/** those of all keys >= PIVOT are to the right.        **/
/** Return the index at which the second group starts. **/
int partition( FLIGHT *array[], int size, char pivot[], int flag )
{
  void  swap( FLIGHT **address1, FLIGHT **address2 );
  int   left = 0;
  int   right = size - 1;

  while ( left <= right )
    switch ( flag ) {
    case 1:
      while ( strcmp( array[ left ] -> fnum, pivot ) < 0 )
        ++left;
      while ( strcmp( array[ right ] -> fnum, pivot ) >= 0 )
        --right;
      if ( left < right )
        swap( &array[ left++ ], &array[ right-- ] );
      break;
    case 2:
      while ( strcmp( array[ left ] -> orig, pivot ) < 0 )
        ++left;
      while ( strcmp( array[ right ] -> orig, pivot ) >= 0 )
        --right;
      if ( left < right )
        swap( &array[ left++ ], &array[ right-- ] );
      break;
    case 3:
      while ( strcmp( array[ left ] -> dest, pivot ) < 0 )
        ++left;
      while ( strcmp( array[ right ] -> dest, pivot ) >= 0 )
        --right;
      if ( left < right )
        swap( &array[ left++ ], &array[ right-- ] );
      break;
    }
  return ( left );
}
/** Swap two elements in an array of addresses. **/
void  swap( FLIGHT **address1, FLIGHT **address2 )
{
  FLIGHT  *temp;
```

```
  temp = *address1;
  *address1 = *address2;
  *address2 = temp;
}

/** Prompt user about querying the FLIGHTS database, and accept **/
/** search key. If search succeeds, print out record(s), else   **/
/** failure message. Loop as long as user wishes.               **/
void  query_flights( void )
{
  int   binary_search( char item[], int choice );
  void  print_finds( char item[], int index, int choice );

  int   choice, flag, response;
  char  item[ 4 ];

  printf( "\n\n\tEnter 1 to make a query, 0 to exit.\n\t" );
  scanf( "%d", &response );

  while( response > 0 ) {
    printf( "\n\n\tDo you wish to search for:\n\n" );
    printf( "\t\tFNUM :: 1\n" );
    printf( "\t\tORIG :: 2\n" );
    printf( "\t\tDEST :: 3\n\n\t\t" );
    scanf( "%d", &choice );
    printf( "\n\n\tPlease enter item:\n\n\t" );
    scanf( "%s", item );

    flag = binary_search( item, choice );

    if ( flag >= 0 )
      print_finds( item, flag, choice );
    else
      printf( "\n\n\tItem not found.\n" );

    printf( "\n\n\tEnter 1 to make a query, 0 to exit.\n\t" );
    scanf( "%d", &response );
  }
}

/** Search one of the sorted arrays FNUMPTR, ORIGPTR, or DESTPTR **/
/** for a given item, which is either an FNUM, ORIG, or DEST.    **/
/** Return the item's index if successful, else -999.           **/

#define  NO_FIND    -999

int  binary_search( char item[], int choice )
{
  int    first = 0;
  int    last = SIZE - 1;
  int    mid;
  int    comp;

  /* search a sorted array */
  while ( first <= last ) {
    mid = ( first + last ) / 2;
```

```c
    switch ( choice ) {
    case 1:
      comp = strcmp( item, fnumptr[ mid ] -> fnum );
      break;
    case 2:
      comp = strcmp( item, origptr[ mid ] -> orig );
      break;
    case 3:
      comp = strcmp( item, destptr[ mid ] -> dest );
      break;
    }
    if ( comp == 0 )
      return ( mid );                /* Item found. */
    else if ( comp > 0 )
      first = mid + 1;               /* Search top. */
    else
      last = mid - 1;                /* Search bottom. */
  }
  return ( NO_FIND );
}

/** Print all records that match a given item. (In case **/
/** the item is a FNUM, only one record gets printed.)  **/

void    print_finds( char item[], int index, int choice )
{
  void  print_fields( int choice, int index );
  int  left = index - 1;

  switch ( choice ) {
    /* fnum */
  case 1:
    print_fields( choice, index );
    break;
    /* orig */
  case 2:
    while ( left >= 0 &&
            strcmp( origptr[ left ] -> orig, item ) == 0 )
      print_fields( choice, left-- );
    while ( index < SIZE &&
            strcmp( origptr[ index ] -> orig, item ) == 0 )
      print_fields( choice, index++ );
    break;
    /* dest */
  case 3:
    while ( left >= 0 &&
            strcmp( destptr[ left ] -> dest, item ) == 0 )
      print_fields( choice, left-- );
    while ( index < SIZE &&
            strcmp( destptr[ index ] -> dest, item ) == 0 )
      print_fields( choice, index++ );
```

```
      break;
   }
}
/** Print all the fields in a given record. **/
void print_fields( int choice, int index )
{
   FLIGHT  *ptr;

   switch ( choice ) {
   case 1:
      ptr = fnumptr[ index ];
      break;
   case 2:
      ptr = origptr[ index ];
      break;
   case 3:
      ptr = destptr[ index ];
      break;
   }

   printf( "\n\n\tFNUM:\t\t%s",      ptr -> fnum );
   printf( "\n\tORIGIN:\t\t%s",      ptr -> orig );
   printf( "\n\tDESTINATION:\t%s", ptr -> dest );
   printf( "\n\tDEPARTURE:\t%s",    ptr -> depart );
   printf( "\n\tARRIVAL:\t%s",      ptr -> arrive );
   printf( "\n\tFARES:" );
   printf( "\n\t\t1ST REGULAR:\t%.2f",    ptr -> fares.regular1st );
   printf( "\n\t\t1ST DISCOUNT:\t%.2f",   ptr -> fares.discount1st );
   printf( "\n\t\t2ND REGULAR:\t%.2f",    ptr -> fares.regular2nd );
   printf( "\n\t\t2ND DISCOUNT:\t%.2f",   ptr -> fares.discount2nd );
   printf( "\n\tCAPACITIES:" );
   printf( "\n\t\t1ST CLASS:\t%d",        ptr -> seats.seats1st );
   printf( "\n\t\t2ND CLASS:\t%d\n",      ptr -> seats.seats2nd );
}
/***** end main.c *****/
```

Discussion

The database consists of an array of structures, each of which represents a record. Each structure variable has the typedef FLIGHT and contains two nested structures: One has the typedef FARE, and the other has the typedef SEAT for seating capacities. The program reads data from the file *flights.dat* into the array of structures. Records in the data file occur in random order. Our sample data file contains 600 records.

While reading in the data, the program stores the address of each structure variable into three arrays:

```
   fnumptr
   origptr
   destptr
```

The three arrays then are sorted by the following keys: flight number, origin, and destination. This supports fast queries against the database, but without requiring us to rearrange the structure variables themselves. The program uses quicksort for sorting and binary search for searching. (For a review of binary search, see Section 5.10.) We discuss quicksort next.

Quicksort

The PHONE program of Section 5.10 uses selection sort to sort an array of strings. Although selection sort works reasonably well on small numbers of items, it becomes prohibitively slow on large numbers of items. Because our database contains 600 records, sorted on three separate keys, we use quicksort for efficiency. In comparison-based sorting, efficiency typically is measured in terms of how many comparisons or exchanges of items are required. For example, we say that the average-case time of selection sort for N items is $\Theta(N^2)$, thereby indicating that, on the average, selection sort requires about CN^2 comparisons and exchanges to sort N items, for some constant C. By contrast, quicksort has an average-case time of only $\Theta(N \log N)$; on the average, quicksort requires about $C'N \log N$ comparisons and exchanges to sort N items, for some constant C'. For large N, $\log N$ is significantly less than N; so for large N, quicksort is usually significantly faster than selection sort.

Quicksort takes a *divide-and-conquer* approach to sorting. In the FLIGHTS program, we do one sort on flight numbers. Suppose that the following flight numbers are to be sorted into ascending order:

157   243   219   351   749   109   245

To keep our discussion general, we call the items to be sorted *keys*.

The first step is to choose a *pivot*. We then divide the list into two sublists. Each key in the first sublist is less than the pivot, and each key in the second sublist is greater than or equal to the pivot. For example, if we take 243 as the pivot, we obtain the following sublists:

157   109   219   351   749   243   245

  1st sublist   2nd sublist

There are various ways to select the pivot. The FLIGHTS program uses a simple method. (In Programming Exercise 9.9, we discuss an improvement.) The simple method is to compare the first key with the next key that differs from it and to take the larger of the two as the pivot. If all the keys are equal, we do not need a pivot, as the keys are already sorted. For example, given the keys

157   243   219   351   749   109   245

we compare the first key, 157, with the next key, 243, that differs from it and take as the pivot 243, the larger of 157 and 243.

The next step is to partition the list of keys. We start from the left and search until we find the first key greater than or equal to the pivot. We mark its spot in the list. We then start from the right until we find the first key less than the pivot. We use L and R as markers. Beginning with the list

157   243   219   351   749   109   245

we obtain

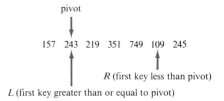

```
                    pivot
                     ↓
      157   243   219   351   749   109   245
             ↑                       ↑
                         R (first key less than pivot)
 L (first key greater than or equal to pivot)
```

On this first iteration, the pivot itself is the first key greater than or equal to the pivot, and 109 is the first key less than the pivot. Next, we swap 243 and 109. The swap may not put either key in its final position, but at least it puts the two in the correct order relative to each other and to the pivot: 109 is to the left of the pivot, and 243 either is the pivot or is to the right of the pivot. The swap produces the following configuration:

```
 157   109   219   351   749   243   245
        ↑                  ↑
        L                  R
```

We leave the markers L and R, for the search now resumes. We first move the L marker right in search of the next key greater than or equal to the pivot, and then we move the R marker left in search of the next key less than the pivot. The configuration becomes

```
       157   109   219   351   749   243   245
                    ↑     ↑
 R (next key less than pivot) |
                    L (next key greater than or equal to pivot)
```

Note that L is now to the right of R; the markers have crossed. This indicates that nothing else needs to be swapped on the current iteration, although the list is not yet sorted. If L were still to the left of R, we would repeat the preceding steps, first moving L to the right and then moving R to the left.

What has the current pass accomplished? Look at the L marker, which now points to key 351. All the keys to its left are less than the pivot; it and all the keys to its right are greater than or equal to the pivot. So the list has been partially sorted. We now divide the list into two sublists. The first sublist begins at the extreme left and ends just before the L marker. The second sublist begins at the L marker and ends at the extreme right.

```
 157   109   219   351   749   243   245
 _____/  _____/
    left sublist         right sublist
```

We now quicksort the left sublist and then the right sublist. Quicksort thus divides and conquers. It breaks the original list into two lists, and each of these into two other lists, and so on. Note that a list with only one key is already sorted and so does not require any further sorting. Finally, the original list is sorted when all the sublists have been sorted.

In our implementation, `quicksort` is a recursive function—a function that invokes itself. On the preceding sample data, `quicksort` would be invoked as follows:

Call *to* quicksort	Array Argument						
1	157	243	219	351	749	109	245
2	157	109	219				
3	109						
4	157	219					
5	157						
6	219						
7	351	749	243	245			
8	351	245	243				
9	243	245					
10	243						
11	245						
12	351						
13	749						

Calls 3, 5, 6, 10, 11, 12, and 13 involve sorting an already sorted array, which happens to be an array with just one element. Note that this sequence of calls also gives the sorted order for keys 109, 157, 219, 243, 245, 351, 749.

Recursion is often a convenient way to implement a divide-and-conquer algorithm. In Chapter 10, we give other examples.

†9.8 Unions and Bit Fields

Unions and bit fields offer a way to economize on storage. Both are more popular in systems than in applications programs, but we include them here for completeness.

Unions

The storage referenced by a union variable can hold data of different types subject to the restriction that at any one time, the storage holds data of a single type. The declaration and definition of unions are syntactically the same as for structures.

Example 9.8.1.   The following code declares a union:

```
/* declare a union */
union numbers {
     char    letter;
     int     number;
     float   dec_number;
     double  precise_dec_number;
};
```

The meaning of the declaration is that any variable of type union numbers can hold a char, an int, a float, or a double. The names letter, number, dec_number, and precise_dec_number inform the system of which type of data we wish to reference.

To define a variable of type union numbers, we write

†This section can be omitted without loss of continuity.

```
/* define a variable of type union numbers */
union numbers   num1;
```

If we want to assign a char to num1, we write

```
num1.letter = 'A';
```

On the other hand, if we want to assign an int to num1, we write

```
num1.number = 5529;
```

The assignment of 5529 to num1 cancels the assignment of 'A' to num1 because, at any one time, num1 holds data of a single type. Similarly, we could write

```
num1.dec_number = 99.2;
```

or

```
num1.precise_dec_number = 2.883910029e-8;
```

Again, each new assignment cancels the previous assignment.

For a union variable, the system allocates an amount of storage equal to that required for its largest member. This storage then can be used for all the smaller members as well. In Example 9.8.1, the system allocates *n* bytes of storage for num1, where

$$n = max \{ \; \text{sizeof (char), sizeof (int),} \\ \text{sizeof (float), sizeof (double) } \}$$

A union can have, as a member, a variable or array of any legal data type, including unions and structures. So we can nest either structures or unions inside unions.

Example 9.8.2. This example illustrates that a union may have composite objects, including structures, among its members.

```
/* declare three structures */
typedef struct lawyer {
            char      clothing_stores[ 10 ][ 25 ];
            char      regular_home_address[ 50 ];
            char      summer_home_address[ 50 ];
            char      winter_home_address[ 50 ];
            char      law_firm[ 30 ];
            int       number_of_partners;
            float     annual_income;

} LAWYER;

typedef struct doctor {
            char      practice1_address[ 50 ];
            char      practice2_address[ 50 ];
            char      malpractice_law_firm[ 25 ];
            char      golf_courses[ 5 ][ 30 ];
            int       number_of_specialties;
            short     house_call_flag;
            float     annual_income;
} DOCTOR;
```

```
typedef struct college_prof {
          char    employer[ 25 ];
          int     tenure_flag;
          short salary;
} PROF;

/* a union with structure variables as members */
typedef union career {
          DOCTOR   career1;
          LAWYER   career2;
          PROF     career3;
} CAREER;
```

To define a union variable `person` of type CAREER, we write

```
CAREER person;
```

At any one time, `person` can hold a structure of type LAWYER, a structure of type DOCTOR, or a structure of type PROF. The system allocates *n* bytes of storage for `person` where

$$n = max \, \{ \; \texttt{sizeof (LAWYER),}$$
$$\texttt{sizeof (DOCTOR),}$$
$$\texttt{sizeof (PROF) \}}$$

Bit Fields

Bit fields serve two purposes. First, they economize on the storage for a structure's members. In this respect, they serve the same general purpose as unions. Second, they enable the programmer to access individual bits of storage. In this respect, they serve the same general purpose as bitwise operators.

A structure's members may be packed together by using bit fields. The syntax is clarified best by an example.

Example 9.8.3. The following code declares a structure with bit fields as members:

```
struct example1 {
     unsigned int   field1   : 4;
     unsigned int   field2   : 8;
     unsigned int   field3   : 4;
};
```

A bit field member is declared just as any other is except that the data type must be `int`, `signed int`, or `unsigned int` and is followed by a colon and an integer constant. The integer constant gives the *width* of the bit field. The width cannot exceed the size in bits of the integer type specified. For example, if

```
sizeof ( unsigned int ) = 4
```

and a byte is 8 bits, the width of an `unsigned int` bit field cannot exceed 4*8 = 32. In the preceding code, `field1` is declared to occupy the first four bits of an `unsigned int`, `field2` the next eight bits, and `field3` the next four bits. If a system implements an `unsigned int` as 32 bits, the three fields together use only half the storage of an `unsigned int`. Finally, a structure may have a mix of regular members and bit fields. Storage for regular members is not compacted.

Operations on bit fields are restricted. The address operator cannot be applied to a bit field, and a bit field cannot be referenced via a pointer. The syntax for accessing bit fields is the same as for ordinary members.

Example 9.8.4. The following code shows how to access bit fields in a structure:

```
/* define a structure with both regular and bit field members */
struct sample2 {
        unsigned int  num1 : 16;   /* num1 and num2 are packed */
        unsigned int  num2 : 16;
        int           num3;        /* num3 is a regular member */
        char          letter;      /* letter is a regular member */
} var;
var.num1 = 99;
var.num2 = 11;
var.num3 = -99;
var.letter = 'A';
```

If our system has a 32-bit `unsigned int`, the bit fields num1 and num2 are compacted into one `unsigned int`.

Exercises

1. Consider the following code:

```
union either_or {
        int   number;
        char  letter;
} var;
var.number = 6;
var.letter = 'A';
```

Would it make sense, at this point, to print both var.number and var.letter? Explain.

2. What is the key difference between a structure and a union?

3. Can one union be nested in another?

4. Can a structure be nested in a union?

5. Under what circumstances would you prefer a union to a structure?

6. Assume that an `int` and a `float` each occupy four bytes and that a `short` occupies two bytes. How many bytes of storage are allocated for the variable `person` in Example 9.8.2? (Assume that the structure members follow one another with no gaps.)

7. What is the error in this intended declaration of a structure with a pair of bit field members?

```
struct saving_space {
        unsigned int  num1    16;
        unsigned int  num2    16;
} var;
```

8. Correct the error in Exercise 7 and assign values to `var.num1` and `var.num2`.

9. What is the principal difference between a bit field and other members of a structure?

10. May a structure be declared with a mix of bit field and regular members?

9.9   Enumerated Types

An enumerated type is a data type with user-specified values. The syntax is similar to that of structures and unions. To declare an enumerated type, we write

- The keyword `enum`, followed by
- An optional identifier of the enumerated type (called a **tag**), followed by
- A list of names that are permissible values for this data type. The values are enclosed in braces and separated by commas.

Example 9.9.1.   The following code declares an enumerated type called `marital_status`:

```
/* declare an enumerated type */
enum marital_status { single, married,
                        divorced, widowed };
```

The tag is `marital_status`. The user-defined data type is `enum marital_status`. Possible values for any variable of type `enum marital_status` are `single`, `married`, `divorced`, and `widowed`. Although the tag is not required, we recommend that it be included.

Like structure variables, variables of an enumerated type may be defined in the declaration by listing them between the terminating brace and the semicolon.

Example 9.9.2.   The following code shows two ways to define variables of an enumerated type. It also assigns values to selected variables.

```
                    /* first way */
/* declare the enumerated type and define the variables
   separately */
enum marital_status { single, married, divorced, widowed };
enum marital_status status1, status2, status3;

/* assign values */
status1 = married;
status3 = single;

                    /* second way */
/* declare an enumerated type and simultaneously
   define the variables */
enum marital_status { single, married, divorced, widowed }
    status_A, status_B;

/* assign values */
status_A = divorced;
status_B = widowed;
```

Declaring an enumerated type does not allocate storage but only describes the user-specified data type and associates integer constants with the values given in braces. (Storage is allocated when variables of the enumerated type are defined.) By default, the first value is associated with 0, the second with 1, the third with 2, and so on. A value of an enumerated type may be used anywhere an integer value is expected.

Example 9.9.3. The following code shows how the system associates integer constants with the values of an enumerated type. We use a `typedef` in this illustration.

```
/* declare an enumerated type */
typedef enum marital_status
        { single, married, divorced, widowed } MARITAL;

/* define two variables of this type */
MARITAL   status1, status2;

/* assign values */
status1 = divorced;
status2 = single;
printf( "\n%d\n", status1 );   /* 2 is printed */
printf( "\n%d\n", status2 );   /* 0 is printed */
```

The next example shows how the programmer can specify the integer values associated with the values of an enumerated type.

Example 9.9.4. We associate specified integer values with the enumerated values in declaring an enumerated type.

```
/* declare an enumerated type */
typedef enum marital_status
    { single = 99, married, divorced, widowed = 376 } MARITAL;

/* define two variables of this type */
MARITAL   status1, status2;

/* assign values */
status1 = divorced;
status2 = widowed;
printf( "\n%d\n", status1 );   /* 101 is printed */
printf( "\n%d\n", status2 );   /* 376 is printed */
```

This example illustrates what happens if the programmer does not provide integer values for each of the enumerated values. The system assigns consecutive integer values until it encounters another explicitly provided value. In this example, we specify 99 as the value to associate with `single`, but we provide no value for `married` and `divorced`, and so the system associates 100 with `married` and 101 with `divorced`. It then associates 376 with `widowed`.

Enumerated types are of limited usefulness in C (unlike, for example, sets in Pascal) because the enumerated values are not tightly bound to the user-defined data type. For example, if we declare the enumerated type MARITAL, as in Example 9.9.4, there is no way to check whether a value, such as `single`, is a value of type MARITAL. As another example, suppose that we define `status1` to be of type MARITAL (as declared in Example 9.9.3) and that we also declare

```
enum sport { baseball, boxing, chess };
```

After we execute

```
status1 = single;
```

the expression

```
status1 == baseball
```

is true, as both `single` and `baseball` are associated with the integer 0. Further, C does *not* enforce the assignment of only enumerated values to variables of an enumerated type, as the next example shows.

> *Example 9.9.5.*   This example illustrates that the programmer can ignore the enumerated values in assignments to variables of an enumerated type.
>
> ```
> /* declare an enumerated type */
> typedef enum marital_status
>       { single, married, divorced, widowed } MARITAL;
>
> /* define a variable of this type */
> MARITAL  status1;
>
> /* assign a value outside the enumerated ones */
> status1 = -9999;
> printf( "\n%d\n", status1 ); /* -9999 is printed */
> ```

The integer values associated with `single`, `married`, `divorced`, and `widowed` are 0, 1, 2, and 3. Nonetheless, we may assign −9999 to a variable of this type. No error results at either compile time or run time. The example shows that the programmer, not C, is responsible for constraining variables of an enumerated type to take a value from among the enumerated ones.

Exercises

1. What is printed?

   ```
   enum good_jobs { tinker, tailor, soldier, spy }
         job1, job2;
   job1 = tinker;
   job2 = spy;
   printf( "\n%d\n%d", job1, job2 );
   ```

2. What is printed?

   ```
   enum good_jobs { tinker = 9, tailor, soldier = 99, spy }
         job1, job2;
   job1 = tailor;
   job2 = spy;
   printf( "\n%d\n%d", job1, job2 );
   ```

3. Use a `typedef` to declare an enumerated type called GOOD_FOODS with at least a dozen possible values.

4. Define a variable of type GOOD_FOODS, and assign it a value (see Exercise 3).

5. Is the following code legal?

```
enum good_jobs { tinker = 1, tailor = 2 } job1, job2;
job1 = 99;
job2 = -99;
```

6. Write the header of a function that returns a structure `struct job_description` with three parameters of types `enum good_jobs`, pointer to `struct job_description`, and `int`. You may assume that `good_jobs` and `job_description` have been previously declared.

Changes from Traditional C

1. Traditional C does not allow a structure as an argument to a function, although it does allow as an argument to a function a pointer to a structure. Also, traditional C does not allow a function to return a structure, although again, it does allow a function to return a pointer to a structure. Further, traditional C does not allow the assignment of a structure. All of these enhancements have been available in most implementations for some time.

2. Traditional C permits only `extern` and `static` structures to be initialized in the definition.

3. Enumerated types have been widely implemented, although they were not described in the original definition of C. Some prestandard versions of C implement enumerated types in a way different from that specified by the standard. The standard requires that the values of an enumerated type be symbolic integer constants. Some nonstandard versions of C refuse to compile a program that uses an enumerated value as an integer (e.g., as an index into an array) without casting it to an integer type.

Common Programming Errors

1. In declaring a structure, it is an error to omit the semicolon after the terminating brace:

```
struct car {
    char    *make;
    char    *model;
    float price;
}   /******* ERROR: missing ; *******/
```

2. If a structure is declared with a tag, the data type is `struct` followed by the tag. It is an error to omit the keyword `struct` when defining a variable:

```
struct car {
    char    *make;
    char    *model;
    float price;
};
car    car1;    /********** ERROR **********/
```

The data type is `struct car`, not `car`. The same error occurs with unions or enumerated types if the keyword `union` or `enum` is omitted.

3. A structure's tag is not a variable and never occurs without the keyword `struct`:

```
struct car {
     char  *make;
     char  *model;
     float price;
} car1;
car.price = 8909.67;    /******** ERROR *********/
```

Although there is a structure variable named `car1` and a member named `car1.price`, there is no structure variable named `car`.

4. In a `typedef`, the order is as follows: the keyword `typedef`, the data type, and the user-provided name. The following is an error:

```
/* WRONG ORDER--data type should be 1st, name 2nd */
typedef AUTOMOBILE struct car {
     char  *make;
     char  *model;
     float price;
};
```

5. A `typedef` is used only to create a synonym for a data type. In a `typedef`, no variables may be defined, and no storage is allocated. For example, it is an error to write

```
typedef struct car {
     char  *make;
     char  *model;
     float price;
} AUTOMOBILE car car1;    /******** ERROR ********/
```

6. An assignment statement involving two structure variables, such as

```
car1 = car2;
```

is permitted only if the variables are of the same type.

7. The member operator has a higher precedence than the dereferencing operator. If a pointer is used to access a member, the pointer expression should be enclosed in parentheses. For example:

```
struct car {
     char  *make;
     char  *model;
     float price;
} car1, *ptr;
ptr = &car1;
(*ptr).price = 11243.89;
```

It would be an error to remove the parentheses, as the expression `*ptr.price` would then be equivalent to

```
*(ptr.price) = 11243.89; /***** ERROR *****/
```

This expression would make sense only if `ptr` were a structure and `ptr.price` were a pointer.

8. It is an error to nest inside a structure a variable of the same type:

```
struct   employee {
        char                name[ 50 ];
        char                ssnum[ 11 ];
        struct employee boss;   /******* ERROR *******/
};
```

However, a structure may contain a pointer to a structure of the same type:

```
struct   employee {
        char                name[ 50 ];
        char                ssnum[ 11 ];
        struct employee *ptr;   /******* OK *******/
};
```

9. It is an error to nest inside a union a variable of the same type:

```
union   record {
        char                name[ 50 ];
        union record        subrecord; /***** ERROR *****/
};
```

10. It is an error to declare a self-referential structure without a tag.

11. It is an error to declare a self-referential union without a tag.

12. It is an error to define a bit field with a width larger than the data type specified. For example, if `sizeof ( unsigned int )` is 2 and a byte is 8 bits, the following is an error:

```
struct problem {
        unsigned int field1 : 8;
        unsigned int field2 : 20; /***** ERROR *****/
};
```

Programming Exercises

9.1. Software products for personal computers typically specify their hardware and software requirements. For example, a product might list constraints such as

- OS/2 operating system
- 5M bytes of random access memory
- Optical disk drive
- An 80-column parallel-port printer

Define four structure variables, each of which can hold requirements for personal computer software. Write a program that assigns values, read from the screen, for your favorite database, spreadsheet, word processing, and game personal computer products to the members of the structure variables. Print the data read to test your program.

9.2. Many businesses keep records that are put to different uses. For example, a business might use the same file of records for both billing customers and generating mailing lists for advertising. Declare a structure that has members to store a customer's last name, first name, street address, city, state, and zip code. Assume that the business has 250 customers. Write a program that generates a mailing list containing all records with a user-specified zip code.

9.3. Assume that a personnel database consists of records, implemented as structures, which contain the following data on each employee: social security number, last name, first name, middle initial, department, title, salary, and number of dependents. Assume that 100 employees are divided among ten departments. Write a menu-driven program that prints the record containing a user-supplied social security number. The program then allows the user to change any information in the record except the social security number.

9.4. Modify the FILM program of Section 9.2 by replacing Euclidean distance with some other distance. What properties should a distance function have?

9.5. Modify the FILM program of Section 9.2 as follows: Instead of locating the single neighbor nearest to the unknown, locate the three neighbors nearest it; then classify the unknown as belonging to the class most frequently represented among the three samples.

9.6. Write a program that tests the success of the FILM program of Section 9.2 by using the *leaving-one-out method* or *U-method*. The method works as follows. Choose an element X from the sample set and assume, for the moment, that X has an unknown class and is to be classified. Classify X by using, as the sample set, the balance of the original sample set. The correctness of the classifier is defined to be

$$\cdot \quad \frac{\text{number of elements correctly classified}}{\text{number of elements in sample set}}$$

9.7. Write a menu-driven, interactive program that tracks inventory for a grocery store. The program uses a structure whose members represent the following: the current month, an item's name, unique identification code, actual quantity in stock for the current month, desired quantity in stock for the current month, cost, price, supplier, shelf life, average monthly volume, and sales total in dollars for the current month. The store carries at least 20 items. The program prompts the user to make one of five choices:

```
0. Exit
1. Item Sale
2. Daily Report
3. Weekly Check
4. Monthly Update
```

If the user picks 1, the program prompts for an item's unique identification number and the quantity sold. The program then updates the associated structure members (e.g., the program decrements the actual quantity in stock and increments monthly sales total). If the user picks 2, the program generates a report that prints each item's unique identification number, name, and current sales total. If the user picks 3, the program determines whether any item is in low supply and issues a warning message for every such item. An item is in low supply if its actual quantity in stock falls below its desired quantity in stock. If the user picks 4, the program prompts for the current month (a character string), the actual quantity in stock, and the desired quantity in stock. The program then updates the appropriate structure variables (e.g., it sets monthly sales total to zero). Finally, if the user picks 0, the program terminates.

9.8. Write a program that prompts the user for a geometric figure such as a triangle or a square and then asks the user for the appropriate dimensions with which to compute the figure's area. For example, if the user selects `square`, the program asks for a side's length; if the user selects `circle`, the program asks for the radius; and so on. The program computes and prints the figure's area, together with a message that describes the figure (e.g., ''The figure is a circle.''). Use a structure to represent each figure. One of the structure's members should be a pointer to a function that computes the figure's area. For example, the structure that represents a circle has a pointer to a function that expects a circle's radius and returns its area; the structure that represents a square has a pointer to a function that expects a side's length and returns its area; and so on. (Pointers to functions are discussed in Section 7.9.) Use a union named `geometric_figure` whose members are structure variables that represent the geometric figures. The union should have at least three such members.

9.9. Modify the FLIGHTS program of Section 9.7 as follows: In our version of `quicksort`, the function `find_pivot` compares the first key with the next one that differs from it and chooses the larger. An alternative is to compare the first, middle, and last keys and to take as the pivot the median of the three keys obtained. For example, if the keys are

    24 24 17 7 39 12 18

this method will select the first, 24, the middle, 7, and the last, 18, and select as the pivot, 18—the median of 24, 7, and 18. Revise `find_pivot` so that it uses this method. What other changes, if any, need to be made in `quicksort`?

9.10. A company keeps a list of its suppliers, with a record for each supplier that gives the supplier's name, unique code, and address. It keeps a separate list of parts that it purchases, with a record for each part that gives the part's name, unique code, size, weight, and color, as well as a list of at most three suppliers that supply the part. Write a program that enables the purchasing agent to enter a part's unique code and then to receive a list of the suppliers who supply the part.

9.11. Modify the program of Exercise 9.10 so that the purchasing agent may enter either the part's name or its unique code. Different parts may have the same part name (e.g., ''bolt''). In this case, the program lists all the parts with this name, together with their codes. The agent then selects the code, and the program again prints a list of suppliers.

9.12. Use an array of 52 structure variables to represent a deck of cards. Each structure variable has members to represent the card's suit and rank. Then simulate the shuffling of a deck of cards. Swap the first card with the card at a random position; then swap the second card with the card at a random position; and so on. (For a review of random number generators, see Section 4.7.)

9.13. Write a program that tracks a family's interest-bearing checking account. The program updates the balance by handling both deposits and withdrawals, calculates interest, signals overdrafts, and prints a list of the transactions over a month's time. For simplicity, assume that there is at most one transaction per day.

9.14. The Happy-Ever-After Dating Service maintains records of individuals looking for dates. Each record tracks an individual's sex, social security number, name, age, occupation, yearly income, major and minor hobbies, height, weight, and religion. The records are sorted by social security number. The service matches individuals as follows: Two individuals match if they are opposite in gender and either (a) are within ten years of one another's age and within $10,000 of each other's income or (b) share both a major and a minor hobby. Write a program that reads a social security number and writes the names and attributes of all matching individuals.

9.15. The RELATIVE_FILE program of Section 8.7 implements a record as a character string. Revise the program so that a record consists of a structure with the following members: social security number, last name, first name, departmental code, and supervisor's last name. Use the sizeof operator to determine the structure's size in bytes.

9.16. Write functions to add, subtract, multiply, and divide two complex numbers. Also, write functions to compute the reciprocal and the conjugate of a complex number. Represent a complex number as a structure with two double members: real and imag. Each function should return a structure that represents the result of the computation.

9.17. Rewrite the scheduling program of Section 7.9. Use a structure with two int members instead of a string to represent an activity.

Introduction to Data Structures

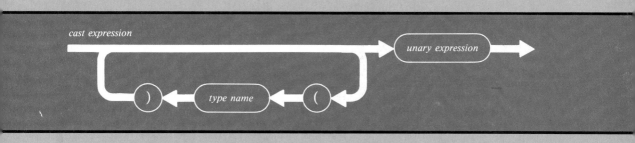

10.1 Compile-Time and Run-Time Storage Allocation

10.2 Linked Lists

10.3 Sample Application: A Text Editor

10.4 Stacks and Queues

10.5 Sample Application: Converting from Infix to Postfix

10.6 Graphs and Trees

10.7 Tree Traversals

10.8 Breadth-First Search and Depth-First Search

10.9 Sample Application: Heuristic Graph Search

Changes from Traditional C

Common Programming Errors

Programming Exercises

All high-level programming languages provide certain built-in data types and operations. For example, C provides the built-in data types `char`, `int`, `float`, and so on and the built-in operations `+`, `==`, `sizeof`, and so on. But many applications demand more complex data types and more sophisticated operations than those supplied by the language. In this case, user-defined data types and user-constructed operations are required. For example, in C the programmer might use a structure to implement the desired complex data type and write functions to provide the required operations. By a **data structure**, we mean a data type together with operations on the data type.

A *stack* is an example of a data structure. (Stacks will be explored in detail in Section 10.4.) The data type is a *list,* which is simply a finite sequence with order taken into account, with one end designated as *top*. For example,

$$23 \quad 87 \quad 2 \quad 10 \quad 9$$
$$\uparrow$$
Top

is an example of the data type under consideration. We define two operations on this data type:

- *Pop*—remove the item from the top. The next item becomes the top.
- *Push*—add an item to the top. The added item becomes the top.

For example, beginning with the previous list, after

> *Pop Pop*

we obtain

$$2 \quad 10 \quad 9$$
$$\uparrow$$
Top

After

> *Push* 88

we obtain

$$88 \quad 2 \quad 10 \quad 9$$
$$\uparrow$$
Top

A *stack* is a list with one end designated as *top* together with the operations *push* and *pop* on the list.

In this chapter, we examine abstract definitions of data structures (that is, definitions such as *stack* that are independent of any language), as well as ways to implement these data structures in C. Separating (1) what data structures do and the data types on which they operate from (2) how they are represented simplifies program development and can be considered as a version of divide-and-conquer applied to the design process.

We can regard certain parts of high-level languages as data structures. For example, in C the data type `int` together with the operations valid for `int` (+, −, %, and so on) is a data structure. Some authors refer to data structures—such as stacks that can be built from the basic data structures available in high-level languages—as *intermediate* data structures.

We can think of data structures as occurring in levels (see the following figure). At the lowest level in our diagram is the machine with primitive data structures available in

Intermediate data structures

```
        ┌─────────────────────────────────┐
        │        Stack, queue, etc.        │
        └─────────────────────────────────┘
                         │
                         ▼
C       ┌─────────────────────────────────┐
        │        Built-in data types       │
        │        Built-in operations       │
        └─────────────────────────────────┘
                         │
                         ▼
Machine ┌─────────────────────────────────┐
        │      Data types provided by      │
        │             hardware             │
        │      Operations provided by      │
        │             hardware             │
        └─────────────────────────────────┘
```

hardware. At the next highest level in our diagram is a high-level language such as C, with its built-in data structures. The compiler can be regarded as a mapping of the data structures in C to the data structures in the machine. At the top level in our diagram are the intermediate data structures that must be mapped into the built-in data structures in C and ultimately into the machine. It is the intermediate data structures with which we are concerned in this chapter.

10.1 Compile-Time and Run-Time Storage Allocation

When we define a variable, storage is allocated, and a name is associated with the allocated storage. For example, if we write

```
int count;
```

the system knows before the program is run that one `int` cell must be allocated and named `count`. We call this kind of storage allocation **compile-time storage allocation** because the system knows at *compile time* the type and amount of storage requested. Of course, the storage itself is not allocated until the program is run. When storage is allocated depends on the storage class of the variable defined (see Chapter 7). It is possible to postpone until run time the decision about the type of storage and the amount to allocate. This method of allocating storage, which we refer to as **run-time storage allocation**, is particularly useful in implementing certain data structures.

To allocate storage at run time, we use the library functions `malloc` and `calloc`. Each allocates an amount of storage specified by the programmer and returns the address of (a pointer to) the storage allocated. The size of the storage requested need not be known until run time. Both `malloc` and `calloc` require the header file *stdlib.h*. We begin by discussing `malloc`.

`malloc`: A Function for Run-Time Storage Allocation

The library function `malloc` expects, as its single argument, the number of bytes to be allocated at run time. If `malloc` successfully allocates the requested storage, it returns a pointer to the allocated storage. If `malloc` is unable to allocate the requested storage, as might happen if insufficient memory is available, it returns NULL, a value recognized as distinct from an actual address. If `malloc` successfully allocates storage, the value returned by `malloc` must be cast so that it points to the type of storage requested. The data type returned by `malloc` is `void *`, pointer to `void`; C guarantees that pointer to `void` can be cast to any other pointer type.

> *Example 10.1.1.*   To allocate one `int` cell and set a pointer to the allocated storage, we first define a pointer to `int`

```
int *ptr;
```

and then invoke `malloc`

```
ptr = ( int * ) malloc( sizeof ( int ) );
```

The argument to `malloc`, `sizeof ( int )`, is exactly the number of bytes necessary to store one `int` on the system in use. Thus `malloc` allocates one `int` cell. The value returned by `malloc` is the address of the allocated cell. This value must be cast to a pointer to `int` by writing

```
( int * )
```

Finally, the address returned by `malloc` is copied into `ptr` (see Figure 10.1.1).

The storage allocation statement

```
ptr = ( int * ) malloc( sizeof ( int ) );
```

of Example 10.1.1 is a typical invocation of `malloc`. In general, the argument to `malloc` is

```
sizeof ( datatype )
```

in which *datatype* describes the type of storage to be allocated. The value returned by `malloc` is cast to point to the type of storage allocated and is, in turn, copied into a variable defined to point to the type of storage allocated.

> *Example 10.1.2.*   The following code allocates run-time storage (see Figure 10.1.2). Depending on the user's response to a prompt, it allocates storage for either a `char` or an `int`. The decision is made at run time.

```
char *letter;    /* pointer to char storage */
int  *number;    /* pointer to int storage */
char response;

printf( "Enter c for character, i for integer: " );
response = getchar();
if ( response == 'c' )
    letter = ( char * ) malloc( sizeof ( char ) );
else
    number = ( int * ) malloc( sizeof ( int ) );
```

ptr

contains `sizeof ( int )` bytes

Figure 10.1.1 Run-time allocation of an `int` cell.

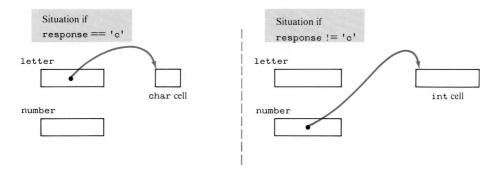

Figure 10.1.2 Run-time storage allocation.

In Example 10.1.2, we could have written

```
letter = ( char * ) malloc( 1 );
```

instead of

```
letter = ( char * ) malloc( sizeof ( char ) );
```

because `sizeof ( char )` has the value 1 on every system.

Example 10.1.3. The following code declares a structure, defines a pointer to this structure, and then allocates one structure at run time by invoking `malloc`. Notice that although the statement that invokes `malloc` looks somewhat complicated, it is syntactically identical to the simpler statements of Examples 10.1.1 and 10.1.2.

```
/* declare a structure */
struct player {
     char    name[ 30 ];
     int     age;
     char    position_code;
     char    team[ 30 ];
     float   salary;
     struct player *link;
};

/* define a pointer to this structure */
struct player *ptr_to_player;

/* allocate one structure at run time and copy the address of the
   allocated storage into the pointer variable */
ptr_to_player =
     ( struct player * ) malloc( sizeof ( struct player ) );
```

`calloc`: **Another Function for Run-Time Storage Allocation**

The library function `calloc` expects two arguments, both integer expressions. The first argument specifies how many storage cells are to be allocated, and the second specifies the size of each. If `calloc` successfully allocates the requested storage, it returns a pointer to the allocated storage. If `calloc` is unable to allocate the requested storage, it returns NULL. If `calloc` successfully allocates storage, the value returned, pointer to void, must be cast so that it points to the type of storage requested. The function calloc is used for the run-time allocation of *contiguous storage cells,* which then may be processed by taking offsets from a starting address. It is convenient to think of calloc as allocating run-time storage for an array, although an array in the strict sense has a name or identifier, whereas the storage allocated by calloc is accessible only by using a pointer. We explain this point in more detail shortly.

Example 10.1.4. The following code uses malloc to allocate storage for 1 int cell and calloc to allocate contiguous storage for 20 int cells:

```
/* define two pointers to int */
int  *ptr1, *ptr2;

/* allocate one int cell */
ptr1 = ( int * ) malloc( sizeof ( int ) );

/* allocate 20 contiguous int cells */
ptr2 = ( int * ) calloc( 20, sizeof ( int ) );
```

Accessing Run-Time Storage

If we allocate a cell by defining a variable, we can access it in two ways: by using the variable's name or by dereferencing a pointer to the cell. On the other hand, if we allocate a cell at run time, we can access it only through a pointer because it has no name.

Example 10.1.5. The following code contrasts access to storage allocated at compile time with access to storage allocated at run time:

```
/* define an int and two pointers to int */
int  num, *ptr1, *ptr2;

/* two ways to access compile-time storage */
num = 10;       /* use the variable's name */
ptr1 = &num;
*ptr1 = 100;    /* use a pointer to it */

/* allocate one int at run time */
ptr2 = ( int * ) malloc( sizeof ( int ) );

/* the only way to access run-time storage */
*ptr2 = 99999;       /* use a pointer */
```

Releasing Run-Time Storage

Compile-time storage of a variable is allocated and released by the system in accordance with its storage class. For example, storage for an auto variable is allocated each time control enters its containing block and released each time control exits its containing block. Storage for a static variable is allocated once, when the program begins executing, and released when the program terminates. With run-time storage, however, the programmer must allocate storage by invoking malloc or calloc; the programmer is also responsible for releasing run-time storage while the program executes. (When the program ends, a reasonable operating system releases all allocated storage.) Release of run-time storage is essential when storage is limited. In any case, good programming practice dictates that run-time storage be released once it is no longer needed.

The library function `free`, which requires the header file *stdlib.h*, is used to release run-time storage. It expects one argument—a pointer to storage allocated by a standard storage allocation function (e.g., `malloc` or `calloc`). After `free` executes, the storage is released and the value of the pointer is no longer meaningful. If the argument to `free` is a pointer to storage allocated by `malloc`, the cell allocated is released. If the argument to `free` is a pointer to storage allocated by `calloc`, all of the storage allocated is released (i.e., if `calloc` allocated *c* cells, the storage for *all c* cells is released). If the argument to `free` is NULL, no action is taken. If the argument to `free` is neither a pointer to storage allocated by a standard allocation function nor NULL, the behavior is system dependent.

Example 10.1.6. The following code allocates one EMPLOYEE structure and later releases this storage:

```
#include <stdlib.h>
/* release of run-time storage */
main()
{
   /* declare a structure */
    typedef struct employee {
             char   lname[ 25 ];
             char   fname[ 15 ];
             char   ssnum[ 12 ];
             int    dept;
             float  salary;
    } EMPLOYEE;

    /* define a pointer to EMPLOYEE */
    EMPLOYEE  *ptr;

    /* allocate an EMPLOYEE structure at run-time */
    ptr = ( EMPLOYEE * ) malloc( sizeof ( EMPLOYEE ) );
    /* process the cell */
           .
           .
           .
    /* release it */
    free( ptr );
}
```

Garbage

If the C programmer does not explicitly release run-time storage, it remains allocated until the program terminates, even if the storage ceases to be accessible. Consider the next example.

Example 10.1.7. The following code allocates run-time storage and then makes it impossible to access that storage (see Figure 10.1.3). The storage remains allocated, however, because the programmer fails to release it.

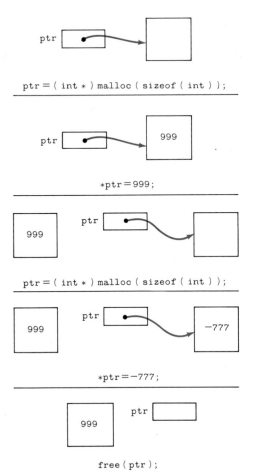

Figure 10.1.3 Generating garbage.

```c
#include <stdlib.h>
/* uncollected garbage */
main( )
{
    int  *ptr;

    /* allocate one int cell */
    ptr = ( int * ) malloc( sizeof ( int ) );

    /* store something there */
    *ptr = 999;

    /* allocate another int cell */
    ptr = ( int * ) malloc( sizeof ( int ) );

    /* store something there */
    *ptr = -777;
    printf( "\n%d\n", *ptr );     /* -777 is printed */

    /* release an int cell */
    free( ptr );     /* cell holding -777 is released */
}
```

The cell holding 999 cannot be accessed once the pointer `ptr` has been reassigned the address of the second cell allocated by `malloc`. The cell holding 999 remains allocated, but the programmer cannot access it. Such a cell is known as **garbage.**

Some languages (e.g., LISP) have built-in routines to recognize and release garbage. In short, they collect garbage. C does not collect garbage. In C, the programmer is responsible for not generating garbage in the first place. If run-time storage is no longer needed, it should be released before access to it is lost.

Exercises

1. What are the main differences between compile-time and run-time storage?

2. Is the storage allocated for defined variables at compile time, run time, or either?

3. Explain why it would be misleading to talk about variables allocated at run time instead of storage allocated at run time.

4. What is the error in the following code?

```
int   num;
num = ( int * ) malloc( sizeof ( int ) );
```

5. What is the error in the following code?

```
float *ptr;
ptr = malloc( sizeof ( float ) );
```

6. What is the error in the following code?

```
float *ptr;
ptr = ( * float ) malloc( sizeof ( float ) );
```

7. In the following code,

```
char       *c;
float      *f;
c = ( char * ) malloc( 1 );
f = ( float * ) malloc( sizeof ( float ) );
```

should we change the statement

```
c = ( char * ) malloc( 1 );
```

to

```
c = ( char * ) malloc( sizeof ( char ) );
```

to promote code portability?

8. What is the principal difference between the library functions `malloc` and `calloc`?

9. What is printed?

```
int        i;
float      *flptr;
flptr = ( float * ) calloc( 3, sizeof ( float ) );
```

```
for ( i = 0; i < 3; ++i )
    *flptr++ = i * 1.1;
for ( i = 0; i < 3; ++i )
    printf( "\n%f\n", *--flptr );
```

10. What is printed?

```
int        *ptr;
ptr = ( int * ) malloc( sizeof ( int ) );
*ptr = 999;
ptr = ( int * ) malloc( sizeof ( int ) );
*ptr = 123;
printf( "\n%d\n", *ptr );
```

11. In Exercise 10, why is the cell that holds 999 called garbage?

12. Does C collect garbage?

13. Write a `typedef` to declare a structure BOOK with members `title` (pointer to char), `author` (pointer to char), `isbn` (int), and `avail_code` (char). Define two pointers, `book_ptr1` and `book_ptr2`, to BOOK. Allocate 100 contiguous BOOK cells, and store the address of the first cell in `book_ptr1`. Store the address of the 52nd cell in `book_ptr2`.

10.2 Linked Lists

A list is a finite sequence, with order taken into account. A list can be implemented in C in several ways. For example, we can represent a list as an array. Another representation involves linked structures, which we consider in this section. Arrays and linked structures often are used to implement various abstract data types.

A **singly linked list** or, more simply, a **linked list** consists of ordered nodes

$$N_1, N_2, \ldots, N_n$$

together with the address of the first node, N_1. Each node has several fields, one of which is an *address field*. The address field of node N_i contains the address of the following node in the list N_{i+1}, $i = 1, \ldots, n - 1$. The address field of the last node, N_n, contains a special value, called *null*, which is different from an actual address. We also admit the *empty linked list*, which consists of no nodes. In this case, there is no first node, and so the address provided is the *null* address.

Example 10.2.1. Figure 10.2.1 shows a linked list consisting of three nodes. The variable *start* contains the address of the first node in the linked list. We indicate this by the usual arrow notation for pointers. Each node has two fields. The first field contains an integer that indicates the position of the node in the linked list. The second field contains the address of the next node in the linked list. Again, we show the value of the

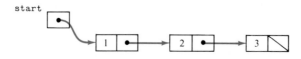

Figure 10.2.1 A linked list.

address fields of the nodes using the arrow notation. The last node has the value *null* in its address field, which is drawn as a diagonal line. This abstract linked list represents the sequence

$$1, 2, 3$$

We can represent a linked list in C by using self-referential structures. Recall that a self-referential structure is a structure that has a member that points to a structure of the same type (see Section 9.5).

Example 10.2.2. The following code generates the linked list shown in Figure 10.2.2. We store NULL, defined in *stdio.h,* in the member `next` of the last node in the linked list. The function `print_elephants`, which prints each elephant's name and gives its position in the linked list, illustrates the simple processing of a linked list.

```
#include <stdio.h>
#include <string.h>

/* declare a self-referential structure */
typedef  struct elephant {
      char              name[ 10 ];
      struct elephant  *next;
} ELEPHANT;

main()
{
      void  print_elephants ( ELEPHANT *ptr );

      /* define 3 ELEPHANT variables and 1 pointer to ELEPHANT */
      ELEPHANT  elephant1, elephant2, elephant3, *start;

      /* store elephants' names */
      strcpy( elephant1.name, "Edna" );
      strcpy( elephant2.name, "Elmer" );
      strcpy( elephant3.name, "Eloise" );

      /* link elephants */
      elephant1.next = &elephant2;   /* Edna points to Elmer */
      elephant2.next = &elephant3;   /* Elmer points to Eloise */
      elephant3.next = NULL;         /* Eloise is last */

      /* start contains the address of the first node */
      start = &elephant1;
      print_elephants( start );
}

void  print_elephants( ELEPHANT *ptr )
{
```

Figure 10.2.2 Representation of a linked list in C.

```
    int count = 1;
    printf( "\n\n\n" );
    while ( ptr != NULL ) {
        printf( "\nElephant number %d is %s.",
            count++, ptr -> name );
        ptr = ptr -> next;
    }
}
```

When `print_elephants` is invoked

```
    print_elephants( start );
```

the value of `start` is copied into the parameter `ptr` (see Figure 10.2.3). Then the variable `count` is initialized to 1:

```
    int count = 1;
```

At the `while` loop

```
    while ( ptr != NULL ) {
```

we first test whether the value of `ptr` is NULL. C guarantees that NULL is not an actual address; so when the value of `ptr` is equal to NULL, we know that `ptr` cannot point to another node and that we are, in fact, at the end of the linked list. In this case, `ptr` is not equal to NULL, and so we execute the body of the `while` loop.

The statement

```
    printf( "\nElephant number %d is %s.",
            count++, ptr -> name );
```

prints

```
    Elephant number 1 is Edna.
```

and increments the value of `count`. Next, we execute

```
    ptr = ptr -> next;
```

The value of `ptr -> next` is the address of `elephant2` (see Figure 10.2.3). Thus we copy the address of `elephant2` into `ptr`. The effect is to cause `ptr` to point to `elephant2` (see Figure 10.2.4). An expression such as

```
    ptr = ptr -> next;
```

occurs frequently when processing linked lists. The effect is to move the pointer `ptr` to the next node in the linked list. We return to the top of the `while` loop.

Again the expression

```
    ptr != NULL
```

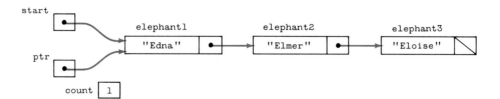

Figure 10.2.3 Beginning of `print_elephants`.

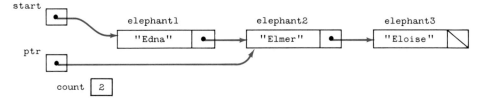

Figure 10.2.4 After one iteration of the while loop in print_elephants.

is true, so we execute the body of the while loop. The first statement

```
printf( "\nElephant number %d is %s.",
    count++, ptr -> name );
```

prints

```
Elephant number 2 is Elmer.
```

and increments the value of count. Next, we execute

```
ptr = ptr -> next;
```

which points ptr to elephant3 (see Figure 10.2.5). We return to the top of the while loop.

Again the expression

```
ptr != NULL
```

is true, so we execute the body of the while loop. The first statement

```
printf( "\nElephant number %d is %s.",
    count++, ptr -> name );
```

prints

```
Elephant number 3 is Eloise.
```

and increments the value of count. Next, we execute

```
ptr = ptr -> next;
```

Because the value of ptr -> next is NULL, we assign to ptr the value NULL (see Figure 10.2.6). We return to the top of the while loop. Because the expression

```
ptr != NULL
```

is false, we terminate the loop, and the function returns. At this point, the program terminates.

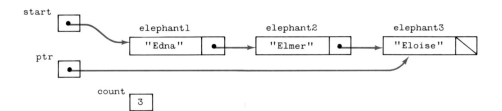

Figure 10.2.5 After two iterations of the while loop in print_elephants.

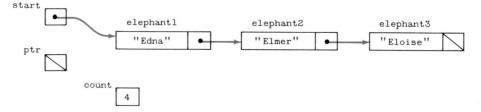

Figure 10.2.6 At the end of the `while` loop in `print_elephants`.

In Example 10.2.2, the nodes in the linked list use compile-time storage, or in different terms, the nodes are implemented as variables. Yet what if we have an indefinite number of elephants to represent? We could define an array of type ELEPHANT with a huge size and hope that we have enough nodes. Of course, if we needed to represent only three nodes, we would waste lots of storage. The solution is to allocate ELEPHANT nodes as we need them, using run-time storage.

Run-Time Allocation of Nodes

We revise Example 10.2.2 to illustrate run-time allocation of nodes in a linked list. The allocation continues as long as the user likes or until memory is exhausted.

Example 10.2.3. The following program constructs a linked list using storage cells allocated at run time:

```
#include <stdio.h>
#include <stdlib.h>

/* declare a self-referential structure */
typedef  struct elephant {
    char             name[ 10 ];
    struct elephant  *next;
} ELEPHANT;

main()
{
    void       print_elephants( ELEPHANT *ptr );
    ELEPHANT   *get_elephants( void ), *start;
    start = get_elephants();
    print_elephants( start );
}

/*   get_elephants allocates run-time storage for nodes. It builds
     the linked list and stores user-supplied names in the name
     members of the nodes. It returns a pointer to the first such
     node. */

ELEPHANT *get_elephants( void )
{
    ELEPHANT   *current, *first;
    int response;

    /* allocate first node */
    current = first = ( ELEPHANT * ) malloc( sizeof ( ELEPHANT ) );
```

```
        /* store name of first elephant */
        printf( "\n\n\tNAME:\t" );
        scanf( "%s", current -> name );

        /* prompt user about another elephant */
        printf( "\n\n\n\tAdd another? (1 == yes, 0 == no)\t" );
        scanf( "%d", &response );

        /* Add elephants to list until user signals halt. */
        while ( response ) {
            /* try to allocate another elephant node */
            if ( ( current -> next =
                ( ELEPHANT * ) malloc( sizeof ( ELEPHANT ) ) ) ==
                NULL ) {
                printf( "Out of memory\nCan't add more elephants\n" );
                return ( first );
            }
            current = current -> next;

            /* store name of next elephant */
            printf( "\n\n\tNAME:\t" );
            scanf( "%s", current -> name );

            /* prompt user about another elephant */
            printf( "\n\n\n\tAdd another? (1 == yes, 0 == no)\t" );
            scanf( "%d", &response );
        }
        /* set link in last node to NULL */
        current -> next = NULL;
        return ( first );
}
/*      print_elephants steps through the linked list pointed to by
        ptr and prints the member name in each node as well as the
        position of the node in the list */

void  print_elephants( ELEPHANT *ptr )
{
    int count = 1;
    printf( "\n\n\n" );
    while ( ptr != NULL ) {
        printf( "\nElephant number %d is %s.",
            count++, ptr -> name );
        ptr = ptr -> next;
    }
}
```

When we execute

```
    current = first = ( ELEPHANT * )
                        malloc( sizeof ( ELEPHANT ) );
```

we allocate one ELEPHANT node and store its address in current and in first (see Figure 10.2.7). Next, we prompt the user for a name and store it in the member name of the node pointed to by current (see Figure 10.2.7). If the user signals that

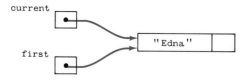

Figure 10.2.7 At the beginning of get_elephants.

another name will be given, the value of response is 1, and we execute the body of the while loop.

When we execute

```
if ( ( current -> next =
       ( ELEPHANT * ) malloc( sizeof ( ELEPHANT ) ) ) ==
     NULL ) {
```

we attempt to allocate another ELEPHANT node and store its address in the member next of the node pointed to by current (see Figure 10.2.8). If malloc is unable to allocate another ELEPHANT node, it returns NULL, which is stored in the member next of the node pointed to by current. In this case, we print a message and return the address of the first node:

```
printf( "Out of memory\nCan't add more elephants\n" );
return ( first );
```

If malloc allocated another node, we execute

```
current = current -> next;
```

which makes current point to the next node (shown as a dotted arrow in Figure 10.2.8). We then read and store the name of the new elephant. If the user now signals that no more elephant names will be given, the response is 0, and we terminate the while loop.

When we execute

```
current -> next = NULL;
```

we store the value NULL in the member next of the node pointed to by current (see Figure 10.2.9). This important step is sometimes inadvertently omitted, with disastrous results. The function get_elephants terminates by returning the address of the first node:

```
return ( first );
```

The function print_elephants is the same function we discussed in Example 10.2.2.

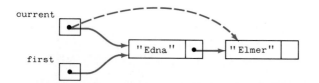

Figure 10.2.8 After one iteration of the while loop in get_elephants.

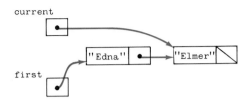

Figure 10.2.9 At the end of get_elephants.

Operations on Linked Lists

In this section, we illustrate some standard operations on linked lists: finding a node in a linked list, adding a node to a linked list, and deleting a node from a linked list. Additional operations on linked lists are given as exercises (see Exercises 12 through 14, 16, and 17). To simplify matters, we use a structure that has only two members: One holds an int and the other a pointer. The typedef is

```
typedef  struct node {
     int          data;
     struct node  *next;
} NODE;
```

We assume that this declaration is contained in the file *structure.h*.

Example 10.2.4. The function find_nth_node expects a pointer to the first node in a linked list and an integer n that specifies a position in the linked list. If n is greater than the number of nodes in the linked list or if n is less than 1, find_nth_node returns NULL; otherwise, it returns a pointer to the nth node.

```
#include <stdlib.h>
#include "structure.h"

NODE  *find_nth_node( NODE *ptr, int n )
{
     if ( n < 1 )
          return ( NULL );
     while ( --n && ptr != NULL )
          ptr = ptr -> next;
     return ( ptr );
}
```

If n < 1, the value of n is invalid, and we return NULL; otherwise, we proceed to the while loop. There are two reasons to terminate the while loop: We have reached the nth node, or we have reached the end of the linked list. The condition

```
--n && ptr != NULL
```

provides the test. After terminating the while loop, we return ptr, which either points to the nth node or is equal to NULL if we reach the end of the linked list.

We illustrate how find_nth_node works for the linked list shown in Figure 10.2.10 with n = 2.

Because n < 1 is false, we proceed directly to the while loop. The value of --n is 1 (true), and ptr is not NULL, so we execute the body of the while loop. The statement

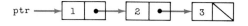

Figure 10.2.10 A linked list.

```
ptr = ptr -> next;
```

moves `ptr` to the next node (see Figure 10.2.11).

The value of −−n is 0 (false), so we terminate the `while` loop. We return `ptr`, the address of the second node in the linked list.

We invite the reader to execute `find_nth_node` for the linked list of Figure 10.2.10 with n = 4 (Exercise 4) to see how it works when n is greater than the number of nodes in the linked list.

Example 10.2.5.   The function `add_at_nth` expects a pointer to the first node in a linked list, a pointer to another node to be added to this linked list, and an integer n that gives the position of the new node after it is inserted. If n is less than 1 or greater than 1 plus the number of nodes in the linked list, `add_at_nth` adds no node and returns NULL; otherwise, it adds the node in the nth position and returns a pointer to the first node of the new linked list.

```c
#include <stdlib.h>
#include "structure.h"
NODE  *add_at_nth( NODE *ptr, NODE *new, int n )
{
     NODE *find_nth_node( NODE *ptr, int n ), *pred;
     if ( n == 1 ) {
          new -> next = ptr;
          return ( new );
     }
     pred = find_nth_node( ptr, n - 1 );

     if ( pred == NULL )
          return ( NULL );

     new -> next = pred -> next;
     pred -> next = new;

     return ( ptr );
}
```

If n is 1, we must add the node at the beginning of the linked list. Because this case requires special handling, we explicitly test for it by writing

```c
if ( n == 1 ) {
     .
     .
     .
```

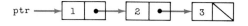

Figure 10.2.11 Executing `find_nth_node`.

If n is not 1, we attempt to find the node preceding the nth:

```
pred = find_nth_node( ptr, n - 1 );
```

If we are not successful, we return NULL; otherwise, we insert the new node and return a pointer to the first node of the new linked list.

We illustrate how `add_at_nth` works for the linked list shown in Figure 10.2.10 with n = 2.

Because n == 1 is false, we proceed to the statement

```
pred = find_nth_node( ptr, n - 1 );
```

which points `pred` to the first node (see Figure 10.2.12). Because `pred` is not NULL, we next execute

```
new -> next = pred -> next;
pred -> next = new;
```

(see Figure 10.2.12, in which the changes are shown with dotted arrows). We then return `ptr`, the pointer to the first node of the new linked list.

We invite the reader to execute `add_at_nth` for the linked list of Figure 10.2.10 with n = 1 (Exercise 5) to see how it works when we add a node at the beginning of the linked list.

Example 10.2.6. The function `delete_nth_node` expects a pointer to the first node in a linked list, an integer n that indicates the position of the node to be deleted, and `success_flag`, a pointer to `int` that is set to 1 or 0 to indicate whether the node was successfully deleted. If n is less than 1 or greater than the number of nodes in the linked list, no node is deleted, and the `int` pointed to by `success_flag` is set to false (0); otherwise, it deletes the nth node and sets the `int` pointed to by `success_flag` to true (1). In any case, the function returns a pointer to the first node in the new linked list.

```
#include <stdlib.h>
#include "structure.h"
NODE *delete_nth_node( NODE *ptr, int n,
                       int *success_flag )
{
        NODE *pred, *old,
             *find_nth_node( NODE *ptr, int n );
        if ( n == 1 ) {
                if ( ptr == NULL ) {
                        *success_flag = 0;
                        return ( ptr );
                }
                old = ptr;
```

Figure 10.2.12 Executing `add_at_nth`.

```
            ptr = ptr -> next;
        }
        else {
            pred = find_nth_node( ptr, n - 1 );
            if ( pred == NULL
                || pred -> next == NULL ) {
                *success_flag = 0;
                return ( ptr );
            }
            old = pred -> next;
            pred -> next = old -> next;
        }
        free( old );
        *success_flag = 1;
        return ( ptr );
    }
```

If n is 1, we must delete the first node in the linked list. Because this case requires special handling, we explicitly test for it by writing

```
if ( n == 1 ) {
        .
        .
        .
```

We cannot delete the node if the linked list is empty, so we test for this case:

```
if ( ptr == NULL ) {
        .
        .
        .
```

If there is a first node, we save its address

```
old = ptr;
```

so that we can free it later; then we delete it:

```
ptr = ptr -> next;
```

If n is not 1, we will attempt to find the node preceding the nth:

```
pred = find_nth_node( ptr, n - 1 );
```

If we are not successful

```
pred == NULL
```

or if there is no nth node

```
pred -> next == NULL
```

we assign *success_flag the value 0 and return; otherwise, we delete the nth node:

```
old = pred -> next;
pred -> next = old -> next;
```

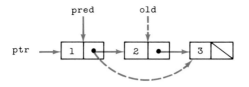

Figure 10.2.13 Executing delete_nth_node.

Finally, we free the deleted node

```
free( old );
```

assign *success_flag the value 1, and return the address of the first node in the new linked list.

In most other high-level languages, the condition

```
pred == NULL || pred -> next == NULL
```

causes a problem when pred is equal to NULL because, in this case, pred -> next is an illegal access. In C, when pred == NULL is true, the expression pred -> next == NULL is *not* evaluated, and there is no illegal access.

We illustrate how delete_nth_node works for the linked list shown in Figure 10.2.10 with n = 2. The statement

```
pred = find_nth_node( ptr, n - 1 );
```

sets pred to the first node (see Figure 10.2.13). We then execute

```
old = pred -> next;
pred -> next = old -> next;
```

(see Figure 10.2.13, in which the changes are shown with dotted arrows). We then free the deleted node, assign *success_flag the value 1, and return a pointer to the first node of the new linked list:

```
free( old );
*success_flag = 1;
return ( ptr );
```

We invite the reader to execute delete_nth_node for the linked list of Figure 10.2.10 with n = 1 (Exercise 8) to see how it works when we delete the first node of a linked list.

Exercises

1. What is printed?

```
struct node {
     char        letter;
     struct node *next;
} a, b, c, *ptr;
a.letter = 'A';
b.letter = 'B';
c.letter = 'C';
```

```
a.next = &b;
b.next = &c;
c.next = NULL;
ptr = a.next;
while ( ptr != NULL ) {
     printf( "\n%c\n", ptr -> letter );
     ptr = ptr -> next;
}
```

2. What is printed when we execute the code of Exercise 1 if we change the line

```
while ( ptr != NULL ) {
```

   to

```
while ( ptr -> next != NULL ) {
```

3. Change Example 10.2.3 so that the user can choose to supply no names.

4. Illustrate how find_nth_node (Example 10.2.4) works for the linked list shown in Figure 10.2.10 with n = 4.

5. Illustrate how add_at_nth (Example 10.2.5) works for the linked list shown in Figure 10.2.10 with n = 1.

6. Illustrate how add_at_nth (Example 10.2.5) works for the linked list shown in Figure 10.2.10 with n = 4.

7. What problems, if any, result from deleting the code

```
if ( n == 1 ) {
     new -> next = ptr;
     return ( new );
}
```

   from add_at_nth (Example 10.2.5)?

8. Illustrate how delete_nth_node (Example 10.2.6) works for the linked list shown in Figure 10.2.10 with n = 1.

9. Illustrate how delete_nth_node (Example 10.2.6) works for the linked list shown in Figure 10.2.10 with n = 4.

10. Why don't we eliminate success_flag and just return NULL in delete_nth_node if we can't delete the node?

11. Change Example 10.2.2 so that the last node in the linked list points back to the first. You now have a *circular linked list*. Write a function that prints each node in a circular linked list exactly once, starting at any node in the list.

12. Write a function last that expects a pointer to the first node in a linked list and returns a pointer to the last node in the linked list or NULL if the list is empty.

13. Write a function length that expects a pointer to the first node in a linked list and returns the number of nodes in the linked list.

14. Write a function append that expects two pointers to the first nodes in two linked lists and returns a pointer to a linked list consisting of the first linked list followed by the second.

15. Explain what will happen if you use your function of Exercise 14 to append a linked list to itself.

16. Write a function `reverse` that expects a pointer to the first node in a linked list and returns a pointer to a linked list that is the reverse of the original linked list. Do not allocate any new nodes; change pointers.

17. Write a function that takes a linked list's third node and makes it the first. For example, suppose that each node in the linked list represents a character string. The first node holds the string `"pictures"`; the second the string `"of"`; the third the string `"pretty"`; and the fourth the string `"pearls"`. If the nodes were processed in their original order, the strings could be printed to form

    pictures of pretty pearls

The idea is to modify the linked list so that instead we would print

    pretty pictures of pearls

18. Revise Example 10.2.3 so that the function `get_elephants` checks whether the system is able to allocate storage for the first ELEPHANT. If the system cannot allocate the storage, `get_elephants` should return NULL.

10.3 Sample Application: A Text Editor

Problem

Implement a text editor. The program begins by requesting the name of the file to edit. If the file exists, it is read into a buffer, and editing begins. If the file does not exist, editing begins with an empty buffer. At the conclusion of the session, the buffer is written to the specified file.

The editor is line oriented; that is, one can enter lines, delete lines, and so on. Text does *not* flow or ''wrap around'' from one line to another.

The editor does not use line numbers. Instead, one moves to a particular line by specifying a substring of the line. The available commands are *find* (the next line containing a given substring), *insert* (lines), *delete* (lines), *type* (display lines at the terminal), *substitute* (a string for a substring in a particular line), *move* (a specified number of lines ahead of the current line), and *quit* (terminate the editor). These commands are specified more formally at the beginning of the C implementation.

Sample Input / Ouptut

There is a dummy first line in the buffer denoted [BOF]. The comments are not part of the input/output but are simply given to help the reader understand how the editor operates. Input is in color; output is in black.

	Comments
Edit which file? pizza.dat	
*** File does not exist	Creating a new file
# i	Insert (# is the editor prompt)
	Editor skips line
I'll have a 10 inch	5 lines are entered
piza. But since	
I'm not	
hungary, just cut	
it into 3 pieces.	

```
Exit                                EOF is generated
# t b                               Type first line
[BOF]                               Dummy first line
# t 3                               Type 3 lines
[BOF]
I'll have a 10 inch
piza. But since
# t                                 Type current line
[BOF]
# m 2                               Move 2 lines forward
piza. But since                     Shows current line
# s 'piza' 'pizza'                  Change piza to pizza in current line
                                    Any delimiters can be used

pizza. But since                    Confirms change
# t b                               Type first line
[BOF]
# f 'hun'                           Find line containing hun
hungary, just cut                   Shows the line
# s /gary/ /gry/                    Change gary to gry in current line
hungry, just cut                    Confirms change
# t b                               Type first line
[BOF]
# m 3                               Move 3 lines forward
I'm not                             Shows current line
# i                                 Insert after current line
                                    Editor skips line
very                                Insert one line
Exit                                EOF is generated
# t b                               Type first line
[BOF]
# t 10                              Type 10 lines
[BOF]
I'll have a 10 inch
pizza. But since
I'm not
very
hungry, just cut
it into 3 pieces.
*** Reached end of buffer           There aren't 10 lines
# m 2                               Move 2 lines forward
pizza. But since                    Shows current line
# s / But since/ //                 Change " But since" to the null
                                    string
pizza.                              Confirms change
# d 4                               Delete 4 lines after current line
# t b                               Type first line
[BOF]
# t 10                              Type 10 lines
```

```
[BOF]
I'll have a 10 inch
pizza.
*** Reached end of buffer          There aren't 10 lines
# q                                Quit editor and write file
```

The file *pizza.dat* is

```
I'll have a 10 inch
pizza.
```

Solution

To make it easy to insert and delete lines, we use a linked list. Each node in the list has two fields. The first field contains storage for a line of text, and the second field contains storage for a pointer to another node.

To store the lines, we define an array of 101 nodes, each capable of storing one line (consisting of 80 or fewer characters, a newline terminator, and a null terminator) and a pointer. Because the first line is the dummy line [BOF], we can store at most 100 * 80 = 8,000 characters (not counting the terminators). We begin by linking the nodes into a list of available nodes.

After reading the file name, we attempt to open the file. If the file cannot be opened, we print a message to that effect and proceed to the editing session; otherwise, we read the file into a linked list. We now have two linked lists—a list of available nodes and a list that contains a copy of the file (or one node containing [BOF] if the file does not exist).

We then cycle through a loop, reading and executing commands. When q (quit) is entered, the program terminates.

We have implemented some, but not all, of the code for the editor. Specifically, we have left to the reader the implementation of some of the commands. We have implemented all of the code necessary to build the linked lists, to read the file, to interpret the commands, to pass the appropriate arguments to the functions that will execute the commands, to insert lines, and to terminate the editor and write the buffer to disk. Implementation of the commands *delete*, *type*, *move*, *find*, and *substitute* is left to the reader (see Programming Exercises 10.8 through 10.12). In our code, when the commands *delete*, *type*, *move*, *find*, and *substitute* are invoked, a message is printed confirming that the appropriate function was entered. (Such dummy functions are called **stubs**.)

C Implementation

```
/*                    ****** LINE EDITOR *****

When the editor is invoked, the user is first prompted for
the name of the file to edit. If the file does not exist, a
message to that effect is written, and the user begins with
an empty buffer. At the conclusion of the editing session,
the specified file is created and the buffer is written to
it. If the file exists, it is read into a buffer and the
editing session begins. At the end of the editing session,
the revised file is written to disk.

The edit prompt is #.

There is always a dummy first line, denoted [BOF], in the
buffer (but not in the file).
```

In the following command list, current refers to the current line. Initially, current is the top line.

The commands available are:

f 'xxxxx' --   Finds the first line after or in the current line containing xxxxx, displays the line, and makes this line the current line. The first character of the second string becomes the delimiter. This delimiter can be anything. (You are not restricted to '.)

i   --   Insert an arbitrary number of lines after the current line. Insert is terminated by generating EOF. Current is unchanged.

d x   --   Delete x lines after the current line.

t b   --   Display the first line [BOF] and make it the current line.

t e   --   Display the last line and make it the current line.

t .   --   Display the current line.

t x   --   Display x lines starting with the current line. The current line is not changed.

s 'xx' 'yy'   Substitute yy for xx in the current line. (The strings xx and yy need not be the same length.) As in find, any character can be used as the delimiter. (You are not restricted to '.)

q   --   Quit the editor and write the revised file to disk.

m x   --   Move current so that it references the line x lines down and display the new current line. Example: Given

                        current -> Line 1
                                   Line 2
                                   Line 3
              after m 2, we would have

                                   Line 1
                                   Line 2
                        current -> Line 3

              and Line 3 would be displayed.

The maximum length of a line is 80 characters (not counting line terminators) and the maximum number of lines in the buffer is restricted to 101 (100 actual lines plus the dummy line [BOF]). */

```
#include <stdio.h>
#include <string.h>
#include <stdlib.h>

#define MAX_LENGTH 82 /* maximum length of line is 80 plus newline
                             terminator plus '\0' string terminator */
#define MAX_LINES 101  /* 1 + maximum number of lines */
#define TRUE 1

typedef struct node {
     char line[ MAX_LENGTH ]; /* text of line */
     struct node *link;  /* pointer to next line */
} NODE;

NODE top[ MAX_LINES ], /* storage for file */
     *bottom,  /* pointer to bottom line */
     *current = top, /* pointer to current line  */
     *avail;  /* pointer to next available unused node */

char inbuff[ MAX_LENGTH ]; /* buffer for input commands */
char file_name[ MAX_LENGTH ];  /* name of file to edit */

main()
{
     void insert( void ),  /* functions to execute commands */
          delet( char *s ),
          type( char *s ),
          move( char *s ),
          quit( void ),
          find( char *s ),
          substitute( char *s, char *t );
     void create( void );  /* creates a linked list of NODEs */
     NODE *read_file( void ); /* reads file into NODEs */

     /* reads buff and stores strings in s2 and s3 */
     int spec_scanf( char *buff, char *s2, char *s3 );

     char err_msg[] = "*** Error. Command is: ";
     char s1[ MAX_LENGTH ]; /* used to store */
     char s2[ MAX_LENGTH ]; /* parts of      */
     char s3[ MAX_LENGTH ]; /* commands      */
     int count; /* counts parts of a command stored */

     create(); /* link the NODEs together */
     bottom = read_file(); /* read file and return pointer to last
                             node used */
     avail = bottom -> link;  /* available list of nodes starts at
                                 node following bottom */
     bottom -> link = NULL; /* NULL link field of last node used */

     while ( TRUE ) {
          printf( "# " ); /* print prompt */
          fgets( inbuff, MAX_LENGTH, stdin ); /* store command */
          /* parse command */
```

```c
count = sscanf( inbuff, "%s%s%s", s1, s2, s3 );
printf( "\n" );

switch ( *s1 ) {
case 'i': /* insert */
     if ( count != 1 )
          printf( "%s i\n", err_msg );
     else
          insert();
     break;
case 'd': /* delete */
     if ( count != 2 )
          printf( "%s d <no of lines>\n", err_msg );
     else
          delet( s2 );
     break;
case 't': /* type */
     if ( count != 2 ) {
          printf( "%s", err_msg );
          printf( "t (b e . or <no of lines>)\n" );
     }
     else
          type( s2 );
     break;
case 'm': /* move */
     if ( count != 2 )
          printf( "%s m <no of lines>\n", err_msg );
     else
          move( s2 );
     break;
case 'q': /* quit */
     if ( count != 1 )
          printf( "%s q\n", err_msg );
     else
          quit();
     break;
case 'f': /* find */
     /* requires reparsing with special function
        spec_scanf because of delimiters of string to
        find */
     count = spec_scanf( inbuff, s2, s3 );
     if ( count != 2 )
          printf( "%s f 'xxx'\n", err_msg );
     else
          find( s2 );
     break;
case 's': /* substitute */
     /* requires reparsing with special function
        spec_scanf because of delimiters of strings to
        substitute */
```

```
                    count = spec_scanf( inbuff, s2, s3 );
                    if ( count != 3 )
                        printf( "%s s 'xx' 'yy'\n", err_msg );
                    else
                        substitute( s2, s3 );
                    break;
            default:
                printf( "*** Unknown command\n" );
                break;
            }
        }
}

/*   create
        Creates a linked list of MAX_LINES NODEs. */

void create( void )
{
    NODE *ptr = top;
    int i;

    for ( i = 1; i < MAX_LINES; i++, ptr++ )
        ptr -> link = ptr + 1;
    ptr -> link = NULL;
}

/*    read_file
        Copies [BOF] into top and then reads a file into the
        linked list starting at the node after top. If the file
        does not exist, the list consists of simply the [BOF]
        node. Returns a pointer to the last node. Does not NULL
        link field of last node. */

NODE *read_file( void )
{
    NODE *temp, *ptr = top;
    FILE *fp;

    strcpy( ptr -> line, "[BOF]\n" ); /* dummy first node */
    printf( "\nEdit which file? " );
    fgets( inbuff, MAX_LENGTH, stdin );
    sscanf( inbuff, "%s", file_name );
    printf( "\n" );

    /* read file, if possible */
    if ( ( fp = fopen( file_name, "r" ) ) != NULL ) {
        for ( temp = ptr -> link; temp != NULL &&
                fgets( temp -> line, MAX_LENGTH, fp ) != NULL;
                temp = temp -> link, ptr = ptr -> link )
                ;
        if ( fgets( inbuff, MAX_LENGTH, fp ) != NULL )
            printf( "*** Not enough room to read entire file\n" );
        fclose( fp);
    }
```

```
        else /* couldn't open file */
            printf( "*** File does not exist\n" );

        return ( ptr );
}

/*   quit writes file and terminates editor. */
void quit( void )
{
        FILE *fp;
        NODE *ptr = top;

        fp = fopen( file_name, "w" );

        for ( ptr = ptr -> link, ptr != NULL; ptr = ptr -> link )
            fprintf( fp, "%s", ptr -> line );

        exit( EXIT_SUCCESS );
}

/* insert
        Inserts lines following current. Gets nodes from avail list. */

void insert( void )
{
        NODE *ptr = avail,     /* ptr is node for next line to read */
            *before_ptr = NULL; /* trails ptr in avail list */

        while ( TRUE ) {
            if ( ptr == NULL ) {
                printf( "*** buffer full--can't add more lines\n" );
                break;
            }
            if ( fgets( ptr -> line, MAX_LENGTH, stdin ) == NULL ) {
                clearerr( stdin ); /* turn off EOF indicator */
                break;
            }
            before_ptr = ptr;
            ptr = ptr -> link;
        }

        /* if no nodes added, just return */
        if ( before_ptr == NULL )
            return;

        /* If nodes were added, insert the added nodes after current.
           before_ptr points to the last node added.
           avail points to the first node added. */
        before_ptr -> link = current -> link;
        current -> link = avail;

        /* update avail */
        avail = ptr;
```

```
        /* if nodes were added at end of buffer, update bottom */
        if ( before_ptr -> link == NULL )
            bottom = before_ptr;
}
/*    delet
            Delete s lines after current. */

void delet( char *s )
{
        printf( "Entered delet\n" );
}

/*    type
            Display lines. */

void type( char *s )
/* Options for s:
    s can be a nonnegative integer
    s can be . (= display current line)
    s can be b (= display top line)
    s can be e (= display last line)

    Only if s is b or e is current reset. */

{
        printf( "Entered type\n" );
}

/*    move
            Move current forward s lines, reset current, and display
            current. */

void move( char *s )
{
        printf( "Entered move\n" );
}

/*    find
            Finds first line after or in current line that contains s,
            prints it, and moves current.   */

void find( char *s )
{
        printf( "Entered find\n" );
}

/*    substitute
            Substitute t for s in current line. */

void substitute( char *s, char *t )
{
        printf( "Entered substitute\n" );
}
```

```
/*    spec_scanf
          Reads from buff and stores strings in s2 and s3, if
          possible. Begin by skipping white space. Then skip
          non-white space (which corresponds to skipping the
          command f or s). Then skip white space. Then store the
          following string between delimiters in s2. Then skip
          white space. Then store the following string between
          delimiters in s3. Return the number of strings skipped
          and stored. (Skipping f or s counts as 1.) */
int spec_scanf( char *buff, char *s2, char *s3 )
{
    /* skip white space and return position of pointer in buffer */
    char *skip_whitesp( char *ptr );

    /* skip non-white space return position of pointer in buffer */
    char *skip_nonwhitesp( char *ptr );

    /* get and store delimited string and return the position
       of the last character scanned */
    char *get_str_delim( char *ptr, char *s );

    buff = skip_whitesp( buff );
    if ( *buff == '\0' )
        return ( 0 );
    buff = skip_nonwhitesp( buff );
    buff = skip_whitesp( buff );
    if ( *buff == '\0' )
        return ( 1 );
    buff = get_str_delim( buff, s2 );
    if ( *buff++ == '\0' )
        return ( 1 );
    buff = skip_whitesp( buff );
    buff = get_str_delim( buff, s3 );
    if ( *buff == '\0' )
        return ( 2 );
    else
        return ( 3 );
}

/*    skip_whitesp
          Move ptr in string as long as it points to a blank,
          tab, or newline. Notice that \0 terminates pointer
          movement. Return final position of pointer. */

char *skip_whitesp( char *ptr )
{
    char c;

    while ( ( c = *ptr ) == ' ' || c == '\t' || c == '\n' )
        ptr++;
    return ( ptr );
}
```

```
/*    skip_nonwhitesp
          Move ptr in string as long as it does not point to a
          blank, tab, newline, or \0. Return final position of
          pointer. */
char *skip_nonwhitesp( char *ptr )
{
     char c;

     while ( ( c = *ptr ) != ' ' && c != '\t' &&
              c != '\n' && c != '\0' )
          ptr++;
     return ( ptr );
}
/*    get_str_delim
          Scan and store delimited string. The string to read is
          pointed to by ptr. The string is stored at the location
          pointed to by s. The delimiter is the first character in
          the string. Return position of second delimiter. If the
          string is improperly delimited, return pointer to the null
          terminator of string. */
char *get_str_delim( char *ptr, char *s )
{
     char delimit = *ptr;
     char c;

     if ( delimit == '\0' )
          return ( ptr );

     ptr++; /* ptr now points to the first character to store */

     /* scan and store until reaching delimiter or end of string */
     while ( ( c = *ptr ) != delimit && c != '\0' ) {
          ptr++;
          *s++ = c;
     }

     *s = '\0';

     return ( ptr );
}
```

Discussion

We declare a structure using a typedef, instances of which can hold lines and pointers:

```
typedef struct node {
     char line[ MAX_LENGTH ];
     struct node *link;
} NODE;
```

The declaration is outside all functions, so it is visible to the entire program. We then define an extern array top of MAX_LINES nodes and three extern pointers:

```
NODE top[ MAX_LINES ],
     *bottom,
     *current = top,
     *avail;
```

which are visible to the entire program. The array furnishes the supply of nodes with which linked lists can be constructed. The pointer constant `top` points to the first node in the linked list that contains the file. The pointer variable `bottom` points to the last node in the linked list that contains the file. Keeping an explicit pointer to the last node makes it possible to move quickly to the last line. The pointer variable `avail` points to the first node in the linked list of available nodes.

We also define an `extern` array `inbuff` to hold the user's command line and an `extern` variable `file_name` to hold the name of the file to edit:

```
char inbuff[ MAX_LENGTH ];
char file_name[ MAX_LENGTH ];
```

The function `main` begins by invoking the function `create` to create a linked list of `MAX_LINES` nodes. The function `create` simply makes each NODE in the array point to the following NODE, except that the last `link` member is set to NULL to signal the end of the linked list (see Figure 10.3.1).

Next, `main` invokes the function `read_file`, which begins by defining the pointers `temp` and `ptr` and setting `ptr` to `top` (see Figure 10.3.2):

```
NODE *temp, *ptr = top;
```

Next, the dummy line [BOF]\n is placed in the first node:

```
strcpy( ptr -> line, "[BOF]\n" );
```

We next prompt for a file name. In `read_file`, as in `main`, we use `fgets` to read the user input into the array `inbuff`. We then use `sscanf` to read the desired parts of `inbuff`. If the file does not exist, we print a message to that effect and return `ptr`. If the file does exist, we read it and store one line per node:

```
for ( temp = ptr -> link; temp != NULL &&
        fgets( temp -> line, MAX_LENGTH, fp ) != NULL;
        temp = temp -> link, ptr = ptr -> link )
     ;
```

In the `for` loop, we begin by assigning `temp` to the second node in the list (see Figure 10.3.2):

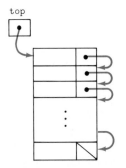

Figure 10.3.1 Executing `create`.

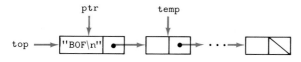

Figure 10.3.2 Initializing `temp`.

```
temp = ptr -> link;
```

There are two reasons to terminate the `for` loop: We can exhaust the supply of nodes, or we can reach the end of the file. The expression

```
temp != NULL
```

tests for the end of the linked list, and the expression

```
fgets( temp -> line, MAX_LENGTH, fp ) != NULL
```

reads a line into `temp -> line` (if there is a line) and also tests for end-of-file. After we successfully read a line into a node, we advance both pointers (see Figure 10.3.3):

```
temp = temp -> link, ptr = ptr -> link
```

After the loop terminates, we test whether the entire file was read

```
if ( fgets( inbuff, MAX_LENGTH, fp ) != NULL )
```

and, if not, we print a message. In any case, we close the file

```
fclose( fp );
```

We return `ptr`, the address of the last node that holds a line of the file.
When we execute

```
bottom = read_file();
```

in `main`, `bottom` points to the last node that holds a line of the file (see Figure 10.3.4).
The available list begins with the node following the last node that contains a line of the file; thus, in `main` we execute

```
avail = bottom -> link;
```

(see Figure 10.3.4). We must also NULL the link field of the last node in the list that contains the file (see Figure 10.3.4):

```
bottom -> link = NULL;
```

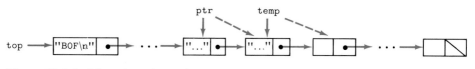

Figure 10.3.3 Advancing `ptr` and `temp`.

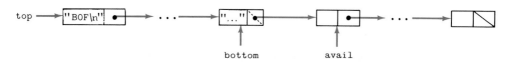

Figure 10.3.4 Initializing `avail` and NULLing `bottom`'s link field.

We are now ready to execute the `while` loop that interprets commands and invokes the appropriate functions. The loop begins by printing the prompt and reading a line of user input:

```
printf( "# " );
fgets( inbuff, MAX_LENGTH, stdin );
```

We next use `sscanf` to parse the command and count the number of arguments delimited by white space in the user buffer:

```
count = sscanf( inbuff, "%s%s%s", s1, s2, s3 );
```

The string `s1` should be one of `"i"`, `"d"`, and so on. A `switch` statement directs us to the appropriate code to execute:

```
switch ( *s1 ) {
case 'i':
      .
      .
      .
```

The `default` alternative traps an unknown command:

```
default:
      printf( "*** Unknown command\n" );
      break;
```

The input buffer contains a varying number of arguments. For example, the `insert` command consists of one argument:

```
i
```

whereas the `substitute` command consists of three arguments:

```
s /gary/ /gry/
```

For each command, we check to be sure that the correct number of arguments is present before invoking the function to execute the command. If the number of arguments is incorrect, we print an error message.

If the command is `find` or `substitute`, a reparsing of the input buffer is required since, in these cases, the arguments that contain the search or replace strings are delimited by the first non–white space character. To store these strings properly, we invoke the function `spec_scanf`.

The function `spec_scanf` begins by invoking `skip_whitesp` to skip white space in the input buffer:

```
buff = skip_whitesp( buff );
```

The function `skip_whitesp` returns the address in the input buffer of the next non–white space character. At this point, if we are at the end of the buffer, `spec_scanf` returns 0 to signal that zero arguments were processed:

```
if ( *buff == '\0' )
      return ( 0 );
```

If we are not at the end of the input buffer, we skip over the non–white space characters that correspond to the command (e.g., `f` or `s`):

```
buff = skip_nonwhitesp( buff );
```

The function `skip_nonwhitesp` returns the address in the input buffer of the next white space character or `'\0'` if the end of the string is reached.

We then invoke `skip_whitesp` again to move to the first delimited string. After checking that we are not at the end of the input buffer, we store the first delimited string by invoking `get_str_delim`:

```
buff = get_str_delim( buff, s2 );
```

The function `get_str_delim` stores the delimited string in `s2`. If `get_str_delim` was able to store a string in `s2`, it returns the address of the last delimiter; otherwise, it returns the address of the null terminator in the input buffer.

If we were not able to store a string in `s2`, we return 1 to signal that we processed one argument (the command):

```
if ( *buff == '\0' )
    return ( 1 );
```

Otherwise, we repeat the preceding steps in order to attempt to store a second delimited string in `s3`. If we are successful, we return 3 to signal that we processed three arguments (the command and two delimited strings); otherwise, we return 2 to signal that we processed two arguments (the command and one delimited string):

```
if ( *buff == '\0' )
    return ( 2 );
else
    return ( 3 );
```

In the function `insert`, we write the added lines in the linked list of available nodes, after which we insert the nodes used into the linked list that represents the file.

The function `insert` begins by defining the pointers `ptr` and `before_ptr`. The pointer `ptr` is initialized to `avail`. The pointer `before_ptr` always points to the node preceding the node pointed to by `ptr` or NULL if there is no predecessor. For this reason, `before_ptr` is initialized to NULL.

In the `while` loop, we first check whether `ptr` is NULL. If `ptr` is NULL, this means that there are no more available nodes, so we terminate the loop. If `ptr` is not NULL, we attempt to read a line into the node pointed to by `ptr`:

```
if ( fgets( ptr -> line, MAX_LENGTH, stdin ) == NULL ) {
    clearerr( stdin ); /* turn off EOF indicator */
    break;
}
```

If the user generates end-of-file, we invoke the library function `clearerr` to clear the end-of-file indicator and then terminate the loop. Some C systems refuse to accept additional input from the standard input after receiving an end-of-file signal. For such systems, it is necessary to clear the end-of-file indicator in order to read additional input from the standard input. Other systems automatically clear the end-of-file indicator when additional input is generated from the standard input. By including the line

```
clearerr( stdin ); /* turn off EOF indicator */
```

we promote portability. If we are successful in reading a line, we update the pointers:

```
before_ptr = ptr;
ptr = ptr -> link;
```

and go to the top of the `while` loop to attempt to read another line.

After we exit the `while` loop, if no nodes were added, `before_ptr` is still NULL. In this case, we simply return.

If nodes were added, we insert the added nodes in the linked list that represents the file and update `avail` (see Figure 10.3.5):

```
before_ptr -> link = current -> link;
current -> link = avail;
avail = ptr;
```

If nodes were added at the end of the file, we must update `bottom`:

```
if ( before_ptr -> link == NULL )
    bottom = before_ptr;
```

The function `quit` reopens the file `file_name` for writing

```
fp = fopen( file_name, "w" );
```

We then step through the linked list, beginning with the node following `top`, and write the lines to the file

```
for ( ptr = ptr -> link; ptr != NULL; ptr = ptr -> link )
    fprintf( fp, "%s", ptr -> line );
```

The function `quit` concludes by invoking the library function `exit` to terminate the program:

```
exit( EXIT_SUCCESS );
```

The function `exit` requires the header file *stdlib.h*. In addition to terminating the program, `exit` writes all output waiting to be written and closes all open files. The function `exit` expects one integer argument called a *status value*. The status value indicates whether the program terminated successfully. Two macros, EXIT_SUCCESS and EXIT_FAILURE, defined in *stdlib.h*, may be used as arguments to `exit` to indicate successful or unsuccessful termination. (A particular implementation may use additional values to signify different kinds of errors.) The status value passed to `exit` can be used by the process that invoked the program to take some action. For example, if the program was invoked from the command line and the status value indicated some type of error, the operating system might display a message.

The editor uses more memory than it needs. (Each line uses 82 bytes, regardless of its actual length.) Efficiency considerations are addressed in Programming Exercise 10.13.

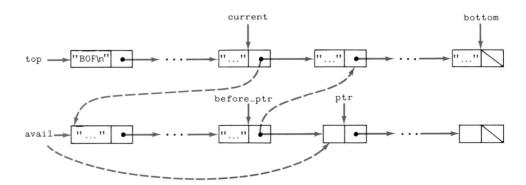

Figure 10.3.5 Executing `insert`.

10.4 Stacks and Queues

In this section, we examine stacks and queues. A **stack** is a list in which insertions and deletions occur at the same end. A **queue** is a list in which insertions occur at one end and deletions occur at the other end. We can implement both stacks and queues using either arrays or linked lists (or, with ingenuity, in other ways as well). We begin by discussing stacks.

Stacks

The end of a stack at which the insertions and deletions occur is known as the **top**. A pile of trays in a cafeteria where a customer takes a tray off the top and later puts it back on the top (after, we hope, cleaning it up) is an example of a stack (see Figure 10.4.1). A stack insertion is called a **push**, and a stack deletion is called a **pop**; that is, we push something onto a stack and pop something off. Because insertions and deletions occur at the same end of a stack, a stack exhibits *last-in, first-out* (LIFO) behavior. We first implement a stack by using an array.

Example 10.4.1.   To implement a stack, we represent the underlying data type on which operations are performed as an array that can hold SIZE variables of type pointer to TRAY. The operations push and pop are implemented as the functions push and pop. The function push checks whether the stack is full before inserting an item, and pop checks whether the stack is empty before deleting an item. The bottom of the stack is fixed at index 0. The variable top marks the current position in the array at which insertions and deletions occur (see Figure 10.4.2).

Storage for items added to the stack is allocated at run time. The array trays holds pointers to the allocated storage. None of these details is evident when the code is run, so the user can manipulate a stack of plates without understanding how the stack has been implemented. In fact, we can change the implementation of the stack (see Example 10.4.2) without changing any of the invoking functions.

```
#include <stdio.h>
#include <stdlib.h>
#define  SIZE  100
```

Figure 10.4.1 A stack of cafeteria trays.

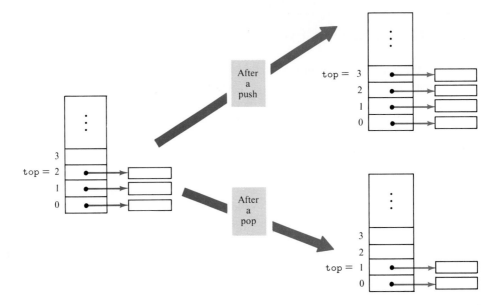

Figure 10.4.2 Implementing a stack using an array.

```
typedef  struct tray {
        char   color[ 10 ];     /* its color */
        int    id;              /* its unique id number */
} TRAY;

TRAY *trays[ SIZE ];    /* array to hold up to SIZE pointers to
                           TRAY */

int    top = -1;        /* index into trays */

main()
{
    void  get_data( TRAY *ptr ), put_data( TRAY *ptr );
    int   ans, flag;
    TRAY  t, *ptr, *pop( void ), *push( TRAY tr );

    /* do stack operations until user signals halt */
    do {
        do {
            printf( "\n\n\tEnter 1 to push, 2 to pop:  " );
            scanf( "%d", &ans );
            printf( "\n" );
            switch ( ans ) {
            case 1: /* get a TRAY and add it to stack */
                get_data( &t );
                if ( push( t ) == NULL )
                    printf( "\n\nSTACK FULL\n\n" );
                break;
            case 2: /* delete a TRAY from stack and print it */
                if ( ( ptr = pop() ) != NULL )
                    put_data( ptr );
```

```
                       else
                              printf( "\n\nSTACK EMPTY\n\n" );
                       break;
                default:
                       printf( "\nIllegal response\n" );
                       break;
                }
          } while ( ans != 1 && ans != 2 );
          printf( "\n\n\n1 to continue, 0 to quit: " );
          scanf( "%d", &flag );
          printf( "\n" );
     } while ( flag );
}
/*   get_data prompts the user for a TRAY's color and id and
     stores it at the address passed.                          */
void  get_data( TRAY *ptr )
{
     printf( "\nenter the tray's color: " );
     scanf( "%s", ptr -> color );
     printf( "\nenter the tray's id: " );
     scanf( "%d", &( ptr -> id ) );
     printf( "\n" );
}
/*   put_data writes the color and id of the TRAY whose address is
     passed.                                                   */
void put_data( TRAY *ptr )
{
     printf( "\ntray's color: %s\n", ptr -> color );
     printf( "\ntray's id: %d\n", ptr -> id );
}
/*   If the stack is full, push returns NULL. Otherwise, push
     allocates storage for a TRAY, copies the data passed into the
     allocated storage, pushes a pointer to the TRAY onto the
     stack, and returns the address of the TRAY passed.        */
TRAY  *push( TRAY tr )
{
     TRAY *ptr;

     if ( top >= SIZE - 1 ) /* stack full? */
          return ( NULL );
     ptr = ( TRAY * ) malloc( sizeof ( TRAY ) ); /* new TRAY */
     *ptr = tr; /* store data */
     trays[ ++top ] = ptr;  /* push it and update top */
     return ( &tr );
}
/*   If the stack is empty, pop returns NULL. Otherwise, pop
     copies the top TRAY to permanent storage, frees the stack
     storage, updates top, and returns the address of the TRAY.  */
```

```
TRAY *pop( void )
{
     static TRAY popped_tray;

     if ( top < 0 ) /* empty stack? */
          return ( NULL );
     popped_tray = *trays[ top ]; /* copy top TRAY */
     free( trays[ top-- ] ); /* collect garbage */
     return ( &popped_tray );
}
```

If the stack is full, push returns NULL. The invoking function can test the value returned by push to determine whether a push did occur. If the stack is not full, push allocates storage for a TRAY structure and copies the data passed to it into the allocated storage. Finally, push moves the index top to the next position in the array, stores the address of the allocated storage in the new position, and returns the address of the TRAY structure passed.

If the stack is empty, pop returns NULL. The invoking function can test the value returned by pop to determine whether a pop did occur. If the stack is not empty, pop copies the data at the top of the stack into the static variable popped_tray. Next, pop frees the storage no longer needed and moves the top index to the previous position in the array. The function pop concludes by returning the address of the popped_tray. It is important that the storage class of the variable popped_tray is static so that the data remain in popped_tray after pop returns.

Example 10.4.2.   Now we implement a stack of trays as a linked list. We add and delete at the beginning of the linked list (see Figure 10.4.3). We modify the structure so that it includes a pointer field and change the extern variables that control the stack. Specifically, the lines that precede main in the revised program are as follows:

```
#include <stdio.h>
#include <stdlib.h>
#define SIZE 100

typedef  struct tray {
        char  color[ 10 ];    /* its color */
        int  id;              /* its unique id number */
        struct tray *below;   /* pointer to successor on stack */
} TRAY;

TRAY *top = NULL;    /* pointer to top TRAY on stack */
int  currsize = 0;   /* number of items on stack */
```

The revised push and pop functions follow.

```
/*   If the stack is full, push returns NULL. Otherwise, push
     allocates storage for a TRAY, copies the data passed into the
     allocated storage, adds the node to the linked list, updates
     top and the current size of the stack, and returns the
     address of the TRAY passed.                                  */

TRAY *push( TRAY tr )
{
     TRAY *ptr;
```

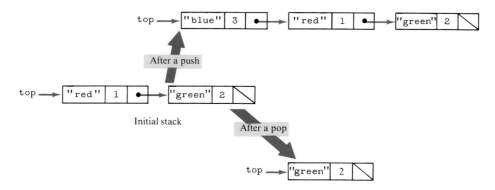

Figure 10.4.3 Implementing a stack using a linked list.

```
    if ( currsize >= SIZE ) /* stack full? */
        return ( NULL );
    ptr = ( TRAY * ) malloc( sizeof ( TRAY ) ); /* new TRAY */
    *ptr = tr; /* store data */
    ptr -> below = top; /* push it on stack */
    top = ptr; /* update top */
    ++currsize; /* update current stack size */

    return ( &tr );
}

/*  If the stack is empty, pop returns NULL. Otherwise, pop
    copies the top TRAY to permanent storage, updates top, frees
    the stack storage, updates the current size of the stack, and
    returns the address of the TRAY.                            */

TRAY *pop( void )
{
    static TRAY popped_tray;
    TRAY *ptr;

    if ( currsize < 1 ) /* empty stack? */
        return ( NULL );
    popped_tray = *top; /* copy data to return */
    ptr = top; /* save address of 1st node for garbage collection */
    top = top -> below; /* update top */
    free( ptr ); /* collect garbage */
    --currsize; /* update current size */

    return ( &popped_tray );
}
```

If the stack is full, push returns NULL. If the stack is not full, push allocates storage for a TRAY structure and copies the data passed to it into the allocated storage. Finally, push adds the allocated node to the beginning of the linked list, updates the current stack size, and returns the address of the TRAY structure passed. Figure 10.4.4 shows the situation just before push returns.

If the stack is empty, pop returns NULL. If the stack is not empty, pop copies the data at the top of the stack into the static variable popped_tray. Next, pop

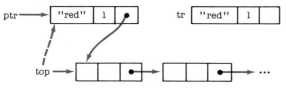

Figure 10.4.4 The function `push`.

saves the address of the first node so that this node can later be freed. We then move `top` to the node that follows it in the linked list. Figure 10.4.5 shows the situation at this point. Finally, we free the first node, update the current stack size, and return the address of `popped_tray`.

Queues

A queue is a list in which insertions and deletions occur at opposite ends. Insertions take place at the **rear** and deletions at the **front**. A line in which people enter at one end and exit at the other is an example of a queue (see Figure 10.4.6). A queue exhibits *first-in, first-out* (FIFO) behavior. As in the preceding subsection, our first implementation uses an array.

Example 10.4.3.   To implement a queue, we represent the underlying data type on which operations are performed as an array that can hold `SIZE` variables of type pointer to `CUSTOMER`. The operations are implemented as the functions `insert` and `remove`. The function `insert` checks whether the queue is full before inserting an item, and `remove` checks whether the queue is empty before deleting an item. Unlike the stack, neither the front nor the rear is fixed (see Figure 10.4.7). We assume that the cell at index 0 follows the last cell. The variable `front` gives the index of the item at the front of the queue. The variable `rear` is 1 more than the index of the item at the rear of the queue (`rear` is 0 if the item at the rear of the queue is in position `SIZE − 1`). The variable `rear` gives the position in the array at which to insert the next item. The `front` and `rear` indexes are initialized to 0 and updated by using the modulus operator.

```
#include <stdlib.h>
#include <stdio.h>
#define  SIZE   100
typedef  struct customer {
          char    lname[ 25 ]; /* last name */
          char    fname[ 15 ]; /* first name */
```

Figure 10.4.5 The function `pop`.

Figure 10.4.6 A queue of customers.

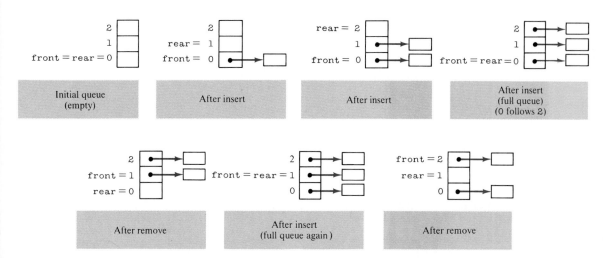

Figure 10.4.7 Implementing a queue using an array.

```
                int      account_no;   /* account number */
                float    balance;      /* balance */
} CUSTOMER;
CUSTOMER  *customers[ SIZE ];
int    front = 0, rear = 0; /* exit and entry positions in queue */
int    count = 0;               /* count of items in queue */
main( )
{
    void  get_data( CUSTOMER *ptr ), put_data( CUSTOMER *ptr );
    int   ans, flag;
    CUSTOMER cu, *ptr, *insert( CUSTOMER cust ), *remove( void );

    /* do queue operations until user signals halt */
    do {
        do {
            printf( "\n\n\tEnter 1 to insert, 2 to remove:   " );
            scanf( "%d", &ans );
            printf( "\n" );
            switch ( ans ) {
            case 1: /* get a CUSTOMER and add to a queue */
                get_data( &cu );
                if ( insert( cu ) == NULL )
                    printf( "\n\nQUEUE FULL\n\n" );
                break;
            case 2: /* delete a CUSTOMER from queue and print */
                if ( ( ptr = remove() ) != NULL )
                    put_data( ptr );
                else
                    printf( "\n\nQUEUE EMPTY\n\n" );
                break;
            default:
                printf( "\nIllegal response\n" );
                break;
            }
        } while ( ans != 1 && ans != 2 );
        printf( "\n\n\n1 to continue, 0 to quit: " );
        scanf( "%d", &flag );
        printf( "\n" );
    } while ( flag );
}
/*  get_data prompts the user for a CUSTOMER's last name, first
    name, account_no, and balance stores the data at the address
    passed.                                                       */

void  get_data( CUSTOMER *ptr )
{
    printf( "\nenter the customer's last name: " );
    scanf( "%s", ptr -> lname );
    printf( "\nenter the customer's first name: " );
    scanf( "%s", ptr -> fname );
```

```
        printf( "\nenter the customer's account number: " );
        scanf( "%d", &( ptr -> account_no ) );
        printf( "\nenter the customer's balance: " );
        scanf( "%f", &( ptr -> balance ) );
        printf( "\n" );
}
/*    put_data writes the last name, first name, account_no, and
      balance of the CUSTOMER whose address is passed.             */
void put_data( CUSTOMER *ptr )
{
        printf( "\ncustomer's name: %s, %s\n", ptr -> lname,
            ptr -> fname  );
        printf( "\ncustomer's account number: %d\n",
            ptr -> account_no );
        printf( "\ncustomer's balance: %f\n", ptr -> balance );
}
/*    If the queue is full, insert returns NULL. Otherwise, insert
      allocates storage for a CUSTOMER, copies the data passed into
      the allocated storage, adds a pointer to the CUSTOMER to the
      array, and returns the address of the CUSTOMER passed.      */
CUSTOMER *insert( CUSTOMER cust )
{
        CUSTOMER *ptr;
        if ( count >= SIZE ) /* queue full? */
            return ( NULL );
        ptr = ( CUSTOMER * )
            malloc( sizeof ( CUSTOMER ) ); /* new CUSTOMER */
        *ptr = cust; /* store data */
        customers[ rear ] = ptr; /* add CUSTOMER to queue */
        rear = ++rear % SIZE; /* update rear */
        ++count; /* update count */

        return ( &cust );
}
/*    If the queue is empty, remove returns NULL. Otherwise, remove
      copies the CUSTOMER at the front to permanent storage, frees
      the queue storage, updates front, and returns the address of
      the CUSTOMER.                                               */
CUSTOMER *remove( void )
{
        static CUSTOMER removed_cust;

        if ( count == 0 ) /* empty queue? */
            return ( NULL );
        removed_cust = *customers[ front ]; /* copy CUSTOMER at front */
        free( customers[ front ] ); /* collect garbage */
        front = ++front % SIZE; /* update front */
        --count;
```

```
      return ( &removed_cust ),
}
```

    If the queue is full, `insert` returns NULL. If the queue is not full, `insert` allocates storage for a CUSTOMER structure and copies the data passed to it into the allocated storage. Next, `insert` stores the address of the allocated storage in the next available position, indexed by `rear`, in the array. The statement

```
      rear = ++rear % SIZE;
```

updates `rear`. If we are at the end of the array, this statement resets `rear` to 0. After updating `count`, `insert` returns the address of the CUSTOMER structure passed.

    If the queue is empty, `remove` returns NULL. If the queue is not empty, `remove` copies the data at the front of the queue, indexed by `front`, into the `static` variable `removed_cust`. Next, `remove` frees the storage no longer needed. The statement

```
      front = ++front % SIZE;
```

updates `front`. If we are at the end of the array, this statement resets `front` to 0. After updating `count`, `remove` returns the address of `removed_cust`.

Example 10.4.4.   Now we represent a queue of customers as a linked list. We add at the end of the linked list and delete from the beginning of the linked list (see Figure 10.4.8). We modify the structure so that it includes a pointer field and change the `extern` variables that control the queue. Specifically, the lines that precede `main` in the revised program are as follows:

```
#include <stdlib.h>
#include <stdio.h>
#define  SIZE  100

typedef  struct customer {
          char    lname[ 25 ];    /* last name */
          char    fname[ 15 ];    /* first name */
          int     account_no;     /* account number */
```

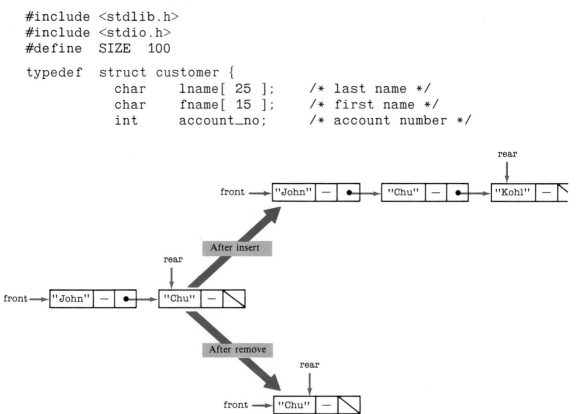

Figure 10.4.8 Implementing a queue using a linked list.

```
        float   balance;         /* balance */
        struct  customer *succ; /* successor on the queue */
} CUSTOMER;
CUSTOMER   *front, *rear; /* exit and entry positions in queue */
int        count = 0;     /* count of items in queue */
```

The revised `insert` and `remove` functions follow:

```
/*  If the queue is full, insert returns NULL. Otherwise, insert
    allocates storage for a CUSTOMER, copies the data passed into
    the allocated storage, adds the node to the rear (last node
    in the linked list), updates rear, NULLs the link field of
    the new node, updates count, and returns the address of the
    CUSTOMER passed. */

CUSTOMER *insert( CUSTOMER cust )
{
    CUSTOMER *ptr;

    if ( count >= SIZE ) /* queue full? */
        return ( NULL );
    ptr = ( CUSTOMER * )
        malloc( sizeof ( CUSTOMER ) ); /* new CUSTOMER */

    *ptr = cust; /* store data */

    if ( count == 0 ) /* empty queue? */
        front = ptr; /* front points to first node in list */
    else
        rear -> succ = ptr; /* if queue not empty, add at end */
    rear = ptr; /* update rear */
    ptr -> succ = NULL; /* NULL last succ field */
    ++count; /* update count */

    return ( &cust );
}

/*  If the queue is empty, remove returns NULL. Otherwise, remove
    copies the CUSTOMER at the front (first node in the linked
    list) to permanent storage, updates front, frees the node,
    updates count, and returns the address of the CUSTOMER.     */

CUSTOMER *remove( void )
{
    static CUSTOMER removed_cust;
    CUSTOMER *next;

    if ( count == 0 ) /* empty queue? */
        return ( NULL );
    removed_cust = *front; /* copy CUSTOMER at front */
    next = front; /* save front node's address for freeing */
    front = front -> succ; /* remove front node */
    free( next ); /* deallocate storage */
    --count; /* update count */

    return ( &removed_cust );
}
```

Exercises

1. Assume that a stack is initially empty. Show the contents of the stack after the following operations are executed: push R, push S, pop, push G, push M, pop, pop, push N, push P, push L, push Q, push Y, pop, push Z, push T.

2. Assume that a queue is initially empty. Show the contents of the queue after the following operations are executed: insert G, delete, insert S, insert M, delete, insert E, insert W, insert A, insert B, delete, insert Q, insert P, insert Y, insert C, delete, delete, insert Z.

3. For each representation in Examples 10.4.1 through 10.4.4, write a function that prints the contents of the stack or queue.

4. The functions insert and remove in Example 10.4.3 use the modulus operator to update front and rear, both of which are initialized to 0. What would happen if we simply incremented rear and front after each invocation?

5. Example 10.4.3 maintains a variable count to test whether the queue is empty or full. Can we determine whether the queue is empty or full by examining the relative locations of front and rear? Explain.

6. Compare the advantages and disadvantages of implementing stacks and queues as arrays and as linked lists.

7. Draw pictures like those of Figures 10.4.4 and 10.4.5 to show how the functions insert and remove work.

8. In the linked-list representation of a queue (Example 10.4.4), why don't we delete at the end of the linked list and add at the beginning of the linked list?

9. Write a function empty_stack that returns 1 if the stack is empty and 0 if the stack is not empty. Use the array representation of Example 10.4.1.

10. Write a function empty_stack that returns 1 if the stack is empty and 0 if the stack is not empty. Use the linked-list representation of Example 10.4.2.

11. Write a function empty_queue that returns 1 if the queue is empty and 0 if the queue is not empty. Use the array representation of Example 10.4.3.

12. Write a function empty_queue that returns 1 if the queue is empty and 0 if the queue is not empty. Use the linked-list representation of Example 10.4.4.

13. Write a function full_stack that returns 1 if the stack is full and 0 if the stack is not full. Use the array representation of Example 10.4.1.

14. Write a function full_stack that returns 1 if the stack is full and 0 if the stack is not full. Use the linked-list representation of Example 10.4.2.

15. Write a function full_queue that returns 1 if the queue is full and 0 if the queue is not full. Use the array representation of Example 10.4.3.

16. Write a function full_queue that returns 1 if the queue is full and 0 if the queue is not full. Use the linked-list representation of Example 10.4.4.

17. Rewrite the function push of Example 10.4.2 so that it checks for a full stack by testing whether the value returned by malloc is NULL.

18. Rewrite the function insert of Example 10.4.4 so that it checks for a full queue by testing whether the value returned by malloc is NULL.

10.5   Sample Application: Converting from Infix to Postfix

Problem

Convert arithmetic expressions in infix notation such as (A + B) % C to equivalent expressions in postfix notation, in this case AB+C%.

Sample Input/Output

The user enters an infix expression, which is converted to postfix. Input is in color; output is in black.

```
Infix (up to 64 chars): A + B * C

Infix:    A + B * C
Postfix: ABC*+

    Another? (y/n)   y

Infix (up to 64 chars): (A+B)*C

Infix:    (A+B)*C
Postfix: AB+C*

    Another? (y/n)   y

Infix (up to 64 chars): ((A + B) - C) * (D / (P + Q))

Infix:    ((A + B) - C) * (D / (P + Q))
Postfix: AB+C-DPQ+/*

    Another? (y/n)   n
```

Solution

Arithmetic expressions in C use **infix notation**, that is, notation in which a (binary) arithmetic operator occurs between its operands. In the expression A + B * C the multiplication operator occurs between the operands B and C, whereas the addition operator occurs between the expressions A and B * C. Because of operator precedence (see Figure 2.4.1), the expression A + B * C is equivalent to A + (B * C).

The occurrence of parentheses in an infix expression such as

((A + B) * (C - D) + (P / Q)) % (((X - Y) / Z) + M)

can render the expression quite complicated. By contrast, **postfix notation** is relatively simple because it dispenses with parentheses and operator precedence. (Postfix notation is also known as *reverse Polish notation* in honor of the logician Lukasiewicz, who invented it.) In postfix, an operator immediately follows its two operands (see Figure 10.5.1). It is common for compilers to convert infix into postfix in the course of translating high-level source code into machine code.

Our program's logic can be clarified by tracing the conversion of the two infix expressions A * B + C and (A + B) * C. We take the examples in order.

Two points need emphasis at the start. The first is that the left-to-right order of *operands* is always the same in infix and postfix expressions. As our program scans the infix buffer from left to right, it copies operands in order into the postfix buffer. It is thus relatively easy to handle operands in the infix-to-postfix conversion. The second point is that the left-to-right order of *operators* need *not* be the same in infix and postfix expres-

Infix	Postfix
A + B	AB+
A + B * C	ABC*+
(A + B) * C	AB+C*
(A + B) * (C − D)	AB+CD−*

Figure 10.5.1 Infix and postfix expressions.

sions. For example, the infix expression A + B * C becomes ABC*+ in postfix. The order of the operators is reversed. However, the infix expression A * B + C becomes AB*C+ in postfix. Here the order of the operators is the same. A relatively tricky part of the conversion is to order the operators. We use a stack for this purpose. Whenever our program encounters an operator while scanning the infix buffer, it pushes the operator onto the stack—but only after popping from the stack any operators of higher precedence. So, in our first example, when the program encounters the * operator, it pushes this operator onto the stack. At that point the stack is empty, as nothing has yet been pushed. When the program encounters the + operator, it first pops the * from the stack because the * has a higher precedence than the +. Figure 10.5.2 traces the conversion. The indexes i and p point to cells in the infix and postfix buffers, respectively. The index t points to the top cell in the stack.

Our second example, (A + B) * C, seems more complicated because of the parentheses. Yet the parentheses appear less intimidating if we keep in mind that they serve only to delimit subexpressions. In our example, the parentheses delimit the subexpression A + B.

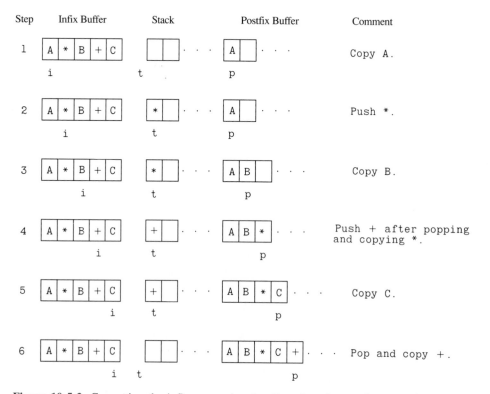

Figure 10.5.2 Converting the infix expression A * B + C to the postfix expression AB*C+.

As our program encounters parenthesized subexpressions, it converts them into postfix and then continues with the remainder of the infix expression. If subexpressions are nested, the program takes such nested subexpressions in order. So the program first converts the subexpression A + B into AB+ and then continues with the remainder of the infix expression to produce AB+C*. Recall that operands are never stacked but that operators are always stacked. Besides operators, only left parentheses are stacked. When the program scans the matching right parenthesis, which marks the end of the subexpression, it pops the stack until it finds a left parenthesis. At this point, the program has converted the entire subexpression. The symbols popped, if any, must be operators. Figure 10.5.3 traces our second example.

Our program allocates `MaxLen chars` for the stack, where `MaxLen` is the maximum number of characters in an input expression. Because only left parentheses and operators

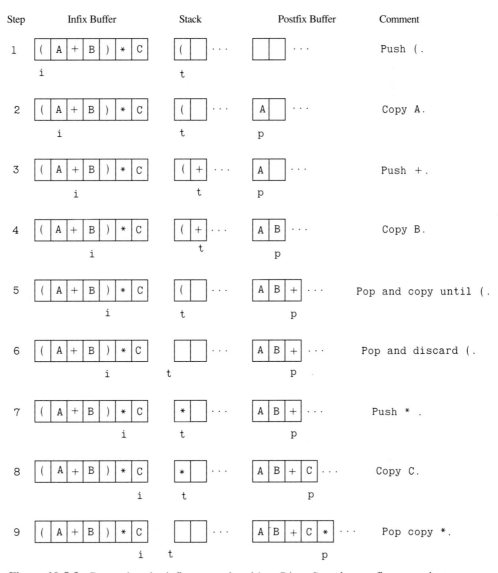

Figure 10.5.3 Converting the infix expression (A + B) * C to the postfix expression AB+C*.

are ever stacked, it is safe to assume that our stack is big enough for the conversion of any input expression of at most MaxLen characters. Further, the program logic prevents us from ever trying to pop an empty stack. Nonetheless, the program includes checks for stack overflow and underflow. A program often contains errors that its programmer thought impossible. Even an error-free program may produce unexpected behavior if later modified. Therefore, to make our program robust, we trap two errors that we do not expect to occur.

C Implementation

```
#include <stdio.h>
#include <ctype.h>
#include <string.h>
#include <stdlib.h>

#define Arnold    '\0'   /* The Terminator */
#define Blank     ' '
#define Tab       '\t'

#define MaxLen 64
static char
    infix[ MaxLen + 1 ],
    stack[ MaxLen ],
    postfix[ MaxLen + 1 ];

#define Empty (-1)        /* empty stack */
static int top;

/* symbol types */
#define Operator    (-10)
#define Operand     (-20)
#define LeftParen   (-30)
#define RightParen  (-40)

static char *symbols = "()+-%*/";

/* symbol precedence */
#define LeftParenPrec 0     /* ( */
#define AddPrec       1     /* + */
#define SubPrec       1     /* - */
#define MultPrec      2     /* * */
#define DivPrec       2     /* / */
#define RemPrec       2     /* % */
#define None          999   /* all else */

main()
{
  void
    read_input( void ),
    infix_to_postfix( void ),
    write_output( void );

  char ans[ 2 ];
```

```
      do {
        /*
         * Read an infix string from stdin,
         * convert it to postfix, and write
         * infix and postfix to stdout.
         */
        top = Empty; /* reset stack */
        read_input();
        infix_to_postfix();
        write_output();

        /* Do another? */
        printf( "\n\t\tAnother? (y/n)  " );
        gets( ans );
      } while ( toupper( ans[ 0 ] ) == 'Y' );
    }

    void infix_to_postfix( void )
    {
      int
        i, p,
        len,
        type, precedence;
      char next;

      void push( char symbol );
      char pop( void );
      int
        get_type( char symbol ),
        get_prec( char symbol ),
        whitespace_p( char symbol );

      /* i for infix, p for postfix */
      i = p = 0;
      len = strlen( infix );

      / Loop through input string. */
      while ( i < len ) {
        /* Ignore whitespace in infix expression. */
        if ( !whitespace_p( infix[ i ] ) ) {
          type = get_type( infix[ i ] );

          switch ( type ) {
          /* Push left paren onto stack. */
          case LeftParen:
            push( infix[ i ] );
            break;

          /* Pop stack until matching left paren. */
          case RightParen:
            while ( ( next = pop() ) != '(' )
              postfix[ p++ ] = next;
            break;
```

```
        /* Transfer operand to postfix string. */
        case Operand:
          postfix[ p++ ] = infix[ i ];
          break;

        /*
         * Pop stack until first operator of higher
         * precedence and then stack this operator.
         */
        case Operator:
          precedence = get_prec( infix[ i ] );

          /* Anything on stack to pop? */
          while ( top > Empty &&
                   precedence <= get_prec( stack[ top ] ) )
            postfix[ p++ ] = pop();
          push( infix[ i ] );
          break;
        }
      }

    i++; /* next symbol in infix expression */
  }

  /* Pop any remaining operators. */
  while ( top > Empty )
    postfix[ p++ ] = pop();

  postfix[ p ] = Arnold;     /* ensure a string */
}

int get_type( char symbol )
{
  switch ( symbol ) {

  case '(':
    return ( LeftParen );

  case ')':
    return ( RightParen );

  case '+':
  case '-':
  case '%':
  case '*':
  case '/':
    return ( Operator );

  default:
    return ( Operand );
  }
}

int get_prec( char symbol )
{
```

```
    switch ( symbol ) {
    case '+':
      return ( AddPrec );

    case '-':
      return ( SubPrec );

    case '*':
      return ( MultPrec );

    case '/':
      return ( DivPrec );

    case '%':
      return ( RemPrec );

    case '(':
      return ( LeftParenPrec );

    default:
      return ( None );
    }
}

int whitespace_p( char symbol )
{
  return ( symbol == Blank   ||
      symbol == Tab      ||
      symbol == Arnold );
}

void push( char symbol )
{
  void full_stack( void );

  /*
   * For program robustness,
   * check for overflow.
   */
  if ( top > MaxLen )
    full_stack();
  else
    stack[ ++top ] = symbol;
}

char pop( void )
{
  void empty_stack( void );

  /*
   * For program robustness.
   * check for underflow.
   */
  if ( top <= Empty )
    empty_stack();
```

```
      else
        return ( stack[ top-- ] );
    }

    /* Exit in case of overflow. */
    void full_stack( void )
    {
      printf( "\n\n\t\tFull stack...exiting.\n\n" );
      exit( EXIT_SUCCESS );
    }

    /* Exit in case of underflow. */
    void empty_stack( void )
    {
      printf( "\n\n\t\tEmpty stack...exiting.\n\n" );
      exit( EXIT_SUCCESS );
    }

    void read_input( void )
    {
      printf( "\n\n\tInfix (up to %d chars): ", MaxLen );
      gets( infix );
    }

    void write_output( void )
    {
      printf( "\n\tInfix:   %s\n", infix );
      printf( "\tPostfix: %s\n", postfix );
    }
```

10.6   Graphs and Trees

In the remainder of this chapter, we consider C implementations of operations on **graphs** and **trees**. In this section, we collect the requisite definitions. Because a tree is a special kind of graph, we begin by discussing graphs.

Figure 10.6.1 shows a graph. Because graphs are typically drawn with dots and lines, they look like road maps. The dots are called **vertices**, and the lines that connect the vertices are called **edges**. The formal definition follows.

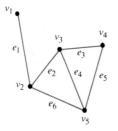

Figure 10.6.1 A graph.

Definition 10.6.1. A *graph* consists of a set V of *vertices* (or *nodes*) and a set E of *edges* (or *arcs*) such that each edge e in E is associated with an unordered pair of distinct vertices. Moreover, for each distinct pair of vertices v and w, there is at most one edge associated with v and w. If the edge e is associated with the pair of vertices v and w, we write $e = (v, w)$ or $e = (w, v)$.

An edge e in a graph that is associated with the pair of vertices v and w is said to be *incident* on v and w, and v and w are said to be *adjacent vertices*.

Example 10.6.1. The graph of Figure 10.6.1 consists of the set

$$V = \{v_1, v_2, v_3, v_4, v_5\}$$

of vertices and the set

$$E = \{e_1, e_2, e_3, e_4, e_5, e_6\}$$

of edges. Edge e_1 is associated with the unordered pair v_1 and v_2 of vertices; thus, we may write $e_1 = (v_1, v_2)$ or $e_1 = (v_2, v_1)$. Edge e_1 is incident on v_1 and v_2. The vertices v_1 and v_2 are adjacent.

Definition 10.6.1 prohibits an edge from being associated with the vertex pair v, w where $v = w$. If such edges were allowed, they would be drawn as shown in Figure 10.6.2. (Such an edge is called a *loop*.) Definition 10.6.1 also prohibits two or more edges from being associated with one vertex pair v, w. If such edges were allowed, they would be drawn as shown in Figure 10.6.3. (Such edges are called *parallel edges*.) Although some definitions of graph permit loops and / or parallel edges, we do not allow such edges in this book.

If we think of the vertices in a graph as cities and the edges as roads, a **path** would correspond to a trip beginning at some city, passing through several cities, and terminating at some city. The formal definition follows.

Definition 10.6.2. Let v_0 and v_n be vertices in a graph. A *path from v_0 to v_n of length n* is a sequence of $n + 1$ vertices

$$(v_0, v_1, \ldots, v_n)$$

where (v_{i-1}, v_i) is an edge for each $i = 1, \ldots, n$.

Example 10.6.2. In the graph of Figure 10.6.1,

$$(v_1, v_2, v_5, v_4, v_3)$$

is a path of length 4 from vertex v_1 to vertex v_3.

A **simple path** from v to w is a path from v to w with no repeated vertices.

Example 10.6.3. In the graph of Figure 10.6.1, the path

$$(v_1, v_2, v_5, v_4, v_3)$$

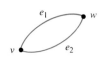

Figure 10.6.2 A loop.   **Figure 10.6.3** Parallel edges.

is a simple path from v_1 to v_3, as it has no repeated vertices. The path

$$(v_2, v_3, v_4, v_5, v_3)$$

is *not* a simple path from v_2 to v_3, as it has repeated vertices.

Sometimes it is convenient to assign values to the edges in a graph (see Figure 10.6.4). Such a graph is called a **network** or a **weighted graph**. We can think of the value of an edge as the *length* of the edge or as the *cost* of the edge. If P is a path in a weighted graph, the **length of the path P** is defined to be the sum of the weights of the edges.

Example 10.6.4.   The weight of the path

$$(v_2, v_3, v_5, v_4, v_3)$$

in the graph of Figure 10.6.4 is 45, the sum of the weights of the edges

$$(v_2, v_3), (v_3, v_5), (v_5, v_4), (v_4, v_3)$$

in the path.

In Section 10.9 we address the problem of finding a minimum-length path in a weighted graph. If the vertices of a graph represent cities and the lengths of the edges represent distances between cities, a minimum-length path from v to w will represent a shortest route from v to w.

We turn next to trees.

Definition 10.6.3.   A (*free*) *tree T* is a graph satisfying the following: If v and w are any vertices in T, there is a unique simple path from v to w. A *rooted tree* is a tree in which a particular vertex is designated as the root.

Example 10.6.5.   The graph T of Figure 10.6.5 is a tree because if v and w are any vertices in T, there is a unique simple path from v to w.

The graph of Figure 10.6.1 is *not* a tree because there is more than one simple path from vertex v_2 to vertex v_5.

The graph of Figure 10.6.6 is *not* a tree because there is no simple path from vertex v_3 to vertex v_5.

If we designate v_4 as the root of the tree of Figure 10.6.5, we obtain a rooted tree. In contrast with natural trees, which have their roots at the bottom, abstract rooted trees are typically drawn with their roots at the top. Figure 10.6.7 shows the way that the tree of Figure 10.6.5 is drawn (with v_4 as the root). First, we place the root v_4 at the top. Under the root and on the same level, we place the vertices v_2 and v_6 that can be reached from the root on a simple path of length 1. Under each of these vertices and on the same level, we

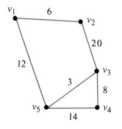

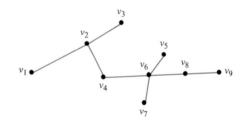

Figure 10.6.4 A network (weighted graph).   Figure 10.6.5 A tree.

Figure 10.6.6 A graph that is not a tree.

place the vertices v_1, v_3, v_5, v_7, and v_8 that can be reached from the root on a simple path of length 2. We continue in this way until the entire tree is drawn. Because the simple path from the root to any given vertex is unique, each vertex is on a uniquely determined level.

Example 10.6.6. If we designate v_8 as the root of the tree of Figure 10.6.5, we obtain the rooted tree shown in Figure 10.6.8.

The following terminology is derived from a family tree.

Definition 10.6.4. Let T be a tree with root v_0. Suppose that x and y are vertices in T and that $(v_0, v_1, \ldots, v_{n-1}, v_n)$ is a simple path in T. Then

1. v_{n-1} is the *parent* of v_n.
2. v_n is a *child* of v_{n-1}.
3. $v_0, \ldots, v_{n-1}$ are *ancestors* of v_n.
4. If x is an ancestor of y, y is a *descendant* of x.
5. If x has no children, x is a *terminal vertex*.
6. The *subtree of T rooted at x* is the graph with vertex set V and edge set E, where V is x together with the descendants of x and

$$E = \{e \mid e \text{ is an edge on a simple path from } x \text{ to some vertex in } V\}$$

Example 10.6.7. In the rooted tree of Figure 10.6.8

1. The parent of v_2 is v_4.
2. The children of v_6 are v_4, v_5, and v_7.
3. The ancestors of v_2 are v_4, v_6, and v_8.
4. The descendants of v_6 are v_1, v_2, v_3, v_4, v_5, and v_7.
5. The terminal vertices are v_1, v_3, v_5, v_7, and v_9.
6. The subtree rooted at v_4 is shown in Figure 10.6.9.

A **binary tree** is a special kind of rooted tree. Every vertex in a binary tree has at most two children. Moveover, each child is designated as either a **left child** or a **right child**.

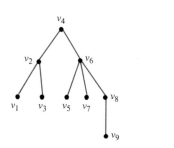

Figure 10.6.7 A rooted tree.

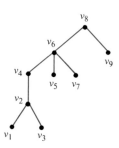

Figure 10.6.8 Another rooted tree.

Figure 10.6.9 A subtree.   **Figure 10.6.10** A binary tree.

When drawing a binary tree, a left child is drawn to the left and a right child is drawn to the right. An example of a binary tree is shown in Figure 10.6.10. The formal definition follows.

Definition 10.6.5. A *binary tree* is a rooted tree in which each vertex has no children, one child, or two children. If a vertex v has one child, that child is designated as either a left child or a right child (but not both). If a vertex v has two children, one child is designated a left child and the other child is designated a right child.

Example 10.6.8. In the binary tree of Figure 10.6.10, vertex v_2 is the left child of vertex v_1 and vertex v_3 is the right child of vertex v_1. Vertex v_4 is the right child of vertex v_2; vertex v_2 has no left child. Vertex v_5 is the left child of vertex v_3; vertex v_3 has no right child.

Exercises

Exercises 1 through 5 refer to the graph

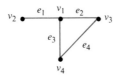

Let V denote the set of vertices and let E denote the set of edges.

1. List the members of V.

2. List the members of E.

3. On which vertices is edge e_3 incident?

4. Find a path of length 5 from v_2 to v_1.

5. Find a simple path of length 2 from v_3 to v_1.

6. Find the length of the path $(v_3, v_1, v_2, v_1, v_6)$ in the weighted graph

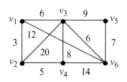

7. Draw the tree of Figure 10.6.5 as a rooted tree with v_9 as the root.

8. Draw the tree of Figure 10.6.5 as a rooted tree with v_6 as the root.

9. The *height* of a rooted tree is the length of a longest simple path from the root to a terminal vertex. Find the heights of the trees of Figures 10.6.7 and 10.6.8.

10. Explain why the graph

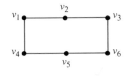

is not a tree.

Answer the questions in Exercises 11 through 16 for the tree in Figure 10.6.7.

11. Find the parent of v_9.

12. Find the children of v_6.

13. Find the ancestors of v_3.

14. Find the descendants of v_6.

15. Find the terminal vertices.

16. Draw the subtree rooted at v_8.

17. What can you say about a vertex in a rooted tree that has no ancestors?

18. What can you say about a vertex in a rooted tree that has no descendants?

Exercises 19 through 21 refer to the binary tree in Figure 10.6.10.

19. Find the left child of v_5.

20. Find the right child of v_5.

21. Draw the binary tree that results from adding a left child v_8 of v_2.

22. What is wrong with the following ''definition'' of a binary tree? A binary tree is a rooted tree in which each vertex has zero, one, or two children.

10.7 Tree Traversals

To **traverse** a tree is to visit each node in the tree. If we traverse the tree in Figure 10.7.1 and print the contents of each node when we visit it, we print the names

Anne Reinhart Olaf Ahmad Katrina Rosa Tyrone

in some order. The order in which the names appear depends on the particular tree traversal algorithm we use. In this section, we discuss three algorithms, **preorder**, **inorder**, and **postorder**, for traversing binary trees as well as C implementations of these algorithms.

Figure 10.7.2 shows an algebraic formula represented as a binary tree. Each node is either a binary operator such as + or * or an operand such as A or B. Each operator has two nonempty subtrees that represent its operands. An operand may be either an expression that consists of an operator and its own nonempty subtrees or a letter.

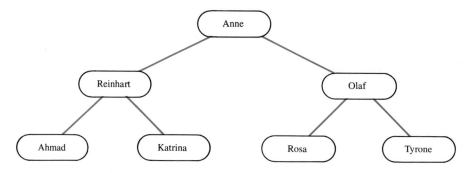

Figure 10.7.1 A binary tree.

Now suppose that we want to traverse the tree in Figure 10.7.2 to print the contents of the nodes. In any traversal, we adopt the following rule:

If a tree is empty, do not traverse it.

The traversals preorder, inorder, and postorder can be characterized as follows when *NODE* is set to the tree's root:

Preorder Traversal

1. Visit *NODE*.
2. Traverse *NODE*'s left subtree in preorder.
3. Traverse *NODE*'s right subtree in preorder.

Inorder Traversal

1. Traverse *NODE*'s left subtree in inorder.
2. Visit *NODE*.
3. Traverse *NODE*'s right subtree in inorder.

Postorder Traversal

1. Traverse *NODE*'s left subtree in postorder.
2. Traverse *NODE*'s right subtree in postorder.
3. Visit *NODE*.

For the tree of Figure 10.7.2, these traversals print the formula as follows:

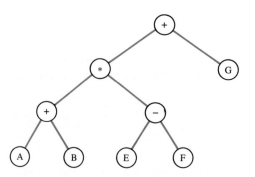

Figure 10.7.2 A binary tree representation of the algebraic formula $(A + B) * (E - F) + G$.

```
+*+AB−EFG          (Preorder Traversal)
A+B*E−F+G          (Inorder Traversal)
AB+EF−*G+          (Postorder Traversal)
```

The formulas correspond to **prefix**, **infix**, and **postfix** notation, respectively. One advantage of prefix and postfix notation is that the expressions require neither parentheses nor precedence conventions. By contrast, the interpretation of an infix expression requires something extra (e.g., parentheses, associativity rules, precedence conventions).

Let us look more closely at inorder traversal. To traverse a tree with a single node using inorder (see Figure 10.7.3), we proceed as follows:

1. We determine that node A's left subtree is empty and so needs no traversal.
2. We visit node A.
3. We determine that node A's right subtree is empty and so needs no traversal.

Now consider a tree with five nodes (see Figure 10.7.4). The inorder traversal is as follows:

  1. We start at node +, which is not empty.
      2. Because node +'s left subtree is not empty, we traverse it using inorder.
         3. Because node *'s left subtree is not empty, we traverse it using inorder.
            4. Because node A's left subtree is empty, we do not traverse it.
            5. We visit node A.
            6. Because node A's right subtree is empty, we do not traverse it.
         7. We visit node *.
         8. Because node *'s right subtree is not empty, we traverse it using inorder.
            9. Because node B's left subtree is empty, we do not traverse it.
           10. We visit node B.
           11. Because node B's right subtree is empty, we do not traverse it.
      12. We visit node +.
      13. Because node +'s right subtree is not empty, we traverse it using inorder.
         14. Because node C's left subtree is empty, we do not traverse it.
         15. We visit node C.
         16. Because node C's right subtree is empty, we do not traverse it.

The problem of traversing a tree using inorder can be broken down into the problem of traversing its left subtree if it is not empty, then processing the tree's root, and then traversing its right subtree if it is not empty. The problem of traversing each subtree can be decomposed in the same way. We thus solve the problem by the divide-and-conquer method. As noted in Section 4.8, recursion is a programming technique well suited to computer solutions of such problems.

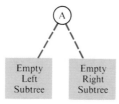

Figure 10.7.3 A binary tree with one node.

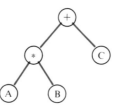

Figure 10.7.4 A binary tree with five nodes.

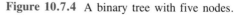

Representing Binary Trees

As with stacks and queues, we represent binary trees using both arrays and linked structures. The array implementation proceeds as follows: The tree's root becomes the array's first element. Its left child becomes the second element, its right child the third element, and so on (see Figure 10.7.5). In general, if a node occurs at index i in the array, its left child will occur at index 2 * i + 1 and its right child at index 2 * i + 2—assuming, as in C, that the first index is 0.

If the node at index i has no left child, the cell at index 2 * i + 1 contains a special code (e.g., zero) to indicate this fact. Similarly, if the node at index i has no right child, the cell at index 2 * i + 2 contains a special code. Thus the array must contain enough storage for both nonempty and empty nodes, which can be wasteful (see Figure 10.7.5).

Example 10.7.1. The following recursive function performs an inorder traversal of a binary tree represented as an array:

```
/*   The recursive function inorder1 traverses a binary tree using
     inorder. It expects an integer that serves as an index into
     the array. This index identifies the root of the tree to be
     traversed. The base condition occurs when the tree is
     EMPTY. */
#include <stdio.h>
#define EMPTY 0

void inorder1( int node, char formula[] )
{
     /* check for terminal */
     if ( formula[ node ] == EMPTY )
         return; /* base condition--no recursion */
     inorder1( 2 * node + 1, formula );   /* traverse left subtree */
     printf( "%c", formula[ node ] );      /* print node */
     inorder1( 2 * node + 2, formula );   /* traverse right subtree */
}
```

We illustrate the calls when the tree of Figure 10.6.5 is passed to inorder1. We use indentation to indicate the levels of recursion.

1. On the first call to inorder1, the argument is 0, which represents the index of the root.
    2. The function calls itself with 1 (i.e., 2 * 0 + 1) as the argument because 1 is the index of node +'s left child (node *).
        3. The function calls itself with 3 (i.e., 2 * 1 + 1) as its argument because 3 is the index of node *'s left child (node A).

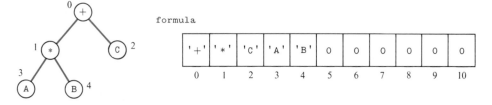

Figure 10.7.5 Representing a binary tree as an array.

4. The function calls itself with 7 (i.e., 2 ∗ 3 + 1) as its argument because 7 is the index of node ∗'s left child. Because A has no left child, the function does not call itself but instead returns to its caller. It resumes execution at the next executable statement in the caller, which is the `printf` instruction.

5. The function prints the contents of the current node, A.

6. The function calls itself with 8 (i.e., 2 ∗ 3 + 2) as its argument because 8 is the index of node A's right child. Because A has no right child, the function does not call itself but instead returns to its caller.

7. The function returns to its caller.

8. The function prints the contents of the current node, ∗.

9. The function calls itself with 4 (i.e., 2 ∗ 1 + 2) as its argument because 4 is the index of node ∗'s right child (node B).

10. The function calls itself with 9 (i.e., 2 ∗ 4 + 1) as its argument because 9 is the index of node B's left child. Because B has no left child, the function does not call itself but instead returns to its caller. It resumes execution at the next executable statement in the caller, which is the `printf` instruction.

11. The function prints the contents of the current node, B.

12. The function calls itself with 10 (i.e., 2 ∗ 4 + 2) as its argument because 10 is the index of node B's right child. Because B has no right child, the function does not call itself but instead returns to its caller.

13. The function returns to its caller.

14. The function returns to its caller.

15. The function prints the current node, +.

16. The function calls itself with 2 (i.e., 2 ∗ 0 + 2) as the argument because 2 is the index of node +'s right child (node C).

17. The function calls itself with 5 (i.e., 2 ∗ 2 + 1) as its argument because 5 is the index of node C's left child. Because C has no left child, the function does not call itself but instead returns to its caller. It resumes execution at the next executable statement in the caller, which is the `printf` instruction.

18. The function prints the contents of the current node, C.

19. The function calls itself with 6 (i.e., 2 ∗ 2 + 2) as its argument because 6 is the index of node C's right child. Because C has no right child, the function does not call itself but instead returns to its caller.

20. The function returns to its caller.

21. The function returns to its caller.

We turn now to linked representations of binary trees. Each node has two pointer fields; one contains the address of the left child and the other the address of the right child (see Figure 10.7.6). If there is no child, the pointer field is set to NULL. We use a `typedef` to declare the structure.

Example 10.7.2. The following recursive function performs an inorder traversal of a binary tree represented as a linked structure. It is interesting to compare this example with the array representation (Example 10.7.1) with respect to clarity and ease of implementation.

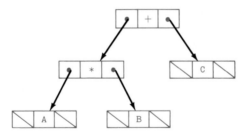

Figure 10.7.6 Representing a binary tree using linked structures.

```
#include <stdio.h>
typedef  struct node {
         char          symbol;
         struct node  *lchild, *rchild;
} NODE;
```

```
/*   The recursive function inorder2 traverses a binary tree using
     inorder. It expects a pointer to the root of the tree to be
     traversed. The base condition occurs when the pointer is
     NULL. */
```

```
void  inorder2( NODE *node )
{
    /* check for empty tree */
    if ( node == NULL )
        return;                    /* base condition--no recursion */

    inorder2( node -> lchild);        /* traverse left subtree */
    printf( "%c", node -> symbol );   /* print node */
    inorder2( node -> rchild );       /* traverse right subtree */
}
```

Exercises

1. Give the order in which the nodes are visited in a preorder, inorder, and
   postorder traversal.

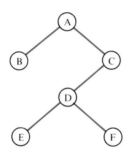

2. Implement preorder as a function using the array implementation of a binary
   tree.

3. Implement postorder as a function using the array implementation of a binary tree.

4. Implement preorder as a function using the linked implementation of a binary tree.

5. Implement postorder as a function using the linked implementation of a binary tree.

6. Find the maximum number of cells that could contain 0 in a 10-node binary tree represented as an array.

7. How many fields are NULL in a 10-node binary tree represented as a linked structure?

8. In the array representation of a binary tree, what is the index of the parent of the node whose index is i?

9. Write a function that prints the data in each node of a binary tree together with the number of descendants of the node.

10. Under what conditions might the array implementation of a binary tree be preferable to the linked representation?

11. Under what conditions might the linked representation of a binary tree be preferable to the array implementation?

10.8   Breadth-First Search and Depth-First Search

Graph search is the analogue of tree traversal. In both cases, the idea is to visit the nodes in a specific order. Two standard ways of searching a graph are **depth-first search** and **breadth-first search**. We clarify both and implement breadth-first search.

Depth-first search begins at a designated vertex V. The search proceeds as follows:

1. Visit V and mark it as visited.
2. Choose an unvisited vertex W adjacent to V. Do a depth-first search, beginning at W.
3. Whenever a vertex U is reached that has no unvisited adjacent vertices, back up to the most recently visited vertex W that does have an unvisited adjacent vertex X. If there is none, terminate the search; otherwise, do a depth-first search beginning at X.

Example 10.8.1. If we designate vertex A as the start vertex in the graph of Figure 10.8.1 and we break ties by choosing the smallest letter (using alphabetical order), depth-first search visits the vertices in the order A, B, D, H, E, F, C, G.

Breadth-first search also begins at a designated vertex, but it differs from depth-first search with respect to the order in which it visits the remaining vertices. If V is the beginning vertex, breadth-first search proceeds as follows.

1. Visit V and mark it as visited.
2. Let W be the least recently visited vertex. Visit and mark as visited each of the unvisited vertices adjacent to W.
3. If all vertices have been visited, terminate the search; otherwise, repeat step 2.

Example 10.8.2. If we again designate vertex A as the start vertex in the graph of Figure 10.8.1 and we break ties by choosing the smallest letter (using alphabetical order), breadth-first search visits the vertices in the order A, B, C, D, E, F, G, H.

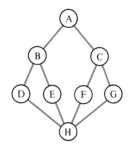

Figure 10.8.1 Graph illustrating breadth-first search and depth-first search.

Representing Graphs

As with stacks, queues, and trees, we represent graphs using both arrays and linked structures. The array representation uses the **adjacency matrix** adj_matrix, which is a two-dimensional array in which each row and column corresponds to a vertex. If vertices i and j are adjacent, we set adj_matrix[i][j] to 1; otherwise, we set adj_matrix[i][j] to 0.

Example 10.8.3.   The following code does a breadth-first search on a graph represented by an adjacency matrix. To illustrate we use the graph in Figure 10.8.2 whose vertices represent the seven deadly sins. The adjacency matrix is as follows:

	anger	lust	envy	gluttony	pride	sloth	covetousness
anger	0	1	1	1	0	0	0
lust	1	0	1	0	0	0	0
envy	1	1	0	0	1	1	0
gluttony	1	0	0	0	0	1	0
pride	0	0	1	0	0	0	0
sloth	0	0	1	1	0	0	1
covetousness	0	0	0	0	0	1	0

We initialize the adjacency matrix in the code to underscore two points. First, each entry represents the presence or absence of an edge between two vertices. Second, adjacency matrices often are *sparse*; that is, they often have far more zero entries than nonzero entries. A sparse matrix thus wastes space.

Because breadth-first search specifies the *least recently visited* vertex as the vertex from which to visit all unvisited adjacent vertices, we use a *queue* to store the visited vertices. We use the array sin_queue to store the items on the queue, and we use the

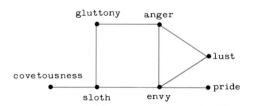

Figure 10.8.2 Graph of the seven deadly sins.

array visited to keep track of which vertices have been visited. Similarly, to implement a depth-first search, we use a *stack*, as a depth-first search specifies the *most recently visited* vertex as the vertex from which to visit an adjacent vertex.

The function bfs1 implements the breadth-first search. We begin by putting the first vertex on the queue and marking it as visited. Then, as long as there is a vertex next on the queue, we delete it. We then visit all of next's unvisited adjacent vertices and put each on the queue. The breadth-first search terminates when the queue is empty.

```c
#include <stdio.h>

typedef  enum seven_deadly_sins { anger, lust, envy, gluttony,
                                  pride, sloth, covetousness }
SINS;

#define  START    anger /* start vertex */
#define  SIZE     7      /* number of vertices */

int visited[ SIZE ];    /* 1 means visited; 0 means not visited */
SINS sin_queue[ SIZE ];

int  adj_matrix[ SIZE ][ SIZE ];

/* queue indexes and counter */
int  front = 0, rear = 0, count = 0;
main()
{
    void  initialize( void ), bfs1( SINS start );

    initialize();
    bfs1( START );
}

/*  The function initialize initializes the array adj_matrix which
    holds SIZE*SIZE integers, each 1 or 0 to indicate the presence
    or absence of an edge. */

void  initialize( void )
{
    adj_matrix[ anger ][ anger ] = 0;
    adj_matrix[ anger ][ lust ] = 1;
    adj_matrix[ anger ][ envy ] = 1;
    adj_matrix[ anger ][ gluttony ] = 1;
    adj_matrix[ anger ][ pride ] = 0;
    adj_matrix[ anger ][ sloth ] = 0;
    adj_matrix[ anger ][ covetousness ] = 0;
    adj_matrix[ lust ][ anger ] = 1;
    adj_matrix[ lust ][ lust ] = 0;
    adj_matrix[ lust ][ envy ] = 1;
    adj_matrix[ lust ][ gluttony ] = 0;
    adj_matrix[ lust ][ pride ] = 0;
    adj_matrix[ lust ][ sloth ] = 0;
    adj_matrix[ lust ][ covetousness ] = 0;
    adj_matrix[ envy ][ anger ] = 1;
```

```
        adj_matrix[ envy ][ lust ] = 1;
        adj_matrix[ envy ][ envy ] = 0;
        adj_matrix[ envy ][ gluttony ] = 0;
        adj_matrix[ envy ][ pride ] = 1;
        adj_matrix[ envy ][ sloth ] = 1;
        adj_matrix[ envy ][ covetousness ] = 0;
        adj_matrix[ gluttony ][ anger ] = 1;
        adj_matrix[ gluttony ][ lust ] = 0;
        adj_matrix[ gluttony ][ envy ] = 0;
        adj_matrix[ gluttony ][ gluttony ] = 0;
        adj_matrix[ gluttony ][ pride ] = 0;
        adj_matrix[ gluttony ][ sloth ] = 1;
        adj_matrix[ gluttony ][ covetousness ] = 0;
        adj_matrix[ pride ][ anger ] = 0;
        adj_matrix[ pride ][ lust ] = 0;
        adj_matrix[ pride ][ envy ] = 1;
        adj_matrix[ pride ][ gluttony ] = 0;
        adj_matrix[ pride ][ pride ] = 0;
        adj_matrix[ pride ][ sloth ] = 0;
        adj_matrix[ pride ][ covetousness ] = 0;
        adj_matrix[ sloth ][ anger ] = 0;
        adj_matrix[ sloth ][ lust ] = 0;
        adj_matrix[ sloth ][ envy ] = 1;
        adj_matrix[ sloth ][ gluttony ] = 1;
        adj_matrix[ sloth ][ pride ] = 0;
        adj_matrix[ sloth ][ sloth ] = 0;
        adj_matrix[ sloth ][ covetousness ] = 1;
        adj_matrix[ covetousness ][ anger ] = 0;
        adj_matrix[ covetousness ][ lust ] = 0;
        adj_matrix[ covetousness ][ envy ] = 0;
        adj_matrix[ covetousness ][ gluttony ] = 0;
        adj_matrix[ covetousness ][ pride ] = 0;
        adj_matrix[ covetousness ][ sloth ] = 1;
        adj_matrix[ covetousness ][ covetousness ] = 0;
}

/*    The function bfs1 does a breadth-first search beginning at
      the vertex start. */

void  bfs1( SINS start )
{
      void  insert( SINS item ), visit( SINS sin );
      SINS delete( void );
      SINS sin, next;

      /* Put start in queue and mark it as visited. */
      insert( start );
      visit( start );
      visited[ start ] = 1;

      /* Search until queue is empty. */
      /* next < 0 means empty queue. */
```

```c
        while ( ( next = delete() ) >= 0 )
            /* Queue up unvisited adjacent vertices. */
            for ( sin = 0; sin < SIZE; ++sin )
                if ( adj_matrix[ next ][ sin ] == 1
                    && !visited[ sin ] ) {
                    /* Put sin in queue and mark it as visited. */
                    insert( sin );
                    visit( sin );
                    /* Mark vertex as visited. */
                    visited[ sin ] = 1;
                }
}
/* Print a visit message. */
void  visit( SINS sin )
{
    switch ( sin ) {
    case anger:
        printf( "\n\nAnger has been visited.\n\n" );
        break;
    case lust:
        printf( "\n\nLust has been visited.\n\n" );
        break;
    case envy:
        printf( "\n\nEnvy has been visited.\n\n" );
        break;
    case gluttony:
        printf( "\n\nGluttony has been visited.\n\n" );
        break;
    case pride:
        printf( "\n\nPride has been visited.\n\n" );
        break;
    case sloth:
        printf( "\n\nSloth has been visited.\n\n" );
        break;
    case covetousness:
        printf( "\n\nCovetousness has been visited.\n\n" );
        break;
    }
}
/* Insert item in queue. */
void insert( SINS item )
{
    if ( count == SIZE )
        printf( "\n\nFULL QUEUE\n\n" );
    else {
        sin_queue[ rear ] = item;
        rear = ++rear % SIZE;
        ++count;
    }
}
```

```
/* Delete an item from queue and return it. */
/* If queue is empty, return -1. */
SINS delete( void )
{
    SINS front_value;

    if ( count == 0 )
        return ( -1 );
    front_value = sin_queue[ front ];
    front = ++front % SIZE;
    --count;

    return ( front_value );
}
```

For the linked representation of a graph, we use **adjacency lists**. In this representation, there is a linked list for each vertex. We store the vertices adjacent to vertex v in the linked list corresponding to v. The addresses of the first nodes in the linked lists are stored in an array. In Figure 10.8.3, we show the adjacency lists for the graph of Figure 10.8.2.

There are two principal advantages to using adjacency lists rather than the adjacency matrix when the adjacency matrix is sparse. First, we save storage, as we store only information about vertices that are actually adjacent. Second, graph algorithms execute faster, as we can directly visit adjacent vertices without "skipping over" zeros, as we must when we use the adjacency matrix.

Example 10.8.4.   We rewrite the program of Example 10.8.3 using adjacency lists. The typedef NODE is the template for a node in an adjacency list. Each node stores a vertex and a pointer. The array graph stores pointers to the first nodes in the lists. To initialize the linked lists, we use the storage allocation function malloc. Figure 10.8.4 shows the result of executing

```
ptr = ( NODE * ) malloc( sizeof ( NODE ) );
ptr -> link = graph[ anger ];
graph[ anger ] = ptr;
ptr -> sin = lust;
```

and Figure 10.8.5 shows the result of then executing

```
ptr = ( NODE * ) malloc( sizeof ( NODE ) );
ptr -> link = graph[ anger ];
```

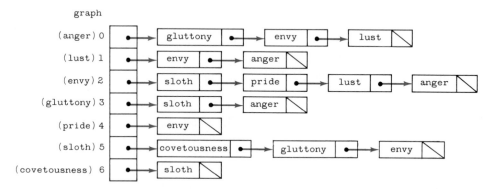

Figure 10.8.3 A graph represented by adjacency lists.

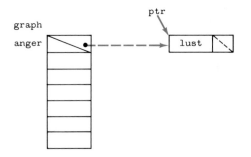

Figure 10.8.4 Adding the node `lust` to `anger`'s linked list.

```
graph[ anger ] = ptr;
ptr -> sin = envy;
```

The functions `visit`, `insert`, and `delete` are identical to those in Example 10.8.3.

```
#include <stdio.h>
#include <stdlib.h>

typedef  enum seven_deadly_sins { anger, lust, envy, gluttony,
                                  pride, sloth, covetousness }
SINS;

#define  START   anger   /* start vertex */
#define  SIZE    7       /* number of vertices */

typedef  struct node {              /* NODE for adjacency lists */
         SINS            sin;
         struct node     *link;
} NODE;

NODE *graph[ SIZE ];   /* array of pointers to adjacency lists */
int visited[ SIZE ];   /* 1 means visited; 0 means not visited */
SINS sin_queue[ SIZE ];

/* queue indexes and counter */
int  front = 0, rear = 0, count = 0;
```

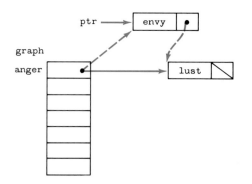

Figure 10.8.5 Adding the node `envy` to `anger`'s linked list.

```
main()
{
    void  initialize( void ), bfs2( SINS next );

    initialize();
    bfs2( START );
}

/* The function initialize constructs the adjacency lists */
void  initialize( void )
{

    int i;
    NODE *ptr;

    for ( i = 0; i < SIZE; i++ )
        graph[ i ] = NULL;

                /* initialize sins */

    /* (anger, lust) */
    ptr = ( NODE * ) malloc( sizeof ( NODE ) );
    ptr -> link = graph[ anger ];
    graph[ anger ] = ptr;
    ptr -> sin = lust;

    /* (anger, envy) */
    ptr = ( NODE * ) malloc( sizeof ( NODE ) );
    ptr -> link = graph[ anger ];
    graph[ anger ] = ptr;
    ptr -> sin = envy;

    /* (anger, gluttony) */
    ptr = ( NODE * ) malloc( sizeof ( NODE ) );
    ptr -> link = graph[ anger ];
    graph[ anger ] = ptr;
    ptr -> sin = gluttony;

    /* (lust, anger) */
    ptr = ( NODE * ) malloc( sizeof ( NODE ) );
    ptr -> link = graph[ lust ];
    graph[ lust ] = ptr;
    ptr -> sin = anger;

    /* (lust, envy) */
    ptr = ( NODE * ) malloc( sizeof ( NODE ) );
    ptr -> link = graph[ lust ];
    graph[ lust ] = ptr;
    ptr -> sin = envy;

    /* (envy, anger) */
    ptr = ( NODE * ) malloc( sizeof ( NODE ) );
    ptr -> link = graph[ envy ];
    graph[ envy ] = ptr;
    ptr -> sin = anger;
```

```
/* (envy, lust) */
ptr = ( NODE * ) malloc( sizeof ( NODE ) );
ptr -> link = graph[ envy ];
graph[ envy ] = ptr;
ptr -> sin = lust;

/* (envy, pride) */
ptr = ( NODE * ) malloc( sizeof ( NODE ) );
ptr -> link = graph[ envy ];
graph[ envy ] = ptr;
ptr -> sin = pride;

/* (envy, sloth) */
ptr = ( NODE * ) malloc( sizeof ( NODE ) );
ptr -> link = graph[ envy ];
graph[ envy ] = ptr;
ptr -> sin = sloth;

/* (gluttony, anger) */
ptr = ( NODE * ) malloc( sizeof ( NODE ) );
ptr -> link = graph[ gluttony ];
graph[ gluttony ] = ptr;
ptr -> sin = anger;

/* (gluttony, sloth) */
ptr = ( NODE * ) malloc( sizeof ( NODE ) );
ptr -> link = graph[ gluttony ];
graph[ gluttony ] = ptr;
ptr -> sin = sloth;

/* (pride, envy) */
ptr = ( NODE * ) malloc( sizeof ( NODE ) );
ptr -> link = graph[ pride ];
graph[ pride ] = ptr;
ptr -> sin = envy;

/* (sloth, envy) */
ptr = ( NODE * ) malloc( sizeof ( NODE ) );
ptr -> link = graph[ sloth ];
graph[ sloth ] = ptr;
ptr -> sin = envy;

/* (sloth, gluttony) */
ptr = ( NODE * ) malloc( sizeof ( NODE ) );
ptr -> link = graph[ sloth ];
graph[ sloth ] = ptr;
ptr -> sin = gluttony;

/* (sloth, covetousness) */
ptr = ( NODE * ) malloc( sizeof ( NODE ) );
ptr -> link = graph[ sloth ];
graph[ sloth ] = ptr;
ptr -> sin = covetousness;
```

```
        /* (covetousness, sloth) */
        ptr = ( NODE * ) malloc( sizeof ( NODE ) );
        ptr -> link = graph[ covetousness ];
        graph[ covetousness ] = ptr;
        ptr -> sin = sloth;
}

/*   The function bfs2 does a breadth-first search beginning at the
     vertex next. */

void  bfs2( SINS next )
{
     void insert( SINS item ), visit( SINS sin );
     SINS delete( void );
     NODE *ptr;

     /* Put next in queue and mark it as visited. */
     insert( next );
     visit( next );
     visited[ next ] = 1;

     /* Search until queue is empty. */
     /* next < 0 means empty queue. */
     while ( ( next = delete() ) >= 0 ) {
          ptr = graph[ next ];
          /* Queue up unvisited adjacent vertices. */
          while ( ptr != NULL ) {
               next = ptr -> sin;
               if ( !visited[ next ] ) {
                    /* Put next in queue and mark it as visited. */
                    insert( next );
                    visit( next );
                    visited[ next ] = 1;
               }
               ptr = ptr -> link;
          }
     }
}
```

Exercises

1. Write the adjacency matrix of the graph.

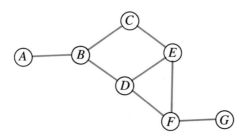

2. For the graph of Exercise 1, list the vertices in the order in which they are visited in a breadth-first search, with vertex *C* designated as the start.

3. For the graph of Exercise 1, list the vertices in the order in which they are visited in a breadth-first search, with vertex *F* designated as the start.

4. Repeat Exercise 2, using depth-first search instead of breadth-first search.

5. Repeat Exercise 3, using depth-first search instead of breadth-first search.

6. What is the output of the program of Example 10.8.3?

7. What is the output of the program of Example 10.8.4?

8. What is the output of the program of Example 10.8.3 if we replace the queue with a stack? Is the traversal a breadth-first search, a depth-first search, or neither?

9. In Examples 10.8.3 and 10.8.4, the array `sin_queue` has `SIZE` elements. In our example, `SIZE` is set to 7. Suppose that someone argues as follows: Each of the seven vertices in the graph could be adjacent to six others, so we need a `sin_queue` of at least 42 to handle the breadth-first search. What is wrong with this argument?

10. Rewrite the program of Example 10.8.3 so that the search is a depth-first search.

11. Rewrite the program of Example 10.8.4 so that the search is a depth-first search.

12. Write a function that, for each vertex in a connected graph, counts the number of vertices adjacent to it. The function should print each vertex's label and count.

10.9 Sample Application: Heuristic Graph Search

Problem

Find an optimal path from a designated vertex START to a designated vertex GOAL in a network (see Figure 10.9.1). The vertices represent cities and the weighted edges represent the distance in miles between any two cities. For example, the edge between vertex Munich and vertex Vienna has a weight of 280, which represents the distance between the two cities. A path's cost is the sum of the costs for the edges in it. A path between two vertices is optimal if no other path between them costs less.

Sample Input / Output

The input comes from two files: *names.dat* contains names of cities together with their estimated distance to the GOAL, which is #defined as Vienna, and *distances.dat* contains the actual distance from a given city to each city adjacent to it. There is also interactive input, as the program prompts the user for the START city. The output has three parts:

- The length of the optimal path from START to GOAL.
- The path itself as a list of the cities visited along the optimal path.
- A list of the cities *expanded,* or explored, as possible vertices in the optimal path.

The following are two sample runs, one with Madrid as START and the other with Paris as START. Our example is adapted from B. Raphael, *The Thinking Computer: Mind Inside Matter* (San Francisco: W. H. Freeman and Co., 1976). Input is in color; output is in black.

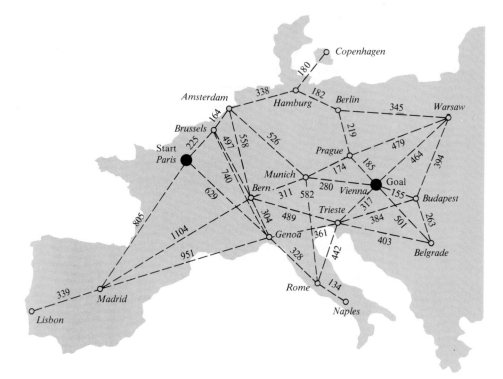

Figure 10.9.1 Map of European cities.

```
Please select a start city.
Enter a number associated with one of the cities.
```

Amsterdam	——— 1		Lisbon	——— 10
Belgrade	——— 2		Madrid	——— 11
Berlin	——— 3		Munich	——— 12
Bern	——— 4		Naples	——— 13
Brussels	——— 5		Paris	——— 14
Budapest	——— 6		Prague	——— 15
Copenhagen	——— 7		Rome	——— 16
Genoa	——— 8		Trieste	——— 17
Hamburg	——— 9		Warsaw	——— 18

```
11

OPTIMAL PATH LENGTH: 1629

OPTIMAL PATH:

madrid
genoa
trieste
vienna

EXPANDED VERTICES:

bern
genoa
```

```
madrid
paris
trieste

          Please select a start city.
          Enter a number associated with one of the cities.

              Amsterdam   ---  1      Lisbon   --- 10
              Belgrade    ---  2      Madrid   --- 11
              Berlin      ---  3      Munich   --- 12
              Bern        ---  4      Naples   --- 13
              Brussels    ---  5      Paris    --- 14
              Budapest    ---  6      Prague   --- 15
              Copenhagen  ---  7      Rome     --- 16
              Genoa       ---  8      Trieste  --- 17
              Hamburg     ---  9      Warsaw   --- 18

              14
OPTIMAL PATH LENGTH: 1195

OPTIMAL PATH:

paris
brussels
amsterdam
munich
vienna

EXPANDED VERTICES:

amsterdam
brussels
genoa
munich
paris
```

Solution

The A∗ algorithm, from the field of artificial intelligence, can be used to solve the problem. The algorithm requires a designated START vertex but may have multiple GOAL vertices. To simplify, we assume one GOAL vertex. Here we indicate briefly how A∗ differs from breadth-first search and depth-first search, leaving further details to the Discussion section.

Suppose that we modify breadth-first search or depth-first search by designating a GOAL as well as a START vertex. If we visit GOAL, we halt the search, reconstruct the path from START to GOAL, and compute the path's cost.

An exhaustive search can become expensive, as the problem of an optimal path shows. To find an optimal path, we first must find every simple path from START to GOAL and then compare them to find an optimal path. If the number of simple paths is large, there is a combinatorial explosion that prevents even the fastest computers from solving the problem. Suppose, for example, that a network has 10 billion simple paths between START and GOAL and that a computer can search 1,000 per second. The computer still needs 10 million seconds, or over three years, to search them all. The A∗ algorithm is designed to find an optimal path, but without an exhaustive search. The algorithm uses a heuristic to reduce the search. A *heuristic* is an informed estimate, the notorious ''educated guess'' about where to search next. Heuristics are not guaranteed to work, for a guess can turn out to be uneducated or even plain dumb. Therefore, the A∗ algorithm, which relies on a heuristic, cannot ensure discovery of an optimal path. Nonetheless, the algorithm lays claim to more modest fame: If its heuristic always underestimates the distance from a given vertex V to the GOAL, then A∗ can find an optimal path from START to GOAL (provided, of course, that there is some path from START to GOAL). Let us call the desired heuristic optimistic because it must underestimate. The trick in A∗ is to use an optimistic heuristic that eliminates as much needless searching as possible. But how can we ensure that a heuristic, a guess, is consistently optimistic? We cannot. So we must be careful about stating what A∗ can do: If it uses a consistently optimistic heuristic and a path exists from START to GOAL, then A∗ can find an optimal path from START to GOAL. For a further discussion of A∗ in particular and heuristics in general, see J. Pearl, *Heuristics: Intelligent Search Strategies for Computer Problem Solving* (Reading, Mass.: Addison-Wesley, 1984).

C Implementation

```c
#include <stdio.h>

#define  SIZE     19    /* number of cities */

int      START;         /* index of start city, set interactively */
#define  GOAL     17    /* index of goal city, Vienna */

#define  CLOSED   0     /* flags for open and closed lists */
#define  OPEN     1

#define  TRUE     1
#define  FALSE    0

typedef  struct city {
         char       name[ 15 ];
         int        ind;            /* position in array cities */
         int        g_val;          /* optimal path to city */
         int        h_est;          /* estimate to goal */
         int        f_est;          /* g_value + h_estimate */
         int        open;           /* open list */
         int        closed;         /* closed list */
         struct city *adjcs[ SIZE ]; /* adjacent cities */
         struct city *backptr;      /* optimal path pointer */
} CITY;

CITY  cities[ SIZE ];

int   distances[ SIZE ][ SIZE ]; /* distances between two cities */
int   open_count = 0;            /* number of items on open list */

main()
{
  void  get_input( void ),
        set_adjacency_lists( void ),
        astar( void );

  get_input();
  set_adjacency_lists();
```

```
   cities[ START ].backptr = NULL; /* path starts here */
   cities[ START ].g_val = 0;

   cities[ START ].open = TRUE;      /* put START on open list */
   ++open_count;

   astar();  /* search */
}
void  astar( void )
{
   void  failure( void ), success( CITY *ptr ),
         expand( int index );
   int   best, get_best_prospect( void );

   if ( open_count == 0 ) /* any more options? */
     failure();                 /* if not, fail */
   else {
     best = get_best_prospect();   /* get most promising city */
     if ( best == GOAL )              /* goal city? */
       success( &cities[ GOAL ] ); /* if so, succeed */
     else {                           /* otherwise: */
       cities[ best ].open = FALSE;    /* remove from open */
       --open_count;
       cities[ best ].closed = TRUE;   /* put on closed */
       expand( best );                 /* expand it */
       astar();                        /* keep searching */
     }
   }
}
int  get_best_prospect( void )
{
   int  i = 0, best;

   /* Find 1st city in open list. */
   while ( cities[ i++ ].open == FALSE )
                   ;
   /* Assume it's the best. */
   best = --i;

   /* Look for something better. */
   for ( i = best + 1; i < SIZE; ++i )
     if ( cities[ i ].open == TRUE  &&
          cities[ i ].f_est <  cities[ best ].f_est )
       best = i;

   return ( best );
}
void  expand( int index )
{
   void  update_values( CITY *ptr ),
         update_path( CITY *ptr, int index );
   int   i = 0;
```

```
    while ( cities[ index ].adjcs[ i ] != NULL {
      /* If adjacent city is not on OPEN or CLOSED, then */
      /* (1) set its backpointer to current city, (2)    */
      /* compute its g_val and f_est, and (3) put it on  */
      /* OPEN.                                            */
      if ( cities[ index ].adjcs[ i ] -> open == FALSE &&
             cities[ index ].adjcs[ i ] -> closed == FALSE ) {
        cities[ index ].adjcs[ i ] -> backptr = &cities[ index ];
        update_values( cities[ index ].adjcs[ i ] );
        cities[ index ].adjcs[ i ] -> open = TRUE;
        ++open_count;
      }
      /* Otherwise, see if its backpointer needs changing. */
      else
        update_path( cities[ index ].adjcs[ i ], index );
      ++i;
    }
}
void  update_values( CITY *ptr )
{
  int    ind1, ind2;
  ind1 = ptr -> backptr -> ind; /* current city */
  ind2 = ptr -> ind;                /* predecessor */
  ptr -> g_val = ptr -> backptr -> g_val  +
                  distances[ ind1 ][ ind2 ];
  ptr -> f_est = ptr -> g_val  +  ptr -> h_est;
}
void  update_path( CITY *ptr, int index )
{
  void  update_values( CITY *ptr );
  CITY  *best;
  /* Assume current path is best. */
  best = ptr -> backptr;
  /* Compare with new path. */
  if ( best != NULL  &&  cities[ index ].g_val  <  best -> g_val ) {
    /* If new path is better than old one,
       then reset backpointer and update g_val and f_est. */
    ptr -> backptr = &cities[ index ];
    update_values( ptr );
    /* Is city on CLOSED? */
    if ( ptr -> closed == TRUE ) {
      /* If so, put back on OPEN. */
      ptr -> closed = FALSE;
      ptr -> open = TRUE;
      ++open_count;
    }
  }
}
```

```
void  get_input( void )
{
  FILE  *fptr;
  int   i, j;
  void  get_start_city( void );

  /* Read cities' names into structure variables. */
  fptr = fopen( "names.dat", "r" );
  for ( i = 0; i < SIZE; ++i ) {
    fscanf( fptr, "%s%d",
            cities[ i ].name, &cities[ i ].h_est );
    cities[ i ].ind = i;
    cities[ i ].open = FALSE;
    cities[ i ].closed = FALSE;
  }
  fclose( fptr );

  /* Read distances between cities into matrix. */
  fptr = fopen( "distances.dat", "r" );
  for ( i = 0; i < SIZE; ++i )
    for ( j = 0; j < SIZE; ++j )
      fscanf( fptr, "%d", &distances[ i ][ j ] );
  fclose( fptr );

  /* Prompt for START city and read its index into START. */
  get_start_city();
}


void  get_start_city( void )
{
  printf( "\n\n\t\tPlease select a start city.\n\t\t" );
  printf( "Enter a number associated with one of the cities.\n" );

  printf( "\n\t\tAmsterdam   ---   1\tLisbon  --- 10" );
  printf( "\n\t\tBelgrade    ---   2\tMadrid  --- 11" );
  printf( "\n\t\tBerlin      ---   3\tMunich  --- 12" );
  printf( "\n\t\tBern        ---   4\tNaples  --- 13" );
  printf( "\n\t\tBrussels    ---   5\tParis   --- 14" );
  printf( "\n\t\tBudapest    ---   6\tPrague  --- 15" );
  printf( "\n\t\tCopenhagen  ---   7\tRome    --- 16" );
  printf( "\n\t\tGenoa       ---   8\tTrieste --- 17" );
  printf( "\n\t\tHamburg     ---   9\tWarsaw  --- 18" );
  printf( "\n\n\t\t" );
  scanf( "%d", &START );

  /* Adjust index for any city except Warsaw, */
  /* whose index is 18. */
  if ( START < 18 )
    --START;
}
```

```
void  failure( void )
{
  printf( "\n\n\n\tYou can't get there from here.\n\n " );
}

void  success( CITY *ptr )
{
  void  print_cities( CITY *ptr );
  int   i;

  printf( "\n\n\n" );
  printf( "\n\n\tOPTIMAL PATH LENGTH: %d\n", ptr -> g_val );
  printf( "\n\n\tOPTIMAL PATH:\n" );
  print_cities( ptr );

  printf( "\n\n\tEXPANDED VERTICES:\n" );
  for ( i = 0; i < SIZE; ++i )
    if ( cities[ i ].closed == TRUE )
      printf( "\n\t%s", cities[ i ].name );
  printf( "\n\n\n" );
}

void  print_cities( CITY *ptr )
{
  if ( ptr -> ind == START )           /* halt backtrack */
    printf( "\n\t%s", ptr -> name );
  else {
    print_cities( ptr -> backptr );  /* backtrack */
    printf( "\n\t%s", ptr -> name );
  }
}

void  set_adjacency_lists( void )
{
  /***          Amsterdam to ...        ***/
  cities[ 0 ].adjcs[ 0 ] = &cities[ 3 ];     /* Bern */
  cities[ 0 ].adjcs[ 1 ] = &cities[ 4 ];     /* Brussels */
  cities[ 0 ].adjcs[ 2 ] = &cities[ 8 ];     /* Hamburg */
  cities[ 0 ].adjcs[ 3 ] = &cities[ 11 ];    /* Munich */

  /***          Belgrade to ...        ***/
  cities[ 1 ].adjcs[ 0 ] = &cities[ 5 ];     /* Budapest */
  cities[ 1 ].adjcs[ 1 ] = &cities[ 16 ];    /* Trieste */
  cities[ 1 ].adjcs[ 2 ] = &cities[ 17 ];    /* Vienna */

  /***          Berlin to ...        ***/
  cities[ 2 ].adjcs[ 0 ] = &cities[ 3 ];     /* Bern */
  cities[ 2 ].adjcs[ 1 ] = &cities[ 8 ];     /* Hamburg */
  cities[ 2 ].adjcs[ 2 ] = &cities[ 14 ];    /* Prague */
  cities[ 2 ].adjcs[ 3 ] = &cities[ 18 ];    /* Warsaw */

  /***          Bern to ...        ***/
  cities[ 3 ].adjcs[ 0 ] = &cities[ 0 ];     /* Amsterdam */
  cities[ 3 ].adjcs[ 1 ] = &cities[ 2 ];     /* Belgrade */
```

```
cities[ 3 ].adjcs[ 2 ] = &cities[ 4 ];      /* Brussels */
cities[ 3 ].adjcs[ 3 ] = &cities[ 7 ];      /* Genoa */
cities[ 3 ].adjcs[ 4 ] = &cities[ 10 ];     /* Madrid */
cities[ 3 ].adjcs[ 5 ] = &cities[ 11 ];     /* Munich */
cities[ 3 ].adjcs[ 6 ] = &cities[ 16 ];     /* Trieste */

/***        Brussels to ...        ***/
cities[ 4 ].adjcs[ 0 ] = &cities[ 0 ];      /* Amsterdam */
cities[ 4 ].adjcs[ 1 ] = &cities[ 3 ];      /* Bern */
cities[ 4 ].adjcs[ 2 ] = &cities[ 7 ];      /* Genoa */
cities[ 4 ].adjcs[ 3 ] = &cities[ 13 ];     /* Paris */

/***        Budapest to ...        ***/
cities[ 5 ].adjcs[ 0 ] = &cities[ 1 ];      /* Belgrade */
cities[ 5 ].adjcs[ 1 ] = &cities[ 16 ];     /* Trieste */
cities[ 5 ].adjcs[ 2 ] = &cities[ 17 ];     /* Vienna */
cities[ 5 ].adjcs[ 3 ] = &cities[ 18 ];     /* Warsaw */

/***        Copenhagen to ...      ***/
cities[ 6 ].adjcs[ 0 ] = &cities[ 8 ];      /* Hamburg */

/***        Genoa to...            ***/
cities[ 7 ].adjcs[ 0 ] = &cities[ 4 ];      /* Brussels */
cities[ 7 ].adjcs[ 1 ] = &cities[ 10 ];     /* Madrid */
cities[ 7 ].adjcs[ 2 ] = &cities[ 13 ];     /* Paris */
cities[ 7 ].adjcs[ 3 ] = &cities[ 15 ];     /* Rome */
cities[ 7 ].adjcs[ 4 ] = &cities[ 16 ];     /* Trieste */

/***        Hamburg to ...         ***/
cities[ 8 ].adjcs[ 0 ] = &cities[ 0 ];      /* Amsterdam */
cities[ 8 ].adjcs[ 1 ] = &cities[ 2 ];      /* Berlin */
cities[ 8 ].adjcs[ 2 ] = &cities[ 6 ];      /* Copenhagen */

/***        Lisbon to ...          ***/
cities[ 9 ].adjcs[ 0 ] = &cities[ 10 ];     /* Madrid */

/***        Madrid to ...          ***/
cities[ 10 ].adjcs[ 0 ] = &cities[ 3 ];     /* Bern */
cities[ 10 ].adjcs[ 1 ] = &cities[ 7 ];     /* Genoa */
cities[ 10 ].adjcs[ 2 ] = &cities[ 9 ];     /* Lisbon */
cities[ 10 ].adjcs[ 3 ] = &cities[ 13 ];    /* Paris */

/***        Munich to ...          ***/
cities[ 11 ].adjcs[ 0 ] = &cities[ 0 ];     /* Amsterdam */
cities[ 11 ].adjcs[ 1 ] = &cities[ 14 ];    /* Prague */
cities[ 11 ].adjcs[ 2 ] = &cities[ 15 ];    /* Rome */
cities[ 11 ].adjcs[ 3 ] = &cities[ 17 ];    /* Vienna */

/***        Naples to ...          ***/
cities[ 12 ].adjcs[ 0 ] = &cities[ 15 ];    /* Rome *

/***        Paris to ...           ***/
cities[ 13 ].adjcs[ 0 ] = &cities[ 4 ];     /* Brussels */
cities[ 13 ].adjcs[ 1 ] = &cities[ 7 ];     /* Genoa */
cities[ 13 ].adjcs[ 2 ] = &cities[ 10 ];    /* Madrid */
```

```
/***           Prague to ...            ***/
cities[ 14 ].adjcs[ 0 ] = &cities[ 2 ];    /* Berlin */
cities[ 14 ].adjcs[ 1 ] = &cities[ 11 ];   /* Munich */
cities[ 14 ].adjcs[ 2 ] = &cities[ 17 ];   /* Vienna */
cities[ 14 ].adjcs[ 3 ] = &cities[ 18 ];   /* Warsaw */

/***           Rome to ...              ***/
cities[ 15 ].adjcs[ 0 ] = &cities[ 7 ];    /* Genoa */
cities[ 15 ].adjcs[ 1 ] = &cities[ 11 ];   /* Munich */
cities[ 15 ].adjcs[ 2 ] = &cities[ 12 ];   /* Naples */
cities[ 15 ].adjcs[ 3 ] = &cities[ 16 ];   /* Trieste */

/***           Trieste to ...           ***/
cities[ 16 ].adjcs[ 0 ] = &cities[ 1 ];    /* Belgrade */
cities[ 16 ].adjcs[ 1 ] = &cities[ 3 ];    /* Bern */
cities[ 16 ].adjcs[ 2 ] = &cities[ 5 ];    /* Budapest */
cities[ 16 ].adjcs[ 3 ] = &cities[ 7 ];    /* Genoa */
cities[ 16 ].adjcs[ 4 ] = &cities[ 15 ];   /* Rome */
cities[ 16 ].adjcs[ 5 ] = &cities[ 17 ];   /* Vienna */

/***           Warsaw to ...            ***/
cities[ 18 ].adjcs[ 0 ] = &cities[ 2 ];    /* Berlin */
cities[ 18 ].adjcs[ 1 ] = &cities[ 5 ];    /* Budapest */
cities[ 18 ].adjcs[ 2 ] = &cities[ 14 ];   /* Prague */
cities[ 18 ].adjcs[ 3 ] = &cities[ 17 ];   /* Vienna */
}
```

Discussion

We shall describe the A* algorithm and then clarify key parts. OPEN and CLOSED are two lists, both at first empty. A vertex's G value is the distance of the currently optimal path from START to it. A vertex's F* value is the (optimistically) estimated distance from START to GOAL through it.

1. Put the START vertex on OPEN.
2. If OPEN is empty, fail.
3. Remove from OPEN and put on CLOSED the vertex V with the minimal F* value.
4. If V is the GOAL, succeed.
5. If V is not the GOAL, expand V by enumerating each of its adjacent vertices. For each adjacent vertex V', take one of the following actions:
   a. If V' is not already on OPEN or CLOSED, put it on OPEN; set its backpointer to V; and calculate its G value and its F* value.
   b. If V' is already on OPEN, determine whether the path through V is cheaper than the current path to it. If so, redirect its backpointer to V and recompute both its G value and its F* value. (This is *backpointer adjustment*.)
   c. If V' is already on CLOSED and requires backpointer adjustment, remove it from CLOSED and put it back on OPEN.
6. Go to step 2.

The OPEN list contains any vertex that is still under consideration as part of an optimal path from START to GOAL. First, only START is on OPEN because it is the only vertex known to us. Thus START is, by default, the most promising vertex. We expand START; that is, we find all the vertices adjacent to it. If these have never been on OPEN, we put

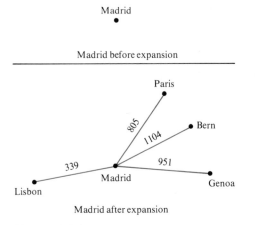

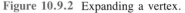

Figure 10.9.2 Expanding a vertex.

them there for the first time. START, which now has been expanded, goes on CLOSED because we now know all the vertices adjacent to it. We repeat the process and choose the most promising vertex from OPEN. For example, suppose that we choose Madrid as START. Figure 10.9.2 depicts OPEN and CLOSED before and after Madrid's expansion.

The vertex on OPEN with the lowest F* value is the most promising, with the F* value computed as follows:

```
F*(vertex) = G(vertex) + H*(vertex)
```

F*(vertex) is the *estimated* cost of a path from START to GOAL that passes through vertex; G(vertex) is the *actual* cost of the optimal path discovered so far from START to vertex; and H*(vertex) is the *estimated cost* of the optimal path from vertex to GOAL. Figure 10.9.3 illustrates. START is Madrid, vertex is Genoa, and GOAL is Vienna. G(Genoa) is 951, the distance of the currently optimal path from Madrid to Genoa. H*(Genoa) is 522, the (optimistically) estimated distance from Genoa to Vienna. Therefore, F*(Genoa) is 1503, or 951 + 552. The vertex on OPEN with the lowest F* value is selected as the most promising. Once selected and expanded, a vertex goes from OPEN to CLOSED. The A* algorithm, as described, has some subtle points offered as problems in the section exercises.

We close with some remarks on the C implementation. We implement each vertex as a structure that includes an array of pointers to all vertices adjacent to it and a single

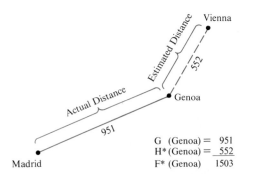

Figure 10.9.3 Estimated cost of the optimal path from vertex to GOAL.

backpointer to its favored predecessor. The predecessor is favored because the optimal path from START to the current vertex *V* passes through this predecessor. We implement OPEN and CLOSED as flags: Each structure variable's flag is set to either TRUE or FALSE to indicate whether it is on the corresponding list.

We store distances between any two cities in a matrix called distances; data are read into this matrix from the file *distances.dat*. The structure variables that represent the cities are in an array called cities. So the expression

```
distances[ index1 ][ index2 ]
```

gives the distance from the city

```
cities[ index1 ]
```

to the city

```
cities[ index2 ]
```

Our implementation is simplified in that any city may be START, but we fix one particular city to be GOAL. This allows us to store in each structure variable the H* value; the file *names.dat* contains a list of the cities together with their optimistically estimated distance from the GOAL, Vienna. A more flexible implementation would allow the user to choose GOAL as well as START; however, this would require another table of estimated distances from any city to any other. We set the H* value for every city to 110 percent of its "crow-flies" distance or "bee-line" from the GOAL. The idea is that the road distance exceeds the air distance, and by at least 10 percent. In sum, we *assume* that "crow-flies" distance optimistically estimates the actual road distance.

The function astar is recursive. It halts on two conditions:

- If the OPEN list is empty, it halts with failure and invokes a function to print a failure message. The search fails because GOAL has not yet been reached and there are no more OPEN vertices to expand.
- If the GOAL vertex is found, it halts with success and invokes a function to print the optimal path, its length, and all vertices on the CLOSED list. This list includes all vertices expanded in the search for the optimal path.

Otherwise, the function finds the most promising node on the OPEN list, expands the vertex and puts any adjacent vertex on OPEN, if it is not already there, and invokes a copy of itself.

Exercises

1. Suppose that at some point in our search for an optimal path from Madrid to Vienna, the most promising city on OPEN happens to be Paris. We expand Paris; that is, we find all cities adjacent to it. These are Madrid itself, Brussels, and Bern. If an adjacent city is not already on OPEN, it simply goes there. If the adjacent city is already on OPEN, we may have to recompute its G value. This is called *backpointer adjustment* and is given as step 5b in our description of the algorithm. Explain why backpointer adjustment may be required.

2. Assume the situation of Exercise 1, in which Paris is selected from OPEN and expanded. Suppose that one of the adjacent cities is on CLOSED rather than

OPEN. Why does this city go back to OPEN if it requires backpointer adjustment? (Note that a city on CLOSED has been *expanded* at least once already.)

3. Assume that we apply A∗ to a particular search problem and that it succeeds in finding a path from START to GOAL. Can we be confident that the path is optimal? Explain.

4. Suppose that we set H∗(vertex) to 0 for every vertex in our search space and that each edge weight is equal to 1. Under these conditions, what search algorithm does A∗ resemble?

Changes from Traditional C

1. In traditional C, there is no type void ∗, pointer to void, so the library functions malloc and calloc return some other kind of pointer (usually a pointer to char), which then is cast to the appropriate type.

2. In some implementations of traditional C, the function cfree is used to free storage allocated by calloc. The standard specifies only the function free, which is used to free storage allocated by either malloc or calloc.

Common Programming Errors

1. C guarantees that NULL is not a legal address. Although a pointer may have NULL as its value, it is an error to dereference a NULL-valued pointer. For example, in the following code, after the while loop terminates, ptr is NULL. Thus the expression ptr −> val attempts to dereference a NULL-valued pointer, which results in an error:

```
while ( ptr != NULL )
    ptr = ptr -> link;
printf( "%d\n", ptr -> val ); /***** ERROR *****/
```

2. Storage allocation functions such as malloc and calloc return pointers. It is a mistake to assign the value that either returns to a nonpointer. For example:

```
int  ptr; /* not a pointer */
ptr = ( int * )
      malloc( sizeof ( int ) );  /*** ERROR ***/
```

3. When we use malloc, we must specify the size of the storage cell to be allocated. When we use calloc, we must specify both the size and number of the cells to be allocated. For example:

```
float   *ptr1, *ptr2;
ptr1 = ( float * )
       malloc( sizeof ( float ) );  /* legal */
ptr2 = ( float * ) malloc();        /* illegal */
ptr1 = ( float * )
       calloc( 10, sizeof ( float ) ); /* legal */
ptr2 = ( float * ) calloc( 10 );  /* illegal */
```

4. Both the functions `malloc` and `calloc` return pointers to `void`. The returned value must be cast to the appropriate type. For example:

```
int  *ptr;
ptr = malloc( sizeof ( int ) );   /* ERROR */

/* correct: */
ptr = ( int * ) malloc( sizeof (int) );
```

Programming Exercises

10.1. Write a function that computes the length of a circular linked list. (A *circular linked list* is a linked list in which the last node points back to the first.)

10.2. Write a function that expects a pointer to the first node of a linked list and returns a pointer to a copy of the list that is the same as the original list except that the nodes are in reverse order.

10.3. Write a function that expects a character string that represents any legal arithmetic expression in C. The function examines the string character by character, putting all operators in one stack and all operands in the other. It ignores parentheses. For example, given the string

$$(7 + 9) * (x - 4)$$

the function will stack the characters as follows:

Operator Stack	Operand Stack
−	4
*	x
+	9
	7

10.4. A *deque* is a list that allows insertions and deletions at either end. Implement a deque using both an array and linked structures, and write insertion and deletion routines for both representations.

10.5. Write a function that expects two arguments: a pointer to a linked list and an integer P representing a position in that list. If possible, the function should switch the nodes at positions P and P + 1. For example, given the list

```
a   b   c   d   e   f   g   h
```

if P = 5, the function alters the list so that it becomes

```
a   b   c   d   f   e   g   h
```

10.6. Write a function that expects pointers to the first nodes of two sorted lists. It then merges the lists into a third list, which also is sorted. For example, if the input is

```
list 1:    a   b   f   k
list 2:      e   g   h   i   p   r
```

the function returns a pointer to the new list

```
a   b   e   f   g   h   i   k   p   r
```

10.7. A *doubly linked list* is like an ordinary linked list except that each node has an extra pointer field that points to the predecessor node. The first node's extra pointer is NULL. Write `find`, `add`, `delete`, `find_last_node`, `length`, and `append` functions for doubly linked lists.

10.8. Implement the function `delet` for the text editor of Section 10.3.

10.9. Implement the function `type` for the text editor of Section 10.3.

10.10. Implement the function `move` for the text editor of Section 10.3.

10.11. Implement the function `find` for the text editor of Section 10.3.

10.12. Implement the function `substitute` for the text editor of Section 10.3.

10.13. Modify the structure used in the text editor of Section 10.3 so that the first member is a pointer to `char`. Add a third member whose value is the length of the line stored. Dynamically allocate storage for the lines so that the storage allocated is exactly equal to the size of the line. Also, allocate nodes only as they are needed. When a node is deleted, free it. When a substitute command is executed that results in a shorter line, allow the extra space to be wasted. When a substitute command is executed that results in a longer line that does not fit in the original node, free the original node and allocate a new node.

10.14. Suppose that we represent a binary tree using linked structures. The node structure is

```
typedef struct node {
    char        label[ 5 ];
    int         descendants;
    struct node *lchild, *rchild;
} NODE;
```

Write a function that traverses the tree and initializes the member `descendants` when a node is visited. The value of `descendants` of a node is the number of descendants of the node.

10.15. A bank has a computer-based appointment system that works as follows: A customer makes a call to a special number that has an answering machine attached. The machine requests the following information:

(a) The customer's unique bank identification number.

(b) The date on which the customer wishes to make an appointment. (The date is entered as six digits; for example, the entry 110293 means November 2, 1993.)

(c) The quarter-hour for which the appointment is desired; for example, 2 * 15 means 2:15.

The customer responds by pressing keys on a touchtone phone. (Those with rotary phones are out of luck.) The customer signals the end of a response by pressing the # key.

The bank is open Monday through Friday from 9:00 until 5:00. Six appointments can be scheduled during one quarter-hour period. Customers are served on a first-come, first-served basis. However, customer traffic is very hard to predict. For some periods, there are only 1 or 2 requests per day, but for others, there are as many as 400.

Simulate this system by writing a program that prompts the user to enter the information as described. Write stub functions that invoke the program to run the speech synthesizer that prompts the customer and that issues error messages. Read each response a character at a time. The system should invoke stub functions that issue messages when no more appointments can be made at a requested time on a given date. The system should be as time and space efficient as possible.

10.16. Extend the simulation of the bank system of Exercise 10.15 to allow a bank employee to check the system to find the next customer waiting for an appointment. If none is available, the employee waits until the next period; otherwise, the employee holds an appointment with the next waiting customer.

10.17. A *binary search tree* is a binary tree T in which data are associated with the nodes. The data are arranged so that for *each* node N in T, each data item in the left subtree of N is less than or equal to the data item in N and each data item in the right subtree of N is greater than the data item in N.

Write a program that uses linked structures allocated at run time to build a binary search tree. Each structure has a key field (a unique character string of length 3) and two pointers, one to its left child and the other to its right child. A string s is inserted into the tree according to the following rules:

1. If the tree is empty, create a node, make it the root, and store s in the root. Stop.

2. Set `ptr` to the root.

3. If s is less than or equal to the string in `ptr`,

> Set `l_ptr` to the left child of `ptr`.
> If `l_ptr` is NULL, create a node, make it the left child of `ptr`, and store s in the left child. Stop.
> Set `ptr` to `l_ptr` and go to step 3.

4. If s is greater than the string in `ptr`,

> Set `r_ptr` to the right child of `ptr`.
> If `r_ptr` is NULL, create a node, make it the right child of `ptr`, and store s in the right child. Stop.
> Set `ptr` to `r_ptr` and go to step 3.

10.18. Add a search function to the program of Exercise 10.17 that expects two arguments: a pointer to the tree's root and a key. The function searches the tree to find a node with that key. If successful, it prints a message to that effect; if not, it allocates a new structure with that key and inserts the structure into the tree.

10.19. Write a function `make_tree` whose argument is a string that represents an expression in prefix form. Assume that valid operators are +, −, *, and / and that valid operands are A through Z. The function returns a pointer to a binary tree that represents the expression. Use linked structures. *Hint*: Let s denote the string. Allocate one node N and store s[0] in it. If the string s is simply an operand, null the link fields and return a pointer to N. Otherwise, the first character s[0] is an operator. Set `count` to 0. Scan the remaining characters from the left, and add 1 to `count` if the character is an operator and subtract 1 from `count` if the character is an operand. Stop when `count` is −1. Assume that we obtain `count == −1` at the character s[i]. Let `left` be the string s[1], . . . , s[i] and let `right` be the remainder of the original string. The left pointer of N should point to make_tree(left), and the right pointer of N should point to make_tree(right). Return N.

10.20. Write a program that simulates a pocket calculator. The input is an arithmetic expression that contains only integers and the arithmetic operators +, −, *, /, and ** (exponentiation). Assume that the input contains no errors and that it is written in infix notation. The expression may be as long as 1,000 characters and as short as 3 characters (e.g., 3 + 2). The program reads input entered at the terminal and prints the expression's value.

10.21. Write a course registration program. The available courses are represented as an array of structures with the following typedef:

```
typedef struct course {
     char      title[ 20 ];
     char      code[ 5 ];
     int       enrollment;
     int       max_enrollment;
     STUDENT   *student;
} COURSE;
```

The user-defined type STUDENT is given by the typedef:

```
typedef struct student {
     char            name[ 30 ];
     int             id;
     struct student  *next;
} STUDENT;
```

The pointer student in each COURSE points to the first student; the pointer next in each STUDENT points to the next enrolled student, if any. All storage for STUDENTs should be allocated at run time.

10.22. A common way to represent a polynomial expression is with linked structures that have three members:
(a) A member to represent the coefficient.
(b) A member to represent the exponent.
(c) A pointer to the next term in the expression.

Write a function that expects pointers to two lists that represent polynomials and returns a pointer to a third list that represents the sum of the polynomials.

10.23. Write a function that implements polynomial multiplication using the representation of Exercise 10.22.

10.24. Given a graph, write a function short_paths with one parameter v that initializes the array len so that for each vertex i, len[i] is the length of a shortest path from v to i. *Hint:* Use a breadth-first search.

10.25. Amend the ASTAR program of Section 10.9 as follows: First, allow the user to choose both the START and the GOAL city. Second, allow the user to set the H* value for each city to either 0 or 110 percent of the straight-line distance to the GOAL.

10.26. Suppose that we are programming in a parallel-processing environment in which instructions can be executed concurrently. Consider, for example, the statements

$$p = x + y \qquad \text{Statement 1}$$
$$q = x * y \qquad \text{Statement 2}$$
$$r = q - p \qquad \text{Statement 3}$$

Two statements may be executed concurrently if the order of their serial execution is irrelevant. For instance, statements 1 and 2 can be executed in either order—1 first and then 2, or 2 first and then 1—with the same result. However, we must execute statement 1 *before* statement 3 because statement 3 uses the value p computed by statement 1, or to put it another way, a variable (p) on the right side of statement 3 appears on the left side of statement 1.

Conditions, known as *Bernstein's conditions,* have been formulated that can be used to determine whether two statements can be executed concurrently. Before stating Bernstein's conditions, we must define two sets of variables for each statement. A statement's *write set* consists of the variables whose values are changed (written) when the statement executes, and a statement's *read set* consists of the variables whose values are unchanged (read) when the statement executes. For a simple assignment statement, the write set is the variable on the left side of the statement, and the read set is the set of variables that appear on the right side of the statement. The write set of statement 1 consists of the single variable p. The write set of statement 3 consists of the single variable r. The read set of statement 1 consists of the variables x and y. The read set of statement 3 consists of the variables p and q.

The *intersection* of two sets consists of the elements that belong to both sets. For example, the intersection of the read sets of statements 1 and 2 consists of the variables x and y. The intersection of the read sets of statements 1 and 3 is empty.

We can now give Bernstein's conditions for concurrent execution. Two statements, S_1 and S_2, can be executed concurrently if and only if they satisfy the following conditions:

1. The intersection of S_1's read set and S_2's write set is empty.
2. The intersection of S_2's read set and S_1's write set is empty.
3. The intersection of S_1's write set and S_2's write set is empty.

Example: For the preceding statements, we have

Read set of statement 1:	$\{x,y\}$
Write set of statement 1:	$\{p\}$
Read set of statement 2:	$\{x,y\}$
Write set of statement 2:	$\{q\}$
Read set of statement 3:	$\{p,q\}$
Write set of statement 3:	$\{r\}$
Intersection of 1's read set and 2's write set:	{ }
Intersection of 2's read set and 1's write set:	{ }
Intersection of 1's write set and 2's write set:	{ }
Intersection of 1's read set and 3's write set:	{ }
Intersection of 3's read set and 1's write set:	$\{p\}$ (Failure)
Intersection of 1's write set and 3's write set:	{ }
Intersection of 2's read set and 3's write set:	{ }
Intersection of 3's read set and 2's write set:	$\{q\}$ (Failure)
Intersection of 2's write set and 3's write set:	{ }

We see that statements 1 and 2 can be executed concurrently but that neither statements 1 and 3 nor statements 2 and 3 can be executed concurrently.

Write a program that prompts the user to enter two assignment statements that are read as character strings. Assume that the statements are correct C statements. The program then builds the read and write sets for each statement and uses Bernstein's conditions to test whether the statements can be executed concurrently. The program prints the following:

1. The read and write sets of each statement.
2. The intersection sets specified by Bernstein's conditions.
3. A message as to whether each intersection is empty.
4. A message as to whether the statements can be executed concurrently.

10.27. Amend the infix to postfix program of Section 10.5 so that it checks for syntax errors. For example, the program currently converts the syntactically incorrect expression A++++B to A+++B+. The program also now accepts an illegal expression such as ((( ), although an illegal expression such as ( ))))) causes the program to terminate because of stack underflow. The revised program should catch these and any other errors in syntax and should print helpful error messages such as Unbalanced parentheses and operator/operand inbalance. *Hint:* The standard arithmetic operators (+, −, *, /, and %) are all binary in that they expect exactly two arguments. An arithmetic expression with *n* operands thus should have $n - 1$ operators. Assign numerical values to operators and operands and keep a running count as you scan an arithmetic expression. For example, you might initialize the running count to zero, increment the count by one for each operand encountered, and decrement the count by two for each operator encountered. The count then can be used to screen for certain types of syntactic error. Also, consider whether it is easier to check for syntactic errors before converting to postfix, to check for such errors while converting to postfix, or to check for the errors only after the conversion is completed.

10.28. A *binary digital picture* (see Programming Exercise 5.17) is a two-dimensional array of 0's and 1's. An element (i,j) (the notation refers to row *i*, column *j*) is called a *pixel* (picture element). The picture is interpreted as consisting of light objects (formed by the 1's) on a dark background (formed by the 0's). An *object* in a binary digital picture is defined in the following way. First, we say that two pixels are *4-neighbors* if they are next to each other horizontally or vertically. For example, pixels (1,1) and (1,2) are 4-neighbors, whereas pixels (1,1) and (2,2) are not 4-neighbors. The terminology arises from the fact that a 4-neighbor of a pixel can occur in at most four positions. (A border pixel may have fewer than four 4-neighbors.) A *4-chain* of pixels is a sequence of pixels, all of which are 1, such that successive pixels in the sequence are 4-neighbors. Pixels are *in the same object* if they are the first and last pixels in some 4-chain. Write a program that uses depth-first search to identify the distinct objects and to label pixels within an object with the same value and pixels in different objects with different values. *Hint:* Consider a graph whose vertices are the pixels with value 1. Put an edge between two vertices if they are 4-neighbors. Now use depth-first search to identify the objects.

Appendix

A   ASCII and EBCDIC Tables

B   Unsigned and Two's Complement Integers

C   Summary of the C Language

D   Syntax Diagrams of C

E   Some C Functions

F   C and UNIX

G   Compiling, Linking, and Running a C Program in Turbo C, VAX/VMS, and UNIX

ASCII and EBCDIC Tables

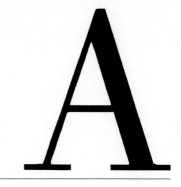

Table A.1 **ASCII Codes**

Decimal	Hexadecimal	Octal	Standard Function
0	00	000	NUL (Null)
1	01	001	SOH (Start of heading)
2	02	002	STX (Start of text)
3	03	003	ETX (End of text)
4	04	004	EOT (End of transmission)
5	05	005	ENQ (Enquiry)
6	06	006	ACK (Acknowledge)
7	07	007	BEL (Ring bell)
8	08	010	BS (Backspace)
9	09	011	HT (Horizontal tab)
10	0A	012	LF (Line feed)
11	0B	013	VT (Vertical tab)
12	0C	014	FF (Form feed)
13	0D	015	CR (Carriage return)
14	0E	016	SO (Shift out)
15	0F	017	SI (Shift in)
16	10	020	DLE (Data link escape)
17	11	021	DC1 (Device control 1)
18	12	022	DC2 (Device control 2)
19	13	023	DC3 (Device control 3)
20	14	024	DC4 (Device control 4)
21	15	025	NAK (Negative acknowledge)
22	16	026	SYN (Synchronous idle)
23	17	027	ETB (End of transmission block)
24	18	030	CAN (Cancel)
25	19	031	EM (End of medium)
26	1A	032	SUB (Substitute)
27	1B	033	ESC (Escape)

Table A.1 **ASCII Codes (*Continued*)**

Decimal	Hexadecimal	Octal	Standard Function
28	1C	034	FS (File separator)
29	1D	035	GS (Group separator)
30	1E	036	RS (Record separator)
31	1F	037	US (Unit separator)
32	20	040	SP (Space)
33	21	041	!
34	22	042	''
35	23	043	#
36	24	044	$
37	25	045	%
38	26	046	&
39	27	047	' (Single quote)
40	28	050	(
41	29	051	)
42	2A	052	*
43	2B	053	+
44	2C	054	, (Comma)
45	2D	055	- (Hyphen)
46	2E	056	.
47	2F	057	/
48	30	060	0
49	31	061	1
50	32	062	2
51	33	063	3
52	34	064	4
53	35	065	5
54	36	066	6
55	37	067	7
56	38	070	8
57	39	071	9
58	3A	072	:
59	3B	073	;
60	3C	074	<
61	3D	075	=
62	3E	076	>
63	3F	077	?
64	40	100	@
65	41	101	A
66	42	102	B
67	43	103	C
68	44	104	D
69	45	105	E
70	46	106	F
71	47	107	G
72	48	110	H
73	49	111	I
74	4A	112	J
75	4B	113	K
76	4C	114	L
77	4D	115	M
78	4E	116	N
79	4F	117	O

Table A.1   **ASCII Codes (*Continued*)**

Decimal	Hexadecimal	Octal	Standard Function
80	50	120	P
81	51	121	Q
82	52	122	R
83	53	123	S
84	54	124	T
85	55	125	U
86	56	126	V
87	57	127	W
88	58	130	X
89	59	131	Y
90	5A	132	Z
91	5B	133	[
92	5C	134	\
93	5D	135	]
94	5E	136	^
95	5F	137	_ (Underscore)
96	60	140	` (Grave accent)
97	61	141	a
98	62	142	b
99	63	143	c
100	64	144	d
101	65	145	e
102	66	146	f
103	67	147	g
104	68	150	h
105	69	151	i
106	6A	152	j
107	6B	153	k
108	6C	154	l
109	6D	155	m
110	6E	156	n
111	6F	157	o
112	70	160	p
113	71	161	q
114	72	162	r
115	73	163	s
116	74	164	t
117	75	165	u
118	76	166	v
119	77	167	w
120	78	170	x
121	79	171	y
122	7A	172	z
123	7B	173	{
124	7C	174	|
125	7D	175	}
126	7E	176	~
127	7F	177	DEL (Delete)

Table A.2 **EBCDIC Codes**

Decimal	Hexadecimal	Octal	Standard Function
0	00	000	NUL (Null)
1	01	001	SOH (Start of heading)
2	02	002	STX (Start of text)
3	03	003	ETX (End of text)
4	04	004	PF (Punch off)
5	05	005	HT (Horizontal tab)
6	06	006	LC (Lowercase)
7	07	007	DEL (Delete)
10	0A	012	SMM (Repeat)
11	0B	013	VT (Vertical tab)
12	0C	014	FF (Form feed)
13	0D	015	CR (Carriage return)
14	0E	016	SO (Shift out)
15	0F	017	SI (Shift in)
16	10	020	DLE (Data link escape)
17	11	021	DC1 (Device control 1)
18	12	022	DC2 (Device control 2)
19	13	023	DC3 (Device control 3)
20	14	024	RES (Restore)
21	15	025	NL (Newline)
22	16	026	BS (Backspace)
23	17	027	IL (Idle)
24	18	030	CAN (Cancel)
25	19	031	EM (End of medium)
26	1A	032	CC (Unit backspace)
28	1C	034	IFS (Interchange file separator)
29	1D	035	IGS (Interchange group separator)
30	1E	036	IRS (Interchange record separator)
31	1F	037	IUS (Interchange unit separator)
32	20	040	DS (Digit select)
33	21	041	SOS (Start of significance)
34	22	042	FS (File separator)
36	24	044	BYP (Bypass)
37	25	045	LF (Line feed)
38	26	046	ETB (End of transmission block)
39	27	047	ESC (Escape)
42	2A	052	SM (Start message)
45	2D	055	ENQ (Enquiry)
46	2E	056	ACK (Acknowledge)
47	2F	057	BEL (Ring bell)
50	32	062	SYN (Synchronous idle)
52	34	064	PN (Punch on)
53	35	065	RS (Record separator)
54	36	066	UC (Uppercase)
55	37	067	EOT (End of transmission)
60	3C	074	DC4 (Device control 4)
61	3D	075	NAK (Negative acknowledge)
63	3F	077	SUB (Substitute)
64	40	100	SP (Space)
74	4A	112	¢
75	4B	113	.
76	4C	114	<

Table A.2   **EBCDIC Codes (*Continued*)**

Decimal	Hexadecimal	Octal	Standard Function
77	4D	115	(
78	4E	116	+
79	4F	117	|
80	50	120	&
90	5A	132	!
91	5B	133	$
92	5C	134	*
93	5D	135	)
94	5E	136	;
95	5F	137	⌐ (Negation)
96	60	140	- (Hyphen)
97	61	141	/
106	6A	152	∧
107	6B	153	, (Comma)
108	6C	154	%
109	6D	155	_ (Underscore)
110	6E	156	>
111	6F	157	?
121	79	171	` (Grave accent)
122	7A	172	:
123	7B	173	#
124	7C	174	@
125	7D	175	' (Single quote)
126	7E	176	=
127	7F	177	''
129	81	201	a
130	82	202	b
131	83	203	c
132	84	204	d
133	85	205	e
134	86	206	f
135	87	207	g
136	88	210	h
137	89	211	i
145	91	221	j
146	92	222	k
147	93	223	l
148	94	224	m
149	95	225	n
150	96	226	o
151	97	227	p
152	98	230	q
153	99	231	r
161	A1	241	~
162	A2	242	s
163	A3	243	t
164	A4	244	u
165	A5	245	v
166	A6	246	w
167	A7	247	x
168	A8	250	y
169	A9	251	z

Table A.2   **EBCDIC Codes (*Continued*)**

Decimal	Hexadecimal	Octal	Standard Function
177	B1	261	\
178	B2	262	{
179	B3	263	}
180	B4	264	[
181	B5	265	]
193	C1	301	A
194	C2	302	B
195	C3	303	C
196	C4	304	D
197	C5	305	E
198	C6	306	F
199	C7	307	G
200	C8	310	H
201	C9	311	I
209	D1	321	J
210	D2	322	K
211	D3	323	L
212	D4	324	M
213	D5	325	N
214	D6	326	O
215	D7	327	P
216	D8	330	Q
217	D9	331	R
226	E2	342	S
227	E3	343	T
228	E4	344	U
229	E5	345	V
230	E6	346	W
231	E7	347	X
232	E8	350	Y
233	E9	351	Z
240	F0	360	0
241	F1	361	1
242	F2	362	2
243	F3	363	3
244	F4	364	4
245	F5	365	5
246	F6	366	6
247	F7	367	7
248	F8	370	8
249	F9	371	9

Unsigned and Two's Complement Integers

In the binary number system, the bit string

$$b_n b_{n-1} \cdots b_1 b_0$$

represents the nonnegative integer

$$b_n * 2^n + b_{n-1} * 2^{n-1} + \cdots + b_1 * 2^1 + b_0 * 2^0$$

For example, the bit string 10010 represents the integer

$$10010 = 1 * 2^4 + 0 * 2^3 + 0 * 2^2 + 1 * 2^1 + 0 * 2^0$$
$$= 16 + 2 = 18 \text{ (decimal)}$$

We call a nonnegative integer represented in the binary number system an **unsigned binary integer,** so as to distinguish it from a **two's complement integer,** to be described later. In the two's complement system, we can represent both negative and nonnegative integers.

To convert a nonnegative decimal integer to an unsigned binary integer, we can subtract the largest power of 2 less than or equal to the number, subtract the largest power of 2 less than or equal to the remainder, and so on. We can then easily write the binary representation.

Example. Write the decimal integer 102 in binary. The largest power of 2 less than or equal to 102 is 64. Thus

$$102 = 64 + 38$$

The largest power of 2 less than or equal to the remainder, 38, is 32. Thus

$$102 = 64 + 32 + 6$$

The largest power of 2 less than or equal to the remainder, 6, is 4. Thus

$$102 = 64 + 32 + 4 + 2$$

The largest power of 2 less than or equal to the remainder, 2, is 2 itself. Now

$$102 = 64 + 32 + 4 + 2$$
$$= 2^6 + 2^5 + 2^2 + 2^1$$
$$= 1100110$$

In the two's complement system, the leftmost bit gives the sign of the integer. If the leftmost bit is 0, the integer is nonnegative; if the leftmost bit is 1, the integer is negative. If the leftmost bit is 0, the unsigned representation and the two's complement representation coincide.

Example. Suppose that we use 8-bit cells to store two's complement integers. Because the leftmost bit of the integer

$$00010010$$

is 0, the integer is nonnegative, and the unsigned representation and the two's complement representation coincide. Thus, the bit string represents the integer decimal 18.

In the two's complement system, if the leftmost bit is 1, the integer is negative. In this case, the absolute value of the integer is the two's complement of the original expression, which is obtained as follows:

1. Change each 0 to 1 and each 1 to 0 in the bit string.
2. Add 1 to the number. Throw away the final carry bit.

The resulting *unsigned* integer is equal to the absolute value of the integer. If the absolute value of the integer is v, the original bit string represents the negative integer $-v$.

Example. Let us convert the 8-bit, two's complement integer

$$10101100$$

to decimal. We first find the absolute value of the integer. We begin by changing each 0 to 1 and each 1 to 0 to obtain

$$01010011$$

We then add 1 to this number to obtain

$$01010100$$

Because

$$01010100 = 4 + 16 + 64 = 84$$

the original bit string 10101100 represents -84.

To convert a negative decimal integer to an n-bit two's complement integer, we compute the two's complement of the n-bit unsigned representation of the absolute value of the integer.

Example. To convert the decimal integer -94 to an 8-bit, two's complement integer, we first write the absolute value 94 as an 8-bit binary integer:

$$94 = 64 + 16 + 8 + 4 + 2 = 2^6 + 2^4 + 2^3 + 2^2 + 2^1 = 01011110$$

Now -94 is represented as the two's complement of 01011110. To compute the two's complement, we first change each 0 to 1 and each 1 to 0:

$$10100001$$

We then add 1 to obtain the 8-bit, two's complement representation of -94:

$$-94 = 10100010$$

The largest positive integer that we can represent as an 8-bit two's complement integer is

$$01111111 = 127$$

The smallest negative integer that we can represent as an 8-bit two's complement integer is

$$10000000 = -128$$

The largest positive integer that we can represent as a 16-bit two's complement integer is

$$0111111111111111 = 32,767$$

The smallest negative integer that we can represent as a 16-bit two's complement integer is

$$1000000000000000 = -32,768$$

The largest positive integer that we can represent as a 32-bit two's complement integer is

$$01111111111111111111111111111111 = 2,147,483,647$$

The smallest negative integer that we can represent as a 32-bit two's complement integer is

$$10000000000000000000000000000000 = -2,147,483,648$$

Two's complement representation simplifies basic arithmetic operations, which explains its popularity. For example, to add two two's complement integers, one simply performs ordinary binary addition without worrying about the sign. Any carry bit is discarded.

Example. To add the 8-bit, two's complement integers 11011100 and 11000001, we compute

$$
\begin{array}{r}
11011100 \\
+ \quad 11000001 \\
\hline
10011101
\end{array}
$$

The carry bit 1 is discarded. The same computation in decimal is

$$
\begin{array}{r}
-36 \\
+ \quad -63 \\
\hline
-99
\end{array}
$$

Example. To subtract the 8-bit, two's complement integer 11011100 from 11000001, we negate 11011100 (by taking two's complement) and add. The two's complement of 11011100 is 00100100. Thus

$$11000001 - 11011100 = 11000001 + 00100100 = 11100101$$

The same computation in decimal is

$$-63 - -36 = -63 + 36 = -27$$

Summary of the C Language

C

In this appendix, we briefly describe the most frequently used parts of C. (The C syntax diagrams are given in Appendix D.) The subsections, listed in alphabetical order, are as follows:

arrays	for	return
break	functions	sizeof
case	goto	standard headers
cast	if	storage classes
comments	initializing in definitions	structures
constants	keywords	switch
continue	labels	typedef
data types	null statement	type qualifiers
do while	pointers	union
enum	precedence of operators	void
		while

Arrays

An array is defined by writing the data type followed by the name followed by the size in brackets as, for example,

```
int x[ 20 ];
```

In this case, the variables x[0], x[1], . . . , x[19] are created.

break

When the statement

```
break;
```

is encountered, the innermost while, do while, for, or switch construct is terminated.

case

See switch.

Cast

The cast operator is written as

(*type*)

where *type* is a data type. When the cast operator is executed, the operand is converted to *type*. As examples, if we write

```
int i = 2;
float x;
x = ( float ) i;
```

the value of i is converted to float and copied into x.
If we write

```
struct node {
    char *data;
    struct node *link;
};
struct node *ptr;
ptr = ( struct node * ) malloc( sizeof ( struct node ) );
```

storage for one structure whose members are data and link is allocated by the library function malloc. The address of this storage is converted to the type pointer to struct node and assigned to ptr.

Comments

A C comment is delimited by /* and */.

Constants

Integer constants may be written in decimal:

130   45   88203

An integer constant that begins with 0 (zero) is an octal number:

0130   045

A sequence of digits preceded by 0X or 0x is a hexadecimal number:

0x90A   0Xf2

Either lowercase f through f or uppercase A through F is acceptable.
    An integer constant may be terminated by u or U, to indicate that it is unsigned, or by l or L, to indicate that it is long. If a decimal constant is not terminated with either u, U, l, or L, it is the first of the types int, long, or unsigned long in which its value can be represented. If an octal or hexadecimal constant is not terminated with either u, U, l, or L, it is the first of the types int, unsigned int, long, or unsigned long in which its value can be represented. If a decimal, octal, or hexadecimal constant is termi-

nated with either u or U, it is the first of the types unsigned int or unsigned long in which its value can be represented. If a decimal, octal, or hexadecimal constant is terminated with either l or L, it is the first of the types long or unsigned long in which its value can be represented. If a decimal, octal, or hexadecimal constant is terminated with either l or L and u or U, it is of type unsigned long.

A floating-point constant consists of a string of digits (integral part) followed by a decimal point followed by a string of digits (fractional part) followed by an integer exponent. The integer exponent is e or E optionally followed by + or − followed by a string of digits. Either the integral part or the fractional part, but not both, may be omitted. Either the decimal point or the integer exponent, but not both, may be omitted. Examples of floating-point constants are

```
2.0   4.3e4   9.21E-9   13.E+4   4e-3   .390
```

A floating-point constant may be terminated by f or F to indicate that it is a float or by l or L to indicate that it is a long double. If a floating-point constant is not terminated with either f, F, l, or L, it is of type double.

A char constant is delimited by single quotation marks, for example, 'g'. C recognizes the following escape sequences:

Constant	Meaning
'\a'	Bell rings
'\\'	Backslash
'\b'	Backspace
'\f'	Form feed
'\n'	Newline
'\t'	Horizontal tab
'\v'	Vertical tab
'\r'	Carriage return
'\''	Single quote
'\ddd'	Octal constant
'\xhh'	Hexadecimal constant

A string constant is delimited by double quotation marks, for example,

```
"This is a string constant."
```

Within a string, C recognizes the escape sequences listed previously, as well as \" (double quotation mark).

continue

When the statement

```
continue;
```

is encountered in a while or do while loop, control passes to the condition that determines whether to execute the body of the loop again.

When the statement

```
continue;
```

is encountered in a `for` loop, control passes to the update statement *expr3* in

```
for ( expr1; expr2; expr3 )
    body
```

Then *expr2* is evaluated to determine whether to execute *body* again.

Data Types

The integer data types are `char`, `short int` (which may be abbreviated to `short`), `int`, and `long int` (which may be abbreviated to `long`). The sizes of these data types satisfy

```
sizeof ( char ) <= sizeof ( short )
               <= sizeof ( int )
               <= sizeof ( long )
```

The signed integer types are `signed char`, `signed short int`, `signed int`, and `signed long int`. In addition, the unsigned integer types `unsigned char`, `unsigned short int`, `unsigned int` (which may be abbreviated to `unsigned`), and `unsigned long int` are available.

The floating-point data types are `float`, `double`, and `long double`. The sizes of these data types satisfy

```
sizeof ( float ) <= sizeof ( double )
                 <= sizeof ( long double )
```

Some other types, defined in standard headers, are given in the following table:

Name	Defined in	Represents
`ptrdiff_t`	*stddef.h*	The difference of two pointers
`size_t`	*stddef.h*	The value of `sizeof`
	stdio.h	
	stdlib.h	
	string.h	
	time.h	
`va_list`	*stdarg.h*	Information needed by macros in *stdarg.h*
`FILE`	*stdio.h*	Information needed to manipulate files
`fpos_t`	*stdio.h*	A position within a file
`clock_t`	*time.h*	Time
`time_t`	*time.h*	Time

See also `enum`.

do while

When we execute

```
do body while ( condition );
```

as long as *condition* is true (nonzero), we execute *body; condition* is tested after *body* is executed. In addition, *body* is enclosed in braces unless it consists of a single statement, in which case it is simply terminated with a semicolon.

`enum`

An enumerated type is a data type with user-specified values. For example, the declaration

```
enum dir { Hitchcock, Huston, Meyer };
```

describes the enumerated type `enum dir`. A variable of type `enum dir` should take one of the values `Hitchcock`, `Huston`, or `Meyer`. To define a variable `name` of type `enum dir`, we write

```
enum dir name;
```

After the preceding definition, the assignment

```
name = Huston;
```

is valid.

`for`

When we execute

```
for ( expr1; expr2; expr3 ) body
```

we first execute *expr1*. Then, as long as *expr2* is true (nonzero), we execute *body* followed by *expr3*; *expr2* is tested before *body* and *expr3* are executed. In addition, *body* is enclosed in braces unless it consists of a single statement, in which case it is simply terminated with a semicolon.

Functions

The definition of a function consists of a header and a body. The header consists of: the data type returned followed by the function's name followed by the data types and names of any parameters in parentheses. If the function returns no value, the keyword `void` occurs in place of the returned data type. If there are no parameters, the keyword `void` occurs in parentheses. No semicolon follows the right parenthesis. The body of the function, that is, the code that implements the function, follows the header and is enclosed in braces.

A declaration of a function resembles a function header. The declaration consists of the data type returned followed by the function's name followed, in parentheses, by the data types and optional names of the expected arguments terminated by a semicolon. If the function returns no value, the keyword `void` occurs in place of the returned data type. If there are no expected arguments, the keyword `void` occurs in the parentheses.

Here is an example of a function definition:

```
int  fun( char letter )     /* header */
{
                .
                .                   /* body */
                .

}
```

Here is a declaration of the preceding function:

```
int  fun( char letter );
```

goto

When the statement

```
goto label;
```

is encountered, control passes to the line

```
label: ...
```

if

When we execute

> if (*condition*) *body*

if *condition* is true (nonzero), we execute *body;* otherwise, we skip to the statement immediately following *body*.

When we execute

> if (*condition*) *body1* else *body2*

if *condition* is true (nonzero), we execute *body1;* otherwise, we execute *body2*. In either case, the next statement executed is the statement immediately following *body2*. In addition, *body1* is enclosed in braces unless it consists of a single statement, in which case it is simply terminated with a semicolon. Similarly, *body2* is enclosed in braces unless it consists of a single statement, in which case it is simply terminated with a semicolon.

Initializing in Definitions

Any variable may be initialized in its definition by writing, for example,

```
int x = 5;
```

An array can be initialized as, for example, by writing

```
int age[ 5 ] = { 4, 32, 5, 27, 29 };
```

A structure can be initialized as, for example, by writing

```
struct date {
    int day;
    char *month;
    int year;
} due_date = { 8, "Jan", 1990 };
```

Keywords

auto	extern	sizeof
break	float	static
case	for	struct
char	goto	switch
const	if	typedef
continue	int	union
default	long	unsigned
do	register	void
double	return	volatile
else	short	while
enum	signed	

Labels

A label is the first identifier on a line and must be followed by a colon:

```
label: ...
```

A line that begins

```
label:
```

is the target of a `goto` statement.

Null Statement

The null statement consists solely of a semicolon.

Pointers

A pointer must be defined so as to point to a particular data type. For example, if we write

```
int *ptr;
```

`ptr` can hold the address of an `int`.
   The syntax

```
*ptr
```

accesses the contents of the cell whose address is `ptr`.

Precedence of Operators

Operators between horizontal lines have the same precedence.

Description	Operator(s)	Associates from the	Precedence
Function expr	( )	left	High
Array expr	[ ]		(Evaluated
`struct` indirection	–>		first)
`struct` member	.		
Incr/decr	++ ––	right	
One's complement	~		
Negation	!		
Address	&		
Dereference	*		
Cast	(*type*)		
Unary minus	–		
Unary plus	+		
Size in bytes	`sizeof`		
Multiplication	*	left	
Division	/		
Remainder	%		
Addition	+		
Subtraction	–		
Shift left	<<		
Shift right	>>		

Description	Operator(s)	Associates from the	Precedence
Less than	<	left	
Less than or equal	<=		
Greater than	>		
Greater than or equal	>=		
Equal	==		
Not equal	!=		
Bitwise and	&	left	
Bitwise exclusive or	^		
Bitwise inclusive or				
Logical and	&&		
Logical or	||		
Conditional	? :	right	
Assignment	= %= += -= *= /= >>= <<= &= ^= |=		(Evaluated last)
Comma	,	left	Low

return

When the statement

```
return;
```

is encountered, the function returns to its invoker without returning a value. When the statement

```
return ( expression );
```

is encountered, the function returns to its invoker the value *expression*. The statement

```
return ( expression );
```

has the same meaning as

```
return expression;
```

sizeof

The value of the `sizeof` operator is the size, in bytes, of its operand. One byte is defined to be `sizeof ( char )`. If a is an array, `sizeof ( a )` is the total size, in bytes, of a. If s is a structure, `sizeof ( s )` is the total size, in bytes, of all of the members of s. Because `sizeof` is an operator and not a function, its value is known at compile time. For this reason, it is legal to write

```
struct date {
        int day;
        char *month;
        int year;
};
#define DATE_SIZE sizeof ( struct date )
```

Standard Headers

The following table lists the header files mandated by standard C and gives a brief description of the purpose of each.

Header File	Purpose
assert.h	Putting diagnostics into programs
ctype.h	Testing and modifying characters
errno.h	Reporting error conditions
float.h	Describing floating-point types
limits.h	Describing integer types
locale.h	Formatting numeric values
math.h	Mathematical functions
setjmp.h	Bypassing default function call and return conventions
signal.h	Handling signals
stdarg.h	Writing functions with an arbitrary number of arguments
stddef.h	Common definitions
stdio.h	Handling input and output
stdlib.h	General utilities
string.h	Handling arrays of characters
time.h	Handling time

Storage Classes

The C storage classes are

```
auto   extern   static   register
```

Because the details are too involved, the reader is directed to Chapter 7.

Structures

A structure declaration consists of `struct` followed by an optional structure tag followed by the declaration of its members in braces. The terminating brace must be followed by a semicolon. For example:

```
struct date {
    int day;
    char *month;
    int year;
};
```

Given a structure declaration, one can define a structure of the given type by writing `struct` followed by the structure tag followed by the name of the variable to be defined. For example, given the preceding structure declaration, we can define a structure called d by writing

```
struct date d;
```

It is possible to declare and define structures simultaneously (see Section 9.1).

A member of a structure can be accessed by using the dot operator. For example, given the preceding declaration and definition, we may access `month` in d by writing

```
d.month
```

The syntax

```
(*s).x
```

is equivalent to

```
s -> x
```

C permits structure assignments using the assignment operator = and permits passing structures to functions and returning structures from functions.

switch

The `switch` statement has the form

```
switch ( expression ) {
case c1:
     statements1
case c2:
     statements2
     .
     .
     .
default:
     def-statements
}
```

When the construct is executed, *expression* is evaluated. Control passes to the line at which *expression* is equal to *ci*. (Each of $c1, c2, \ldots$ must be distinct.) If *expression* is not equal to any of the *ci*'s, control passes to *def-statements*. Execution continues until a `break` statement is encountered, at which point control passes to the first statement after *def-statements*. If no `break` statement is present, execution continues through all the statements, beginning with the first `case` in which *ci* equals *expression*. Normally, each of *statements1, statements2, . . . , def-statements* concludes with

```
break;
```

Each of $c1, c2, \ldots$ must be an integer constant; `default` is optional.

typedef

The use of `typedef` creates a synonym for some other data type. For example, if we write

```
typedef struct x {
     int day;
     char *month;
     int year;
} DATE;
```

the types `struct x` and `DATE` are synonyms. Given the preceding `typedef`, writing

```
DATE d;
```

is the same as writing

```
struct x {
     int day;
     char *month;
     int year;
} d;
```

Type Qualifiers

Type qualifiers are specified by the keywords `const` and `volatile` and are used to inform the compiler about the behavior of variables and parameters. The type qualifier `const` ("constant") indicates to the compiler that a variable or parameter is not to have its value reset. Any attempt to reset the value of a `const` variable or parameter results in an error. The type qualifier `volatile` indicates to the compiler that a variable or parameter may have its value set by something (e.g., an operating system call) outside the C program. In effect, the `volatile` type qualifier warns an optimizing compiler against making assumptions about how the value of the variable or parameter will be set.

The type qualifiers may occur together in variable definitions and parameter declarations. However, the type qualifiers always come after the storage class and before the data type. Here are two examples:

```
static const volatile int    num;   /* variable definition */
void fun( const float   real )      /* parameter declaration */
```

union

The union construct is syntactically identical to the structure construct (see Structures). A union may, at different times, hold one, and only one, of the types defined. For example, if we define

```
union num {
     int x;
     float y;
} u;
```

u may hold an `int` or a `float`, but not both. Storage is allocated for the largest of the data types specified. A member of union u is accessed syntactically exactly as a member of a structure.

void

The keyword `void` shows that a function returns no value or expects no arguments. For example,

```
void f( int x, int y )
```

is the header of a function with two parameters, both of type `int`, that returns no value. As another example,

```
float g( void )
```

is the header of a function with no parameters that returns a value of type `float`. Also, certain library functions such as `malloc` return a pointer to `void`, `void *`, which can be cast to any appropriate pointer type.

while

When we execute

```
while ( condition ) body
```

as long as *condition* is true (nonzero), we execute *body; condition* is tested before *body* is executed. In addition, *body* is enclosed in braces unless it consists of a single statement, in which case it is simply terminated with a semicolon.

Syntax Diagrams of C

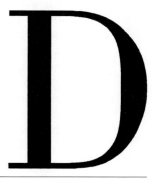

These syntax diagrams are based on the standard but are not an official part of the standard.

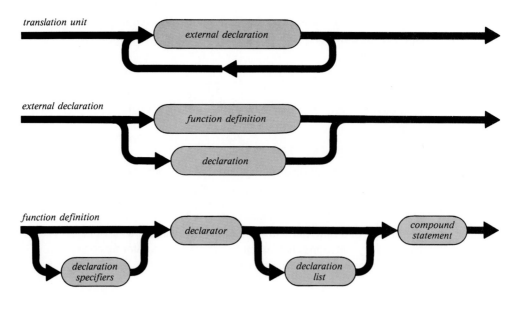

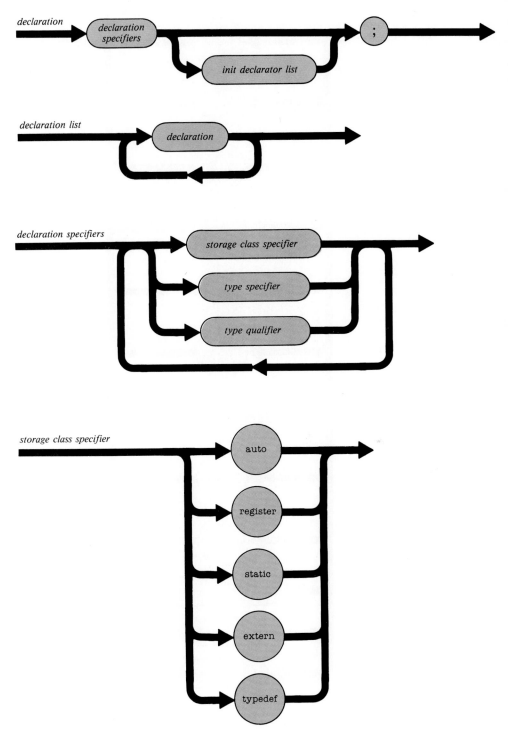

type specifier

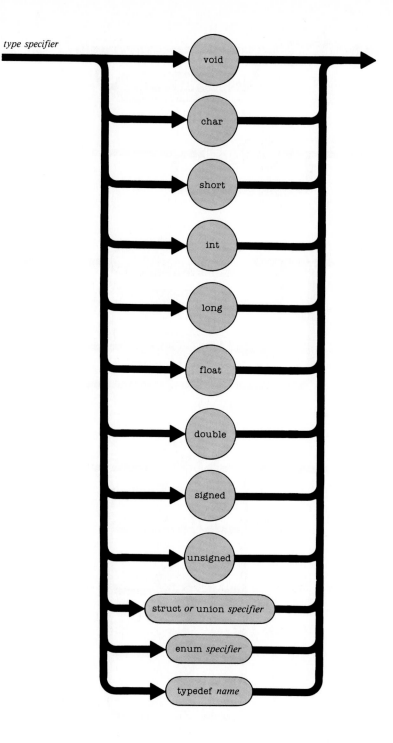

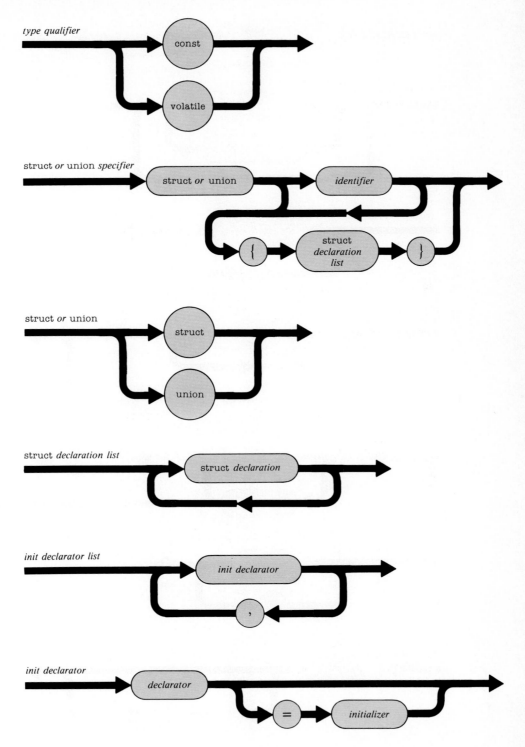

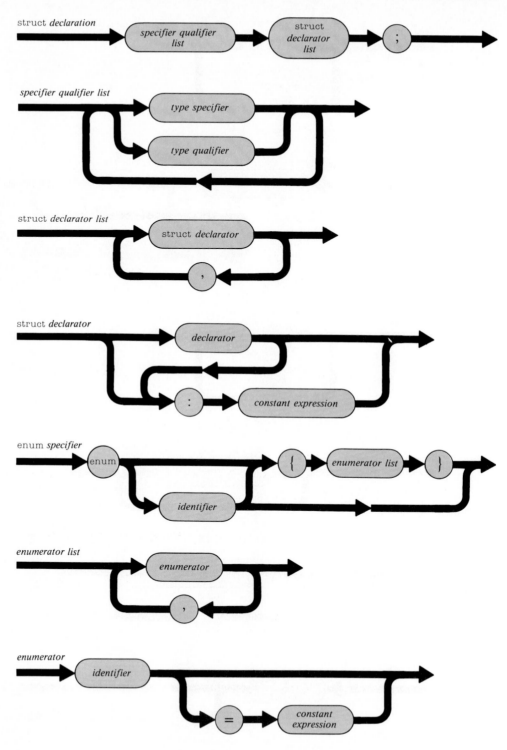

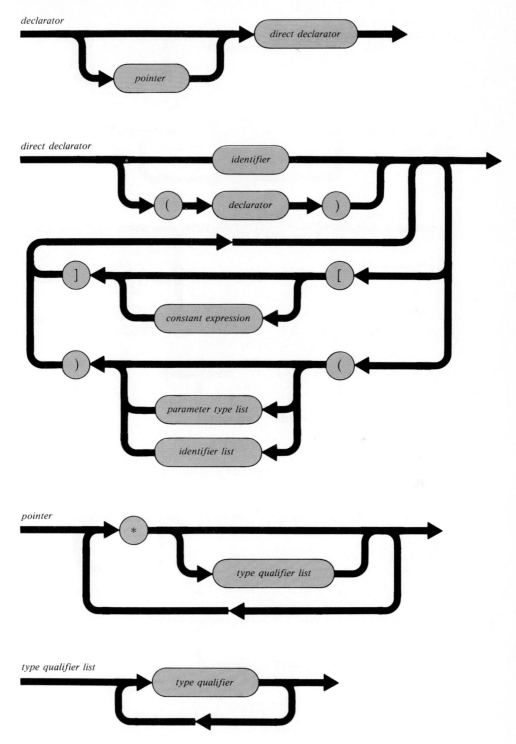

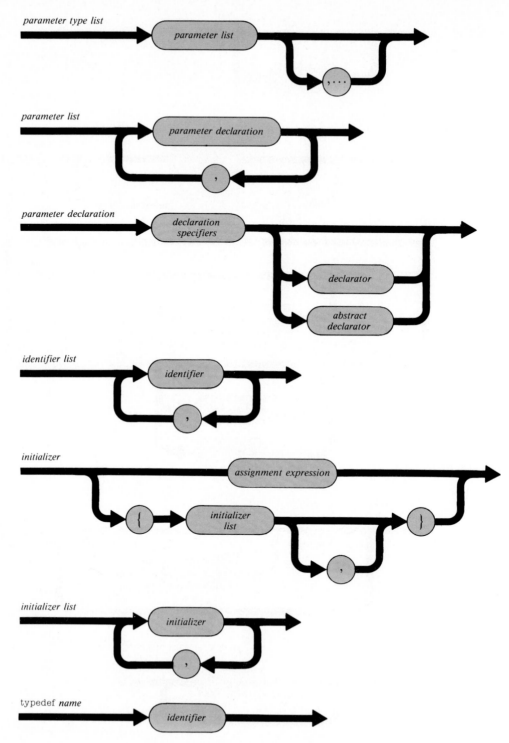

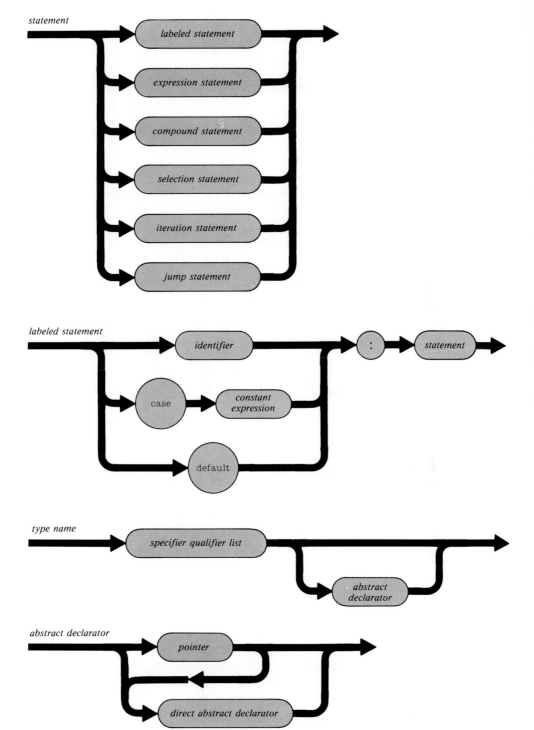

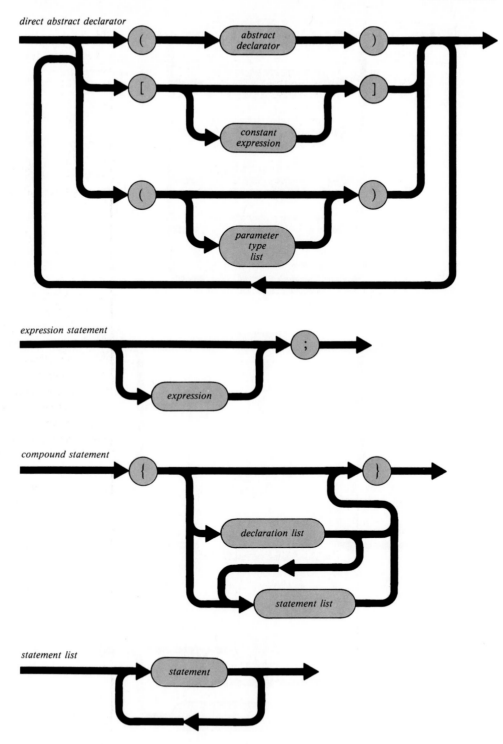

direct abstract declarator

expression statement

compound statement

statement list

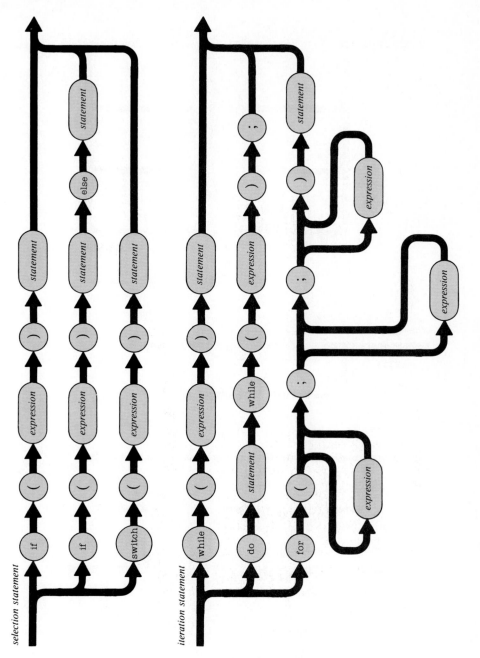

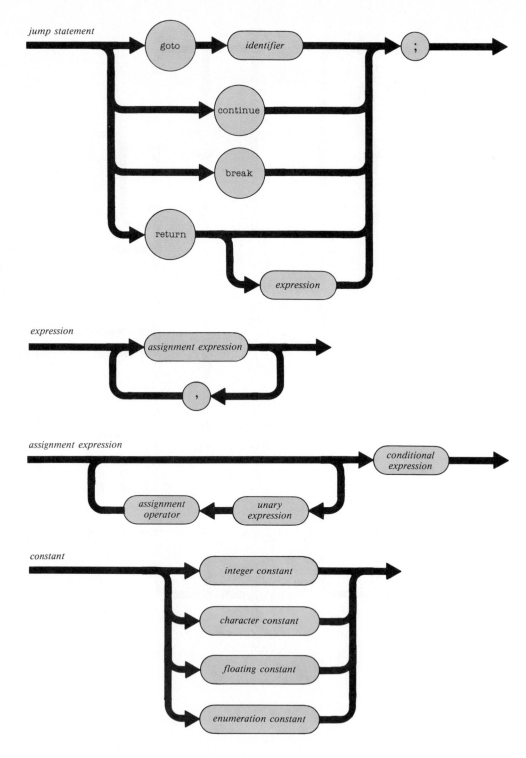

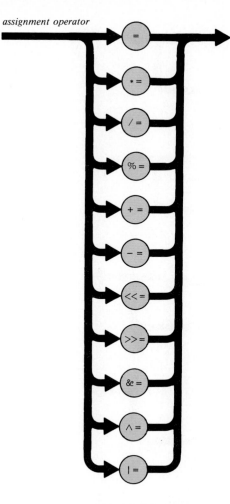

assignment operator

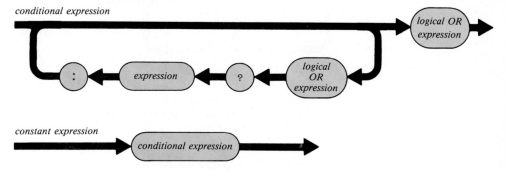

conditional expression

constant expression

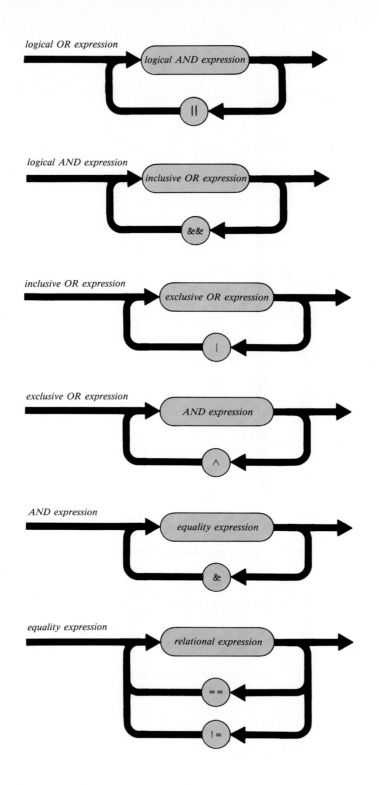

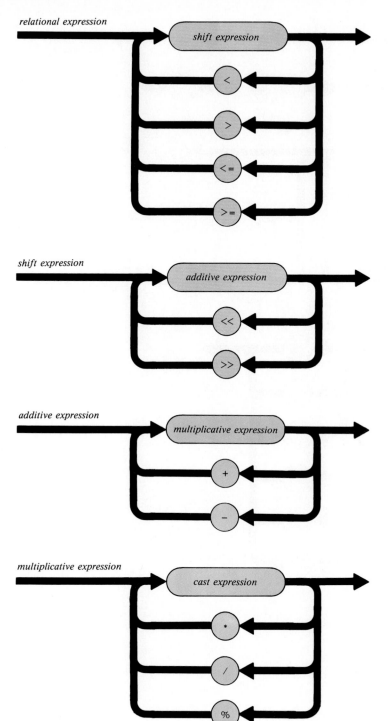

cast expression

unary expression

unary operator

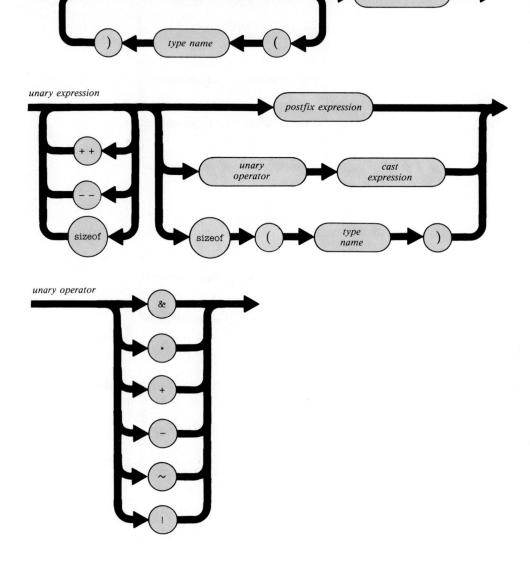

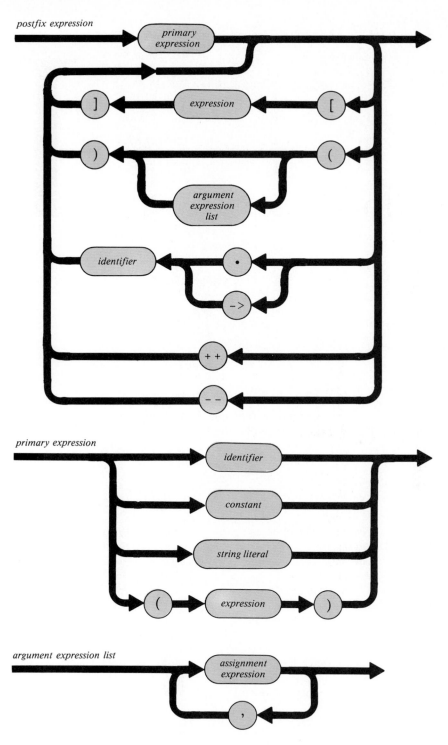

Some C Functions

Before summarizing in detail several useful library functions, we briefly describe each. Except for certain input/output functions (which are flagged), each is specified by the standard. The following lists group the functions by type:

.

Math Functions

abs	Absolute value of an int	floor	Floor
acos	Arccosine	labs	Absolute value of a long
asin	Arcsine	log	$\log_e x$
atan	Arctangent	log10	$\log_{10} x$
atof	Convert string to double	pow	x^y
atoi	Convert string to int	rand	Generate a random integer
atol	Convert string to long	sin	Sine
ceil	Ceiling	sinh	Hyperbolic sine
cos	Cosine	sqrt	Square root
cosh	Hyperbolic cosine	srand	Seed the random number generator
exp	e^x	tan	Tangent
fabs	Absolute value of a double	tanh	Hyperbolic tangent

Memory Allocation Functions

calloc	Allocate storage
free	Free storage
malloc	Allocate storage

Input/Output Functions

†close	Close a file	getchar	Read a character
†creat	Create a file	gets	Read a string
fclose	Close a file	†lseek	Move within a file
fgetc	Read a character	†open	Open a file
fgets	Read a string	printf	Write formatted output
fopen	Open a file	putc	Write a character
fprintf	Write formatted output	putchar	Write a character
fputc	Write a character	puts	Write a string
fputs	Write a string	†read	Read from a file
fread	Read several items	rewind	Move to beginning of file
fscanf	Read formatted input	scanf	Read formatted input
fseek	Move within a file	sprintf	Write formatted output
ftell	Find position within a file	sscanf	Read formatted input
fwrite	Write several items	ungetc	Return a character to a buffer
getc	Read a character	†write	Write to a file

†Input/output function not specified by the standard.

Type and Conversion Functions

atof	Convert string to double
atoi	Convert string to int
atol	Convert string to long
isalnum	Alphanumeric?
isalpha	Alphabetic character?
iscntrl	Control character?
isdigit	Decimal digit?
isgraph	Nonblank, printable character?
islower	Lowercase character?
isprint	Printable character?
ispunct	Punctuation character?
isspace	Space character?
isupper	Uppercase character?
isxdigit	Hexadecimal character?
tolower	Convert from uppercase to lowercase
toupper	Convert from lowercase to uppercase

String Functions

memchr	Find leftmost character in object
memcmp	Compare objects
memcpy	Copy object
memmove	Copy object
strcat	Concatenate strings
strchr	Find leftmost character in string
strcmp	Compare strings
strcpy	Copy string
strcspn	Complement of span
strlen	Length of string
strncat	Concatenate strings
strncmp	Compare strings
strncpy	Copy string
strpbrk	First break character
strrchr	Find rightmost character in string
strspn	Span
strstr	Find substring

Miscellaneous Functions

bsearch	Binary search
clearerr	Clears end-of-file and error indicators
difftime	Compute difference between times
exit	Terminate program
qsort	Quicksort
signal	Invoke a function to handle a signal
system	Execute a command
time	Find time

We now list the functions alphabetically. Each description consists of the file to include, the function's declaration, and a few sentences that describe what the function does. All character codes are given in ASCII. When we write string, it is the address of (pointer to) a sequence of null-terminated, contiguous chars. Each nonstandard input/output function is designated as such, and a warning to consult the documentation of the particular system is included.

abs

```
#include <stdlib.h>
int abs( int integer );
```

Returns the absolute value of integer. See also fabs and labs.

acos

```
#include <math.h>
double acos( double real );
```

Returns the arccosine (in radians) of real. The value returned is between 0 and π.

asin

```
#include <math.h>
double asin( double real );
```

Returns the arcsine (in radians) of real. The value returned is between $-\pi/2$ and $\pi/2$.

atan

```
#include <math.h>
double atan( double real );
```

Returns the arctangent (in radians) of real. The value returned is between $-\pi/2$ and $\pi/2$.

atof

```
#include <stdlib.h>
double atof( const char *string );
```

Converts a real number, represented as `string`, to `double`. Returns the converted number; `string` consists of optional tabs and spaces followed by an optional sign followed by digits followed by an optional decimal point followed by an optional exponent. The optional exponent is `e` or `E` followed by an integer. See also `atoi` and `atol`.

atoi

```
#include <stdlib.h>
int atoi( const char *string );
```

Converts an integer, represented as `string`, to `int`. Returns the converted number; `string` consists of optional tabs and spaces followed by an optional sign followed by digits. See also `atof` and `atol`.

atol

```
#include <stdlib.h>
long atol( const char *string );
```

Converts an integer, represented as `string`, to `long`. Returns the converted number; `string` consists of optional tabs and spaces followed by an optional sign followed by digits. See also `atof` and `atoi`.

bsearch

```
#include <stdlib.h>
void *bsearch( const void *key,
               void *start,
               size_t no_elts,
               size_t size_elt,
               int (*cmp) (const void *, const void *) );
```

Searches for `*key` in a sorted array of size `no_elts` whose initial cell is at address `start`. The parameter `size_elt` is the size in bytes of one cell of the array. The parameter `cmp` is a pointer to a function that compares `*key` and an element in the array and returns an integer to signal the result of the comparison. The first argument to the comparison function `*cmp` is `key` and the second is a pointer to an item in the array. The value of the expression `*cmp( *first, *second )` is negative if `*first` is to the left of `*second` in the sorted order; `*cmp( *first, *second )` is zero if `*first` is equal to `*second`; and `*cmp( *first, *second )` is positive if `*first` is to the right of `*second` in the sorted order. If `*key` is in the array, `bsearch` returns a pointer to a cell containing `*key`; if `*key` is not in the array, `bsearch` returns NULL.

calloc

```
#include <stdlib.h>
void *calloc( size_t n, size_t size );
```

Allocates `n * size` bytes of contiguous storage and sets all bits in the storage to zero. Returns the address of the first byte allocated. If the storage cannot be allocated, `calloc` returns NULL. See also `malloc`.

ceil

```
#include <math.h>
double ceil( double real );
```

Returns the least integer (as a `double`) greater than or equal to `real`.

clearerr

```
#include <stdio.h>
void clearerr( FILE *file_pointer );
```

Clears the end-of-file and error indicators in the file referenced by `file_pointer`.

close

```
int close( int file_descriptor );
```

Closes the file referenced by `file_descriptor`. If successful, `close` returns 0; otherwise, it returns −1. Consult your system documentation for more on this nonstandard input/output function. See also `fclose`.

cos

```
#include <math.h>
double cos( double real );
```

Returns the cosine of `real`; `real` must be in radians.

cosh

```
#include <math.h>
double cosh( double real );
```

Returns the hyperbolic cosine of `real`.

creat

```
int creat( char *string, int mode );
```

Creates the file whose name is pointed to by `string`. The file receives the protection mode given by `mode`; `creat` returns a file descriptor that references the file, or in case of error, it returns −1. The `int` returned can be used in subsequent calls involving nonstandard input/output functions such as `read` and `lseek`. Consult your system documentation for more on this nonstandard input/output function.

difftime

```
#include <time.h>
double difftime( time_t end, time_t begin );
```

Returns the difference (end − begin), in seconds, between the times `end` and `begin`. See also `time`.

exit

```
#include <stdlib.h>
void exit( int status_value );
```

Terminates the program and sends the value status_value to the invoking process (operating system, another program, etc.). The constants EXIT_SUCCESS and EXIT_FAILURE, defined in *stdlib.h*, may be used as arguments to exit to indicate successful or unsuccessful termination. The function exit flushes all buffers and closes all open files.

exp

```
#include <math.h>
double exp( double real );
```

Returns e^{real}, where e (2.71828 . . .) is the base of the natural logarithm. See also pow.

fabs

```
#include <math.h>
double fabs( double real );
```

Returns the absolute value of real. See also abs and labs.

fclose

```
#include <stdio.h>
int fclose( FILE *file_pointer );
```

Closes the file referenced by file_pointer. Flushes all buffers. If successful, fclose returns 0; otherwise, it returns EOF.

fgetc

```
#include <stdio.h>
int fgetc( FILE *file_pointer );
```

Returns the next character from the file referenced by file_pointer, or if the end of the file is reached or an error occurs, it returns EOF. Equivalent to the function getc. See also getc, getchar, and ungetc.

fgets

```
#include <stdio.h>
char *fgets( char *storage, int max_line,
             FILE *file_ pointer );
```

Reads the next line from the file referenced by file_pointer and stores it at address storage. The "next line" consists of

The next max_line − 1 characters.

or

All characters up to and including the next newline character.

or

All characters up to the end of the file.

whichever is shortest. If at least one character is stored, `fgets` adds a terminating null `'\0'` to the end of the line. Notice that `fgets` stores the newline character if it was read, and that `fgets` never stores more than `max_line` characters (including newline and `'\0'`). If no characters are stored or an error occurs, `fgets` returns NULL; otherwise, `fgets` returns the address `storage`. See also `gets`.

floor

```
#include <math.h>
double floor( double real );
```

Returns the greatest integer (as a `double`) less than or equal to `real`.

fopen

```
#include <stdio.h>
FILE *fopen( const char *string, const char *mode );
```

Opens the file whose name is pointed to by `string`. In addition, `fopen` returns the address of a structure that allows access to the file, or in case of error, it returns NULL. The pointer returned can be used in subsequent input/output calls involving functions such as `fread` and `fprintf`.

If mode is `"r"` and the file exists, the file is opened as a text file for reading. Reading commences at the beginning of the file. If the file does not exist, `fopen` returns NULL.

If mode is `"w"`, the file is opened as a text file for writing. A new (initially empty) file is created whether the file exists or not.

If mode is `"a"`, the file is opened as a text file for appending (writing at the end of the file). If the file does not exist, it is created.

If mode is `"r+"` and the file exists, the file is opened as a text file for reading and writing. Reading and writing commence at the beginning of the file. If the file does not exist, `fopen` returns NULL.

If mode is `"w+"`, the file is opened as a text file for reading and writing. A new (initially empty) file is created whether the file exists or not.

If mode is `"a+"`, the file is opened as a text file for reading and writing. Reading and writing commence at the end of the file. If the file does not exist, it is created.

The modes `"ab"`, `"rb"`, and `"wb"` have the same effect as `"a"`, `"r"`, and `"w"` except that the file is opened as a binary file. (See Section 8.1 for a discussion of the distinction between text and binary files.) The modes `"ab+"`, `"rb+"`, and `"wb+"` have the same effect as `"a+"`, `"r+"`, and `"w+"` except that the file is opened as a binary file. The mode `"ab+"`, `"rb+"`, or `"wb+"` may be written `"a+b"`, `"r+b"`, or `"w+b"`, respectively.

fprintf

```
#include <stdio.h>
int fprintf( FILE *file_pointer, const char *string,... );
```

Writes formatted output to the file referenced by file_pointer. The parameter string points to characters to be copied to the output, as well as format specifications for the following arguments. The function fprintf returns the number of characters written, or in case of error, it returns a negative number. See also printf and sprintf.

fputc

```
#include <stdio.h>
int fputc( int character, FILE *file_pointer );
```

Writes character to the file referenced by file_pointer. In addition, fputc returns the character written, or in case of error, it returns EOF. Equivalent to the function putc. See also putc and putchar.

fputs

```
#include <stdio.h>
int fputs( const char *string, FILE *file_pointer );
```

Writes string to the file referenced by file_pointer. The function fputs does *not* add a newline or copy the null terminator to the output. If successful, fputs returns a nonnegative value; in case of error, it returns EOF. See also puts.

fread

```
#include <stdio.h>
size_t fread( void *storage, size_t size,
              size_t count, FILE *file_pointer );
```

Reads up to count items, each of size bytes, from the file referenced by file_pointer. The items are stored in memory, beginning at address storage. The function fread returns the number of items (*not* bytes) read.

free

```
#include <stdlib.h>
void free( void *storage );
```

Frees the area beginning at storage previously allocated by calloc or malloc.

fscanf

```
#include <stdio.h>
int fscanf( FILE *file_pointer, const char *string,... );
```

Reads formatted input from the file referenced by file_pointer. The converted data are stored at addresses given by the arguments that follow string, which contains the format specifications for the data read. If the end of the file is reached before any conversion, fscanf returns EOF; otherwise, it returns the number of items read and stored. See also scanf and sscanf.

fseek

```
#include <stdio.h>
int fseek( FILE *file_pointer, long offset, int base );
```

Repositions the file position marker in the file referenced by file_pointer. In a binary file, fseek repositions the file position marker offset bytes from the beginning of the file (if base is equal to SEEK_SET), from the current position of the file position marker (if base is equal to SEEK_CUR), or from the end of the file (if base is equal to SEEK_END). In a text file, base must be equal to SEEK_SET and offset must be either zero (in which case the file position marker is moved to the beginning of the file) or a value returned previously by ftell (in which case the file position marker is moved to a previously saved position). If successful, fseek returns 0; otherwise, it returns a nonzero value. See also ftell and rewind.

ftell

```
#include <stdio.h>
long ftell( FILE *file_pointer );
```

Returns the location of the file position marker in the file referenced by file_pointer, or in case of error, it returns -1. If the file is a binary file, the location is measured in bytes from the beginning of the file. If the file is a text file, the value returned by ftell is useful only as an argument to fseek. See also fseek.

fwrite

```
#include <stdio.h>
size_t fwrite( const void *storage, size_t size,
               size_t count, FILE *file_pointer );
```

Writes count items from address storage (unless an error occurs), each of size bytes, to the file referenced by file_pointer. Returns the number of items written.

getc

```
#include <stdio.h>
int getc( FILE *file_pointer );
```

The function getc is equivalent to fgetc, except that getc is usually implemented as a macro. The function getc returns the next character from the file referenced by file_pointer, or if the end of the file is reached or an error occurs, it returns EOF. See also fgetc, getchar, and ungetc.

getchar

```
#include <stdio.h>
int getchar( void );
```

Returns the next character from the standard input, or if the end of the file is reached or an error occurs, it returns EOF. See also fgetc, getc, and ungetc.

gets

```
#include <stdio.h>
char *gets( char *storage );
```

Reads the next line from the standard input. The "next line" consists of all characters up to and including the next newline character or the end of the file, whichever comes first. If at least one character is read, gets stores at address storage all characters read except the newline that is discarded and adds a terminating null to the end of the line. Notice that gets never stores a newline character. If no characters are stored or an error occurs, gets returns NULL; otherwise, gets returns the address storage. See also fgets.

isalnum

```
#include <ctype.h>
int isalnum( int character );
```

Returns a nonzero integer if character is an alphanumeric character ('a' through 'z', 'A' through 'Z', or '0' through '9'); otherwise, it returns 0.

isalpha

```
#include <ctype.h>
int isalpha( int character );
```

Returns a nonzero integer if character is an alphabetic character ('a' through 'z' or 'A' through 'Z'); otherwise, it returns 0.

iscntrl

```
#include <ctype.h>
int iscntrl( int character );
```

Returns a nonzero integer if character is a control character (integer value decimal 127 or less than decimal 32); otherwise, it returns 0.

isdigit

```
#include <ctype.h>
int isdigit( int character );
```

Returns a nonzero integer if character is a decimal digit ('0' through '9'); otherwise, it returns 0.

isgraph

```
#include <ctype.h>
int isgraph( int character );
```

Returns a nonzero integer if character is a nonblank printing character (integer value greater than or equal to decimal 33 and less than or equal to decimal 126); otherwise, it returns 0.

islower

```
#include <ctype.h>
int islower( int character );
```

Returns a nonzero integer if `character` is a lowercase character ('a' through 'z'); otherwise, it returns 0.

isprint

```
#include <ctype.h>
int isprint( int character );
```

Returns a nonzero integer if `character` is a printable character (integer value greater than or equal to decimal 32 and less than or equal to decimal 126); otherwise, it returns 0.

ispunct

```
#include <ctype.h>
int ispunct( int character );
```

Returns a nonzero integer if `character` is a punctuation character (integer value decimal 127 or integer value less than decimal 33); otherwise, it returns 0.

isspace

```
#include <ctype.h>
int isspace( int character );
```

Returns a nonzero integer if `character` is a space character (space, tab, carriage return, form feed, vertical tab, or newline—decimal 32 or greater than decimal 8 and less than decimal 14); otherwise, it returns 0.

isupper

```
#include <ctype.h>
int isupper( int character );
```

Returns a nonzero integer if `character` is an uppercase character ('A' through 'Z'); otherwise, it returns 0.

isxdigit

```
#include <ctype.h>
int isxdigit( int character );
```

Returns a nonzero integer if `character` is a hexadecimal digit ('0' through '9', 'a' through 'f', or 'A' through 'F'); otherwise, it returns 0.

labs

```
#include <stdlib.h>
long labs( long integer );
```

Returns the absolute value of `integer`. See also `abs` and `fabs`.

log

```
#include <math.h>
double log( double real );
```

Returns the natural logarithm (log to the base *e*) of `real`.

log10

```
#include <math.h>
double log10( double real );
```

Returns the logarithm to the base 10 of `real`.

lseek

```
long lseek( int file_descriptor, long offset, int base );
```

Repositions the file position marker in the file referenced by `file_descriptor` `offset` bytes from the beginning of the file (if `base` is 0), from the current position of the file position marker (if `base` is 1), or from the end of the file (if `base` is 2). In addition, `lseek` returns the number of bytes from the beginning of the file to the new position of the file position marker, or in case of error, it returns -1. Consult your system documentation for more on this nonstandard input/output function. See also `fseek`.

malloc

```
#include <stdlib.h>
void *malloc( size_t size );
```

Allocates `size` bytes of contiguous storage. Returns the address of the first byte allocated. If the storage cannot be allocated, `malloc` returns NULL. See also `calloc`.

memchr

```
#include <string.h>
void *memchr( const void *block,
              int character,
              size_t numb );
```

Returns the address of the first occurrence of `character` in the first numb bytes of the object at address `block`, or if `character` does not appear in the first numb bytes of the object, it returns NULL. On some systems, `memchr` may execute faster than `strchr`. See also `strchr` and `strrchr`.

memcmp

```
#include <string.h>
int memcmp( const void *block1,
            const void *block2,
            size_t numb );
```

Compares the first numb bytes of the object at address `block1` with the first numb bytes of the object at address `block2`. Returns zero if the item at `block1` is equal to the item at block2. Returns a negative integer if the item at block1 is less than the item at block2. Returns a positive integer if the item at block1 is greater than the item at block2. On some systems, memcmp may execute faster than strncmp. See also strcmp and strncmp.

memcpy

```
#include <string.h>
void *memcpy( void *block1,
              const void *block2,
              size_t numb );
```

Copies the first numb bytes of the object at address block2 into the object at address block1 and returns block1. The copy may not work if the objects overlap. On some systems, memcpy may execute faster than memmove and strncpy. See also memmove, strcpy, and strncpy.

memmove

```
#include <string.h>
void *memmove( void *block1,
               const void *block2,
               size_t numb );
```

Copies the first numb bytes of the object at address block2 into the object at address block1 and returns block1. The objects are allowed to overlap. On some systems, memmove may execute faster than strncpy. See also memcpy, strcpy, and strncpy.

open

```
int open( char *string, int mode );
```

Opens the file whose name is pointed to by string. If mode is 0, the file is opened for reading. If mode is 1, the file is opened for writing. If mode is 2, the file is opened for reading and writing. In addition, open returns a file descriptor that allows access to the file, or in case of error, it returns −1. The int returned can be used in subsequent calls involving nonstandard input/output functions such as read and lseek. Consult your system documentation for more on this nonstandard input/output function. See also fopen.

pow

```
#include <math.h>
double pow( double real1, double real2 );
```

Returns $real1^{real2}$. An error occurs if real1 is negative and real2 is not an integer. See also exp.

printf

```
#include <stdio.h>
int printf( const char *string,... );
```

Writes formatted output to the standard output. The parameter string points to characters to be copied to the output, as well as format specifications for the following arguments. The function printf returns the number of characters written, or in case of error, it returns a negative number. See also fprintf and sprintf.

putc

```
#include <stdio.h>
int putc( int character, FILE *file_pointer );
```

The function putc is equivalent to fputc, except that putc is usually implemented as a macro. The function putc writes character to the file referenced by file_pointer. In addition, putc returns the character written, or in case of error, it returns EOF. See also fputc and putchar.

putchar

```
#include <stdio.h>
int putchar( int character );
```

Writes character to the standard output. In addition, putchar returns the character written, or in case of error, it returns EOF. See also fputc and putc.

puts

```
#include <stdio.h>
int puts( const char *string );
```

Writes string followed by a newline to the standard output. The function puts does *not* copy the null terminator to the output. If successful, puts returns a nonnegative value; in case of error, it returns EOF. See also fputs.

qsort

```
#include <stdlib.h>
void qsort( void *start, size_t no_elts, size_t size_elt,
            int ( *cmp ) ( const void *, const void * ) );
```

Sorts an array of size no_elts whose initial cell is at address start. The parameter size_elt is the size of one cell of the array in bytes. The parameter cmp is a pointer to a function that compares two elements whose data type is the same as that of the array and returns an integer to signal the result of the comparison. The arguments to the comparison function *cmp are pointers to the two items to be compared. The value of the expression *cmp(*first, *second) is negative if *first is to the left of *second in the sorted order; *cmp(*first, *second) is zero if *first is equal to *second; and *cmp(*first, *second) is positive if *first is to the right of *second in the sorted order.

rand

```
#include <stdlib.h>
int rand( void );
```

Returns a pseudorandom integer in the range 0 to RAND_MAX (a macro defined in *stdlib.h*). See also `srand`.

read

```
int read( int file_descriptor, void *storage, int count );
```

Reads `count` bytes from the file referenced by `file_descriptor`. The items are stored in memory beginning at address `storage`. In addition, `read` returns the number of bytes actually read, or in case of error, it returns -1. Consult your system documentation for more on this nonstandard input/output function. See also `fread`.

rewind

```
#include <stdio.h>
void rewind( FILE *file_pointer );
```

Repositions the file position marker in the file referenced by `file_pointer` to the beginning of the file. See also `fseek`.

scanf

```
#include <stdio.h>
int scanf( const char *string,... );
```

Reads formatted input from the standard input. The converted data are stored at addresses given by the arguments that follow `string`, which contains the format specifications for the data read. If the end of the file is reached before any conversion, `scanf` returns EOF; otherwise, it returns the number of items read and stored. See also `fscanf` and `sscanf`.

signal

```
#include <signal.h>
void ( *signal( int sig, void ( *handler ) ( int ) ) )
        ( int );
```

Catches a signal and invokes a function to handle the signal. Signals are sent, for example, when a user interrupts a program and when certain programming errors occur. The function that handles the signal can be either a user-written function or a system function. If the request can be handled, `signal` returns the value of `handler` for the previous call to `signal` for the given `sig`; otherwise, it returns SIG_ERR. For more information, see Appendix F.

sin

```
#include <math.h>
double sin( double real );
```

Returns the sine of `real`, which must be in radians.

sinh

```
#include <math.h>
double sinh( double real );
```

Returns the hyperbolic sine of real.

sprintf

```
#include <stdio.h>
int sprintf( char *storage, const char *string,... );
```

Writes formatted output to memory beginning at address storage. sprintf adds a null terminator to the end of the output. The parameter string points to characters to be copied, as well as format specifications for the following arguments. The function sprintf returns the number of characters written (not counting the added null terminator), or in case of error, it returns a negative number. See also fprintf and printf.

sqrt

```
#include <math.h>
double sqrt( double real );
```

Returns the square root of real.

srand

```
#include <stdlib.h>
void srand( unsigned int seed );
```

Seeds the random number generator. Calling srand with seed equal to 1 is equivalent to calling the random number function rand without first invoking srand. See also rand.

sscanf

```
#include <stdio.h>
int sscanf( const char *string1,
        const char *string2,... );
```

Reads formatted input from string1. The converted data are stored at addresses given by the arguments that follow string2, which contains the format specifications for the data read. If the end of string1 is reached before any conversion, sscanf returns EOF; otherwise, it returns the number of items read and stored. See also fscanf and scanf.

strcat

```
#include <string.h>
char *strcat( char *string1, const char *string2 );
```

Copies string2 to the end of string1. Returns string1 (the address of the first string). See also strncat.

strchr

```
#include <string.h>
char *strchr( const char *string, int character );
```

Returns the address of the first occurrence of character in string, or if
character does not occur in string, it returns NULL. See also strrchr,
strstr, and memchr.

strcmp

```
#include <string.h>
int strcmp( const char *string1,
           const char *string2 );
```

Returns a negative integer if string1 is (lexicographically) less than string2. Returns 0 if string1 is equal to string2. Returns a positive integer if string1 is
greater than string2. See also strncmp and memcmp.

strcpy

```
#include <string.h>
char *strcpy( char *string1, const char *string2 );
```

Copies string2 to string1. Returns string1 (the address of the first string). See
also strncpy, memcpy, and memmove.

strcspn

```
#include <string.h>
size_t strcspn( const char *string1,
               const char *string2 );
```

Returns the number of consecutive characters in string1, beginning with the first, that
do not occur anywhere in string2. See also strspn.

strlen

```
#include <string.h>
size_t strlen( const char *string );
```

Returns the length of string (not counting the null terminator).

strncat

```
#include <string.h>
char *strncat( char *string1, const char *string2,
              size_t max_len );
```

Copies string2 or max_len characters from string2, whichever is shorter, to the
end of string1. In either case, a terminating null is placed at the end. Returns
string1 (the address of the first string). See also strcat.

strncmp

```
#include <string.h>
int strncmp( const char *string1,
            const char *string2, size_t max_len );
```

Let s denote the string obtained by choosing string2 or max_len characters from string2, whichever is shorter. Returns a negative integer if string1 is (lexicographically) less than s. Returns 0 if string1 is equal to s. Returns a positive integer if string1 is greater than s. See also strcmp and memcmp.

strncpy

```
#include <string.h>
char *strncpy( char *string1, const char *string2,
               size_t max_len );
```

Copies exactly max_len characters (counting the null terminator '\0') from string2 to string1. If the length of string2 is less than max_len, null terminators are used to fill string1. The resulting string is *not* null terminated if the length of string2 is greater than or equal to max_len. Returns string1 (the address of the first string). See also strcpy, memcpy, and memmove.

strpbrk

```
#include <string.h>
char *strpbrk( const char *string1,
               const char *string2 );
```

Returns the address of the first character in string1 that occurs anywhere in string2, or if no character in string1 is also in string2, it returns NULL.

strrchr

```
#include <string.h>
char *strrchr( const char *string, int character );
```

Returns the address of the last occurrence of character in string, or if character does not occur in string, it returns NULL. See also strchr, strstr, and memchr.

strspn

```
#include <string.h>
size_t strspn( const char *string1,
               const char *string2 );
```

Returns the number of consecutive characters in string1, beginning with the first, that occur somewhere in string2. See also strcspn.

strstr

```
#include <string.h>
char *strstr( const char *string1,
              const char *string2 );
```

Returns the address of the first occurrence in string1 of string2, or NULL if string2 is not a substring of string1. See also strchr and strrchr.

system

```
#include <stdlib.h>
int system( const char *string );
```

Executes the command `string`. The value returned is implementation dependent. (The value returned usually indicates the exit status of the command executed.)

tan

```
#include <math.h>
double tan( double real );
```

Returns the tangent of `real`, which must be in radians.

tanh

```
#include <math.h>
double tanh( double real );
```

Returns the hyperbolic tangent of `real`.

time

```
#include <time.h>
time_t time( time_t *storage );
```

Returns the time (typically measured in seconds elapsed since midnight, January 1, 1970 GMT). If `storage` is not equal to NULL, `time` stores the current time at address `storage`. See also `difftime`.

tolower

```
#include <ctype.h>
int tolower( int character );
```

Converts `character` from uppercase to lowercase and returns the converted value. If `character` is not `'A'` through `'Z'`, `tolower` simply returns `character`.

toupper

```
#include <ctype.h>
int toupper( int character );
```

Converts `character` from lowercase to uppercase and returns the converted value. If `character` is not `'a'` through `'z'`, `toupper` simply returns `character`.

ungetc

```
#include <stdio.h>
int ungetc( int c, FILE *file_pointer );
```

Writes c to the buffer of the file referenced by `file_pointer` (opposite of `getc`). If c is equal to EOF, the buffer is unchanged. If successful, `ungetc` returns c; otherwise, it returns EOF. See also `fgetc`, `getc`, and `getchar`.

`write`

```
int write( int file_descriptor, void *storage,
           int count );
```

Writes `count` bytes from address `storage` to the file referenced by `file_descriptor`. In addition, `write` returns the number of bytes actually written, or in case of error, it returns −1. Consult your system documentation for more on this nonstandard input/output function. See also `fwrite`.

C and UNIX

C is independent of any particular operating system but has close ties to UNIX. For example, most of UNIX is written in C. UNIX provides utilities, such as `make` and `cb`, to aid program development in C, and C programs have straightforward access to the UNIX run-time libraries and system calls. In this appendix, we illustrate some connections between C and UNIX.

UNIX is not standardized as is C, and so UNIX's support for C may differ from one UNIX system to another. Among the widely used UNIX dialects are Berkeley UNIX, AT&T UNIX, and Ultrix. Each dialect itself usually has several versions. Despite UNIX's lack of standardization, many features such as `make` and pipes are nearly standard across UNIX systems and have even been brought over to some non-UNIX systems. Our examples were run under AT&T UNIX System 5, Release 2. This appendix serves as an introduction to C under UNIX, but you should consult your user's manual for your particular system.

On-line Help

`man`

UNIX systems usually furnish an on-line UNIX manual with clarification of its commands. For example, the command `man` (''manual'')

```
% man cc
```

asks the system to display to the standard output the manual pages on the `cc` command. (We are using % as the system prompt.) The `man` command also may be used with benign self-reference. The command

```
% man man
```

asks the system to display information about the man command itself. If you want more information about the commands discussed in this appendix, you may find it convenient to use the man command.

Producing Executable C Programs Under UNIX

C source code is translated into an executable program in three stages under UNIX. In the first stage, the C preprocessor reads one or more source files, processes these files in accordance with directives such as #define and #include, and produces one or more output files that are then ready for the compiler. A source file typically has a *.c* extension, for example, *main.c*. In the second stage, the C compiler takes as input one or more preprocessed files and produces as output the same number of *object modules*. An object module receives a *.o* extension by default, for example, *main.o*. In the third stage, the C linker takes as input one or more object modules and produces as output a single *load module*. The load module receives the name *a.out* by default. Only the load module is executable. To run a C program under UNIX is to execute a load module.

UNIX provides a single command to accomplish the three stages of translation. Suppose that the program ROBOT has its component functions spread among three files: *main.c, sensors.c,* and *plans.c.* If we invoke the command cc (''compile c'') and reference the files *main.c, sensors.c,* and *plans.c,*

```
% cc main.c sensors.c plans.c
```

a single load module is produced. (The files can be listed in any order.) The object modules produced along the way, *main.o, sensors.o,* and *plans.o,* are deleted automatically once the load module has been produced. The load module is named *a.out* by default. To execute the load module, the user enters its name

```
% a.out
```

at the system prompt. This simple method of producing a load module requires that the cc command reference files that contain, among them, the *entire* program. Of course, #include directives may be used to access functions or macros from both standard and user-created files and libraries.

The second way of producing a load module from source code involves separate compilation. Suppose that we want to compile each source file in the ROBOT program after it is written. After completing the file *plans.c,* we can compile it separately by issuing the command

```
% cc −c plans.c
```

The −c (''compile'' only) flag specifies that an object module, rather than a load module, should be produced as output. In this case, the object module is named *plans.o,* with *.o* as the standard extension for an object module. After separately compiling each of *main.c, sensors.c,* and *plans.c,* we have the object modules *main.o, sensors.o,* and *plans.o.* These object modules can then be linked by issuing the command

```
% cc main.o plans.o sensors.o
```

The load module is named *a.out.* The cc command can be invoked with any mix of *.c* and *.o* files. For example, the command

```
% cc main.c plans.o sensors.c
```

produces a load module from the source files *main.c* and *sensors.c* and the object module *plans.o*. The load module is again named *a.out*.

The `cc` command allows other options besides −c:

Option	Meaning
−c	Compile separately, producing an object module rather than a load module.
−lm	Load referenced modules from the mathematics library.
−o *name*	Name the resulting load module *name* instead of *a.out,* the default.
−w	Suppress warning messages.
−C	Stop the preprocessor from eliminating comment lines.
−E	Have the preprocessor, but not the compiler, pass over the file and print the result to the standard output.
−O	Use the object-module optimizer.

The flags may be used in combination. For example, the command

```
% cc −o robot −w −O main.c plans.o sensors.o
```

directs UNIX to produce a load module from the files *main.c, plans.o,* and *sensors.o*; to give the load module the name *robot*; to suppress warning messages; and to optimize the object modules. The flags can occur in any order, but the `cc` command must come first, and the file names must follow the flags.

Directories and Paths

UNIX has a hierarchical directory structure. The root directory, whose identifier is the character /, has no parent directory but may have any number of child directories or subdirectories. Any child directory has exactly one parent directory and none or more child directories of its own. Figure F.1 depicts a directory structure with the root directory and various subdirectories.

A file resides in a directory. Its **full path name** lists the names of directories from the root down to the directory in which the file resides. For example,

   /users/fred/robotplans.c

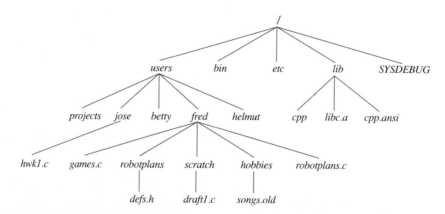

Figure F.1 UNIX directory structure.

is the full path name of the file *robotplans.c*, which resides in the child directory *fred* whose parent directory is *users*, which in turn is a child directory of root (see Figure F.1). A **working directory** is the directory in which you currently find yourself. For example, after you have just logged onto the system, you may find that your working directory is */users/fred*. We next consider some UNIX commands for navigating its directory structure.

pwd, cd

The command pwd ("print working directory") displays the working directory. For example, if the working directory is */users/fred/robotplans*, then

```
% pwd
```

displays

```
/users/fred/robotplans
```

The command cd ("change directory") changes the working directory. For example, if the working directory is */users/fred/robotplans*, then

```
% cd roughdraft
```

changes the working directory to */users/fred/robotplans/roughdraft*, assuming that *roughdraft* is a child directory of */users/fred/robotplans*. The command

```
% cd /users/fred/robotplans/roughdraft
```

has the same effect regardless of what the working directory is, as the command specifies the full path name.

mkdir, rmdir

Directories may be created with the mkdir ("make directory") command and destroyed with the rmdir ("remove directory") command. If the working directory is */users/fred*, then the command

```
% mkdir scratch
```

creates a child directory whose full path name is */users/fred/scratch*. The command

```
% mkdir /users/fred/scratch
```

would accomplish the same thing regardless of the working directory, assuming that the directory */users/fred/scratch* did not already exist because it is an error to create a directory that already exists. The command

```
% rmdir /users/fred/scratch
```

removes the directory */users/fred/scratch* if the directory contains no files, including subdirectories of its own. (Technically, a UNIX directory is a special kind of file.)

rm

Files may be removed with the rm ("remove") command. The command

```
% rm /users/fred/scratch/draft1.c
```

removes the file *draft1.c* from the directory */users/fred/scratch*. The more dangerous command

```
% rm /users/fred/scratch/*
```

removes all files, but not subdirectories, from */users/fred/scratch*. The star * is a wildcard character that matches any file name that is not itself a subdirectory name. The extremely powerful and comparably dangerous command

```
% rm -r /users/fred
```

removes all files in */users/fred*—including all files and subdirectories that have */users/fred* in their full path name. For example, the command would remove all files from */users/fred/scratch*, */users/fred/goodstuff*, and */users/fred/robotplans*—and apply the `rmdir` command to these subdirectories in the process. The −r in the command stands for "recursive" to suggest that the `rm` command works its way down the subdirectories starting at the specified directory.

ls, cat, pr, lp, more

UNIX provides various commands for displaying files, finding files, finding contents of files, and copying or moving files. The command `ls` ("list") lists files in the working directory, except those such as *.profile* or *.login* whose names begin with the period. The command

```
% ls -a
```

lists all such files, including those such as *.profile* whose names do begin with the period. The `ls` command also can be used with the wildcard character and with full path names. For example, the command

```
% ls /users/fred/robotplans/*.h
```

lists all files with a *.h* extension in the subdirectory */users/fred/robotplans*, whatever the working directory may be.

The command `cat` ("concatenate")

```
% cat walk.c talk.c chew_gum.c
```

displays to the standard output the contents of files *walk.c, talk.c*, and *chew_gum.c* if these files reside in the working directory. Again, `cat` may specify the full path name, as in

```
% cat /users/fred/robotplans/defs.h
```

The `pr` ("print") command behaves similarly to the `cat` command, except that it does some formatting. For example, `pr` breaks the displayed text into numbered pages, whereas `cat` does not. Either command may be used with wildcard characters as, for example, in the command

```
% pr /users/fred/robotplans/*.h
```

which formats and displays the contents of all files with a *.h* extension in the specified directory.

If we `cat` or `pr` a file that has too many lines to be displayed all at once, UNIX simply displays the lines without pausing so that the top lines cannot be seen when the bottom ones are finally displayed. A solution is to use the `more` command, which stops after displaying as many lines as will fit on the display. An example is

```
% more /users/fred/scratch/draft1.c
```

After the screen fills, to advance one line, the user hits *Return*; to advance one full screen, the user hits the space bar.

The command `lp` ("line printer") sends a designated file to the line printer. For example, the command

```
% lp /users/fred/robotplans/defs.h
```

requests that the file */users/fred/robotplans/defs.h* be printed. Later in this appendix we explain how the `pr` and `lp` commands may be combined.

grep, find

The command `grep` ("grab regular expression") can be used to search a file for a pattern, and the command `find` ("find") can be used to find a file. Suppose, for example, that we want to find all occurrences of the pattern

```
misanthrope
```

in any file with a *.txt* extension in the working directory. The command

```
% grep misanthrope *.txt
```

does the job by displaying to the standard output any line in the file that contains the pattern `misanthrope`. If the pattern contains white space, it should be enclosed in single quotation marks. For example, the command

```
% grep 'My Blue Heaven' /users/fred/hobbies/songs.old
```

searches the file */users/fred/hobbies/songs.old* for the pattern

```
My Blue Heaven
```

and displays to the standard output any lines containing this pattern.

The `find` command can be used to locate a file. Suppose, for example, that we want to find the file *plans.c*. We are not sure in which directory it resides but suspect that the directory begins */users*. The command

```
% find /users -name plans.c -print
```

asks UNIX to search for the file named *plans.c*, starting at the directory */users*, and to print the file's full path name if it is found. (On some systems, the `-print` option may not be required.) The search begins at directory */users* and descends through all subdirectories.

cp, mv

UNIX has commands to copy and move files. The command `cp` ("copy") makes a copy of a specified file, whereas the command `mv` ("move") moves a specified file. For example, the command

```
% cp /users/fred/games.c /tmp/hide.c
```

copies the file */users/fred/games.c* to the file */tmp/hide.c*. If the latter file does not already exist, UNIX creates it; if it does exist, UNIX overwrites the previous contents with */users/fred/games.c*. Accordingly, cp should be used with caution.

The command

```
% mv /users/fred/games.c newgames.c
```

moves */users/fred/games.c* to the file *newgames.c* in the working directory. Again, UNIX creates *newgames.c* if it does not exist already and overwrites it otherwise. After the mv command, the file */users/fred/games.c* ceases to exist; after the cp command, */users/fred/games.c* continues to exist.

Program Development Under UNIX

UNIX provides several utilities to help the programmer develop source code. We consider two such utilities here: cb ("C beautifier") and make.

cb

Consider the following source code, which fails to use indentation and other conventions that make programs more readable:

```
main(){ int number; int odd_or_even( void );
printf( "\n\n\tEnter a number\n" ); scanf( "%d",
&number );
if ( odd_or_even( number ) == 0 )
printf( "even" ); else printf( "odd" ); }
```

If the code resides in file *ugly.c,* the command

```
% cb ugly.c
```

writes the following version to the standard output:

```
main() {
    int number;
    int odd_or_even( void );
    printf( "\n\n\tEnter a number\n" );
    scanf( "%d", &number );
    if ( odd_or_even( number ) == 0 )
        printf( "even" );
    else printf( "odd" );
}
```

Although the preceding code might be beautified even further, it greatly improves the original version.

make

Suppose that you are working on a large program that has many component functions. You could put all the functions in a single file and simply recompile the entire file every time you add a new function, correct an error, or make any other changes; but if you make only a minor change to the file, it will become tedious to have to recompile the entire file. On the other hand, if you divide the functions among various files and then make changes to only a few files, you must remember exactly which files to recompile; then you have to link all the object modules to produce a load module. The UNIX make utility (also available in Turbo C) addresses just this problem. It allows you to divide a program's component functions among various files. Whenever you alter a file, it takes note of the fact and recompiles only the altered file. It then links the resulting object module with the others to produce an executable program. We clarify this with a short example.

Suppose that you have a program that computes your taxes and has the following modules:

Module	Sketch of Its Role
globals.h	Definitions of macros; referenced in all functions.
defs.h	Definitions used only in *expenses.c*.
taxes	The load module (executable program).
main.c	Invokes income and expenses.
income.c	Computes income.
expenses.c	Computes expenses.

To use the make utility, we first create a file called *makefile*, which looks like

```
taxes: main.o income.o expenses.o
     cc -o taxes main.o income.o expenses.o
main.o: globals.h main.c
     cc -c main.c
income.o: globals.h income.c
     cc -c income.c
expenses.o: globals.h defs.h expenses.c
     cc -c expenses.c
```

The file has two types of commands. The unindented commands, such as

```
taxes: main.o income.o expenses.o
```

are *dependency descriptions*. A dependency description shows which modules depend on other modules in the sense that certain modules are needed to produce another module. This particular dependency description shows that the (load) module *taxes* depends on the object modules *main.o, income.o,* and *expenses.o*. The indented commands, such as

```
cc -o taxes main.o income.o expenses.o
```

are *compile-link descriptions*. A compile-link description shows what needs to be compiled and/or linked to obtain the required module. This particular compile-link description shows the command that links *main.o, income.o,* and *expenses.o* to obtain *taxes*. Our example *makefile* also shows that *main.o* depends on *globals.h* and *main.c; income.o* depends on *globals.h* and *income.c*; and *expenses.o* depends on *globals.h, defs.h,* and *expenses.c*. Furthermore, we obtain *main.o* by compiling *main.c*; we obtain *income.o* by compiling *income.c*; and we obtain *expenses.o* by compiling *expenses.c*.

On most UNIX systems, a dependency description must begin in column 1 of *makefile*, and the entire description must occur on a single line. The compile-link description occurs on its own line but on most systems must begin with a tab character.

Once *makefile* has been built, we invoke the `make` utility by entering

```
% make
```

at the command level. If nothing needs to be done, the system responds

```
'taxes' is up to date
```

Otherwise, the utility recompiles and links any modules that have been changed since the last invocation of `make`. In our example, any change to *globals.h* would result in the recompilation and relinking of all modules. By contrast, a change to *main.c* would result only in the recompilation of the module *main.c* and the relinking of *main.o* with the other object modules.

The *make* utility compiles all files with the −0 option for optimization. On most UNIX systems, the `make` command itself usually can be invoked with various options. For example, the command

```
% make −f XyZ
```

invokes the `make` utility, but the utility uses the file named *XyZ* instead of the file named *makefile*. The `make` utility also can be used in place of a command such as

```
% cc −o games games.c
```

which compiles and links the source file *games.c* to produce the load module *games*. An equivalent but more convenient command is

```
% make games
```

Executing UNIX Commands from Within a C Program

In Section 6.8, we showed how a C program could interact with the operating system by passing command line arguments to a C program. UNIX provides additional interfaces between UNIX and C programs. We focus on the library function `system` and show how it can be used to execute UNIX commands. The function `system` is declared in the header *stdlib.h* and is mandated by the standard.

Consider the following program:

```c
#include <stdio.h>
#include <stdlib.h>
#define  NL      putchar( '\n' )
#define  FORMAT  NL, NL, NL
main()
{
    /* Print user's login name; show other users logged on;    */
    /* print current month's calendar; pause five minutes for   */
    /* coffee; and exit.                                        */
    FORMAT;
    printf( "YOUR LOGNAME:" );
    NL;
    system( "logname" );      /* print user's login name */
    FORMAT;
    printf( "YOUR FELLOW USERS:" );
```

```
NL;
system( "who" );      /* print login names of other users */
FORMAT;
printf( "CURRENT MONTH'S CALENDAR:" );
NL;
system ( "cal" );           /* print calendar */
FORMAT;
printf( "5 MINUTE BREAK FOR COFFEE:" );
NL;
printf( " SLEEPING... PLEASE DO NOT DISTURB..." );
system( "sleep 300" );    /* pause 300 seconds */
FORMAT;
printf( "5 MINUTES ARE UP—TIME TO START WORKING!" );
}
```

Each argument to the function `system` is a string that specifies the UNIX command to execute. For example, the line

```
system( "sleep 300" );
```

executes the UNIX command

```
% sleep 300
```

Of course, when we enter a UNIX command in response to the UNIX prompt, we do not enclose it in quotation marks; however, we must enclose the command in quotation marks when we pass it as an argument to the function `system`.

Handling Exceptions

An *exception* is an unusual event that occurs during processing. For example, an exception occurs if the result of a floating-point computation is too large or too small to store in a floating-point cell. Computer systems generate a *signal* to indicate the occurrence of an exception. When a signal is generated, the operating system responds to the signal in some appropriate way (e.g., by aborting the program and printing an error message). A C program under UNIX can detect signals and then invoke its own functions, known as *exception handlers,* to respond to the exception in a user-defined way.

The UNIX header file *sys/signal.h* contains macros whose values are integers that represent signals. (On some systems and in standard C, the header file is simply *signal.h*.) The list of macros together with their values and meanings for UNIX 5.2 follows:

Symbolic Constant	Value	Meaning
SIGHUP	01	Hang up
SIGINT	02	Interrupt
SIGQUIT	03	Quit
SIGILL	04	Illegal instruction
SIGTRAP	05	Trace trap
SIGIOT	06	IOT instruction
SIGEMT	07	EMT instruction
SIGFPE	08	Floating-point exception
SIGKILL	09	Kill
SIGBUS	10	Bus error

Symbolic Constant	Value	Meaning
SIGSEGV	11	Segmentation violation
SIGSYS	12	Bad argument to system call
SIGPIPE	13	Pipe with no reader
SIGALRM	14	Alarm clock
SIGTERM	15	Software termination signal
SIGUSR1	16	User-defined signal 1
SIGUSR2	17	User-defined signal 2
SIGCLD	18	Death of a child process
SIGPWR	19	Power failure

The library function `signal` can be used to catch a signal. (The function `signal` is also specified by the standard.) The first argument to `signal` is one of the mnemonics in the preceding table. The second argument is a function that handles the exception. This function can be a user-written function or either SIG_DFL or SIG_IGN, which are defined in *sys/signal.h*. The meaning of these terms is given in the following table:

Symbolic Constant	Meaning
SIG_DFL	Terminates program when a specified signal is caught.
SIG_IGN	Ignores a specified signal. (SIGKILL cannot be ignored, however.)

A C program that traps a signal may handle it one of three ways:

- Terminate itself if the response to the signal is set to SIG_DFL.
- Ignore the signal, except for SIGKILL, if the response to the signal is set to SIG_IGN.
- Invoke a user-definition function that responds to the signal in its own way.

We illustrate with two examples.

Example.   Suppose that we have a data entry program and expect the user occasionally to hit a wrong key. Under UNIX, hitting a key such as "break" or "rubout" causes a currently executing program to terminate. We want our data entry program to ignore a user-generated interrupt of this kind. The following program sketch illustrates a method of trapping this exception:

```
#include <stdio.h>
#include <sys/signal.h>
main( )
{
     /* variable and function declarations */
          .
          .
          .

     /* Ignore keyboard-generated interrupts. */
     signal( SIGINT, SIG_IGN );
     /* data entry tasks */
          .
          .
          .
}
```

An alternative to using a system-provided interrupt handler is to write our own. For example, we might caution the user about striking the "break" or "rubout" keys. (Such a caution, if repeated too often, may be very bad for morale, of course.) We illustrate with an example.

Example.   The following program shows a user-written interrupt handler:

```c
#include <stdlib.h>
#include <stdio.h>
#include <sys/signal.h>
main()
{
    /* variable and function declarations */
    int  handler( int sig ); /* interrupt handlers return an int */
        .
        .
        .

    /* Invoke handler() in case of keyboard-generated interrupt. */
    signal( SIGINT, handler );
    /* data entry tasks */
        .
        .
        .

}
int  handler( int sig )
/* the signal SIGINT automatically passed to handler */
{
    /* Print cautionary message. */
    printf( "\nPlease take care not to hit the BREAK"
            "\nor RUBOUT keys as this terminates the"
            "\nprogram. You must restart." );
    exit( EXIT_SUCCESS );
}
```

The interrupt handler of the preceding example terminates the program with a call to the library function `exit`. What if we want the program to resume by having the interrupt handler return to its invoking function? This can be done under UNIX, but the specifics are implementation dependent. On some systems, for example, the function that invoked the interrupt handler resumes execution at the instruction that generated the interrupt. Solving the problem may require the programmer to mark where execution should be resumed after the interrupt handler returns and explicitly to resume execution at that mark. In sum, you need to consult the user's manual for the specifics about resuming execution after trapping exceptions.

Pipes

Suppose that we have an executable program *stock_tips* that reads from the standard input, processes the data read, and then writes to the standard output. The UNIX command

```
% stock_tips < market.dat
```

causes *stock_tips* to read from the file *market.dat* instead of from the standard input. The input has been redirected (see Section 1.9). The command

```
% stock_tips > tips.dat
```

causes *stock_tips* to write to the file *tips.dat* instead of to the standard output. The output has been redirected. The command

```
% stock_tips < market.dat > tips.dat
```

causes *stock_tips* to read from the file *market.dat* instead of from the standard input and to write to the file *tips.dat* instead of to the standard output. Both the input and the output have been redirected.

UNIX also supports the *pipe,* a utility through which one program's output becomes another program's input. For example, suppose that we have an executable program *report_tips* that can generate a report from the output of *stock_tips.* We could combine the programs by executing the following UNIX commands:

```
% stock_tips > temp.dat
% report_tips < temp.dat
```

stock_tips reads from the standard input and writes to *temp.dat,* after which *report_tips* reads from *temp.dat* and writes to the standard output. A pipe accomplishes the same result, but more conveniently:

```
% stock_tips | report_tips
```

The vertical bar | designates a pipe. *stock_tips* pipes its output into *report_tips,* which then writes to the standard output.

A *pipeline* may be built out of individual pipes. Suppose that we want the output of *stock_tips* to be sorted before it is formatted by *report_tips* and written to the standard output and that we have a program *sort_tips* that does the sorting. We could build a pipeline as follows:

```
% stock_tips | sort_tips | report_tips
```

The input to *stock_tips* is the standard input. Because of the first pipe, the output of *stock_tips* is the input to *sort_tips.* Because of the second pipe, the output of *sort_tips* is the input to *report_tips,* and *report_tips* writes to the standard output.

Pipes can be combined with redirection. The following command is the same as the preceding command except that the report is written to the file *report.dat*:

```
% stock_tips | sort_tips | report_tips > report.dat
```

As we have previously seen, any UNIX command can be invoked from within a C program by using the library function `system`. The following program sketch shows how we might execute the previous command from within a C program:

```
#include <stdio.h>
#include <stdlib.h>
main()
{    /* variable definitions and function declarations */
         .
         .
         .

    /* the pipeline */
```

```
system( "stock_tips | sort_tips | report_tips > report.dat" );
         .
         .
         .
}
```

Pipes may be combined with various other commands in quite powerful ways. Consider the `pr`, `lp`, `more`, and `man` commands discussed earlier. To format the file */users/fred/robotplans/defs.h* and print it, we pipe the output of `pr` to `lp`:

```
% pr /users/fred/robotplans/defs.h | lp
```

Similarly, to format the file */users/project/large.c* and display it a screen at a time, we pipe the output of `pr` to `more`:

```
% pr /users/project/large.c | more
```

As a final example, suppose that we want a printed copy of the UNIX manual pages on the command `grep`. The command

```
% man grep | lp
```

redirects the output of `man` to `lp`, which gives us a printed copy. UNIX encourages its users to become pipers.

Run-Time Libraries

System header files such as *math.h* usually contain function declarations in addition to macros and `typedef`s. For example, the header file *math.h* includes declarations such as

```
extern double pow( double, double );
extern double floor( double );
extern double ceil( double );
```

because the standard requires that an implementation provide these three functions, among others. The implementation typically provides the functions themselves as object modules collected in a run-time library, that is, a library of functions that an applications program can access at run time but for which the source code is not available. For example, the functions declared in *math.h* are available in most UNIX systems in the run-time library *libm.a*. To access the functions in this library, an applications program typically must be linked explicitly with this library. This can be done by using the −lm option in the `cc` command. For instance, if we wrote statistics functions that needed mathematics functions such as `pow`, `floor`, and `ceil`, and placed these functions in the file *stats.c*, our `cc` command might look like this:

```
% cc -c stats.c -lm
```

The −lm option in the command directs the linker to the library named *libm.a*. If the `cc` command succeeds, the object module produced, *stats.o*, contains not only the functions defined in *stats.c* but also any functions in *libm.a*, such as `pow`, invoked in *stats.c*.

In general, run-time libraries have names of the pattern *libNAME.a*, where *NAME* identifies the particular library. To take a second example, most UNIX implementations provide a library named *libcurses.a*, which contains functions for screen management and basic graphics. This library, too, can be linked through the −l option in the `cc` command:

```
% cc -c cusses_with_curses.c -lcurses
```

In the two preceding examples, the −1 option does not give the full path name for a library because UNIX searches one or more default directories to find a specified library. Many run-time libraries, such as *libm.a* and *libcurses.a*, reside in the directory */usr/lib*.

Programmers often find it useful to build run-time libraries of their own, thereby allowing the component functions to be shared among many different applications programs. It is common for each such library to have its own header file that contains declarations for the functions implemented in the library. The library and the header file could be located in any directory, but it is convenient to place them in default directories so that their full path names need not be given in #include directives or −1 options. The C preprocessor, when encountering an #include directive with a header file name in angle brackets, searches one or more default directories for the header file. A familiar example is

```
#include <stdio.h>
```

Many system header files, such as *stdio.h*, reside in the directory */usr/include*. If our header files reside in a default directory, angle brackets may be used in the corresponding #include directive. If our run-time library's name follows the pattern *libNAME.a* and resides in a default directory, the −1 option in the cc command need not give the library's full path name. We illustrate with a short example that assumes */usr/include* is a default directory for header files and that */usr/lib* is a default directory for run-time libraries.

Suppose that we want to build a library of statistical functions for use in a variety of applications programs. We create a header file */usr/include/stats.h*, which contains function declarations such as

```
/* median of n doubles */
extern double median( double nums[], int n );

/* mean of n doubles */
extern double mean( double nums[], int n );

/* variance of n doubles */
extern double var( double nums[], int n, double mean );
```

An applications program now can #include our header file with the directive

```
#include <stats.h>
```

Definitions for our statistical functions, which invoke mathematics functions such as pow and floor, reside in the file *stats.c*. Accordingly, we compile *stats.c* with the −1m option:

```
% cc −c stats.c −lm
```

The object module produced, *stats.o*, contains our functions and ones from the mathematics library. Next, we use the object module to create a run-time library named, say, *libstats.a* and we move *libstats.a* to a default library directory such as */usr/lib*. (On most UNIX systems, a run-time library is created from one or more object modules by using the ld command with specified flags.) An applications program that needs to access our run-time library should have the #include directive for *stats.h* in the appropriate source files and should use the −1 option in the cc command:

```
% cc −o small_lies source.c −lstats
```

Note that the application sees no distinction between our run-time library and one furnished by a UNIX system.

Compiling, Linking, and Running a C Program in Turbo C, VAX/VMS, and UNIX

G

This appendix summarizes the commands for compiling, linking, and running a C program in Turbo C, VAX/VMS, and UNIX. We first discuss the situation when the entire program resides in one file.

Turbo C++ 1.0 Under MS-DOS (One File)

Turbo C++, version 1.0, includes ANSI C as a subset. Turbo C++ provides two different ways to compile programs. One is similar to the other systems described here. Suppose that we have a program that resides in the file *convert.c*. To compile and link the program, we issue the command

```
C> tcc convert.c
```

(We assume that C> is the system prompt.) The executable file is named *convert.exe*. To run the program, we type

```
C> convert
```

Turbo C++ also provides an integrated environment, which is a menu-driven system that includes a compiler, linker, editor, and debugger. The integrated environment is invoked by issuing the command

```
C> tc
```

The user is presented with a screen divided into two windows—a window at the top to edit a file and a window at the bottom for messages (see Figure G.1). In addition, a menu is given at the top of the screen and a reference line is given at the bottom. Main menu items can be selected by using a mouse or by pressing *Alt* and the identifying letter (usually the first letter) of the desired item simultaneously. For example, to select the compile option, press *Alt-c*.

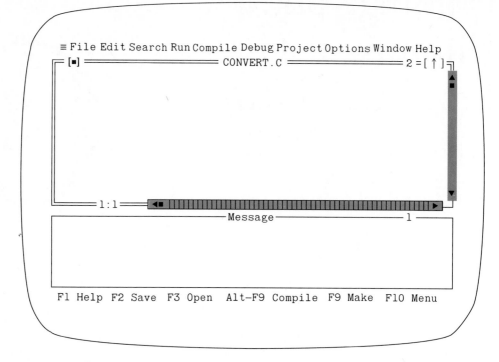

Figure G.1 Turbo C++ 1.0 integrated environment screen.

To create the file *convert.c,* choose *File* in the main menu. (Select *File* by pressing *Alt-f.*) Another menu pops up with several options. Select *Open* by hitting *o* (the "oh" key). In the box provided, type *convert.c,* the name of the file to edit, and hit *Return.* At this point, Turbo C++ transfers control to the editor and the screen will be that shown in Figure G.1. Type in the program. Figure G.2 summarizes some of the most commonly used editor commands.

After typing in the program, to compile, link, and run it, select *Run* on the main menu by pressing *Alt-r.* Another menu pops up with several options. Select *Run* by hitting *r.* Turbo C++ tries to compile and link the program and, if successful, it then runs the program. When the program is run, the screen clears, the program executes, and control is returned to the Turbo C++ screen. To view the previous screen in which the program was run, hit *Alt-F5.* To return from the program screen to the Turbo C++ screen, hit any key.

If an error is detected by the compiler or linker, a message will be displayed in a special window that gives information about the compilation and linking process. To correct the errors, first leave the compiler by hitting any key. To correct the first error, hit *Return.* You will automatically be placed into the editor, and the cursor will be at the position in the file that caused the error message to be generated. You can now correct this error.

To correct the next error, hit *Alt-F8,* which moves the cursor to the line that caused the next error message. Since you remain in the editor, the next error can immediately be corrected. *Alt-F7* moves to the previous error and *Alt-F8* moves to the next error. After correcting all the errors, the program can be rerun by typing *Alt-r* and then *r.*

To save the editor file, hit *F2.* To leave any pop-up menu, hit *Esc.* To leave the integrated environment and return to MS-DOS, type *Alt-x.*

Cursor Movement

Movement	Command
Character left	Left arrow
Character right	Right arrow
Line up	Up arrow
Line down	Down arrow
Word left	Ctrl-a
Word right	Ctrl-f
Start of line	Home
End of line	End
Page up	PgUp
Page down	PgDn
Beginning of file	Ctrl-qr
End of file	Ctrl-qc

Insert/Delete

Action	Command
Insert mode on/off	Ins
Delete character	Del
Del char left	Backspace
Del word right	Ctrl-t
Delete line	Ctrl-y

Find/Replace/Block Commands

Action	Command
Find	Ctrl-qf
Find/replace	Ctrl-qa
Begin block	Ctrl-kb
End block	Ctrl-kk
Copy block	Ctrl-kc
Delete block	Ctrl-ky
Hide/display block	Ctrl-kh
Move block	Ctrl-kv

Figure G.2 Commands for the Turbo C++ editor.

When the *convert* program is successfully compiled and linked, the executable file *convert.exe* is created. This file can be run from the MS-DOS command line by typing

```
C> convert
```

VAX-11 C Under VMS (One File)

Suppose that we have a program that resides in the file *convert.c*. To compile the program, we issue the command

```
$ cc convert
```

(We assume that $ is the system prompt.) We must then link the output of the compiler by issuing the command

```
$ link convert
```

To run the program, we type

```
$ run convert
```

C Under UNIX (One File)

Suppose that we have a program that resides in the file *convert.c*. To compile and link the program, we issue the command

```
% cc convert.c -o convert
```

(We assume that % is the system prompt.) The output of the compiler is the file named after −o. In this case, the output of the compiler is the file *convert*. To run the program, we type

```
% convert
```

We next discuss the commands to compile, link, and run a C program in Turbo C, VAX/VMS, and UNIX when a program resides in multiple files. In each example, we assume that a program resides in the files *series.c, sum.c,* and *transform.c* and that the goal is to create an executable module named *series* with an extension appropriate for the particular operating system.

Turbo C++ 1.0 Under MS-DOS (Multiple Files)

To compile and link the three modules from the command line, we issue the command

```
C> tcc series.c sum.c transform.c
```

(We assume that C> is the system prompt.) This command produces the load module *series.exe*. To run the program, we type

```
C> series
```

It is also possible to compile each file individually and then link the resulting object files. In this case, we issue the commands

```
C> tcc -c series.c
C> tcc -c sum.c
C> tcc -c transform.c
```

At this point, we have the object modules *series.obj, sum.obj,* and *transform.obj*. To link these object modules and produce the load module *series.exe*, we issue the command

```
C> tcc series.obj sum.obj transform.obj
```

To compile, link, and run a C program divided among two or more source files in the Turbo C++ integrated environment, we first use the editor to create the files *series.c, sum.c,* and *transform.c* as described previously. We then create a ''project'' that tells Turbo C++ the names of the files that make up the program. To open a project, type *Alt-p* to select *Project* on the main menu and then type *o* (''oh''). In the space provided, type the name of the project. In this example, we might select the name *series*. (By default, all projects have extension *.prj*, so we could just as well have typed *series.prj*.) At this point, the message window at the bottom of the screen is replaced by the project window. To add files to the project, type *Alt-p* to again select *Project*. This time, type *a* (add). A window pops up into which the names of the files that make up the project can be entered. Type in the file names, *series.c*, *sum.c*, and *transform.c*, and terminate each with *Return*. After each file name is entered, it is also displayed in the project window. After all the files are added, hit *Esc* to leave the add pop-up window. To compile the program, select *Compile* by typing *Alt-c*. Then in the compile pop-up window, type *m* (make). Turbo C++ attempts to compile and link all files in the project into an executable file. Errors are flagged and corrected, as described previously. When the files are successfully compiled and linked, hit *Return* to leave the compile message window. To run the program, hit *Alt-r* and then *r*.

When the program is successfully compiled and linked, the executable file *series.exe*, whose name is derived from the project name *series.prj*, is created. This file can be run from the MS-DOS command line by typing

```
C> series
```

(assuming that C> is the system prompt).

VAX-11 C Under VMS (Multiple Files)

To compile the three modules, we issue the command

```
$ cc series + sum + transform
```

(We assume that $ is the system prompt.) We must then link the output of the compiler by issuing the command

```
$ link series
```

To run the program, we type

```
$ run series
```

It is also possible to compile each file individually and then link the resulting object files. In this case, we issue the commands

```
$ cc series
$ cc sum
$ cc transform
```

At this point, we have the object modules *series.obj*, *sum.obj*, and *transform.obj*. To link these object modules and produce the load module *series.exe,* we issue the command

```
$ link series, sum, transform
```

C Under UNIX (Multiple Files)

To compile and link the three modules, we issue the command

```
% cc series.c sum.c transform.c -o series
```

(We assume that % is the system prompt.) This command produces the load module *series*. To run the program, we type

```
% series
```

It is also possible to compile each file individually and then link the resulting object files. In this case, we issue the commands

```
% cc -c series.c
% cc -c sum.c
% cc -c transform.c
```

At this point, we have the object modules *series.o, sum.o,* and *transform.o.* To link these object modules and produce the load module *series,* we issue the command

```
% cc series.o sum.o transform.o -o series
```

Appendix F discusses the UNIX compiler in more detail.

Hints and Solutions to Odd-Numbered Exercises

Section 1.2

1.

```
/*   The program reads a weight in pounds from the keyboard,
     representing it as an integer. It converts the weight to
     ounces, and prints it. */

#include <stdio.h>

main()
{
    int  pounds;
    /* Read first weight in pounds. */
    printf( "\n\n\tWeight in pounds?  " );
    scanf( "%d", &pounds );
    /* Loop until user signals halt with negative integer. */
    while ( pounds >= 0 ) {
        printf( "\n\n\tEquivalent weight in ounces: %d",
            pounds * 16 );
        printf( "\n\n\tWeight in pounds?  " );
        scanf( "%d", &pounds );
    }
}
```

Section 1.3

1. The identifiers name and NAME are distinct because C distinguishes between lowercase and uppercase characters.

3. Legal

5. Illegal—while is a C keyword
7. Illegal—contains a dash, which is an illegal character
9. Illegal—initial tree contains white space (i.e., a blank)
11. No—only the first 31 characters are significant

Section 1.4

1. 7
   5
   3
   1
3. −1
5. 0

Section 1.5

1. x = 2
   x = 0

Section 1.7

1. 5
3. 3
   5
5. The condition in an if statement must be enclosed in parentheses and thus should read:

   ```
   if ( x >= 2 )
   ```

7. Mathematician
   Computer Scientist

Section 1.8

1. 15
3. Yes, the fragments always produce the same output given the same input. The first form is preferable, since it is more efficient when code is 1 or 2. In the second form, each expression, code == 1, code == 2, code == 3, is always evaluated.
5. No, the fragments do not always produce the same output given the same input. For example, if the value of code is 1, the first fragment prints

   ```
   Freshman
   ```

   whereas the second fragment prints

   ```
   Freshman
   Sophomore
   Junior
   ```

Section 1.9

1. The UNIX command with a percent sign % as the system prompt:

```
% convert <data.dat >output.dat
```

3. The VAX/VMS commands with a dollar sign $ as the system prompt:

```
$ define/user sys$input data.dat
$ define/user sys$output output.dat
$ run convert
```

Section 1.10

1. The C statements that open the file *infile.dat* for reading:

```
#include <stdio.h>
main()
{
    FILE *fptr;
    fptr = fopen( "infile.dat", "r" );
        .
        .
        .
}
```

3. The C statements that write the statement

```
Delinquent Taxpayer
```

to the file *output.dat*:

```
#include <stdio.h>
main()
{
    FILE *fp;
    fp = fopen( "output.dat", "w" );
    fprintf( fp, "Delinquent Taxpayer" );
        .
        .
        .
}
```

5.

```
/*  This program modifies the Sample Application of Section 1.2
    as follows:

    1.   The input comes from the file length.dat instead of from
         the keyboard.

    2.   The output goes to the file cvt.dat instead of to the
         display.

    The program stops reading from length.dat when it detects
    EOF. */
```

```c
#include <stdio.h>

main()
{
    FILE *infile, *outfile;
    int  yard, feet, inch;
    infile = fopen( "length.dat", "r" );   /* open length.dat */
    outfile = fopen( "cvt.dat", "w" );      /* open cvt.dat */
    /* Read from length.dat until encountering EOF. Write
       conversion to cvt.dat.  */
    while ( fscanf( infile, "%d", &yard ) != EOF ) {
        feet = 3 * yard;
        inch = 36 * yard;
        fprintf( outfile, "\n%d yd =\n", yard );
        fprintf( outfile, "%d ft\n", feet );
        fprintf( outfile, "%d in\n", inch );
    }
    fclose( infile );       /* close length.dat */
    fclose( outfile );      /* close cvt.dat */
}
```

7.

```c
/*  This program reads integers from scores.dat until it
    encounters EOF. It tracks the sum of the nonnegative
    integers, printing it when all the scores have been read. */

#include <stdio.h>

main()
{
    FILE *infile;
    int  integer, sum;
    infile = fopen( "scores.dat", "r" );  /* open scores.dat */
    sum = 0;
    /* Read and sum scores until EOF. */
    while ( fscanf( infile, "%d", &integer )  != EOF )
        if ( integer >= 0 )
            sum = sum + integer;
    fclose( infile );       /* close scores.dat */
    printf( "\n\n\tThe sum is:  %d\n", sum );
}
```

Section 2.1

    1. 64

    3. -32 through 31, inclusive

Section 2.2

    1. int a, b, c;

    3. int   a = 9, b = -23, c = 0;

5. There are two main differences: (1) Cell storage for a variable of type `char` must be exactly one byte, where the size of a byte depends on the particular computer system; cell storage for a variable of type `int` must not be smaller than one byte and typically is larger. (2) Variables of type `int` hold numbers that usually represent integers, whereas variables of type `char` hold numbers that usually represent characters.

7. Z

9. 90

11. Because the ASCII code of the character 2 is 32 (hex), after

```
int i = '2';
```

we have

i | 00 32 |

Because of the format descriptor `%c`, the code 33 (hex) of the character read by `scanf` is deposited at the address of i, giving us

i | 33 32 |

When we execute

```
printf( "%c\n", i );
```

we print the character 2, whose code 32 is in the least significant byte in cell i. When we execute

```
printf( "%d\n", i );
```

we print 33 32 (hex) in decimal.

Section 2.3

1. `3.99481772e+5`

3. `2.281500e-10`

5. `i = 8`

```
        c = 10
x = 4.249070e+01          x = 42.490700
```

Section 2.4

1. 15

3. 1.433333

5. 13.536978

7. 13

9. 3

11. 8

13. 3

Section 2.5

1.

Expression	Value	Value of Variables
x + y >= z	1	Unchanged
y == x − 2 * z − 1	1	Unchanged
6 * x != x	1	Unchanged
c > d	0	Unchanged
x = y == 4	1	x = 1
(x = y) == 4	1	x = 4
(x = 1) == 1	1	x = 1
2 * c > d	1	Unchanged

3. The programmer probably meant to write && rather than &. A double ampersand denotes the logical and operator, whereas a single ampersand denotes the bitwise and operator (see Section 3.9).

Section 2.6

1. No, because the lines

```
if ( x > max )
      max = x;
else
      min = x;
```

assign x to min if x is less than or equal to the current value of max, and we want to assign x to min only if x is less than the current value of min.

Section 2.7

1. 2
3
4
5
6

3. 6
6

5.
```
#include <stdio.h>

main()
{
      int i;
      int sum = 0;

      for ( i = 2; i <= 100; i += 2 )
            sum += i;
      printf( "sum = %d\n", sum );
}
```

Section 2.8

1. i's value is 4, k's value is 4

3. i's value is 2, k's value is 2

5. i's value is 0, k's value is −1

7. 12

9. x−− −−y   It is not a legal expression.

Section 2.9

1. Input files (b) and (c) work correctly, but input file (a) does not. With file (a) as the input file, the `do while` loop echoes the line (including 48):

```
Action Comics 48
```

Input file (b) works correctly since the first title is on a line by itself, as it should be. After `scanf` reads 48, the next text to read is correctly `Marvel Mystery Comics` (terminated by a newline). Input file (c) works correctly since after `scanf` reads the last value, 43, the `while` loop detects end-of-file and the program terminates normally. (The blank in the format string `" %c"` matches white space if it is present. If there is no white space to match, the blank is, in effect, ignored.)

3. If the blank in the format string were omitted, the next character read would be the newline that follows the integer representing the value of the comic. In this case, the body of the `do while` loop would print an extra newline before echoing the title. Also, the last row of stars would be printed twice, since after printing the last title and the last row of stars, when we next execute

```
while ( scanf( "%c", &c ) != EOF ) {
```

we would read the newline that follows the last integer (which is the last character in the file). In the `do while` loop, we would print the newline and attempt to read another character. Since there are no more characters to read, the value of `c` would be unchanged and the `do while` loop would terminate. Similarly, the attempt to read another integer would fail and the `for` loop would reuse the previous value read, after which the `while` loop would terminate.

Section 3.1

1. 2
bottom of loop
4
bottom of loop
6
bottom of loop

3. 3
bottom of loop
4
bottom of loop
5
bottom of loop

5. 2
4
5

7.
```
#include <stdio.h>
main()
{
    float x, sum;
    int count;

    sum = 0.0;
    count = 0;

    while ( scanf( "%f", &x ) != EOF )
        if ( x > 0.0 ) {
```

```
            sum += x;
            count++;
        }

    if ( count > 0 )
        printf( "\naverage = %f\n", sum / count );
    else
        printf( "\nno positive numbers read\n" );
}
```

Section 3.2

1. Suppose that no integer k satisfying

$$2 \le k \le \sqrt{i}$$

divides i. We show that i is prime. Suppose, by way of contradiction, that i is not prime. Then i has a divisor $d \ge 2$. Now i/d is also a divisor of i. Because no integer k satisfying

$$2 \le k \le \sqrt{i}$$

divides i, we must have

$$d > \sqrt{i} \quad \text{and} \quad i/d > \sqrt{i}$$

We may multiply to obtain

$$i = d(i/d) > \sqrt{i} \cdot \sqrt{i} = i$$

which is a contradiction. Therefore, i is prime.

    If i is prime, obviously no integer k satisfying

$$2 \le k \le \sqrt{i}$$

can divide i.

3. Except for 2 itself, no prime has 2 as a divisor. So, once beyond 2, we generate only odd numbers as both possible primes and possible divisors.

Section 3.3

```
1. Cubs
   *** End of baseball team listing
3. No team
   *** End of baseball team listing
5. Mets
   *** End of baseball team listing
   Royals
   *** End of baseball team listing
   Strike three!
   Strike three!
```

Section 3.5

```
1. 1
   4
   3
```

Section 3.6

1. We need to change only the condition in the do while loop:

```
do {
    printf( "Enter day and leap year codes: " )
    scanf( "%d%d", &day_code, &leap_year );
} while ( day_code < 0 || day_code > 6 ||
            leap_year < 0 || leap_year > 1 );
```

Section 3.7

1. z = (double) x / (double) y;

Section 3.8

1. klm

3.

```
/* This program checks whether the standard input has the same
   number of left as right brackets. */
#include <stdio.h>
main()
{
    int next_char, left_count = 0, right_count = 0;

    while ( ( next_char = getchar() ) != EOF )
        if ( next_char == '[' )
            ++left_count;
        else if ( next_char == ']' )
            ++right_count;

    if ( left_count == right_count )
        printf( "\nYes\n" );
    else
        printf( "\nNo\n" );
}
```

5. 1
1
1

Section 3.9

1. 111
111
−67

3. 194
244

5. The int read is odd if and only if its rightmost bit is 1. As a bit string, mask is equal to 00 . . . 001; thus, the value of

```
input & mask
```

is equal to mask if the rightmost bit of input is 1, and has all bits 0 if the rightmost bit of input is 0. To put it another way, the value of input & mask is 1 if input is odd and 0 if input is even.

7. Using the ideas of Exercise 6, we may write

```
int min_int = 1, max_int;
while ( min_int > 0 )
      min_int << = 1;
max_int = ~min_int;
```

Because min_int is 100...00, max_int is 011...11.

9. The values of a and b are interchanged.

11.

```
#include <stdio.h>
main( )
{
      int mask, input, i;

      while ( scanf( "%d", &input ) != EOF ) {
            mask = -32768; /* mask is 1000...00 */

            /*   Print 1 if the leftmost bit of input is 1 and 0
                 otherwise. The leftmost bit of input is 1 if and only
                 if mask & input is not zero. !!x is 1 if x is nonzero
                 and 0 if x is zero. */
            printf( "\n%d", !!( mask & input ) );

            mask = 16384; /* mask is 01000...00 */

            for ( i = 1; i < 16; i++ ) {
                  /* Print 1 if the next bit of input is 1 and 0
                     otherwise. */
                  printf( "%d", !!( mask & input ) );

                  /* shift the 1 in mask one place right */
                  mask >>= 1;
            }
            printf( "\n" );
      }
}
```

Section 4.1

1. True   **3.** False   **5.** False   **7.** False   **9.** True   **11.** True

13. To define a function is to create it by giving its header and its body. To declare a function is to give its name, the data types of its parameters (and, optionally, names), and the data type of the value that the function returns. The declaration of a function occurs inside or before a function that invokes it. A function definition never occurs inside another function's body.

15. A function's header is not terminated with a semicolon. The definition should be written

```
void fun1( int parm1, float parm2 )
{
      .
      .
      .
}
```

17. The names should follow the data types. The correct declaration is

```
int status( char code, float time );
```

19.

```
#include <stdio.h>

int echo_chars( void )
{
      int count = 0, c;
      while ( ( c = getchar() ) != EOF ) {
            count++;
            putchar( c );
      }
      return ( count );
}
```

21.

```
#include <stdio.h>

int echo_some_chars( int max_echo )
{
      int count = 0, c;
      while ( ( c = getchar() ) != EOF
            && count < max_echo ) {
            count++;
            putchar( c );
      }
      if ( count > 0 )
            return ( count );
      else
            return ( EOF );
}
```

23. One argument is passed to h. The *expression* a, b, c evaluates to c, so that the value of c is passed to h. (Here , is the comma operator.)

Section 4.2

1. False

3. True

5. When a function is invoked, all the function's arguments are evaluated before control is passed to the invoked function. Although C guarantees that all arguments will be evaluated before control passes to the invoked function, it does not guarantee the order of evaluation.

Section 4.3

1. False

3. The value `arg1` is stored in a cell named `parm1`. (The cell named `parm1` is distinct from the cell named `arg1`.) Similarly, the value `arg2` is stored in a cell named `parm2` and the value `arg3` is stored in a cell named `parm3`.

Section 4.4

1. The modification requires changes to both `print_codes` and `decode_char`. The lines

```
printf( "\tGold--------------------> D\n" );   /* golD */
printf( "\tSilver------------------> S\n" );   /* Silver */
```

should be added to `print_codes`. (The letter G is used already for green.) The lines

```
case 'D':
        return ( −1.0 );
case 'S':
        return ( −2.0 );
```

should be added to `decode_char` in the `case` statement.

Section 4.5

1. True

3. A variable may not have the same name as a parameter.

Section 4.6

1. False

3. `#include "structures.h"`

5. The C preprocessor replaces the `#include` line with the contents of the indicated file.

7. False

9. 3

11. `#define dbl( x ) ( 2 * ( x ) )`

13. The second macro is preferable. Indeed, for some arguments the results may be unexpected. For example, if we execute either

```
j = MAX1( i = 3, 5 );
j = MAX2( i = 3, 5 );
```

we would expect i to be assigned the value 3 and j to be assigned the value 5. This is indeed what happens when we execute

```
j = MAX2( i = 3, 5 );
```

However, when we execute

```
j = MAX1( i = 3, 5 );
```

i and j are both assigned the value 5.
The previous line expands to

```
j = ( i = 3 > 5 ? i = 3 : 5 );
```

Since "greater than" has a higher precedence than the assignment operator or the conditional operator, we first evaluate $3 > 5$, which is false. The conditional operator is evaluated before the assignment operator, so we next evaluate the conditional expression. Because $3 > 5$ is false, the value of the conditional expression

```
3 > 5 ? i = 3 : 5
```

is 5. This value is then assigned to i and then to j.
On the other hand, the line

```
j = MAX2( i = 3, 5 );
```

expands to

```
j = ( (i = 3) > (5) ? (i = 3) : (5) );
```

The parentheses force us to first evaluate $i = 3$, the effect of which is to assign the value 3 to i. The value of the expression

```
i = 3
```

is 3. Since $3 > 5$ is false, the value of the conditional expression

```
(i = 3) > (5) ? (i = 3) : (5)
```

is 5. This value is then assigned to j.

15. It is illegal to put space between the macro's name and the left parenthesis. The correct definition is

```
#define max( x, y ) ( x > y ? x : y )
```

17. A macro is not called at run time, as is a function; rather, a macro is replaced in the source code by its definition prior to compilation.

Section 4.8

1.
```
int fact( int num )
{
    int val;

    if ( num <= 1 )
        return ( 1 );

    val = num;
    while ( --num > 1 )
        val *= num;

    return ( val );
}
```

3.
```
int sum( int n )
{
    if ( n == 1 )
        return ( 2 );
    return ( sum( n - 1 ) + 2 * n );
}
```

5.
```
int walk_three_recursive( int dist )
{
    /* base cases:  1 meter-- 1 way,   (1)
                    2 meters--2 ways, (1,1 or 2)
                    3 meters--4 ways, (1,1,1 or 1,2
                                        or 2,1 or 3) */
    switch ( dist ) {
    case 1:
        return ( 1 );
    case 2:
        return ( 2 );
    case 3:
        return ( 4 );
    }

    return ( walk_three_recursive( dist - 1 )
            + walk_three_recursive( dist - 2 )
            + walk_three_recursive( dist - 3 ) );
}
```

7. The base cases ($n = 5, 6$) can be directly verified. For the inductive step, assume that $n > 6$. Then

$$
\begin{aligned}
\text{walk}(n) &= \text{walk}(n - 1) + \text{walk}(n - 2) \\
&> \left(\frac{3}{2}\right)^{n-1} + \left(\frac{3}{2}\right)^{n-2} \\
&= \left(\frac{3}{2}\right)^{n-2}\left(1 + \frac{3}{2}\right) \\
&> \left(\frac{3}{2}\right)^{n-2}\left(\frac{3}{2}\right)^{2} = \left(\frac{3}{2}\right)^{n}
\end{aligned}
$$

Section 4.10

1. INT_MIN   **3.** `int scanf( char *format_string, ... );`
5.

```
#include <stdarg.h>
#include <limits.h>

int min( int how_many, ... )
{
    int smallest = INT_MAX;
    int i;
    va_list arg_addr;
    int next_int;
```

```
        va_start( arg_addr, how_many );

        for ( i = 0; i < how_many; i++ )
              if ( ( next_int = va_arg( arg_addr, int ) ) < smallest )
                    smallest = next_int;

        va_end( arg_addr );

        return ( smallest );
}
```

   7. va_arg increases its first argument sizeof (*arg2*) bytes, where *arg2*
      denotes the second argument. For example, if the second argument is int and
      sizeof (int) equals 2, va_arg adds 2 to its first argument.

Section 5.1

   1. 25
   3. int

Section 5.2

   1. True
   3. No
   5. The code swaps the contents of letters[0] and letters[25]. After
      the swap, letters[0] holds 'Z', and letters[25] holds 'A'.
   7. 0 through 25
   9. No. The number of bits per cell is system dependent, but the storage cell for a C
      int must have at least as many bits as the cell for a C char has.
   11. All the elements of an array must have same data type.
   13. The array's size is enclosed in square brackets, not parentheses:

      ```
      float  reals[ 500 ];
      ```

   15. With the exception of an array initialized at definition time, an array's definition
      must specify the number of elements.
   17.

8	−2	20	26	−1003
x[0]	x[1]	x[2]	x[3]	x[4]

   19. 160
   21. 4
   23. The two fragments do not always produce the same output. If a[i] and a[j]
      are 0 and the value of w prior to executing either fragment is 1, the first
      fragment prints No, but the second prints Yes.

Section 5.4

   1. False. For example, the standard library provides functions such as scanf that
      automatically insert the terminating null character when they read a character
      string into an array.

3. A
A

5. urly
u

7. 17

9. fred Hitchcock

11. Error—`printf` with the `%s` conversion code expects an address expression, and an array's name is an address expression. We should write either

```
printf( "%s", s );
```

or, equivalently,

```
printf( "%s", &s[ 0 ] );
```

13. Error—`printf` with the `%c` conversion code does not expect an address expression. We should write

```
printf( "%c", s[ 2 ] );
```

15. Error—to print the first character, we should write

```
printf( "%c", s[ 0 ] );
```

17.

19. Error—`scanf` with the `%s` conversion code expects an address expression, and an array's name is already an address expression. We should write either

```
scanf( "%s", s );
```

or, equivalently,

```
scanf( "%s", &s[ 0 ] );
```

21. Correct—the value `'B'` is stored at index 2 in the array `s`.

23. Error. We should write

```
scanf( "%c", &s[ 0 ] );
```

Section 5.6

1. The address of `sample1`'s first element is passed to `fun1`, whereas the value of `sample1`'s third element is passed to `fun2`. All the elements are floating-point numbers.

3. 2
4
6
8
10
16

5. The program would sum all but the first number in the array.

Section 5.7

1. Base 8 is just like base 10 if you have no thumbs.

3. Negative

5. Far Out

7. Shady Deals

9. string1 > string2

11. 28
23

Section 5.8

1.

```
/* function to compute a string's length    */
int  length( char string[] )
{
     int  count = 0;       /* string's length */
     while ( string[ count ] != '\0' )
          ++count;
     return ( count );
}
```

3.

```
/* homegrown version of strcmp */
int  compare( char str1[], char str2[] )
{
     int  index = 0;
     while ( str1[ index ] != '\0'
          && str1[ index ] == str2[ index ] )
          ++index;
     return ( ( int ) str1[ index ]
               - ( int ) str2[ index ] );
}
```

Section 5.9

1. Yes

3. We multiply together the numbers in brackets in the array's definition.

5. False. The parameter declaration must include the size for every dimension beyond the first.

7. 67
0
84
84
2

9. The following is a sample program. We first store values in the three-dimensional array and then copy them into corresponding cells in the one-dimensional array.

```
#define SIZE1   5
#define SIZE2   2
#define SIZE3   9
main()
{
    int   array1[ SIZE1 ][ SIZE2 ][ SIZE3 ],
          array2[ SIZE1 * SIZE2 * SIZE3 ], i, j, k;
    /* initialize the three-dimensional array */
    for ( i = 0; i < SIZE1; ++i )
        for ( j = 0; j < SIZE2; ++j )
            for ( k = 0; k < SIZE3; ++k )
                array1[ i ][ j ][ k ] = i + j + k;
    /* copy values into corresponding cells in one-dimensional
       array */
    m = 0;
    for ( i = 0; i < SIZE1; ++i )
        for ( j = 0; j < SIZE2; ++j )
            for ( k = 0; k < SIZE3; ++k )
                array2[ (SIZE2 * SIZE3 * i) + (SIZE3 * j) + k ]
                    = array1[ i ][ j ][ k ];
}
```

Section 5.10

1. We still get

> Record: Lauper   Cindi   708-123-9091

Whether we enter Lauper, or Lauper followed by two blanks, since main
pads with blanks, the candidate search string is the same for either input.

3.

```
/*   This recursive implementation of binary search searches the
     sorted array

         array[ left ], array[ left + 1 ],..., array[ right ]

     for candidate, returning the appropriate index if candidate
     is found, and the NO_FIND flag otherwise. */

int binary_search_rec(
    char   candidate[],
    char   array[][ MAX_REC_SIZE + 1 ],
    int    left,
    int    right )
{
    int    mid;  /* midpoint between left and right */
    int    flag; /* holds result of string comparison */

    if ( left > right )  /* nowhere left to look */
        return ( NO_FIND );
```

```
        /* find (approximate) midpoint */
        mid = ( left + right ) / 2;
        flag = strncmp( candidate, array[ mid ], LNAME_SIZE );
        if ( flag == 0 )      /* candidate == array[ mid ] */
            return ( mid );

        if ( flag > 0 )        /* candidate > array[ mid ] */
            /* Recursively search the right half. Return the
               appropriate value computed by the recursive call. */
            return ( binary_search_rec( candidate, array,
                                        mid + 1, right ) );

    /* candidate < array[ mid ]
       Recursively search the left half. Return the appropriate
       value computed by the recursive call. */
    return ( binary_search_rec( candidate, array, left, mid - 1 ) );
}
```

Section 6.1

1. ptr1 is defined incorrectly. The correct definition is

```
char var1, *ptr1;
```

3. The assignment statement is wrong. It should be

```
*p = c;
```

5. 2323

7. 2323

9. T

11. S

13. 2224

15. S

Section 6.2

1. False

3. char

5. 1234.560000

7. Q

9. p2 should hold the address of a float variable, and p1 is defined to hold the address of an address of a float variable. Once p1 has been assigned the address of a float variable, we can write

```
p2 = *p1;
```

11. To print the letter Z using p, we need to dereference p twice. The printf statement should read

```
printf( "%c", **p );
```

Section 6.3

1. True

3. A pointer variable, like any variable, can be the target (left-hand side) of an assignment statement. A pointer constant, like any constant, cannot be the target of an assignment statement. Any variable can hold different values at different times, whereas a constant is a single value.

5. The statement

```
t = p;
```

is incorrect because t, a pointer constant, cannot be the target of an assignment statement. The statement

```
p = t;
```

is correct. It stores the address t in variable p.

7. False. However, an error results if we then dereference p.

9. The assignment statement is wrong. Instead of writing

```
ptr = &reals;
```

we should write either

```
ptr = reals;
```

or

```
ptr = &reals[ 0 ];
```

11. The value of the expression

```
characters + 5
```

is the address of the sixth cell in the array. The value of the expression

```
*( characters + 5 )
```

is the contents of the sixth cell in the array.

13. 111.1

15. 11
11

17. At the end of the while loop, ptr has an illegal value because it points before the beginning of the array.

19. The system interprets either expression as *(a + i).

Section 6.4

1. Yes

3. Yes. The invoked function cannot modify the arguments themselves, which are addresses; however, the invoked function can use the addresses to modify the cells at those addresses.

5. False

7. False

9. B

  C

  D

11. 3

The function f returns the string's length + 1.

13.

```
/* homegrown compare with pointers */
int  compare( char *s1, char *s2 )
{
      while ( *s1 != '\0'  &&  *s1 == *s2 ) {
            ++s1;
            ++s2;
      }
      return ( ( int ) ( *s1 - *s2 ) );
}
```

Section 6.7

1. silly1 is the ragged array, and silly2 is the smooth array.

3. 70 bytes

5. We must access string[1][7]. Because string is an array of arrays, each with 30 cells, we must add 1 * 30 to the address of the first cell to obtain the address of the second string. We then add 7 to obtain the address of 'X'.

7. 'i'   **9.** 'a'   **11.** '\0'

Section 6.8

1. 5   file4.dat   file2.dat

Section 6.9

1. True

3. The header for fun99 could be written:

```
void fun99( void ( *ptr1 )( int, char ),
            void ( *ptr2 )( int * ),
            int ( *ptr3 )( float, float ) )
```

We could declare fun99 as

```
void fun99( void ( *ptr1 )( int, char ),
            void ( *ptr2 )( int * ),
            int ( *ptr3 )( float, float ) );
```

Section 7.1

1. Any variable with storage class auto must be defined inside a function's body.

3. main's i = 0   main's i = 1   **5.** 4.200000   14.500000

   val's i = 100   val's i = 100

7.
```
count = 5          count = 2
count = 4          count = 1
count = 3
```

9.
```
int fib[ 50 ] = { 1, 1, 2 };
int walk_dynamic( int dist )
{
    if ( dist <= 2 )
        return ( dist );

    walk_dynamic( dist - 1 );

    return ( fib[ dist ] = fib[ dist - 1 ] +
                           fib[ dist - 2 ] );
}
```

Section 7.3

1. Each time its containing block is entered

3. False

Section 7.4

1. A `static` variable may be made visible in several functions by placing its definition outside and before the functions.

3. False

5.

Variable	Functions in Which It Is Visible
c	function `main` in file *A*
d	all functions in file *B*
v	function `f2` in file *B*
x	functions `print_prompt` and `far_out` in file *B*; function `main` in file *A*
y	function `f1` in file *A*; function `far_out` in file *B*

Section 7.5

1. Yes

3. No

5. No

Section 7.6

1. A function cannot have `auto` as its storage class, only `static` or `extern`.

3. The functions `fun1`, `fun2`, `fun3`, `fun4`, and `fun5`—and only these functions—should be housed in the same file, and `fun5` should have `static` as its storage class.

Section 7.8

1. The type qualifier must come after the storage class. The correct definition is:

```
static volatile int    fail_flag;
```

3. Yes

5. Yes

7.

```
int compare( const void *first, const void *second )
{
    return ( -( *( ( int * ) first ) - *( ( int * ) second ) ) );
}
```

9.

```
#include <stdio.h>
#include <stdlib.h>
#include <string.h>

#define MAX_SIZE 100
#define MAX_STRING 81

int compare( const void *first, const void *second );

main()
{
    char seq[ MAX_SIZE ][ MAX_STRING ];
    int size, i;

    for ( size = 0;
            size < MAX_SIZE
              && fgets( seq[ size ], MAX_STRING, stdin ) != NULL;
            size++ )
        ;

    qsort( seq, size, sizeof ( seq[ 0 ] ), compare );

    for ( i = 0; i < size; i++ )
        printf( "%s", seq[ i ] );
}
int compare( const void *first, const void *second )
{
    return ( -strcmp( first, second ) );
}
```

Section 7.9

1. 1,6 7,8 10,12 12,16

3. 1,4 3,5 4,7 7,10

Section 8.1

1. False

3. It is correct. We simply read lines from the standard input until end-of-file.

5. The correct definition of file_ptr is

```
FILE *file_ptr;
```

7. The mode "r" opens the file for reading only, whereas the mode "r+" opens the file for reading and writing.

9. The mode "a" opens the file for writing only (at the end of the file), whereas the mode "a+" opens the file for reading and writing (again at the end of the file).

11. The statement declares `ptr` to be a pointer to a function that returns a value of type FILE.

Section 8.2

1.

Incorrect	Correct
`fputc( fp, c );`	`fputc( c, fp );`
`fclose( "out.dat" );`	`fclose( fp );`

3. Advantages: Ease of use; `getchar` skips no white space (unlike `scanf`); `getchar` always reads the next character (unlike `scanf`); and this method provides a common interface to many system utilities that also read from the standard input and write to the standard output. The last point is particularly important in a UNIX environment.

Disadvantages: No formatting conversion is provided; in some cases, the input/output may be unbuffered; the user must redirect the input/output; and only one input file and one output file can be used.

5. ufl ilsdfnt   h sdt
rd   aesot-ivr   tlinadbekoewtreoriepgosutieht

Section 8.4

1. NULL

3. No, `gets` does not store the newline.

5.

```
#include <stdio.h>
#define SIZE          9
#define COUNT        100
main()
{
      FILE *fptr, *fout1, *fout2;
      char array[ ( SIZE + 1 ) * COUNT ];
      char *ptr = array;
      int i, n;
      void print_code( FILE *file_ptr, char *pointer );

      fptr = fopen( "INVENTORY.DAT", "r" );
      fout1 = fopen( "FIRST.DAT", "w" );
      fout2 = fopen( "SECOND.DAT", "w" );

      n = fread( array, SIZE + 1, COUNT, fptr );
```

```
    for ( i = 0; i < n/2; ++i ) {
        print_code( fout1, ptr );
        ptr += SIZE + 1;
    }

    for ( ; i < n; ++i ) {
        print_code( fout2, ptr );
        ptr += SIZE + 1;
    }

    fclose( fptr );
    fclose( fout1 );
    fclose( fout2 );
}

void print_code( FILE *file_ptr, char *pointer )
{
    int i;

    for ( i = 0; i < SIZE; ++i )
        fputc( *pointer++, file_ptr );

    fputc( '\n', file_ptr );
}
```

7.

```
#include <stdio.h>
char *getstr( char *ptr )
{
    int c;
    char *start = ptr;

    if ( ( c = getchar() ) == EOF )
        return ( NULL );

    while ( c != '\n' && c != EOF ) {
        *ptr++ = c;
        c = getchar();
    }
    *ptr = '\0';
    return ( start );
}
```

9.

```
#include <stdio.h>
int putstr( char *ptr )
{
    char c;

    while ( c = *ptr++ )
        putchar( c );
    putchar( '\n' );
    return ( '\n' );
}
```

11.

```c
#include <stdio.h>
int new_write( char *array,
               int output_size,
               int output_count,
               FILE *file_ptr )
{
    int i;

    for ( i = 0; i < output_size * output_count;
          i++ )
        fputc( *array++, file_ptr );
    return ( output_count );
}
```

Section 8.5

1. string1: ABC
string2: pqr34
num: 1.23

3. th   **5.** 19
ca
        na
4

7.

```c
#include <stdio.h>
int getstrdc( char *s, char c )
{
    char format_string[] = " c%[^c]c";

    /* install appropriate delimiter */
    format_string[ 1 ] = c;
    format_string[ 5 ] = c;
    format_string[ 7 ] = c;

    return ( scanf( format_string, s ) );
}
```

9. sscanf(s, "%lx", &val);
11. sprintf(s, "%lo", numb);

Section 8.6

1. ABBQA

Section 9.1

1. An array can aggregate only variables of the same type, whereas a structure can aggregate variables of different types.

3. A structure declaration does not allocate any storage but instead describes the number and type of storage cells that will be allocated when a structure variable is defined.

5. If the structure has a tag, the structure variables need not be defined when the structure is declared; the variables can be defined later.

7. True

9. Here are the variable definitions:

```
struct animal   temp, menagerie[ 200 ];
```

11. Here are sample initializations:

```
menagerie[ 5 ].id = 123321;
strcpy( menagerie[ 5 ].type, "carnivore" );
strcpy( menagerie[ 5 ].name, "leona_the_lioness" );
menagerie[ 5 ].age = 3.5;
```

13. 66

15. 13,200

17. 30

19. We assume the structure declared in Exercise 18 has the tag `student_record`:

```
struct student_record   records[ 300 ];
```

21. The variable `car.model` is a pointer to a `char`, whereas `car.make` is an array of 10 `char` variables.

23. `main` returns a value of type `struct record`.

Section 9.3

1.

```
typedef struct robot {  /* type   declaration */
       char     name[ 15 ];
       int      limbs;
       int      joints;
       float    weight;
       float    max_speed;
       char     bad_habits[ 20 ][ 100 ];
} ROBOT;
ROBOT    r2, d2;     /* variable definitions */
```

3. The lowercase `house` is the structure's tag, whereas the uppercase `HOUSE` is a user-defined data type, which is a synonym for `struct house`.

5. Yes

7. The `typedef` of `BOOK` must occur separately from the definition of the 200 variables of type `BOOK`. In short,

```
BOOK books[ 200 ];
```

should occur as a separate statement.

9. True

Section 9.4

1.

```
bike1.brand_name = "CyclePro";
bike1.spokes_per_wheel = 38;
bike1.links_in_chain = 276;
bike1.height = 24.5;
bike1.length = 70.4;
bike1.price = 324.23;
bike2.brand_name = bike1.brand_name;
bike2.spokes_per_wheel = bike1.spokes_per_wheel;
bike2.links_in_chain = bike1.links_in_chain;
bike2.height = bike1.height;
bike2.length = bike1.length;
bike2.price = bike1.price;
```

3. Yes

5.

```
struct sample {
      char      table[ 2 ][ 2 ];
      int       num1;
      float     num2;
};
struct sample
      s1 = { 'A', 'B', 'C', 'D', 99, 99.9 },
      s2 = { 'p', 'q', 'r', 's', 11, 11.1 };
```

7.

```
#include <stdio.h>
#include <stdlib.h>
#include <string.h>

typedef struct stereo {
   int id;
   char brand[ 80 ];
   float cost;
} STEREO;

int compare( const void *first, const void *second );

main()
{
   STEREO seq[ 100 ];
   int count, i;

   for ( count = 0; count < 100; count++ ) {
      if ( scanf( "%d ", &seq[ count ].id ) == EOF )
         break;
      gets( seq[ count ].brand );
      scanf( "%f", &seq[ count ].cost );
   }
```

```
        qsort( seq, count, sizeof ( seq[ 0 ] ), compare );
        for ( i = 0; i < count; i++ )
            printf( "\nid = %d\n"
                    "brand = %s\n"
                    "cost = %f\n",
                    seq[ i ].id,
                    seq[ i ].brand,
                    seq[ i ].cost );
    }
    int compare( const void *first, const void *second )
    {
        return ( strcmp( ( ( STEREO * ) first ) -> brand,
                         ( ( STEREO * ) second ) -> brand ) );
    }
```

Section 9.5

1. `ptr = &soldier3;`

3. `printf( "%s", (*ptr).rank );`

5.

```
Audie Murphy
A
A
i
```

7. We assume the following declarations from Exercise 6:

```
struct employee {
    char      *name;
    char      *ssnum;
    float     salary;
};
struct department {
    struct employee  manager;
    char             *dept_name;
    float            budget;
};
```

Here are sample initializations:

```
struct department   accounting;
accounting.manager.name = "Jessica Cruz";
accounting.manager.ssnum = "111-22-3333";
accounting.manager.salary = 68987.09;
accounting.dept_name = "ACCT.";
accounting.budget = 671239.98;
```

9. We use `printf` statements to illustrate the access:

```
printf( "%d", car1.motor.number_of_cyls );
printf( "%d", ptr -> motor.number_of_cyls );
printf( "%d", car1.motor_ptr -> number_of_cyls );
```

11. The structure `struct node` has members, `next` and `last`, that are pointers to variables of type `struct node`.

Section 9.6

1. By value

3. We assume that the `typedef` for TV_SHOW occurs at the top of a file that contains both `main` and `get_tv_data`, which `main` invokes. Here is `get_tv_data`'s definition:

```
TV_SHOW  get_tv_data( void )
{
     TV_SHOW temp;
     printf( "\nShow's title--" );
     gets( temp.title );
     printf( "\nNetwork--" );
     gets( temp.network );
     printf( "\nRating--" );
     scanf( "%f", &temp.rating );
     printf( "\nMarket share--" );
     scanf( "%f", &temp.share );
     return ( temp );
}
```

5. We make the same assumptions as in Exercise 3 and assume further that `main` invokes `get_tv_data2` with a pointer to a structure variable of type TV_SHOW. Here is `get_tv_data2`'s definition:

```
void  get_tv_data2( TV_SHOW *show )
{
     printf( "\nShow's title--" );
     gets( show -> title );
     printf( "\nNetwork--" );
     gets( show -> network );
     printf( "\nRating--" );
     scanf( "%f", &( show -> rating ) );
     printf( "\nMarket share--" );
     scanf( "%f", &( show -> share ) );
}
```

7. If an array occurs as a member of a structure variable, the array—along with all other members—can be passed by value to a function. The programmer, in declaring a structure with only an array as a member, presumably wants to pass the array by value.

Section 9.8

1. No, because the union variable `var` uses the same storage for the member `number` as for the member `letter`. Because the assignment of `'A'` to `var.letter` occurs after the assignment of 6 to `var.number`, this shared storage currently holds only `'A'`.

3. Yes

5. If storage is at a premium and only one member variable is needed at any given time, a union might be preferred to a structure.

7. A colon must precede each bit-field size. The correct declaration is

```
struct saving_space {
    unsigned int  num1  : 16;
    unsigned int  num2  : 16;
} var;
```

9. Only a bit-field member has a size that the user can specify.

Section 9.9

1. 0
   3

3.

```
typedef enum good_foods { twinkies, tootsie_rolls,
                          fritos, greasy_chips,
                          fat_fries, pretzel_bars,
                          big_steaks, medium_steaks,
                          small_steaks, ice_cream,
                          fudge, cotton_candy }
GOOD_FOODS;
```

5. Yes (unfortunately)

Section 10.1

1. The system knows at compile time the type and amount of compile-time storage requested, whereas the system knows only at run time the type and amount of run-time storage requested. The amount of compile-time storage must be determined in advance. The amount of run-time storage can be determined when the program is running and can depend on the data. Compile-time storage is obtained by defining variables. Run-time storage is obtained by invoking library functions such as `malloc` and `calloc`.

3. Run-time storage is referenced by pointers only.

5. The pointer returned by `malloc` must be cast to the appropriate type:

```
ptr = ( float * ) malloc( sizeof ( float ) );
```

7. No. On any system, the value of `sizeof ( char )` is 1.

9. 2.200000
   1.100000
   0.000000

11. The cell that holds 999 is inaccessible.

13.
```
typedef struct book {
    char *title;
    char *author;
    int isbn;
    char avail_code;
} BOOK;
```

```
            BOOK *book_ptr1, *book_ptr2;
            book_ptr1 = ( BOOK * )
                        calloc( 100, sizeof ( BOOK ) );
            book_ptr2 = book_ptr1 + 51;
```

Section 10.2

    1. B
       C

    3.

```
#include <stdio.h>
#include <stdlib.h>
ELEPHANT *get_elephants( void )
{
    ELEPHANT  *current, *first;
    int response;

    /* allocate extra node */
    current = first = ( ELEPHANT * ) malloc( sizeof ( ELEPHANT ) );

    /* prompt user for an elephant */
    printf( "\n\n\n\tAdd one? (1 == yes, 0 == no)\t" );
    scanf( "%d", &response );

    /* Add elephants to list until user signals halt. */
    while ( response ) {
        /* allocate another elephant node */
        current -> next =
            ( ELEPHANT * ) malloc( sizeof ( ELEPHANT ) );
        current = current -> next;
        /* store name of next elephant */
        printf( "\n\n\tNAME:\t" );
        scanf( "%s", current -> name );
        /* prompt user about another elephant */
        printf( "\n\n\n\tAdd another? (1 == yes, 0 == no)\t" );
        scanf( "%d", &response );
    }

    /* set link field of last node to NULL */
    current -> next = NULL;

    /* save extra first node for freeing */
    current = first;

    /* chop off extra first node */
    first = first -> next;

    /* free extra node */
    free( current );

    return ( first );
}
```

5. Because n is 1, we simply execute

```
new -> next = ptr;
```

which makes the new node point to the original first node in the list. We then return the address of the new node.

7. If we delete the indicated lines and n is 1, we first execute

```
pred = find_nth_node( ptr, n - 1 );
```

Because the second argument is 0, find_nth_node returns NULL. Because pred is NULL, when we execute

```
if ( pred == NULL )
    return ( NULL );
```

we return NULL. We did not add the new node.

9. Because n is not 1, we first execute

```
pred = find_nth_node( ptr, n - 1 );
```

which points pred to the node whose data field is 3. Because pred -> next is NULL, we set *success_flag to 0 and return ptr.

11.
```
#include <stdio.h>
void  print_elephants( ELEPHANT *ptr )
{
    int count = 1;
    ELEPHANT *temp = ptr;
    printf( "\n\n\n" );
    do {
        printf( "\nElephant number %d is %s.",
            count++, ptr -> name );
        ptr = ptr -> next;
    } while ( ptr != temp );
}
```

13. We assume that NODE is the typedef of a structure for a node in a linked list.

```
#include <stdio.h>
int length( NODE *ptr )
{
    int count = 0;
    while ( ptr != NULL ) {
        count++;
        ptr = ptr -> next;
    }
    return ( count );
}
```

15. You obtain a circular linked list.

17. We assume that NODE is the typedef of a structure for a node in a linked list.

```
NODE *third_to_first( NODE *ptr )
{
    NODE *second = ptr -> link;
    NODE *third = second -> link;
```

```
                second -> link = third -> link;
                third -> link = ptr;
                return ( third );
        }
```

Section 10.4

1. (top) T Z Q L P N R

3. (Example 10.4.1 only)

```
#include <stdio.h>
void dump_stack( void )
{
    int i = top;
    while ( i >= 0 ) {
        printf( "\ntray's color: %s\n", trays[ i ] -> color );
        printf( "\ntray's id: %d\n", trays[ i ] -> id );
        i--;
    }
}
```

5. No. An empty and a full queue have front and rear at the same relative positions. However, if we define a queue to be full if there is exactly one empty cell in the array, we can test for full and empty by examining the relative positions of front and rear.

7.

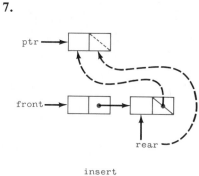

insert

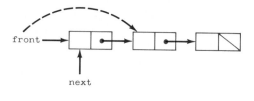

remove

9.

```
    int empty_stack( void )
    {
        if ( top < 0 )
            return ( 1 );
        return ( 0 );
    }
```

11.

```
    int empty_queue( void )
    {
        if ( count == 0 )
            return ( 1 );
```

```
                return ( 0 );
        }
```

13.

```
    int full_stack( void )
    {
        if ( top >= SIZE - 1 )
            return ( 1 );
        return ( 0 );
    }
```

15.

```
    int full_queue( void )
    {
        if ( count >= SIZE )
            return ( 1 );
        return ( 0 );
    }
```

17. This function uses the fact that if `malloc` cannot allocate the requested storage, it returns NULL.

```
    #include <stdlib.h>
    TRAY *push( TRAY tr )
    {
        TRAY *ptr;
        ptr = ( TRAY * ) malloc( sizeof ( TRAY ) );
        if ( ptr == NULL )
            return ( NULL );
        *ptr = tr;
        ptr -> below = top;
        top = ptr;
        ++currsize;
        return ( &tr );
    }
```

Section 10.6

1. $V = \{v_1, v_2, v_3, v_4\}$ **3.** v_1 and v_4 **5.** (v_3, v_4, v_1)

7.

9. (Figure 10.6.7) 3   **11.** v_8 **13.** v_2, v_4
(Figure 10.6.8) 4

15. v_1, v_3, v_5, v_7, v_9 **17.** It is the root.   **19.** v_6

21.

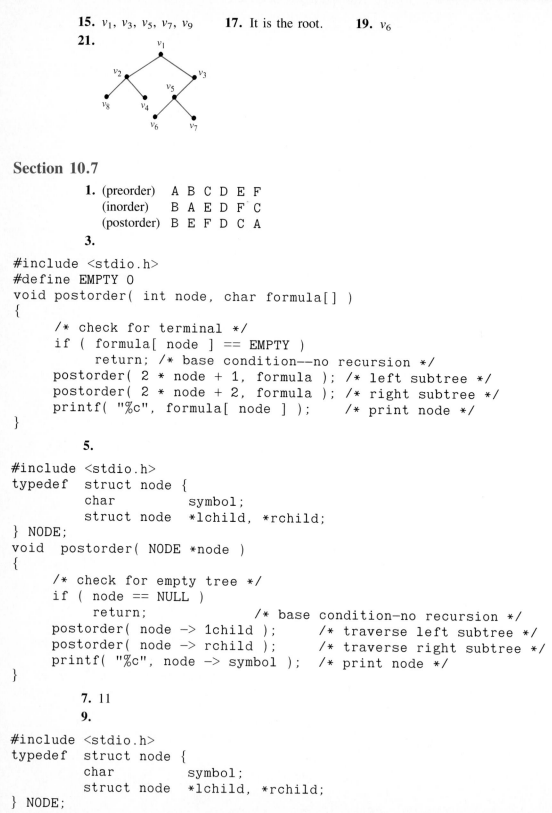

Section 10.7

1. (preorder)   A B C D E F
(inorder)   B A E D F C
(postorder) B E F D C A

3.

```
#include <stdio.h>
#define EMPTY 0
void postorder( int node, char formula[] )
{
    /* check for terminal */
    if ( formula[ node ] == EMPTY )
        return; /* base condition--no recursion */
    postorder( 2 * node + 1, formula ); /* left subtree */
    postorder( 2 * node + 2, formula ); /* right subtree */
    printf( "%c", formula[ node ] );    /* print node */
}
```

5.

```
#include <stdio.h>
typedef  struct node {
        char           symbol;
        struct node  *lchild, *rchild;
} NODE;
void  postorder( NODE *node )
{
    /* check for empty tree */
    if ( node == NULL )
        return;                    /* base condition-no recursion */
    postorder( node -> lchild );   /* traverse left subtree */
    postorder( node -> rchild );   /* traverse right subtree */
    printf( "%c", node -> symbol ); /* print node */
}
```

7. 11

9.

```
#include <stdio.h>
typedef  struct node {
        char           symbol;
        struct node  *lchild, *rchild;
} NODE;
```

```
int   descendants( NODE *node )
{
      int count = 0;
      /* check for empty tree */
      if ( node == NULL )
          return ( 0 );         /* base condition--no recursion */
      if ( node -> lchild != NULL )
          count += 1 + descendants( node -> lchild );
      if ( node -> rchild != NULL )
          count += 1 + descendants( node -> rchild );
      printf( "Node %c has %d descendants\n",
              node -> symbol, count );
      return ( count );
}
```

11. The linked representation of a binary tree is usually preferable to the array implementation. The exceptional case occurs when we can guarantee nodes at consecutive indexes 0, 1, . . . so that little or no space is wasted in the array.

Section 10.8

1.

	A	B	C	D	E	F	G
A	0	1	0	0	0	0	0
B	1	0	1	1	0	0	0
C	0	1	0	0	1	0	0
D	0	1	0	0	1	1	0
E	0	0	1	1	0	1	0
F	0	0	0	1	1	0	1
G	0	0	0	0	0	1	0

3. F D E G B C A

5. F D B A C E G

7.
```
anger
gluttony
envy
lust
sloth
pride
covetousness
```

9. Because the array sin_queue contains distinct vertices, it can hold at most SIZE elements at one time.

11. We assume the existence of a stack that can hold pointers to NODE and functions push, pop, and stack_not_empty. The last function returns 1 if the stack is not empty and 0 if the stack is empty.

```
#include <stdio.h>
void dfs( SINS next )
{
      void push( SINS item ), visit( SINS sin );
      int stack_not_empty( void );
      NODE *pop( void );
```

```
NODE *ptr;

push( graph[ next ] );
visit( next );
visited[ next ] = 1;

while ( stack_not_empty() ) {
    ptr = pop();
    while ( ptr != NULL ) {
        next = ptr -> sin;
        if ( !visited[ next ] ) {
            push( ptr -> link );
            visit( next );
            visited[ next ] = 1;
            ptr = graph[ next ];
        }
        else
            ptr = ptr -> link;
    }
}
}
```

Section 10.9

1. We clarify with an example. Suppose that starting from some designated start city, we reach CITY3 by way of CITY2A, and suppose further that the only path to CITY3 goes through CITY2A.

   ```
   START ->...-> CITY2A -> CITY3
   ```

   CITY3's backpointer points to CITY2A, which currently belongs to the optimal (indeed, the only) path. Now suppose that we discover an alternative path to CITY3:

   ```
   START ->...-> CITY2B -> CITY3
   ```

   There are now two paths to CITY3, one through CITY2A and the other through CITY2B, and, by assumption, the one through CITY2B is shorter than the one through CITY2A. We accordingly have to adjust CITY3's backpointer so that it points to CITY2B rather than CITY2A.

3. If our heuristic is consistently optimistic (namely, if it consistently underestimates the distance from a given city to the goal city), A* will find an optimal path from START to GOAL. However, there usually is no way to ensure that a heuristic is consistently optimistic.

Index

A

A* algorithm, 541
a.out, 617
abs, 598
Ackermann's function, 177
acos, 598
Addition operator (+), 48
Address
  of a cell, 35
  operator (&), 5, 6, 35, 243
  relative, 382
Adjacency list, 534
Adjacency matrix, 530
Adjacent vertices, 519

Airline flight database program, 436
American National Standards Institute
  (ANSI), vii, 2
American Standard Code for Information
  Interchange (ASCII), 37, 53
Ancestor, 521
And operator
  bitwise (&), 100
  logical (&&), 52
ANSI (American National Standards Insti-
  tute), vii, 2
Arc, 519
argc, 285
Argument, 109, 118
argv, 285

Arithmetic operations, 48
Arithmetic shift, 102
Array, 180, 248, 569
  and pointer, 185
  definition of, 181
  dimension of, 215
  extern, 225
  function argument, 201, 217
  index, 181
  initializing, 184, 195, 226, 574
  multidimensional, 215
  of char, 194, 249
  offset in, 181
  one-dimensional, 215
  ragged, 282
  smooth, 282
  static, 226
Array syntax
  equivalence to pointer syntax, 258
Artificial intelligence, 541
ASCII (American Standard Code for Information Exchange), 37, 53, 560
asin, 598
Assignment operator, 5, 15, 52, 55, 65
Assignment suppression operator, 365
atan, 598
atof, 598
atoi, 598
atol, 598
auto, 304, 315

B

B programming language, 2
Base case, 149
BCPL (Basic Combined Programming Language), 2
Berlekamp, E. R., 177
Bernstein's conditions, 556
Binary file, 352, 377, 379, 393
Binary operator, 48
Binary search, 224
Binary search tree, 554
Binary tree, 521, 526
  left child in, 521
  right child in, 521
Bit field, 450
Bitwise operator, 99
  and operator (&), 99
  complement operator (~), 99
  exclusive or operator (^), 100
  left shift operator (<<), 101
  or operator (|), 100
  right shift operator (>>), 101
Block, 304
  containing, 304
  nested, 322
Body of a function, 110
Breadth-first search, 529, 541
break statement, 76, 81, 87, 569, 578

Breaking text into pages program, 311
bsearch, 599
Buffer, 97
Byte, 34

C

Call by reference, 123, 264
  for structures, 433
Call by value, 120, 264
  for structures, 430
Calling a function, 109
calloc, 464, 599
Carroll, Lewis, 233
case statement, 83, 570
Cast operator, 94, 570
cat, 620
cb, 622
cc, 617
cd, 619
ceil, 600
Cell, 34
  address of, 34
  size, 34, 35
Cell-mapping function, 217
char, 36–42, 168
  array of, 194, 249
  pointer to, 249
Character, 36
  constant, 570
  conversion function, 375, 597
  input/output, 356
  string, 194
  testing function, 375, 597
Child, 521
  left, 521
  right, 521
Chu, I. P., 163, 177
Circular linked list, 482, 552
clearerr, 497, 600
close, 392, 600
Closing a file, 352
Collision, 383
Collision resolution policy, 383
Comma operator (,), 61, 62
Command line, 285
Command line argument, 285
Comment, 2, 570
Comparing sorting algorithms program, 289
Compile-link description, 623
Compile-time storage, 463
Compiler optimization, 336
Compiling
  in Turbo C, 631, 634
  in UNIX, 617, 634, 635
  in VAX/VMS, 633, 635
Complement operator (~), 99
Computing a string's length program, 214
Computing income tax programs, 12, 29
Computing resistance in ohms program, 124

Concatenation, 205
  of string constants, 7
Conditional compilation, 137
Conditional expression (? :), 90
const, 331, 344, 379
Constant
  character, 570
  floating-point, 570
  hexadecimal, 570
  integer, 570
  octal, 570
  pointer, 287
  string, 571
Containing block, 304
continue statement, 76, 571
Conversion of lengths program, 4
Conway, J. H., 177, 231
cos, 600
cosh, 600
Cost of an edge, 520
cp, 97
creat, 600
ctype.h, 130, 375

D

Data structure, 462
Data type, 572
  range of, 34
DBL_MAX, 415
Declaration
  of an extern variable, 317
  of a function, 112
  of a structure, 402–408, 417
  of a variable, 317
Decrement operator (−−), 64
Default action, 25, 86
#define, 131, 333, 416
defined, 138
Definition
  of an array, 181
  of an extern variable, 316, 344
  of a function, 112
  and initialization of a variable, 34
  of a structure, 403–408
  of a variable, 5, 34, 317
Dependency description, 623
Depth-first search, 529, 541
Deque, 552
Dereference operator (*), 237
Descendant, 521
Determining a source file's size in bytes
    program, 358
difftime, 293, 600
Dimension of an array, 215
Directory, UNIX, 618
Divide-and-conquer, 446
Division operator (/), 48
Division-remainder hashing, 382
double, 44, 76, 168

Doubly linked list, 553
do while statement, 11, 76, 572

E

EBCDIC (Extended Binary Coded Decimal
    Interchange Code), 37, 53, 563
Edge, 518
  cost of, 520
  incident, 519
  length of, 519
  parallel, 519
#elif, 138
#else, 137
enum, 452, 573
Enumerated type, 452, 455, 573
  tag, 452
EOF, 13, 31, 95, 129
Epp, H., 382
Equals operator (==), 7, 15, 52
#error, 139
Exception handler, 625
Exclusive-or operator (^), 99
exit, 601, 627
exp, 601
Exponential notation, 44
extern array, 225
extern function, 326
extern variable, 305, 316, 344
  declaration of, 316
  definition of, 316, 344

F

fabs, 601
Factorial, 146
fclose, 28, 29
Feigenbaum, M., 74
fgetc, 135, 356, 601
fgets, 225, 359, 601
Fibonacci, L., 153
Fibonacci sequence, 153
Field width, 367, 372
FILE, 28, 30, 352
File, 28
  binary, 352, 377, 379, 393
  closing, 352
  descriptor, 391
  FILE, 28, 30, 352
  header, 3, 30
  inclusion directive, 129
  load factor of, 383
  opening, 352
  pointer, 28, 352
  position marker, 353
  random access, 381
  relative, 381
  text, 352, 377, 379, 393
FILENAME_MAX, 415
float, 44, 70, 168

float.h, 47, 70, 130, 415
Floating-point constant, 571
floor, 602
fopen, 28, 352, 602
FOPEN_MAX, 353
Format string, 5, 365, 370
Formatted input/output, 364
Formatting text with a given line length program, 199
for statement, 61, 76, 573
fprintf, 28, 29, 370, 603
fputc, 135, 356, 603
fputs, 361, 603
fread, 362, 603
free, 467, 603
Free tree, 520
fscanf, 28, 29, 364, 603
fseek, 377, 393, 604
ftell, 379, 604
Function, 3, 108, 573
    Ackermann's, 177
    with an arbitrary number of arguments, 164
    argument, 109, 118
    array argument in, 201, 217
    body, 109, 573
    call, 109
    cell-mapping, 217
    character conversion, 375, 597
    character testing, 375, 597
    declaration, 112, 597
    definition, 112, 573
    extern, 326
    factorial, 146
    hash, 382
    header, 109, 573
    high-level, 393
    input/output, 597
    invoking, 109
    low-level, 393
    mathematics, 597
    memory allocation, 597
    parameter, 109, 110
    pointer to, 287
    prototype form, 112, 113, 168
    recursive, 146
    static, 326
    storage class of, 326
    string, 598
    strung-handling, 205
    and structures, 430
    visibility of, 326
fwrite, 363, 604

G

Garbage, 467
Generating prime numbers program, 80
getc, 356, 604
getchar, 95, 135, 356, 604

gets, 359, 604
Goldbach's conjecture, 233
goto statement, 89, 574
Graph, 518
    arc in, 519
    edge in, 519
    heuristic search, 539
    loop in, 519
    network, 520
    node in, 519
    optimal path in, 541
    parallel edges in, 519
    path in, 519
    representation of, 530
    simple path in, 519, 541
    vertex in, 519
    weighted, 520
Greater than operator (>), 7, 52
Greater than or equal operator (>=), 7, 52
Greedy algorithm, 339
grep, 621
Guy, R. K., 177

H

Hash function, 382
Header file, 3, 30, 576
Header of a function, 109
Height of a tree, 523
Heuristic graph search program, 539
Hexadecimal constant, 570
Hexadecimal notation, 39, 42
Hierarchical storage system, 336
High-level function, 393

I

Identifier, 8
#if, 137
if statement, 14–25, 574
#ifdef, 137
#ifndef, 137
Incident, 519
#include, 3, 130
Increment operator (++), 64
Index into an array, 181
Infix, 511, 524
Infix to postfix program, 511
Initializing
    arrays, 184, 195, 226, 574
    pointers, 242
    structures, 419, 574
    variables, 305–309, 574
Inorder traversal, 524
Input
    character, 356
    formatted, 364
    function, 594
    nonstandard, 392
    redirecting, 27

standard, 26, 354
  string, 359
Insertion sort, 297
`int`, 35–42, 168
Integer, 35
Integer constant, 570
`INT_MAX`, 146
Invoking a function, 109
`isalnum`, 375, 605
`isalpha`, 375, 605
`iscntrl`, 375, 605
`isdigit`, 375, 605
`isgraph`, 375, 605
`islower`, 375, 606
`isprint`, 375, 606
`ispunct`, 375, 606
`isspace`, 375, 606
`isupper`, 375, 606
`isxdigit`, 375, 606

J

Johnsonbaugh, R., vii, 163, 177

K

Kalin, M., vii
Kernighan, B. W., 2
Key, 382
Keyword, 8, 574

L

Label, 89, 575
`labs`, 606
Leading separate numeric string, 301
Leaving-one-out method, 458
Left child, 521
Left shift operator (<<), 101
Length
  edge, 519
  path, 519
Less than or equal operator (<=), 7, 55
Less than operator (<), 7, 55
Level of indirection, 244
Lexicographic order, 207
Library, run-time, 629
Life, 231
limits.h, 41, 70, 130, 146
`#line`, 138
Linear probing, 383
Linked list, 470
  circular, 482, 552
  doubly, 553
  singly, 470
Linking
  in Turbo C, 631, 634
  in UNIX, 617, 634, 635
  in VAX/VMS, 633, 635
Lipinski, W., 73

List, 462
Load factor, 383
Local variable, 127
`log`, 607
`log10`, 607
Logical and operator (&&), 52
Logical not operator (!), 52
Logical or operator (| |), 52
Logical shift, 102
`long double`, 44, 76
`long float`, 76
`long int`, 41
Loop, 519
Low-level function, 393
`ls`, 620
`lseek`, 604
Lucas, É., 150
Lukasiewicz, 511

M

Macro, 131
  parameterized, 132
Magic square, 300
`main`, 3, 108, 285
`make`, 677
`malloc`, 463, 607
`man`, 616
math.h, 60, 125, 129, 331
Mathematics functions, 597
Mean, 58
Member of a structure, 402
Member operator (.), 404
`memchr`, 607
`memcmp`, 607
`memcpy`, 608
`memmove`, 608
Memory allocation functions, 596
Mid-square hashing, 399
`mkdir`, 619
Modulus operator (%), 49
`more`, 620
Morse code, 175
MS-DOS, 97, 631, 634
  redirecting input and output in, 27
Multidimensional array, 215
Multiplication operator (*), 5, 48
`mv`, 621

N

Nearest-neighbor algorithm, 411, 415
Negation operator (!), 52
Nested block, 322
Nested structures, 426
Network, 520
Newline, 3
`NEW_PHONE` program, 276
Newton's method, 175
Node, 518

Nonstandard input/output, 392
Not equal operator (!=), 7, 52
Not operator (!), 52
NULL, 210, 225, 360
Null directive (#), 139
Null statement, 19, 575
Null terminator, 194

O

Octal constant, 570
Octal notation, 39, 42
Offset in an array, 181
One's complement operator (~), 99
open, 392, 608
Opening a file, 352
Operator
  binary, 48
  precedence of, 51, 575
  unary, 49
Optimization of a compiler, 336
Or operator
  bitwise (|), 100
  logical (||), 52
Output
  character, 356
  formatted, 364
  function, 597
  nonstandard, 392
  redirecting, 27
  standard, 27, 354
  string, 359

P

Packed decimal array, 301
Parallel edges, 519
Parameter, 109, 118
  with type qualifiers, 334
Parameterized macro, 132
Parent, 521
Parse, 64
Path, 519
  length of, 519
  optimal, 541
  simple, 519, 541
Pattern recognition, 415
Pattern recognition program, 411
Paulos, J. P., 74
Pearl, J., 542
PHONE program, 221
Pipe, 627
Pivot, 446
Pointer, 185, 236, 575
  and arrays, 185, 248
  arithmetic, 251
  to char, 249
  constant, 186
  dereferencing, 237
  file, 28, 352

to a function, 287
  initializing, 242
  operations, 255
  operator (->), 424
  range of, 255
  to a structure, 423
  syntax, 251
  variable, 186, 236
  to void, 237, 293, 463
Pop a stack, 462, 499
Population variance, 58
Postfix, 511, 524
Postorder traversal, 524
pow, 125, 331, 608
Power-lifting, 73
pr, 620
#pragma, 139
Precedence of operators, 51, 575
Precision, 370
Prefix, 525
Preorder traversal, 524
Preprocessor, 129
Preprocessor directive, 3, 30, 129
Prime number, 80
printf, 3, 5-7, 35, 36-40, 45-46, 369,
  608
Printing a bar graph program, 68
Printing a calendar program, 90
Prototype form, 112, 113, 168
Push on a stack, 462, 499
putc, 356, 609
putchar, 95, 135, 356, 609
puts, 361, 609
pwd, 619

Q

qsort, 335, 609
Queue, 449, 504, 530
Quicksort, 446

R

Ragged array, 282
rand, 146, 293, 609
Random access file program, 381
RAND_MAX, 146, 293
Range
  of a data type, 34
  for pointers, 255
Raphael, B., 539
read, 392, 610
Real variables, 44
Recursion, 146; see also Recursion
  base case, 149
  tail, 155
Recursive tiling program, 156
Redirecting input and output
  in MS-DOS, 27
  in UNIX, 27, 627
  in VAX/VMS, 27

`register`, 315, 337
Relational operator, 52
Relative address, 382
Relative file, 382
Representation
   binary tree, 526
   graph, 530
   queue, 499
   stack, 499
`return` statement, 111, 576
Reverse Polish notation, 511
Reversing a string in place program, 273
`rewind`, 377, 610
Richards, M., 2
Right child, 521
Right shift operator (>>), 101
Right tromino, 156
Ritchie, D., 2
`rm`, 619
`rmdir`, 619
Root, 520
Rooted tree, 520
   ancestor in, 521
   child in, 521
   descendant in, 521
   parent in, 521
   root in, 520
   subtree of, 521
   terminal vertex in, 521
Run-time library, 629
Run-time storage, 463
Running a program
   in Turbo C, 631, 634
   in UNIX, 617, 634, 635
   in VAX/VMS, 634, 635

S

Sample set, 411
Savings account transactions program, 328
`scanf`, 5, 14, 35, 36, 46, 196, 361, 364, 610
Scheduling problem program, 339
Scientific notation, 44
Scope of variables, 127
Search
   binary search tree, 554
   breadth-first, 529, 541
   depth-first, 529, 541
   heuristic graph, 539
`SEEK_CUR`, 378, 394
`SEEK_END`, 378, 394
`SEEK_SET`, 377, 394
Selection sort, 223
Self-referential structure, 428
Seven deadly sins, 530
Shift operators, 101
`short int`, 41, 168
`signal`, 610, 626
Signal, 625

signal.h, 625
`signed`, 42, 71
Simple path, 519, 541
Simulating a dice game program, 140
`sin`, 610
Singly linked list, 470
`sinh`, 611
`sizeof` operator, 34, 187, 576
   and structures, 407
`size_t`, 336
`sleep`, 146
Smooth array, 282
Sorting
   comparing sorting programs, 289
   insertion sort, 297
   quicksort, 446
   selection sort, 223
   sorting and searching program, 219, 276
Sorting and searching program, 219, 276
`sprintf`, 369, 611
`sqrt`, 611
`srand`, 147, 611
`sscanf`, 364, 611
Stack, 298, 461, 499, 530
Standard deviation, 58
Standard error, 354
Standard input, 26, 354
Standard output, 26, 354
`static` array, 226
`static` function, 326
`static` variable, 306, 320
Statistical measures program, 58
stdarg.h, 130, 164, 168
`stderr`, 354
`stdin`, 135, 354
stdio.h, 3, 13, 28, 131, 135, 352, 377, 415
stdlib.h, 146, 293, 463, 467, 624
`stdout`, 354
Storage class, 577
   of a function, 326
   of a variable, 304, 316
`strcat`, 206, 611
`strchr`, 210, 612
`strcmp`, 207, 612
`strcpy`, 208, 612
`strcspn`, 612
String, 194
   comparison, 207
   concatenation, 206
   constant, 571
   format, 5, 364, 369
   function, 206, 597
   input/output, 359
String-handling functions, 206
string.h, 130, 206
`strlen`, 209, 612
`strncat`, 206, 612
`strncmp`, 207, 612
`strncpy`, 208, 613
`strpbrk`, 613

`strrchr`, 210, 613
`strspn`, 613
`strstr`, 210, 613
`struct`, 402
Structure, 28, 401, 577
    declaration, 402–408, 417
    definition, 403–408, 417
    and functions, 430
    initializing, 419, 574
    member, 403
    member operator, 404
    nested, 426
    passing by reference, 433
    passing by value, 430
    pointer to, 423
    pointer operator, 424
    self-referential, 428
    and `sizeof` operator, 407
    tag, 403
Subtraction operator (−), 48
Subtree, 521
`switch` statement, 76, 83, 578
Syntax diagram, 580
`system`, 614, 624

T

Tag, 403, 452
Tail recursion, 155
`tan`, 614
`tanh`, 614
Terminal vertex, 521
Text editor program, 483
Text file, 352, 377, 379, 393
Thompson, K., 2
Tiling, 156
`time`, 290, 614
time.h, 130, 293
Token, 64, 71
`tolower`, 375, 614
`toupper`, 375, 614
Tower of Hanoi, 150
Tracking and reporting car sales program,
    189
Traversal tree, 523
Tree, 518, 520
    binary, 521, 526
    binary search, 554
    free, 520
    height of, 523
    rooted, 520
    subtree of, 521
    traversals, 523
Tromino, 156
Turbo C, 14, 35, 44, 46, 137, 293, 333,
    392, 631–633, 634
    editor, 631–632
    integrated environment, 632
Two's complement integer, 566
`typedef`, 416, 578

Type qualifier, 331, 344, 579
    and compiler optimization, 336
    parameter with, 334

U

U-method, 458
Unary minus operator (−), 49
Unary plus operator (+), 49, 71
`#undef`, 135
`ungetc`, 314, 614
Union, 448, 579
UNIX, 13, 97, 98, 392, 616, 634, 635
    and C, 616
    directories and paths, 618
    exception handling, 625
    on-line help, 616
    pipes, 627
    program development in, 622
    redirecting input and output in, 27, 627
    run-time libraries, 629
`unsigned`, 41, 71
Unsigned binary integer, 566

V

`va_arg`, 164
`va_end`, 166
`va_list`, 165
Variable
    declaration, 317
    declaration of `extern`, 317
    defining and initializing, 34
    definition, 5, 34, 317
    definition of `extern`, 317, 344
    `extern`, 305, 315–316, 344
    initializing, 305–309, 574
    local, 127
    pointer, 186, 236
    real, 44
    scope of, 127
    `static`, 306, 320
    storage class of, 304, 316
    visibility of, 127, 305–309, 316–321,
        322–326
Variance
    population, 58
`va_start`, 164
VAX-11 C, 35, 315, 392, 633, 635
VAX/VMS, 14, 97, 98
    redirecting input and output in, 27
Vertex, 519
    adjacent, 519
    ancestor of, 521
    child of, 521
    descendant of, 521
    parent of, 521
    terminal, 521
Visibility
    of a function, 326

of a variable, 127, 305–309, 316–321, 322–326
VMS, 633
`void`, 112, 168, 579
   pointer to, 237, 293, 463
`volatile`, 331, 344, 579

W

Washington, H., 73

Weighted graph, 520
`while` statement, 5, 9, 63, 76–77, 579
`write`, 393, 615

X

X3J11 standardization committee, vii

Codes for printf, fprintf, and sprintf

Code	Interpretation	Example of Output	Corresponding Argument Must Be
c	a character	p	char, short, int
s	a character string	pie	address of char
d, i	integer written in signed decimal notation	−999	char, short, int
ld, li	long written in signed decimal notation	2964775	long
o	integer written in unsigned octal notation	7031	char, short, int
lo	long written in unsigned octal notation	7255547	long
x	integer written in unsigned hexadecimal notation	fe4	char, short, int
X	integer written in unsigned hexadecimal notation	FE4	char, short, int
lx	long written in unsigned hexadecimal notation	2d3d27	long
lX	long written in unsigned hexadecimal notation	2D3D27	long
u	unsigned decimal	287092	unsigned char, unsigned short, unsigned int
lu	unsigned long	3775287092	unsigned long
e	float or double written in the form m.nnnnnne±xx	3.141590e+03	float, double
E	float or double written in the form m.nnnnnnE±xx	3.141590E+03	float, double
f	float or double written in the form m.nnnnnn	2.718282	float, double
g	number written in the d, e, or f format, whichever is shortest	33.900000	float, double
G	number written in the d, E, or f format, whichever is shortest	33.900000	float, double
Le	long double written in the form m.nnnnnne±xx	3.141590423e+03	long double
LE	long double written in the form m.nnnnnnE±xx	3.141590423E+03	long double
Lf	long double written in the form m.nnnnnn	3.141592654	long double
Lg	number written in the d, Le, or Lf format, whichever is shortest	43.9000001	long double
LG	number written in the d, LE, or Lf format, whichever is shortest	43.9000001	long double
p	address	(implementation dependent)	pointer to void
n	number of characters written so far is stored in int whose address is passed	(none)	address of int
hn	number of characters written so far is stored in short whose address is passed	(none)	address of short
ln	number of characters written so far is stored in long whose address is passed	(none)	address of long
%	write the character %	%	(none)